Black Americans
and
White Business

Dickenson Series on Business Management
David R. Hampton, Consulting Editor

Finance Problems: Basic Business Finance
  John R. Kreidle
Money, Financial Markets and the Economy
  Michael DePrano
Modern Management
  David R. Hampton
Black Americans and White Business
  Edwin M. Epstein and David R. Hampton
Management Perspectives in Marketing
  Louis E. Boone

Dickenson Series on Contemporary Thought in Management
David R. Hampton, Series Editor

Behavioral Concepts in Management
  David R. Hampton
Management and Society
  Lynn H. Peters
International Management
  Richard N. Farmer
Management: A Decision-Making Approach
  Stanley Young
Quantitative Disciplines in Management Decisions
  Richard I. Levin and Rudolph P. Lamone
Organization Concepts and Analysis
  William G. Scott

BLACK AMERICANS
AND
WHITE BUSINESS

Edwin M. Epstein
University of California, Berkeley

David R. Hampton
San Diego State College

Dickenson Publishing Company, Inc.
Encino, California, and Belmont, California

Library of Congress Catalog Card Number: 71-154819

Printed in the United States of America

1   2   3   4   5   6   7   8   9   10

Eastern
8-51

To Our Children
Mimi and Danny Epstein
and
Davy Hampton
and to Ricky and Laura Seed

Contents

From philosopher Alfred North Whitehead's belief that "A great society is a society in which its men of business think greatly of their functions"[1] to rock singer Ray Steven's warning, "You better take care of business, Mr. Businessman," runs a common understanding and a rising sense of urgency. What is commonly understood is that business and society are interdependent—that economic activity is an inextricable part of a total social system. What has become urgent is that racial injustice imperils the system's stable existence.

For a long time, the social consequences of the plight of black[2] Americans have been remote from the businessman's concern. But recent years of turbulence have demonstrated graphically the relatedness of parts within a system. Business's well-being depends utterly upon a stable society and social stability will vanish without racial peace. Business has discovered not only what it stands to lose from social turmoil and destruction, but also has begun to discover what a positive force for social change it can be. Not only can be, but must be! As Kenneth B. Clark, a prominent black social psychologist, has stated, "Other areas in our society—government, education, churches, labor—have defaulted in dealing with Negro problems. It is now up to business."[3]

The purpose of this book can be stated very simply: to inform students, businessmen, and members of the general public about the contemporary and historical relationship between black Americans and the white business community and to suggest possible directions for restructuring this relationship from one of negative imbalance to one of economic and social equality. It is our belief that this important subject has been treated but cursorily elsewhere, and that a text is needed that focuses sharply on the issues presented here.

We approach the subject from an environmental perspective, examining the interaction of business organizations and economic institutions, and a particular segment of American society—the black community. We believe this book will be of particular interest to students and teachers in a variety of disciplines and courses including the Social and Political Environment of Business, Business and Society, Industrial Relations, Business and Public Policy, Black Studies, Economic Sociology, Race Relations, Minority Economic Development, and Urban Economics. This work is also highly pertinent for business managers responsible for the conduct of corporate urban affairs and for operating executives. Hopefully, awareness and concern on the part of present and future businessmen will result in substantial changes in the relationship between the business and black communities.

We decided upon the format of a text combining readings drawn from a variety of sources with our own introductory and integrative essays. It seemed to us at the beginning of this project that there existed materials focusing upon specific aspects of the general subject matter, which, if brought together, organized, edited, and examined in a competent fashion, would constitute a coherent and comprehensive work which would fill a gap in the existing literature and merit serious attention. While there is a clear need for a scholarly and analytical monographic treatment of this subject, we consider a textbook to be an excellent vehicle for an initial examination of the field. Moreover, we feel time to be of importance, and, here, too, a textbook has considerable advantages over a monograph. We hope this book will stimulate sufficient concern among our colleagues to result in substantial scholarly attention to the subject. In the meantime, we hope we can reach students *now* and can contribute to their education by means of the materials presented here.

In selecting readings we have preferred to use primary materials where possible, particularly source materials which are in the public domain. This enabled us to reproduce at length essential documents or studies rather than simply rely on brief discussions of them in secondary sources such as books or articles. Moreover, primary sources tend to possess greater life and vitality than discursive writings. We have also emphasized fewer but longer selections rather than a large number of short excerpts or fragments. Rather than simply offering a patchwork quilt or collage of brief readings which provide a general but somewhat hazy overview of limited substance, we have striven to paint a picture of the subject which highlights critical themes and develops them fully. At the same time we have sought to avoid being repetitive of other books or collections of readings concerning themselves with the economic conditions of black Americans, for example, omitting materials suggesting alternatives to current marketing practices in the ghetto and those relating to the role of labor unions as influences upon the employment of blacks.[4]

A decision we were required to make early in this project was whether to deal with the relationship between the business community and minority groups generally or to focus upon one specific group and its experience in the American economy. We opted for the latter approach, once again, to permit us to deal in depth with a particular minority—the black community—rather than simply to "cover the waterfront." It is our view that it is better to omit all treatment of other minorities and to concentrate on one group rather than to include a few token selections relating to the others which would permit only a superficial treatment of their unique situations.

It is appropriate to point out that the definition of a minority group is itself a matter of no small controversy. In a numerical sense, Italian Americans, Irish Americans, Scandinavian Americans, Jewish Americans, Greek Americans and Slavic Americans, to cite some obvious examples, are also minority group members. By way of example, the approximately six million Jews in the United States constitute only slightly more than 25 percent of the black population of this country which totaled over 22 million persons in 1968. If quantitative measures alone are determinative, Jewish Americans clearly comprise a minority group. However, we submit, Jews are not "minority Americans" within the contemporary meaning of the term.

For our purposes we are defining a minority group as a body of Americans characterized by a history of oppression and exploitation in America; collective economic, political, and social disadvantages; a lack of ownership and control of significant economic resources; and a particular ethnic or racial identity which they seek to maintain and by which they are differentiated from the society as a whole (usually with negative connotations and consequences). Today this definition is virtually conterminous with the various people of color present within American society. We recognize, however, this definition is subject to criticism. It is arguable, for example, that as a result of a fairly general economic and social mobility, Japanese Americans should not be included within the definition, while residents of Appalachia (who indeed possess a unique culture although not a special pigmentation), because of their overall poverty, powerlessness, and distinctive life style, should be. Since this is not an appropriate forum for a detailed discussion of the question of ethnicity, race, and minority group status, we refer the reader to a number of discussions of the subject.[5]

In summary, we consider ethnicity, color, poverty, economic and political powerlessness, oppression and exploitation, group identity, and relative social immobility to be critical determinants of minority status. It is recognized, however, if one views American society as an inherently pluralistic society in which there exists no "host" (usually defined as white, Protestant, Anglo Saxon) group but simply an agglomeration of people from many diverse sources, it can be argued that there are no minority groups but simply people of various origins, some of whom have larger numerical representation in the population and others less representation. While some black intellectuals have offered such an interpretation of American society, there is usually an implicit assumption among both blacks and whites that blacks live in what, by definition, has been a white society.

Black Americans and White Business is organized into three discrete but related sections: The first part, A Primer on America, Black and White, contains materials examining from a broad environmental perspective the historical and contemporary conditions of blacks in American society. Following this introduction (Chapter 1), Chapter 2 highlights, in several short selections, a variety of moods and viewpoints felt and expressed by recent and current black spokesmen, and then proceeds to an examination of the past and present socioeconomic conditions of the black community within the United States. Chapter 3 explores the contemporary racial attitudes of blacks and whites in American society, and the social and psychological implications of these attitudes.

Part two, Business Institutions and the Black Community, emphasizes specific areas of economic interface between the business community and black Americans, employment (Chapter 4), housing (Chapter 5), retail merchandising (Chapter 6) and financing practices (Chapter 7). In Chapter 8, we look at a somewhat different type of relationship by examining the nature, extent, history, and success of efforts by black Americans to establish business enterprises within the United States. We consider the inclusion of this topic to be appropriate because of the impact of white institutions upon the development of black business.

In part three, The Role of Business in Social Change, we examine a variety of alternatives available to the business community *vis-à-vis* black Americans. In Chapters 9 (employment), 10 (housing), and 11 (finance), we reconsider the areas of interface treated in the preceding part of the book and suggest a number of possible directions by which business can alter its traditional relationship of negative imbalance with the black community and help, thereby, to ensure that blacks—just as whites—have a vested economic interest in the survival of the society. Chapter 12 (black economic development) analyzes a number of the suggestions offered for what has popularly (albeit, unfortunately) come to be known as "Black Capitalism," and explores the potential for establishing a substantial number of black-owned and -managed enterprises. Part four, Whither an American Dilemma?, consists of the final chapter, or conclusion (13). It examines the future relationship of black Americans and white business in the context of the alternatives confronting American society as it deals with its dilemma: peaceful social change in keeping with democratic traditions, or maintenance of the status quo with the attendant violence and repression characteristic of a totalitarian social order.

This book has benefited from the assistance of a number of individuals and institutions. The Institute of Business and Economic Research of the University of California at Berkeley provided typing and other facilities which have been of great help. More importantly, it funded the research assistance of Stanley Kowalczyk, a doctoral student in the Graduate School of Business Administration at the University of California, Berkeley, and of Peter Ekeh, a doctoral student in sociology at Berkeley, which was indispensable to this project. Roy Finkle, a graduate student at the School of Business Administration, San Diego State College, also provided invaluable research assistance. Daniel G. Hill, Director, Human Rights Commission, Ontario, Canada, helped locate source material on the problem of cultural bias in employment testing. A number of our colleagues, including Marcus Alexis, Richard F. America, Jr., Robert Blauner, Cleveland Chandler, Richard W. Roehl, Thaddeus Spratlen, and Dow Votaw, took the pains to read and comment upon parts of the manuscript. Their contributions are gratefully acknowledged. They are, of course, to be absolved from criticism for limitations of this book. The Berkeley author wishes to thank the administration of the Schools of Business Administration, particularly Dean Richard H. Holton, which afforded him the opportunity of observing and participating directly in the area of interface between black Americans and white business during his tenure as Director of the Office of Urban Programs within the Schools. This experience in the field of the economic development of minority communities provided invaluable insights in preparing of the book. Our thanks also to John T. Crain of Dickenson Publishing Company for bringing together the two participants in this collaborative venture and for his encouragement and unstinting assistance. We are indebted to Elaine Linden of Dickenson for enhancing the readability of this book. The typing assistance of Pat Chatham, Joan Nielsen, and Helen Way is greatly appreciated. Finally, we are especially grateful to our respective wives, Sandra P. Epstein and Dorothy A. Hampton, who handled the permissions correspondence and numerous additional research and editorial chores, and, most importantly, maintained the morale of their spouses throughout this project.

Edwin M. Epstein

David R. Hampton

NOTES

[1]Alfred North Whitehead, *Adventures of Ideas* (New York: The Macmillan Company), p. 124.

[2]Throughout this book, we shall use the adjective "black" and the noun "blacks" rather than "Negro" or "Negroes" in referring to Afro-Americans, although the latter terms are employed in many of the selections which appear here. We are aware that within the black (or Negro, or Afro-American) community, there is considerable disagreement regarding which term to use. Since, however, "black" appears to be most favored by the young to whom this book is primarily addressed and since "black" has come to be associated with the peaceful revolution of the 1960s and 1970s to alter the historical status quo of inequality between white Americans and those of African origin, it seems particularly appropriate to use it in this book, concerned as it is with the subject of social and economic change in American society.

[3]Kenneth B. Clark, "What Business Can Do for the Negro," *Nation's Business,* Vol. 55 (October, 1967), p. 68.

[4]See Frederick D. Sturdivant (ed.), *The Ghetto Market Place* (New York: The Free Press, 1969); Herbert Hill (with Arthur M. Ross), *Employment, Race and Poverty* (New York: Harcourt Brace & World, 1967); Herbert R. Northrup, *Organized Labor and the Negro* (New York: Harper & Row, 1944); Ray Marshall, *The Negro and Organized Labor* (New York: John Wiley & Sons, 1965); and Louis A. Ferman, Joyce L. Kornbluh, and J. A. Miller (eds.), *Negros and Jobs: A Book of Readings* (Ann Arbor: The University of Michigan Press, 1968).

[5]See Milton M. Gordon, *Assimilation in American Life* (New York: Oxford University Press, 1964); Nathan Glazer and Daniel Patrick Moynihan, *Beyond the Melting Pot: The Negroes, Puerto Ricans, Jews, Italians, and Irish of New York City* (Cambridge, Mass: M.I.T. Press, 1963); Oscar and Mary Handlin, *The Uprooted* (Little Brown, 1951); Oscar Handlin, *Race and Nationality in American Life* (Garden City, N.Y.: Doubleday, 1957); John Hope Franklin (ed.), *Color and Race* (Boston: Beacon Press, 1968, 1969); Louis Wirth, "The Problem of Minority Groups," in Ralph Linton (ed.), *The Science of Man in the World Crisis* (New York: Columbia University Press, 1945), pp. 347-372; and George Easton Simpson and J. Milton Yinger, *Racial and Cultural Minorities: An Analysis of Prejudice and Discrimination,* 3rd ed., (New York: Harper & Row, 1965).

PART 1

A PRIMER ON AMERICA: BLACK AND WHITE

A generation ago Gunnar Myrdal characterized the historical relationship existing in the United States between blacks and whites as "an American Dilemma."[1] The dilemma suggested by Myrdal was the struggle between the democratic ideals of equality basic to the American creed and the chronic inequality in the treatment of the black 10 (now approximately 11) percent of American society.[2] While this dilemma has been manifest in all aspects of the American scene, perhaps nowhere has its existence been more obvious—and more paradoxical—than in the economic life of the United States. In the words of one observer:

The Negro lives and works in the backwaters and eddies of the national economy in the United States. This has been true since he arrived on these shores long before the colonies became a nation. In recent years, Negroes have made a number of vigorous advances in their efforts to enter the mainstream of economic activity. However, they remain at best a marginal factor in virtually every field, except those protected by the legacy of racial segregation and discrimination.[3]

No matter what measure is used to compare the relative economic statuses of black and white Americans—employment rates, occupation, income, union membership, business ownership, consumer costs, financing charges—blacks as a cohort within American society come off a clear second best. While in recent years, a few blacks have achieved certain economic "firsts," as a recent federal document emphasized, "it should be noted—and stressed—that Negroes generally remain very far behind whites in most social and economic categories."[4]

America has frequently been called a "business civilization"—a society in which economic values, economic institutions, and economic considerations assume profound importance in structuring the life, culture, and social priorities of the nation. Although this characterization of the United States is somewhat less accurate today than in the past, there is no gainsaying that Americans have tended generally to be "econocentric" in perspective—that is, we Americans have been prone to view as axiomatic (in terms of both social necessity and legitimacy) the central role of the economy in shaping the total character and in determining the priorities of the society. During this nation's history, business needs have frequently been assigned higher national priority than competing social claims. American business ideology has always stressed the view that the greatness of American society is directly attributable to the characteristics of our economic system.[5] Indeed, the explicit criteria commonly used by politicians and the popular press alike for measuring national "greatness" or "success" have been economic, for example, productivity, efficiency, per capita income, growth in GNP.

The most important reason for America's greatness, according to business ideology, is the existence of a free market system in which maximum economic (and social) utility results from each individual seeking to maximize his economic interests. Indeed, the emergence of a capitalistic system in its American context is considered to be the apogee of individual freedom. Social class and mobility are, supposedly, based on *achievement* rather than *ascription* as in traditional, nonindustrial societies such as feudal or royalist Europe or some contemporary Middle East countries where social status is ascribed or determined at birth. In describing and analyzing this system, economists generally have ignored factors such as social class, ethnicity, or race as being irrelevant to the functioning of the economy.[6] The economic system is presumed to be neutral—or color blind—with regard to the economic roles of the individuals within the society; the only critical factor, theoretically, is that economic tasks essential for the survival of the society must be performed. And, by and large, social mobility in America has been on the basis of achievement, although, most certainly, not to the extent that our folk ideology of a "classless" society would have us believe. At least this is how it has operated for many white Americans. As sociologist Neil J. Smelser notes, however, "In practice, of course, ascribed characteristics, especially racial ones, prevent the operation of this system in pure form."[7]

ECONOMICS AND RACISM: A PARADOX

Indeed, the failure of this system to operate in "pure form" is both a manifestation and a consequence of the existence of racism among white Americans throughout our national history. By racism we mean (1) the distribution of status, power, and wealth within a society on the basis of color, ethnicity, or other ascribed group characteristics; and (2) the subordination of, maintenance of control over, and oppression of low status color, ethnic, or otherwise differentiated groups by those not possessing the particular (negative) characteristics.[8]

America has been characterized throughout its history, in the words of historian John Hope Franklin, by the existence of "the two worlds of race,"[9] with regard to both the attitudes and behavior of individuals and the operations of American institutions. It is no accident that the National Commission on Civil Disorders viewed white racism as being "essentially responsible for the explosive mixture which has been accumulating in our cities since the end of World War II."[10]

The paradoxical quality of the relationship between the black American and the American economy is that although the economic model assumes the mobility of the human factors of production and although American democratic ideology assumes the right—and indeed the obligation—of each man to maximize his economic and, consequently his social position, neither the model nor the ideology have included the black American. Despite his continued presence within the society and his role in performing some of its essential economic tasks since the second decade of the seventeenth century, he has been viewed as being somehow extraneous to the society—in but not of the society.

The black man was brought to America as a slave and his inferior position was explicitly recognized in the United States Constitution, particularly in Article 1, Section 2 which provided that for purposes of representation and direct taxes, slaves should be counted as three-fifths of a person. His economic role was to serve as a cheap source of labor for agricultural and, later on, manufacturing interests located predominantly in the South but spread across the United States. Recent students of American economic history have recognized the important contribution of slavery to the rapid growth of the American economy during the antebellum period.[11]

Following Emancipation, the economic role of the black American continued to be determined by his status as a black man, not by the requirements of a racially neutral economic system. Although some blacks in the South had become an important part of the skilled nonagricultural labor force before the Civil War, working as artisans and mechanics in a variety of crafts and trades after Reconstruction, blacks were virtually excluded from such occupations and restricted to "colored" jobs which were always the worst available in any given labor market. While this condition was particularly true in the South, it was almost as pronounced in the North, especially after the heavy influx of immigrant labor from Europe began in the 1870s[12] It can be argued convincingly that as a purely economic proposition, discrimination was and is suboptimal in terms of national economic growth; however, economic optimization has been subsidiary to other considerations.[13]

Racial job patterns had a strong caste element about them. Slavery and color marked the Negro as an inferior person; therefore, whites considered it improper for Negroes to compete directly with them for the better jobs. It was especially unthinkable that Negroes should hold supervisory positions over whites.[14]

The pattern of economic subordination described above has persisted to this day, although its specific manifestations have changed.

Ironically, those who wished to justify the relegation of the black American to a position of inferiority considered themselves to have received the imprimatur of one leading spokesman of the black community when in 1895 Booker T. Washington, in his famous "Atlanta Compromise" speech delivered at the Atlanta Cotton States and International Exposition, urged his fellow blacks to "cast down your bucket where you are . . . in agriculture, mechanics, in commerce, in domestic service, and in the professions . . . [and to recognize that] . . . it is at the bottom of life we must begin, and not at the top."[15] However, it was Washington who urged blacks to strive for economic mobility as the means for achieving social equality and sought to stimulate the establishment and growth of black enterprise by founding the National Negro Business League in 1900.

During the twentieth century blacks began slowly to enter the mainstream of the industrial economy. Several factors have been critical to the meager progress which has occurred. They include the rapid expansion of industrialization and the economic growth of the United States since the turn of the century; the shutting off of the immigration of foreign labor during the 1920s; the swelling migration of blacks from the South to the North and West; and the need by manufacturers of alternative sources of manpower during the world wars and periods of industrial unrest (as strike breakers). As in all relations with the white world, however, the economic position of the black has remained marginal and precarious—he is still the "last to be hired and the first to be fired." While, as a group, blacks today may be better off in terms of socioeconomic status relative to blacks living a half century ago, or to the poor of underdeveloped nations, when compared with contemporary white Americans (the only relevant reference point), blacks have experienced but little improvement in their condition. As economist Rashi Fein has pointed out:

In many respects the Negro is today living in a world the white has long since left behind. The gains the Negro has made and is making are substantial—all indicators are advancing. The real situation today is better than it once was. Nevertheless, we dare not overestimate the extent of these gains or underestimate the distance still to be covered.

Though the gains are large relative to where an earlier generation of Negroes stood, they are often more limited if the comparison is made of non-white indicators relative to those for whites. In such comparisons . . . we often find that the differential between white and non-whites has been widening in recent years. [16]

CHANGING BLACK SELF-PERCEPTION

The self-perception of the black man in the overall context of American society is critical to any discussion of the relative socioeconomic condition of blacks and whites in the United States. Historically, the experience of being black in a white and fundamentally hostile environment continually reinforced a negative self-image. The structural inability of the black male to fulfill the normal masculine function of breadwinner and economic head of household and the endemic subordinate position of the black community contributed to a feeling of powerlessness and low self-esteem together with a seeming acquiescence in what was viewed as an immutable system. At the same time, the black man repressed, for his own safety, a sense of rage over the inequities of the situation in which he found himself. Black psychiatrists William H. Grier and Price M. Cobbs stressed this critical fact in their recent study, *Black Rage*, stating, "Of the things that need knowing, none is more important than that all blacks are angry. White Americans seem not to recognize it." [17] This anger was typically inner-directed; however, its primary focus, though seldom externalized, was upon the white man.

Examining specifically the economic implications of this negative black self-perception, we can see that while the black American looked enviously upon the more favorable socioeconomic condition of the white man, and, indeed, in the case of the black middle class, emulated white life styles, he did not until recently envision himself sharing in the largesse of the system, except for occasional scraps. He was basically in the position of an outsider looking longingly into the window of the white world, while compelled realistically to view his socioeconomic position solely in relation to that of other blacks, present and past. In his classic analysis of the black middle class, *Black Bourgeoisie*, the late E. Franklin Frazier made the point with great impact:

The black bourgeoisie in the United States is an essentially American phenomenon. Its emergence and its rise to importance within the Negro community are closely tied up with economic and social changes in the American community. Its behavior as well as its mentality is a reflection of American modes of behavior and American values. What may appear as distortions of American patterns of behavior and thought are due to the fact that the Negro lives on the margin of American society. The very existence of a separate Negro community with its own institutions within the heart of the American society is indicative of its quasi-pathological character, especially since the persistence of this separate community has been due to racial discrimination and oppression. [18]

At best the black bourgeoisie was historically a marginal middle class on the periphery of the larger white society. What is equally as important, in their heart of hearts most of the members of this class and their poorer black brethren saw little alternative to the seemingly immutable white-dominated social order.

Since the end of World War II, however, the psychological situation of black Americans has altered dramatically. Acquiescence to "the system" has given way to increasingly aggressive efforts to confront it and to change it. We recognize there were antecedents to this development in the period between the two great wars.

Particularly significant among them were the organization and growth of the Universal Negro Improvement Association under the leadership of Marcus Moses Garvey; the Harlem Renaissance of the 1920s (also known as the Black Renaissance or New Negro Movement); the increasingly aggressive activities, particularly on the legal front, of such organizations as the National Association for the Advancement of Colored People and the National Urban League; and the continuous impact of the activist-intellectual Dr. W. E. B. DuBois during the entire period. However, in the main, these factors (with the exception of Garvey's U.N.I.A.) mobilized relatively few blacks, particularly outside of the North, and did not result in dramatic and concerted efforts to confront the white society. The emergence of a widespread psychological readiness to confront white America awaited the decades of the 1950s and 1960s.[19]

The reasons underlying the change of attitude on the part of many black Americans from acquiescence to aggressiveness have been analyzed in innumerable books and essays.[20] We will only summarize those factors which to us appear most important.

1. The psychological impact of World War II resulted in many blacks leaving the South for the first time to enter military service and being thrust into a world in which old taboos and traditional forms of social control were no longer operative. Upon returning home some blacks were unwilling to bend to old constraints.

2. A second but related impact of the war was that many blacks became even more acutely aware of the paradoxical fact that while fighting abroad, so they were told, to preserve democracy and oppose totalitarianism, they lacked at home much of the freedom and many of the rights which they were expected to obtain for others. If the Four Freedoms (freedom of speech, freedom of religion, freedom from want, and freedom from fear) were to be fought for abroad, they should, many blacks reasoned, be practiced at home. It is noteworthy that a succeeding generation of blacks (and whites) has adopted this reasoning with regard to the Southeast Asian conflict.[21]

3. World War II also had a number of subsidiary effects:

    a.   The Armed Services were a decidedly masculine environment and provided more opportunity for sanctioned aggressiveness than the society itself.

    b.   Military service resulted in some blacks acquiring skills in a variety of occupations and crafts which subsequently they sought to utilize in civilian life.

    c.   Blacks were employed in defense and war jobs in industries not previously open to them during peacetime. Although their positions were generally at the bottom of the employment ladder, for the first time they obtained access to substantial numbers of industrial positions.

    d.   A number of blacks remained in the military at the conclusion of World War II, and eventually achieved senior enlisted ranks or middle levels of officer status. Accordingly, the armed services offered, at least for some blacks, an opportunity for economic security and social mobility not present in civilian society.

    e.   Some few blacks were able to benefit from the G.I. Bill and thereby obtain a college education which, otherwise, would have been unavailable to them. This educated cadre has begun to play a significant leadership role within the black community.

4. The migration of blacks from the South to the North and West reached its highest levels in the decade and a half following World War II. Left behind were the rigid constraints of the South for the relatively more relaxed racial mores and prohibitions of the rest of the country. As a consequence, blacks began to see

themselves more in the perspective of the total society and not simply as a caste apart from the rest of Americans. Another consequence of migration was to increase the potential political power of blacks in the metropolitan centers where they were located. Recently, blacks have begun to utilize the power to elect officials and representatives at the local, state, and federal levels.

5. The emergence of the new African nations presented blacks (and whites) with a more positive image of the abilities and potential of people of color than they had entertained before. As a result, positive group identity and pride in color began to develop among blacks in America, along with an emboldened vision regarding the realm of possible achievement within this country.

6. The genesis of these new nations, together with the spread of nationalism in predominantly nonwhite areas of Asia, the Middle East, and Latin America, made it necessary for the federal government to concern itself increasingly with the position of minorities (particularly blacks) at home in an effort to woo the allegiance of the "third world" in the cold war competition with Russia. Discrimination against or repression of black Americans could hardly endear the United States to black Africans or other peoples of color. The United States could, moreover, ill afford to have African and other nonwhite diplomats treated poorly while in this country.

7. Signal advances by blacks in a number of highly visible fields have increased the expectation level of the black population as a whole. Professional major league and collegiate sports, television, motion pictures, the stage, concert hall and opera, both houses of Congress, the federal and state benches, the United States cabinet and the Supreme Court have, since 1946, come to include black Americans.

8. As a result of federal, state, and local legislation, judicial decisions, and executive orders, significant advances in the legal status of black Americans have taken place. The developments have resulted in the elimination of state-sanctioned discriminatory practices and have proclaimed as governmental policy that all men—including blacks—are considered to be equal before the law. While the various civil rights acts, voter registration laws, fair housing, equal opportunity acts, reapportionment decisions, civil rights cases, and presidential proclamations have not resulted in the elimination of discrimination, they have at least created an environment in which discriminatory practices are viewed as wrong and illegal. In this context, the political and psychological impact of the 1954 decision of the Supreme Court in *Brown v. Board of Education of Topeka, Kansas,* 347 U.S. 483 (1954), overthrowing the "separate but equal" doctrine which had constituted the judicial rationale for state-enforced segregation for over a half century, has been monumental. This is true notwithstanding the fact that in many communities the court's mandate has yet to be implemented.

9. The postwar dispersion of blacks within the United States and the singular impact of the television medium has exposed white America and its wealth to black eyes as never before, and has heightened yet further black desires to share in this wealth. The impact of media is likely to be even more important in the years ahead.

10. Particular combinations of men and events have acted as catalytic agents to changing black attitudes—the sit-ins and freedom marches of black college students; charismatic leaders such as the Rev. Dr. Martin Luther King, Jr. and Malcolm X; and black intellectuals and writers ranging from James Baldwin to Eldridge Cleaver. In different ways, this leadership group has energized collective (and frequently militant) black action, increased black pride, and has created an awareness that whites are neither omnipotent nor free from fear of the black potential. In turn, this awareness has resulted in increased confidence among blacks in their relations with whites.

In the economic sphere especially the black American no longer judges his position simply in terms of other blacks. Rather, his point of reference is now the larger white society in which he is situated and his basis for comparison is how his lot stacks up against whites whom he sees around him. In short, he sees himself as entitled to be a full participant in the American economy and to enjoy the fruits of affluence which he observes about him. Comparisons with how favorably he is doing relative to the average Bolivian, Ghanaian, or Egyptian are irrelevant; his concern is with how his socioeconomic status places him alongside the average white citizen in the community where he lives, be it Atlanta, Boston, Houston, or San Diego.

One result of this new and broadened perspective is that blacks have been experiencing what social psychologists term a sense of "relative deprivation." Thomas F. Pettigrew explains the concept:

> When we talk about social motivation, we are not talking of hunger, thirst, or the other basic physiological drives, but what an individual has, not in absolute terms, but in relation to what he aspires to. It refers to what he realistically and rightfully expects to attain . . . thus after twenty years of progress, particularly in certain areas, the Negro is nevertheless considerably more frustrated today than he was at the beginning of this period of change because, while his absolute standard has been going up, his aspiration level has been rising much faster. His relative deprivation level, the difference between what he has and what he expects to have and what he thinks is his right to have is now probably greater than at any other time in American history.[22]

Blacks compared with blacks have indeed made some progress over the last few years; compared with whites, however, the improvement has not been impressive.[23]

This new perspective of black progress, while frustrating, is a very healthy development since it indicates that many blacks are striving for collective social mobility within the society and view it as attainable. For whites, the new relationship constitutes both a threat and a challenge: a threat since if their aspirations are not fulfilled, many blacks are determined to seek economic and social change through any effective means—including, as a last resort, violence; a challenge since the time is upon us to see, once and for all, if American society and its institutions are sufficiently open to accommodate to pressure for social change "with all deliberate speed" and in a peaceful fashion. A black sociologist put it succinctly in a recent book:

> The extent to which the society is able to avoid increased racial conflict depends upon the willingness of white Americans to come to terms with the reality of the Negro's status and the requirements for improving this status.[24]

These remarks are particularly pertinent to our business institutions because of their overriding importance to the social and economic life of this country.

THE PAST ROLE OF THE BUSINESS COMMUNITY

In the above pages we have made some general comments concerning the relationship between black Americans and the United States economy. However, the emphasis of this volume is upon a particular sector of the economy—the business community. By "business" we mean those institutions and organizations for the conduct of economic activity which are privately as opposed to governmentally owned, and whose ordinary decisions are made by owners or managers rather than by public officials. By way of illustration, we consider McDonnell-Douglas, the Bank of America, United Airlines, and Federated Department Stores to be business organizations, while we do not so consider the National Aeronautical and Space Administration, the Federal Reserve Bank of Cleveland, the Military Air Transport

Service, and the General Services Administration, although they may perform economic functions which are rather similar. We are aware, however, that the viability of the distinction between "business" (private) and "governmental" (public) organizations has been particularly subject to question in recent years with the growth of the "interdependent," "pluralistic," or "mixed" economy, or, to use John Kenneth Galbraith's term, the "industrial state" in which privately owned firms perform what are essentially public tasks.[25]

We do not wish to suggest that the business sector is monolithic, comprised only of large, national or multinational firms. The corner grocery, gasoline station, realtor, insurance agency, appliance dealer, and brokerage house also constitute "business" and are integral components of the economic life of the nation. However, our emphasis upon the activities of large corporations reflects their overriding importance to our society in performing the productive, distributive, and service tasks which are essential to the maintenance of an industrial nation. It also reflects the fact that the past and, unfortunately, often the present operations of these firms as employers and as provider of goods, services, housing, and capital have contributed to the unfavorable condition in which the great majority of black Americans find themselves. Finally, it suggests that the present and future policies of large enterprises will go a long way toward determining whether black America will, indeed, achieve economic parity with the white society. As *Fortune* editor Max Ways stated a few years ago, "In the United States, the role of business is so important that it cannot escape a large share of responsibility for the health of the society."[26] It is ironic that these words were written not by a Marxist theoretician but by a writer for a respected business publication seeking to preserve a capitalistic socioeconomic order.

BUSINESS AND THE BLACK COMMUNITY: A RELATIONSHIP OF NEGATIVE IMBALANCE

It is our contention that the relationship between black Americans and the business community has been one of *negative imbalance*. In all aspects of business life—as employees, as consumers of goods, services, capital and housing, as entrepreneurs establishing businesses in the far-flung sectors of the American economy—blacks, as we have seen, have historically occupied an inferior and subordinate position. Just as they have been relegated to marginal roles in all other aspects of American life, blacks have been shunted to the nether world of the United States economy. Indeed, it is arguable that it is this very economic subordination which today underlies much of the pathology which characterizes black life in white America. The above statements are not written to create a sense of guilt in our white readers but to indicate our perception of the reality of the economic position of the black American. Lest, however, whites reading this book have any doubts concerning this matter, the black community does, indeed, adjudge white business guilty of creating and perpetuating the social and economic negative imbalance from which it has suffered.

A corollary proposition is that the historical relationship of negative imbalance which has existed between black Americans and white business must be redressed. This inequity is so patently obvious and so manifestly borne out by the materials presented in this book that it is unnecessary to belabor it here. We wish to assure the reader that we have not sought to "stack the deck" by selecting only materials which present the white business community in an unfavorable light. Rather, we are attempting to "tell it like it is," and, unfortunately, the tale is not a pleasant one. On purely moral grounds, therefore, we consider it beyond cavil that the business community must redress its relationship with black Americans if American democratic ideology is to retain any validity.

We stated earlier that (moral considerations aside) the present condition of negative imbalance between black Americans and the business community is unhealthy for the total society. Let us more closely examine its consequences. It is bad business, since it has limited the economic potential of black Americans as consumers—as a market—and as producers—both as employees of white business firms and as businessmen who could establish and build substantial economic enterprises. Thus, in the above ways, business discrimination against the black man is economically dysfunctional. More importantly, however, it is a source of exacerbation which has contributed to the social tension manifest between blacks and whites in the United States today. Black Americans have clearly demonstrated in the past few years that they no longer feel obligated or willing to acquiesce to the historical pattern of economic and social subordination. On the contrary, they are prepared to do all that is necessary to obtain full equality within the system or—failing this goal because of the intransigence of white society in general and the business community in particular—to seek the destruction of the existing economic order. The cliché of the times is "a fair share of the pie—or, no pie at all." It is questionable that blacks could, by themselves, destroy our economic institutions. It is, however, indisputable that the governmental efforts necessary to thwart such an attempt would be so repressive— amounting to civil war—that they would have untoward effects extending far beyond the realm of economics—would, indeed, corrupt the very character of American life.

Thus, it appears to us, the business community has the alternative of being an agent of positive and peaceful social change, or a prime catalyst of the forces of social upheaval. It is our hope that by sensitizing the businessman and the prospective businessman to the critical issues at stake, we can contribute to the realization of the first alternative and minimize the possibility of the latter.

SUMMARY

We are not suggesting that all of the problems experienced by black Americans are economic in origin or are to be placed upon the doorstep of American business. Nor are we suggesting that if the economic status of blacks was to improve dramatically that the total pathology characteristic of their situation in American society would be corrected overnight. One needs only to consider the exacerbations which would remain in such areas as health and mortality; access to and quality of education; residential segregation; police relations and the operations of our legal system; the anachronisms and inequities of the welfare system; and the persistence of racist attitudes on the part of some (white and black) Americans. We are suggesting, however, that there is a large economic component in each of these social problem areas. Social mobility and political effectiveness in American society are in large measure a function of economic success. Indicative of the social health of any group— and of the society as a whole—is its economic condition.

In the past, the functioning of our business institutions has both reflected and constituted racism in the economic context. Race has been *the* prime determinant of the relationship of negative imbalance between black Americans and whites in what is commonly designated as our "free enterprise" system. Accordingly, this system must bear its fair share of accountability for the social malaise which has afflicted black Americans and white society.

The manner and rate in which the economic advancement of black Americans will take place will be largely determined by the almost totally white business community.[27] If business's responsibility is borne well then the prediction of the Kerner Commission that "our nation is moving toward two societies, one black, one white— separate and unequal,"[28] will be disproved and we shall have a society in which blacks and whites alike will share equally in the enjoyment of, and control over, our national wealth. At such time as this objective is achieved, the title of this book will be rendered absurd, and the dichotomy upon which it is premised will have disappeared.

NOTES

[1]Gunnar Myrdal, with the assistance of Richard Sterner and Arnold Rose, *An American Dilemma* (New York: Harper & Row, 1944), esp. pp. LXIX-LXXXIII. While Myrdal's description of the condition of the black American has received virtually unanimous acceptance, his thesis concerning the existence of an "American Dilemma" has been challenged. See, e.g., Oliver Cromwell Cox, *Caste, Class and Race: A Study in Social Dynamics* (New York: Monthly Review Press, 1959) esp. pp. 509-538.

[2]One caveat is necessary. We are aware that, as is true with all group generalizations, our continuous references to a collective entity, *black Americans,* does not portray accurately the socioeconomic status, aspirations, state of mind, or other salient factors of particular members of the group. Blacks, no more than whites, do not constitute a hundred percent monolithic block within our society. However, we are convinced on the basis of our research that the facts, observations, and materials appearing in the following pages present a valid description and analysis of the condition of the overwhelming majority of blacks living within the United States. Accordingly, for the purposes of this book, we consider our generalizations to be warranted.

[3]Andrew F. Brimmer, "The Negro in the National Economy," in John P. Davis (ed.), *The American Negro Reference Book* (Englewood Cliffs, N.J.: Prentice-Hall, 1966), p. 251.

[4]U.S. Department of Labor, Bureau of Labor Statistics and U.S. Department of Commerce, Bureau of the Census, *Recent Trends in Social and Economic Conditions of Negroes in the United States,* Current Population Reports, series P-23, No. 26 BLS Report No. 347 (Washington, D.C.: U.S. Government Printing Office, July 1968), p.v.

[5]For a discussion of this point see, e.g., Francis X. Sutton, *et al, The American Business Creed* (New York: Schocken Books, 1962), esp. Chapter 2.

[6]In recent years, however, economists have paid increasing attention to the importance of slavery and racial discrimination to the economic development of the United States. See, e.g., various numbers of Working Paper Series—Southern Economic History Project, Richard C. Sutch and Roger L. Ransom (Principal Investigators) published by The Institute of Business and Economic Research, University of California, Berkeley. See also sources cited in footnotes 11 and 13.

[7]Neil J. Smelser, *The Sociology of Economic Life* (Englewood Cliffs, N.J.: Prentice-Hall, 1963), p. 66.

[8]For discussions of the nature and sources of racism, see: John Hope Franklin (ed.) *Color and Race* (Boston: Beacon Press, 1968); Talcott Parsons and Kenneth B. Clark (eds), *The Negro American* (Boston: Beacon Press, 1965, 1966); Robin M. Williams, Jr. *American Society: A Sociological Interpretation,* 3rd ed. (New York: Alfred A. Knopf, 1970), pp. 498-500; Gunnar Myrdal, *An American Dilemma,* esp. pp. 3-153; Gordon W. Allport, *The Nature of Prejudice* (Cambridge, Mass.: Addison-Wesley, 1954); Winthrop D. Jordan, *White Over Black: American Attitudes Toward the Negro, 1550-1812* (Baltimore, Md: Penguin Books, 1968); Kenneth M. Stampp, *The Peculiar Institution: Slavery in the Ante-Bellum South* (New York: Vintage Books, 1956); Hannah Arendt, *The Origins of Totalitarianism* (Cleveland: The World Publishing Company, 1958); Oscar Handlin, *Race and Nationality in American Life* (Garden City, N.Y.: Doubleday & Company, 1957); George Eaton Simpson and Milton J. Yinger, *Racial and Cultural Minorities: An Analysis of Prejudice and Discrimination,* 3rd ed. (New York: Harper & Row, 1965); Thomas F. Gossett, *Race: The History of an Idea in America* (New York: Schocken Books, 1963); John Dollard, *Caste and Class in a Southern Town* (Garden City, N.Y.: Doubleday and Company, 1949); Stokely Carmichael and Charles V. Hamilton, *Black Power: The Politics of Liberation in America* (New York: Vintage Books, 1967), pp. 2-32; *Report of the National Advisory Commission on Civil Disorders,* Kerner Commission Report (New York: Bantam Books, 1968), pp. 203-206; and W. J. Cash, *The Mind of the South,* (New York: Vintage Books, 1941).

[9]John Hope Franklin, "The Two Worlds of Race," in Parsons and Clark, *The Negro American,* pp. 47-68.

[10]*Report,* National Advisory Commission on Civil Disorders, p. 203.

[11]The issue of the profitability of slavery and the contribution of the institution to American economic development has long been a concern of economists and historians. Several recent essays summarize the discussion. See, e.g., Stanley L. Engerman, "The Effects of Slavery Upon the Southern Economy: A Review of the Recent Debate," *Explorations in Entrepreneurial History/ Second Series,* V.4, N.2 (Winter 1967), pp. 71-97, and essays in "The Structure of the Cotton Economy of the Antebellum South," *Agricultural History,* V. XLIV, N 1. (January 1970), pp. 1-165. See also, Alfred H. Conrad and John R. Meyer, *The Economics of Slavery: And Other Studies in Econometric History* (Chicago: Aldine Publishing Company, 1964), pp. 43-114; Eugene D. Genovese, *The Political Economy of Slavery: Studies on the Economy and*

Society of the Slave South (New York: Pantheon Books, 1965); Ulrich B. Phillips, *American Negro Slavery* (New York: Appleton, 1918); Douglas C. North, *The Economic Growth of the United States 1790-1860* (Englewood Cliffs, N.J.: Prentice-Hall, 1961); Kenneth M. Stampp: *The Peculiar Institution: Slavery in the Ante-Bellum South* (New York: Vintage Books, 1956), pp. 383-418; Robert W. Fogel and Stanley L. Engerman, *The Reinterpretation of American Economic History* (New York: Harper & Row, Forthcoming); Robert S. Starobin, "The Economics of Industrial Slavery in the Old South," *Business History Review*, V. XLIV, N.2 (Summer 1970), pp. 131-174; and ——, *Industrial Slavery in the Old South* (New York, Oxford University Press, 1970); and Richard C. Wade, *Slavery in the Cities: The South 1820-1860* (New York; Oxford University Press, Inc, 1964).

[12] For accounts of the establishment of "job ceilings," see W. E. B. DuBois, *The Philadelphia Negro: A Social Study* (New York: Schocken Books, 1967), pp. 97-146 and 322-355; St. Clair Drake and Horace R. Cayton, *Black Metropolis: A Study of Negro Life in a Northern City*, VI, Rev. ed. (New York: Harper & Row, 1962), pp. 214-262; Allan H. Spear, *Black Chicago: The Making of a Negro Ghetto, 1890-1920* (Chicago: University of Chicago Press, 1967), pp. 29-49; and Herman D. Bloch, *The Circle of Discrimination: An Economic and Social Study of the Black Man in New York* (New York: New York University Press, 1969).

[13] Lester C. Thurow, *Poverty and Discrimination* (Washington, D.C.: The Brookings Institution, 1969), esp. pp. 111-138. See also, Gary A. Becker, *The Economics of Discrimination*, (Chicago: University of Chicago Press, 1957); Harold Demetz, "Minorities in the Market Place," *North Carolina Law Review*, V. 43, N. 2 (February 1965), pp. 271-297, esp. p. 277; John Paul Formby, "The Economics of Discrimination—A Normative Approach," (Unpublished Ph.D. Dissertation, University of Colorado, 1965); and Albert and Roberta Wohlstetter, "Third Worlds Abroad and at Home," *The Public Interest*, N. 14 (Winter 1969), pp. 88-107.

[14] Ray Marshall, *The Negro Worker*, (New York: Random House, 1967), pp. 8-9.

[15] Booker T. Washington, "The Atlanta Exposition Address," quoted in Hugh Hawkins (ed.), *Booker T. Washington and His Critics: The Problem of Negro Leadership* (Lexington, Mass.: D. C. Heath and Company, 1962), p. 16. The portrayal of Booker T. Washington as a black accommodationist of white racism has been challenged by both his contemporaries and historians. See, e.g., essays in Hawkins (ed.) *Booker T. Washington and his Critics;* August Meier, "Toward a Reinterpretation of Booker T. Washington," *Journal of Southern History*, XXIII, (May 1957), pp. 220-227; and Harold Cruse, *Rebellion or Revolution* (New York: William Morrow & Company, 1968), pp. 74-96 and 193-258.

[16] Rashi Fein, "An Economic and Social Profile of the Negro American," *Daedalus*, V. 94, N. 4 (Fall 1965), p. 839; reprinted in Parsons and Clark, *The Negro American*, p. 126.

[17] William H. Grier and Price M. Cobbs, *Black Rage* (New York: Basic Books, 1968), p. 4.

[18] E. Franklin Frazier, *Black Bourgeoisie: The Rise of a New Middle Class*, (New York: The Free Press, 1957), pp. 233-234.

[19] For additional historical discussion, we refer the reader to sources cited in note 20.

[20] For readers interested in additional discussion of the causes underlying altered expectations among blacks following World War II, we recommend the following works: John P. Davis, (ed.), *The American Negro Reference Book* (Englewood Cliffs, N.J.: Prentice-Hall, 1966); John Hope Franklin, *From Slavery to Freedom: A History of Negro Americans*, 3rd ed. (New York: Vintage Books, 1967); Talcott Parsons and Kenneth B. Clark, *The Negro American*, (Boston: Houghton Mifflin Company, 1966); Kenneth Clark, *Dark Ghetto*, (New York: Harper & Row, 1965); Eldridge Cleaver, *Soul on Ice*, (New York: McGraw-Hill Book Company, 1968); Robert L. Allen, *Black Awakening in White America* (Garden City, N.Y.: Doubleday & Company, 1969); Malcolm X, *The Autobiography of Malcolm X*, (New York: Grove Press, 1964); Stokely Carmichael and Charles Hamilton, *Black Power: The Politics of Liberation in America* (New York: Vintage Books, 1967); Robin M. Williams, Sr., "Social Change and Social Conflict: Race Relations in the United States, 1944-1964," *Sociological Inquiry*, V. 35, N. 1 (Winter 1965), pp. 8-25; Harold Cruse, *The Crisis of the Negro Intellectual* (New York: William Morrow and Company, 1967), and *Rebellion or Revolution* (New York: William Morrow and Company, 1968); William H. Grier and Price M. Cobbs, *Black Rage* (New York: Basic Books, 1968); Nathan Wright, Jr., *Black Power and Urban Unrest* (New York: Hawthorn Books, 1967); James Baldwin, *Notes of a Native Son* (Boston: Beacon Press, 1955), and *The Fire Next Time* (New York: Dial Press, 1963); W. E. B. DuBois, *The Souls of Black Folk* (Greenwich, Conn.: Fawcett Publications 1961); Leonard Broom and Norval Glenn, *Transformation of the Negro American* (New York: Harper & Row, 1965); Charles E. Silberman, *Crisis in Black and White* (New York: Vintage Books, 1964); "Protest in the Sixties," *The Annals of Social Science*, V. 382 (March 1969); Thomas F. Pettigrew, *A Profile of the Negro American* (Pendleton, N.J.: Van Nostrand and Company, 1964); "The Negro Protest," *The Annals of the American Academy of Political and Social Science*, V. 357 (January 1965); Lewis Killian and Charles Grigg, *Racial Crisis in America: Leadership in Conflict* (Englewood Cliffs, N.J.: Prentice-Hall, 1964); Alphonso Pinkney, *Black Americans* (Englewood Cliffs, N.J.: Prentice-Hall, 1969); and *Report of the National Advisory Commission on Civil Disorders*, Kerner Commission (New York: Bantam Books, 1968); Louis E. Lomax, *The Negro Revolt* (New York: Signet Books, 1962, 1963); E. U. Essiem-Udom, *Black Nationalism: A Search for Identity in America* (New York: Dell Publishing Co., 1962); C. Eric Lincoln, *The Black Muslims in America* (Boston: Beacon Press, 1961); Arthur I. Waskow, *From Race Riot to Sit-In, 1919 and the 1960's*, (New York: Doubleday and Company, 1966); Jerome H. Skolnick, *The Politics of Protest* (New York: Ballantine Books, 1969); Harold W. Pfautz, "The New 'New Negro': Emerging American" in *Phylon* (Winter 1963), V. XXIV, N.4, pp. 360-368; August Meier and

Elliott Rudwick (eds.), *The Making of Black America: The Black Community in Modern America,* V. II (New York: Atheneum, 1969); Francis L. Broderick and August Meier (eds.), *Negro Protest Thought in the Twentieth Century* (Indianapolis: Bobbs-Merrill, 1965); St. Clair Drake and Horace R. Cayton, *Black Metropolis: Study of Negro Life in a Northern City,* Vols. I and II, Rev. ed. (New York: Harper & Row, 1945, 1962); August Meier (ed.), *The Transformation of Activism* (Chicago: Trans-Action Books, published and distributed by Aldine Publishing Company, 1970); Harold R. Isaacs, "The Changing Identity of the Negro American," in Leonard J. Duhl (ed.), *The Urban Condition: People and Policy in the Metropolis* (New York: Simon and Schuster, 1963), pp. 275-294. This list does not purport to be all-inclusive, but is suggestive of the available literature on the subject.

[21]See, e.g., James Fendrich and Michael Pearson, "Black Veterans Return," *Trans-Action,* V. 7, N.5 (March 1970), pp. 32-37.

[22]Thomas Pettigrew, "Negro-White Confrontations," in Eli Ginsberg (ed.) *The Negro Challenge to the Business Community* (New York: McGraw-Hill Book Company, 1964), pp. 40-41. See also, Pettigrew, *A Profile of . . . ;* Robert K. Merton, *Social Theory and Social Structure,* 1968 enlarged ed. (New York: The Free Press, 1968), pp. 279-334; and S. A. Stouffac, E. A. Suchman, L. C. DeVinney, Shirley A. Star, and R. M. Williams, *The American Soldier: Studies in Social Psychology in World War II.* Vol. I, *Adjustment During Army Life* (Princeton, N.J.: Princeton University Press, 1949).

[23]The reader should appreciate there exists an inherent paradox in this sense of relative deprivation on the part of contemporary blacks. On the one hand, as was suggested previously, racial pride and a spirit of fraternity with people of color—particularly black Africans—have become important aspects of the black psyche. To this extent, black Americans consciously seek to distinguish themselves from whites and to view themselves in more global terms. At the same time, however, in evaluating the equity of their share of economic wealth, political power and social status, American blacks continue to compare themselves primarily with white Americans, their co-inhabitants within the United States. For these purposes, therefore, blacks have tended to remain parochially American, rather than worldwide in perspective. My thanks to Peter Ekeh for contributing to this insight. (E.M.E.)

[24]Alphonso Pinkney, *Black Americans,* p. 216.

[25]For additional discussion of this point see Edwin M. Epstein, *The Corporation in American Society* (Englewood Cliffs, N.J.: Prentice-Hall, 1969), pp. 38-46.

[26]Max Ways, "The Deeper Shame of the Cities," *Fortune,* V. LXXVII, N.1 (January 1968), p. 208.

[27]We do not intend by these observations to detract from the critically important role which local, state, and, particularly, the federal government will play in the futures of black Americans. Governmental policies relating to such problems as taxation, income redistribution, provision of essential social services (for example, education and training, health facilities, and low-cost housing), urban development and restoration, and minority economic development constitute the environmental context within which American business operates. It should also be pointed out, however, that business frequently influences these policies.

[28]*Report,* National Advisory Commission . . ., p 1.

2 Black Americans, Yesterday and Today: A Social and Economic Perspective

Prerequisite to understanding is perspective. Essential to perspective is a sense of history and the ability to discern relationships among seemingly disassociated social phenomena. The readings in this chapter explore some aspects of the social, political, economic, and historical background essential for a comprehension of the status of black Americans in contemporary society, providing an environmental perspective on the critical roles which economic activity and business institutions have played in shaping the life chances and life style of the black 11 percent of the population of the United States.

In the first section of the chapter, "A Mosaic of Black Views," we have included selections which convey in the words of past and present day black leaders and intellectuals, including W. E. B. DuBois, Malcolm X, William H. Grier and Price M. Cobbs, Louis E. Lomax, Ralph Ellison, LeRoi Jones, Whitney M. Young, Jr. and the Rev. Martin Luther King, Jr., recurring views and feelings concerning the condition of black men and women in American society. They serve to acquaint the reader with some of the significant social and psychological themes underlying what has been called the "Black Revolution." It is particularly significant that while the men whose views are presented here hold differing philosophical positions, ranging from pronounced militancy to quiet moderation, all express a sense of deep frustration and anger regarding the socioeconomic status of black Americans.

Although the selection "Economic Inequality," from Gunnar Myrdals' classic, *An American Dilemma*, first appeared nearly three decades ago, and a few minor factual points are slightly dated, particularly the importance of agriculture as a primary source of black employment and the overwhelming geographical concentration of America's black population in the southern United States, it is totally contemporary and insightful in analyzing the roots and manifestations of the social and economic inequality which black people experience in American society. The reading reprinted from the *Report of the National Commission on Civil Disorders* (the Kerner Commission) constitutes a source of pertinent data and an excellent summary of the quality of life in the racial ghetto measured in terms of crime rates, conditions of health, and environmental factors. Unfortunately, the conditions described in the Kerner *Report* have not altered perceptively since its publication in 1968. The final selection, "Internal Colonialism and Ghetto Revolt" by sociologist Robert Blauner, is an insightful analysis of the frequently drawn analogy between the status of blacks in the United States and the position of the subjugated peoples in areas colonized by Western nations.

When considered together with the discussion in Chapter 1, these materials constitute a comprehensive environmental matrix within which specific aspects of the complex relationship between black Americans and white business can be examined.

A MOSAIC OF BLACK VIEWS

[T]he Negro is a sort of seventh son, born with a veil, and gifted with second-sight in this American world,—a world which yields him no true self-consciousness, but only lets him see himself through the revelation of the other world. It is a peculiar sensation, this double-consciousness, this sense of always looking at one's self through the eyes of others, of measuring one's soul by the tape of a world that looks on in amused contempt and pity. One ever feels his two-ness,—an American, a Negro; two souls, two thoughts, two unreconciled strivings; two warring ideals in one dark body, whose dogged strength alone keeps it from being torn asunder.

The history of the American Negro is the history of this strife,—this longing to attain self-conscious manhood, to merge his double self into a better and truer self. In this merging he wishes neither of the older selves to be lost. He would not Africanize America, for America has too much to teach the world and Africa. He would not bleach his Negro soul in a flood of white Americanism, for he knows that Negro blood has a message for the world. He simply wishes to make it possible for a man to be both a Negro and an American, without being cursed and spit upon by his fellows, without having the doors of Opportunity closed roughly in his face.—W. E. B. DuBois, *The Souls of Black Folk* (New York: Fawcett Publications, Inc., 1961), pp. 16-17. Reprinted by permission of Mrs. Shirley Graham DuBois.

Human rights! Respect as *human beings!* That's what America's black masses want. That's the true problem. The black masses want not to be shrunk from as though they are plague-ridden. They want not to be walled up in slums, in the ghettoes, like animals. They want to live in an open, free society where they can walk with their heads up, like men and women!—*The Autobiography of Malcolm X* (New York: Grove Press, Inc., 1964), Black Cat Edition, p. 272. Copyright © 1964 by Alex Haley and Malcolm X; copyright © 1965 by Alex Haley and Betty Shabazz. Reprinted by permission of the publisher.

People bear all they can and, if required, bear even more. But if they are black in present-day America they have been asked to shoulder too much. They have had all they can stand. They will be harried no more. Turning from their tormentors, they are filled with rage.—William H. Grier and Price M. Cobbs, *Black Rage* (New York: Basic Books, Inc., 1968), pp. 1-2. Reprinted by permission of the publisher.

All American Negroes "pay dues." "Dues" is the fee one pays for being black in America. If you are a musician, "dues" is the price you pay when you see white musicians take tunes and concepts you created and make millions while you tramp the country on one-nighters; if you are a writer, "dues" is the price you pay for being relegated to "Negro" themes when your real interest could very well lie somewhere else; if you are a college professor, "dues" is what you pay for being confined, for the most part, to Negro colleges which don't afford you the academic challenge every scholar wants; if you are a college professor on an "integrated" campus, "dues" are what you pay when students make you a specialist on the Negro and approach you with sympathetic condescension; if you are just a common man—and that is what most of us are—"dues" are what you pay when rents are high, apartments are filthy, credit interest is exorbitant and white policemen patrol your community ready to crack heads at any moment. In a phrase, "dues" are the day-to-day outlay—psychological and economic—every black American must make simply because he is black. And a "lodge member," as anyone who stopped laughing at Amos and Andy long enough to think should realize, is a fellow Negro who, of course, also pays dues. Soul music and soul food are the mystical oneness with certain rhythms and the cooking we have enjoyed while forging ourselves into a people welded together by common suffering.—Louis E. Lomax, *The Negro Revolt* (New York: Harper & Row, 1962), pp. 42-43. Reprinted by permission of the publisher.

For this is a world in which the major energy of the imagination goes not into creating works of art, but to overcome the frustrations of social discrimination. Not quite citizens and yet Americans, full of the tensions of modern man but regarded as primitives, Negro Americans are in desperate search for an identity. Rejecting the second-class status assigned them, they feel alienated and their whole lives have become a search for answers to the questions: Who am I, What am I, Why am I, and Where? Significantly, in Harlem the reply to the greeting, "How are you?" is very often, "Oh, man, I'm *nowhere*"—a phrase revealing an attitude so common that it has been reduced to a gesture, a seemingly trivial word. Indeed, Negroes are not unaware that the conditions of their lives demand new definitions of terms like *primitive* and *modern, ethical* and *unethical, moral* and *immoral, patriotism* and *treason, tragedy* and *comedy, sanity* and *insanity.*—Ralph Ellison, "Harlem Is Nowhere," in *Shadow and Act* (New York: Random House, Inc., 1953), p. 297. Reprinted by permission of the publisher.

This society, for as long as it has functioned, was never meant to be equitable as far as black men were concerned. It was made for the white man, and the black man was brought here only to be *used*, to promote the luxury of the white man. That was the only reason. It still is the only reason the black man is alive in the West today, that continued exploitative use. But one day, and very soon, the white man might just look up, hip again, and see that the black man has outlived his usefulness. Then the murders will break out in earnest.—LeRoi Jones, "The Last Days of the American Empire (Including Some Instructions for Black People)" from *Home: Social Essays.* Reprinted by permission of William Morrow and Company, Inc. Copyright © 1964, 1966 by LeRoi Jones.

The discrimination gap is real and is explosive. It must be recognized that our Negro citizens, after only grudgingly receiving the barest minimum in health, education, welfare, housing, economic, and cultural opportunities, cannot conceivably compete equally for, or share in, the full rewards and responsibilities of our society simply by an announcement, with impressive flourishes, that now a state of equal opportunity exists. Equal opportunity, if it is to be more than a hollow mockery, must also mean the opportunity to be equal; to be given a fair chance to achieve equality. Anything less is simply the exercise by the white majority of a concern that all too clearly is only skin deep. For the individual it represents a shallow attempt to salve one's conscience and remove the symbols that disturb.—Whitney M. Young, Jr., *To Be Equal* (New York: McGraw-Hill Book Company, 1964), p. 23. Reprinted by permission of the publisher.

We have waited for more than 340 years for our constitutional and God-given rights. The nations of Asia and Africa are moving with jetlike speed toward gaining political independence, but we still creep at horse-and-buggy pace toward gaining a cup of coffee at a lunch counter. Perhaps it is easy for those who have never felt the stinging darts of segregation to say "Wait." But when you have seen vicious mobs lynch your mothers and fathers at will and drown your sisters and brothers at whim; when you have seen hate-filled policemen curse, kick and even kill your black brothers and sisters; when you see the vast majority of your twenty million Negro brothers smothering in an airtight cage of poverty in the midst of an affluent society; when you suddenly find your tongue twisted and your speech stammering as you seek to explain to your six-year-old daughter why she can't go to the public amusement park that has just been advertised on television, and see tears welling up in her eyes when she is told that Funtown is closed to colored children, and see ominous clouds of inferiority beginning to form in her little mental sky, and see her beginning to distort her personality by developing an unconscious bitterness toward white people; when you have to concoct an answer for a five-year-old son who is asking: "Daddy, why do white people treat colored people so mean?"; when you take a cross-country drive and find it necessary to sleep night after night in the uncomfortable corners of your automobile because no motel will accept you; when you are humiliated day in and day out by nagging signs reading "white" and "colored"; when your first name becomes "nigger," your middle name becomes "boy" (however old you are) and your last name becomes "John," and your wife and mother are never given the respected title "Mrs."; when you are harried by day and haunted by night by the fact that you are a Negro, living constantly at tiptoe stance, never quite knowing what to expect next, and are plagued with inner fears and outer resentments; when you are forever fighting a degenerating sense of "nobodiness"—then you will understand why we find it difficult to wait. There comes a time when the cup of endurance runs over, and men are no longer willing to be plunged into the abyss of despair. I hope, sirs, you can understand our legitimate and unavoidable impatience.—Martin Luther King, Jr., "Letter from Birmingham Jail," in *Why We Can't Wait* (New York: Harper & Row, 1963), pp. 83-84. Reprinted by permission of Harper & Row, Publishers and Joan Daves. Copyright © 1963, 1964 by Martin Luther King. Jr.

ECONOMIC INEQUALITY

Gunnar Myrdal

NEGRO POVERTY

The economic situation of the Negroes in America is pathological. Except for a small minority enjoying upper or middle class status, the masses of American Negroes, in the rural South and in the segregated slum quarters in Southern and Northern cities, are destitute. They own little property; even their household goods are mostly inadequate and dilapidated. Their incomes are not only low but irregular. They thus live from day to day and have scant security for the future. Their entire culture and their individual interests and strivings are narrow.

These generalizations will be substantiated and qualified in the following chapters. For this purpose the available information is immense, and we shall, in the main, be restricted to brief summaries. Our interest in this part of our inquiry will be to try to unravel the causal relations underlying the abnormal economic status of the American Negro. We want to understand how it has developed and fastened itself upon the economic fabric of modern American society. It is hoped that out of a study of trends and situations will emerge an insight into social and economic dynamics which will allow inferences as to what the future holds for the economic well-being of the American Negro people. This future development will depend in part upon public policy, and we shall discuss the various alternatives for induced change. Certain value premises will be made explicit both in

order to guide our theoretical approach and to form the basis for the practical analysis.

Before we proceed to select our specific value premises, let us ask this question: Why is such an extraordinarily large proportion of the Negro people so poor? The most reasonable way to start answering this question is to note the distribution of the Negro people in various regions and occupations. We then find that the Negroes are concentrated in the South, which is generally a poor and economically retarded region. A disproportionate number of them work in agriculture, which is a depressed industry. Most rural Negroes are in Southern cotton agriculture, which is particularly over-populated; backward in production methods; and hard hit by soil exhaustion, by the boll weevil, and by a long-time fall in international demand for American cotton. In addition, few Negro farmers own the land they work on, and the little land they do own is much poorer and less well-equipped than average Southern farms. Most Negro farmers are concentrated in the lowest occupations in agriculture as sharecroppers or wage laborers. In the North, there are practically no Negroes in agriculture.

Nonagricultural Negro workers are, for the most part, either in low-paid service occupations or have menial tasks in industry. Few are skilled workers. Most of the handicrafts and industries in the South where they have a traditional foothold are declining. The majority of manufacturing industries do not give jobs to Negroes. Neither in the South nor in the North are Negroes in professional, business, or clerical positions except in rare instances and except when serving exclusively the Negro public—and even in this they are far from having a monopoly.

The unemployment risk of Negroes is extraordinarily high. During the depression, government relief became one of the major Negro "occupations." Indeed, the institution of large-scale public relief by the New Deal is almost the only bright spot in the recent economic history of the Negro people.

Such a survey, however, even when carried out in greater detail, does not, by itself, explain why Negroes are so poor. The question is only carried one step backward and at the same time broken into parts: Why are Negroes in the poorest sections of the country, the regressive industries, the lowest paid jobs? Why are they not skilled workers? Why do they not hold a fair proportion of well-paid middle class positions? Why is their employment situation so precarious?

We can follow another approach and look to the several factors of economic change. In most cases changes in the economic process seem to involve a tendency which works against the Negroes. When modern techniques transform old handicrafts into machine production, Negroes lose jobs in the former but usually do not get into the new factories, at least not at the machines. Mechanization seems generally to displace Negro labor. When mechanized commercial laundries replace home laundries, Negro workers lose jobs. The same process occurs in tobacco manufacture, in the lumber industry and in the turpentine industry. When tractors and motor trucks are introduced, new "white men's jobs" are created out of old "Negro jobs" on the farm and in transportation. Progress itself seems to work against the Negroes. When work becomes less heavy, less dirty, or less risky, Negroes are displaced. Old-fashioned, low-paying, inefficient enterprises, continually being driven out of competition, are often the only ones that employ much Negro labor.

Although there are no good data on employment trends by race, it seems that the business cycles show something of the same tendency to work against Negroes as do technical changes. It is true that Negroes, more than whites, are concentrated in service industries, and in certain maintenance occupations (janitors, floor-sweepers, and so forth) which are relatively well-protected from depressions. On the other hand, the Negro agricultural laborer is more likely to be forced out by depressions than is the white farmer and farm worker. In fact, in almost every given occupation Negroes tend to be "first fired" when depression comes. Even in the service and maintenance occupations, Negroes are fired to give jobs to white workers. When prosperity returns, the lost ground is never quite made up. As cycle succeeds cycle, there is a tendency toward cumulative displacement of Negroes. The general level of unemployment, depression or no depression, is always higher for Negroes than for whites, and the discrepancy is increasing.

Likewise the organization of the labor market by trade unions has, most of the time, increased the difficulties for Negroes to get and to hold jobs. Even social legislation instituted in order to protect the lowest paid and most insecure workers—among whom the Negroes ordinarily belong—is not an undivided blessing to Negro workers. When the employer finds that he has to take measures to protect his workers' health and security and to pay them higher wages, he often substitutes, voluntarily or under pressure, white workers for Negroes. Sometimes sweatshop industries, existing only because of low-paid Negro labor, are actually driven out of business by legislation or union pressure, and the Negro is again the victim instead of the beneficiary of economic and social progress.

Of course, Negroes are pressing hard in all directions to get jobs and earn a living. The number of job-seeking Negroes is constantly increased, as the shrinkage of the international cotton market, the national agricultural policy under the A.A.A. program, and the displacement of Negroes from traditional jobs, all create a growing unemployment. Negroes are willing—if it were allowed them—to decrease their demand for remuneration, and they are prepared to take the jobs at the bottom of the occupational hierarchy. But still their unemployment is growing relative to that of the whites.

Again we are brought to ask: Why are the Negroes always the unlucky ones? What is this force which, like gravitation, holds them down in the struggle for survival and economic advance? To these questions—as to the closely related questions stated above—we shall find the detailed answers as diverse as the structure of modern economic life itself. But there will be a common pattern in the answers.

OUR MAIN HYPOTHESIS: THE VICIOUS CIRCLE

This common pattern is the vicious circle of cumulative causation outlined . . . [elsewhere in the book].

There is a cultural and institutional tradition that white people exploit Negroes. In the beginning the Negroes were owned as property. When slavery disappeared, caste remained. Within this framework of adverse tradition the average Negro in every generation has had a most disadvantageous start. Discrimination against Negroes is thus rooted in this tradition of economic exploitation. It is justified by the false racial beliefs we studied . . . [earlier]. This depreciation of the Negro's potentialities is given a semblance of proof by the low standards of efficiency, reliability, ambition, and morals actually displayed by the average Negro. This is what the white man "sees," and he opportunistically exaggerates what he sees. He "knows" that the Negro is not "capable" of handling a machine, running a business or learning a profession. As we know that these deficiences are not inborn in him—or, in any case, in no significant degree—we must conclude that they are caused, directly or indirectly, by the very poverty we are trying to explain, and by other discriminations in legal protection, public health, housing, education and in every other sphere of life.

This scheme of causal interrelation is as important in explaining why Negroes are so poor and in evaluating the wider social effects of Negro poverty, as it is in attempting practical planning to raise the economic level of the Negro people. The dynamics of the problem is this: A primary change, induced or unplanned, affecting any one of three bundles of interdependent causative factors—(1) the economic level; (2) standards of intelligence, ambition, health, education, decency, manners, and morals; and (3) discrimination by whites—will bring changes in the other two and, through mutual interaction, move the whole system along in one direction or the other. No single factor, therefore, is the "final cause" in a theoretical sense. From a practical point of view we may, however, call certain factors "strategic" in the sense that they can be controlled.

The statistics of the system can be illustrated by the following comments on the Negro share-cropper in the rural South:

Shiftlessness and laziness are reported as reasons for the dependent state, whereas, in fact, in so far as they exist, they are not necessarily inherent, but are caused by the very conditions of the share-cropping system. . . . It is a notorious and shameful fact that the stock arguments employed against any serious efforts to improve the lot of the cotton tenant are based upon the very social and cultural conditions which tenancy itself creates. The mobility of the tenant, his dependence, his lack of ambition, shiftlessness, his ignorance and poverty, the lethargy of his pellagra-ridden body, provide a ready excuse for keeping him under a stern paternalistic control. There is not a single trait alleged which, where true, does not owe its source and continuance to the imposed status itself.[1]

The same type of vicious circle controls the situation for the poverty-stricken Negroes outside of cotton agriculture. Poverty itself breeds the conditions which perpetuate poverty.

The vicious circle operates, of course, also in the case of whites. Few people have enough imagination to visualize clearly what a poor white tenant or common laborer in the South would look like if he had had more opportunities at the start. Upper class people in all countries are accustomed to look down upon people of the laboring class as inherently inferior. But in the case of Negroes the deprecation is fortified by the elaborate system of racial beliefs, and the discriminations are organized in the social institution of rigid caste and not only of flexible social class.

THE VALUE PREMISES

The system of social ideals which we have called the American Creed, and which serves as the source of the instrumental value premises in this study, is less specified and articulate in the economic field than, for instance, in regard to civic rights. There is, in regard to economic issues, considerable confusion and contradiction even *within* this higher plane of sanctified national ideals and not only—as elsewhere—*between* those ideals and the more opportunistic valuations on lower planes. In public discussion opposing economic precepts are often inferred from the American Creed. A major part of the ideological battle and of political divisions in the American nation, particularly in the decade of the Great Depression, has concerned this very conflict of ideals in the economic sphere. "Equality of opportunity" has been battling "liberty to run one's business as one pleases."

Meanwhile the battle-front itself has been moving—on the whole definitely in favor of equality of opportunity. American economic liberalism was formerly characterized by "rugged individualism"; it is now gradually assimilating ideals of a more social type. There was always the vague popular ideal of "an American standard of living," but now a more definite and realistic conception is growing out of it. A new kind of "inalienable rights"—economic and social—is gradually taking shape within the great political canon of America and is acquiring the respectability of common adherence even if not of immediate realization. As an exemplification of the new way of thinking, without assuming that it has advanced to the level of a national ideal, we may quote the following statement by the National Resources Planning Board, which is an elaboration of President Roosevelt's pronouncement of "freedom from want" as one of the human liberties:

We look forward to securing, through planning and cooperative action, a greater freedom for the American people. . . . In spite of all . . . changes, that great manifesto, the Bill of Rights, has stood unshaken 150 years and now to the old freedoms we must add new freedoms and restate our objectives in modern terms . . . .

Any new declaration of personal rights, any translation of freedom into modern terms applicable to the people of the Unites States, here and now must include:

1. The right to work, usefully and creatively through the productive years.

2. The right to fair pay, adequate to command the necessities and amenities of life in exchange for work, ideas, thrift, and other socially valuable service.

3. The right to adequate food, clothing, shelter, and medical care.

4. The right to security, with freedom from fear of old age, want, dependency, sickness, unemployment, and accident.

5. The right to live in a system of free enterprise, free from compulsory labor, irresponsible private power, arbitrary public authority, and unregulated monopolies.

. . . . . .

9. The right to rest, recreation, and adventure; the opportunity to enjoy life and take part in an advancing civilization.[2]

The most convenient way of determining our value premises for the economic part of our inquiry is, perhaps, to start from the viewpoint of what the American does *not* want. The ordinary American does not, and probably will not within the surveyable future, raise the demand for full *economic equality* in the meaning of a "classless society" where individual incomes and standards of living would become radically leveled off. Such an ideal would be contrary to the basic individualism of American thinking. It could hardly be realized while upholding the cherished independence of the individual. It would nullify the primary responsibility of the individual for the economic fate of himself and his family. It would rob the individual of his chance to rise to wealth and power. It would thus bury the American Dream. It runs contrary to the common belief that it is the individual's hope for economic advancement which spurs him to do his utmost and at the same time acts as the main driving force behind progress in society. The strength of these individualistic ideals is extraordinary in America even today, in spite of the important changes of basic conditions which we shall presently consider.

Although there is a great deal of inequality of income and wealth in America, the American Creed has always been definitely adverse to class divisions and class inequalities. Americans are, indeed, hostile to the very concept of class. But the observer soon finds that this hostility is generally directed only against a rigid system of privileges and social estates in which the individual inherits his status, and not against differences in wealth as such. The American demand is for *fair opportunity and free scope for individual effort*.

In a new nation with rapid social mobility—which is practically always in an upward direction as new immigrants always fill the lower ranks—this way of reconciling liberty with equality is understandable. Social mobility permitted a relative uniformity of social forms and modes of thinking to exist side by side with a great diversity of economic levels of living.

Cultural heterogeneity within the nation and huge geographical space also permitted a measure of anonymity and ignorance of distress. On account of the rapid tempo of economic progress and the rapidly growing market, economic adversities never did appear so final and hopeless. Land was abundant and practically free, and there was at least an avowed national ideal of free education for all individuals.

The principle of noninterference on the part of the State in economic life, therefore, did not seem incompatible with the principle of equality of opportunity. This ideal has had, of course, more influence in America than in any comparable European country. There have always been qualifications, however, even in this country. In recent times the qualifications have been increasing in relative importance, slowly remolding the entire configuration of this part of the American Creed. Probably most Americans are today prepared to accept a considerable amount of *public control* for the purpose of preserving natural resources. Land and other natural assets are today almost entirely occupied and are no longer free. In the whole nation, a vivid realization has grown up of the waste and damage done to these national assets in reckless exploitation and speculation.

In regard to the personal resources of the nation, Americans are not as willing to have public control. But in the one field of education, they have been the pioneering radical interventionists of the world bent upon improving the human material by means of proper schooling. The spirit of interventionism by education is continually gaining in momentum. It early became a self-evident qualification of American economic liberalism. Within the last decades this spirit has spread to other fields. Social legislation has been instituted to regulate children's and women's work, safety measures, and other working conditions in industry, and— later—wages, hours and labor organizations. A system of social insurance has gradually been taking form.

The mass unemployment during the depression of the 'thirties—mounting higher than ever before and higher over a long period than in any other country—and the realization that whole regions and occupational groups can be brought to destitution through no fault of their own caused the development to full conscious-

ness of a sense of public responsibility for these things. For the first time America saw itself compelled to organize a large-scale system of public relief. For the first time also, America made substantial exertions in the field of public housing. The school lunch program, the food stamp plan, and the direct distribution of surplus commodities represent other activities in the same direction, as do also the attempts to induce Southern farmers and sharecroppers to have year-round gardens. Public health programs were expanded, and the nation is even gradually facing the task of organizing the care of the sick in a more socially protective way than hitherto.

Behind this great movement there is an unmistakable trend in social outlook and political valuations. As articulate opinion is gradually taking form that there is *a minimum standard of living* below which no group of people in the country should be permitted to fall. This idea, of course, is not new in America; it is a development of the spirit of Christian neighborliness which has been present in the American Creed from its beginning. But the emphasis is new. Now it is not only a question of humanitarianism; it is a question of national social and economic welfare. Neither the political conflicts raging around the proper means of providing help by public measures nor the widespread uncertainty and disagreement concerning the actual height of the minimum standard to be protected by those measures should conceal the important fact that *the American Creed is changing to include a decent living standard and a measure of economic security among the liberties and rights which are given this highest moral sanction.*

As usual in America, the ideals are running far ahead of the accomplishments. The new belief that the health, happiness, and efficiency of the people can be raised greatly by improved living conditions is already just as much in the forefront of public attention in America as in most progressive countries in Europe and the British Dominions. Nowhere are so many housing investigations carried out to demonstrate the correlation between bad housing conditions and juvenile delinquency, tuberculosis, and syphilis as in America.

Contrary to *laissez-faire* principles, various industries have long been given government protection in the United States—most often by means of the tariff. The recent development has shifted the motivation from "assistance-to-business" terms to "social welfare" terms. This change in motivation is not always carried out in the measures actually taken. The agricultural policy may be pointed to as an example. If we except the work of the Farm Security Administration, there are only weak attempts to administer the public assistance given the farmers in accordance with their individual needs; those farmers who have the highest incomes most often also get the highest relief benefits from the A.A.A. If the trend does not change its course, however, all economic policy is bound to come under the orbit of social welfare policy.

At the same time, social welfare policy proper—by an increasing stress upon the preventive instead of the merely curative aspects—is becoming integrated with economic policy. *Social welfare policy is bound to become looked upon in terms of the economic criterion of national investment.*

Another change is that of an increasing interest in the distribution of income and wealth as such. The rise of taxation to pay for social policy—and now also for the War—is forcing public attention to this problem. The old idea in public finance that taxation should leave the distribution of incomes and wealth between individuals and classes "unchanged" has become impractical. There is a strong tendency to expect some leveling off of the differences through taxation. It is rationalized by giving a new meaning to the old normative formula that taxes should be imposed according to "ability to pay." Similarly, there is a trend away from the attempt to construct social welfare policies in such a manner that they would not have any influence on the labor market.

All of these trends are gradually decreasing the sanctity of individual enterprise, which is slowly coming under public control, although not necessarily public ownership. The American public has been critical of the huge "monopoly" and the "holding company" for over fifty years. The general trend for big business and corporate finance to grow at the expense of small business—which will be accentuated by the present War—has made Americans more and more willing to have government restrictions on private business. Even if big business still

utilizes the old individualistic formulas for its purposes, the observer feels that its success in this is declining. Private property in business itself seems less holy to the average American when it is no longer connected to individually-run enterprise and when large-scale interferences are necessitated by international crises and when taxation is mounting and its burden must be placed somewhere. In agriculture, the increase in tenancy and migratory labor and the decline of the independent farmer are having a similar effect.

In all these respects the American Creed is still in flux. The change has, however, only strengthened the basic demand for equality of opportunity. But it is becoming apparent to most Americans that conditions have so changed that this demand will require more concerted action and even state intervention to become realized. It is commonly observed that the closing of the frontier and the constriction of immigration tend to stratify the social order into a more rigid class structure. Occupational mobility and social climbing are tending to become possible mainly by means of education, and a significant shift now takes two generations instead of one. The self-made man is a vanishing social phenomenon.

The perfection of the national educational system, while increasingly opening up fairer chances for individuals starting out even from the lowest social stratum, is at the same time restricting opportunities to move and to rise for individuals who have passed youth without having had the benefit of education and special training. If they are in the laboring or farming classes they will, in all probability, have to stay there. As this situation is becoming realized among the masses, and as cultural heterogeneity is decreasing, a new impetus is given toward mass organizations. Throughout America collective interest groups are gradually getting the sanction of public approval. The growth of labor unions is on the verge of becoming looked upon as a realization of the American belief in the independence and integrity of the individual.

When all these trends have reached their maturity, the meaning of economic individualism in the American Creed will have changed considerably. For the time being, however, the American Creed is somewhat disorganized in respect to economic life. For our present purpose of selecting, out of the main stream of national thinking, the relevant value premises for studying the economic aspects of the American Negro problem, a satisfactory minimum of clear-cut economic ideals seems to be available in spite of this state of flux.

We shall, in our inquiry, assume that the following norms are generally and explicitly held on the higher or national plane of the valuation sphere in the hearts of ordinary Americans:

1. *There is nothing wrong with economic inequality by itself.* The mere fact that the Negro people are poorer than other population groups does not *per se* constitute a social problem. It does not challenge the American Creed. This first value premise will not be conspicuous in our inquiry. Its main significance is the negative one of keeping our study within the conservative reformist limits of average American economic discussion.

2. Somewhat less precise is our second value premise: *that no American population group shall be allowed to fall under a certain minimum level of living.* This premise also assumes Negro poverty and all other poverty as a matter of fact. It insists only that poverty shall not go too far without being given public attention and amelioration. It offers a means of evaluating the social effects of poverty and affords a motivation for social welfare policy. Even if the general principle of a minimum level of living must now be considered as established in national thinking, it is still undecided how high or low this minimum level should be.

3. Our third value premise is bound to be the most significant one for our inquiry as it brings out the principal chasm between American ideals and practices: *that Negroes shall be awarded equal opportunities.* In so far as Negro poverty is caused by discrimination, the American Creed is challenged in one of its most specific and longest established precepts. Equality of opportunity, fair play, free competition—"independent of race, creed or color"—is deeply imprinted in the nationally sanctioned social morals of America. This value premise must direct every realistic study of the Negroes' economic status in America.

Discrimination is, for this reason, the key term in such a study. This term is *defined in relation to the norm of equality of opportunity* in the American Creed. In this sense it is, naturally, a "value-loaded" term, and rightly so. But it lacks nothing in scientific preciseness and definiteness. An inquiry into the Negro problem in America which shrinks from this valuation is devoid of social perspective and, indeed, interest. Discrimination will be our central concept for our analysis of both the utilization of Negro productivity and the distribution of goods and services for Negro consumption.

THE CONFLICT OF VALUATIONS

By formulating these value premises, and particularly the third one, demanding fair play, we again confront the split in American personality and the ambivalence in American social morals. Our central problem is neither the exploitation of the Negro people nor the various effects of this exploitation on American society, but rather the moral conflict in the heart of white Americans.

In passing we might glance at some of the standard rationalizations by which the American white man tries to build a bridge of reason between his equalitarian Creed and his nonequalitarian treatment of the Negroes. It should be understood that the popular theories are based upon what the ordinary white man conceives to be his own observations and upon what he believes to be common knowledge. We shall first refer to the folklore in the South.

Sometimes a mere reference to custom is advanced as a reason for economic discrimination against Negroes. A report on teachers' salaries prepared by a university in one of the Border states reads:

An additional argument in favor of the salary differential is the general tradition of the South that negroes and whites are not to be paid equivalent salaries for equivalent work. The attitude may be considered wrong from whatever angle it is viewed, but the fact remains that the custom is one that is almost universal and one that the practical school administrator must not ignore.[3]

For not a few, this moral logic that "what was and is, shall be and ought to be" seems sufficient.

Interestingly enough, only rarely will a white man in the South defend economic discrimination in terms of white people's interest to have cheap labor available. Nearest to such a motivation come oblique statements like: "This is a white man's country"; or more expressively: "We don't have money enough to pay our white workers decent wages"; or, in regard to discrimination in the school system: "The appropriations do not suffice even to give the white children good schools."

Such statements are common in the whole South. They are made even by intellectuals. Often there is a further rationalization behind such pronouncements to the effect that "Negroes are the wards of the white people"—an American version of the doctrine of English imperialism about "the white man's burden." "Negroes couldn't live at all without the aid and guidance of the white people," it is said. "What little they have, they have got from the whites." Their own sacrifices apparently do not count. Their poverty itself becomes, in fact, the basis of the rationalization. "The whites give them all the jobs." "Actually, they live on us white people." "They couldn't sustain themselves a day if we gave them up." "The whites pay all the taxes, or don't they?"

Then, too, economic inequality "has to" be maintained, for it is the barrier against "social equality": "you wouldn't let your sister or daughter marry a nigger." The sister or the daughter comes inevitably even into the economic discussion.

This is the ordinary Southerner explaining the matter in plain words to the inquisitive stranger. He is serious and, in a sense, honest. We must remember that the whole white Southern culture, generation after generation, is laboring to convince itself that there is no conflict between the equalitarianism in the American Creed and the economic discrimination against Negroes. And they can never get enough good reasons for their behavior. They pile arguments one on top of the other.

The most important intellectual bridge between the American Creed and actual practices in the economic sphere is, of course, the complex of racial beliefs discussed above. . . . Their import in the economic sphere is that the Negro is looked upon as inherently inferior as a worker and as a consumer. God himself has made the Negro to be only a servant or a laborer employed for menial, dirty, heavy and disagreeable

work. And, since practically all such work is badly paid, it is God's will that the Negro should have a low income. Also, any attempt to raise Negro incomes goes against "the laws of supply and demand" which are part of the order of nature. The Negro is bad as a consumer too. "If you give him more pay, he will stop working"; he will "drink it up and start a row." "Higher wages will make the nigger lazy and morally degraded." This last belief particularly, but also many of the others, bears a striking similarity to ideas about the laboring class as a whole developed in a systematic form by European mercantilist writers in the seventeenth and eighteenth centuries. (The whole ideology displays a static, precapitalistic tendency. When white Southerners object to a conspicuous rise in Negro levels of living, they act much like the upper classes in most European countries centuries ago when they frowned upon lower class people's rise to higher levels of consumption, and even instituted legal regulations forbidding the humbler estates to have servants, to own certain types of dress, and so on. An American Negro in a luxurious car draws unfavorable comment, and so—in previous times—did a Swedish maid who "dressed like a lady." In the static pre-competitive society, tradition was in itself a value.)

On the other hand, it is said that the Negro is accustomed to live on little. "It is a marvel how these niggers can get along on almost nothing." This would actually imply that the Negro is a careful consumer—but the conclusion is never expressed that way.

This touches upon the second main logical bridge between equalitarianism and economic discrimination: the cost-of-living and the standard-of-living arguments. The first of these two popular theories is—again quoting the already mentioned university publication—presented in the following way:

. . . observation alone would suggest to the unbiased observer that the negro teacher will be able to purchase within her society a relatively higher standard of living than the white teacher will be able to secure with the same amount of money.[4]

Statistical investigations are referred to which seem to indicate the remarkable fact that Negro teachers with smaller salaries spend less money for various items of the cost-of-living budget than better paid white teachers.

Scientifically, this is nonsense, of course. A cost-of-living comparison has no meaning except when comparing costs for equivalent budget items and total budgets. That poor people get along on less has nothing to do with the cost of living. They *must* get along on less, even when cost of living, in the proper sense, is higher for them. We have quoted this statement only to illustrate a popular theory which, though it now seldom gets into respectable print, is widespread in the South and constitutes a most important rationalization among even educated people.

Sometimes an attempt is made to give the theory greater logical consistency by inserting the idea that "Negroes don't have the same demands on life as white people." "They are satisfied with less." It should be remembered that equal pay for equal work to women has been objected to by a similar popular theory in all countries. The underlying assumption of a racial differential in psychic wants is, of course, entirely unfounded.

Others are heard expressing the theory of lower demands on life in the following way: "Their cost of living is obviously lower since they have a lower standard of living." Lower wages and lower relief grants are generally motivated in this way. A great number of more or less confused notions are held together in such expressions. Having "a low standard of living," for one thing, means to many to be a "no-account" person, a worthless individual. It also means that, being able to live as they are living, Negroes have a peculiar ability to manage a household. Oblique statements to this effect are often made when discussing this type of popular theory; one social worker in a responsible position came out straight with the argument. It probably also means that people accustomed to suffer from want do not feel poverty so much as if they had seen better days. This, of course, is a much more common popular theory: all over the world the "people who have seen better days" are believed to be worse off than other paupers. In the case of the Negro there is the additional belief that he has a particularly great capacity to be happy in his poverty. He is a child of nature. And he has his religion. He can sing and dance.

The rationalizations amount to this: since Negroes are poor and always have been poor, they are inferior and should be kept inferior. Then they are no trouble but rather a convenience. It is seldom expressed so bluntly. Expressions like "standard of living" and "cost of living" are employed because they have a flavor of scientific objectivity. They avoid hard thinking. They enable one to stand for the *status quo* in economic discrimination without flagrantly exposing oneself even to oneself. For their purpose they represent nearly perfect popular theories of the rationalization type.

These are only a few examples to illustrate the way of thinking utilized in the South of today to justify economic discrimination. In the North there exists practically nothing of these piled-up, criss-crossing, elaborated theories. In matters of discrimination the ordinary Northerner is unsophisticated. Most Northerners, even in those parts of the country where there are Negroes, know only vaguely about the economic discriminations Negroes are meeting in their communities. They are often uninformed of the real import of those discriminations in which they themselves participate.

It is generally held in the North that such discrimination is wrong. When the matter occasionally comes up for public discussion in newspapers and legislatures, it is assumed that discrimination shall be condemned. Some states have, as we shall see, made laws in order to curb discrimination in the labor market. The present writer is inclined to believe that, as far as such discriminations are concerned, a large majority of Northerners would come out for full equality if they had to vote on the issue and did not think of their own occupations. Nothern states and municipalities, on the whole, hold to the principle of nondiscrimination in relief, and this is probably not only due to considerations of the Negro vote but also in obedience to the American Creed.

As we shall find, however, there is plenty of economic discrimination in the North. In situations where it is acute and where it becomes conscious, the average Northerner will occasionally refer to the interest of himself and his group in keeping away Negro competition—a thing which seldom or never happens in the South. On this point he might be cruder. His rationalizations will seldom go much further than presenting the beliefs in the Negroes' racial inferiority and the observation that he "just does not want to have Negroes around" or that he "dislikes Negroes." Southern-born white people in the North usually keep more of the complete defense system and also spread it in their new surroundings. Even in the North it happens occasionally, when economic discrimination is discussed, that the "social equality" issue and the marriage matter are brought up, though with much less emotion.

A main difference between the types of rationalization in the two regions seems to be that the Southerners still think of Negroes as their former slaves, while the association with slavery is notably absent from the minds of Northern-ers. To Northerners, the Negro is, more abstractly, just an alien, felt to be particularly difficult to assimilate into the life of the community. But in the South, the master-model of economic discrimination—slavery—is still a living force as a memory and a tradition.

NOTES

[1] Charles S. Johnson, Edwin R. Embree, and W. W. Alexander, *The Collapse of Cotton Tenancy* (1935), pp. 14-15 and 21-22.

[2] National Resources Planning Board, *National Resources Development, Report for 1942* (1942), p. 3.

[3] *Bulletin of the Bureau of School Service, University of Kentucky*, "A Salary Study for the Lexington Public Schools" (March, 1935), p. 26.

[4] "A Salary Study for the Lexington Public Schools," *op. cit.*, p. 25.

CONDITIONS OF LIFE IN THE RACIAL GHETTO

National Advisory Commission on Civil Disorders

The conditions of life in the racial ghetto are strikingly different from those to which most Americans are accustomed—especially white, middle-class Americans. We believe it important to describe these conditions and their effect on the lives of people who cannot escape from the ghetto.

We have not attempted here to describe conditions relating to the fundamental problems of housing, education and welfare, which are treated in detail in later chapters.

CRIME AND INSECURITY

Nothing is more fundamental to the quality of life in any area than the sense of personal security of its residents, and nothing affects this more than crime.

In general, crime rates in large cities are much higher than in other areas of our country. Within such cities, crime rates are higher in disadvantaged Negro areas than anywhere else.

The most widely-used measure of crime is the number of "index crimes" (homicide, forcible rape, aggravated assault, robbery, burglary, grand larceny, and auto theft) in relation to population. In 1966, 1,754 such crimes were reported to police for every 100,000 Americans. In cities over 250,000, the rate was 3,153, and in cities over one million, it was 3,630—or more than double the national average. In suburban areas alone, including suburban cities, the rate was only 1,300, or just over one-third the rate in the largest cities.

Within larger cities, personal and property

Reprinted from *Report of the National Advisory Commission on Civil Disorders* (Washington, D.C.: U.S. Government Printing Office, March, 1968), pp. 133-139. Footnotes omitted.

insecurity has consistently been highest in the older neighborhoods encircling the downtown business district. In most cities, crime rates for many decades have been higher in these inner areas than anywhere else, except in downtown areas themselves where they are inflated by the small number of residents.

High crime rates have persisted in these inner areas even though the ethnic character of their residents continually changed. Poor immigrants used these areas as "entry ports," then usually moved on to more desirable neighborhoods as soon as they acquired enough resources. Many "entry port" areas have now become racial ghettos.

The difference between crime rates in these disadvantaged neighborhoods and in other parts of the city is usually startling, as a comparison of crime rates in five police districts in Chicago for 1965 illustrates. Taking one high-income, all-white district at the periphery of the city, two very low-income, virtually all-Negro districts near the city core, both including numerous public housing projects, and two predominantly white districts, one with mainly lower-middle-income families, the other containing a mixture of very high-income and relatively low-income households, the table shows crime rates against persons and against property in these five districts, plus the number of patrolmen assigned to them per 100,000 residents.

These data suggest the following conclusions:
- Variations in the crime rate against persons within the city are extremely large. One very low-income Negro district had 35 times as many serious crimes against persons per 100,000 residents as did the high-income white district.
- Variations in the crime rate against property

Incidence of Index Crimes and Patrolmen Assignments per 100,000
Residents in 5 Chicago Police Districts, 1965

Number	High Income White District	Low-Middle-Income White District	Mixed High and Low-Income White District	Very Low Income Negro District No. 1	Very Low Income Negro District No. 2
Index crimes against persons	80	440	338	1,615	2,820
Index Crimes against property	1,038	1,750	2,080	2,508	2,630
Patrolmen assigned	93	133	115	243	291

are much smaller. The highest rate was only 2.5 times larger than the lowest.

• Both income and race appear to affect crime rates: the lower the income in an area, the higher the crime rate there. Yet low-income Negro areas have significantly higher crime rates than low-income white areas. This reflects the high degree of social disorganization in Negro areas described in the previous chapter, as well as the fact that poor Negroes, as a group, have lower incomes than poor whites, as a group.

• The presence of more police patrolmen per 100,000 residents does not necessarily offset high crime in certain parts of the city. Although the Chicago Police Department had assigned over three times as many patrolmen per 100,000 residents to the highest-crime area shown as to the lowest, crime rates in the highest-crime area for offenses against both persons and property combined were 4.9 times as high as in the lowest-crime area.

Because most middle-class Americans live in neighborhoods similar to the more crime-free district described above, they have little comprehension of the sense of insecurity that characterizes the ghetto resident. Moreover, official statistics normally greatly understate actual crime rates because the vast majority of crimes are not reported to the police. For example, a study conducted for the President's Crime Commission in three Washington, D.C. precincts showed that six times as many crimes were actually committed against persons and homes as were reported to the police. Other studies in Boston and Chicago indicated that about three

times as many crimes were committed as were reported.

Two facts are crucial to understand the effects of high crime rates in racial ghettos: most of these crimes are committed by a small minority of the residents, and the principal victims are the residents themselves. Throughout the United States, the great majority of crimes committed by Negroes involve other Negroes as victims, just as most crimes committed by whites are against other whites. A special tabulation made by the Chicago Police Department for the President's Crime Commission indicated that over 85 percent of the crimes committed by Negroes between September 1965 and March 1966 involved Negro victims.

As a result, the majority of law-abiding citizens who live in disadvantaged Negro areas face much higher probabilities of being victimized than residents of most higher-income areas, including almost all suburbs. For nonwhites, the probability of suffering from any index crime except larceny is 78 percent higher than for whites. The probability of being raped is 3.7 times higher among nonwhite women, and the probability of being robbed is 3.5 times higher for nonwhites in general.

The problems associated with high crime rates generate widespread hostility toward the police in these neighborhoods for reasons described elsewhere in this Report. Thus, crime not only creates an atmosphere of insecurity and fear throughout Negro neighborhoods but also causes continuing attrition of the relationship between Negro residents and police. This bears a direct relationship to civil disorder.

There are reasons to expect the crime situation in these areas to become worse in the future. First, crime rates throughout the United States have been rising rapidly in recent years. The rate of index crimes against persons rose 37 percent from 1960 to 1966, and the rate of index crimes against property rose 50 percent. In the first nine months of 1967, the number of index crimes was up 16 percent over the same period in 1966, whereas the United States population rose about one percent. In cities of 250,000 to one million, index crime rose by over 20 percent, whereas it increased four percent in cities of over one million.

Second, the number of police available to combat crime is rising much more slowly than the amount of crime. In 1966, there were about 20 percent more police employees in the United States than in 1960, and per capita expenditures for police rose from $15.29 in 1960 to $20.99 in 1966, a gain of 37 percent. But over the six-year period, the number of reported index crimes had jumped 62 percent. In spite of significant improvements in police efficiency, it is clear that police will be unable to cope with their expanding workload unless there is a dramatic increase in the resources allocated by society to this task.

Third, in the next decade the number of young Negroes aged 14 to 24 will increase rapidly, particularly in central cities. This group is responsible for a disproportionately high share of crimes in all parts of the nation. In 1966, persons under 25 years of age comprised the following proportions of those arrested for various major crimes: murder—37 percent; forcible rape—60 percent; robbery—71 percent; burglary—81 percent; larceny—about 75 percent; and auto theft—over 80 percent. For all index crimes together, the arrest rate for Negroes is about four times higher than that for whites. Yet the number of young Negroes aged 14 to 24 in central cities will rise about 63 percent from 1966 to 1975, as compared to only 32 percent for the total Negro population of central cities. (Assuming those cities will experience the same proportion of total United States Negro population growth that they did from 1960 to 1966.)

HEALTH AND SANITATION CONDITIONS

The residents of the racial ghetto are significantly less healthy than most other Americans. They suffer from higher mortality rates, higher incidence of major diseases, and lower availability and utilization of medical services. They also experience higher admission rates to mental hospitals.

These conditions result from a number of factors.

POVERTY

From the standpoint of health, poverty means deficient diets, lack of medical care, inadequate shelter and clothing, and often lack of awareness of potential health needs. As a result, about 30 percent of all families with incomes less than $2,000 per year suffer from chronic health conditions that adversely affect their employment—as compared with less than 8 percent of the families with incomes of $7,000 or more.

Poor families have the greatest need for financial assistance in meeting medical expenses. Only about 34 percent of families with incomes of less than $2,000 per year use health insurance benefits, as compared to nearly 90 percent of those with incomes of $7,000 or more.

These factors are aggravated for Negroes when compared to whites for the simple reason that the proportion of persons in the United States who are poor is 3.5 times as high among Negroes (41 percent in 1966) as among whites (12 percent in 1966).

MATERNAL MORTALITY

Maternal mortality rates for nonwhite mothers are four times as high as those for white mothers. There has been a sharp decline in such rates since 1940, when 774 nonwhite and 320 white mothers died for each 100,000 live births. In 1965, only 84 nonwhite and 21 white mothers died per 100,000 live births—but the *relative* gap between nonwhites and whites actually increased.

INFANT MORTALITY

Infant mortality rates among nonwhite babies are 58 percent higher than among whites for those under one month old, and almost three times as high among those from one month to one year old. This is true in spite of a large drop in infant mortality rates in both groups since 1940.

Number of Infants Who Died per 1,000 Live Births

	Less Than One Month Old		One Month to One Year Old	
Year	White	Nonwhite	White	Nonwhite
1940	27.2	39.7	16.0	34.1
1950	19.4	27.5	7.4	17.0
1960	17.2	26.9	5.7	16.4
1965	16.1	25.4	5.4	14.9

LIFE EXPECTANCY

To some extent because of infant mortality rates, life expectancy at birth was 6.9 years longer for whites (71.0 years) than for non-whites (64.1 years) in 1965. Even in the prime working ages, life expectancy is significantly lower among nonwhites than among whites. In 1965, white persons 25 years old could expect to live an average of 48.6 more years; whereas nonwhites 25 years old could expect to live another 43.3 years, or 11 percent less. Similar but smaller discrepancies existed at all ages from 25 through 55, and these discrepancies actually became wider between 1960 and 1965.

LOWER UTILIZATION OF HEALTH SERVICES

A fact that also contributes to poorer health conditions in the ghetto is that Negroes with incomes similar to those of whites spend less on medical services and visit medical specialists less often.

Since the lowest income group contains a much larger proportion of nonwhite families than white families, the overall discrepancy in medical care spending between these two groups is very significant, as shown.

Percent of Family Expenditures Spent for Medical Care 1960-61

Income Group	White	Nonwhite	Ratio White: Nonwhite
Under $3,000	9	5	1.8:1
$3,000 to $7,499	7	5	1.4:1
$7,500 & over	6	4	1.5:1

These data indicate that nonwhite families in the lower income group spent less than half as much per person on medical services as white families with similar incomes. This discrepancy sharply declines but is still significant in the higher income group, where total nonwhite medical expenditures per person equal, on the average, 74.3 percent of white expenditures.

Negroes spend less on medical care for several reasons. Negro households generally are larger, requiring larger nonmedical expenses for each household, and leaving less money for meeting medical expenses. Thus lower expenditures per person would result even if expenditures per household were the same. Negroes also often pay more for certain other basic necessities such as food and consumer durables, as is discussed in other sections of this Report. In addition, fewer doctors, dentists, and medical facilities are conveniently available to Negroes—especially to poor families—than to most whites. This is a result both of geographic concentration of doctors in higher income areas in large cities and of discrimination against Negroes by doctors and hospitals. A survey in Cleveland indicated that there were 0.45 physicians per 1,000 people in poor neighborhoods, compared to 1.13 per 1,000 in nonproverty

Health Expenses per Person per Year for the Period From July to December 1962

Income Racial Group	Total Medical	Expenses			
		Hospital	Doctor	Dental	Medicine
Under $2,000 per family per year:					
White	$130	$33	$41	$11	$32
Nonwhite	63	15	23	5	16
$10,000 and more per family per year:					
White	$179	$34	$61	$37	$31
Nonwhite	133	34	50	19	23

Percent of Population Making One or More
Visits to Indicated Type of Medical
Specialist from July 1963 to June 1964

Type of Medical Specialist	Family Incomes of $2,000 to $3,999		Family Incomes of $7,000 to $9,999	
	White	Nonwhite	White	Nonwhite
Physician	64	56	70	64
Dentist	31	20	52	33

areas. The result is fewer visits to physicians and dentists.

Although widespread use of health insurance has led many hospitals to adopt nondiscriminatory policies, some private hospitals still refuse to admit Negro patients or to accept doctors with Negro patients. And many individual doctors still discriminate against Negro patients. As a result, Negroes are more likely to be treated in hospital clinics than whites, and they are less likely to receive personalized service.

This conclusion is confirmed by the following data:

Percent of All Visits to Physicians from July 1963 to June 1964
Made in Indicated Ways

Type of Visit to Physician	Family Incomes of $2,000 to $3,999		Family Incomes of $7,000 to $9,999	
	White	Nonwhite	White	Nonwhite
In Physician's Office	68	56	73	66
Hospital clinic	17	35	7	16
Other (mainly telephone)	15	9	20	18
Total	100	100	100	100

ENVIRONMENTAL FACTORS

Environmental conditions in disadvantaged Negro neighborhoods create further reasons for poor health conditions there. The level of sanitation is strikingly below that which is prevalent in most higher income areas. One simple reason is that residents lack proper storage facilities for food—adequate refrigerators, freezers, even garbage cans which are sometimes stolen as fast as landlords can replace them.

In many areas where garbage collection and other sanitation services are grossly inadequate—commonly in the poorer parts of our large cities, rats proliferate. It is estimated that in 1965, there were over 14,000 cases of rat-bite in the United States, mostly in such neighborhoods.

The importance of these conditions was outlined for the Commission as follows:

Sanitation Commissioners of New York City and Chicago both feel this [sanitation] to be an important community problem and report themselves as being under substantial pressure to improve conditions. *It must be concluded that slum sanitation is a serious problem in the minds of the urban poor and well merits, at least on that ground, the attention of the Commission.* A related problem, according to one Sanitation Commissioner, is the fact that residents of areas bordering on slums feel that sanitation and neighborhood cleanliness is a crucial issue, relating to the stability of their blocks and constituting an important psychological index of "how far gone" their area is.

. . . . There is no known study comparing sanitation services between slum and nonslum areas. The experts agree, however, that there are more services in the slums on a quantitative basis, although perhaps not on a per capita basis. In New York, for example, garbage pickups are supposedly scheduled for about six times a week in slums, compared to three times a week in other areas of the city; the comparable figures in Chicago are two-three times a week versus once a week.

The point, therefore, is not the relative quantitative level of services, but the peculiarly intense needs of ghetto areas for sanitation services. This high demand is the product of numerous factors including: (1) higher population density; (2) lack of well managed buildings and adequate garbage services provided by landlords, number of receptacles, carrying to curbside, number of electric garbage disposals; (3) high relocation rates of tenants and businesses, producing heavy volume of bulk refuse left on streets and in buildings; (4) different uses of the streets—as outdoor living rooms in summer, recreation areas—producing high visibility and sensitivity to garbage problems; (5) large numbers of abandoned cars; (6) severe rodent and pest problems; (7) traffic congestion blocking garbage collection and (8) obstructed street cleaning and snow removal on crowded car-choked streets. Each of these elements adds to the problem and suggests a different possible line of attack.

INTERNAL COLONIALISM AND GHETTO REVOLT

Robert Blauner

It is becoming almost fashionable to analyze American racial conflict today in terms of the colonial analogy.[1] I shall argue in this paper that the utility of this perspective depends upon a distinction between colonization as a process and colonialism as a social, economic, and political system. It is the experience of colonization that Afro-Americans share with many of the nonwhite people of the world. But this subjugation has taken place in a societal context that differs in important respects from the situation of "classical colonialism." In the body of this essay I shall look at some major developments in Black protest—the urban riots, cultural nationalism, and the movement for ghetto control—as collective responses to colonized status. Viewing our domestic situation as a special form of colonization outside a context of a colonial system will help explain some of the dilemmas and ambiguities within these movements.

The present crisis in American life has brought about changes in social perspectives and the questioning of long accepted frameworks. Intellectuals and social scientists have been forced by the pressure of events to look at old definitions of the character of our society, the role of racism, and the workings of basic institutions. The depth and volatility of contemporary racial conflict challenge sociologists in particular to question the adequacy of theoretical models by which we have explained American race relations in the past.

For a long time the distinctiveness of the Negro situation among the ethnic minorities

was placed in terms of color, and the systematic discrimination that follows from our deep-seated racial prejudices. This was sometimes called the caste theory, and while provocative, it missed essential and dynamic features of American race relations. In the past ten years there has been a tendency to view Afro-Americans as another ethnic group not basically different in experience from previous ethnics and whose "immigration" condition in the North would in time follow their upward course. The inadequacy of this model is now clear—even the Kerner Report devotes a chapter to criticizing this analogy. A more recent (though hardly new) approach views the essence of racial subordination in economic class terms: Black people as an underclass are to a degree specially exploited and to a degree economically dispensable in an automating society. Important as are economic factors, the power of race and racism in America cannot be sufficiently explained through class analysis. Into this theory vacuum steps the model of internal colonialism. Problematic and imprecise as it is, it gives hope of becoming a framework that can integrate the insights of caste and racism, ethnicity, culture, and economic exploitation into an overall conceptual scheme. At the same time, the danger of the colonial model is the imposition of an artificial analogy which might keep us from facing up to the fact (to quote Harold Cruse) that "the American black and white social phenomenon is a uniquely new world thing."[2]

During the late 1950's, identification with African nations and other colonial or formerly colonized peoples grew in importance among Black militants.[3] As a result the U.S. was increasingly seen as a colonial power and the concept of domestic colonialism was introduced

Reprinted from *Social Problems*, Vol. 16, No. 4 (Spring 1969), pp. 393-408, by permission of the author and the publisher.

into the political analysis and rhetoric of militant nationalists. During the same period Black social theorists began developing this frame of reference for explaining American realities. As early as 1962, Cruse characterized race relations in this country as "domestic colonialism."[4] Three years later in *Dark Ghetto*, Kenneth Clark demonstrated how the political, economic, and social structure of Harlem was essentially that of a colony.[5] Finally in 1967, a full-blown elaboration of "internal colonialism" provided the theoretical framework for Carmichael and Hamilton's widely read *Black Power*.[6] The following year the Colonial analogy gained currency and new "respectability" when Senator McCarthy habitually referred to Black Americans as a colonized people during his campaign. While the rhetoric of internal colonialism was catching on, other social scientists began to raise questions about its appropriateness as a scheme of analysis.

The colonial analysis has been rejected as obscurantist and misleading by scholars who point to the significant differences in history and social-political conditions between our domestic patterns and what took place in Africa and India. Colonialism traditionally refers to the establishment of domination over a geographically external political unit, most often inhabited by people of a different race and culture, where this domination is political and economic, and the colony exists subordinated to and dependent upon the mother country. Typically the colonizers exploit the land, the raw materials, the labor, and other resources of the colonized nation; in addition a formal recognition is given to the difference in power, autonomy, and political status, and various agencies are set up to maintain this subordination. Seemingly the analogy must be stretched beyond usefulness if the American version is to be forced into this model. For here we are talking about group relations within a society; the mother country—colony separation in geography is absent. Though whites certainly colonized the territory of the original Americans, internal colonization of Afro-Americans did not involve the settlement of whites in any land that was unequivocably Black. And unlike the colonial situation, there has been no formal recognition of differing power since slavery was abolished outside the South. Classic colonialism

involved the control and exploitation of the majority of a nation by a minority of outsiders. Whereas in America the people who are oppressed were themselves originally outsiders and are a numerical minority.

This conventional critique of "internal colonialism" is useful in pointing to the differences between our domestic patterns and the overseas situation. But in its bold attack it tends to lose sight of common experiences that have been historically shared by the most subjugated racial minorities in America and non-white peoples in some other parts of the world. For understanding the most dramatic recent developments on the race scene, this common core element—which I shall call colonization—may be more important than the undeniable divergences between the two contexts.

The common features ultimately relate to the fact that the classical colonialism of the imperialist era and American racism developed out of the same historical situation and reflected a common world economic and power stratification. The slave trade for the most part preceded the imperialist partition and economic exploitation of Africa, and in fact may have been a necessary prerequisite for colonial conquest—since it helped deplete and pacify Africa, undermining the resistance to direct occupation. Slavery contributed one of the basic raw materials for the textile industry which provided much of the capital for the West's industrial development and need for economic expansionism. The essential condition for both American slavery and European colonialism was the power domination and the technological superiority of the Western world in its relation to peoples of non-Western and non-white origins. This objective supremacy in technology and military power buttressed the West's sense of cultural superiority, laying the basis for racist ideologies that were elaborated to justify control and exploitation of non-white people. Thus because classical colonialism and America's internal version developed out of a similar balance of technological, cultural, and power relations, a common *process* of social oppression characterized the racial patterns in the two contexts—despite the variation in political and social structure.

There appear to be four basic components of the colonization complex. The first refers to how the racial group enters into the dominant society (whether colonial power or not). Colonization begins with a forced, involuntary entry. Second, there is an impact on the culture and social organization of the colonized people which is more than just a result of such "natural" processes as contact and acculturation. The colonizing power carries out a policy which constrains, transforms, or destroys indigenous values, orientations, and ways of life. Third, colonization involves a relationship by which members of the colonized group tend to be administered by representatives of the dominant power. There is an experience of being managed and manipulated by outsiders in terms of ethnic status.

A final fundament of colonization is racism. Racism is a principle of social domination by which a group seen as inferior or different in terms of alleged biological characteristics is exploited, controlled, and oppressed socially and psychically by a superordinate group. Except for the marginal case of Japanese imperialism, the major examples of colonialism have involved the subjugation of non-white Asian, African, and Latin American peoples by white European powers. Thus racism has generally accompanied colonialism. Race prejudice can exist without colonization—the experience of Asian-American minorities is a case in point—but racism as a system of domination is part of the complex of colonization.

The concept of colonization stresses the enormous fatefulness of the historical factor, namely the manner in which a minority group becomes a part of the dominant society.[7] The crucial difference between the colonized Americans and the ethnic immigrant minorities is that the latter have always been able to operate fairly competitively within that relatively open section of the social and economic order because these groups came voluntarily in search of a better life, because their movements in society were not administratively controlled, and because they transformed their culture at their own pace— giving up ethnic values and institutions when it was seen as a desirable exchange for improvements in social position.

In present-day America, a major device of Black colonization is the powerless ghetto. As Kenneth Clark describes the situation:

Ghettoes are the consequence of the imposition of external power and the institutionalization of power- lessness. In this respect, they are in fact social, political, educational, and above all—economic colonies. Those confined within the ghetto walls are subject peoples. They are victims of the greed, cruelty, insensitivity, guilt, and fear of their masters. . . .

The community can best be described in terms of the analogy of a powerless colony. Its political leadership is divided, and all but one or two of its political leaders are shortsighted and dependent upon the larger political power structure. Its social agencies are financially precarious and dependent upon sources of support outside the community. Its churches are isolated or dependent. Its economy is dominated by small businesses which are largely owned by absentee owners, and its tenements and other real property are also owned by absentee landlords.

Under a system of centralization, Harlem's schools are controlled by forces outside of the community. Programs and policies are supervised and determined by individuals who do not live in the community . . . [8]

Of course many ethnic groups in America have lived in ghettoes. What make the Black ghettoes an expression of colonized status are three special features. First, the ethnic ghettoes arose more from voluntary choice, both in the sense of the choice to immigrate to America and the decision to live among one's fellow ethnics. Second, the immigrant ghettoes tended to be a one and two generation phenomenon; they were actually way-stations in the process of acculturation and assimilation. When they continue to persist as in the case of San Francisco's China- town, it is because they are big business for the ethnics themselves and there is a new stream of immigrants. The Black ghetto on the other hand has been a more permanent phenomenon, although some individuals do escape it. But most relevant is the third point. European ethnic groups like the Poles, Italians, and Jews gener- ally only experienced a brief period, often less than a generation, during which their residen- tial buildings, commercial stores, and other enterprises were owned by outsiders. The Chi- nese and Japanese faced handicaps of color prejudice that were almost as strong as the Blacks faced, but very soon gained control of their internal communities, because their tradi- tional ethnic culture and social organization had not been destroyed by slavery and internal colonization. But Afro-Americans are distinct in the extent to which their segregated communities have remained controlled economically, politically, and administratively from the outside. One indicator of this difference is the estimate that the "income of Chinese-Americans from Chinese-owned businesses is in proportion to their numbers 45 times as great as the income of Negroes from Negro owned businesses."[9] But what is true of business is also true for the other social institutions that operate within the ghetto. The educators, policemen, social workers, politicians, and others who administer the affairs of ghetto residents are typically whites who live outside the Black community. Thus the ghetto plays a strategic role as the focus for the administration by outsiders which is also essential to the structure of overseas colonialism.[10]

The colonial status of the Negro community goes beyond the issue of ownership and decision-making within Black neighborhoods. The Afro-American population in most cities has very little influence on the power structure and institutions of the larger metropolis, despite the fact that in numerical terms, Blacks tend to be the most sizeable of the various interest groups. A recent analysis of policy-making in Chicago estimates that "Negroes really hold less than 1 percent of the effective power in the Chicago metropolitan area. [Negroes are 20 percent of Cook County's population.] Realistically the power structure of Chicago is hardly less white than that of Mississippi."[11]

Colonization outside of a traditional colonial structure has its own special conditions. The group culture and social structure of the colonized in America is less developed; it is also less autonomous. In addition, the colonized are a numerical minority and furthermore they are ghettoized more totally and are more dispersed than people under classic colonialism. Though these realities affect the magnitude and direction of response, it is my basic thesis that the most important expressions of protest in the Black community during the recent years reflect the colonized status of Afro-America. Riots, programs of separation, politics of community control, the Black revolutionary movements, and cultural nationalism each represent a different strategy of attack on domestic colonialism in America. Let us now examine some of these movements.

RIOT OR REVOLT?

The so-called riots are being increasingly recognized as a preliminary if primitive form of mass rebellion against a colonial status. There is still a tendency to absorb their meaning within the conventional scope of assimilation-integration politics: some commentators stress the material motives involved in looting as a sign that the rioters want to join America's middle-class affluence just like everyone else. That motives are mixed and often unconscious, that Black people want good furniture and television sets like whites is beside the point. The guiding impulse in most major outbreaks has not been integration with American society, but an attempt to stake out a sphere of control by moving against that society and destroying the symbols of its oppression.

In my critique of the McCone Report I observed that the rioters were asserting a claim to territoriality, an unorganized and rather inchoate attempt to gain control over their community or "turf."[12] In succeeding disorders also the thrust of the action has been the attempt to clear out an alien presence, white men and officials, rather than a drive to kill whites as in a conventional race riot. The main attacks have been directed at the property of white business men and at the police who operate in the Black community "like an army of occupation" protecting the interests of outside exploiters and maintaining the domination over the ghetto by the central metropolitan power structure.[13] The Kerner Report misleads when it attempts to explain riots in terms of integration: "What the rioters appear to be seeking was fuller participation in the social order and the material benefits enjoyed by the majority of American citizens. Rather than rejecting the American system, they were anxious to obtain a place for themselves in it."[14] More accurately, the revolts pointed to alienation from this system on the part of many poor and also not-so-poor Blacks. The sacredness of private property, that unconsciously accepted bulwark of our social arrangements, was rejected; people who looted apparently without guilt generally remarked that they were taking things that "really belonged" to them anyway.[15] Obviously the society's bases of legitimacy and authority have been attacked. Law and order has long been viewed as the white man's law and order by Afro-Americans; but now this perspective characteristic of a colonized people is out in the open. And the Kerner Report's own data question how well ghetto rebels are buying the system: In Newark only 33 percent of self-reported rioters said they thought this country was worth fighting for in the event of a major war; in the Detroit sample the figure was 55 percent.[16]

One of the most significant consequences of the process of colonization is a weakening of the colonized's individual and collective will to resist his oppression. It has been easier to contain and control Black ghettoes because communal bonds and group solidarity have been weakened through divisions among leadership, failures of organization, and a general disspiritment that accompanies social oppression. The riots are a signal that the will to resist has broken the mold of accommodation. In some cities as in Watts they also represented nascent movements toward community identity. In several riot-torn ghettoes the outbursts have stimulated new organizations and movements. If it is true that the riot phenomenon of 1964-68 has passed its peak, its historical import may be more for the "internal" organizing momentum generated than for any profound "external" response of the larger society facing up to underlying causes.

Despite the appeal of Frantz Fanon to young Black revolutionaries, America is not Algeria. It is difficult to foresee how riots in our cities can play a role equivalent to rioting in the colonial situation as an integral phase in a movement for national liberation. In 1968 some militant groups (for example, the Black Panther Party in Oakland) had concluded that ghetto riots were self-defeating of the lives and interests of Black people in the present balance of organization and gunpower, though they had served a role to stimulate both Black consciousness and white awareness of the depths of racial crisis. Such militants have been influential in "cooling" their communities during periods of high riot potential. Theroretically oriented Black radicals see riots as spontaneous mass behavior which must be replaced by a revolutionary organization and consciousness. But despite the differences in objective conditions, the violence of the 1960's seems to serve the same psychic function, assertions of dignity and manhood for young Blacks in urban ghettoes, as it did for the colonized of North Africa described by Fanon and Memmi.[17]

CULTURAL NATIONALISM

Cultural conflict is generic to the colonial relation because colonization involves the domination of Western technological values over the more communal cultures of non-Western peoples. Colonialism played havoc with the national integrity of the peoples it brought under its sway. Of course, all traditional cultures are threatened by industrialism, the city, and modernization in communication, transportation, health, and education. What is special are the political and administrative decisions of colonizers in managing and controlling colonized peoples. The boundaries of African colonies, for example, were drawn to suit the political conveniences of the European nations without regard to the social organization and cultures of African tribes and kingdoms. Thus Nigeria as blocked out by the British included the Yorubas and the Ibos, whose civil war to day is a residuum of the colonialist's disrespect for the integrity of indigenous cultures.

The most total destruction of culture in the colonization process took place not in traditional colonialism but in America. As Frazier stressed, the integral cultures of the diverse African peoples who furnished the slave trade were destroyed because slaves from different tribes, kingdoms, and linguistic groups were purposely separated to maximize domination and control. Thus language, religion, and national loyalties were lost in North America more more completely than in Caribbean and Brazil where slavery developed somewhat differently. Thus on this key point America's internal colonization has been more total and extreme than situations of classic colonialism. For the British in India and the European powers in Africa were not able—as outnumbered minorities—to destroy the national and tribal cultures of the colonized. Recall that American slavery lasted 250 years and its racist aftermath another

100. Colonial dependency in the case of British Kenya and French Algeria lasted only 77 and 125 years respectively. In the wake of this more drastic uprooting and destruction of culture and social organization, much more powerful agencies of social, political, and psychological domination developed in the American case.

Colonial control of many peoples inhabiting the colonies was more a goal than a fact, and at Independence there were undoubtedly fairly large numbers of Africans who had never seen a colonial administrator. The gradual process of extension of control from the administrative center on the African coast contrasts sharply with the total uprooting involved in the slave trade and the totalitarian aspects of slavery in the United States. Whether or not Elkins is correct in treating slavery as a total institution, it undoubtedly had a far more radical and pervasive impact on American slaves than did colonialism on the vast majority of Africans.[18]

Yet a similar cultural process unfolds in both contexts of colonialism. To the extent that they are involved in the larger society and economy, the colonized are caught up in a conflict between two cultures. Fanon has described how the assimilation-oriented schools of Martinique taught him to reject his own culture and Blackness in favor of Westernized, French, and white values.[19] Both the colonized elites under traditional colonialism and perhaps the majority of Afro-Americans today experience a parallel split in identity, cultural loyalty, and political orientation.[20]

The colonizers use their culture to socialize the colonized elites (intellectuals, politicians, and middle class) into an identification with the colonial system. Because Western culture has the prestige, the power, and the key to open the limited opportunity that a minority of the colonized may achieve, the first reaction seems to be an acceptance of the dominant values. Call it brainwashing as the Black Muslims put it; call it identifying with the aggressor if you prefer Freudian terminology; call it a natural response to the hope and belief that integration and democratization can really take place if you favor a more commonsense explanation, this initial acceptance in time crumbles on the realities of racism and colonialism. The colonized, seeing that his success within colonialism is at the expense of his group and his own inner

identity, moves radically toward a rejection of the Western culture and develops a nationalist outlook that celebrates his people and their traditions. As Memmi describes it:

Assimilation being abandoned, the colonized's liberation must be carried out through a recovery of self and of autonomous dignity. Attempts at imitating the colonizer required self-denial; the colonizer's rejection is the indispensible prelude to self-discovery. That accusing and annihilating image must be shaken off; oppression must be attacked boldly since it is impossible to go around it. After having been rejected for so long by the colonizer, the day has come when it is the colonized who must refuse the colonizer.[21]

Memmi's book, *The Colonizer and the Colonized,* is based on his experience as a Tunisian Jew in a marginal position between the French and the colonized Arab majority. The uncanny parallels between the North African situation he describes and the course of Black-white relations in our society is the best impressionist argument I know for the thesis that we have a colonized group and a colonizing system in America. His discussion of why even the most radical French anti-colonialist cannot participate in the struggle of the colonized is directly applicable to the situation of the white liberal and radical vis-à-vis the Black movement. His portrait of the colonized is as good an analysis of the psychology behind Black Power and Black nationalism as anything that has been written in the U.S. Consider for example:

Considered *en bloc* as *them, they,* or *those,* different from every point of view, homogeneous in a radical heterogeneity, the colonized reacts by rejecting all the colonizers *en bloc.* The distinction between deed and intent has no great significance in the colonial situation. In the eyes of the colonized, all Europeans in the colonies are de facto colonizers, and whether they want to be or not, they are colonizers in some ways. By their privileged economic position, by belonging to the political system of oppression, or by participating in an effectively negative complex toward the colonized, they are colonizers. . . . They are supporters or at least unconscious accomplices of that great collective aggression of Europe.[22]

The same passion which made him admire and absorb Europe shall make him assert his differences; since those differences, after all, are within him and correctly constitute his true self.[23]

The important thing now is to rebuild his people,

whatever be their authentic nature; to reforge their unity, communicate with it, and to feel that they belong.[24]

Cultural revitalization movements play a key role in anti-colonial movements. They follow an inner necessity and logic of their own that comes from the consequences of colonialism on groups and personal identities; they are also essential to provide the solidarity which the political or military phase of the anti-colonial revolution requires. In the U.S. an Afro-American culture has been developing since slavery out of the ingredients of African world-views, the experience of bondage, Southern values and customs, migration and the Northern lower-class ghettoes, and most importantly, the political history of the Black population in its struggle against racism.[25] That Afro-Americans are moving toward cultural nationalism in a period when ethnic loyalties tend to be weak (and perhaps on the decline) in this country is another confirmation of the unique colonized position of the Black group. (A similar nationalism seems to be growing among American Indians and Mexican-Americans.)

THE MOVEMENT FOR GHETTO CONTROL

The call for Black Power unites a number of varied movements and tendencies.[26] Though no clear-cut program has yet emerged, the most important emphasis seems to be the movement for control of the ghetto. Black leaders and organizations are increasingly concerned with owning and controlling those institutions that exist within or impinge upon their community. The colonial model provides a key to the understanding of this movement, and indeed ghetto control advocates have increasingly invoked the language of colonialism in pressing for local home rule. The framework of anti-colonialism explains why the struggle for poor people's or community control of poverty programs has been more central in many cities than the content of these programs and why it has been crucial to exclude whites from leadership positions in Black organizations.

The key institutions that anti-colonialists want to take over or control are business, social services, schools, and the police. Though many spokesmen have advocated the exclusion of white landlords and small businessmen from the ghetto, this program has evidently not struck fire with the Black population and little concrete movement toward economic expropriation has yet developed. Welfare recipients have organized in many cities to protect their rights and gain a greater voice in the decisions that affect them, but whole communities have not yet been able to mount direct action against welfare colonialism. Thus schools and the police seem now to be the burning issues of ghetto control politics.

During the past few years there has been a dramatic shift from educational integration as the primary goal to that of community control of the schools. Afro-Americans are demanding their own school boards, with the power to hire and fire principals and teachers and to construct a curriculum which would be relevant to the special needs and culture style of ghetto youth. Especially active in high schools and colleges have been Black students, whose protests have centered on the incorporation of Black Power and Black culture into the educational system. Consider how similar is the spirit behind these developments to the attitude of the colonized North African toward European education:

He will prefer a long period of educational mistakes to the continuance of the colonizer's school organization. He will choose institutional disorder in order to destroy the institutions built by the colonizer as soon as possible. There we will see, indeed, a reactive drive of profound protest. He will no longer owe anything to the colonizer and will have definitely broken with him.[27]

Protest and institutional disorder over the issue of school control came to a head in 1968 in New York City. The procrastination in the Albany State legislature, the several crippling strikes called by the teachers union, and the almost frenzied response of Jewish organizations makes it clear that decolonization of education faces the resistance of powerful vested interests.[28] The situation is too dynamic at present to assess probable future results. However, it can be safely predicted that some form of school decentralization will be institutionalized in New York, and the movement for community control of education will spread to more cities.

This movement reflects some of the problems and ambiguities that stem from the situation of colonization outside an immediate colonial context. The Afro-American community is not parallel in structure to the communities of colonized nations under traditional colonialism. The significant difference here is the lack of fully developed indigenous institutions besides the church. Outside of some areas of the South there is really no Black economy, and most Afro-Americans are inevitably caught up in the larger society's structure of occupations, education, and mass communication. Thus the ethnic nationalist orientation which reflects the reality of colonization exists alongside an integrationist orientation which corresponds to the reality that the institutions of the larger society are much more developed than those of the incipient nation.[29] As would be expected the movement for school control reflects both tendencies. The militant leaders who spearhead such local movements may be primarily motivated by the desire to gain control over the community's institutions—they are anti-colonialists first and foremost. Many parents who support them may share this goal also, but the majority are probably more concerned about creating a new education that will enable their children to "make it" in the society and the economy as a whole—they know that the present school system fails ghetto children and does not prepare them for participation in American life.

There is a growing recognition that the police are the most crucial institution maintaining the colonized status of Black Americans. And of all establishment institutions, police departments probably include the highest proportion of individual racists. This is no accident since central to the workings of racism (an essential component of colonization) are attacks on the humanity and dignity of the subject group. Through their normal routines the police constrict Afro-Americans to Black neighborhoods by harassing and questioning them when found outside the ghetto; they break up groups of youth congregating on corners or in cars without any provocation; and they continue to use offensive and racist language no matter how many intergroup understanding seminars have been built into the police academy. They also shoot to kill ghetto residents for alleged crimes such as car thefts and running from police officers.[30]

Police are key agents in the power equation as well as the drama of dehumanization. In the final analysis they do the dirty work for the larger system by restricting the striking back of Black rebels to skirmishes inside the ghetto, thus deflecting energies and attacks from the communities and institutions of the larger power structure. In a historical review, Gary Marx notes that since the French revolution, police and other authorities have killed large numbers of demonstrators and rioters; the rebellious "rabble" rarely destroys human life. The same pattern has been repeated in America's recent revolts.[31] Journalistic accounts appearing in the press recently suggest that police see themselves as defending the interests of white people against a tide of Black insurgence; furthermore the majority of whites appear to view "blue power" in this light. There is probably no other opinion on which the races are as far apart today as they are on the question of attitudes toward the police.

In many cases set off by a confrontation between a policeman and a Black citizen, the ghetto uprisings have dramatized the role of law enforcement and the issue of police brutality. In their aftermath, movements have arisen to contain police activity. One of the first was the Community Alert Patrol in Los Angeles, a method of policing the police in order to keep them honest and constrain their violations of personal dignity. This was the first tactic of the Black Panther Party which originated in Oakland, perhaps the most significant group to challenge the police role in maintaining the ghetto as a colony. The Panther's later policy of openly carrying guns (a legally protected right) and their intention of defending themselves against police aggression has brought on a series of confrontations with the Oakland police department. All indications are that the authorities intend to destroy the Panthers by shooting, framing up, or legally harassing their leadership—diverting the group's energies away from its primary purpose of self-defense and organization of the Black community to that of legal defense and gaining support in the white community.

There are three major approaches to "police colonialism" that correspond to reformist and revolutionary readings of the situation. The most elementary and also superficial sees colonialism in the fact that ghettoes are overwhelmingly patrolled by white rather than by Black officers. The proposal—supported today by many police departments—to increase the number of Blacks on local forces to something like their distribution in the city would then make it possible to reduce the use of white cops in the ghetto. This reform should be supported, for a variety of obvious reasons, but it does not get to the heart of the police role as agents of colonization.

The Kerner Report documents the fact that in some cases Black policemen can be as brutal as their white counterparts. The Report does not tell us who polices the ghetto, but they have compiled the proportion of Negroes on the forces of the major cities. In some cities the disparity is so striking that white police inevitably dominate ghetto patrols. (In Oakland 31 percent of the population and only 4 percent of the police are Black; in Detroit, the figures are 39 percent and 5 percent; and in New Orleans 41 and 4.) In other cities, however, the proportion of Black cops is approaching the distribution in the city: Philadelphia 29 percent and 20 percent; Chicago 27 percent and 17 percent.[32] These figures also suggest that both the extent and the pattern of colonization may vary from one city to another. It would be useful to study how Black communities differ in degree of control over internal institutions as well as in economic and political power in the metropolitan area.

A second demand which gets more to the issue is that police should live in the communities they patrol. The idea here is that Black cops who lived in the ghetto would have to be accountable to the community; if they came on like white cops then "the brothers would take care of business" and make their lives miserable. The third or maximalist position is based on the premise that the police play no positive role in the ghettoes. It calls for the withdrawal of metropolitan officers from Black communities and the substitution of an autonomous indigenous force that would maintain order without oppressing the population. The precise relationship between such an independent police, the city and county law enforcement agencies, a ghetto governing body that would supervise and

finance it, and especially the law itself is yet unclear. It is unlikely that we will soon face these problems directly as they have arisen in the case of New York's schools. Of all the programs of decolonization, police autonomy will be most resisted. It gets to the heart of how the state functions to control and contain the Black community through delegating the legitimate use of violence to police authority.

The various "Black Power" programs that are aimed at gaining control of individual ghettoes—buying up property and businesses, running the schools through community boards, taking over anti-poverty programs and other social agencies, diminishing the arbitrary power of the police—can serve to revitalize the institutions of the ghetto and build up an economic, professional and political power base. These programs seem limited; we do not know at present if they are enough in themselves to end colonized status.[33] But they are certainly a necessary first step.

THE ROLE OF WHITES

What makes the Kerner Report a less-than-radical document is its superficial treatment of racism and its reluctance to confront the colonized relationship between Black people and the larger society. The Report emphasizes the attitudes and feelings that make up white racism, rather than the system of privilege and control which is the heart of the matter.[34] With all its discussion of the ghetto and its problems, it never faces the question of the stake that white Americans have in racism and ghettoization.

This is not a simple question, but this paper should not end with the impression that police are the major villains. All white Americans gain some privileges and advantage from the colonization of Black communities.[35] The majority of whites also lose something from this oppression and division in society. Serious research should be directed to the ways in which white individuals and institutions are tied into the ghetto. In closing let me suggest some possible parameters.

1. It is my guess that only a small minority of whites make a direct economic profit from ghetto colonization. This is hopeful in that the ouster of white businessmen may become politically feasible. Much more significant, however,

are the private and corporate interests in the land and residential property of the Black community; their holdings and influence on urban decision-making must be exposed and combated.

2. A much larger minority have occupational and professional interests in the present arrangements. The Kerner Commission reports that 1.3 million non-white men would have to be upgraded occupationally in order to make the Black job distribution roughly similar to the white. They advocate this without mentioning that 1.3 million specially privileged white workers would lose in the bargain.[36] In addition there are those professionals who carry out what Lee Rainwater has called the "dirty work" of administering the lives of the ghetto poor: the social workers, the school teachers, the urban development people, and of course the police.[37] The social problems of the Black community will ultimately be solved only by people and organizations from that community; thus the emphasis within these professions must shift toward training such a cadre of minority personnel. Social scientists who teach and study problems of race and poverty likewise have an obligation to replace themselves by bringing into the graduate schools and college faculties men of color who will become the future experts in these areas. For cultural and intellectual imperialism is as real as welfare colonialism, though it is currently screened behind such unassailable shibboleths as universalism and the objectivity of scientific inquiry.

3. Without downgrading the vested interests of profit and profession, the real nitty-gritty elements of the white stake are political power and bureaucratic security. Whereas few whites have much understanding of the realities of race relations and ghetto life, I think most give tacit or at least subconscious support for the containment and control of the Black population. Whereas most whites have extremely distorted images of Black Power, many—if not most—would still be frightened by actual Black political power. Racial groups and identities are real in American life; white Americans sense they are on top, and they fear possible reprisals or disruptions were power to be more equalized. There seems to be a paranoid fear in the white psyche of Black dominance; the belief that Black autonomy would mean unbridled license

is so ingrained that such reasonable outcomes as Black political majorities and independent Black police forces will be bitterly resisted.

On this level the major mass bulwark of colonization is the administrative need for bureaucratic security so that the middle classes can go about their life and business in peace and quiet. The Black militant movement is a threat to the orderly procedures by which bureaucracies and suburbs manage their existence, and I think today there are more people who feel a stake in conventional procedures than there are those who gain directly from racism. For in their fight for institutional control, the colonized will not play by the white rules of the game. These administrative rules have kept them down and out of the system; therefore they have no necessary intention of running institutions in the image of the white middle class.

The liberal, humanist value that violence is the worst sin cannot be defended today if one is committed squarely against racism and for self-determination. For some violence is almost inevitable in the decolonization process; unfortunately racism in America has been so effective that the greatest power Afro-Americans (and perhaps also Mexican-Americans) wield today is the power to disrupt. If we are going to swing with these revolutionary times and at least respond positively to the anti-colonial movement, we will have to learn to live with conflict, confrontation, constant change, and what may be real or apparent chaos and disorder.

A positive response from the white majority needs to be in two major directions at the same time. First, community liberation movements should be supported in every way by pulling out white instruments of direct control and exploitation and substituting technical assistance to the community when this is asked for. But it is not enough to relate affirmatively to the nationalist movement for ghetto control without at the same time radically opening doors for full participation in the institutions of the mainstream. Otherwise the liberal and radical position is little different than the traditional segregationist. Freedom in the special conditions of American colonization means that the colonized must have the choice between participation in the larger society and in their own independent structures.

NOTES

[1]This is a revised version of a paper delivered at the University of California Centennial Program, "Studies in Violence," Los Angeles, June 1, 1968. For criticisms and ideas that have improved an earlier draft, I am indebted to Robert Wood, Lincoln Bergman, and Gary Marx. As a good colonialist I have probably restated (read: stolen) more ideas from the writings of Kenneth Clark, Stokely Carmichael, Frantz Fanon, and especially such contributors to the Black Panther Party (Oakland) newspaper as Huey Newton, Bobby Seale, Eldridge Cleaver, and Kathleen Cleaver than I have appropriately credited or generated myself. In self-defense I should state that I began working somewhat independently on a colonial analysis of American race relations in the fall of 1965; see my "Whitewash Over Watts: The Failure of the McCone Report," *Trans-action*, 3 (March-April, 1966), pp. 3-9, 54.

[2]Harold Cruse, *Rebellion or Revolution*, New York: 1968, p. 214.

[3]Nationalism, including an orientation toward Africa, is no new development. It has been a constant tendency within Afro-American politics. See Cruse, *ibid*, esp. chaps. 5-7.

[4]This was six years before the publication of *The Crisis of the Negro Intellectual*, New York: Morrow, 1968, which brought Cruse into prominence. Thus the 1962 article was not widely read until its reprinting in Cruse's essays, *Rebellion or Revolution, op. cit.*

[5]Kenneth Clark, *Dark Ghetto*, New York: Harper and Row, 1965. Clark's analysis first appeared a year earlier in *Youth in the Ghetto*, New York: Haryou Associates, 1964.

[6]Stokely Carmichael and Charles Hamilton, *Black Power*, New York: Random, 1967.

[7]As Eldridge Cleaver reminds us, "Black people are a stolen people held in a colonial status on stolen land, and any analysis which does not acknowledge the colonial status of black people cannot hope to deal with the real problem." "The Land Question," *Ramparts*, 6 May, 1968), p. 51.

[8]*Youth in the Ghetto, op. cit.*, pp. 10-11; 79-80.

[9]N. Glazer and D. P. Moynihan, *Beyond the Melting Pot*, Cambridge, Mass.: M.I.T., 1963, p. 37.

[10]"When we speak of Negro social disabilities under capitalism, . . . we refer to the fact that he does not own anything—*even what is ownable in his own community*. Thus to fight for black liberation *is to fight for his right to own*. The Negro is politically compromised today because he owns nothing. He has little voice in the affairs of state because he owns nothing. The fundamental reason why the Negro bourgeois-democratic revolution has been aborted is because American capitalism has prevented the development of a black class of capitalist owners of institutions and economic tools. To take one crucial example, Negro radicals today are severely hampered in their tasks of educating the black masses on political issues because Negroes do not own any of the necessary means of propaganda and communication. The Negro owns no printing presses, he has no stake in the networks of the means of communication. Inside his own communities he does not own the house he lives in, the property he lives on, nor the wholesale and retail sources from which he buys his commodities. He does not own the edifices in which he enjoys culture and entertainment or in which he socializes. In capitalist society, an individual or group that does not own anything is powerless."—H. Cruse.

"Behind the Black Power Slogan," in Cruse, *Rebellion or Revolution, op. cit.*, pp. 238-39.

[11]Harold M. Baron, "Black Powerlessness in Chicago," *Trans-action*, 6 (Nov., 1968), pp. 27-33.

[12]R. Blauner, "Whitewash Over Watts," *op. cit.*

[13]"The police function to support and enforce the interests of the dominant political, social, and economic interests of the town" is a statement made by a former police scholar and official, according to A. Neiderhoffer, *Behind the Shield*, New York: Doubleday, 1967 as cited by Gary T. Marx, "Civil Disorder and the Agents of Control," *Journal of Social Issues*, forthcoming.

[14]Report of the National Advisory Commission on Civil Disorders, N.Y.: Bantam, March, 1968, p. 7.

[15]This kind of attitude has a long history among American Negroes. During slavery, Blacks used the same rationalization to justify stealing from their masters. Appropriating things from the master was viewed as "*taking* part of his property for the benefit of another part; whereas *stealing* referred to appropriating something from another slave, an offense that was not condoned." Kenneth Stampp, *The Peculiar Institution*, Vintage, 1956, p. 127.

[16]Report of the National Advisory Commission on Civil Disorders, *op. cit.*, p. 178.

[17]Frantz Fanon, *Wretched of the Earth*, New York: Grove, 1963; Albert Memmi, *The Colonizer and the Colonized*, Boston: Beacon, 1967.

[18]Robert Wood, "Colonialism in Africa and America: Some Conceptual Considerations," December, 1967, unpublished paper.

[19]F. Fanon, *Black Skins, White Masks*, New York: Grove, 1967.

[20]Harold Cruse has described how these two themes of integration with the larger society and identification with ethnic nationality have struggled within the political and cultural movements of Negro Americans. *The Crisis of the Negro Intellectual, op. cit.*

[21]Memmi, *op. cit.*, p. 128.

[22]*Ibid*, p. 130.

[23]*Ibid*, p. 132.

[24]*Ibid*, p. 134.

[25]In another essay, I argue against the standard sociological position that denies the existence of an ethnic Afro-American culture and I expand on the above themes. The concept of "Soul" is astonishingly parallel in content to the mystique of "Negritude" in Africa; the Pan-African culture movement has its parallel in the burgeoning Black culture mood in Afro-American communities. See "Black Culture: Myth or Reality" in Peter Rose, editor, *Americans From Africa*, Atherton, 1969.

[26]Scholars and social commentators, Black and white alike, disagree in interpreting the contemporary Black Power movement. The issues concern whether this is a new development in Black protest or an old tendency revised; whether the movement is radical, revolutionary, reformist, or conservative; and whether this orientation is unique to Afro-Americans or essentially a Black parallel to other ethnic group strategies for collective mobility. For an interesting discussion of Black Power as a modernized version of Booker T. Washington's separatism and economism, see Harold Cruse, *Rebellion or Revolution, op. cit.*, pp. 193-258.

[27]Memmi, *op. cit.*, pp. 137-138.

[28]For the New York school conflict see Jason Epstein, "The Politics of School Decentralization," *New York Review of Books,* June 6, 1968, pp. 26-32; and "The New York City School Revolt," *ibid,* 11, no. 6, pp. 37-41.

[29]This dual split in the politics and psyche of the Black American was poetically described by Du Bois in his *Souls of Black Folk,* and more recently has been insightfully analyzed by Harold Cruse in *The Crisis of the Negro Intellectual, op. cit.* Cruse has also characterized the problem of the Black community as that of underdevelopment.

[30]A recent survey of police finds "that in the predominantly Negro areas of several large cities, many of the police perceive the residents as basically hostile, especially the youth and adolescents. A lack of public support—from citizens, from courts, and from laws—is the policeman's major complaint. But some of the public criticism can be traced to the activities in which he engages day by day, and perhaps to the tone in which he enforces the "law" in the Negro neighborhoods. Most frequently he is 'called upon' to intervene in domestic quarrels and break up loitering groups. He stops and frisks two or three times as many people as are carrying dangerous weapons or are actual criminals, and almost half of these don't wish to cooperate with the policeman's efforts." Peter Rossi *et al,* "Between Black and White—The Faces of American Institutions and the Ghetto," in Supplemental Studies for The National Advisory Commission on Civil Disorders, July 1968, p. 114.

[31]"In the Gordon Riots of 1780 demonstrators destroyed property and freed prisoners, but did not seem to kill anyone, while authorities killed several hundred rioters and hung an additional 25. In the Rebellion Riots of the French Revolution, though several hundred rioters were killed, they killed no one. Up to the end of the Summer of 1967, this pattern had clearly been repeated, as police, not rioters, were responsible for most of the more than 100 deaths that have occurred. Similarly, in a related context, the more than 100 civil rights murders of recent years have been matched by almost no murders of racist whites." G. Marx, "Civil Disorders and the Agents of Social Control," *op. cit.*

[32]Report of the National Advisory Commission on Civil Disorders, *op. cit.,* p. 321. That black officers nevertheless would make a difference is suggested by data from one of the supplemental studies to the Kerner Report. They found Negro policemen working in the ghettoes considerably more sympathetic to the community and its social problems than their white counterparts. Peter Rossi *et al,* "Between Black and White—The Faces of American Institutions in the Ghetto," *op. cit.,* chap. 6.

[33]Eldridge Cleaver has called this first stage of the anti-colonial movement *community* liberation in contrast to a more long-range goal of *national* liberation. E. Cleaver, "Community Imperialism," Black Panther Party newspaper, 2 (May 18, 1968).

[34]For a discussion of this failure to deal with racism, see Gary T. Marx. "Report of the National Commission: The Analysis of Disorder or Disorderly Analysis," 1968, unpublished paper.

[35]Such a statement is easier to assert than to document but I am attempting the latter in a forthcoming book tentatively titled *White Racism, Black Culture,* to be published by Little Brown, 1970.

[36]Report of the National Advisory Commission on Civil Disorders, *op. cit.,* pp. 253-256.

[37]Lee Rainwater, "The Revolt of the Dirty-Workers," *Trans-action,* 5 (Nov., 1967), pp. 2, 64.

ADDITIONAL READINGS FOR CHAPTER 1*

"The American Underclass: Red, White and Black," *Trans-action,* V. 6, N. 4 (February 1969).

Lerone Bennett, Jr., *Before the Mayflower* (Chicago: Johnson Publishing Co., 1964).

Herman D. Bloch, *The Circle of Discrimination: An Economic and Social Study of the Black Man in New York* (New York: New York University Press, 1969).

Kenneth B. Clark, *Dark Ghetto: Dilemmas of Social Power* (New York: Harper & Row, Publishers, 1965).

Harold Cruse, *Rebellion or Revolution* (New York: William Morrow & Company, 1968).

John P. Davis (ed.), *The American Negro Reference Book* (Englewood Cliffs, N.J.: Prentice-Hall, 1966).

St. Clair Drake and Horace R. Cayton, *Black Metropolis: A Study of Negro Life in a Northern City,* Rev. ed. (New York: Harper & Row, Publishers, 1962), Vs. I & II.

W. E. B. DuBois, *The Philadelphia Negro: A Social Study* (New York: Schocken Books, 1967).

Otis Dudley Duncan, "Discrimination Against Negroes," *Annals of the American Academy of Political and Social Science,* V. 371 (May 1967), pp. 85-103.

Stanley M. Elkins, *Slavery: A Problem in American Institutional and Intellectual Life* (New York: Grosset & Dunlap, 1963).

John Hope Franklin, *From Slavery to Freedom: A History of Negro Americans,* 3rd ed. (New York: Vintage Books, A Division of Random House, 1967).

E. Franklin Frazier, *The Negro Family in the United States,* Rev. and abr. ed. (Chicago: The University of Chicago Press, 1966).

——, *The Negro in the United States,* Rev. ed. (New York: The Macmillan Company, 1957).

Kenneth G. Goode, *From Africa to the United States And Then . . . ,* (Glenview, Ill.: Scott, Foresman and Company, 1969).

John F. Kain (ed.), *Race and Poverty: The Economics of Discrimination* (Englewood Cliffs, N.J.: Prentice-Hall, 1969).

Charles Keil, *Urban Blues* (Chicago: The University of Chicago Press, 1966).

Elliot Liebow, *Tally's Corner: A Study of Negro Streetcorner Men* (Boston: Little, Brown and Company, 1967).

Seymour Martin Lipset, *The First New Nation* (New York: Basic Books, 1963).

The Negro Family: The Case for National Action (Moynihan Report) (Washington, D.C.: Office of Policy Planning and Research, U.S. Department of Labor, March 1965).

Talcott Parsons and Kenneth B. Clark (eds.), *The Negro American* (Boston: Beacon Press, 1965).

Thomas F. Pettigrew, *A Profile of the Negro Ameri-*

can (Princeton, N.J.: D. Van Nostrand Company, 1964).

Alphonso Pinkney, *Black Americans* (Englewood Cliffs, N.J.: Prentice-Hall, 1969).

Lee Rainwater (ed.), *Soul* (Chicago: Aldine Publishing Company, 1970).

Lee Rainwater and William L. Yancey, *The Moynihan Report and the Politics of Controversy* (Cambridge, Mass.: The M.I.T. Press, 1967).

Arnold Rose, *The Negro in America* (Boston: Beacon Press, 1948).

Paul M. Siegel, "On the Cost of Being a Negro," *Sociological Inquiry,* V. 35, N. 1 (Winter 1965), pp. 41-58.

Charles E. Silberman, *Crisis in Black and White* (New York: Vintage Books, A Division of Random House, 1964).

Kenneth M. Stampp, *The Peculiar Institution: Slavery in the Ante-Bellum South* (New York: Vintage Books, A Division of Random House, 1956).

Karl and Alma Taeuber, *Negroes in Cities* (Chicago: Aldine Publishing Company, 1965).

U.S. Bureau of the Census, *Changing Characteristics of The Negro Population,* by Daniel O. Price (A 1960 Census Monograph) (Washington, D.C.: U.S. Government Printing Office, 1969).

U.S. Department of Labor (Bureau of Labor Statistics) and U.S. Department of Commerce (Bureau of the Census), *Social and Economic Conditions of Negroes in the United States (1969),* BLS Report No. 375 and Current Population Reports, Series P-23, No. 29 (Washington, D.C.: U.S. Government Printing Office, 1969).

Max Way, "The Deeper Shame of the Cities," *Fortune,* V. LXXVII, N. 1 (January 1968), pp. 122-132, 205-209.

Eric Williams, *Capitalism and Slavery* (New York: Russell & Russell, 1961).

Albert and Roberta Wohlstetter, "'Third Worlds' Abroad and at Home," *The Public Interest,* N. 14 (Winter 1969), pp. 88-107.

*The works listed above and at the conclusion of succeeding chapters should be consulted *in addition* to the sources from which the selections in this book are drawn. Further references for this chapter can be obtained by consulting the works cited in Chapter 1. The reader may also wish to refer to the excellent bibliography appearing at the conclusion of Andrew F. Brimmer and Harriet Harper, "Economists' Perception of Minority Economic Problems: A View of Emerging Literature," Journal of Economic Literature, V. VIII, N. 3 (September 1970), esp. pp. 788-806.

3 Contemporary Racial
Their Social and

In a country in which racial factors play such an important part in determining the opportunities (life chances) and mode of life (life style) of its citizens, it is important to examine the impact of racial attitudes upon the relationship of one group of citizens to "the other Americans." Attitudes, in and of themselves, are not necessarily significant; what is critical is how attitudes are manifested in behavior—in the activities and interactions of human beings. Although there exists some disagreement among scholars concerning this point, it can be argued that discrimination (manifested behavior) is prejudice (an attitudinal phenomenon) made operational.[1] If, on the subject of race, both blacks and whites were both attitudinally and behaviorally neutral—that is, if race were not a salient factor in the individual's or group's evaluative and decision-making processes—racial considerations would be irrelevant in determining the socioeconomic position of all members of the society. Other criteria might emerge which would be no less objectionable and uncontrollable by the individual—for example, the size of his ears or the length of his foot—but race would cease to be a determinative social factor.

In addition to the economic consequences of racial attitudes are their social and psychological effects upon individuals and groups. It is valuable to examine these factors in order to understand the past and contemporary relationship between blacks and whites and to permit some assessment of the likelihood of significant changes in this relationship in the years ahead.

The first selection, "Black Views of Racial Issues," prepared by Angus Campbell and Howard Schuman of the Survey Research Center of the University of Michigan and published as a Supplementary Study for the National Commission on Civil Disorders (Kerner Commission), examines the attitudes of black Americans *vis à vis* whites regarding a variety of racial issues. The data reported here (drawn from a survey of approximately 2,500 blacks in fifteen cities throughout the nation) present a picture of black perceptions of racial reality within the United States. The study is, therefore, of value both for suggesting plausible explanations of racially significant events of the recent past and indicating possible directions that social action by the black community may take in the near future. The reader should be aware that individual and collective attitudes are not permanently fixed. In times of rapid social change, attitudes may change in response to events, and, indeed, may help shape events. The attitudinal studies reprinted in this chapter present views current at the time the survey research was conducted in early 1968 among the particular sample surveyed—although we believe that the data continues to reflect predominant racial views.

In the selection from Thomas F. Pettigrew's *A Profile of the Negro American*, "Psychological Gains and Psychological Losses," the author, a Harvard social psychologist, explores the psychological importance of the feeling of "relative

Attitudes, Black and White:
Psychological Implications

deprivation" held by many blacks. By this term, Pettigrew refers to a sense of increased frustration and dissatisfaction among blacks concerning their life's condition at a time when some significant improvements have taken place. On the basis of his examination of black attitudes and beliefs, he also ventures four predictions concerning likely future patterns of action among blacks as they continue and intensify their striving for full equality in American society. Although the importance which Pettigrew attributed to nonviolent direct activity by blacks and the apparent receptivity of the nation to dramatic social change was probably more true of the early 1960s than of today, his overall analysis remains valid.

Equally important as black attitudes concerning whites—indeed, arguably, even more important, since whites constitute an overwhelming majority of the American population and maintain a virtual monopoly of power within the society—are white views concerning blacks. In "White Beliefs About Negroes," which also appeared as one of the Supplemental Studies for the National Advisory Commission on Civil Disorders, Professors Campbell and Schuman have provided the complement of the first selection in this chapter. Based upon approximately 2,500 respondents in fifteen cities throughout the United States, the data explore the feeling of whites towards blacks on a variety of subjects, including governmental policy toward blacks. It will come as little surprise to the reader that significant disparities exist between blacks and whites in their perceptions of social reality.

In "Why Did It Happen? The Basic Causes," drawn from the Report of the National Advisory Commission on Civil Disorders, the Commission ventures some opinions concerning the reasons underlying the outbreak of civil disorder in a number of cities during the summer of 1967. Many of the themes presented in several of the earlier readings in this chapter recur in the selection from the Kerner Commission Report, making it of great value in drawing together seemingly disparate but actually related ideas in the context of specific social events.

The reader will notice that the selections in this chapter fall into two distinct categories. The excerpts from the Kerner Report and Supplemental Studies can be considered sociological "macroanalysis" in that they present data and make observations concerning blacks and whites as total populations. On the other hand, the Pettigrew essay constitutes "microanalysis" in that it focuses upon the individual as the unit of examination. We have selected material from both categories to present an overview of the subject.

NOTES

[1]Recent research has suggested that intervening variables such as perceived reference group support, social constraint and social distance may serve as mediating influences between racial attitudes and overt

behavior. See, e.g., James M. Fendrich, "Perceived Reference Group Support: Racial Attitudes and Overt Behavior," *American Sociological Review,* V. 32, N. 6, (December 1967), pp. 960-970; and Lyle G. Warner and Melvin L. DeFleur, "Attitude As an Interactional Concept: Social Constraint and Social Distance as Intervening Variables Between Attitudes and Action," *American Sociological Review,* V. 34, N. 2 (April 1969), pp. 153-169. See also, Irwin Deutscher, "Words and Deeds: Social Science and Social Policy," *Social Problems,* V. 13. N. 3 (Winter 1966), pp. 235-254; Lawrence S. Linn, "Verbal Attitudes and Overt Behavior: A Study of Racial Discrimination," *Social Forces,* V. 43, N. 3 (March, 1965); and Milton Rokeach, "Attitude Change and Behavioral Change," *Public Opinion Quarterly,* V. 30, N. 4 (Winter 1967) pp. 529-540.

BLACK VIEWS OF RACIAL ISSUES

Angus Campbell and Howard Schuman

A group of Negro college students at a major northern university in May, 1968, demanded the provision of separate dormitory accommodations. To some ears it sounded like a call for segregation by race, another example of recent repudiations by some Negroes of the goal of integration. In the first section of this chapter we will describe the extent to which integration remains a goal of black Americans in the 15 cities we studied. We will also examine the *meaning* attached by Negroes to integration in such concrete contexts as schools. The second section attempts to look for possible signs of change in our data, so that we do not too quickly impose a static view on what is obviously a volatile period in American racial history. In the third section we present fragmentary but interesting evidence on a type of change in Negro aspirations that is not really located on a simple separatist-integrationist dimension. The fourth section turns to an account of the appeal militant leaders have to nonseparatist followers. Negro perceptions of discrimination and prejudice are described and a preliminary attempt is made to locate these in terms of the dimensions of age and education. The chapter ends with a brief consideration of some of the main strategies adopted by Negroes in confronting obstacles perceived as due to white racial attitudes and practices.

Reprinted from "Racial Attitudes in Fifteen American Cities," Angus Campbell and Howard Schuman, *Supplemental Studies for the National Advisory Commission on Civil Disorders* (Washington, D.C.: U.S. Government Printing Office, July 1968), pp. 15-28. Footnotes omitted.

RACIAL INTEGRATION AND BLACK SEPARATISM

We did not ask many general questions about the desirability of integration, but posed the issue concretely in terms of several specific areas of life. For example, the following table (Table 1) gives the results of a question concerned with residential integration.

Table 1. *"Would you personally prefer to live in a neighborhood with all Negroes, mostly Negroes, mostly whites, or a neighborhood that is mixed half and half?"*

[In percent]

	Negro		
	Men	Women	Total
All negro	7	8	8
Mostly Negro	7	4	5
Mostly White	1	1	1
Mixed half and half	47	48	48
Makes no difference	37	37	37
Don't know	1	2	1
	100	100	100

Nearly half the Negro sample indicate a preference for a mixed neighborhood and another third claim that the racial character of the neighborhood makes no difference to them. Only one Negro respondent out of eight in our sample favors residential separation. The overwhelming majority prefer "integration" either in the positive sense of "racial balance" or in the nondiscriminatory sense of race being irrelevant to decisions about neighborhood.

These percentages must not be taken too literally: they are influenced not only by general attitudes toward integration or separation, but by the particular subject matter of the question, in this case, residence, and by peculiarities of wording. A better idea of the range of answers to questions on integration and separation is provided in Table 2, which lists all the questions we included within this area broadly defined. The questions are ordered in terms of the percentage giving an answer that seems in a "separatist" direction—that is, show some rejection of whites or some preference for racial exclusiveness.

Table 2. *Percentage of Negroes Favoring Separatist Response to Each of Ten Questions*

	Men	Women	Total
Believe stores in "a Negro neighborhood should be owned and run by Negroes"	21	15	18
Believe school with mostly Negro children should have Negro principal	17	12	14
Prefer to live in all Negro or mostly Negro neighborhood	14	12	13
Believe school with mostly Negro children should have mostly Negro teachers	13	7	10
Agree that "Negroes should have nothing to do with whites if they can help it"	11	8	9
Believe whites should be discouraged from taking part in civil rights organizations	9	6	8
Prefer own child to go to all or mostly Negro school	7	6	6
Believe close friendship between Negroes and whites is impossible .	6	5	6
Agree that "there should be a separate black nation here"	7	4	6
Prefer child to have only Negro friends, not white friends too ...	6	4	5

The findings from this table are clear-cut. When Negro respondents are asked whether they wish their children to have only Negro friends, they reject this possibility by 19 to 1. When asked whether they favor "a separate black nation here" (the exact location unspecified), they again reject this by 19 to 1. Both in their personal lives and on issues concerning public institutions, Negroes in these 15 cities oppose black separatism by an overwhelming margin. The largest support for racial exclusiveness turns on the ownership by Negroes of stores in a Negro neighborhood, which is supported by nearly one out of five members of the sample; yet even on this highly publicized current issue, four out of five respondents refuse to introduce race as a criterion for ownership or control.

It may be argued that responses implying integration are chosen largely for pragmatic reasons. Negroes tend to perceive neighborhood services in white or mixed residential areas as better than those in largely Negro areas. White businessmen may be seen as having capital to maintain a wider range of merchandise. White schools may be regarded as having the benefit of better facilities or less crowded conditions. Because of such real social and economic differences, Negroes might lean toward "mixed" or "white" responses for purely practical reasons.

In order to explore this issue, we asked respondents to explain their answers to several of the questions given in Table 2. The results of two such follow-up inquiries are shown in Tables 3 and 4. They point in two directions. First, a sizable proportion of the Negro sample do, in fact, mention a "practical" reason for preferring mixed schools and mixed neighbor-

Table 3. *"Why do you feel that way?"*
[Follow-up Question to Preference for Racial Composition of School]

[In percent]

	Negro		
	Men	Women	Total
Type of Explanation Given by Those Preferring "Mixed" Schools:			
Mixed schools have better facilities (e.g., "teachers take more time in a mixed school")	24	25	24
Learn to get along with each other (e.g., "kids should grow up together and learn to get along")	30	29	30
Other (e.g., "race shouldn't be that important")	6	6	6
Inapplicable—Already said race should not make any difference— not asked follow-up question	30	29	30
Prefer Negro school	7	6	6
Don't know	3	5	4
	100	100	100

hoods—24 percent in the former case and 14 percent in the latter. But second, as large or an even larger proportion give a more purely integrationist response (30 percent for schools and 18 percent for neighborhoods) which emphasizes the desirability of Negroes and whites learning "to get along with each other." To these latter integrationist respondents, we should add the more than a third of the sample who claimed that race should not make any difference at all, since such people can hardly be seen as individuals who would favor racial exclusiveness. The results then indicate that a majority of Negro respondents not only favor integration, but that they do so because of either a commitment to racial harmony or a conviction that racial considerations should be transcended entirely.

The desire for better school and neighborhood facilities and a belief in integration as an end in itself are, of course, not mutually exclusive. The high percentage of Negroes (95 percent) in Table 2 who would like their children to have white as well as Negro friends suggests

that many respondents who mention "practical facilities" to other questions are not intending to rule out an interest in integration for its own sake. On the other hand, . . . Negroes in these 15 cities have many specific dissatisfactions about their cities that have little to do directly with issues of integration.

It is also worth noting that even responses which suggest an apparent desire for "black power" may in reality reflect a somewhat different concern. Although 14 percent of the Negro sample believe a mostly Negro school should have a Negro principal, only a tiny proportion explain this in terms of black control of black institutions. Most speak in terms of the better understanding Negro principals will have of Negro children, or their superior ability to work closely with the parents of their pupils. And, of course, despite these quite practical reasons for wanting Negro principals in all-Negro schools, *most* Negroes in our sample do *not* believe that race should enter into the selection process.

In summary, it is clear that in early 1968 the major commitment of the great majority of the Negro population in these 15 cities was not to racial exclusiveness insofar as this meant personal rejection of whites or an emphasis on racial considerations in running community institutions. Negroes hold strongly, perhaps more strongly than any other element in the American population, to a belief in nondiscrimination and racial harmony.

WINDS OF CHANGE?

The conclusions of the previous section do not provide much support for the sense of radical change that comes from listening to new and more militant voices from the black community. One possibility is that these new leaders have no following. However, another possibility is that our data reflect well enough the inertia of opinion in this large urban Negro population, but not at all well the potentiality for change growing rapidly within it. In this section we will attempt to look hard at the data both for signs of such growth and for the importance of what change may already have occurred. This will

Table 4. *"Why do you feel that way?"* (Follow-up Question to Preference for Racial Composition of Neighborhood)

[In percent]

	Negro		
	Men	Women	Total
Type of Explanation Given by Those Preferring "Mixed" Neighborhood			
Mixed neighborhood has better services (e.g., "schools are better")	5	4	4
Mixed neighborhood better place to live (e.g., "less crime," "quieter")	9	12	10
Learn to get along with each other (e.g., "we should learn to live together")	18	17	18
Other (e.g., "race should not make any difference in choosing a place to live")	9	8	9
Inapplicable—Already said race should not make any difference—not asked follow-up question	37	37	37
Prefer Negro neighborhood	14	12	13
Don't know	8	10	9
	100	100	100

require a somewhat more speculative orientation than we follow in most other parts of this report.

First, it is reasonable to argue that the small percentage of separatist thinking that does appear in the preceding tables deserves to be taken seriously in its own right. Small percents can represent large numbers of people. In this study, one percent of the Negro sample stands for approximately 33,000 people, ages 16 to 69, in the 15 cities in which we interviewed. A finding of 10 percent represents 330,000, or nearly one-third of a million persons. (This counts only Negroes in the 15 cities, there being an unknown but undoubtedly large number of individuals with similar beliefs in other American cities.) Thus when we say that six percent of the sample advocates the formation of a separate black nation, we are implying that some 200,000 Negroes in these 15 cities feel so little a part of American society that they favor withdrawing allegiance from the United States and in some sense establishing a separate national entity.

Unlike election polls where it is usually correct to focus on majority or at least plurality figures, "small" percentages in this study must not be disregarded as unimportant. In a formal election six percent of the vote means little, but in a campaign to change minds and influence policies, six percent of a population can represent a considerable force. This is particularly true when the six percent represents deviation from a traditional position, since it is likely that many of those who hold to the majority position do so with little thought or commitment. To deviate from a very widely held norm probably requires more conviction than to hold to it, and if we could estimate this extra factor and weight it into the results we might well find the force behind black nationalism to be considerably greater than its numbers suggest. Finally, the high degree of residential and general social segregation in these cities promotes communication and association among such individuals, and provides them with easy access to just the audience they wish to reach.

In addition to appreciating the absolute size and strength of separatist opinion, there is the equally important question of how fast it is growing, if indeed it is growing at all. A single survey, however, is like a single photograph, and

there is no direct way it can measure recent rates of change, let alone predict with precision future rates. There is no past survey of this 15-city population with which we can closely compare our present results, and we must rely on age as an indirect indication of change. We make the assumption that what change there is in the long-term goal of integration is likely to occur most rapidly among the young. It was a relatively young minister, Martin Luther King, who at the age of 27 led the Montgomery bus boycott in 1957. College students were the main participants in the "sit-ins" of the early 1960's. Today, as we near the end of the decade, it appears to be black youth in colleges and black youth on ghetto streets who are least satisfied with America as it is, or perhaps even as their parents wish it to be. This fits the common assumption that the young are less conservative in the generic sense of the word: satisfaction with the currently traditional ways of doing things. If the youth in our sample show more separatist thinking than the older men and women, one can interpret this as a sign of change, using the shape and steepness of the age curve as a rough measure of the rate of change.

The use of age as an indicator in this way has definite problems. One is the difficulty of separating the trend movement in which we are interested from youthful rebellions that have no lasting effect but subside into middle-aged acceptance. Nor, on the other hand, can we be sure that the "rate of change" one estimates by comparing young and old is itself unchanging; if the rate accelerates, young children coming of "interview age" will differ more from their teenage fellows than the latter do from present adults. More generally, the projection of present trends to describe the future is full of risk, since unforeseen events—an assassination, a war, a major racial clash—can always alter the direction or speed of change. The following discussion must be read with these reservations in mind.

Five of the ten questions discussed earlier were selected as conceptually closest to "separatism," and the relation of each to age is shown in Table 5. The overall trend seems clear: younger people are somewhat more accepting of separatist beliefs than are older people. The trend is more consistent for men than for women, with the latter showing little perceptible

Table 5. *Percentage in Each Age Category Showing Separatist Thinking on Five Questions*

	Negro men					
	16-19	*20-29*	*30-39*	*40-49*	*50-59*	*69-69*
Believe stores in "a Negro neighborhood should be owned and run by Negroes"	28	23	20	18	14	18
Believe school with mostly Negro children should have mostly Negro teachers	22	15	13	6	5	15
Agree that "Negroes should have nothing to do with whites if they can help it"	18	14	6	12	4	13
Believe whites should be discouraged from taking part in civil rights organizations	19	12	8	6	3	5
Agree that "there should be a separate black nation here" . . .	11	10	5	5	4	10
	Negro women					
Believe stores in "a Negro neighborhood should be owned and run by Negroes"	18	16	16	15	13	8
Believe school with mostly Negro children should have mostly Negro teachers	11	9	6	5	5	12
Agree that "Negroes should have nothing to do with whites if they can help it"	11	7	7	8	5	7
Believe whites should be discouraged from taking part in civil rights organizations	11	7	7	5	7	3
Agree that "there should be a separate black nation here" . . .	9	3	2	6	4	3

change on the more extreme items (defined as those with the smallest percentage of separatist response for the sample as a whole). There is also one quite consistent reversal of the main trend: the oldest males "double-back" and are much more separatist than would be expected from the primary direction of change. We suspect this involves an irrelevent artifact, but cannot explore the problem in the present report.

Table 6 presents broad age trends in conjunction with educational groupings. The latter show little relation to separatist response, but the age differences continue to hold within almost all educational groups. There is a hint in the table, which will need further investigation, that institutional self-rule appeals to more educated Negroes, while wholesale rejection of whites appeals to the less educated.

In general, then, younger Negroes do assert separatist beliefs more strongly than do older Negroes. If one ignores the oldest age group (60-69) as artifactual, the change between the 50 to 59 group and the 16 to 19 represents at least a doubling of percent separatist thinking for women and a tripling for men. If the 60 to 69 cohort is included, as caution dictates, the increase is about .50 over the total age span contained in the table. The largest jump is from individuals in their 20s to the 16 to 19 category.

If we were to assume that the younger people will hold to their beliefs, then in a little more than a generation separatism would rise noticeably over the whole population. *Even then,* however, it would remain a distinctly minority position within the Negro community. Instead of being represented by five or ten percent of the Negro population, it would characterize 15 or at most 20 percent of the adult Negroes in these 15 cities. The majority would still have to be described as "integrationist" in goal and sentiment.

It would be possible to project more dramatic change in Negro opinion if one introduced one or both of two additional assumptions. For example, if we assumed that the rate of change for maturing age groups continued for those cohorts entering the adult population, rather than remaining at the level we have observed in this survey, there would obviously be a long-term increment in separatist thinking. Thus we would have to assume that the attitudes of the new generation entering the 16 to 19 year-old category departed even further from the general average of the total Negro population than the present 16 to 19 year-old group does. Our data showing the rate of change from one age group to the next might be interpreted as suggesting some such increment but the evidence could only be taken as inferential and does not dem-

56   A PRIMER ON AMERICA

Table 6. *Percentage in Each Age and Education Group Showing Separatist Thinking*
[Results for Negro Men and Women Averaged]

	Age 16-19*	Age 20-39					Age 40-69				
		8th grade or less	9-11 grades	12 grades	Some college	College graduate	8th grade or less	9-11 grades	12 grades	Some college	College graduate
Believe stores in "a Negro neighborhood should be owned and run by Negroes"	22	19	18	18	20	30	16	13	13	17	13
Believe school with mostly Negro children should have mostly Negro teachers	16	8	11	10	10	20	10	4	5	5	3
Agree that "Negroes should have nothing to do with whites if they can help it"	14	18	11	6	6	0	14	5	5	5	4
Believe whites should be discouraged from taking part in civil rights organizations	15	14	7	8	11	10	5	5	5	5	5
Agree that "there should be a separate black nation here"	10	8	5	6	2	4	8	3	2	5	0

*This group combines all educational categories.

onstrate the validity of the assumption in question.

A second assumption which might be considered would project an increase in separatist opinion in those age cohorts where such thought is now least popular, the older generations. If separatist thinking increases among the young and is "taken up" by popular leaders and the influential mass media, one might assume that it would diffuse in some degree into the larger Negro population.[1] To the extent that this diffusion was successful the separatist position might change from the clearly deviant one it is today to one of far greater influence.

We must emphasize again, however, that these speculations go far beyond what our data tell us. Even the age trends on which much of this speculation is based are not as steep or consistent as many readers might have expected. In fact, sharper age differences are reported ... on another subject (the use of violence) but evidence is also presented there that casts doubt on how much the differences represent long-term shifts in orientation; they seem at least as much to represent youthful boldness, much of which may not persist with maturation.

At this point, then, it is useful to reiterate the main findings presented earlier in the chapter. Most Negroes of all age groups today reject separatist thinking both in the political and in the personal sense. Commitment to the values of nondiscrimination and racial harmony are paramount for Negroes in these 15 cities.

PLURALISM: AN ALTERNATE PATH

"Black separatism," both as preached and as practiced, actually has two clearly distinguishable aspects. One side is largely political and social, calling for black control of institutions that serve the black population and for concentration of all informal social relationships within the black community. We have already seen that this program has relatively little support at present within the Negro population of these 15 cities. The other aspect of the program is cultural in the sociological sense of the term and attempts to encourage the growth of a positive black identity, a realization of the significance of black achievement, both in Africa and in America, and a desire to contribute to the development of the black community. We find in our data some important evidence that this cultural emphasis has wide appeal within the urban Negro population.

The results of four questions that point in this direction are presented in Table 7. It is perhaps no surprise to learn that 96 percent of the sample affirm that "Negroes should take more pride in Negro history," or that nearly as many agree "there should be more Negro business, banks, and stores." But it is striking indeed that 42 percent of this sample believe "Negro school children should study an African language." Unfortunately, we had no other question that so clearly taps positive identification with a black heritage without at the same time implying rejection of whites. But the support for this single proposition, which a few years ago was scarcely discussed by most Negroes and still seems exotic and impractical to most white ears, is so impressive that it suggests a considerable potential for the growth of black cultural identity in America. It also suggests that the more frequently voiced demand for more Negro history in public schools probably has very broad support in the Negro population.

The gap between the 42 percent agreement with this item and the 9 percent agreement reported earlier with the item "Negroes should

Table 7 *Percentage of Negroes Approving Each of Four Positive Cultural Identity Statements*

	Men	Women	Total
"Negroes should take more pride in Negro history"	96	96	96
"There should be more Negro business, banks, and stores" . . .	95	92	94
"Negroes should shop in Negro owned stores whenever possible"	70	69	70
"Negro school children should study an African language" . . .	46	38	42

not have anything to do with whites if they can help it" (Table 2) is a good indication of the difference in appeal between programs emphasizing positive cultural identity and programs espousing rigid social separation. The positive character of this interest in having children study African languages is further brought out by some of the explanations respondents gave for agreeing with the item:

Since all races have a language of their own it would be good if we had one too. Italians, Germans, Jews have one, why not us?

The majority of the explanations are in fact universalistic, offering a reason that is very much in keeping with general American values:

I feel they should study all languages.

They teach every other language, an African language could be taught too.

And a few responses carry a negative edge:

In school you are only taught the white man's language. You are not taught the Negro native language.

The proposal thus has appeal to many segments of the Negro population.

Results of the African language item by age and education are shown in Table 8. They indicate a slight trend for agreement to be associated with *lower* education, but no consistent relation to age. This is somewhat puzzling and suggests that the item represents not so much a new idea, but more an appeal to rather long-standing needs within the Negro community. Its greater attraction to the less-educated

may also indicate that its importance is mostly symbolic, since those least able to add such an extra language burden to their education are most willing to approve a proposal to do so. It may also indicate that the item appeals especially to those in the Negro community who are furthest from having achieved a middle-class American way of life. The item also has one of the highest "don't know" percentages of any question in the interview; while not surprising, the exact meaning of this will have to be clarified through further analysis.

There is one other finding in Table 7 that is of interest but also somewhat puzzling. Over two-thirds of the sample agree with the statement that "Negroes should shop in Negro owned stores whenever possible." This was intended as an indicator of separatism and might well have been listed in Table 2. The precentage agreement, however, is so far out of line with any question in the separatism set that we feel it was understood by many people in a way different than intended. Note, for example, that in Table 2, 80 percent of the sample rejected giving Negroes the exclusive right to own stores in Negro areas. Our assumption is borne out by explanations of those who indicated agreement. They talk for the most part in terms of offering positive support for the struggling Negro businessman who is trying to make a success of his business. They seldom relate this to not patronizing white-owned stores. Perhaps having just earlier indicated their agreement that "there should be more Negro business, banks, and stores," the need to patronize such stores to make them successful was especially salient to respondents. In any case, we interpret the result here as more an emphasis on promoting positive Negro achievement than on separatism or rejection of whites, though it obviously is a somewhat ambiguous item.

In summary, this section suggests strongly the value of further study of the interest of urban Negroes in positive racial symbols of achievement and identity, without confounding this interest with more social or political issues involving separatism. As in the case of religious and ethnic groups in America, there seems to be wide support for cultural individuality *within* a larger interracial social structure. Such affirmation of black identity is in keeping with American pluralism and should not be termed

Table 8. *"Negro School Children Should Study an African Language"*
[Percentages for Men and Women Averaged]

	Age 16-19*	Age 20-39					Age 40-69				
		8th grade or less	9-11 grades	12 grades	Some college	College graduate	8th grade or less	9-11 grades	12 grades	Some college	College graduate
Approve	44	54	41	39	43	28	43	44	38	33	33
Disapprove ...	46	33	47	46	44	61	37	38	51	49	42
Don't know**..	8	7	11	12	12	9	17	17	10	18	24
Other	2	6	1	3	1	2	3	1	1	0	1
	100	100	100	100	100	100	100	100	100	100	100

*This group combines all educational categories.
**The "don't know" category is quite large and probably of substantive importance in indicating uncertainty, hence it has been distinguished from other miscellaneous responses.

"separatism." It does, however, contain a source from which leaders advocating separatism can draw, especially if there is wide disillusionment with the possibility of making integration work in social and political contexts.

SOURCES OF DISSATISFACTION

The rise of angry and militant black leaders, like the outbursts of urban rioting, are not only disturbing to many white Americans, but puzzling as well. Considering the improvements for Negroes over the past 15 years—visible in Supreme Court decisions, in civil rights legislation, in appointments to high offices, and perhaps most of all in the appearance for the first time of black faces in restaurants and airplanes, on television and movie screens—why aren't black Americans more satisfied? Why, indeed, are they not gratified by the enormous progress that has occurred in race relations during and since what a distinguished author referred to as "a revolutionary decade, 1954 to 1964," one that the "most far-seeing of men standing at the beginning of the period, would have been quite unlikely to predict. . . ."

The following that "black nationalist" spokesmen have can easily be exaggerated, of course. In our survey, as in all previous studies we know of, their popular support is much less than that for the NAACP or for the late Dr. Martin Luther King (Table 9). Nevertheless, the at least partial support they have is not small, particularly when one considers that the mili-

tant figures mentioned in Table 9 were hardly known at all several years ago. Stokely Carmichael's "stand" is approved or partly approved by 35 percent of the sample, the same percentage that show clear disapproval. H. Rap Brown wins less support, but nevertheless more than a quarter of the sample gives general or partial approval to what he "stands for," and slightly less than half the sample disapproves. The names of both men seem to be slightly better known than the name of Roy Wilkins, Executive Director of the NAACP.

Approval or partial approval for a man does not necessarily mean approval for his specific programs—the connections are frequently hazy to the average respondent. We have already seen that there is little support for black separatism as a political movement. . . . We will show that support for violence is somewhat greater, but still quite limited in percentage terms. The main attraction that men like H. Rap Brown and Stokely Carmichael have to the wider Negro community is probably their emphasis on the serious difficulties Negroes face and the vociferous attribution of these difficulties to white America.

Our interest here lies not so much in the amount of support for any particular spokesman, but rather in the extent to which *racial* conditions are seen by Negroes as cause for profound and justified criticism. We will look at this in terms of two general areas of possible criticism: first, the extent of overt discrimination that is perceived to exist today in America,

Table 9. *"Now I want to read you a list of people active in civil rights. For each one, please tell me whether you approve or disapprove of what the person stands for, or don't know enough about him to say?"*

[In percent]

	Negro		
	Men	Women	Total
STOKELY CARMICHAEL			
Approve	18	10	14
Partly approve and partly			
disapprove	24	17	21
Disapprove	34	36	35
Don't know	24	37	30
	100	100	100
MARTIN LUTHER KING			
Approve			
Partly approve and partly	70	74	72
disapprove	22	16	19
Disapprove	5	4	5
Don't know	3	6	4
	100	100	100
ROY WILKINS			
Approve	54	46	50
Partly approve and partly			
disapprove	13	11	12
Disapprove	4	2	3
Don't know	29	41	35
	100	100	100
H. RAP BROWN			
Approve	17	10	14
Partly approve and partly			
disapprove	14	12	13
Disapprove	46	44	45
Don't know	23	34	28
	100	100	100
HOW ABOUT THE NAACP?			
Approve	77	74	75
Partly approve and partly			
disapprove	12	10	11
Disapprove	3	3	3
Don't know	8	13	11
	100	100	100

and second, Negro perceptions of white racial attitudes of a more intangible nature.

AN END TO DISCRIMINATION?

We began this chapter by noting that a large proportion of the white population probably believe that much progress has been made over the last 15 years in eliminating overt racial discrimination in the United States. No single question about such change was asked of whites and we state this as an assumption of what we would find. We did ask Negroes such a question,

however, and the results are illuminating. The question (Table 10) concerns the amount of progress that has been made over the past ten or fifteen years "in getting rid of racial discrimination" in America. Although a majority of the Negro sample believes that substantial progress has been made, the more striking finding is that one out of every three respondents agrees that there has not been "much real change for most Negroes" over a period that dates roughly from the 1954 Supreme Court decision on school desegregation. The basic assumption of major improvement, so seemingly obvious to many white Americans, is not accepted by many black Americans.

One might expect denial that progress has occurred to come especially from younger people. They did not experience the more blatant forms of discrimination characteristic of America in 1950, nor did they see one type of racial segregation after another outlawed over a relatively short time. The age trends for the data provide some support for this expectation. Of teenagers, 43 percent of the males and 37 percent of the females disclaim progress, but in the 60 to 69 year old groups the percentages drop to 28 and 26 percent, respectively. The age trend is smooth for men, but somewhat irregular for women. Among younger people (ages 20 to 39), the more educated of both sexes recognize more change; there is little relation of education to perception of change for persons over 40. Taken together these results suggest that those who are older and those who have more education are better able to recognize the broad movement of events of the last decade and a half. Negroes too young to have person-

Table 10. *"Some people say that over the past 10 or 15 years there has been a lot of progress in getting rid of racial discrimination. Others say that there hasn't been much real change for most Negroes over that time. Which do you agree with most?"*

[In percent]

	Negro		
	Men	Women	Total
A lot of progress	63	60	62
Hasn't been much real change	34	36	35
Don't know	3	4	3
	100	100	100

ally experienced the break-up of many traditional racial patterns and those with less general awareness of recent history (or perhaps simply lower incomes, a correlate of education not yet explored) are more likely to deny that meaningful change has occurred.

But these effects are only moderate. Even among the oldest and among the best educated, a quarter still report that there has not been much real change for most Negroes. They do this apparently because from their perspective there has indeed been little visible change, whatever may have occurred elsewhere in the country. Respondents who said "no change" explained their responses in the following way:

We can do the same job as whites but get unequal pay. Education is different in white and colored schools.

... We bought this nice furniture, thought we were going to buy a house. When they found out we were Negroes they wouldn't sell to us.

There has been some but not much. There are still a lot of jobs that Negroes can't get and there are a lot of houses that Negroes can't rent or buy.

On the whole the prejudice of people is still the same. They are just pretending today.

The question just discussed speaks of discrimination in the abstract. Most of our inquiries in this area were more specific. Table 11 presents the results of nine questions dealing with employment. The first two questions indicate that more than a third of the Negro males in the sample claim to have *personally* experienced racial discrimination in employment. The figure is somewhat smaller for women, probably because fewer have been in the labor force. To avoid confusing recent with ancient history, we asked how long ago the last such incident had happened. For those mentioning any discrimination at all, the majority report an incident of discrimination within the past five years, and nearly three-quarters report an incident within the past ten years. We have no way, of course, to verify these reports. Even in a current situation it is often difficult to prove or disprove that job discrimination occurred. What is clear, however, is that a great many Negroes believe that discrimination not only happens, but that it has happened personally to them during the same

"past ten or fifteen years" referred to in the earlier question on change.

When job discrimination is asked about in more general terms, Table 11 indicates that about 70 percent of the sample believe that "many" or "some" Negroes (as against "few") miss out on good jobs because of their race. (Only about 40 percent, however, choose the term "many," rather than the vague word "some.") Approximately 40 percent of the sample believe that Negroes are discriminated against in federal employment, and the figure rises to over 50 percent when city employment is considered. The claim by some large private companies that they are looking for all capable Negroes they can find to put into good jobs has also not made a great impression in these 15 cities: nearly 80 percent of the sample believe that such hiring is only of a token nature. There is little difference by sex on any of these questions on perceptions of extent of discrimination, unlike the reports of personal experience mentioned above.

Discriminatory personal experience in the job area is reported most frequently by persons in their 20's and 30's, and less both by teenagers and by persons over 40 and especially over 50

Table 11. *Percentage of Negroes Perceiving Discrimination in Employment*

	Men	Women	Total
Report having been refused a job because of racial discrimination ..	34	25	30
Report having been refused promotion on a job because of racial discrimination	18	9	14
Believe many or some Negroes miss out on jobs today because of discrimination	72	70	71
Believe many or some Negroes miss out on promotions today because of race	68	67	68
Believe there is discrimination in hiring by the federal government	40	40	40
Believe there is discrimination in hiring by their city government	51	49	50
Believe there is discrimination in hiring in teaching	35	33	34
Believe big companies hire a few Negroes only for show purposes, to appear to be non-discriminatory	78	76	77
Believe discrimination in hiring and promotions is increasing or not changing	42	43	42

Table 12. *Age Trends Among Negroes for Four Questions on Employment Discrimination*

[Percentages for Men and Women Averaged*]

	Age					
	16-19	20-29	30-39	40-49	50-59	60-69
Have been personally discriminated against in employment	21	33	37	30	24	18
Have been personally discriminated against for promotions	4	12	17	18	12	13
Believe many Negroes miss out on good jobs because of discrimination	34	38	44	42	40	26
Believe many Negroes miss out on promotions because of discrimination . .	29	37	46	41	37	24

*Trends are very similar for men and women considered separately.

(Table 12). The lower rate in the former group is presumably due to the large proportion still in school. The lack of reporting in the older groups is less easily accounted for; these people may never have attempted to get jobs in competition with whites, or may be settled in their jobs and have forgotten early instances of discrimination, or may have been less ready to define an ambiguous situation as discriminatory. However, exactly the same trends occur for all the questions on extent of job discrimination. (Age trends for two such general items are shown in Table 12, along with the personal experience questions.) The mild curvilinear relationship that is repeated over all four questions in the table is difficult to account for. Rephrasing the explanation given above, we might hypothesize that those who are in their prime working years have the most involvement with employment and promotion and therefore the most immediate opportunity to perceive discrimination. This explanation does not seem to us wholly satisfactory, and further analysis will be required to support it or to arrive at a more adequate interpretation of the data.

Most knowledgeable white Americans agree that job discrimination is still a problem in American cities, but some comfort is often taken in the belief that such discrimination is decreasing. Whatever the truth of the matter, this belief is shared by only half the Negro respondents in our sample (Table 11 above). In fact, 20 percent of the sample believe job discrimination to be on the increase, the remaining 30 percent perceiving no change at all. Education makes some difference in this case for women—the more educated see a decrease in job discrimination—but there is no such relation for men. A better understanding of this difference will require analysis using employment status, and must be reserved for later reports.

Discrimination in housing is seen in dimensions that are roughly similar to those for employment (Table 13). We did not ask about *personal experience* in this area because much residential segregation is self-perpetuating: few Negroes seek housing in all-white areas which they think will prove inhospitable. Instead we asked whether there were "many, some, or just a few places" in the city where the respondent believed he "could *not* rent or buy a house because of racial discrimination." It should be noted that the question referred directly to the city itself and did not ask about the much more highly segregated suburban areas. Two out of five respondents believed there were many such places in their city, and another quarter felt there were "some" rather than few.

About the same proportion answered a more general question on whether Negroes "miss out on good housing" in their city because of race: 45 percent say "many" do and 30 percent that "some" do. Finally, a little over 50 percent of the sample see no decrease in residential discrimination underway at present. There are no differences by sex on any of these questions; age and education trends have not yet been studied.

Our questionnaire did not deal in detail with other social areas, for example, education. But Table 13 does sample two quite different public spheres. Judicial behavior, in theory far removed from racial bias, is seen as discrimina-

Table 13. *Percentage of Negroes Perceiving Discrimination in Housing and Other Areas*

	Men	Women	Total
Believe "many" or "some" Negroes (as against "few") in this city miss out on good housing because of racial discrimination	75	76	76
Believe there are "many" places (as against "some" or "none") in this city where they could not rent or buy a house because of discrimination	42	44	43
Believe that racial discrimination in housing is increasing or not changing	54	53	54
Believe judges in this city are harder on Negroes than on whites	25	19	22
Believe "city officials" pay less attention to a request from a Negro than a white person	62	59	60

tory by 22 percent of the sample. A much larger porportion—three out of five—expect unequal treatment when they go as citizens to make a request to "city officials." Indeed, this question produces the most widespread perception of discrimination of any item of the questionnaire. Both from it and from the earlier question on employment opportunities in city government, it seems that city hall does not ordinarily represent a model of social justice in the eyes of the majority of Negroes in our sample.

Although the percentages vary depending on the particular question, in general about 40 percent to 50 percent of the Negroes interviewed emphasize the seriousness of current discrimination to as great an extent as a given question allows. (This range does not apply to questions about personal experience or about rate of change.) The other half do not by any means discount discrimination as a force acting upon Negroes, but they qualify their answers somewhat where qualification is provided. This is especially true for the quarter of the sample that take the *least* emphatic way of describing discrimination, e.g., say that there are *"few* places" in the city where they could not rent or buy a house because of race.

From a descriptive standpoint, these results may come as a surprise to readers of several viewpoints. To those who feel deeply the existence of racial discrimination in the United States, it will be surprising that half the Negro

population in these 15 cities are somehow unable or unwilling to stress discrimination as an overwhelming factor in their lives. Yet clearly many Negroes either do not perceive much discrimination or deny it to be a serious problem. Indeed, had we presented our data from the opposite direction, we could have shown that about a quarter of the sample see job and housing discrimination as applying to only a few Negroes, not to "many" or even to "some." Not all black urban Americans see the world as does Stokely Carmichael, or indeed even as does a "moderate" civil rights organization such as the NAACP.

But white Americans who would like to believe that discrimination, at least in employment if not in housing, is an "out of date issue" in 1968, must face the fact that half the Negro population in 15 major cities see discriminatory treatment as a major obstacle to getting a good job, finding a good house, or even having complaints listened to by officials of one's own city. For a substantial proportion of the Negro sample, discontent can find a basis not only in economic deprivation and psychological dissatisfaction, but in the belief that basic improvement in one's condition of life is barred by overt white discrimination.

BLACK PERCEPTIONS OF WHITE ATTITUDES

Overt discrimination in such crucial areas as hiring is the side of racial tension in the United States easiest to condemn, easiest to legislate against, and easiest to ask survey questions about. Yet it seems clear that beyond initial decisions to employ, promote, or rent to another person, more personal actions and expressed attitudes are fundamental to black-white relations in 1968. What Negroes think whites think about Negroes (and vice versa) may in the end be as important as more clearcut issues of discrimination and economic advancement.

A good introduction to this complex issue is provided by a question that lies somewhere between explicit discrimination and the subtler expression of attitudes. We chose an area of social life where "integration" has been widespread for many years in most of the 15 cities, and where at least superficially pleasant relations between Negroes and whites are clearly called for by the official norms of the situation.

Table 14. *"Do you think Negro customers who shop in the big downtown stores are treated as politely as white customers, or are they treated less politely?"*

[Results for Negro Men and Women Averaged, in Percent]

	Age					
	16-19	*20-29*	*30-39*	*40-49*	*50-59*	*60-69*
As politely	60	56	60	67	66	64
Less politely	35	36	30	22	23	16
Don't know	5	8	10	11	11	20
	100	100	100	100	100	100

The question concerns politeness to customers in downtown department stores, and is shown by age categories in Table 14. More than a quarter of the sample responded that Negro customers receive less courtesy than white customers in major stores. This feeling is a good deal stronger among younger people, where the percentage perceiving discourtesy is twice that of the oldest age category. More than one out of three Negroes in their teens and twenties expect to be the object of discourteous behavior when they shop in downtown stores. This applies equally to men and women and it applies at all educational levels.

A much more direct question about white attitudes is shown in Table 15, having to do with perceptions of the extent to which black Americans are disliked by white Americans. One out of eight Negroes in the sample perceive a world where almost all white people dislike Negroes. (This includes one and a half percent who volunteered that *all* white people, not just almost all, dislike Negroes.) Again it is worthwhile to remind ourselves that these percentages stand for a great many people—in the present instance some 400,000 adults who face what they think of as an almost totally hostile white America.

Table 15. *"Do you think only a few white people in (City) dislike Negroes, many dislike Negroes or almost all white people dislike Negroes?"*

[In percent]

	Negro		
	Men	*Women*	*Total*
Few white people dislike Negroes .	38	37	38
Many dislike Negroes	44	46	45
Almost all dislike Negroes	13	11	12
Don't know	5	6	5
	100	100	100

Moreover they are supported in their beliefs by another 45 percent of the sample who anticipate dislike from "many" whites, which in the context of the other alternatives probably means at least half the white population. Altogether in these 15 cities, nearly two million Negro adults from 16 to 69 see themselves as a widely disliked racial minority.

The word "dislike" was a compromise among several terms—distrust, fear, depreciate, hate—that might have been chosen in phrasing the above question. One specification of it may be seen in a question about whether most white people want to see Negroes get a better break, want to keep Negroes down, or don't care one way or the other (Table 16).

Table 16. *"On the whole, do you think most white people in (City) want to see Negroes get a better break, or do they want to keep Negroes down, or don't they care one way or the other?"*

[In percent]

	Negro		
	Men	*Women*	*Total*
Most whites want to see Negroes get a better break	30	28	29
Most whites want to keep Negroes down	28	26	27
Most whites don't care	34	34	34
Don't know	8	12	10
	100	100	100

The results of this question are more polarized than the previous one. Three Negro respondents out of ten believe most white people are basically sympathetic to Negro advancement, but nearly the same proportion believe that most whites want to keep Negroes down. Another third see whites as indifferent to the fate of Negro Americans. Note that the selection of the sympathetic response did not require a belief

Table 17. *Age and Education Trends in Negro Perception of White Attitudes*

[Results for Men and Women Averaged, In Percent]

	16-19*	Age 20-39					Age 40-69				
		8th Grade or Less	9-11 Grades	12 Grades	Some College	College Graduate	8th Grade or Less	9-11 Grades	12 Grades	Some College	College Graduate
QUESTION ON NUMBER OF WHITES WHO DISLIKE NEGROES											
Few white people dislike Negroes	38	28	36	33	36	38	39	39	38	49	60
Many dislike Negroes	47	42	45	51	48	53	40	45	47	42	34
Almost all dislike Negroes	12	22	11	12	9	6	11	9	8	4	5
Don't know	3	8	8	4	7	3	10	7	7	5	1
	100	100	100	100	100	100	100	100	100	100	100
QUESTION ON WHITE STANCE TOWARD NEGRO ADVANCEMENT											
Most whites want to see Negroes get a better break	27	18	27	28	19	17	31	30	39	46	46
Most whites want to keep Negroes down	29	32	29	29	28	16	26	29	24	18	15
Most whites don't care	40	38	33	36	39	64	27	31	30	28	29
Don't know	4	12	11	7	14	3	16	10	7	8	10
	100	100	100	100	100	100	100	100	100	100	100

*This group combines all educational categories.

that whites were willing to *do* anything about improving conditions of Negroes, but only that whites "want" to see Negroes get a better break. The finding that seven out of ten Negroes reject such a statement points to a wide gulf, in Negro eyes, between black aspirations and white desire to support such aspirations.

Age and education trends for the two previous questions are somewhat complex, as shown in Table 17. Putting together the results for both questions, we can summarize the trends as follows: Negro adults in their 20's and 30's—the generation that came of age in the years following World War II—perceive more hostility and less sympathy from whites than does the older prewar generation. The differences are not great, but they are consistent over most educational levels and for both questions. However, there is no evidence that the loss of faith in whites is increasing even more with the Negro adults of tomorrow: youth 16 to 19 answer these two questions in much the same way as does the 20 to 29 year old category. Whether they will remain at this level we have no way of knowing.

There is a hint in the data that college-level education in earlier years was associated with a more optimistic view of white attitudes, but if this was indeed the case it is apparently not so with the post-World War II generation. Among the young adults college experience is not associated with a more positive view of whites. What college training does seem to do, and this is true of educational effects in the two tables more generally, is to modulate perceptions of whites, so that the respondent gives a less extreme response. More educated respondents are less likely to assert that all whites dislike Negroes or want to keep Negroes down, and more likely to see whites as indifferent or to recognize that there may be some genuine white support for Negroes. But education does not increase the proportion of Negroes who see *most* whites as sympathetic. These effects of education may be largely the result of greater sophistication, which makes a person less likely to choose an extreme response when a somewhat more qualified one is available.[2]

In summary, the three questions reviewed in this section provide evidence that the majority of Negroes expect little from whites other than hostility, opposition, or at best indifference. On the common-sense assumption that people who feel themselves the object of dislike will in turn feel dislike toward the perceived source, we would expect a great deal of black hostility toward whites. This return hostility might or might not be expressed openly, of course, depending upon a number of factors. We saw in the first section of this chapter that only some 10 percent of the Negro sample express open rejection of whites. At a more indirect attitudinal level we asked respondents whether they felt "they could trust Negroes more than white people, the same as white people, or less than white people." About a quarter of the sample (23 percent) indicated greater trust of Negroes than whites, while the rest reported no difference (68 percent) or claimed they trusted whites more than Negroes (7 percent). Age trends are quite similar to those just reported, but even sharper: the proportion (31 percent) of young people who trust Negroes more than whites is twice as great as the proportion (14 percent) among persons in their 60's. Figure 1 shows the trend to be generally smooth, but it is interesting to note again that the teenage group is not more extreme than the age 20 to 29 cohort. There is also a slight trend for the more educated respondents to say they trust members of both races the same.

The question on trust and the questions dealt with at the beginning of this chapter are the only ones that attempted to assess black antipathy toward whites. There is certainly evidence of such antagonism, but it is less great in these data than one would expect on the basis of the "mirror-image" assumption. It may be that our interview simply did not pick up such emotional hostility very well, but it is also possible that other factors serve to dilute the simple reciprocity implied by the assumption.

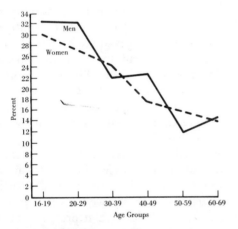

Figure 1. Percentages of Negroes Trusting Other Negroes More Than Whites

STRATEGIES FOR CHANGE

We have seen thus far that about half the Negro sample perceive serious problems with discrimination in areas such as employment. Roughly the same proportion expect hostility from whites at a more personal level. What then are the solutions Negroes see to racial problems in 1968?

Only a small minority, although not a trivial one in numbers, has moved very far toward separatist solutions. Most Negroes appear to have incorporated too strongly the values of equal opportunity regardless of race to change

suddenly to criteria that make racial considerations a major factor in decisions. Indeed, most Negroes reject the imposition of black political control even in areas of life where Negroes clearly predominate and where other ethnic groups have often demanded and received at least informal control.

Perhaps a supporting factor here is the belief that the race of the person in control has not in itself always been of decisive importance. We asked several questions about the effects of race on treatment and discovered only limited support for the notion that replacement of whites by blacks will make any great difference to most Negroes. With regard to whether black policemen treat Negroes better than do white policemen, 73 percent of the sample could not see any difference; the rest were divided somewhat more in favor of white policemen than of Negro policemen.[3] With regard to stores in Negro neighborhoods, Negro and white owned stores are thought to be about the same in terms of fair pricing. Black storekeepers are seen as somewhat more respectful of Negro customers than are white storekeepers (15 percent to 7 percent), but nonetheless 70 percent of the sample feel there is no difference by race.

The one question that does suggest some faith in the benefits of substituting black for white control asked whether the election of Negro mayors in Cleveland and Gary would make things better, worse, or not make any difference. More than three-fifths of the sample expected an improvement in those two cities. There is some reason to wonder, however, whether this response does not reflect less the race of the mayor and more the knowledge or suggestion that he is a crusader for Negro rights. A white political leader with such a reputation might well draw as large an indication of support. If this is the case, it indicates considerable backing for political action in traditional spheres, rather than a strong leaning toward black leadership as such.

Our study did uncover unexpectedly strong support for a kind of cultural pluralism, symbolized by the study of Negro history and of African languages. This seems to turn not so much on the rejection of whites as on the acceptance of things black. It involves a commitment to the development of Negro identity as a valid basis for cultural life within a larger interracial and if possible integrated society. Such a movement from race to ethnicity may help Negroes in a number of ways, but it does not promise quick relief to problems of perceived discrimination and unfair treatment.

There would seem to be two directions which point toward a solution, and Negroes appear to have a commitment to both. One is to work within the system through individual advancement, trusting that it is possible by effort to overcome all barriers. A question concerned with the validity of this approach—that a young Negro who works hard enough "can usually get ahead in this country in spite of prejudice and discrimination"—finds nearly four out of five Negroes (78 percent) in agreement. Faith in the system then is very strong, being held even by many who perceive a great deal of discrimination.

An analysis by age and education reveals clear regularities which have, by now, familiar and contradictory implications. The results are presented separately by sex in Table 18, since they show some differences in clarity if not in trend. Education has a clear *positive* association with belief that a Negro can get ahead in America despite prejudice and discrimination. The relation is sharpest for men in their 20's and 30's, where the belief in individual accomplishment is held by 93 percent of the college graduates but only 68 percent of those with grade school education. We cannot, of course, tell what is cause and what is effect here— whether the more ambitious go on with their education, or whether those obtaining more education gain more confidence, or whether

there is a third factor such as ability that underlies both, or finally whether some mix of all these occurs.

The age trends are more complex and also less certain. But it appears that for men these age differences are concentrated largely among the less educated: there is little difference by age for those with 12 or more years of education, but among those who failed to complete high school, the younger men are more willing to attribute lack of success to prejudice and discrimination than are the older men. The teenage male group in this instance, unlike other cases discussed earlier, continues the general age trend—that is, is even more inclined to see failure to get ahead as caused by racial injustice. Among women, younger people at all levels of education are more inclined to blame the system for failure to get ahead.

The age and education trends taken together suggest that for males a belief in the value of individual initiative and in the possibility of individual achievement continues to reinforce the person who manages to go through school. The more he gets ahead, the more he thinks he should be able to get ahead. But what is often called the school drop-out lacks the possibility of achievement, and apparently in a growing proportion of cases he believes that it is society that is at fault, not he himself.

When a belief in individual accomplishment fails, to what can an individual turn? He can try to reform the system or he can try to destroy it. Reform actions were not well covered in our questionnaire, and we have at present little to report about types of individuals who attempt to

Table 18. *"If a Young Negro Works Hard Enough, Do You Think He or She Can Usually Get Ahead in This Country in Spite of Prejudice and Discrimination, or That He Doesn't Have Much Chance No Matter How Hard He Works?"*

[In Percent]

| | | Negro Men | | | | | | | | |
| | | Age 20-39 | | | | | Age 40-60 | | | |
	Age 16-19*	8th Grade Or Less	9-11 Grades	12 Grades	Some College	College Graduate	8th Grade Or Less	9-11 Grades	12 Grades	Some College	College Graduate
Can get ahead	72	68	75	82	81	93	79	83	81	85	91
Doesn't have much chance	26	27	24	15	16	7	19	16	14	15	6
Don't know	2	5	1	3	3	0	2	1	5	0	3
	100	100	100	100	100	100	100	100	100	100	100
		Negro Women									
Can get ahead	76	72	72	79	76	72	74	80	80	93	89
Doesn't have much chance	18	72	25	18	18	13	20	18	18	4	4
Don't know	6	6	3	3	6	15	6	2	2	3	7
	100	100	100	100	100	100	100	100	100	100	100

change the system in important but specific ways. We did include substantial material on the urban riots, and we shall review much of it in . . . [a later chapter]. This approach may seem to focus solely on attempts to destroy the American system, yet as we will see, the riot itself is viewed by most Negroes not as an attempt to destroy America, but as a loud protest, the culmination of many protests, calling for reform rather than revolution.

NOTES

[1] There are some indications of such a shift in some sections of the Negro press. For example, the *Michigan Chronicle,* the major Negro newspaper for Detroit, has changed in tone since the 1967 riot. The word "black" has been substituted for "Negro," a regular column of commentary by a leading militant spokesman has been added, and more regular coverage is given to groups advocating separation. Much of the change, however, fits better the type of cultural shift discussed in our next section, rather than being fully separatist.

[2] Since younger Negroes are more educated, age and education tend to work against each other in this population. Youth is associated with greater perceived distance from whites, but greater education makes it more difficult to classify all whites as hostile. This suggests a "tension" which might be especially great for Negro college students in mixed university settings.

[3] The above results do not mean lack of support for more Negroes in the police force. In the "pretest" to this study we found almost unanimous support for the idea of there being more Negro policemen. But the reasons had to do largely with jobs—the more Negroes who can get jobs as police the better—and not with the effect of having Negro policemen on the fairness of law enforcement. Perhaps the explanations would have been different if we had asked the question about higher ranking police officers or about a Negro police commissioner.

ACTUAL GAINS AND PSYCHOLOGICAL LOSSES

Thomas F. Pettigrew

The late Samuel Stouffer, one of America's greatest sociologists, always became incensed when a layman blithely reacted to a finding of behavioral science with, "Who didn't know that?" He countered with a simple true-false test of ten items, the "obvious, common sense" answers to which had all been demonstrated to be incorrect by rigorous social research. Most of those who take Stouffer's test miss every item. The moral is clear: many behavioral science findings appear obvious only after the fact.

Stouffer's favorite illustration involved the relative morale of the Air Corps and the Military Police in World War II. Promotions were rapid and widespread in the Air Corps, but slow and piecemeal in the Military Police. Conventional wisdom predicts that the Air Corpsmen should have been more satisfied with their chances for promotion, for the "obvious" reason that they were in absolute terms moving ahead faster in their careers. But, as a matter of empirical fact, Stouffer found in his famous studies of *The American Soldier* that the Air Corpsmen were considerably more frustrated over promotions than the Military Police. What was not so obvious was that the fliers' wide-open system of promotions led them to assume exceedingly high aspirations; most of them expected such swift elevation that even the generous promotions of their service left them *relatively* dissatisfied. By contrast, morale was reasonably high among the Military Police. The MP's did not expect rapid promotions and learned to be content with what few advances they did achieve. It was not the absolute level of

attainment that made for poor morale so much as relative deprivation—the discrepancy between what one anticipates and what one attains.

Likewise, conventional wisdom dictates that Negro Americans should be more content today than any previous point in America's history. After all, have Negro gains not been faster in recent decades than any period since Emancipation? Why, then, are many Negroes so unusually restive, so openly angry, so impatient for further gains? Relative, not absolute, deprivation once again provides a social-psychological explanation. The great majority of Negroes in past years dared not cherish high aspirations. While never satisfied with their lot, they, like the Military Police, expected very little of life, and they had to be content with what crumbs they did receive. But Negro Americans in recent years hunger for much more than crumbs. Like the Air Corpsmen, they have tasted significant progress and can fully appreciate what further progress could mean. Indeed, Negro aspirations have risen far more swiftly than Negro advances. Thus, while better off in absolute terms than ever before, Negroes today are relatively more deprived than they were before the last twenty-five years of racial progress.

This important social-psychological principle underlies the Negro American protest of the 1960's. . . .

Slowly, imperceptibly, the frame of reference for many Negro Americans has shifted during the past few decades. While formerly most Negroes judged how well off they were by their own previous conditions, the rising expectations of the present are increasingly framed in terms of the wider society. Negro protest today is moving away from an exclusive emphasis upon desegregation and equal opportunity toward a broader demand for a "fair share" and advantages directly comparable to those of whites. This shift merits special attention, for the actual gains just reviewed were all relative to previous Negro conditions. But such advances are not enough to meet the hopes of a people beginning to contrast their still-lowly position with the rich abundance surrounding them. The hard truth is that the Negro's recent progress does not begin to close the gap between the two races. Consider once again each of the realms in which changes have occurred. . . .

Thus, in each interrelated realm—health, employment, business, income, housing, voting, and education—the absolute gains of the 1950's pale when contrasted with current white standards. Numerous spokesmen for the status quo have boasted of the present status of the Negro in glowing international comparisons. Negroes in the United States today, goes one boast, have a consumer buying power comparable to that of similarly-populated Canada. And a larger percentage of Negroes, goes another, attends college than residents of the British Isles. But such glittering statements must not blind us to the fact of greatest psychological importance. Negro American standards have their psychological meaning relative to the standards of other Americans, not of Canadians or the British. The Negro American judges his living standards, his opportunities, indeed, even judges himself, in the only cultural terms he knows—those of the United States and its "people of plenty." Dr. Martin Luther King, Jr. made the point bluntly in his Washington March address: "The Negro lives on a lonely island of poverty in the midst of a vast ocean of material prosperity . . . and finds himself an exile in his own land."

The resulting relative deprivation is the fundamental basis of mass Negro American dissatisfaction today. But it is not the only factor. Special frustrations are created by the appearance of proud new African nations upon the world scene. Emerging Africa has a dual psychological effect upon Negro Americans. On the one hand, it generates racial pride and lifts self-esteem—especially among the darkest members of the group. On the other hand, it lends a desperate urgency to protest at home. Heretofore, Negro Americans have been the most sophisticated and respected black group in the Western world—regardless of their lowly position by American standards. But now many Africans can claim complete freedom, while Negro Americans still seek theirs. In this sense, then, independent African nations add to the Negro's keen sense of relative deprivation.

A similar phenomenon occurs regionally within the United States. Negro Northerners have typically prided themselves on being the products of the big-city North, on being superior to their Southern "country cousins." Yet Negro Southerners today lead the struggle for racial justice; many of them have willingly faced fire hoses, dogs, jail, and police brutality in order to demand and assert their rights; and one of them, Dr. King, has become the symbol of the protest movement throughout the country. A few Negro leaders in the South even hint wryly that the day may come when Negro Northerners will have to migrate southward to obtain true equality. And when Negroes in the North contrast their slow progress against de facto segregation in housing, schools, and employment with the dramatic desegregation of public facilities in many parts of the South, they must wonder if such wry hints do not possess some basis in truth.

Thus, the present-day Negro's feeling of being left behind springs from three sources. It derives partly from relating his situation to emerging Africa. For the Negro Northerner, it also stems from comparing his gains with those of his on-rushing Southern relatives. But its primary source is from contrasting his still meager lot with the abundance of other Americans.

ALL, HERE, NOW!

Intense relative deprivation in an age of rising expectations is the stuff out of which revolutions are made. But this revolution of 1963, with its ringing demand for "all, here, now," is a revolution only in a sense special to the Negro's unique role in American society.[1] An understanding of this special form of revolution is requisite to any meaningful projection of the Negro American's status into the future.

This non-violent revolution does resemble more typical revolutions in some ways. The present movement has shifted in emphasis from legalism to direct action, from narrow objectives to a full-scale attack, from pockets of protest to a genuine mass movement cutting across divisions within the Negro community. And like other mass movements, it has achieved a heightened militancy and urgency, a new sense that "even yesterday was too late." It also exhibits some of the irrationality common to all revolutions.

Nevertheless, this is a revolution with a basic difference. It aims to modify, not to overturn, the society it confronts; it seeks to amend, not to ravage. Negro Americans are so firmly rooted in and shaped by their land that their revolution is attempting merely to guarantee full participation in the society as it otherwise exists. In short, they do not wish to deprecate or destroy that which they wish to join. It is, then, a peculiarly conservative revolution, a fact that in many ways gives it a special force.

Such a conservative revolution acts out the culture's most cherished values; it dramatizes the "American dilemma" between high ideals and lowly practices. It does not offer new values, but demands that old values be realized. To suppress such a revolution would be to surrender the very foundations of the United States. There is in the long run, then, but one viable alternative—to move with history and achieve a racially integrated society in which skin color loses all relevance. This alternative is already recognized in the support given the protest by the federal government—a strange ally for true revolutionaries. Even if federal authorities have sometimes been too late with too little help, as in Albany, Georgia, and other Black Belt sites, the fact remains that the current Negro protest takes place within a generally permissive national atmosphere.

Moreover, this special type of revolution is supported to a considerable degree by white American opinion. There is a hard core of whites marching in demonstrations, going to jail, even facing death with Negroes. Though a small minority, these whites serve the vital function of keeping the confrontation from becoming a purely black versus white conflict. To be sure, there is also a hard core of white dead-enders, those who resist even token desegregation by burning crosses, exploding bombs, and assassinating Negro leaders. But the majority of white Americans range somewhere in between, and, while their attitudes often do not measure up to Negro expectations, they nevertheless contribute to the permissive atmosphere in a number of ways.

To begin with, there is solid approval outside of the South of the Supreme Court's 1954 school desegregation ruling. Gallup polls show that 62 per cent of the nation, Negro and white, approves of the decision, with the proportion among non-Southerners reaching almost three out of four. School desegregation itself wins general approval outside of the South, as long as Negro children are not in the majority. In the South, although racial change is still widely opposed by white Southerners, such change is increasingly seen as inevitable. Gallup polls have repeatedly asked Southerners of both races if they thought "the day will ever come when white and Negro people will be going to the same schools, eating in the same restaurants, and generally sharing the same public accommodations." In 1957, only 45 per cent of the South answered "yes"; by 1958, 53 per cent did so; by 1961, 76 per cent; and by 1963, 83 per cent. In addition, among the 83 per cent who saw desegregation as inevitable in 1963, half believed it would come about completely within five years and another fourth believed it would occur within ten years. Thus, the majority of white Southerners clearly expects racial progress even while opposing it, and this widespread feeling of inevitability contributes importantly to the present milieu in which the Negro protest is operating.

The ground was prepared for these white opinions before the current revolution. During and since World War II, the stereotype of the Negro has undergone drastic modification. Witness the erosion of the racist contention that Negroes are innately stupid. The National Opinion Research Center asked Americans in a series of representative polls: "In general, do you think Negroes are as intelligent as white people—that is, can they learn just as well if they are given the same education and training?" In 1942, only 42 per cent of white Americans believed the two groups to be equally intelligent; by 1944, the figure was 44 per cent; by 1946, 53 per cent; by 1956, 78 per cent. This fundamental alteration of the image of the Negro acts to sharpen further white guilt over the "American dilemma."

There remain, however, serious limitations to white understanding of the Negro American. The majority of white Americans as yet neither identifies with Negro Americans nor senses the urgency of the present revolution. Most whites believe that Negroes are being treated fairly in the United States and that gradualism should be the rule in effecting desegregation. Since these beliefs assuage guilty consciences, it is not surprising that Negro demonstrations which boldly challenge them are resented. In 1961, for example, national samples questioned by Gallup pollsters indicated that 64 per cent disapproved of the freedom rides and 57 per cent believed the rides would "hurt the Negro's chance of being integrated in the South. Similarly, 65 per cent of white Northerners and 73 per cent of white Southerners interviewed in 1963 thought that "mass demonstrations by Negroes are likely to hurt the Negro's cause for racial equality." Without denying the basic justice of the protest, many whites handle their guilt by complaining that Negroes are "pushing too hard too fast." Yet some of these same people realize upon reflection that Negroes do in fact make maximum progress only when they confront the nation directly with their demands.

Within this social-psychological context—severe relative deprivation among Negroes, an urgent, but basically conservative, protest revolution, a supportive federal government, and a guilty, if gradualistic, dominant climate of white opinion—four predictions for the future can be ventured.

First, Negro protests will continue to grow both in intensity and depth. As demonstrations persist, advances will occur ever more rapidly. These advances serve to reward the protest and stimulate its continuance. "The leaders sitting down together would, of course, be the best way," frankly confided one Negro lady, "but we found it didn't work and sit-ins did." Advances also serve to highlight further racial changes that are needed. These effects are part of a widely-studied psychological phenomenon known technically as "goal gradient" and popularly as "running for home." As subjects in an experiment approach their final goal, they typically gain a "second wind" and speed up their performance. Or in relative deprivation terms, protest success enlarges aspirations faster than actual gains can meet; the result is deeper frustration and more insistent demands. "The closer we come to the achievement of our ideals," shrewdly observed a Civil Rights Commissioner, "the more obvious and galling is the disparity."

Apart from its success, the current revolution will become increasingly intense because of the psychological effects of the demonstrations themselves, mentioned in the previous chapter. No protester, Negro or white, comes out of a racial demonstration the same person he was when he entered. Personal participation publicly commits the protester; it gives him a new sense of actively influencing events rather than passively accepting them; and it can provide him with greater confidence and an enhanced self-image. All of these changes aid him in undertaking additional protest. In short, demonstrations are both a symptom and a cause of psychological health. "My feets is tired," remarked an elderly Negro lady in the midst of the Montgomery bus boycott, "but my soul is rested."

Furthermore, demonstrations instruct both participants and by-standers that segregation is a two-way street, a process of role reciprocation. It takes two to tango, and it requires the complicity of both whites and Negroes to maintain patterns of segregation and discrimination. If Negroes disengage themselves from these patterns, racial barriers cannot long be maintained. This insight, achieved in the midst of demonstrations, also makes further protest inevitable. "We the Negro people are now not afraid," announced a grocery store owner in a small Alabama town, "we have woke up."

Second, the protests will increasingly attract a larger proportion of lower-income Negroes and shift from status to economic goals. The direct action phase of the revolution began in earnest when Southern college students initiated in 1960 a wave of mass sit-in demonstrations aimed at the desegregation of lunch-counters. The fact that college students sparked this phase and that public facilities were the initial targets is important; but direct action weapons are now spreading and will continue to spread to diverse segments of the Negro population with primarily economic targets.

The fact that Negro college students ignited the direct action fuse involves a special irony. These youngsters benefited from the best schools the South ever provided Negroes. Though still not the equal of white education, this improved training produced a relatively more sophisticated, self-confident generation. It also kindled, through the mechanism once again of relative deprivation, a greater frustration over racial barriers that finally exploded into militant social action. Like oil and water, education and oppression do not mix.

The student presented the perfect symbol as the initiator of public demonstrations. Well-dressed and well-behaved, the Negro student epitomized the group's aspirations for social mobility and integration. His nonviolent movement flew in the face of the segregationist stereotype of the Negro as violent yet subservient, degraded yet happy with his lot. The student was also less encumbered with fears from past mistreatment and less vulnerable to economic retaliation. In short, he was uniquely situated to transform public protest and going to jail into not only socially respectable acts but badges of high honor.

To become a full-fledged revolution, however, the movement has to incorporate all elements of the Negro community. The Montgomery bus boycott in 1955-1956 provided a preview of the power of a unified effort across class lines. But it required Bull Connor's police dogs and fire hoses in Birmingham in 1963 to capture the imagination of all segments of Negro America. Data from a national poll of Negroes in the summer of 1963 tell the story. Fifty per cent felt the pace of racial change was far too slow; 80 per cent felt certain demonstrations were effective; 4 per cent had already personally been jailed in the cause or had family members who had been; 40 per cent had already personally, or had family members who had taken part in a sit-in, marched in a mass protest, or engaged in picketing; and 48 per cent reported a willingness to participate in mass protests even if it meant going to jail. Clearly the revolution is an authentic mass movement that unites many different Negro elements, and shows every promise of recruiting more adherents in the future.

As the proportion of lower-income participators climbs, the nature of the struggle's primary goals necessarily shifts from status to economic concerns. Poor Negroes are not importantly affected by the desegregation of the opera, expensive restaurants, or golf courses; they are chiefly interested in getting good jobs and sharing in the material abundance surrounding them. "Freedom" for them signifies inseparably both dollars and dignity. Yet relative occupational and income gains, it will be recalled, were the most disappointing indices of the 1950's. Consequently, 1963's wave of building-site demonstrations against racial discrimination in the building trades is sure to be merely the forerunner of attacks upon a variety of employment fields and economic problems.

Third, a more extensive use of local and national boycotts of consumer products will be made. The consumer boycott is a weapon yet to be fully exploited. But a number of localities, like Philadelphia and Nashville, have learned what well-organized Negro boycotting can accomplish. And national advertisers have made agreements with protest organizations to include Negroes in their television programs and advertisements in order to avert national campaigns against their products. A 1963 poll of Negroes reports that because of employment discrimination 29 per cent of its sample stopped buying in certain stores and 19 per cent stopped buying certain companies' products. But this barely touches the potential. Sixty-three per cent of the sample stated that it would stop buying at a store if asked, including over two-thirds of the highest-income Negroes.

This mass willingness to participate in boycotts stems from two factors. The first is economic; boycotts are unusually well-suited for achieving the employment breakthroughs so desperately desired by low-income Negroes.[2] The second factor is psychological . . . [T]here are three major types of responses human beings can make to oppression: they can move toward the oppressor and seek acceptance as an equal; they can move against the oppressor and aggressively express their frustration; and they can move away from the oppressor and seek to minimize painful contacts. Boycotts have the distinct psychological advantage of appealing to all three of these basic responses. Such campaigns move toward the oppressor by seeking to achieve desegregation; they move against the oppressor by encouraging group unity and aggressively upsetting the white-controlled economy; and they move away from the oppressor by requesting the participators merely to avoid the scene of conflict. For these reasons, it seems highly probable that boycotts will increase in number and scope.

Four, as the revolution proceeds through the coming years, some basic structural changes in American society will have to occur before viable race-relations solutions are possible. . . . The problems facing Negro American protest are considerably more complicated than merely battering down the walls of segregation. The skill with which the movement addresses itself to these structural issues, particularly the economic ones, is a critical determinant of its success in the near future. Indeed, success is dependent upon all of the factors mentioned in these predictions. Should the protest movement cool, should the involvement of lower-income Negroes and the shift in emphasis to economic goals not take place, should nationwide boycotts not be effectively mounted, should all types of necessary and decisive structural changes needed now by the American society be blocked, then obviously significant progress will not occur.

This is precisely what makes the 1960's and 1970's such crucial, yet promising, years for American race relations. The gravest danger is not interracial violence, as the mass media endlessly assert, but that this golden opportunity will not be fully utilized. The nation is ripe for sweeping racial change and is in fact changing. Except for the Black Belt South, the formal desegregation of public facilities will soon be a mopping-up operation. The critical question, then, is: Can the revolution deal with *de facto* segregation and the vast educational and economic issues still impeding Negro progress as effectively as it has dealt with local segregation?

FREEDOM!

In Mississippi there is a tall, black-skinned young woman, Annelle Ponder, who contributes to the revolution as a voter registration worker. For her efforts she was once beaten by police and thrown in jail in the little town of Winona. When friends visited her, they found her sitting in her cell, her face swollen and bruised, barely able to speak. She looked up at them, and managed to whisper one word: "Freedom!"

As in many revolutions, *freedom* has assumed a definition special to the situation. Freedom for protesting Negro Americans means a complete casting off of the inferior role of "Negro"; it means the cessation of all of the disabilities traditionally placed upon black skin by American society. It means the stilling of self-hatred. Freedom also means an end to claims of white superiority. to dire poverty, to the social conditions permitting inflated rates of disease and inadequate medical care, low intelligence test scores, and heightened crime rates. Freedom means, in short, the right to participate fully in American society with the dollars and dignity of other Americans.

NOTES

[1] In the technical language of social science, the Negro American protest is a reform movement and not a revolution. This is true because the protest aims to change norms—the accepted rules of societal operation—and not to overturn basic values. The term "revolution" is used here, then, only in the popular sense of a major social movement demanding fundamental reforms.

[2] Not all boycotts, of course, gain effective leverage on economic problems. Thus, boycotts against whole industries (e.g., new automobiles) or the entire economy (e.g., no Christmas buying) may serve other protest aims, but are not ideally styled for battering down employment barriers. More directed are selective boycotts, campaigns to restrict sales of one particular company's stores or products. Such selective campaigns have the dual advantage of: (1) greater likelihood of success, for followers must make fewer alterations in their daily living; and (2) both firms whose sales decline and those whose sales correspondingly rise achieve healthy respect for the Negro's ability to influence profit margins.

WHITE BELIEFS ABOUT NEGROES

Angus Campbell and Howard Schuman

Although the National Advisory Commission on Civil Disorders observes in its opening paragraphs that "our nation is moving toward two societies, one black, one white," the fact is, of course, that these two societies have existed, separate and unequal, in this country for over three hundred years. The long period of slavery set a pattern of division which remains in modified form a century later.

One of the results of this separation is a barrier of psychological distance between the races which makes it difficult for either race to form an accurate picture of the other and makes it easy for each to develop misunderstanding, apprehension, and mistrust. The preceding chapter has reviewed the perceptions and attitudes of Negroes regarding whites; we now examine the beliefs and attitudes the white population holds toward Negroes.

WHITE BELIEFS REGARDING NEGROES

Although the relative disadvantage of Negroes in virtually every economic, educational, social, and political aspect of American life has been documented many times over it cannot be assumed that these facts are fully comprehended by the white population. Several questions were asked of the white respondents of our survey specifically intended to reveal their perceptions of the status of Negroes and their appreciation of the presence of racial discrimination. The first of these had to do with job

Reprinted from "Racial Attitudes in Fifteen American Cities," Angus Campbell and Howard Schuman, *Supplemental Studies for the National Advisory Commission on Civil Disorders* (Washington, D.C.: U.S. Government Printing Office, July 1968), pp. 15-28.

opportunities; do white people believe discrimination against Negroes in the work situation is prevalent or relatively infrequent (Table 1)?

As we see, about one-fifth of the white sample expressed the belief that many Negroes suffer from discrimination in the job situation and an additional third agreed that this was the case for "some" Negroes. Perhaps more impressive is the fact that nearly four out of ten white people apparently believe that few if any Negroes are subject to discrimination in hiring or promotions. One white respondent in eight specifically denied the presence of any such discrimination even though this option was not given in the alternatives presented in the question.

A somewhat stronger sense of the special problems Negroes face was found when we directed our question toward discrimination in housing. In this case two-thirds of the white sample agreed that "many" or "some" Negroes have difficulties in renting or buying houses from white owners (Table 2).

A rather different distribution appeared when we asked our white respondents about the

Table 1. *"Do you think that in (Central City) many, some, or only a few Negroes miss out on jobs and promotions because of racial discrimination?"*

[In percent]

	White		
	Men	Women	Total
Many	23	20	22
Some	33	35	34
Only a few	25	26	26
None	12	13	12
Don't know or not ascertained ...	7	6	6
	100	100	100

Table 2. *"Do you think that in (Central City) many, some, or only a few Negroes miss out on good housing because white owners won't rent or sell to them?"*

[In percent]

	White		
	Men	Women	Total
Many	38	38	38
Some	30	29	30
Only a few	21	22	22
None	4	5	4
Don't know	7	6	6
	100	100	100

treatment they thought Negroes received from the police. Only a small fraction of our white sample accepted without reservation the suggestion that Negroes might be more subject to rough treatment and disrespect from the police than white people and over half of them rejected it as probably or unqualifiedly untrue (Table 3). As we will see later, when we asked our white and Negro samples whether they had actually experienced disrespect or rough treatment from police, Negroes were far more likely to report such incidents. It is apparent, however, that many of our white respondents do not want to accept this implied reflection on the even-handedness of American justice.

In order to assess the perception white people have of the relative status of Negroes in contrast to themselves, we asked our white respondents to compare their income to what they thought Negroes of the same educational achievement as themselves would have. It may have been difficult for some of our respondents to abstract

Table 3. *"It is sometimes said that the things we have just been talking about, such as unnecessary roughness and disrespect by the police, happen more to Negroes in (Central City) than to white people. Do you think this is definitely so, probably so, probably not so, or definitely not so?"*

[In percent]

	White		
	Men	Women	Total
Definitely so	11	7	9
Probably so	29	28	29
Probably not so	27	33	30
Definitely not so	27	25	26
Don't know	6	7	6
	100	100	100

from the total Negro population just those whose educational level was comparable to their own; however, most of them answered the question (Table 4). Nearly half of these saw themselves as better off than Negroes of comparable education; only five percent classed themselves as worse off. Since these figures would be equal if there were no difference in white perceptions of the comparative economic status of whites and Negroes of equal training, this discrepancy again reflects recognition within a part of the white population of the effects of discrimination.

Finally, we confronted our white respondents with the fact that Negroes as a whole in their city have poorer jobs, education, and housing than they themselves do and asked them whether they thought these differences were primarily the result of racial discrimination or mainly due to some failure in Negroes themselves. As we see in Table 5, the majority of our white respondents felt that Negroes themselves were responsible for their disadvantaged situation and an additional fraction believed that both discrimination and Negro inadequacies contributed to their circumstances.

We asked those respondents who told us they thought the deprived conditions of Negroes in their city were due mainly to failures among Negroes themselves or to a combination of such failures and racial discrimination, "What it is about Negroes themselves that makes them have worse jobs, education, and housing?" While it is not possible to present the full detail of answers which this open question evoked, it is clear that those white people who placed some or all of the responsibility for the deficiencies of Negro life on Negroes themselves (approximately three-

Table 4. *"I would like you to think of Negroes who have the same education you have. As far as the present income of your family goes, do you think you are better off, worse off, or in about the same position as the average Negro with the same education?"*

[In percent]

	White		
	Men	Women	Total
Better off	43	41	42
About the same	45	46	46
Worse off	6	5	5
Don't know	6	8	7
	100	100	100

Table 5. *"On the average, Negroes in (Central City) have worse jobs, education and housing than white people. Do you think this is due mainly to Negroes having been discriminated against, or mainly due to something about Negroes themselves?"*

[In percent]

	White		
	Men	Women	Total
Mainly due to discrimination	18	19	19
Mainly due to Negroes themselves .	56	57	56
A mixture of both	20	17	19
Don't know	6	7	6
	100	100	100

quarters of the total white sample) tended to think in terms of failures of motivation among Negroes. Nearly half of them spoke of the Negro's presumed laziness, lack of ambition, or unwillingness to take advantage of opportunities. Very few made any reference to supposed innate inferiority or other inherited racial differences.

In order to pursue this latter consideration specifically we asked these same people whether they thought the inadequacies they saw in Negroes were the consequence of some inborn trait, or were characteristics which were subject to change (Table 6). We find that only a very small proportion (six percent of the total white sample) were prepared to accept the belief common in earlier years that Negroes are subject to some inherent defect which is beyond the possibility of change.

In responding to the question "What is it about Negroes" that explains their deprived

Table 6. *"Do you think Negroes are just born that way and can't be changed, or that changes in the Negro are possible?"*

[In percent]

	White		
	Men	Women	Total
Those who felt Negro conditions are mainly or partly due to Negroes themselves:			
Negroes are born that way	7	4	6
Changes are possible	66	66	66
Don't know	3	4	3
Those who felt Negro conditions are due to discrimination or did not know what they are due to	24	26	25
	100	100	100

situation and to various other questions in the interview which invited a full answer, a certain proportion of the white respondents revealed overtly hostile attitudes toward Negroes. These ranged from full-blown expressions of racial bigotry to more moderate statements of exasperation with the insistence of Negro demands for change. We cannot summarize these comments in this report; we mention them here to remind the reader that many of the opinions which are brought together in the tables of this report are held with great intensity.

Some indication of the impression white people themselves have of white attitudes toward Negroes may be obtained from the question from the interview which reads "Do you think that only a few white people in the (City) area dislike Negroes, many dislike Negroes, or almost all dislike Negroes?" About a quarter of our white respondents said they thought only a few white people dislike Negroes, nearly six in ten thought many do, and one in ten thought almost all do. The rest would not offer an opinion. We offset this question with a corresponding question regarding Negro attitudes toward whites, "How about the reverse: Do you think only a few Negroes dislike white people, many dislike white people, or almost all dislike white people?" In this case the proportion of the white sample who thought nearly all Negroes dislike white people is about one in five, twice as large as the corresponding estimate of white opinion, and the other categories are somewhat smaller.

We cannot say precisely how these people interpreted the word "dislike" and we cannot assume that the actual distribution of white dislike of Negroes or of Negro dislike of whites corresponds to our sample's perception of them. However, it is evident from the answers to our questions that two-thirds of our white respondents sense some degree of negative feeling toward Negroes as widespread among the white population and their sense of Negro dislike of whites is if anything even stronger.

A simple cross-tabulation of the answers to the two questions reveals a substantial association between white perception of widespread dislike of Negroes among whites and their perception of widespread dislike of whites among Negroes. The relationship can be seen in the following comparisons:

Of those whites who think few white people dislike Negroes: 53 percent believe few Negroes dislike whites. 8 percent believe almost all Negroes dislike whites.

Of those whites who think almost all white people dislike Negroes: 8 percent believe few Negroes dislike whites. 67 percent believe almost all Negroes dislike whites.

It seems evident that our white respondents tend strongly to hold a rather general view of racial hostility; what they see on one side they also see on the other side. We did not ask these people to report their own degree of liking or dislike of Negroes; it seems very probable that their perceptions of much or little dislike among others reflect their own feelings in some part.

In order to assess the extent to which generational differences exist within the white population in the way they perceive and respond to these issues of race relations, we have divided the men and women of the sample according to the decade of their age. The youngest age category in Table 7 contains those respondents less than 20 years old and the succeeding categories represent the succeeding decades.

The general pattern of Table 7 is clear. There is a consistent tendency for the younger age cohorts to express a stronger appreciation of the discrimination to which Negroes are subject and to accept the presumption that Negro disadvantages in jobs, education and housing are primarily the result of this discrimination. The folk belief that Negroes "are born that way and can't be changed" is accepted by very few people but by a much larger proportion of older people than younger.

From these seven tables we may draw the following conclusions regarding prevailing white beliefs concerning the prevalence and consequence of discrimination against Negroes:

1. Although a majority of white people are prepared to admit that Negroes are handicapped by discriminatory practices in employment and housing, there is a minority of significant size which denies the existence of such practices or regards them as infrequent.

2. Most white people do not accept the suggestion that Negroes are subjected to rougher treatment by the police than are whites themselves. A quarter of the white sample specifically deny this charge.

Table 7. White Beliefs Regarding Negroes Among Age Categories

[In Percent]

	Men by Age					
	16-19	20-29	30-39	40-49	50-59	60-69
Think many Negroes miss out on jobs because of discrimination	36	28	24	14	18	19
Think many Negroes miss out on housing because of discrimination . .	47	45	41	32	31	33
Think Negroes are definitely or probably more subject to police roughness than white people	55	48	48	27	36	25
Think Negro disadvantages are due mainly to discrimination	30	22	20	10	15	25
Think Negroes are born that way and can't be changed	1	1	4	8	12	13
	Women by Age					
	16-19	20-29	30-39	40-49	50-59	60-69
Think many Negroes miss out on jobs because of discrimination	26	29	21	21	11	15
Think many Negroes miss out on housing because of discrimination . .	49	47	45	36	31	27
Think Negroes are definitely or probably more subject to police roughness than white people	40	45	36	33	26	30
Think Negro disadvantages are due mainly to discrimination	30	28	20	11	11	22
Think Negroes are born that way and can't be changed	2	1	3	6	7	5

3. While admitting the presence of discrimination white people show a strong tendency to blame the disadvantaged circumstances of Negro life on Negroes themselves. Although they do not subscribe to genetic theories of racial inferiority, they find much to criticize in the attitudes and behavior patterns they see as characteristic of Negroes and apparently feel that it is within the power of Negroes to improve their own situation.

4. These beliefs regarding racial discrimination vary systematically by age among white people. The overall distribution of beliefs is similar in the different generations but younger people are clearly more willing to agree that discrimination exists and that it has deleterious effects on Negroes. The direction of the generational differences we see in our data strongly suggests that a long-term shift is occurring in the white population away from the traditional racial attitudes of an earlier time in this country. While this appears to be a significant movement, it cannot be said that a dramatic reversal of the pattern of racial attitudes has occurred even among the youngest age group.

INTEGRATION AND SEGREGATION

The pattern of interracial relations in a society depends for the most part on the willingness of individual citizens to enter into personal contact of one kind or another with members of the other race. The patterns which have evolved in this country over the past generations are very complex and we cannot hope to represent them fully in this survey. We have limited our inquiry to a series of questions regarding white attitudes toward racial integration in housing, work, children's play, and related situations.

The issue of open housing is at present the focus of legislative attention throughout the country. The Civil Rights Act of 1968 laid down federal regulations on the sale of homes, and various states and municipalities have recently passed, rejected, or considered ordinances of a similar vein. Although it is not likely that any of these legislative acts will have any immediate effect on the housing pattern in American cities, the issue has taken on a certain symbolic importance. When we asked our white respondents their opinions on the "rights" of whites and Negroes regarding housing we found a strong

Table 8. *"Which of these statements would you agree with: First, white people have a right to keep Negroes out of their neighborhoods if they want to, or Second, Negroes have a right to live wherever they can afford to just like white people?"*

[In percent]

	White		
	Men	Women	Total
Whites have a right to keep Negroes out	27	32	30
Negroes have a right to live anywhere	64	59	62
Negroes have a right to live anywhere if they are the "right kind"	3	2	2
Other	3	3	3
Don't know	3	4	3
	100	100	100

majority who supported the basic principle of open housing (Table 8).

It is certainly not surprising that when confronted with a question implying equal rights a majority of white Americans give their verbal support. Many earlier inquiries have demonstrated the willingness of large majorities of the American public to approve statements of democratic principle of this sort.

Those respondents who expressed some degree of approval of the right of Negroes to live wherever they wish were asked a subsequent question intended to measure their willingness to convert this sentiment into a specific legal requirement (Table 9). We now discover that a significant fraction of those who support the principle of open housing are opposed to specific legislation to prevent discrimination in housing. If we combine those who are forthrightly opposed to neighborhood integration with those who are not ready to accept laws to

Table 9. *"How about laws to prevent discrimination against Negroes in buying or renting houses and apartments? Do you favor or oppose such laws?"*

[In percent]

	White		
	Men	Women	Total
Favor such laws	42	38	40
Oppose such laws	23	19	21
Undecided, don't know	8	11	9
Feel whites have a right to keep Negroes out	27	32	30
	100	100	100

bring it about we find that they outnumber those who favor such laws.

On the assumption that some of these whites who favored open occupancy in principle but rejected the suggestion of laws to enforce it might have felt such laws were unnecessary, we asked this fraction of the sample (slightly over one-fifth of the total white sample) if they would favor such legislation if there were "no way for Negroes to get enough good housing without such laws." Although the majority of this group maintained their opposition in the face of this contingency, a substantial number accepted the necessity of a law under these terms and their change of vote brought the division of attitude of the total sample to virtually an even balance of those favoring and opposing legislation in support of open housing.

In order to approach this complicated issue in a more specific way we asked our respondents to visualize a situation in which the first Negro family had moved into an otherwise white neighborhood. Would they favor setting a limit on the number of Negro families who might move into the neighborhood—a quota of some sort to prevent the neighborhood from changing from all white to all black. This proposal divided our white respondents very closely (Table 10).

Table 10. "Suppose there are 100 white families living in a neighborhood. One white family moves out and a Negro family moves in. Do you think it would be a good idea to have some limit on the number of Negro families that move there, or to let as many move there as want to?"

[In percent]

| | White | | |
	Men	Women	Total
There should be some limit	45	52	48
Let as many move there as want	44	36	40
Don't know	11	12	12
	100	100	100

Nearly half of those who expressed an opinion felt there should be some limit; of these one in five specified that no additional families should be admitted and half of the remainder would limit the addition to no more than 10 percent. Of those people who felt there should be a limit but set their quota at some point higher than zero, about half felt that a limit of the kind they proposed would make them more

willing to have Negro families in the neighborhood. The other half (about 16 percent of the total sample) did not feel such a quota would make any significant difference to them.

Our final inquiry in this series on housing brought the issue down to the more specific question of how the respondent would feel about having a Negro "with about the same education and income" as himself living next door. Approximately half of the sample felt this would cause them no concern at all; about one in five seemed seriously disturbed by the prospect (Table 11). It is of interest that of the small number of white respondents who were in fact living next door to a Negro family at the time of the interview most said this caused them no concern and about one in ten said they "minded it a lot." (About one in seven of the white respondents reported in answer to another question that they or someone in their families had at one time moved from a neighborhood because Negroes were moving in.)

Table 11. "If a Negro family with about the same income and education as you moved next door to you, would you mind it a lot, a little or not at all?"

[In percent]

| | White | | |
	Men	Women	Total
Mind a lot	17	21	19
Mind a little	25	26	25
Not at all	53	44	49
There is already a Negro family next door	3	5	4
Don't know	2	4	3
	100	100	100

From the problem of housing, our questions moved to the area of employment. We first asked whether our white respondents felt there should be preference given to white applicants in filling desirable jobs. This blunt statement of discrimination went too far for most of our sample; 95 percent of them chose the alternative that "race should not make any difference one way or the other." We then asked these people how they would feel about laws to prevent discrimination on the job. A substantial majority declared themselves in favor of such legislation, perhaps realizing that fair employment practice laws have been in force for some years (Table 12). Nonetheless, one respondent in five

Table 12. *"Do you favor or oppose laws to prevent discrimination against Negroes in job hiring and promotion?"*

[In percent]

	White		
	Men	Women	Total
Favor	68	66	67
Oppose	20	18	19
Don't know	8	12	10
Favor preference for whites	4	4	4
	100	100	100

declared himself opposed to such laws, a much larger number than had earlier accepted the proposal of outright discrimination in favor of hiring white job applicants.

Again bringing the issue to a question of direct personal contact we asked the white respondents how they would feel about having a "qualified Negro" as their supervisor on a job. Although there was a very small minority who thought they would find this situation difficult, the great majority of the sample classified themselves as being not at all concerned with this prospect (Table 13).

Table 13. *"Suppose you had a job where your supervisor was a qualified Negro. Would you mind that a lot, a little, or not at all?"*

[In percent]

	White		
	Men	Women	Total
Mind a lot	4	4	4
Mind a little	7	9	8
Mind not at all	87	84	86
Don't know	2	3	2
	100	100	100

In order to assess white opinion regarding a proposal which has been put forward by some leaders of the Negro community we asked the sample of white respondents how they would feel about reserving the various kinds of service jobs in Negro neighborhoods exclusively for Negroes. This proposal drew a divided response. Although a third of the respondents were ready to agree with this suggestion, over half, especially of the men, were not (Table 14). Apparently they saw this suggestion as a violation of the principle of equal treatment in job placement which they had earlier supported so overwhelmingly.

Table 14. *"Some Negro leaders think all the teachers, bus drivers, store clerks, and other employees in Negro neighborhoods should be Negroes. Would you agree with that idea or would you disagree?"*

[In percent]

	White		
	Men	Women	Total
Agree	30	39	34
Disagree	66	55	60
Other	0	1	1
Don't know	4	5	5
	100	100	100

One further question was asked regarding attitudes toward personal contact between the races, in this case contact among young children. Although, as we see in Table 15, well over half of the white respondents say either that they would prefer for their children to have Negro friends or that they don't care one way or the other, there is a solid one-third of the white sample who say they would prefer for their children to have exclusively white friends. We cannot say as yet whether these people who object to interracial contact among "small children" are simply expressing a general rejection of any form of integration or whether the prospect of contact among children holds some special threat. Our question did not specify Negro children of comparable class background and it may be that our white respondents thought in terms of a stereotype of lower-class children with rough language and manners. Or the suggestion of Negro friends may have implied the presence of Negro families in the neighborhood, a prospect which we know to be disturbing to many white people. Our survey did not inquire into the rationale behind this specific attitude although subsequent analysis of our data may help us understand it.

Table 15. *"If you had small children would you rather they had only white friends, or would you like to see them have Negro friends too, or wouldn't you care one way or the other?"*

[In percent]

	White		
	Men	Women	Total
Only white friends	30	37	33
Negro friends too	19	19	19
Don't care one way or the other ..	48	43	46
Don't know	3	1	2
	100	100	100

In order to assess attitudes in one additional area of urban life, an area which is becoming more significant as the Negro population of the cities increases, we asked our white respondents how they would feel about voting for a Negro for mayor in their city. This question requires the assumption that the Negro candidate is of the respondent's party and that he be a capable man and under these conditions most of the respondents felt that they would support him. There was a visible minority, however, who found this prospect unacceptable (Table 16). When we asked the respondents in Cleveland and Gary how they had actually voted in their recently held mayorality elections a large majority reported that they had supported the white candidates, especially in Gary. These reports coincide with the evidence of racial voting in these cities obtained from precinct records.

Table 16. *"If a capable Negro ot your own party preference was running for Mayor of (Central City), would you vote for him or not?"*

[In percent]

	White		
	Men	Women	Total
Yes; if he were the better man	61	58	60
No	20	21	20
Not eligible to vote	10	10	10
Don't know	4	6	5
Live in Cleveland or Gary	5	5	5
	100	100	100

When we again divide our sample by age categories we find that integrationist attitudes are stronger in the younger cohorts than they are in the older. This is particularly true in the question posing the principle of open housing. Differences between age groups in response to some of the other questions were not as great and there are some inconsistencies, especially among the men, but the overall pattern of Table 17 is unmistakable.

If we carry this analysis one step further by dividing our sample by both age and education simultaneously, we find a pattern which was not apparent in the simple comparison of age groups. We see that years of formal education exert an influence on racial perceptions and attitudes but it is not a simple cumulative effect and it is much stronger among younger people than among older people. We present in Figure

1 the data from two of the questions we have reviewed in this chapter; it may be seen that the pattern of findings is very similar in Parts 1 and 2 of Figure 1.

Among people over 40 years of age, those with higher levels of education are no more or less likely to support an open housing law or to express lack of concern at having a Negro family next door than people of lower educational attainment. The picture is quite different among people age 20 through 39. Here we see that the attitudes expressed by young people whose formal education has not gone beyond high school do not differ from older people of similar educational level. But those who have gone on to college differ substantially both from less educated people of their own generation and from college-educated people of the older generation. More of them believe that there should be a law guaranteeing open housing and

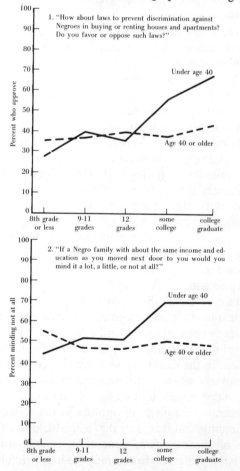

Figure 1. Relation of Racial Attitudes to Educational Levels Among White Men

more of them say they are not at all disturbed at the prospect of a Negro neighbor.

The general pattern of these two figures recurs when we plot the answers to a wide variety of questions regarding perceptions, attitudes, and opinions. There are many irregularities, due in part to the small number of respondents in some of these educational categories. The educational contrasts are not always as sharp as those shown in Parts 1 and 2 of Figure 1. In some cases the college graduates of the older generation show something of the same movement away from the prevailing attitudes of their age group as the younger college people do. But there is a persistent configuration in the data: (1) In the older generation educational level has a consistently weaker relationship to racial attitudes than it has in the younger generation, and (2) in the younger generation attitudes of people of various educational levels below college do not vary greatly but there is a strong swing among college people toward clearer recognition of racial discrimination, greater acceptance of racial integration, and stronger support of Negro civil rights.

These findings raise questions regarding the nature of social change which we will not be able to consider fully here. It appears from the data that prior to about 1945, the educational experience of white Americans in the schools had relatively little effect on their perceptions and attitudes regarding race. Great individual differences were present, of course, but these apparently developed out of family background, community norms, or personal experience and were not systematically deflected one way or the other by what these people were exposed to in school. The schools appear to have accepted without question the prevailing culture of race relations. Since World War II those white students who have gone on to college have evidently been exposed to influences which have moved their attitudes away from the traditional pattern in the directions we have observed. We cannot say whether this resulted from specific instruction regarding questions of race or from a general atmosphere of opinion in the college community but it is clear that a sizable proportion of these postwar generation college students were affected. In contrast, the high schools which our respondents attended during the postwar years seem to have been little more involved in the nation's racial problems than they were in the prewar period. Or, to be more precise, their involvement has been so peripheral that it has had relatively little influence on the racial attitudes of their graduates.

We have explored the possibilities of long-term changes in racial attitudes in the preceding chapter ["Black Views of Racial Issues"] and we do not propose to repeat that discussion here. Our survey has shown a significant deflection in the points of view of young white college people from the prevailing attitudes of their parents' generation. As these younger cohorts move through the life cycle, replacing their elders and being followed by generations with even larger proportions of college-exposed people, the potential for massive change in the traditional pattern of white racial attitudes in this country seems great. However, this is a projection based on simple assumptions of persistence and takes no account of events which may intervene to bring about unforeseeable alteration in the pace and even the direction of this change.

The conclusions which we may draw from these questions regarding white attitudes toward these various aspects of racial integration or segregation are necessarily rather general, but they give some sense of the willingness of white people in these northern cities to accept specific patterns of racial contact.

1. When white people are asked to respond to the concept of the right of Negroes to equal treatment they come down strongly against discrimination. This is especially true in the job situation and it is true in lesser degree in the apparently more sensitive area of neighborhood integration.

2. The prospect of passing laws to protect Negro rights to equal treatment is less warmly supported by white people than the abstract right itself. Even so, a substantial majority approve of laws to ensure fair employment practices. Opinion on the desirability of an open housing law seems about evenly divided.

3. The prospect of close personal contact with Negroes in a job situation seems to disturb relatively few white people, even when a subordinate relationship to a "qualified Negro" is proposed. Living arrangements are clearly more sensitive; although half of the white sample

Table 17. *White Attitudes Toward Integration and Segregation Among Age Categories*

[In Percent]

	Men by Age					
	16-19	20-29	30-39	40-49	50-59	60-69
Believe Negroes have a right to live where they choose	70	67	68	60	65	55
Favor laws preventing discrimination in housing	49	47	45	36	38	38
Favor letting as many Negroes as want move into a neighborhood	50	48	45	37	42	41
Would not mind at all having Negro family next door	55	59	55	42	45	60
Favor laws preventing discrimination against Negroes in jobs	68	78	73	65	60	64
Would not mind at all having a Negro supervisor	89	89	85	83	88	86
Oppose idea of all-Negro employment in Negro neighborhoods	70	62	72	61	63	74
Would like to see their children have Negro friends	27	24	24	16	14	14
Would vote for a qualified Negro mayor		70	74	58	59	66
	Women by Age					
Believe Negroes have a right to live where they choose	80	69	57	52	50	57
Favor laws preventing discrimination in housing	60	42	40	32	33	30
Favor letting as many Negroes as want move into a neighborhood	58	45	33	31	27	33
Would not mind at all having Negro family next door	54	46	40	42	40	48
Favor laws preventing discrimination against Negroes in jobs	78	68	70	58	66	64
Would not mind at all having a Negro supervisor	91	86	85	83	76	87
Oppose idea of all-Negro employment in Negro neighborhoods	59	58	59	49	56	53
Would like to see their children have Negro friends	30	24	18	13	18	15
Would vote for a qualified Negro mayer		67	66	65	55	57

declared themselves free of any concern about having a Negro neighbor of their own income and educational class, there were almost as many who expressed some degree of opposition to this prospect.

4. Attitudes toward various aspects of racial integration are clearly more favorable among young people than among the older generations. The differences are not extreme; they do not approach a reversal of attitudes from one generation to the next. But they indicate a movement over time away from the traditional pattern of racial segregation. An important component of this movement is contributed by those members of the below-40 generation who have attended college.

PROPOSALS FOR ACTION

Our survey attempted not only to assess white attitudes toward various aspects of interracial contact but also to measure white reaction to proposals to improve the circumstances of life in the urban centers. Several questions were asked in our interviews, some suggesting general governmental programs dealing with unemployment, schools and housing, and others concerned with specific actions intended to alleviate the conditions which may have led to the urban riots.

The first of these questions dealt with the issue of full employment; do white people in the northern cities accept the proposition that the federal government has some responsibility to see to it that everyone who seeks a job should have one? The answer is that well over half of the sample accept this proposal (Table 18). Although no reference is made to Negro unemployment in the question and we cannot assume that our respondents had Negroes in mind in answering the question, there is no doubt that such a policy would have special meaning to the urban Negro.

Table 18. *"Some people say that if there are not enough jobs for everyone who wants one, the government should somehow provide the extra jobs needed. Others say that the government should not do this. What is your opinion?"*

[In percent]

	White		
	Men	Women	Total
Government should do this	58	60	59
Government should not do this ...	38	35	37
Don't know	4	5	4
	100	100	100

A second question proposing governmental action to improve the quality of the public schools in depressed areas of the cities attracted even stronger support (Table 19). The implication of the question that all schools in the city should come up to an equal standard apparently had particular appeal to our respondents.

Table 19. *"Some neighborhoods in and around (Central City) have public schools with better buildings and more trained teachers than others. Do you think the government should provide money to bring the poorer schools up to the standard of the better schools, or that the government shouldn't do this?"*

[In percent]

	White		
	Men	Women	Total
Government should do this	75	81	78
Government should not do this ...	19	12	15
Don't know	6	7	7
	100	100	100

The third question in this series dealt with housing and here again a majority of the white respondents accepted the proposal that the federal government take an active role in the urban problem (Table 20).

Table 20. *"There are areas in cities like (Central City) where the housing is rundown and overcrowded. Some say the government should provide money to help improve the housing in such places. Others don't think the government should do this. What is your opinion?"*

[In percent]

	White		
	Men	Women	Total
Government should do this	58	60	59
Government should not do this ...	38	35	36
Don't know	4	5	5
	100	100	100

In each of these instances the white respondents favored the intervention of the federal government to help solve the difficulties of the cities. We later asked a question which summarized the content of the previous questions and specifically related the proposed governmental programs to the improvement of the conditions of urban Negroes in order "to prevent riots" (Table 21). Two-thirds of the respondents answered this omnibus proposal favorably, a proportion very comparable to those found for the individual questions.

Table 21. *"If top government officials in Washington said that a program of spending more money for jobs, schools, and housing for Negroes is necessary to prevent riots, would you go along with such a program or would you oppose it?"*

[In percent]

	White		
	Men	Women	Total
Go long with it	64	67	66
Oppose it	32	25	28
Don't know	4	8	6
	100	100	100

We followed this question with a probe intended to compel the respondents to face the financial implications of a program of governmental assistance. Even when threatened with a tax increase of ten percent to finance the proposed program, slightly over half of the sample still were willing to support the proposal (Table 22). This is no doubt an unrealistically high estimate of the support such a tax would actually receive in any of these cities; we intend the question merely as a measure of concern with the problem involved.

Table 22. *"Suppose the program increased your own taxes by ten percent—that is, if you were paying $300 last year, you would pay $330 this year, and so forth. Would you be willing in that case?"*

[In percent]

	White		
	Men	Women	Total
Yes, would be willing	53	53	53
No, would not be willing	10	16	13
Don't know	5	6	6
Oppose such a program	32	25	28
	100	100	100

Finally we asked the respondents to face the problem of what to do about the urban riots and to choose between the alternative of tighter police control or a greater effort to improve the condition of Negroes in the cities. The responses to this question are generally consistent with those given to the more generally phrased questions. Relatively few white respondents saw the answer to the urban problem exclusively in terms of more effective police control. For the most part the respondents felt the solution was more likely to be found in "trying harder" to improve the conditions of urban Negroes (Table 23).

Table 23. *"Thinking about the next five to ten years, what do you think would be the best thing to do about the problem of riots—build up tighter police control in the Negro areas, or try harder to improve the condition of Negroes?"*

[In percent]

	White		
	Men	Women	Total
Tighter police control	17	15	16
Improve Negro conditions	53	56	54
Do both	28	27	28
Don't know	2	2	2
	100	100	100

Comparison of the reactions of the younger and older age groups to these proposals for action reveals the same pattern we have seen in the earlier tables. There is a consistent but not remarkable tendency among the younger white people to give stronger support to these proposals to improve the conditions of the urban Negro than among the older generations (Table 24).

Table 24. *White Attitudes Toward Proposals for Action Among Age Categories*

[In Percent]

	Men by Age					
	16-19	20-29	30-39	40-49	50-59	60-69
Agree that government should provide needed jobs	63	62	60	55	55	54
Agree that government should improve schools	89	83	71	72	70	69
Agree that government should improve slum housing	69	66	58	53	63	51
Would go along with program of spending to help Negroes.	72	71	64	56	64	59
Willing to pay more taxes for program to help Negroes	59	55	50	42	56	54
Prefer to try harder to improve condition of Negroes	58	57	54	57	44	49
	Women by Age					
	16-19	20-29	30-39	40-49	50-59	60-69
Agree that government should provide needed jobs	79	59	50	55	62	68
Agree that government should improve schools	95	91	77	81	73	73
Agree that government should improve slum housing	78	65	51	57	59	53
Would go along with program of spending to help Negroes	77	74	61	66	61	63
Willing to pay more taxes for program to help Negroes	61	57	48	54	49	48
Prefer to try harder to improve condition of Negroes	71	68	55	49	46	54

These questions in our survey have in effect asked our sample of white citizens to respond to a plebiscite on several proposals regarding public action to be taken on the urban problem. We cannot be sure, of course, that the distributions of opinions we have reported would be precisely the same as those that might be obtained in a referendum vote in these cities with all the attendant political pressures that might be involved. However, two conclusions from the data we have reviewed seem firm and important.

1. There is a willingness among the white population of these northern cities to see government play a strong hand in helping bring about improvement in the conditions of the cities. This opinion is not unanimous; there is a substantial minority who oppose the suggestion of such programs. But there is a consistent majority on all these proposals who accept the necessity of governmental assistance and this approval is not reduced when the purpose of the assistance is specifically related to the needs of the Negro population and the prevention of riots.

2. The superficially simple solution to the problem of urban riots—more rigid police control of the Negro areas— is not generally seen by white urban residents as an adequate answer.

The large majority of these people accept the proposition that there must be an improvement in the conditions of Negro life.

THE WHITE SUBURBS

When we compare the beliefs of white suburbanites concerning the prevalence of racial discrimination to those we have just reviewed we find no differences of any consequence. White people in the suburbs are somewhat more likely to feel they are better off economically than Negroes of similar educational status and this probably reflects the fact that their own economic situation is on the average better than that of white people within the cities. Suburban white people also differ very little from whites within the city limits in their attitudes on most aspects of racial integration and in their acceptance of the desirability of governmental programs to improve conditions within the cities. The one point at which suburban people show a special sensitivity is in the area of segregated housing. They are more likely to support the proposition that white people may properly keep Negroes out of their neighborhood if they wish and they show more resistance to the prospect of having a Negro family living next door. These differences are small, less than ten percentage points, but they are not chance.

WHY DID IT HAPPEN? THE BASIC CAUSES

National Advisory Commission on Civil Disorders

We have seen what happened. Why did it happen?

In addressing this question we shift our focus from the local to the national scene, from the particular events of the summer of 1967 to the factors within the society at large which have brought about the sudden violent mood of so many urban Negroes.

The record before this Commission reveals that the causes of recent racial disorders are imbedded in a massive tangle of issues and circumstances—social, economic, political, and psychological—which arise out of the historical pattern of Negro-white relations in America.

These factors are both complex and interacting; they vary significantly in their effect from city to city and from year to year; and the consequences of one disorder, generating new grievances and new demands, become the causes of the next. It is this which creates the "thicket of tension, conflicting evidence and extreme opinions" cited by the President.

Despite these complexities, certain fundamental matters are clear. Of these, the most fundamental is the racial attitude and behavior of white Americans toward black Americans. Race prejudice has shaped our history decisively in the past; it now threatens to do so again. White racism is essentially responsible for the explosive mixture which has been accumulating in our cities since the end of World War II. At the base of this mixture are three of the most bitter fruits of white racial attitudes:

Pervasive discrimination and segregation. The first is surely the continuing exclusion of great

Reprinted from the *Report of the National Advisory Commission on Civil Disorders* (Washington, D.C.: U.S. Government Printing Office, March 1968), pp. 91-93.

numbers of Negroes from the benefits of economic progress through discrimination in employment and education, and their enforced confinement in segregated housing and schools. The corrosive and degrading effects of this condition and the attidues that underlie it are the source of the deepest bitterness and at the center of the problem of racial disorder.

Black migration and white exodus. The second is the massive and growing concentration of impoverished Negroes in our major cities resulting from Negro migration from the rural South, rapid population growth and the continuing movement of the white middle-class to the suburbs. The consequence is a greatly increased burden on the already depleted resources of cities, creating a growing crisis of deteriorating facilities and services and unmet human needs.

Black ghettos. Third, in the teeming racial ghettos, segregation and poverty have intersected to destroy opportunity and hope and to enforce failure. The ghettos too often mean men and women without jobs, families without men, and schools where children are processed instead of educated, until they return to the street—to crime, to narcotics, to dependency on welfare, and to bitterness and resentment against society in general and white society in particular.

These three forces have converged on the inner city in recent years and on the people who inhabit it. At the same time, most whites and many Negroes outside the ghetto have prospered to a degree unparalleled in the history of civilization. Through television—the universal appliance in the ghetto—and the other media of mass communications, this affluence has been endlessly flaunted before the eyes of the Negro poor and the jobless ghetto youth.

As Americans, most Negro citizens carry within themselves two basic aspirations of our society. They seek to share in both the material resources of our system and its intangible benefits—dignity, respect and acceptance. Outside the ghetto many have succeeded in achieving a decent standard of life, and in developing the inner resources which give life meaning and direction. Within the ghetto, however, it is rare that either aspiration is achieved.

Yet these facts alone—fundamental as they are—cannot be said to have caused the disorders. Other and more immediate factors help explain why these events happened now.

Recently, three powerful ingredients have begun to catalyze the mixture.

Frustrated hopes. The expectations aroused by the great judicial and legislative victories of the civil rights movement have led to frustration, hostility and cynicism in the face of the persistent gap between promise and fulfillment. The dramatic struggle for equal rights in the South has sensitized Northern Negroes to the economic inequalities reflected in the deprivations of ghetto life.

Legitimation of violence. A climate that tends toward the approval and encouragement of violence as a form of protest has been created by white terrorism directed against nonviolent protest, including instances of abuse and even murder of some civil rights workers in the South; by the open defiance of law and federal authority by state and local officials resisting desegregation; and by some protest groups engaging in civil disobedience who turn their backs on nonviolence, go beyond the constitutionally protected rights of petition and free assembly, and resort to violence to attempt to compel alteration of laws and policies with which they disagree. This condition has been reinforced by a general erosion of respect for authority in American society and reduced effectiveness of social standards and community restraints on violence and crime. This in turn has largely resulted from rapid urbanization and the dramatic reduction in the average age of the total population.

Powerlessness. Finally, many Negroes have come to believe that they are being exploited politically and economically by the white "power structure." Negroes, like people in poverty everywhere, in fact lack the channels of communication, influence and appeal that traditionally have been available to ethnic minorities within the city and which enabled them—unburdened by color—to scale the walls of the white ghettos in an earlier era. The frustrations of powerlessness have led some to the conviction that there is no effective alternative to violence as a means of expression and redress, as a way of "moving the system." More generally, the result is alienation and hostility toward the institutions of law and government and the white society which controls them. This is reflected in the reach toward racial consciousness and solidarity reflected in the slogan "Black Power."

These facts have combined to inspire a new mood among Negroes, particularly among the young. Self-esteem and enhanced racial pride are replacing apathy and submission to "the system." Moreover, Negro youth, who make up over half of the ghetto population, share the growing sense of alienation felt by many white youth in our country. Thus, their role in recent civil disorders reflects not only a shared sense of deprivation and victimization by white society but also the rising incidence of disruptive conduct by a segment of American youth throughout the society.

Incitement and encouragement of violence. These conditions have created a volatile mixture of attitudes and beliefs which needs only a spark to ignite mass violence. Strident appeals to violence, first heard from white racists, were echoed and reinforced last summer in the inflammatory rhetoric of black racists and militants. Throughout the year, extremists crisscrossed the country preaching a doctrine of black power and violence. Their rhetoric was widely reported in the mass media; it was echoed by local "militants" and organizations; it became the ugly background noise of the violent summer.

We cannot measure with any precision the influence of these organizations and individuals in the ghetto, but we think it clear that the intolerable and unconscionable encouragement of violence heightened tensions, created a mood of acceptance and an expectation of violence, and thus contributed to the eruption of the disorders last summer.

The Police. It is the convergence of all these factors that makes the role of the police so difficult and so significant. Almost invariably the incident that ignites disorder arises from police action. Harlem, Watts, Newark and Detroit—all the major outbursts of recent years— were precipitated by routine arrests of Negroes for minor offenses by white police.

But the police are not merely the spark. In discharge of their obligation to maintain order and insure public safety in the disruptive conditions of ghetto life, they are inevitably involved in sharper and more frequent conflicts with ghetto residents than with the residents of other areas. Thus, to many Negroes police have come to symbolize white power, white racism and white repression. And the fact is that many police do reflect and express these white attitudes. The atmosphere of hostility and cynicism is reinforced by a widespread perception among Negroes of the existence of police brutality and corruption, and of a "double standard" of justice and protection—one for Negroes and one for whites.

To this point, we have attempted only to identify the prime components of the "explosive mixture." In the chapters that follow we seek to analyze them in the perspective of history. Their meaning, however, is already clear:

In the summer of 1967, we have seen in our cities a chain reaction of racial violence. If we are heedless, we shall none of us escape the consequences.

ADDITIONAL READINGS FOR CHAPTER 3

T. W. Adorno, Else Frenkel-Brunswik, Daniel J. Levinson, and R. Nevitt Sanford, *The Authoritarian Personality* (New York: John Wiley & Sons, 1964).

Gordon W. Allport, *The Nature of Prejudice* (Reading, Mass.: Addison-Wesley Publishing Co., 1954).

Roger Beardwood, "The New Negro Mood;" *Fortune*, V. LXXVII, N. 1 (January 1968) pp. 146-151, 230, 232, 234.

Bernard Berelson and Gary A. Steiner, *Human Behavior: An Inventory of Scientific Findings* (New York: Harcourt, Brace & World, 1964), pp. 493-525.

Bruno Bettleheim and Morris Janowitz, *Social Change and Prejudice* (New York: The Free Press, 1964).

William Brink and Louis Harris, *Black and White: A Study of U.S. Racial Attitudes Today* (New York: Simon & Schuster, 1966).

——, *The Negro Revolution in America* (New York: Simon & Schuster, 1964).

Kenneth B. Clark, *Dark Ghetto: Dilemmas of Social Power* (New York: Harper & Row, Publishers, 1965).

W. J. Cash, *The Mind of the South* (New York: Alfred A. Knopf, 1941).

Irwin Deutscher, "Words and Deeds: Social Science and Social Policy," *Social Problems,* V. 13 (Winter 1966), pp. 235-254.

Frantz Fanon, *Black Skins, White Masks* (New York: Grove Press, 1967).

William H. Grier and Price M. Cobbs, *Black Rage* (New York: Basic Books, 1968).

Herbert H. Hyman and Paul B. Sheatsley, "Attitudes Toward Desegregation," *Scientific American* V. 211, N. 1 (July 1964), pp. 16-23.

——, "Attitudes Towards Desegregation," *Scientific American* V. 195, N. 6 (December 1956), pp. 35-39.

Winthrop D. Jordan, *White Over Black: American Attitudes Toward the Negro, 1550-1812* (Baltimore, Md.: Penguin Books, 1968).

John C. Leggett, *Class, Race, and Labor: Working-Class Consciousness in Detroit* (New York: University Press, 1968).

Lawrence S. Linn, "Verbal Attitudes and Overt Behavior: A Study of Racial Discrimination," *Social Forces,* V. 43, N. 3 (March 1965), pp. 353-364.

Gary T. Marx, *Protest and Prejudice: A Study of Belief in the Black Community* (Harper & Row, Publishers, 1967).

Gunnar Myrdal, with the assistance of Richard Sterner and Arnold Rose, *An American Dilemma: The Negro Problem and Modern Democracy* (New York: Harper & Row, Publishers, 1944).

Milton Rokeach, *Beliefs, Attitudes and Values* (San Francisco: Jossey-Bass, Publishers, 1969).

——, "Attitude Change and Behavioral Change," *Public Opinion Quarterly,* V. 30 (Winter 1966-1967), pp. 529-550.

Mildred A. Schwartz, *Trends in White Attitudes Toward Negroes* (Chicago: National Opinion Research Center, 1967).

Paul B. Sheatsley, "White Attitudes Toward the Negro," in Talcott Parson and Kenneth B. Clark (eds.), *The Negro American* (Boston: Beacon Press, 1965).

Jerome H. Skolnick, *The Politics of Protest: The Skolnick Report to the National Commission on the Causes and Prevention of Violence* (New York: Ballantine Books, 1969) pp. 177-209.

Lyle G. Warner and Melvin L. DeFleur, "Attitude as an Interactional Concept: Social Constraint and Social Distance as Intervening Variables Between Attitudes and Action," *American Sociological Review,* V. 34, N. 2 (April 1969), pp. 153-169.

PART 2

BUSINESS INSTITUTIONS
AND THE BLACK COMMUNITY

$4.$ *E m p l o y m e n t*

Malcolm X. suggested that the two white men who had most aided the conditions of Negroes in America were Adolph Hitler and Joseph Stalin.[1] The point he was making was that not until the requirements of World War II and the cold war made it necessary for the United States to commit its manpower heavily to the armed services were blacks able to secure employment in industrial jobs (especially in the semiskilled and operative categories) which previously had been the sacred preserves of whites.[2] Thus, external pressures—not a change of heart on the part of white Americans— resulted in some slight advancements for blacks in the labor market. The sentiments expressed by Malcolm X. come as a shock to a people accustomed to thinking of itself as the benevolent agent of its own progress. But before we dismiss his ideas as the overstatement of impassioned rhetoric, we should note the observation of urbanologist Daniel P. Moynihan, Special Assistant for Urban Affairs to President Richard M. Nixon: "The fundamental, overwhelming fact is that *Negro unemployment*, with the exception of a few years during World War II and the Korean War, has continued at disaster levels for 35 years."[3]

Just what is the status and pattern of the employment of blacks in the United States? What kind of jobs do blacks obtain? What changes have taken place in the distribution of black employment in the last decade? What is the impact of unemployment and underemployment (employment below the training responsibilities or skill level of the employee) upon the individual? Finally, how does the employment status of blacks compare with that of whites with comparable training and experience?

The first group of selections in this chapter responds directly to these questions. The opening article, by labor economist Claire C. Hodge, provides statistics to answer the question, "The Negro Job Situation: Has it Improved?" Sociologist Paul M. Siegel's contribution, "On the Cost of Being a Negro," examines income differentials between blacks and whites within the same occupational and educational groupings. On the basis of his analysis of census data, he concludes that blacks pay a premium of over a thousand dollars annually in reduced earnings as a result of their blackness, irrespective of their comparable training and job classifications. The next selection, excerpted from a research study by Herbert R. Northrup of the Industrial Research Unit of the University of Pennsylvania, investigates the same issue in the aerospace industry. On the whole, it indicates some improvements in the employment status of blacks occurred during the mid- and late sixties, at a time when both the federal government and private industry were stressing "affirmative action" in employment as a result of persistent and increasingly militant pressure from the black community. While minority employment programs such as JOBS, sponsored by the National Alliance of Businessmen, and Plans for Progress facilitated to some extent the recruitment of blacks into industrial positions, they never realized the potential their publicity suggested for them. In all industries (including aerospace), blacks continue to predominate at the bottom levels of the employment ladder with least seniority and lowest wages.[4]

The next selection portrays another aspect of employment of blacks by business: the impact of employers' personnel policies and practices. What employers perceive as potential problems associated with the hiring of blacks and the means by which employers recruit manpower all bear upon the prospect of blacks securing useful, remunerative jobs—indeed, any jobs—within the private sector labor market. "Testing of Minority Group Applicants for Employment," by Phyllis Wallace, Beverly Kissinger, and Betty Reynolds, all formerly of the United States Equal Employment Opportunity Commission, discusses the special impact of tests validated for the white majority culture on the employment selection of minority culture blacks.

Next, a set of firsthand reports of discrimination in employment, drawn from hearings before the U.S. Equal Employment Opportunity Commission, enables the reader to better understand the experience of black Americans in the job market. When, in the next chapter, we read of Captain Lanier's experience in trying to rent an apartment, we shall have a chance to ask ourselves, "How would I feel if I were he?" We can ask ourselves the same question as we read the testimony of Miss Saundra Sharp and Mr. Emanual Robinson before the Commission. The concluding selection, "Sex, Status, and Underemployment of the Negro Male," by Kenneth B. Clark, discusses the psychological and sociological effects of unemployment and underemployment upon black men and women.

In the past few years, there have been a number of highly publicized instances of blacks achieving employment "firsts" in business—that is, of becoming the first black to obtain a particular high level position. The readings in this chapter focus upon the *overall status* of the black employee in the private sector labor market. Only by assessing the totality of the employment situation of the black population within the United States, rather than concentrating on the dramatic breakthroughs of selected individuals (important though they may be) can we obtain a clear picture of the current state of employment for black Americans.

NOTES

[1] See Malcolm X., *Malcolm X. Speaks* (New York: Grove Press, 1965), pp. 80 and 141.

[2] In early 1941, A. Philip Randolph, president of the Brotherhood of Sleeping Car Porters, began plans for a march on Washington to secure government action to insure the employment of blacks in federal and defense industry jobs. The march was subsequently called off when, prior to its scheduled date, President Roosevelt issued an Executive Order prohibiting discrimination in employment in defense industries and government.

[3] U.S. Department of Labor, *The Negro Family: The Case for National Action* (Washington, D.C.: U.S. Government Printing Office, March 1965) p. 20.

[4] In the executive suite and corporate board room, blacks are virtually nonexistent. A study released in late 1970 by the Race Relations Information Center indicated that of the 3182 senior officers and directors of 50 of the nation's largest corporations as listed in *Fortune* magazine, only three were black. All three were nonofficer directors of leading financial institutions—Chase Manhattan Bank, the Metropolitan Life Insurance Company, and the Equitable Life Assurance Society. See "Executive Suites—A White Domain," San Francisco Chronicle, October 1, 1970, p. 4.

THE NEGRO JOB SITUATION: HAS IT IMPROVED?

Claire C. Hodge

The past decade has seen a marked improvement in the number and kinds of jobs held by black Americans. Some of this occupational upgrading occurred between 1957 and 1962, but the trend accelerated sharply in the 1962-67 period, as nearly 1.1 million Negroes moved into jobs offering higher pay and status. Furthermore, during the past 5 years, the employment growth has been concentrated among full-time workers, while the number involuntarily on short workweeks—one measure of underemployment—has declined sharply.

Despite these recent substantial gains, however, the Negro today still holds a disproportionate share of jobs at the lower end of the occupational ladder and is underrepresented in the higher-skilled, better-paying jobs. In 1967, nearly half the employed Negroes were in unskilled, service, or farm jobs, compared with a fifth of the white workers. Conversely, nearly half of the employed whites held white-collar jobs, but less than one-fourth of the Negroes. Nevertheless, over the past decade, there has been improvement in the occupational configuration of Negro employment, with a concomitant increase in pay, status, and security.

EMPLOYMENT-UNEMPLOYMENT TRENDS

In 1967, employment of Negroes age 16 and over averaged 8 million, a 20-percent increase over a decade earlier. The number of Negroes employed increased by about 400,000 from 1957 to 1962 (5.4 percent) and by 1 million

Reprinted from *Monthly Labor Review*, U.S. Department of Labor, Bureau of Labor Statistics (Washington, D.C.: U.S. Government Printing Office, January 1969), pp. 20-28. Footnotes omitted.

from 1962 to 1967 (14.4 percent)—in both periods a faster rate of growth than that of white workers. Major factors contributing to these gains included an exceptional increase in the total number of job opportunities provided by the rapid economic expansion of most of the decade, new and expanded programs for retraining the existing workforce and for training prospective new entrants to the labor force, higher levels of educational attainment, and the decline in discrimination in hiring. Some of this, of course, can also be attributed to increases in the Negro labor force and the fact that in 1962 unemployment among Negroes was very high, thus providing an ample supply of workers for employers.

The 1-million gain in the past 5 years was accompanied by a sharp drop in the Negro unemployment rate—from 10.9 percent in 1962 to 7.4 percent in 1967—which, even so, was about double the white rate, a differential that has persisted for more than a decade. For most color and age-sex groups, unemployment rates have fallen sharply since 1962, but the rate for Negro teenagers has remained between 25 and 30 percent. (Statistics for nonwhite workers are used to indicate the situation for Negro workers. Negroes constitute about 92 percent of all nonwhites in the United States.)

One encouraging development has been the decline in long-term unemployment of Negro workers. In 1962, 300,000 Negroes, or about one-third of the Negro unemployed, were out of a job 15 weeks or more. By 1967, the number of long-term unemployed had been cut significantly, and an average of only 100,000 Negroes (about one-sixth of total Negro unemployment) were jobless 15 weeks or more—about the same proportion as among white workers.

The 1962-67 period was also marked by a concentration of employment growth among full-time workers and a substantial decline in the number of workers who were on short workweeks for economic reasons. Over 90 percent of the increase in the total number of Negroes at work was in those on full-time job schedules (35 hours or more a week). By 1967, 5.8 million Negro nonagricultural workers were on full-time schedules, compared with 4.7 million 5 years earlier. During the same period, the number of nonagricultural Negro workers employed part time for economic reasons—such as slack work, material shortage, inability to find full-time work, and so forth—fell from 615,000 to 475,000.

Still another encouraging aspect during the past 5 years was the expansion of Negro employment into those industries considered to offer the best jobs in terms of pay, advancement, security, and status. Negro employment grew especially rapidly—by one-third or more—in the fields of education, public administration, and durable-goods manufacturing. The number of Negroes at work in these industries rose from 1.3 million in 1962 to 2.1 million in 1967, a pickup of nearly 60 percent, compared with an increase of about 25 percent for whites. Meanwhile, substantial reductions in Negro employment were noted in two lower-paying fields of work in which Negro workers have been concentrated in the past—agriculture and private household work.

MOVEMENT TOWARD BETTER JOBS

An evaluation of Negro occupational employment changes during the past decade points up clearly the significant upgrading of the black worker and his movement toward better jobs. As table 1 illustrates, the Negro made substantial gains between 1957 and 1962 but there was a sharp acceleration of this trend in the 1962-67 period.

From 1962 to 1967, the number of Negroes moving into better jobs reached sizable proportions among professional and technical workers, clerical workers, craftsmen and foremen, and operatives in the steel, automobile, and other durable goods manufacturing industries. In total (including small increases in management,

sales, and protective service positions), there was an increase of nearly 1.1 million jobs in fields that generally offer higher pay and status, 3 times the increase in the previous 5 years. In addition, there was a substantial increase in the employment of Negro operatives in nondurable-goods manufacturing and nonmanufacturing industries. Many of these semiskilled jobs (truck and taxi drivers, deliverymen, assemblers, etc.) offer good pay and steady work.

In the less attractive, lower paying, and less secure occupations, Negro employment declined about 600,000 from 1962 to 1967. There was a drop of about 200,000 private household workers, 60,000 industrial (nonfarm) laborers, and 360,000 farm workers. In the remaining occupational group—which consists of a diverse group of service-worker occupations that are difficult to classify according to quality—Negro employment increased by about 230,000.

The rise in Negro professional and technical workers has been about equally divided between men and women. The increase in clerical and service jobs (except protective services) has been greatest among women. On the other hand, the advance in salaried managerial, crafts, durable goods operatives, and protective service occupations has been mostly among men.

One way of evaluating the extent to which Negro workers have succeeded in gaining entry into higher status or better paying occupations is to examine the changes that have taken place in the proportion of such jobs held by black workers in relation to the total proportion of Negroes in the labor force. In 1967, Negroes constituted 10.8 percent of total employment; therefore, while their share of white-collar jobs, for example, increased from 4.0 percent in 1962 to 5.4 percent in 1967, they were still underrepresented in the white-collar jobs. It is significant, however, that in this 5-year period they moved at least part of the distance between the 4-percent level of 1962 and the 10.8 percent that would equal their proportion in the employed labor force. The gain of 1.4 percentage points represents about one-fifth of the distance they would have had to gain to move from 4.0 to 10.8 percent.

This way of evaluating occupational gains is illustrated in table 2. The computation, of course, is useful only to provide a rough measure of relative gains in different occupations.

Table 1. *Nonwhite Workers by Occupation, Annual Averages: 1957, 1962, and 1967*

[Numbers in Thousands]

Occupation Group	1957[1][2]	1962[1]	1967	Change 1957 to 1962 (Percent)	Change 1962 to 1967 (Percent)
Total, 16 years of age and over	6,647	7,004	8,011	5.4	14.4
Total, 14 years of age and over	6,749	7,097	—	5.2	12.9[3]
Professional, technical and kindred	246	373	592	51.6	58.7
Medical and health	42	72	120	71.4	66.7
Teachers, excluding college	88	138	202	56.8	46.4
Other	116	163	271	40.5	66.3
Managers, officials, and proprietors	140	188	200	34.3	11.2
Salaried	35	77	115	120.0	49.4
Self-employed, retail trade	61	59	51	-3.3	-13.6
Self-employed, excluding retail trade	44	52	43	18.2	-17.3
Clerical	401	512	899	27.7	75.6
Stenographers, typists, and secretaries	80	95	163	18.8	71.6
Other	321	417	736	29.9	76.5
Sales	78	115	138	47.4	20.0
Retail trade	62	77	99	24.2	28.6
Other	16	38	39	137.5	2.6
Craftsmen and foremen	380	427	617	12.4	44.5
Carpenters	35	44	52	25.7	18.2
Construction excluding carpenters	92	111	157	20.7	41.4
Mechanics and repairmen	119	133	192	11.8	44.4
Metal craftsmen excluding mechanics	35	36	69	2.9	91.7
Other craftsmen	76	76	100	0.0	31.6
Foremen, not elsewhere classified	23	27	49	17.4	81.5
Operatives and kindred workers	1,411	1,412	1,882	0.1	33.3
Drivers and deliverymen	314	303	354	-3.5	16.8
Other	1,097	1,110	1,528	1.2	37.7
Durable goods manufacturing	342	359	575	5.0	60.2
Nondurable goods manufacturing	286	306	484	7.0	58.2
Other industries	469	445	469	-5.1	5.4
Nonfarm laborers	1,007	962	899	-4.5	-6.5
Construction	—	225	197	—	-12.4
Manufacturing	—	264	285	—	8.0
Other industries	—	473	416	—	-12.1
Service workers	2,159	2,326	2,353	7.7	1.2
Private households	1,008	1,040	835	3.2	-19.7
Service workers, excluding private household	1,151	1,286	1,519	11.7	18.1
Protective service workers	32	37	67	15.6	81.1
Waiters, cooks, bartenders	239	253	304	5.9	20.2
Other service workers	880	996	1,149	13.2	15.4
Farm workers	927	782	423	-15.6	-45.9
Farmers and farm managers	276	195	107	-29.3	-45.1
Farm laborers and foremen	651	587	317	-9.8	-46.0
Paid	463	444	281	-4.1	-36.7
Unpaid family workers	188	143	38	-23.9	-27.8

[1]Beginning in 1967, occupational data cover persons 16 years of age and over. Prior to 1967, occupational data have not been revised to exclude persons 14-15 years of age except for the figures on total employment shown here for comparison with 1967 total employment.

[2]1957 averages based on observations for January, April, July, and October; 1962 and 1967 are based on 12-month averages.

[3]Based on change between 1962 including persons 14 years of age and over, and 1967 including persons 16 years and over.

Note: Dashes indicate data not available.

Table 2. *Nonwhite Workers as a Proportion of All Workers in Higher Status Occupations*

| Occupation | Nonwhite workers as a proportion of all workers in the occupation | | | Increase in proportion of nonwhite workers required to reach 10.8 percent of all workers in occupation[1] | Actual increase, 1962-67, as a percent of the increase required to reach 10.8 percent |
| | Percent | | Increase, 1962-67 | | |
	1962	1967	(Percentage points)	(Percentage points)	(Percent)
Professional, technical and kindred workers	4.6	6.0	1.4	6.2	23
Medical and health	5.3	7.6	2.3	5.5	42
Teachers except college	8.1	9.4	1.3	2.7	48
Others	3.3	4.4	1.1	7.5	15
Managers, officials, and proprietors	2.5	2.8	0.3	8.3	4
Salaried	1.9	2.2	0.3	8.9	3
Self-employed, retail trade	3.7	4.7	1.0	7.1	14
Self-employed, other	2.9	3.8	0.9	7.9	11
Clerical and kindred workers	5.1	7.3	2.2	5.7	39
Stenographers, typists and secretaries	3.8	5.1	1.3	7.0	19
Others	5.5	8.0	2.5	5.3	47
Sales workers	2.6	3.0	0.4	8.2	5
Retail trade	3.0	3.6	0.6	7.8	8
Other	2.1	2.2	0.1	8.7	1
Craftsmen, foremen, and kindred workers. .	4.9	6.3	1.4	5.9	24
Carpenters	5.4	6.2	0.8	5.4	15
Construction craftsmen except carpenters .	6.5	8.2	1.7	4.3	40
Mechanics and repairmen	6.2	7.6	1.4	4.6	30
Metal crafts except mechanics	3.4	5.5	2.1	7.4	28
Other craftsmen	4.3	5.4	1.1	6.5	17
Foremen, not elsewhere classified	2.2	3.4	1.2	8.6	14
Protective service workers	4.6	7.0	2.4	6.2	39

[1]Difference between 1962 level and 10.8 percent (the proportion of Negroes in the employed labor force in 1967).

Note: Operatives and kindred workers are not included in this table because the nonwhite proportion was greater than 10.8 percent of all workers in the occupation in 1967. (See Table 4.)

There is no reason to expect the members of any one ethnic group to be distributed among occupations exactly like every other group; even if all racial discrimination in employment and all inequalities in educational and training opportunity were removed, the traditional interests, personal preferences, and geographic location of various ethnic groups might lead to a somewhat different mix of occupations. Keeping these qualifications in mind, however, one can compare the Negroes' proportion of jobs in each occupation with their proportion of total employment to give a rough measure of progress.

As noted above, Negroes made substantial progress in white-collar jobs in the 5-year period 1962 to 1967. Most noteworthy are their gains in medical and health occupations and clerical occupations—in each case they moved about two-fifths of the way toward the theoretical goal of 10.8 percent. Already relatively well-represented in the teaching profession, Negroes covered nearly half of the distance in teaching jobs. The slowest upgrading, and the smallest

relative progress, was found in the managerial and sales occupations, in which Negroes moved less than 5 percent of the distance.

In the skilled crafts, Negroes also made substantial gains, moving nearly one-quarter of the way toward the 10.8 figure. Notable gains were made in the construction trades (where a modest gain among carpenters was far outdistanced by progress in other trades), mechanics and repairmen, and metal crafts. Notable progress was made in protective service occupations, which include policemen, firemen, guards, and watchmen. Negroes increased their share of these jobs sharply in the 5-year period, moving nearly two-fifths of the distance toward a proportionate number of jobs.

Negroes thus have made substantial progress in a relatively short period toward better representation in some of the major higher status, better paid occupational fields. This is a significant record, even if it has to be qualified in two major respects: First, within any of the broad occupation groups for which data are available there are occupations with a wide range of earnings levels and status, and Negroes may have entered the lower levels in greater proportions than the higher levels; second, differences in pay and status exist even within a specific occupation, and this, too, could result in a greater degree of occupational inequality than is apparent from the broad occupational group data.

CHANGES IN PATTERNS

The changes in Negro occupational patterns are summarized in chart 1 and described in greater detail below.

About two-thirds of the net increase in employment of all Negro workers from 1962 to 1967 was in professional and technical, managerial, clerical, and sales occupations. As a result, the proportion of all Negro workers who were employed in white-collar jobs rose substantially, from 16.7 percent in 1962 to 22.9 percent in 1967. Nevertheless, Negroes still represented only 5.4 percent of all white-collar workers in 1967, a moderate rise from the 4.0 percent in 1962.

The most substantial gains in Negro employment were among professional and technical workers (an increase of 59 percent) and clerical workers (76 percent).

Black workers in professional and technical occupations numbered 600,000 in 1967, a gain of 200,000 jobs since 1962. The proportion of all Negro workers who were employed in such jobs advanced significantly during this period, from 5.3 to 7.4 percent. (See chart 2.)

Within the professional fields, teaching remained a primary field of employment for Negro college graduates, and, as a result, Negroes made up a relatively large proportion of all teachers—8.1 percent in 1962 and 9.4 percent in 1967. Negroes have also made substantial advances in medical and health jobs.

Negro employment opportunities grew even more rapidly in the clerical occupations. From 1962 to 1967, Negro clerical worker employment grew by 400,000 to 900,000. Although these are fast-growing occupations for whites as well as for Negroes, the proportion of Negro workers nonetheless increased sharply, both as a percent of their total employment and within the occupational group. The largest part of the gain occurred in clerical occupations other than stenographers, typists, and secretaries, in jobs such as cashiers, shipping and receiving clerks, stock clerks and storekeepers, mail carriers, postal clerks, and so forth.

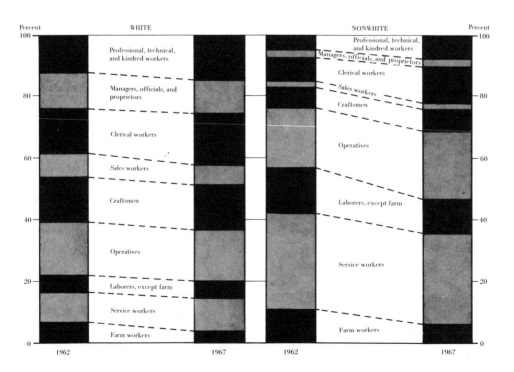

Chart 1. Change in Distribution of Workers, by Occupational Group, 1962-67

MANAGERS AND SALESWORKERS

In managerial and sales occupations, little occupational improvement occurred in the 1962-67 period. There were increases of less than 25,000 each in the number of Negroes in these two fields, and the proportion of all Negro workers who were employed in these occupations remained virtually unchanged.

One reason for so little progress in these two groups is that it is easier to gain access to faster growing fields, where openings are more plentiful, than to move into relatively stable occupations such as managers or more slowly growing occupations such as sales workers.

A second reason may be educational and skill requirements that make it difficult for many Negroes to qualify for these jobs. In 1966, the median educational attainment for persons employed in these two groups was about 12.5 years, higher than for any other group except professional workers. Another reason may be that Negroes often lack the experience that would permit upgrading or, as in the case of managers of small businesses, the financial resources to start their own enterprises. Also, the fact that a large proportion of sales jobs offer only part-time work and its corresponding low income may have discouraged Negro workers from entering sales jobs. Many qualified Negroes, women in particular, may prefer to seek full-time jobs elsewhere because they need the added earnings to augment their generally low family incomes.

One encouraging recent development is the progress of Negroes into salaried managerial positions, often in large companies or in government. The number of Negro salaried managers rose by about 40,000 from 1962 to 1967, nearly a 50-percent increase. This is a rapidly growing field (the exception within this major group) for both Negro and white workers, and the Negro proportion of all such jobs edged up only from 1.9 to 2.2 percent. (See tables 3 and 4.)

In the self-employed group of managers, on the other hand, the number of Negroes declined, as did the number of white workers in the occupation. These self-employed managerial positions differ greatly from salaried jobs. Many self-employed managers (both white and Negro) are proprietors of small marginal businesses. Moreover, opportunities in this type of work have been declining rapidly; the number

of self-employed managers fell by about one-third from 1962-67. However, special new programs designed to assist Negro small businessmen to remain in operation and the push for Negro-owned and managed businesses in ghettos may offset some of these recent declines.

CRAFTSMEN AND OPERATIVES

Two blue-collar groups—craftsmen and foremen, and operatives and kindred workers—have also provided additional well-paying higher status jobs for Negroes over the last 5 years. The number of Negro craftsmen and operatives increased about 35 percent, and the proportion of all Negro workers who were employed in these occupations also rose, equaling the proportion of all white workers in these occupations. However, the bulk of the employment gain occurred in the operative group, where Negroes were already employed in large numbers.

In the higher skilled craftsmen group, Negro employment rose 45 percent. Because of large gains for white workers, however, Negro workers still remain underrepresented in craftsmen jobs. Nevertheless, progress in the occupational group has kept pace with the proportionate increase in professional and technical occupations.

The picture differs sharply among individual craftsmen occupations, however. The most improved situation was for construction workers (except carpenters), mechanics and repairmen, and metal craftsmen (except mechanics). The occupations of construction craftsmen and mechanics and repairmen provided the largest number of additional opportunities for Negro jobseekers—an increase of more than 100,000 workers, or 43 percent, during the 5-year period.

Negro operatives had increased opportunities in both durable and nondurable-goods manufacturing, a rise of about 200,000 jobs in each. Operative jobs in steel, automotive, and other durable-goods manufacturing offer better pay and status than operative jobs in nondurable goods, and are usually filled by men. Between 1962 and 1967, Negroes in operative jobs increased from 1.4 to 1.9 million. By 1967, nearly one-quarter of all Negroes were employed as operatives.

Despite the gains enumerated above, in 1967 41 percent of all Negro workers were still

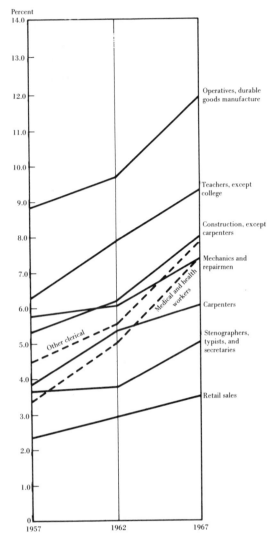

Chart 2. Nonwhite Workers as a Percent of all Workers in Selected Occupations, 1957, 1962, and 1967

employed in unskilled or service jobs. This compared with only 15 percent of all white workers.

In the nonfarm labor group, Negro employment declined between 1962 and 1967. The proportion of all Negro workers who were in this occupational group also fell, as declines in the number of Negro laborers in construction and other industries offset an increase in the number of Negro laborers in manufacturing. However, because manual labor is a declining occupation for both whites and Negroes, the proportion of Negro workers to the total in the occupation was practically unchanged between 1962 and 1967.

SERVICE WORKERS

Declines in the number of Negro service workers in private households and farm workers have made a further contribution to the overall upgrading of Negro workers. It would appear that most workers leaving these fields during the last 5 years have found better opportunities elsewhere, since their numbers were at least not added to the unemployed rolls.

The number of Negro service workers (not including private household workers) rose by nearly 250,000 in the 1962-67 period, to a total of 1.5 million, keeping pace with the overall increase in service-worker employment. As a result, Negro employment as a proportion of the occupational group was unchanged from 1962 to 1967. Because there are a variety of jobs in the group with different rates of pay, hours of work, benefits, security and status, these developments are difficult to evaluate in terms of upgrading.

There are several tentative conclusions that can be drawn, however. Negro workers continue to be concentrated in the less desirable service occupations. For example, the latest available data (1966) show that black workers made up 30 percent or more of the employment of chambermaids and maids and janitors and sextons. On the other hand, Negroes constituted less than 10 percent of those more desirable service occupations—bartenders, hairdressers, firemen, policemen, and guards. Negro workers have nonetheless made gains in these better jobs during the last 5 years. For example, job opportunities have been good in the protective service category—policemen, firemen and guards—and the number of Negroes employed has increased from less than 40,000 to nearly 70,000. Except for the protective service group, the rise in service-worker employment has been among women.

The largest Negro job increase in the service occupations (150,000) was in the less favorable "other service workers" category. Typically, Negro men in these jobs were janitors and sextons, porters, and kitchen workers. Negro women held more than half of all jobs in this category, typically as hospital attendants, chambermaids and maids, kitchen workers not elsewhere classified, and practical nurses. Except for practical nurses, most of these jobs pay very low

Table 3. *Employed Persons by Occupation and Color, Annual Averages, 1962 and 1967*
[Numbers in Thousands]

Occupation Group	1962[1]				1967			
	White		Nonwhite		White		Nonwhite	
	Number	Percent	Number	Percent	Number	Percent	Number	Percent
Total	60,749	100.0	7,097	100.0	66,361	100.0	8,011	100.0
Professional, technical, and kindred	7,667	12.6	373	5.3	9,287	14.0	592	7.4
Managers, officials, and proprietors	7,220	11.9	188	2.6	7,287	11.0	209	2.6
Clerical	9,594	15.8	512	7.2	11,435	17.2	899	11.2
Sales	4,231	7.0	115	1.6	4,387	6.6	138	1.7
Craftsmen and foremen	8,250	13.6	427	6.0	9,229	13.9	617	7.7
Operatives and kindred	10,629	17.5	1,412	19.9	12,002	18.1	1,882	23.5
Nonfarm laborers	2,597	4.3	962	13.6	2,635	4.0	899	11.2
Service workers	6,476	10.6	2,326	32.8	6,971	10.5	2,353	29.4
Private household	1,301	2.1	1,040	14.7	934	1.4	835	10.4
Service, excluding private household	5,175	8.5	1,286	18.1	6,037	9.1	1,519	19.0
F. m workers	4,084	6.7	782	11.0	3,130	4.7	423	5.3
Farmers and farm managers	2,400	4.0	195	2.7	1,862	2.8	107	1.3
Farm laborers and foremen	1,684	2.8	587	8.3	1,268	1.9	317	4.0

[1]Beginning in 1967, data cover persons 16 years of age and over. Prior to 1967, persons 14 years of age and over included.

wages and offer little in the way of advancement. Thus, increased employment in these occupations does not necessarily reflect an upgrading of the Negro worker.

During the past 5 years, both whites and Negroes have been leaving domestic service jobs in large numbers. Employment of Negro private household workers (nearly all women) fell by 200,000. However, the number of white workers in this category also declined, and the proportion of Negro workers to the total in the occupation was basically unchanged.

The number of Negro farm workers continued to decline, dropping by more than 350,000 between 1962 and 1967, with Negroes leaving the farms at twice the white rate. As a result, the proportion of all Negro workers employed as farm workers was halved by 1967, and farm work now accounts for about the same proportion of black as white employment. However, Negro farm workers were primarily farm laborers and foremen, while three-fifths of all white farm workers were farmers and farm managers.

TOWARD OCCUPATIONAL PROGRESS

If Negro occupational upgrading is to continue, efforts must continue to improve employment opportunities for Negroes in many occupations, industries, and geographic areas. And, since job requirements are rising in the labor force as a whole, the educational and skill level of black workers must continue to rise at a faster

than average rate if they are to catch up with their white counterparts.

The substantial gains noted above in the occupational upgrading of the Negro workforce are encouraging, but they cannot mask the fact that Negroes still constitute a disproportionate share of the workers in most low-paying, low-level occupations. It is not postulated here that Negroes, or any other population group, could or should achieve exactly proportional representation in each occupation. Many factors must be considered in understanding Negro occupational distributions—education, experience, training, geographic location, motivation, status, personal desires. Nevertheless, it is clear that the Negro's movement into better-paying, better-quality jobs must continue if equality of opportunity is to become a reality.

The importance of continuing the progress of the past several years can be brought into sharper focus by an examination of what the situation would be today if Negro workers had *not* improved their occupational status in recent years. If Negroes in 1967 made up the same proportion of each occupational group as they did in 1962, that is, if there had been no occupational upgrading, Negro workers would be in a significantly worse position than they are today. For example, they would have 140,000 fewer professional jobs than they actually had in 1967 and 270,000 fewer clerical positions. By way of contrast, they would have 115,000 more farm jobs and 90,000 more laborer jobs. Even more important, total employment of Negroes

Table 4. *Nonwhite Workers as a Percent of Total Employment by Occupation, Annual Averages*

[Numbers in Thousands]

Occupation Group	1957[1][2] Total Employment	1957[1][2] Percent Nonwhite	1962[1] Total Employment	1962[1] Percent Nonwhite	1967 Total Employment	1967 Percent Nonwhite
Total	65,100	10.4	67,846	10.5	74,372	10.8
Professional, technical, and kindred	6,476	3.8	8,040	4.6	9.879	6.0
Medical and health	1,157	3.6	1,353	5.3	1,578	7.8
Teachers, excluding college	1,351	6.5	1,713	8.1	2,159	9.4
Other	3,968	2.9	4,974	3.3	6,143	4.4
Managers, officials, and proprietors	6,705	2.1	7,408	2.5	7,495	2.8
Salaried	3,045	1.1	4,053	1.9	5,284	2.2
Self-employed — retail trade	1,835	3.3	1,583	3.7	1,074	4.7
Self-employed, excluding retail trade	1,825	2.4	1,773	2.9	1,137	3.8
Clerical	9,172	4.4	10,107	5.1	12,333	7.3
Stenographers, typists, and secretaries	2,170	3.7	2,511	3.8	3,190	5.1
Other	7,002	4.6	7,596	5.5	9,144	8.0
Sales	4,137	1.9	4,346	2.6	4,525	3.0
Retail trade	2,495	2.5	2,529	3.0	2,761	3.6
Other	1,642	1.0	1,817	2.1	1,765	2.2
Craftsmen and foremen	8,663	4.4	8,678	4.9	9,845	6.3
Carpenters	899	3.9	812	5.4	840	6.2
Construction, excluding carpenters	1,673	5.5	1,705	6.5	1,923	8.2
Mechanics and repairmen	2,032	5.9	2,145	6.2	2,539	7.6
Metal crafts, excluding mechanics	1,182	3.0	1,046	3.4	1,260	5.5
Other craftsmen	1,709	4.4	1,751	4.3	1,858	5.4
Foremen, not elsewhere classified	1,168	2.0	1,218	2.2	1,427	3.4
Operatives and kindred	12,542	11.3	12,041	11.7	13,884	13.6
Drivers and deliverymen	2,330	13.5	2,352	12.9	2,511	14.1
Other	10,212	10.7	9,689	11.5	11,372	13.4
Durable goods manufacturing	3,805	9.0	3,611	9.9	4,751	12.1
Nondurable goods manufacturing	3,458	8.3	3,314	9.2	3,761	12.9
Other industries	2,949	15.9	2,764	16.1	2,861	16.4
Nonfarm laborers	3,682	27.3	3,559	27.0	3,533	25.4
Construction	N.A.	N.A.	747	30.1	732	26.9
Manufacturing	N.A.	N.A.	1,017	26.0	1,107	25.7
Other Industries	N.A.	N.A.	1,796	26.3	1,694	24.6
Service workers	7,653	28.2	8,802	26.4	9,325	25.3
Private household	2,108	47.8	2,341	44.4	1,769	[3]47.2
Service workers excluding private household	5,545	20.8	6,461	19.9	7,556	20.1
Protective service workers	742	4.3	805	4.6	954	7.0
Waiters, cooks, bartenders	1,593	15.0	1,774	14.3	2,061	14.8
Other service workers	3,210	27.4	3,882	25.7	4,541	26.3
Farm workers	6,070	15.3	4,866	16.1	3,554	11.9
Farmers and farm managers	3,326	8.3	2,595	7.5	1,970	5.4
Farm laborers and foremen	2,744	23.7	2,271	25.8	1,584	20.0
Paid	1,495	31.0	1,382	32.1	1,049	26.8
Unpaid family workers	1,249	15.1	889	16.1	536	6.7

[1]Beginning in 1967, occupational data cover persons 16 years of age and over. Prior to 1967, persons 14 years of age and over are included.

[2]1957 averages based on observations for January, April, July, and October.

N.A. — Not available.

[3]The change in definition of employment eliminating persons 14 and 15 years of age affects comparisons of white-nonwhite employment in this category. If allowances are made for these changes, the proportion of Negroes in this occupation would be slightly lower in 1967 than in 1962.

would have been one-half million less than it actually was in 1967. On this basis, and assuming the same labor force as in 1967, the hypothetical unemployment rate for Negroes would have been nearly double the actual rate of 7.4 percent.

Despite its importance, continuing the progress of the last 5 or 10 years will not be easy.

ECONOMIC GROWTH IS A MUST

The pace of improvement in employment for any worker, of course, is governed by the rate at which the Nation's economy grows and the demand for workers. But for Negro workers, a continuing strong demand for workers is critical, for it is often in the rapidly growing occupations that they can gain real ground. In growing occupations, or in occupations with high turnover, hiring needs are greater and upgrading is more prevalent than in declining fields. Furthermore, for Negro workers to gain a larger share of jobs in declining occupations might not necessarily be considered a favorable development if in the long run it led to unemployment or dead end jobs. Similarly, Negro gains of the recent past could be lost if the economy fails to grow. The situation for Negro workers has long been one of "last hired-first fired." When employers need workers, on the other hand, discriminatory barriers are more quickly let down.

Geographic factors are also a consideration, since a disproportionate number of Negroes live in the Southern region of the United States and in rural areas, where fewer high-level jobs are readily available. Nevertheless, in recent years, millions of Negroes have migrated to other areas in search of better jobs and opportunities.

It is also important to note that the education and skill levels of the entire workforce continue to rise, so that the black worker must continue to advance even more rapidly in education and training if he is to make up for past handicaps.

Upgrading educational attainment of an employed workforce is a slow process. In recent years, a great many workers have been the beneficiaries of special training and retraining courses, both government and private. For many of the older Negro workers, the gap between employers' job requirements and their educational attainment is wide. Accelerated movement into better jobs depends on improving the opportunities for and the qualifications of younger workers. Today, nearly one black teenager in four is unemployed and a high proportion of employed Negro youth are in unskilled occupations. To acquire the skill and experience which will qualify them for highly skilled positions in the future, these young people must have the opportunity and the training for meaningful jobs now.

ON THE COST OF BEING A NEGRO

Paul M. Siegel

Arguing that racial prejudice can be understood only if the process by which racial groups form images of themselves and others is viewed as a *collective* phenomenon, Herbert Blumer had occasion to identify four types of feeling always present in racial prejudice by a majority group. These he specified as: (1) a feeling of superiority, (2) a feeling that the subordinate group is intrinsically alien and different, (3) a feeling of proprietary claim to certain areas of privilege and advantage, and (4) a fear and suspicion that the subordinate race harbors designs on the prerogatives of the dominant group. While Blumer makes it amply clear that the "sense of group position" which these four types of feeling comprise is not the same as objective social status, the two are not altogether independent of each other. Since the sense of group position is a historical product, originally formed out of the conditions of initial contact between the two groups, "subsequent experience in the relation of the two racial groups, especially in the area of claims, opportunities, and advantages may mold the sense of group position in many diverse ways."

The source of race prejudice lies in a felt challenge to the sense of group position.

The challenge, one must recognize, may come in many different ways. It may be in the form of an affront to feelings of group superiority; it may be in the form of attempts at familiarity or transgressions of the boundary line of group exclusiveness; it may be in the form of encroachment at countless points of proprietary claim; it may be a challenge to power and privilege; it may take the form of economic competi-

tion. Race prejudice is a defensive reaction to such challenging of the sense of group position. . . . It functions, however shortsightedly, to preserve the integrity and the position of the dominant group.[1]

In recent years, in North and South, schools and churches, public and private places, Negro leaders and their white collaborators have not challenged but *assaulted* the established order of relations between the two racial groups. There can be little question that the Negro has improved his objective social condition over the past half century. His occupational attainment is higher, his death rate lower, and his educational attainment greater than fifty, nay ten, years ago. These aspects of the Negro's progress are well known, but they do not necessarily indicate a reduction in white-nonwhite differentials. In large part improvements in the Negro's status are reflections of secular trends in the whole society. The more delicate question of how white-nonwhite *differentials* in education, occupation, and income have been affected by these secular trends is another matter, and the subject of this paper. Although we cannot trace the full impact of objective conditions upon the "sense of group position," we can provide a context of objective relations within which the collective process of racial identification must occur. It is inconceivable that the state of the *collective conscience* should be independent of the shape of objective relations. Indeed, we will be able to identify a number of critical objective relations which can only provide an impetus to the current protest movement.

One major concern of the current civil rights movement is for equal jobs and job opportunities. When the *Newsweek* Poll asked Negroes how discrimination had affected them person-

Reprinted from "On the Cost of Being a Negro," by Paul M. Siegel, *Sociological Inquiry*, V. 35, N 1. (Winter 1965), pp. 41-57, by permission of the author and the publisher. Some footnotes omitted.

ally, about a third of those interviewed said it had kept them from getting the kinds of jobs they wanted. It is fitting then that we begin our investigation with an examination of the occupational segregation of whites from nonwhites and the changes that have occurred in this segregation in the decade from 1950 to 1960. For each of four age cohorts and at each of eight educational levels we can establish the index of dissimilarity[2] between the white and nonwhite major occupation distributions. The index of dissimilarity indicates the percentage of nonwhites (or of whites) who would have to change their major occupation group in order that the occupational distributions of whites and nonwhites within that age-education group be the same. Table 1 sets forth indices of this type for both 1950 and 1960.[3]

In Table 1 we note that there are two kinds of comparisons which can be made. These are indicated in the second panel of the table, for those with no years of schooling completed. The curved arrow represents "inter-cohort" comparisons, i.e., comparisons between two distinct groups of persons of similar education, but reaching a given age at two different points in time. Thus from the second panel of Table 1 we see that the index of dissimilarity between the occupational distribution of whites and nonwhites with no years of schooling completed and who were aged 25-34 in 1950 was 23.2. For the group reaching these ages in 1960, again with no years of schooling completed, the index of dissimilarity was slightly lower, 18.6. There are a total of 32 inter-cohort comparisons possible in Table 1, each specific to age and education. Of these 32 independent comparisons, 25 show that the occupational segregation of the two races was lower in 1960 than in 1950. Although the indices of dissimilarity are not vastly lower in 1960 than in 1950, there is nevertheless some indication of slight occupational desegregation. At almost every educational level, younger nonwhite cohorts are finding slightly less occupational segregation than was found by the cohort born ten years earlier at comparable ages.

The inter-cohort comparisons are complemented by the "intra-cohort" comparisons indicated by the diagonal arrows in the second panel of Table 1. The intra-cohort comparisons contrast the occupational segregation of the same

group of people at two points in time. Thus in the second panel of Table 1 we see as before that the index of dissimilarity between the occupational distributions of whites and nonwhites with no years of schooling completed and who were aged 25-34 in 1950 is 23.2. Following the diagonal arrow we see that ten years later, when this same group of people is aged 35-44, the index of dissimilarity has fallen to 18.0. In all there are 24 intra-cohort comparisons specific to age and education in this table. Of these 24 contrasts, 18 show a decline between 1950 and 1960 in the occupational segregation of a given age-education cohort of whites and nonwhites. This improvement, ignoring differential mortality, it appears, can only result from differential mobility on the part of nonwhites: they must have moved in such a way as not only to make their occupational distributions more similar to those of whites, but also in such a way as to compensate for the intra-generational mobility experienced by their white peers between 1950 and 1960.

One might be tempted to summarize the findings in Table 1 as indicating slight but consistent tendencies towards occupational desegregation within educational groupings over the ten year period. Such a conclusion, while accurate to some extent, overlooks the most basic pattern in the table, a pattern of white-nonwhite differentials persistent at least since 1940, and one to which we shall return several times in the course of this paper. Inspection of the table reveals that in both 1950 and 1960 there was a tendency for dissimilarity to increase with level of education and taper off at the highest levels: in both 1950 and 1960 the highest indices of dissimilarity occur at the high school and some college levels. Inspection of [Nathaniel] Hare's tables reveals a similar pattern for 1940. Persons with so much education are qualified for supervisory, craft, sales, and managerial duties. These are, however, the very occupations denied to Negroes by social mores governing race relations, especially the norm which proscribes the supervision of white workers by Negroes. Nonwhites who complete college can take up professional occupations servicing Negro clientele. Both Negroes and whites at the lower levels of education cannot achieve much more than operative level jobs. It is at the high school and some college levels that non-

Table 1. *Indices of Dissimilarity Between White and Nonwhite Occupational Distributions For Males Aged 25-64 in the United States, 1950 and 1960, By Age and Education* *

Years of School Completed and Census Year	Age Group			
	25-34	35-44	45-54	55-64
Total				
1950	36.5	39.1	39.6	36.7
1960	35.4	37.3	38.5	38.9
No school years				
1950	23.2	20.8	22.2	32.2
1960	18.6	18.0	15.7	19.8
Elementary 1-4 years				
1950	22.8	24.2	25.6	29.7
1960	19.9	21.2	23.6	24.8
Elementary 5-7 years				
1950	26.2	28.8	29.0	26.4
1960	26.1	26.6	28.6	30.4
Elementary 8 years				
1950	28.9	32.6	34.2	31.4
1960	27.0	26.9	30.3	33.5
High School 1-3 years				
1950	29.0	36.0	39.6	38.4
1960	28.2	31.4	33.4	37.8
High School 4 years				
1950	33.8	39.1	40.5	36.9
1960	33.4	34.1	35.8	38.7
College 1-3 years				
1950	38.8	39.5	39.3	29.2
1960	34.4	38.2	37.6	34.8
College 4 or more years				
1950	17.8	17.8	21.6	17.2
1960	18.6	19.1	18.7	19.0

*Source: U.S. Bureau of the Census, U.S. Census of Population: 1950, 4, Special Report, Part 5, Chapter B, Education, Table 11; and U.S. Census of Population: 1960, Subject Reports, Educational Attainment, Table 8.

Note: Data pertain to the "Employed" in 1950 and to the "Experienced Civilian Labor Force" in 1960.

whites are most segregated from whites. Yet *these are the very educational levels which Negroes are now reaching in large numbers* for the first time. In 1940 only 19 percent of all Negro males aged 25-34 fell into the categories 1-3 years of high school, 4 years of high school completed, and 1-3 years of college. By 1950, 34 percent of all Negro males aged 25-34 were in these educational categories. And in 1960 the corresponding figure was 54 percent. Thus in each of the last two decades a considerably increasing proportion of young Negroes have been able to upgrade themselves educationally, only to arrive at the very educational levels where occupational segregation is the greatest.

It is not hard to see the importance, in the current reformation of race relations, of this change in educational attainment and its resultant exposure to greater occupational segrega-

tion. While the pattern is not historically unique to the current decade, it is a pattern to which more and more of the Negro population is being exposed, and it can only serve to add acrimony to Negro-white relations. It was Hare's failure to see this basic relation of educational achievement and patterns of occupational segregation, that led him to expect education to play a vital role in easing the tensions of inequality between the races. Focusing on the group with the highest level of education, college graduates—where occupational segregation is at a relative minimum—he projected that, as the secular trend of increasing education brought more and more Negroes to this level, occupational segregation would disappear. The data so far reviewed suggest that as more and more Negroes gain higher and higher educational levels, fewer and fewer Negroes will be able to profitably employ their education. Thus, it is likely that while whites' image of the Negro must reflect Negroes' increasing educational attainment, this improvement in educational status not only increases the possibility of whites perceiving a Negro threat to white prerogatives: it creates greater motivation for Negroes to demand equal treatment both inside and outside the labor market, and it provides reinforcement of an image of Negroes as inferior and unable to realize the potential of their education. A further and more detailed picture of Negro-white differentials in this basic aspect of the group condition—making a living—is offered by the consideration of income as determined within occupational groups by education. While they are unable to provide the historical perspective we have used here, the data discussed below go a long way towards amplifying the findings reported here—that Negroes are just beginning to be exposed to a whole new area of segregation.

Prior to the publication of the 1960 Census of Population, simultaneous tabulations of income by education *and* occupation were not available. Tabulations of this kind are now available, specific to region and race, for a five percent sample of the male civilian experienced labor force aged 25-64 in 1960. These data provide a unique opportunity for examining white-nonwhite differentials in average earnings within major occupation groups at every educational level, for both the South and the non-South (which will be called the North). Figures 1 to 10 show the relationship between mean earnings in 1959 and educational attainment separately for whites and nonwhites in the North and South. A separate figure is presented for each Census major occupation group; a capital N is used to identify curves for nonwhites and a capital W identifies those for whites; and solid lines indicate incomes in the North while dashed lines indicate those in the South.

The pattern of relationships illustrated in Figures 1 to 10 is remarkably consistent. With the single exception of nonwhite farmers in the North, the figures show that at *every* educational level in every occupational group, and in the North as well as the South, nonwhites have average earnings less than those of whites. This finding has long been anticipated but until the appearance of the 1960 Census data it was not possible to demonstrate it comprehensively. The figures also enable one to see the magnitude of the differentials, which are frequently in excess of $1000. Indeed, not only are differences of this magnitude observed between white and nonwhite earnings within each of the geographic regions under consideration: differences in excess of $1000 are observed between the earnings of nonwhites in the South and nonwhites elsewhere in the United States.

While one might choose to interpret these differences as due to quality differences in education, or to differences in detailed occupational distributions within major occupation groups, it seems unlikely that either factor alone, or both in conjunction, could produce differentials as large as those shown in the charts. This point is perhaps amply documented by reading some of the more dramatic differentials from the charts. For example, Figure 1 shows that a white professional in the North, with fewer than eight years of school completed, earns on the average a thousand dollars more per year than a nonwhite professional in the South with four or more years of college. Figure 2 indicates that on the average a nonwhite Northern manager who has completed four or more years of college earns no more than his white counterpart with less than eight years of school completed. This latter difference reflects, no doubt, the etiquette of retail relationships, wherein Negro managers are largely restricted to servicing Negro clientele and are restricted from achieving supervisory positions superior to whites. Other striking contrasts can be found in each of the figures.

Many of the striking contrasts one can extract from the figures might of course be "explained away" by differences in the detailed occupational pursuits of whites and nonwhites within major occupational categories. But since we have previously argued that at some educational levels Negroes cannot *get* the same jobs as whites, to invoke detailed occupational differentiation of those Negroes who do gain employment comparable with that of their white educational peers is to change the argument from "Negroes are paid less than whites with the same training in the same jobs," to "Negroes are not allowed into the high paying jobs within major occupational groups." The latter argument could be buttressed by reference to the rules of race relations which exclude Negroes

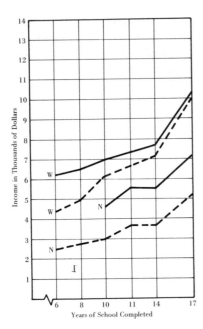

Figure 1. Professional, Technical, and Kindred Workers

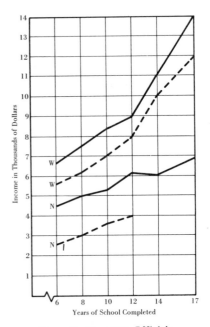

Figure 2. Managers, Officials, and Proprietors

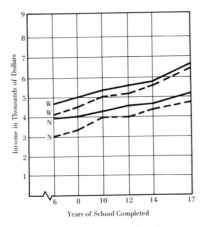

Figure 3. Clerical and Kindred Workers

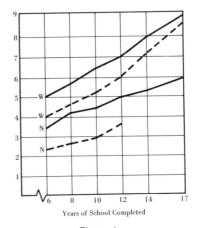

Figure 4. Sales Workers

from positions of authority over whites, or from entry into trades governed by discriminatory unions. The point is, of course, that the income differentials displayed in Figures 1 to 10 do not necessarily reflect white-nonwhite pay differentials for similar work and similar training: various features of the social organization of the relations between the races may also account for the differentials. But regardless of what final account is given of the differentials here displayed, an individual Negro cannot expect to earn as much as a white person with the same number of years of school completed and at the same general level of employment.

Inspection of the figures also reveals that the white-nonwhite differentials in earnings at most occupational and educational levels are greater inside than outside the South. Although the differential is occasionally as great as $1000, for most occupation-education combinations the white-nonwhite income difference is on the order of $100 to $500 greater in the South.

Apart from racial and regional differences in income, we can also derive some understanding of how the occupational structure itself affects the differential incomes of Negroes and whites. All of the figures are plotted in the same scale, so comparisons between them can readily be made.

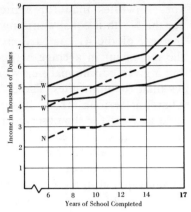

Figure 5. Craftsmen, Foremen, and Kindred Workers

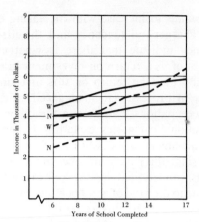

Figure 6. Operatives and Kindred Workers

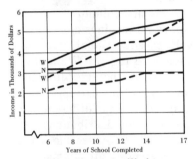

Figure 7. Service Workers, Including Private Household

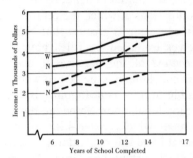

Figure 8. Laborers, Except Farm and Mine

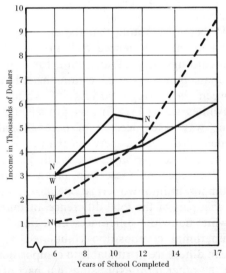

Figure 9. Farm Owners and Managers

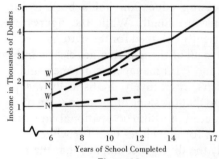

Figure 10. Farm Laborers and Foremen

and nonwhites to be most similar, these comparisons tend to confirm our previous suspicion that part of the white-nonwhite income differential observed at the higher status occupational levels reflected differences in detailed occupational affiliation.

Close inspection of the figures also reveals that there is both a general tendency for income to increase with education and two subtendencies: (1) for income to increase *more* rapidly with increasing education in some occupations than in others; and (2) for white-nonwhite

Comparisons of this kind will show that the differentials between whites and nonwhites average least among clerical and kindred workers, service workers, and unskilled laborers. Since these are the very levels at which one might expect the detailed occupations of whites *differentials* to increase with increasing education. The general tendency and the first sub-tendency indicate that there is what can be thought of as a return on investment in education and that the return on this investment is higher in professional, managerial, sales, and craft occupations than among the other major occupational categories, excluding farmers and farm managers (a special case). This is not too surprising: the payoff on investment in education is conditioned by the relevance of the training to the kind of work performed. One can easily see that in this respect the white and nonwhite occupational hierarchies are roughly parallel. This phenomenon is, of course, quite relevant to the matter at hand, for it is from the very occupations at which the return on investment in education is greatest that Negroes find themselves excluded by rules governing the *social context* of the practice of occupations. Thus we conclude that the Negro who manages to upgrade himself educationally is apt to find the occupational door closed at the levels of employment which enable him to realize his investment in educational attainment, a conclusion to which we have been drawn before.

The tendency for income differentials between whites and nonwhites to increase with increasing education holds both inside and outside the South. While the figures are not sufficiently enlarged for the pattern to be clearly seen in all of them, it emerges clearly in Figures 2, 5, and 7, for managers, craftsmen, and service workers, respectively. Statistically the pattern means that the slope of the regression of income on education within occupational categories will be less for nonwhites than for whites. Substantively the divergence implies that the return in income for completing a given educational step is less for nonwhites than it is for whites. Since they are independent, if we compare the slopes of the curves for whites and nonwhites at each educational step, within regions and major occupational groups, we can summarize the patterns of return upon investment in education by counting the number of comparisons in which the income increment for completing a given educational step is larger for whites than for nonwhites. Within the South there are 33 such comparisons. In 29, or 87.2 percent of these 33 comparisons the increment in average earnings for completing a given education step

is less for nonwhites than for whites. The pattern for the North is equally striking: in 34, or 82.9 percent of the 41 comparisons in the North, the increment in average earnings for completing a given educational step was larger for whites than for nonwhites. These findings suggest, barring serious errors of reporting which could account for the observed pattern, that the rate of return upon educational investment is appreciably less for Negroes than for whites. Thus the Negro not only starts out with a financial handicap, but in most occupations the handicap is *accentuated* with increasing education.

In order to summarily display this disadvantageous aspect of increasing education, we present in the first column of Table 2 the mean white-nonwhite earnings difference for each of six levels of educational attainment for all occupations and regions. While the tabled values clearly show that the difference between white and nonwhite earnings increases with increasing education, differences in occupational and regional distributions—shown in the figures to account for sizeable white-nonwhite earnings differences—are not taken into account in the first column of the table. A simple procedure will enable us to remedy this confounding.

We begin by noting that for all males aged 25-64 in the experienced civilian labor force with earnings in 1959 and with, for example, less than eight years of education, the difference between the average earnings of whites and nonwhites was $1421. This is a gross figure and in no way takes account of occupational or residential differences between the two groups. We can, by simple algebraic manipulation of the difference of these two mean incomes, decompose it into two terms: one term expressing that part of the total difference attributable to white-nonwhite differences in regional and occupational composition (tabulated as the "mean difference attributable to composition"), and the other term expressing that part of the total difference attributable to white-nonwhite earnings differences specific to occupation region (the "mean difference net of composition").[4] This particular formula is not unique; it is only one of numerous similar relationships which enable one to ascertain the components of a difference between two rates.

Table 2. *Decompositions of Mean Differences Between White and Nonwhite Earnings in 1959 For Males Aged 25-64 in the United States, 1966, Specific to Education Groups* *

Years of School Completed	Mean Difference White-Nonwhite Earnings	Mean Difference Attributable to Occupational-Regional Composition	Mean Difference Net of Composition	Mean Nonwhite Earnings
Elementary 0-7 years	$1,421	$ 725	$ 696	$2,562
Elementary 8 years	1,519	601	918	3,318
High School 1-3 years	2,033	757	1,276	3,522
High School 4 years	2,229	823	1,406	4,021
College 1-3 years	3,199	1,441	1,758	4,355
College 4 or more years	4,567	767	3,800	5,671

*Source: U.S. Bureau of the Census, U.S. Census of Population: 1960, Subject Reports, Occupation by Earnings and Education, Washington, D.C.: U.S. Government Printing Office, 1963. Table 1.

Working out the suggested decomposition of the total earnings difference among those with less than eight years of schooling, we see that $725 of the total difference of $1421 can be attributed to differences in the proportions of whites and nonwhites in particular occupational-regional categories. On the other hand $696 of the total difference in white-nonwhite earnings can be attributed to white-nonwhite differences in rates of earnings within region and occupation combinations for this particular educational group. These rate differences can be interpreted as reflecting the money costs to nonwhites of discrimination, though they may to some extent be influenced by quality differences in education or occupation which are too fine to be discerned by our gross measures. It is quite apparent in Table 2 that, while earnings differences due to composition do not vary systematically with education, when the effects of occupational and regional composition are removed the remaining earnings differences increase regularly as level of educational achievement increases. This means that, even if whites had the same occupational and regional configuration as nonwhites, there would remain rather large income differences; and these would be accentuated with increasing education.

We have seen that over the past twenty years there has been a slight tendency towards occupational desegregation and that this tendency appears whether we follow a particular group of people through the period or look at the experience of people at particular age-education conjunctions at different points in time. We also have found evidence of persistent high levels of occupational segregation at all ages among those who completed high school or attended less than four years of college. Thus, while evidence from the longitudinal data seems to indicate a pattern of gradually lessening occupational segregation, there is one finding which agrees with the more pessimistic conclusions to be drawn from our more extensive cross-sectional analysis. These data suggest a bleak picture from the viewpoint of the nonwhite, no matter how they are regarded. The figures show that Negroes earn less than whites at almost all educational levels in almost all occupations, both in the North and the South, and these differentials are greater in the South. While there are some occupational groups in which these differentials are minimized, the minima are rather large. The return upon investment in education appears to be less for nonwhites than for whites in almost all occupational groups.

The data provide no support for the view that education will immediately remove the financial and occupational handicaps imposed on the Negro. On the contrary, they suggest that increasing the level of educational attainment of the Negro may lead to higher white-nonwhite income differentials, at least in the short run. Since this is a statement about longitudinal trends inferred from cross-sectional data, it is intended to be taken with great caution. However, the data certainly warrant the conclusion that there is no closing of the income gap at higher levels of education.

Findings like these clearly suggest part of what current racial protest movements are about. Before we proceed to assess the import of these objective relations in terms of the subjective processes that underlie race relations, it might be well to attempt to provide a single figure which expresses the impost referred to in the title of this paper.

We have thus far avoided the question of the cost of being a Negro for two reasons. First, we wanted to demonstrate that white-nonwhite income differentials appear at most educational and occupational levels and that little progress in occupational desegregation has been made since 1940. These findings, of course, imply that the cost of being a Negro is itself a variable. Consequently, any single figure must be an average taken over widely different circumstances. Second, we avoided preparing such an estimate because *any* evaluation of the average cost of being a Negro is necessarily arbitrary at certain points owing to (1) decisions about methods of calculation and (2) limitations imposed by the available data. Although the estimate we present below has some appeal, it ignores differences in white-nonwhite age structure and, of course, suffers from being taken over major instead of detailed occupational categories. Therefore, it must be treated as but one of several such estimates that could be made.

We have already discussed the method by which we shall estimate the cost of being a Negro, for it consists of modifying the decomposition equation already discussed to take account of education as a compositional variable in addition to occupation and region. Applying this new equation to the mean difference in white-nonwhite earnings for the total population of males aged 25-64 with earnings in 1959, we shall again derive two terms, one corresponding to the amount of the difference attributable to occupational, educational, and regional differences between the two groups, and the other expressing the difference in earnings net of composition. We shall interpret this second term as the cost of being a Negro.

Working out the suggested decomposition of the total difference in average white-nonwhite earnings, we find that only $1097 of the total difference of $2852 can be attributed to white-nonwhite differences in mean earnings within region, occupation, and education combinations. Thus, net of regional, educational, and occupational effects, the cost of being a Negro is

roughly a thousand dollars. On the other hand, 61.5 percent of the total difference in white and nonwhite mean earnings can be attributed to compositional differences with regard to region, occupation, and education. This suggests that the current discrepancy might be appreciably reduced if Negroes could bring their educational, occupational, and geographical distribution more into line with that of whites. We have tried to argue here that changes along the first two dimensions would *not* be particularly efficacious, and there are good arguments that equalization of the geographic distributions of the races would not ameliorate the income distributions. In any case such herculean metamorphoses would not eliminate income differentials—for 38.5 percent of the current difference in average earnings of whites and nonwhites is apparently *independent of the achievement* of nonwhites! To put it baldly, about two-fifths of the difference in average earnings of whites and nonwhites is what it costs to be black.

The relations discussed in this paper between education, occupation, and income are not new, they are not even newly uncovered. The only new thing here is the data which enable us for the first time simultaneously to "control" for the effects of educational and occupational composition while assessing white-nonwhite income differentials. It should not be surprising, then, that rather than state stunning new hypotheses about Negro-white relations we are merely able to shore-up platitudes, or at least supply an argument from data in place of arguments from common sense. If, as Blumer suggests, race relations are founded upon the "sense of group position," which in turn reflects to some extent the actual situation, then we should expect these objective relationships to have their representations in the sense of position of each of the two racial groups. There is scattered evidence that they do.

Certainly an important class of such representations are those which arrogate to whites the right to the supervisory, managerial, and service occupations currently denied to Negroes. We have repeatedly referred to these norms in the course of this paper to explain occupational segregation. The data suggest the basis of a white sense of superiority to Negroes who are apparently incapable of realizing the potential for advancement which lies dormant in their new educational attainments. And, finally, although economic competition need not always prove threatening to the competitors, in this case we might expect whites to see their prerogatives threatened by this encroaching, inferior group. Thus, we have the bases of feelings of "prerogatives," "moral superiority," and "threat:" the stuff of prejudice.

On the Negro side we might advance a simple investment model to account for the differentially high Negro school-dropout rate as reflecting investor choices of other, better paying investments. We might speak of the motivation provided the civil rights movement by the discovery on the part of thousands of young Negroes that their coveted education wasn't worth much on the open market.

Despite our ability to translate our findings into statements in the terms of Blumer's scheme, the findings are most satisfactory as a simple summary of what the Negro has to overcome to achieve economic equality. As the majority of Negroes interviewed by the *Newsweek* Poll put it, "If you do the same work as a white man, you will probably be paid less than he will." And, we can now say how much less: about a thousand dollars a year.

NOTES

[1] Herbert Blumer, "Race Prejudice as a Sense of Group Position," in Jitsuichi Masuoka and Preston Valien, editors, *Race Relations: Problems and Theory*, Chapel Hill: University of North Carolina Press, 1961.

[2] The index of dissimilarity, or *delta*, is defined by

$$\Delta = 1/2 \sum_{i=1}^{n} |x_i - y_i|,$$

where x^1 is the percentage of one population in the ith of n categories and y^1 is the corresponding percentage for another population. So defined,

$$\sum_{i=1}^{n} x_i = \sum_{i=1}^{n} y_i = 100.$$

In the present case x^1 and y^1 are just the percentages of whites and nonwhites of given ages and educational attainments which are in the ith major occupational group.

[3] Some minor points to be noted in the discussion of Table 1: the 1950 indices are computed on the employed male population, while the 1960 data pertain to the experienced civilian labor force. This incomparability would tend to make the 1960 indices somewhat larger than the 1950 indices if no change had occurred. In analyzing Table 1 we make use of a convenient assumption: that educational attainment is fixed subsequent to age 25. This assumption enables us to study changes within *educational* as well as age cohorts. Although errors of reporting in the two censuses and actual increases in educational attainment of those over 25 imply that the assumption is not always valid, it is nevertheless reasonable in the majority of cases.

[4] Letting W represent mean income to whites and w represent mean income of nonwhites, we can represent the gross mean difference by:

$$(1) \quad W - w = \sum_{i,j} N_{ij} W_{ij} - \sum_{i,j} n_{ij} w_{ij}$$

Where N^{ij} is the proportion of all whites who are in the ith region (South or non-South) and the jth occupation and n^{ij} and w^{ij} are the corresponding proportions and mean wage rates f nonwhites and the summation is over all combinations. The value W - w will not be changed by adding and then subtracting the same term, so we can write

$$(2) \quad W - w = \sum_{i,j} N_{ij} W_{ij} + \sum_{i,j} n_{ij} W_{ij} - \sum_{i,j} n_{ij} W_{ij} - \sum_{i,j} n_{ij} w_{ij}$$

This can be regrouped and rewritten thus:

$$(3) \quad W - w = \sum_{i,j} n_{ij}(W_{ij} - w_{ij}) + \sum_{i,j} W_{ij}(N_{ij} - n_{ij})$$

Note that the first term on the right-hand side of (3) is merely the sum over all nonwhites of white-nonwhite mean earning differences within region and white-nonwhite mean earning differences within region. The second term on the right side of (3) is the portion of the gross differences due to compositional differences. See Evelyn M. Kitagawa, "Components of a Difference between Two Rates," *Journal of the American Statistical Association*, 50 (December, 1955), pp. 1168-1194.

THE NEGRO IN AEROSPACE WORK

Herbert R. Northrup

Seven months before the Japanese attack on Pearl Harbor, *Fortune* magazine reported that the aircraft industry had "an almost universal prejudice against Negroes. . . . you almost never see Negroes in aircraft factories. . . ." Today few industries are working more assiduously than aircraft and related aerospace companies to expand Negro employment opportunities. Yet it is the unusual aerospace company which has been able to raise its percentage of Negroes to 8 or 10 percent of a particular facility. The reasons for this tell us a great deal about problems of Negro employment, upgrading and intraplant movement, and variations from industry to industry or plant to plant.

The aerospace industry employed an average of 1,298,000 persons in 1966 or 6.8 percent of the total manufacturing payroll. Plants of this industry are located in all major regions of the country. Four-fifths of the product of these plants are purchased by the Department of Defense, the National Aeronautical and Space Agency, and other governmental bodies. Commencing in World War II, the pressure of these government agencies (especially since 1961) has been heavy on the industry, first to open jobs to Negroes, then by "affirmative action" to increase Negro participation in the better jobs. The progress has been great, but disappointing to those who might expect a greater percentage of Negroes. The reasons are several.

© 1969 by The Regents of the University of California. Reprinted from *California Management Review*, Vol. XI, No. 4, pp. 11-26, by permission of The Regents. Footnotes have been omitted. The article is a summary of an expanded and updated work which has been published in the book by Herbert R. Northrup and others, *Negro Employment in Basic Industry*, Industrial Research Unit, Wharton School of Finance and Commerce, University of Pennsylvania, 1970.

Table 1 shows the number and proportion of Negroes in the aerospace industry by sex and occupational group for late 1966, based upon a sample including about two-thirds of the industry's employees. Less than 5 percent of the total employees are Negro. This is about one-third of the Negro ratio in steel and even less than that in the automobile industry. There are several reasons for the relatively lower representation of minority groups in aerospace.

SPECIAL PROBLEMS

Job structure. First and foremost is the character of work in aerospace. Much of the work is of a high job shop precision level. Jobs are not broken down to semiskilled components when one builds a few Mercury capsules, a short-run order of missiles, or one-half dozen experimental planes. Yet much of the industry does just this. Such work requires highly trained mechanics, and unfortunately the Negro community has few of these.

There is some long-run work, to be sure. Companies having such orders are able to break down jobs into semiskilled components and train relatively unskilled personnel as sheet metal workers or machine tenders to handle the repetitive work. It is noteworthy that our research indicates that in general the more repetitive the operations, the higher the percentage of Negroes. But where high-precision shop skills are required, few Negroes make it up the occupational ladder.

Finding either Negro craftsmen or apprenticeship candidates is a frustrating search. Past discriminatory practices, lack of Negro family connections to "pick up a trade," absence of a craft tradition in the Negro community except

Table 1. *Aerospace Industry Employment by Race, Sex, and Occupational Group for the Total United States in 1960**

	All Employees			Male			Female		
	Total	Negro	Per Cent Negro	Total	Negro	Per Cent Negro	Total	Negro	Per Cent Negro
Officials and managers	71,328	292	0.4	70,638	289	0.4	690	3	0.4
Professionals	179,436	1,435	0.8	175,513	1,375	0.8	3,923	60	1.5
Technicians	63,999	1,209	1.9	57,284	1,128	2.0	6,715	81	1.2
Sales workers	720	2	0.3	673	2	0.3	47	–	–
Office and clerical	130,261	3,692	2.8	51,289	1,986	3.9	78,972	1,706	2.2
Craftsmen (skilled)	164,991	7,595	4.6	158,623	7,050	4.4	6,368	545	8.6
Operatives (semiskilled)	155,167	18,417	11.9	122,869	13,566	11.0	32,298	4,851	15.0
Laborers (unskilled)	8,065	1,804	22.4	6,344	1,619	25.5	1,721	185	10.7
Service workers	14,055	3,124	22.2	12,015	2,792	23.2	2,040	332	16.3
Total	788,022	37,570	4.8	655,248	29,807	4.5	132,774	7,763	5.8

Source: Data in author's possession.

*21 companies; 127 establishments.

in the southern trowel trades, and now the mores of the community pressing youngsters, white or black, to a mediocre college education instead of a more useful craft training leaves highly paid maintenance jobs with little Negro representation. Negro applicants from the South or from urban slums lack the necessary arithmetical or communications skills to qualify for apprenticeships. In aerospace, as in most industries, skilled maintenance work, except for a few welders, carpenters, and trowel tradesmen, remains largely a white man's preserve.

Aerospace companies have scoured the country looking for professional and technical employees. But Negroes have traditionally not been oriented to engineering as a profession. Bright Negroes seeking professional education and attainment have only recently gone into either engineering or work in industry. Considering this fact, the few who are found in the aerospace industry are a sizeable percentage of those available. Several have very responsible positions, but many who graduated from segregated schools find their background insufficient for advancement and probably would not even be employed were it not for governmental pressure.

The push to managerial jobs is slow. Negro supervisors are no longer rare, but not commonplace either. They now supervise mixed crews all over the country, but advancement beyond the first or second line is still relatively rare. Few Negroes have the modern "plumbers' license"

for managerial development—the MBA from a prestigious graduate business school—and as those of us from such institutions know so regretfully, few are enrolled although our efforts to improve our position rivals that of the aerospace industry.

Locational factors. We have already noted that the aerospace industry is located in every major region of the country. It is, therefore, found near the great concentrations of the Negro population in both the South and in the major industrial centers of the North and West. This superficially would appear to make the industry accessible to the Negro who desires employment in the industry. In actual fact, the locational problems are severe.

The very nature of the aerospace industry requires most plants to be located on the outside perimeters of cities, preferably near an airport. In some cases, the facility must be even more remote. Martin's Denver missile operations are actually twenty-five miles outside of the city in a semiarid pasture. Moreover, the need for remote test facilities draws plants away from cities. Again Martin's development of the Denver site, and Martin's United Aircraft's Florida plants located near Canaveral are illustrations of expansion that would have been more helpful to Negro employment if they had occurred in Baltimore or Hartford, Connecticut. Similarly, when World War II ended, a number of Southern California aircraft manufacturers abandoned facilities in older, heavily populated areas of Los Angeles and moved all their operations to those outside the city limits.

The significance of the plant location problem is well illustrated in the Southern California industry. The few plants located either close to Watts or on direct public transportation routes generally have two or three times the proportion of Negroes that those have which are located in the outer county areas. The same companies and policies are involved. Interestingly enough, however, the outlying plants have a less skewed in-plant distribution of Negroes. These outlying plants are either new or newly integrated. The practice of confining Negroes to certain jobs never existed and was easier to avoid than where it had become institutionalized. Moreover, the type of Negro who can find a home in the suburbs, or is willing to commute great distances for a job, is usually highly motivated as well as able and therefore capable of accepting or gaining promotion and upgrading opportunities.

Despite some exceptions, however, the farther from the inner city the aerospace plant, the fewer Negroes found on its employment rolls. Workers who have had little experience, motivation, or.assistance do not know enough to look for work at long commuting distance, and superior workers usually do not have to commute long distances to obtain good jobs with promotion possibilities. Consequently, both employment and upward plant movement in the industry are restricted by the necessities of plant location in relation to the central city where Negroes are concentrated.

Seniority systems. The seniority systems in the aerospace system are quite varied but in general do not appear to restrict Negro advancement. In a few cases, the lines are long and narrow, but mostly seniority districts tend to be broad with families of jobs clustered in one district. There are occasionally plant-wide applications, and sometimes transfers among plants of one company are part of the collective agreement. The volatility of employment as a result of government contract awards and cancellations insures maximum interest in job security and a general approach to a broad seniority policy.

In general, the wider the seniority district, the greater the opportunity for Negroes for upgrad-

ing and advancement. As the most recently hired and the group which most likely has the fewest skills, Negroes profit substantially from broad opportunities for movement. But, of course, a wide seniority progression system has its corollary disadvantages, too. When employment turns downward, it provides the broadest opportunities for bumping. With Negroes both relatively new and still overly concentrated in the semiskilled and relatively unskilled jobs, they are then especially vulnerable.

Job bidding is widely used in the industry to fill higher jobs. Company officials have repeatedly complained that Negroes appear more reluctant to bid on jobs than whites and often require great encouragement if they are to bid. Lack of experience in industrial practices, fear of moving from a job situation which is acceptable to white fellow workers to one which is not, or lack of motivation are possible reasons for this.

At least one company in the industry does not apply straight seniority in either promotion or layoffs. One of this company's facilities is under considerable government pressure to increase its percentage and distribution of Negro employment. Recently employment declined in this facility, but the percentage of Negroes increased. Whether this resulted from "affirmative action" or discrimination in reverse, or whether these terms are distinctions without differences, could not be ascertained.

Training. The aerospace industry is accustomed to training because of its sudden employment shifts. Vestibule training—teaching basic shop behavior, arithmetic, and English—is frequently done by the companies themselves or indirectly through the support of school programs or those of such organizations as the Opportunities Industrialization Center. Closely related are the programs for training on simple sheet metal assembly or other entry jobs which often continue as long as employment is expanding. Special efforts have been made by the industry to include Negroes in these classes since 1962. Their success is indicated by a steadily increasing percentage of Negroes in most aerospace plants.

In addition, however, few industries offer so much training for advancement and upgrading.

The rapidly evolving technology compels much of this if the work force and supervision are to be kept current. But this training also provides tremendous opportunities for those who wish to move up the occupational ladder. Negro involvement in such programs is substantial, but nowhere near the ratio one might hope or expect. Motivational factors appear very important. Willingness to contribute one's time to train for a better future depends on background, expectations, and genuine belief in opportunity. That all three are lacking to some degree in the Negro community is not difficult to understand. Until training opportunities are grasped, however, Negro upgrading will not achieve its potential in aerospace or in any other industry.

REGIONAL EMPLOYMENT

Tables 2 through 7 show Negro employment in the aerospace industry by occupational groups for all major regions of the country in 1966, except for the South, which is discussed later. These tables utilize the same data which are summarized in Table 1, but divide them on a regional basis by establishment. Many companies are thus represented by plants in several regions.

Turning first to the Northeast (Table 2), we find Negro employment ratios and in-plant distributions fairly close to national averages throughout the entire occupational hierarchy. In this region, Negro females have a higher ratio of jobs than the industry's national average, and Negroes are somewhat less concentrated in the bottom two categories. They are, however, also less well represented in the craftsmen category but hold almost an identical share of the salaried positions as they do nationally.

The Northeast region is divided into two areas, New England (Table 3) and Middle Atlantic (Table 4). The high proportion of operatives in New England is attributable to the location there of major engine plants of United Aircraft, Avco, and General Electric, which utilize a much higher proportion of such labor than do many other aerospace plants. The Negro representation here is very similar to the national average, but the high proportion of operatives offsets the lag of Negroes in the craftsmen classification and raises the over-all Negro percentage to slightly above 5 percent. Negro women make up an even larger percentage of female employment in New England than they do in the total Northeast area. A heavy migration of Negroes from both the South and from New York City, particularly to cities in Connecticut, has been a strong factor in the increased representation of Negroes in New England aerospace plants. In addition, United Aircraft, the region's major aerospace employer, has long had a deserved reputation for practicing equal employment, a factor which,

Table 2. *Aerospace Industry Employment by Race, Sex, and Occupational Group for the Northeast Region in 1966* *

	All Employees			Male			Female		
	Total	Negro	Per Cent Negro	Total	Negro	Per Cent Negro	Total	Negro	Per Cent Negro
Officials and managers	13,740	50	0.4	13,605	49	0.4	135	1	0.7
Professionals	34,604	247	0.7	34,027	242	0.7	577	5	0.9
Technicians	13,287	255	1.9	12,121	234	1.9	1,166	21	1.8
Sales workers	174	—	—	172	—	—	2	—	—
Office and clerical	21,575	571	2.6	8,193	245	3.0	13,382	326	2.4
Craftsmen (skilled)	35,073	1,165	3.3	34,592	1,079	3.1	481	86	17.9
Operatives (semiskilled)	42,188	4,554	10.8	35,626	3,312	9.3	6,562	1,242	18.9
Laborers (unskilled)	3,988	563	14.1	2,958	474	16.0	1,030	89	8.6
Service workers	4,174	791	19.0	3,656	727	19.9	518	64	12.4
Total	168,803	8,196	4.9	144,950	6,362	4.4	23,853	1,834	7.7

Source: Data in author's possession.

*Northeast region includes New England and the Middle Atlantic states.

Table 3. *Aerospace Industry Employment by Race, Sex, and Occupational Group for the New England Region in 1966**

	All Employees			Male			Female		
	Total	Negro	Per Cent Negro	Total	Negro	Per Cent Negro	Total	Negro	Per Cent Negro
Officials and managers	8,121	29	0.4	8,052	29	0.4	69	—	—
Professionals	17,689	54	0.3	17,420	53	0.3	269	1	0.4
Technicians	6,098	53	0.9	5,259	40	0.8	839	13	1.5
Sales workers	170	—	—	168	—	—	65	—	—
Office and clerical	11,177	192	1.7	3,491	65	1.9	7,686	127	1.7
Craftsmen (skilled)	18,366	357	1.9	18,301	341	1.9	65	16	24.6
Operatives (semiskilled)	34,681	3,946	11.4	28,622	2,761	9.6	6,059	1,185	19.6
Laborers (unskilled)	3,329	382	11.5	2,422	310	12.8	907	72	7.9
Service workers	2,001	198	9.9	1,689	159	9.4	312	39	12.5
Total	101,632	5,211	5.1	85,424	3,758	4.4	16,208	1,453	9.0

Source: Data in author's possession.

*New England region includes Maine, Vermont, New Hampshire, Massachusetts, Connecticut, and Rhode Island.

with the opportunity of good jobs at high wages, has attracted many Negroes to jobs in the area.

The Middle Atlantic data (Table 4) again hold close to the national average in all categories. Female employment of Negroes is considerably less than in New England, but the type of work which predominates does not offer the same opportunities. In the Middle Atlantic region craftsmen outnumber operatives two to one; in New England, the ratios are almost reversed. Large missile and space operations and considerable job and machine work are found in this area. The one great aircraft production facilities of Martin-Marietta near Baltimore have been greatly reduced and with them have gone numerous semiskilled jobs of

which Negroes once held a good share. Boeing's Vertol Division near Philadelphia employs a large number of both craftsmen and operatives and has done a very capable job of training and upgrading Negroes in the machining skills. The higher than average craftsmen representation of Negroes in this area testifies to the results of such programs.

The Midwest (Table 5) has the highest percentage of Negroes of any area—6.8 as compared with 4.8 nation-wide. Since the data also include the few installations in the Rocky Mountain and Northern Plains areas where few Negroes live, the data in Table 5 understate, if anything, Negro representation in the traditional Midwest area.

Table 4. *Aerospace Industry Employment by Race, Sex, and Occupational Group for the Middle Atlantic Region in 1966**

	All Employees			Male			Female		
	Total	Negro	Per Cent Negro	Total	Negro	Per Cent Negro	Total	Negro	Per Cent Negro
Officials and managers	5,619	21	1.4	5,553	20	0.4	66	1	1.5
Professionals	16,915	193	1.1	16,607	189	1.1	308	4	1.3
Technicians	7,189	202	2.8	6,862	194	2.8	327	8	2.4
Sales workers	4	—	—	4	—	—	—	—	—
Office and clerical	10,398	379	3.6	4,702	180	3.8	5,696	199	3.5
Craftsmen (skilled)	16,707	808	4.8	16,291	738	4.5	416	70	16.8
Operatives (semiskilled)	7,507	608	8.1	7,004	551	7.9	503	57	11.3
Laborers (unskilled)	659	181	27.5	536	164	30.6	123	17	13.8
Service workers	2,173	593	27.3	1,967	568	28.9	206	25	12.1
Total	67,171	2,985	4.4	59,526	2,604	4.4	7,645	381	5.0

Source: Data in author's possession.

*Middle Atlantic region includes New York, Pennsylvania, New Jersey, Maryland, and Delaware.

Table 5. *Aerospace Industry Employment by Race, Sex, and Occupational Group
for the Midwest Region in 1966**

	All Employees			Male			Female		
	Total	Negro	Per Cent Negro	Total	Negro	Per Cent Negro	Total	Negro	Per Cent Negro
Officials and managers	11,231	73	0.6	11,148	73	0.7	83	—	—
Professionals	18,318	146	0.8	17,941	140	0.8	377	6	1.6
Techninians	8,160	120	1.6	7,528	123	1.6	632	6	0.9
Sales workers	120	2	1.7	117	2	1.7	3	—	—
Office and clerical	18,723	639	3.4	9,690	464	4.8	9,033	175	1.9
Craftsmen (skilled)	32,697	2,043	6.2	31,454	1,929	6.1	1,243	114	9.2
Operatives (semiskilled)	23,893	3,637	15.2	18,595	2,373	12.8	5,298	1,264	23.9
Laborers (unskilled)	1,825	660	36.2	1,438	589	41.0	387	71	18.3
Service workers	2,066	637	30.8	1,563	529	33.8	503	108	21.5
Total	117,033	7,966	6.8	99,474	6,222	6.3	17,559	1,744	9.9

Source: Data in author's possession.

*Midwest includes all midwestern and Rocky Mountain states. The actual plants exist only in Colorado and the midwestern states, except for small military installations.

The three great aerospace employment locations in the Midwest are Evendale, near Cincinnati, Ohio, where General Electric has its large jet engine facility; St. Louis, the home of McDonnell; and Wichita, Kansas, which contains a large facility of Boeing and the manufacturing facilities of Cessna, Beech, and Lear-Jet. The heaviest Negro concentrations are found in the McDonnell and General Electric plants.

McDonnell, as noted earlier, has long been a practitioner of equal employment opportunity. Located near a center of Negro population, although a long commute from the St. Louis North Side, it has made strenuous efforts to recruit Negro employees. The great success of its Phantom jet fighter has enabled it to break down jobs into semiskilled components and has thus enabled it to develop entry jobs that have attracted large numbers of Negro men and women who have previously not worked in industry. McDonnell has also been quite successful in upgrading Negroes. Its long record of Negro employment has facilitated this, for Negroes employed many years ago have been able to work up or to train for higher jobs. McDonnell's ratio of Negro employees is more than twice that of the industry, with a higher than average percentage in the skilled category.

General Electric likewise has a forceful program of equal opportunity and has applied it at Evendale where many Negroes are migrants from the South. The result is that Evendale has a relatively high proportion of Negroes in the skilled categories.

At Wichita, Negro representation in the major plants has lagged, although both Boeing and Beech have made very strenuous efforts to improve minority group work participation. Beech has been quite successful over the years in integrating its minority work force throughout its light plane manufacturing facility. The Negro population of Wichita, 8 percent in 1960 and estimated at about 12 percent today, is of course considerably less than that in the St. Louis or Cincinnati areas.

The most significant aspect of the favorable attitudes and programs in the major Midwest facilities is the high Negro representation in the craftsmen and office and clerical occupational groups. In the former, the Negro percentage in the Midwest region is 6.2, as compared with the 4.6 national average; in the office and clerical group, the Midwest percentage is 3.4, the national, 2.8. Negro females also are much better represented in the Midwest than in the country as a whole. A combination of favorable employer attitudes and policies of long standing, character of work and work mix, and the heavy Negro migration to the area have combined to make the Midwest aerospace centers among the most favorable in the industry to Negro employment.

The West Coast, and particularly Southern California, ranks with the Midwest as the area giving Negroes the best employment opportunities qualitatively and quantitatively. Total West Coast data (Table 6) includes, besides Southern California, the great Boeing plants in Seattle

Table 6. *Aerospace Industry Employment by Race, Sex, and Occupational Group for the West Coast Region in 1966**

	All Employees			Male			Female		
	Total	Negro	Per Cent Negro	Total	Negro	Per Cent Negro	Total	Negro	Per Cent Negro
Officials and managers	35,016	134	0.4	34,615	132	0.4	401	2	0.5
Professionals	96,055	858	0.9	93,561	817	0.9	2,494	41	1.6
Technicians	32,115	679	2.1	27,856	638	2.3	4,259	41	1.0
Sales workers	284	—	—	242	—	—	42	—	—
Office and clerical	68,319	1,824	2.7	23,547	888	3.8	44,772	936	2.1
Craftsmen (skilled)	73,318	3,831	5.2	69,099	3,490	5.1	4,219	341	8.1
Operatives (semiskilled)	62,630	8,031	12.8	45,292	5,882	13.0	17,338	2,149	12.4
Laborers (unskilled)	1,711	353	20.6	1,467	335	22.8	244	18	7.4
Service workers	5,917	1,022	17.3	4,969	896	18.0	948	126	13.3
Total	375,365	16,732	4.5	300,648	13,078	4.3	74,717	3,654	4.9

Source: Data in author's possession.

*West Coast region includes Washington, Oregon, California, Idaho, and Nevada.

and the various installations near San Jose, south of San Francisco. At Seattle, where only about 5 percent of the population is Negro, Boeing has done extensive recruiting and upgrading and has many Negro engineers and technicians as well as lower-rated personnel. Both Lockheed and United Aircraft in Northern California have extensively recruited and trained Negroes, especially those from the Oakland area.

Southern California (Table 7) has about the same percentage of Negro operatives and craftsmen as the Midwest region and thus is ahead of the national average in these important groups. The Negro employment and Negro female employment in the lowest two job categories in Southern California is almost identical with the national average.

In the office and clerical group, Southern California is slightly better (3.0 to 2.8) than the national percentage, but its superiority is greater with the male clerical group. Undoubtedly, the proportion of Negro female office and clerical employees is reduced because of commuting problems between Negro residential areas and plant locations in Southern California.

Southern California is the leading region in the industry, both numerically and in proportion, of Negro officials and managers, professionals, and technicians. Perhaps, like their white counterparts, Negroes in this group flock to the balmy weather of the area. It is also true,

Table 7. *Aerospace Industry Employment by Race, Sex, and Occupational Group for the Southern California Region in 1966*

	All Employees			Male			Female		
	Total	Negro	Per Cent Negro	Total	Negro	Per Cent Negro	Total	Negro	Per Cent Negro
Officials and managers	21,056	99	0.5	20,748	97	0.5	308	2	0.6
Professionals	64,600	648	1.0	62,839	612	1.0	1,761	36	2.0
Technicians	18,336	496	2.7	16,067	470	2.9	2,269	26	1.1
Sales workers	271	—	—	236	—	—	35	—	—
Office and clerical	44,284	1,336	3.0	14,744	620	4.2	29,540	716	2.4
Craftsmen (skilled)	48,342	3,035	6.3	45,412	2,771	6.1	2,930	264	9.0
Operatives (semiskilled)	43,241	6,557	15.2	29,521	4,788	16.2	13,720	1,769	12.9
Laborers (unskilled)	1,462	331	22.6	1,235	313	25.3	227	18	7.9
Service workers	4,244	873	20.6	3,517	780	22.2	727	93	12.8
Total	245,836	13,375	5.4	194,319	10,451	5.4	51,517	2,924	5.7

Source: Data in author's possession.

however, that the Southern California industry has a long record of utilizing Negro personnel in these areas.

Southern California is the headquarters of Lockheed, North American, Douglas, Hughes, Northrop, the Convair Division of General Dynamics, and Aerojet-General, as well as of many smaller companies. All are now firmly committed to strong affirmative action, and several like Lockheed, Douglas, and North American have done so for a number of years. If the industry continues to expand its employment in this region, Negroes can expect continued gains.

SOUTHERN DEVELOPMENT

Southern developments in the 1960's. The South (Tables 8 to 10) offers in some ways a more discouraging picture than other areas, but in other ways one of increasing promise. Table 8, which includes both the Southeast and the Southwest, shows excessively heavy concentrations of Negroes in the lowest two occupational groups—concentrations one and one-half to twice the national average—but under-representation in the operative and craftsmen level compared with the national picture. Surprisingly, the salaried groups show representation of Negroes very close to the national average and, in the case of office and clerical groups, actually superior to the national average. The significance of, and reasons for, these interesting Negro gains in the salaried area can best be explained by examining the data for the Southeast in Table 9.

To one who is not familiar with developments in the Southeast, the picture presented by Table 9 will come as a great surprise. To be sure, about one-third of the laborers and service workers are Negroes, as compared with less than one-fourth nationally. But Negro representation among the semiskilled operatives is almost identical with that nationally (11.7 to 11.9%), and the same is true among craftsmen (4.1 to 4.6%). Then one finds that Negro office and clerical employees comprise 4.2 percent of those in the Southeast, but only 2.8 percent of those nationally! Moreover, representation among the officials and managers, professionals, and technicians for Negroes in the Southeast is nearly identical with that nationally.

CHANGES IN SOUTHEAST

What has happened in the Southeast is that a number of major aerospace companies have opened facilities and, partially because they have practiced equal employment, and partially under federal government prodding, they have changed the employment practices of the region in a major manner. Despite the high skill content of their work, they have done much more in this regard than many other industries, for example, the automobile industry, which has tended much more to maintain the status quo. Many of these companies have installations at space centers like Huntsville, Alabama, Cape

Table 8. *Aerospace Industry Employment by Race, Sex, and Occupational Group for the South in 1966*

	All Employees			Male			Female		
	Total	Negro	Per Cent Negro	Total	Negro	Per Cent Negro	Total	Negro	Per Cent Negro
Officials and managers	11,341	35	0.3	11,270	35	0.3	71	–	–
Professionals	30,459	184	0.6	29,984	176	0.6	475	8	1.7
Technicians	10,437	146	1.4	9,779	133	1.4	658	13	2.0
Sales workers	142	–	–	142	–	–	–	–	–
Office and clerical	21,644	658	3.0	9,859	389	3.9	11,785	269	2.3
Craftsmen (skilled)	23,903	556	2.3	23,478	552	2.4	425	4	0.9
Operatives (semiskilled)	26,456	2,195	8.3	23,356	1,999	8.6	3,100	196	6.3
Laborers (unskilled)	541	228	42.1	481	221	45.9	60	7	11.7
Service workers	1,898	674	35.5	1,827	640	35.0	71	34	49.9
Total	126,821	4,676	3.7	110,176	4,145	3.8	16,645	531	3.2

Source: Data in author's possession.

Kennedy, Florida, Bay St. Louis, Mississippi, or Michaud, Louisiana. Others, such as Martin-Marietta or United Aircraft established facilities near these. A third group, Lockheed at Marietta, Georgia, or Avco at Nashville, Tennessee, operated plants which had their genesis in World War II. All of them have brought with them a new urgency for equal employment opportunity and are constantly pushed further into affirmative action by governmental presence and prodding.

In space center areas, for example, special councils of the major employers conduct training, recruit at Negro schools, scour the areas for potential employees, and otherwise do what they can to increase Negro representation in the plant. Moreover, their programs to upgrade and to train persons have had great success—as the percentage of Negro craftsmen demonstrates.

Special mention needs to be made of the work of Lockheed since 1961. In 1951, when it took over the huge facility at Marietta, Georgia, near Atlanta, it did not eliminate the segregation practices. Then Lockheed became the first company to join Plans for Progress and embarked on a vigorous affirmative action program which soon obtained for it a reputation as the region's most active and interested employer of Negroes. Lockheed, already operating the largest facility in the area, has been aided by an expanding business. Its recruiting, training, and upgrading of Negroes are strongly reflected in the data in

Table 9, because Lockheed is by far the largest employer in the Southeast.

Negro women lag somewhat in the Southeast, but not in the office and clerical group where their percentage exceeds the national average of Table 1 (3.0 to 2.2%). Here again, active recruiting and training of the aerospace companies have produced results and promise continued progress.

The data for the Southeast show the great strides which have been made and promise of even greater improvement, but those for the Southwest are rather discouraging. Table 10 shows that in this area in 1966 Negroes were most heavily overconcentrated in the bottom two occupational classifications; that they had only one-half the representation among the semiskilled operatives that they hold nationally (5.6 to 11.9%); that their share of craftsmen's work was less than 1 percent as compared with 4.6 percent nationally, and of office and clerical jobs only 1.6 percent as compared with 2.8 percent nationally; and that in the top three categories, the Southwest also lagged. Finally, Negro female employees had fewer jobs in the Southwest than in any other region.

There are several reasons for this situation. A few of the southwestern plants are located in places like Tucson, Arizona, or White Sands, New Mexico, where few Negroes live. These, however, are relatively small, and the major plants of the area are in the Dallas—Fort Worth

Table 9. *Aerospace Industry Employment by Race , Sex, and Occupational Group for the Southeast Region in 1966**

	All Employees			Male			Female		
	Total	Negro	Per Cent Negro	Total	Negro	Per Cent Negro	Total	Negro	Per Cent Negro
Officials and managers	6,158	24	0.4	6,126	24	0.4	32	–	–
Professionals	18,221	147	0.8	17,952	141	0.8	269	6	2.2
Technicians	6,669	116	1.7	6,288	106	1.7	381	10	2.6
Sales workers	115	–	–	115	–	–	–	–	–
Office and clerical	12,022	501	4.2	5,259	298	5.7	6,763	203	3.0
Craftsmen (skilled)	11,441	468	4.1	11,263	465	4.1	178	3	1.7
Operatives (semiskilled)	11,857	1,383	11.7	10,541	1,253	11.9	1,316	130	9.9
Laborers (unskilled)	292	92	31.5	236	85	36.0	56	7	12.5
Service workers	722	261	36.1	671	244	36.4	51	17	33.3
Total	67,497	2,992	4.4	58,451	2,616	4.5	9,046	376	4.2

Source: Data in author's possession.

*Southeast region includes Virginia, West Virginia, North Cafolina, South Carolina, Georgia, Florida, Alabama, Mississippi, Louisiana, Tennessee, and Kentucky.

Table 10. *Aerospace Industry Employment by Race, Sex, and Occupational Group for the Southwest Region in 1966 ** *

	All Employees			Male			Female		
	Total	Negro	Per Cent Negro	Total	Negro	Per Cent Negro	Total	Negro	Per Cent Negro
Officials and managers	5,183	11	0.2	5,144	11	0.2	39	–	–
Professionals	12,238	37	0.3	12,032	35	0.3	206	2	1.0
Technicians	3,768	30	0.8	3,491	27	0.8	277	3	1.1
Sales workers	27	–	–	27	–	–	–	–	–
Office and clerical	9,622	157	1.6	4,600	91	2.0	5,022	66	1.3
Craftsmen (skilled)	12,462	88	0.7	12,215	87	0.7	247	1	0.4
Operatives (semiskilled)	14,599	812	5.6	12,815	746	5.8	1,784	66	3.7
Laborers (unskilled)	249	136	54.6	245	136	55.5	4	–	–
Service workers	1,176	413	35.1	1,156	396	34.3	20	17	85.0
Total	59,324	1,684	2.8	51,725	1,529	3.0	7,599	155	2.0

Source: Data in author's possession.

*Southwest region includes Texas, Oklahoma, New Mexico, and Arizona.

area of Texas. These plants are now all committed to equal employment opportunity, but they have been slow both to run short of labor and to adopt affirmative action programs. The General Dynamics plant at Fort Worth, where the F-111 is being built, is now working at capacity, but was not prior to 1967. In 1967, it added more than 8,000 persons to its payroll. Similarly, employment at the former Chance-Vought plant (now a Ling-Temco-Vought facility) rose 6,000 in 1967 and that at Bell Helicopter by a sizable amount also. General Dynamics and L-T-V in particular began the 1960's with a small labor force and a huge number of employees with recall rights. The fact that little integration occurred prior to the mid-1960's was thus the joint product of lack of progress in the 1950's and a slow buildup in the 1960's.

There are other reasons for the lack of progress in the Southwest as of 1966. Some of the southwestern plants did little training; one until recently required six months' experience for entry jobs above laborer and service workers, which obviously meant some other company had to do its training and that few Negroes would qualify. Until prodded by the aerospace companies the schools (in the Fort Worth area, especially) do not seem to have provided much incentive or training for Negroes to enter into industry. Unlike the Atlanta, Georgia, area, where a sizable Negro middle class exists and housing is available for Negro professional, business, and other middle-class personnel, the Dallas-Fort Worth area lags in both such a

middle class and in proper or even adequate housing. One company in particular believes housing has been a major block in recruiting Negro engineers for its Fort Worth facility.

Some progress has been made in the Dallas-Fort Worth area since 1966. Table 11 contains the racial-occupational employment data for the three major companies there in 1967. These data show substantial increases in the percentage of Negroes in the craftsmen and operatives categories over 1966 (Table 10). (Table 10 includes data for several small installations not found in Table 11.) Progress is also indicated by the manner in which Fort Worth and Dallas companies have moved to employ hard-core unemployed and to participate in recent months in other programs designed to improve minority participation in industry. General Dynamics has opened a new facility at San Antonio which is employing hard-core unemployed minorities almost exclusively.

Nevertheless, the Southwest still lags in the employment of Negroes, both quantitatively and qualitatively, behind other regions in the aerospace industry. Progress is likely to continue, but the slow start will probably cause the area to continue to lag for many years.

THE LABOR UNIONS

Union influence has in general not been the significant factor in aerospace racial policies that it has been on the positive side in such industries as automobiles or meatpacking, or on

Table 11. *Aerospace Industry Employment by Race, Sex, and Occupational Group for Three Major Southwest Companies in 1967*

	All Employees			Male			Female		
	Total	Negro	Per Cent Negro	Total	Negro	Per Cent Negro	Total	Negro	Per Cent Negro
Officials and managers	4,895	18	0.4	4,867	18	0.4	28	–	–
Professionals	10,637	28	0.3	10,439	27	0.3	198	1	0.5
Technicians	2,294	17	0.7	2,112	14	0.7	182	3	1.6
Sales workers	21	–	–	21	–	–	–	–	–
Office and clerical	8,738	144	1.6	4,525	103	2.3	4,213	41	1.0
Craftsmen (skilled)	14,673	261	1.8	14,347	257	1.8	326	4	1.2
Operatives (semiskilled)	12,714	963	7.6	11,434	888	7.8	1,280	75	5.9
Laborers (unskilled)	313	127	40.6	271	119	43.9	42	8	19.0
Service workers	748	320	42.8	739	311	42.1	9	9	100.0
Total	55,033	1,878	3.4	48,755	1,737	3.6	6,278	141	2.2

Source: Data in author's possession.

the negative side in such industries as building construction, railroads, or pulp and paper. The two dominant unions in the industry, the International Association of Machinists and Aerospace Workers (IAM) and the United Automobile, Aerospace and Agricultural Implement Workers (UAW) originally avowed very different policies. The IAM, founded in the railroad shops of Atlanta during the latter half of the nineteenth century, at first limited membership to white workers by constitutional provision and later accomplished the same thing by a secret ritual which pledged members to admit only competent white mechanics.

In the 1930's, the IAM expanded into the aircraft industry. During World War II its anti-Negro ritual became a source of embarrassment to its top officials, but not till the late 1940's was it repealed. In some cases, IAM union policies proved a bar to Negro employment in the industry during World War II, but in most cases the IAM did not have a compulsory union membership contract and therefore could not adversely affect Negro employment.

In recent years, the IAM attitude on race has been basically a passive one. Locals of the IAM are very independent, with the international exercising only limited interference. As a result, there is little or no affirmative action in support of Negro employment and no national union interference when local unions either drag their feet or oppose affirmative action programs.

The UAW has had a militant program of equal opportunity for many years. In aerospace, it has supported company programs, but at the local union level this support varies considerably. Unlike the situation in both automobiles and agricultural implements, Negroes comprise only a small part of the membership in the aerospace industry and have not been able to exert influences in local unions as they have in these other industries. Consequently, although most managements feel that the UAW has given sound support to programs aimed at Negro advancement, it is also true that Negroes play a very minor role in local unions, have few offices above shop steward, and seem to me to be generally much more inactive than in the automobile industry.

There have been some rank-and-file Negro rumblings against union lack of leadership in the industry. A group led by CORE (Congress of Racial Equality) picketed the UAW and North American in the Los Angeles area in 1966, claiming inadequate promotions for Negroes. Generally, however, such demonstrations have been rare, especially since, in recent years there has been a great upward movement of Negroes.

In aerospace, the dynamics of racial policies do not seem to be radically influenced by unions. The companies have taken the lead, as they have in employee relations generally, and the unions, although occasionally challenging, supporting, or encouraging, have been the followers. Neither the official indifference of the IAM nor the loud affirmance of the UAW seem to have had any decisive effects. Union-management seniority clauses are not aimed at hindering Negro upgrading, and, as in the case of Lockheed in Georgia, the attempts of local unions to obtain discriminatory clauses do not seem to have hindered Negro job movement. Moreover, job bidding, which is widely used, permits considerable movement within the plant.

GOVERNMENT PRESSURES

The government is the aerospace industry's big customer, and government pressure is always a factor that aerospace companies must consider. There can be no doubt that the affirmative action plans which are so prominent in the industry stem from heavy (often heavy-handed) government pressure which motivates employers, keeps the problem in the forefront, and constantly pushes the industry to take further affirmative action. But the government is not a single-dimensioned pressure force. The government is also the customer, and it is the policeman. As customer, it demands, as it should, zero defect work. Life is involved, and the quality of workmanship cannot be compromised. The industry has to certify the capability of workmen on many jobs. Social programs are admirable, but there is no substitute for experience and ability. Affirmative action can go only so far, and educational, cultural, and attitudinal deficiencies cannot be glossed over or overcome quickly. The unfortunate fact is that the higher the qualifications which are required, the fewer Negroes are qualified and the more difficult it is for them to gain qualifications by short-run training or educational programs.

Much aerospace work is under tight security. Jail or arrest records at one time automatically meant clearance denials. Given the facts of city slums and Negro-police relations, this was a powerful bar to Negro advancement or even employment in the industry. Now a more sophisticated approach is the rule. Arrest records are scrutinized and the minor in counted. It appears governmen equal opportunity pressures are synchronized in approach than formerly.

There is now the danger that the government may push companies too far in liberalizing employment policies. Some in the industry are quite concerned about sabotage and poor workmanship. The pressures on both sides are great, but it should be reiterated that overly zealous minority group employment programs should certainly not be allowed to compromise workmanship standards in this industry. Yet the fact remains that government pressure has historically been a prime motivating force in obtaining increased employment opportunities for Negroes, and it is likely to continue. The results must be considered salutary.

Another significant result of government pressure is governmental aid to managers who greatly desire to increase minority employment in continued social engineering in developing training and motivational programs with a resultant increase in Negro employment and upgrading. The aerospace companies now have considerable experience in training those once considered too unskilled to apply—certainly a gain in itself. Of course, only when jobs are broken down by relatively large-scale production can employees so limited be utilized. Fortuitously, the drive for equal employment opportunity has coincided not only with a tremendous expansion of employment in the industry, but an expansion concentrated during 1965-1967 in the manned aircraft portion of the industry which can use much less skilled workers than can missile or space vehicle development and manufacturing. A downturn in this segment of the industry would have a most adverse impact on Negro aerospace employment.

TESTING OF MINORITY GROUP APPLICANTS FOR EMPLOYMENT

Phyllis Wallace, Beverly Kissinger, and Betty Reynolds

INTRODUCTION

The Motorola case[1] and the Tower amendment to Title VII of the Civil Rights Act of 1964 Section 703(h)[2] have dramatized the issue of whether the use of general intelligence tests by employers as selection devices for hiring and promotion deprives Negroes and members of other minority groups of equal employment opportunity. Individuals from culturally disadvantaged backgrounds perform less well on these tests on the average than do applicants from middle class environments and consequently may be screened out of training programs and/or excluded from jobs. Differences in culture, in opportunity, and in experience can have a devastating effect on test performance. Since many Negroes, Mexican-Americans, Indians, and lower-class whites have not shared the middle class culture, they may perform in an inferior manner on tests of general intelligence, particularly paper and pencil, but not necessarily on performance for which the tests are supposed to be predictive.

Consistent and significant differences on mean scores are also found between age, sex, educational, and urban-rural groups, but the focus of this report is the effect of testing on the culturally disadvantaged, many of whom are Negroes. This report is not concerned with the willful misuse of tests to discriminate such as giving tests to Negroes but not to whites, or requiring Negroes to achieve higher scores than whites, or failing Negroes regardless of their actual performance. These practices are clearly unlawful. The question to be considered here is whether many "professionally developed ability tests" used by employers to select qualified applicants do in fact discriminate *inadvertently*.

Authorities in the field of psychological testing have suggested several proposals for mitigating the effects of *unintentional* types of discrimination against minority groups. We have examined the various proposals and have concluded that careful selection and administering of tests and validation of the testing instrument within an industrial setting, may be the most desirable means to achieve the goal of full utilization of the nation's human resources. The implications of this affirmative conclusion are discussed from the viewpoint of the Equal Employment Opportunity Commission, private employers, and the research psychologists who would have to assume the major responsibility for formulating suitable standards for selection of testing programs.

TYPES OF TESTS

The major types of tests most commonly used in employee selection are: (1) general intelligence tests, (2) tests of specific intellectual abilities, (3) knowledge and skill tests, (4) measures of dexterity and coordination, and (5) inventories of personality traits.

Intelligence tests such as the Wonderlic, Stanford-Binet, and Otis Quick-Scoring are designed primarily to measure the ability of the individual to understand and to reason with words and numbers. Such tests are most useful

Reprinted from *Testing of Minority Group Applicants for Employment*, Phyllis Wallace, Beverly Kissinger, Betty Reynolds (Washington, D.C.: Office of Research and Reports, U.S. Equal Employment Opportunity Commission, March, 1966) pp. 1–9. Footnotes omitted.

in selection for jobs where learning from and understanding verbal academic material is important.

Specific intellectual abilities tests determine potential for learning certain kinds of work and for solving certain kinds of problems. The tests are not designed to test for a specific job, but to measure the skills for understanding and reasoning with words, numbers and symbols, visualizing of spatial relationships, word fluency, visual speed and accuracy, and creative abilities.

Knowledge and skill tests are usually specific to a job or job family. Knowledge tests are designed to measure the understanding of blueprint reading, electronics, accounting, etc., while skill tests measure one's ability to type, to take dictation, to drive, etc. These tests measure the degree or level of knowledge or skill already attained by candidates at the time of the test.

Dexterity and coordination tests measure speed and accuracy of physical movements. These tests must be very specific to the movements required in the job and are usually constructed by the employer. Examples of such tests are spatial and mechanical abilities, perceptual accuracy, motor abilities.

Personality and interest tests are intended to indicate how a person typically acts and feels, and to determine the type of activities he likes. Tests of this nature have been developed primarily for use in either vocational guidance or clinical use. *It is extremely important for a highly trained professional psychologist to evaluate and interpret the results of these tests.*

Tests may be further categorized as aptitude versus proficiency. Aptitude tests are designed to measure potential while achievement tests measure skill level at the time of testing.

HOW TESTS DISCRIMINATE AGAINST MINORITY GROUPS

An aptitude test that fails to predict job performance in the same way for both Negroes and whites, or fails to predict job performance at all is not a valid test. If such a test is weighted to differentiate between Negroes and whites, it is similarly invalid and similarly discriminatory. Tests may be held to discriminate in the *social sense* if they deny equal opportunity for consideration. A test may operate in this manner (a) when scores on it tend to differentiate between identifiable sub-groups, where the sub-grouping itself is not a relevant selection factor, and either (b) scores for the lower group underpredict performance on the job when the standards of the upper-group are applied, or (c) scores on the test do not predict job performance for either group.

It is known that Negroes on the average do less well on paper and pencil tests than whites. The mean scores for Negroes are lower than the mean scores[3] for whites on most paper and pencil tests of general ability, intelligence, aptitude, learning ability, or overall ability. The distribution of scores overlap, often considerably, but the average scores differ significantly in most studies.

More research has been done on the testing of minority group children than workers, but the information which has resulted from this research offers insight into why Negro adults achieve a lower mean score than job applicants from a more middle class background. Newton S. Metfessel, psychologist at the University of Southern California, in his research on children and youth who live in the culture of poverty, found that cultural factors such as home and family structure, personality and social characteristics, learning characteristics, and general school relationships handicap performance on tests.

These children usually come from a home environment where there is such a paucity of objects that the child's conceptual formation development is adversely affected. They also lack curiosity, and this affects both motivational patterns and the development of creative behavior. The culturally disadvantaged child is characterized by weak ego-development, a lack of self-confidence, and a negative self-concept. These conflicting feelings about himself frequently result in exaggerated positive and negative attitudes toward others.

Many aspects of learning characteristics are affected by the culturally poor background. The culturally disadvantaged typically have a cognitive style which responds more to visual and kinesthetic signals than to oral or written stimuli. Also, these children learn more readily by inductive than deductive approaches. Learning experiences which move from the part to the whole rather than from the whole to the part are invariably more successful. Significant gaps in knowledge and uneven patterns of learning are typical of this type of background.

Children from the culture of poverty have had little experience in receiving approval for success in learning a task, an assumption on which the school culture is organized. "The cycle of skill mastery which demands that successful experiences generate more motivation to perform which in turn guarantees levels of skill sufficient to prevent discouragement, and so on, may be easily reversed in direction and end the achievement habit prior to its beginning."

In general school relationships and school characteristics, these children from the background of cultural deprivation are placed at a marked disadvantage on standardized tests, which for the most part have been designed to test the white, middle class child. The shortcomings of the standardized tests when they are used with disadvantaged minority groups are discussed below.

RELIABILITY OF DIFFERENTIATION

Standardized tests may not provide reliable differentiation in the range of the minority group's scores. The reliability coefficient for a particular test is strongly affected by the spread of test scores in the group for which the reliability is established. In general, the greater the spread of scores in the reliability samples, the higher the reliability coefficient. For many tests, there is evidence "that children from the lower socioeconomic levels tend to have a smaller spread of scores than do children from middle-income families, and such restriction in the distribution of scores tends to lower reliability so far as differentiation of measurement with such groups is concerned."

PREDICTIVE VALIDITY

Second, the predictive validity of tests for minority groups may be quite different from that for the standardization and validation groups. Factors which may impair a test's predictive validity are:

1. *Test-related factors*, that is, test-taking skills, anxiety, motivation, speed, understanding of test instructions, degree of item or format novelty, examiner-examinee rapport which may

affect test scores but have little relation to the criterion.

2. *Complexity of criteria.* It is important to recognize the influence of other factors, not measured by tests, which may contribute to criterion success. Since disadvantaged groups tend to do poorly on general intelligence and achievement tests of the paper and pencil type, one should explore background, personality, and motivation of members of such groups for compensatory factors, untapped by the test, which may be related to criterion performance.

While certain aptitude and proficiency tests may have excellent criterion validity for some purposes, even the best of them are unlikely to reflect the true capacity of underprivileged children. They tap abilities that have been molded by the cultural setting. The test content, mode of communication involved in responding to test items, and the motivation needed for making responses are intrinsically dependent upon the cultural context.

VALIDITY OF TEST INTERPRETATION

Third, the validity of the interpretation of tests is strongly dependent upon an adequate understanding of the social and cultural background of the group in question. Sources of error in test interpretation stemming from lack of recognition of the special features of culturally disadvantaged groups are: (1) deviation error—tendency to infer maladjustment from responses which are deviant from the viewpoint of a majority culture, but which may be typical of a minority group; (2) simple determinant error-thinking of the test content as reflecting some absolute or pure trait, process, factor, or construct, irrespective of conditions of measurement or the population being studied; (3) failure barriers—requiring minority group individuals to solve problems with unfamiliar tools.

Job applicants from lower socioeconomic levels may be characterized in contrast to their middle class counterparts as being less verbal, more fearful of strangers, less confident, less motivated toward scholastic and academic achievement, less conforming to middle class norms of behavior and conduct, less knowledgeable about the world outside their immediate neighborhood. To the extent that these subcultural differences affect test performance adversely, these persons may be denied the opportunity to employment and a more productive contribution to society. Selection instruments often call for responses that are influenced by the culture of the applicant's community or quality of his educational opportunity. Since such tests are "culturally loaded" against persons from a lower socioeconomic status, they may operate as instruments of racial discrimination. The crucial question is whether employers use techniques that *unwittingly* eliminate persons who might perform satisfactorily on the job. The relationship between test performance and cultural deprivation on the one hand, and job performance on the other, must be investigated for both white and nonwhite job applicants.

NOTES

[1] *Motorola, Inc., V. Illinois Fair Employment Practices Commission, et al,* 34 Ill. 2d 266, 215 N.E. 2d 286 (1966). (Footnote added).

[2] ". . . nor shall it be an unlawful employment practice for an employer to give and to act upon the results of any professionally developed ability test provided that such test, its administration or action upon the results is not designed, intended or used to discriminate because of race, color, religion, sex or national origin." Sec. 703(h)

[3] Raw scores are converted to norms in order to compare an individual performance with a specific group.

HEARINGS ON DISCRIMINATION IN WHITE COLLAR EMPLOYMENT

U.S. Equal Employment Opportunity Commission

TESTIMONY OF MISS SAUNDRA SHARP

CHAIRMAN [CLIFFORD L.] ALEXANDER. We'll ask Mr. Steiner to proceed with some questions.

MR. [DANIEL] STEINER. Could you tell us what you are doing now? Are you employed?

MISS SHARP. Yes, I have currently two jobs. I'm employed as a singer and actress in the "Hello, Dolly" company on Broadway, and I'm also employed as a per diem substitute teacher for the Board of Education of New York City.

MR. STEINER. I see. What subjects are you teaching when you act as a substitute teacher?

MISS SHARP. My license is music. However, under the current strained situation in the system, I teach just about every subject. I go in and I work wherever they need me.

MR. STEINER. You've been teaching a wide variety of subjects—music, mathematics—

MISS SHARP. Yes, music, science, math, art, girl's gym, the whole gamut.

MR. STEINER. Were you born in New York, Miss Sharp?

MISS SHARP. No. I was born in Cleveland, Ohio, where I lived for 21 years, and I've been a resident of New York City for three and a half years.

MR. STEINER. Did you receive your secondary education in Cleveland?

MISS SHARP. Yes, and college education at

Reprinted from *Hearings Before The United States Equal Employment Opportunity Commission on Discrimination in White Collar Employment*, Jan. 15-18, 1968 in New York City (Washington, D.C.: U.S. Government Printing Office), pp. 14-22, 199-204, 204-207, 383-390.

Bowling Green State University. I graduated from Bowling Green in 1964.

MR. STEINER. And what did you major in?

MISS SHARP. I majored in music education, and I minored in radio and television production and speech.

MR. STEINER. I see. Then after graduating college you came to New York City?

MISS SHARP. Yes, I did. In July of 1964.

MR. STEINER. And what kind of work were you interested in finding?

MISS SHARP. When I first came to New York I was looking for work in the radio-television production area. And I looked for it for quite a while before I finally gave up in this particular field. My first job in New York was as a copywriter for *TV Guide* magazine, which was not the field that I came to work in.

MR. STEINER. What sort of firms did you go to in your attempt to find a job in the radio and television area?

MISS SHARP. Prior to coming to New York I wrote letters, about 30 or 40, requesting interviews; I came to New York for one week, during which time I had about 26 interviews with a lot of the major advertising agencies and production companies, from which I could see basically that nothing developed.

They were encouraging. They referred me to Negroes who were in the business who had jobs already, and this was about the extent of it. And the idea was kind of—well, this Negro has already made it, perhaps he can give you a hint of some type.

MR. STEINER. But you received no job offers from any of these agencies in the field that you were interested in?

MISS SHARP. Not in the field. The general trend was that—"Well, we see your resume, we see that you have training and experience in radio-television production. Now tell us how many words you type a minute and do you take shorthand?" And I received a number of offers to be a secretary and with the possibility—no promise—but the possibility that "in two or three years you can work your way into a position which you are already qualified to fill."

MR. STEINER. Well, had you had any practical experience in radio and television while in college, or had you just studied?

MISS SHARP. No, I studied and I also had practical experience. I had a children's radio show in Cleveland, Ohio, on a commercial station. This was a weekly series. I also had a weekly children's radio series on WBGU-FM, which was a college commercial station, for a year, and I had a music documentary series on this same station; in television I worked in most of the technical areas, directing, writing, producing, and what you call the "back-stage" of television for about a year and a half on a UHF station. So I had had commercial and paid experience in all of these areas.

MR. STEINER. Your job offers, however, at advertising agencies in New York were limited to secretarial . . .

MISS SHARP. I was offered nothing beyond secretarial work. Correct.

MR. STEINER. I see.

MISS SHARP. The only white collar job offer was the one I took, which was in copywriting, but not from an advertising agency.

MR. STEINER. What did you then do, Miss Sharp? Did you make a change in career plans at that point?

MISS SHARP. I worked doing copywriting and a few miscellaneous things for ten months, and then I decided to go to the other side of the fence, to the performing area, and here I found again the "How many words do you type a minute?" and I found it necessary to go back and get my teaching license for New York City in order to have income for rent and food. I also did secretarial work, part-time and temporary, until I was able to gain regular employment as I have on Broadway now, which has been a period of about two years trying to acquire this.

MR. STEINER. What kind of performing work were you interested in finding?

MISS SHARP. Well, I sing and have been modeling professionally for 10 years, and I also had some experience in acting, so I was interested in any of these three areas, where I might be able to gain sufficient employment and sufficient income.

MR. STEINER. Have you had any specific instances, in terms of looking for jobs in the modeling area, that you would—

MISS SHARP. Yes, I have had several. I was working with a contact through one of the city employment agencies, one of the government employment agencies, who sent me out on several jobs which worked quite successfully, and we've had one or two, of course, which did not.

In September of 1966 she referred me to a job, which was working in one of the major department stores. The employment was not being handled by the department store, it was being handled by a food store company, which was selling a British candy product. She said that the person conducting the interview was blind, and that therefore the interview would be by telephone.

This gentleman contacted me, and he asked about my measurements, because it involved wearing a costume, and he said this was satisfactory; and he said that my telephone voice and personality sounded fine, that he thought he definitely could use me, and he told me when to report to work and when I would start, and what the salary would be, and so forth.

And then he said: "You realize—I don't know whether they told you or not, but I'm blind," and I said: "Yes, I was told that" and he said: "In view of this, would you mind giving a physical description of yourself."

I said: "Certainly." I said: "I'm five foot six, a medium brown-skinned Negro, with long black hair and brown eyes."

And there was a long pause at the end, and he said: "They didn't tell me you were a Negro," I said: "And—" And he said: "Well, I don't think we're going to be able to use you." I said: "What's the problem?" and he said: "Well, you see, it's a *British* candy." I said: "yes." And he said: "Well, I just don't think we're going to be able to use you."

And I said: "Well, they have Negroes in Great Britain, you know," and he kind of doubted whether there were Negroes in Great

Britain. At any rate, he also brought up the fact that it was supposed to be a girl and boy sales team, and that a white male had already been hired for the job, and through his stuttering and stammering, he just couldn't seem to get beyond the point that he "wouldn't be able to use me." And that was the end of it, and I reported the incident to the agency which had referred me to the job.

MR. STEINER. What happened when you reported what happened to this governmental employment agency?

MISS SHARP. They told me that a report was being filed and that the company would no longer be referred to or be used at all by the government agency.

And then they sent me on another job which involved demonstrating cosmetic products, which could be used by men or women, but it was being demonstrated by women, and the appointment for the interview was made by telephone. When I arrived for the appointment, the woman who was in charge of the product took one look at me and she began to try to immediately convince me that I would never be able to successfully demonstrate this product, and at the time I had not worked for some time and, to put it point blank, I was hungry. And so I just kind of sat down in the chair and made it clear that I was not moving until she at least gave me the opportunity, because I hadn't even seen the product.

So she talked to someone else in the office and they brought the product out, demonstrated it to me, and the first time that I tried to do it, I did it successfully. So she hired me, and she made an appointment for me to meet her, to work for one of the national trade shows. She made an appointment for me to meet her at the booth at the opening of the trade show. I was there and she was not.

She called me later that evening and accused me of not having shown up for the appointment. So the official opening day of the convention I appeared, prepared to work, and there was a kind of, at that point, nothing too much that she could do. When she did permit me to go ahead and demonstrate the product, she found I was doing very well with it, and then she began to broadcast all over the place: "Look at this wonderful Negro girl I've got, what a beautiful

job she's doing." But this, of course, was after my practically fighting for the job.

And the same person called me a year later and asked me to do the same job again for about eight additional hours, for less money than I had worked for the year before.

MR. STEINER. Have you done any television commercial work, Miss Sharp?

MISS SHARP. Yes, I have. I have worked as an extra—for those who are not sure what an extra is, an extra is a person who works in the background of a particular movie or television commercial, and does not have any words or handle the product, and he's usually paid about the minimum salary. They don't have any lines and you just see them kind of passing by. I've worked as an extra in four major, or national, product commercials.

MR. STEINER. What of the person who appears as the lead, so to speak, in a commercial.

MISS SHARP. They're called the principal.

MR. STEINER. What is the difference in pay between a principal and an extra on a television commercial, generally speaking?

MISS SHARP. If it's what we call a "buy-out extra," which means that there are no residuals for a performance, the extra receives an average of $60 a day before taxes are taken out. A principal receives a minimum of $230 or $250 a day, and can receive more depending on how many hours they work, whether it's out of New York City, the costume involved, etc., but usually a minimum of somewhere between $200 and $300 for the same amount of work.

MR. STEINER. So there's quite a difference in terms of economic earning power—

MISS SHARP. Right.

MR. STEINER (continuing). Between being an extra and being the principal.

MISS SHARP. Also it's very possible that the principal might receive residuals where he can earn up to $1,000 to $2,000 or more on that one commercial, depending on how long it runs on television.

MR. STEINER. I see. Have you generally found it easy to be interviewed at modeling agencies in terms of just getting a chance—a crack at getting a job?

MISS SHARP. Generally you send in your picture and your resume and then you call back for an appointment. Now this is where the catch comes, because quite often they can say over the telephone: "Oh, we're not interviewing any-one," or "We have plenty of models," or "We're going to be very busy and we won't see anyone for the next few months. Our file is complete."

And there's not too much you can do when you hear this, other than wait a few weeks and contact them again and try to bug them to death until finally they will see you. I have run into instances, and I think this is important to bring out, where people other than the person seeing you make it very difficult for you.

For example, I do have one instance that happened to me recently. I went to an agency which deals in specialized types of modeling, using only hands, or legs, or your hair, this type of thing, and the receptionist—it was very crowded that day, there were about five or six people ahead of me—she asked them for their names and wrote down their names, and handed them an application. They were all white. I was the only Negro in the office. When she got to me, she asked me quite a few questions and did her best not to give me an application. In other words, I cannot say that she was speaking for the policy-makers of the company; she might have been speaking from her own personal preju-dices. I think that this happens quite often—that the company is not able to regulate all of its employees, or perhaps they do not make an attempt to, and therefore you run into a recep-tionist, or a doorman, or any position other than the top brass, who use their own personal prejudice and try to stop you from getting the job. And in many cases they are able to, because very often without an application, if you have to go through a big rigamarole, then you never get to see the person in charge. And this quite often is done.

MR. STEINER. Were the types of questions that were asked you in this particular situation designed to show whether you had qualifica-tions or what your experience was? What type of questions were these? Do you remember?

MISS SHARP. Well, yes. She wanted to know if I had done any prior modeling and if I had had experience before, and she tried to tell me that if I hadn't had particular experience as a hand model I could not work for this agency as a hand model, whereas none of these questions had been asked of any of the other people who walked up and just gave their names and asked for an application.

MR. STEINER. I see. Thank you very much, Miss Sharp. There may be some other questions.

CHAIRMAN ALEXANDER. Commissioner Jackson?

COMMISSIONER [SAMUEL C.] JACKSON. No, I don't have any.

CHAIRMAN ALEXANDER. Commissioner Xi-menes.

COMMISSIONER [VINCENTE T.] XIMENES. One question. Miss Sharp, with your looks, I don't see how anybody would dare turn you down for any kind of employment—

MISS SHARP. Thank you very much.

COMMISSIONER XIMENES (continuing). But I do want to ask you one question. How do you, when faced with this kind of situation where you know that the employer has told you that he will not hire you because you are a Negro, how do you overcome this kind of humiliation, and what do you do? Do you go to an agency and complain, or do you try to—or do you say to yourself: "Well, I'll try again."

MISS SHARP. That's a kind of difficult ques-tion. I try to maintain my dignity, because you do run into some very embarrassing situations once in a while.

For example, I went in to one place where I had an appointment, and the office boy went into the back, and I heard him say "Hey, so-and-so, there's a colored girl out here to see you." And the fellow came out and acted like I had come to scrub the floors or something, rather than coming for a high-fashion model position.

So if you can do that and kind of act like it doesn't bother you, rather than falling to pieces over it, then the next thing is that we tend to spread the word, among each other, "don't bother going to such-and-such an agency," or "don't give them any business, if possible," or "don't waste your time sending your picture or resume there because they're not going to use you." And the same way, if there is an agency or a company that does use Negroes, we spread the word also.

"Go see so-and-so at such-and-such a com-pany because they will at least interview you. I went to see them and they were very nice," or "they did take a few minutes, they were inter-ested in my resume."

So this, in a way, kind of helps so that those who are following behind us do not go to the same companies again and run into the same humiliation and embarrassment.

As far as reporting it to someone, one of the unions which I am a member of, Equity, does have a minority board, which does try to investigate this type of thing, but they are limited, I'm afraid, in what they can do; because if the person will not let you in the door, or if they will give you two or three minutes to interview you and then when you walk out they throw your picture and resume and application in the wastebasket and you don't know about it, then there's not too much you can do about it.

COMMISSIONER XIMENES. So, in other words, as soon as the word gets around that a company does act that way toward a minority applicant, it's kind of unlikely that a minority applicant's going to walk up to that company.

MISS SHARP. Again unless we hear that there is a change of personnel. I generally feel that it is a matter of individuals within a company, particularly in advertising agencies where they are constantly changing casting directors.

So I keep an eye on the trade papers, and if I see that the particular person that I had trouble with has moved to another agency, then I will resubmit by picture and my resume and my application to that company again, and see what happens. This way I can determine whether it is the company policy or whether it was just that one person in that position.

CHAIRMAN ALEXANDER. So would you say that for a company that has discriminated in the past, that there is an effort that should be made on their part, not just to subtly convey to the public that it no longer discriminates, but overtly and aggressively to let the minority public know that in fact it is an open employer. Do you think that some kind of effort like that is necessary?

MISS SHARP. I think some kind of effort like that would help if they are sincere. Now there are many companies which have called a lot of Negro performers down in the past year or year and a half because it's "the thing" now to have at least one Negro, you know, and if you're too light in skin color, this has also gotten to be "a thing." You must really *look* Negro now, particularly in television areas. (Laughter.)

Just being a Negro isn't enough. You've got to have the right look. You have to look very Negro so that it comes agross on television or sound very Negro, so that it comes across on radio. And a lot of the large agencies have called us down, they have made videotapes, they have had us sing and dance and act, and do cold readings for them, and they're extremely enthused. They don't know where we've been all of their lives, and they're definitely going to use us, and a year later you still haven't heard anything from them.

If they in their intention did not plan to use you, did not plan to use your work, no matter how good they thought you were, then it's a waste of your time, you see. I would rather they remained prejudiced and not call me (laughter), than to decide for the benefit of the public, or for the benefit of their records, to say that they interviewed so-and-so many percentage of Negroes. If they're not using you, it's a great waste of the Negro's time when he could be looking for employment from someone who is going to use him.

CHAIRMAN ALEXANDER. I think this Commission is interested not in the percentage that they interview, but in the percentage that they hire.

MISS SHARP. That they *use*, right.

CHAIRMAN ALEXANDER. I think that's the most important thing. One other question concerning television ads: are you a television watcher yourself?

MISS SHARP. To a small degree.

CHAIRMAN ALEXANDER. You'd be watching here in the New York area.

MISS SHARP. Yes.

CHAIRMAN ALEXANDER. Do you often see Negroes in principal roles in television ads?

MISS SHARP. No. I know of one Negro girl who is working in principal roles has had one principal for a soap commercial. I know of one Negro male, and most of us in the business know each other. And this is it.

CHAIRMAN ALEXANDER. This is it for all Negro girls?

MISS SHARP. This is it for principals, yes. I know my theatrical director has made four commercials, two for cigarette companies, one for a car company, and one for an airplane ad, in which he was a principal. He was paid the $200 or $300 for the day's work. However, none of these commercials were ever run.

Consequently, he does not receive any residuals. Often the agency can say to you, the

Commission, "Yes, we did use such-and-such a person, he was a Negro; we used him in four ads," but these ads have never yet run on television. And he's made four of them within the past two years. None of the four have ever run. They're not being seen by the public, but the agency is saying, "Yes, we use Negroes."

CHAIRMAN ALEXANDER. So from what you say, would it be true that a survey that was done, I think by City College, that indicated in sports shows in this town, that 44 percent of the pro basketball players being Negro and at least 26 percent of pro football players being Negro, that less than 5 percent of those on camera were Negroes, in not only principal roles, but any kind of role? Would that be typical of your television advertising watching?

MISS SHARP. Yes, it would be. I guess the general assumption is that Negroes don't use tooth paste and soap and hair oils and things, because you don't see them.

Another point that I did want to bring out was something that one runs into. For example, the cosmetic products that I mentioned, where they seemed to function on the negative stereotypes of Negroes. They make an appointment by telephone and they don't know that you're a Negro until they see you. And when they see you, immediately all sorts of things that they've heard and read of the negative stereotype of the Negro come into mind, and they immediately assume that you are not capable of doing the job, rather than giving you a chance to do it; this happens very frequently.

CHAIRMAN ALEXANDER. Miss Sharp, thank you very much. We appreciate your taking the time to come down here.

MISS SHARP. Thank you.

TESTIMONY OF MR. EMANUAL ROBINSON

CHAIRMAN ALEXANDER. Ladies and gentlemen, we have another witness from the minority community. As with previous witnesses, there will be no reference to specific individuals or employers. Our witness is Mr. Emanual Robinson, who has kindly agreed to come and testify before the Commission. Mr. Robinson.

MR. STEINER. Mr. Robinson, you are a native New Yorker, sir?

MR. ROBINSON. No, I was born in Atlantic City, New Jersey.

MR. STEINER. And did you receive your education in Atlantic City?

MR. ROBINSON. I went to grammar school and high school in Atlantic City.

MR. STEINER. And where did you go for further education after high school?

MR. ROBINSON. To Rutgers University. I did some additional graduate work at Columbia University here in New York.

MR. STEINER. I see, and when did you graduate from Rutgers?

MR. ROBINSON. 1954.

MR. STEINER. And what field did you major in?

MR. ROBINSON. Psychology.

MR. STEINER. And roughly what kind of an average did you have at Rutgers?

MR. ROBINSON. B.

MR. STEINER. What did you do your graduate work in at Columbia?

MR. ROBINSON. Psychology, also.

MR. STEINER. Now, while you were doing graduate work, were you employed at the time?

MR. ROBINSON. Part of the time, yes.

MR. STEINER. What sort of work were you doing?

MR. ROBINSON. I was doing temporary work in a—at a market research outfit.

MR. STEINER. I see. And did you ever try to get a permanent job there?

MR. ROBINSON. Yes.

MR. STEINER. And what happened then?

MR. ROBINSON. Well, in 1957, I obtained a temporary position as a research assistant in the research department of one of the world's largest advertising agencies. This temporary status meant that I was on a weekly salary, receiving no benefits such as sick time, vacations or holidays. And, of course, I could be terminated at such time as their work load slacked off. However, the need to retain me continued for several months. Finally, I started to think about being placed on the permanent payroll, since my work was obviously more than satisfactory and since I already knew the people and procedures of the department. I started putting out feelers toward this end, and since they didn't want to lose me, I was placed in a special category, that is, on a monthly basis, which meant that I was paid for holidays and received other fringe benefits such as participation in the medical plan, but my status was still not that of permanent employee on the payroll, employee as was everybody else in the department. The only reason for this state of "limbo" was that I was the first Negro in the research department, and in fact I do not know whether there were any other Negroes throughout the agency at that time.

MR. STEINER. How do you know that this was the reason, Mr. Robinson? How do you know that this was the reason that you were in a state of "limbo"? Were there any indications that this was the case?

MR. ROBINSON. The head of the research department was known to be opposed to hiring me permanently, both because of his racial prejudices and because he was averse to "breaking new ground," as he put it. The issue of whether to make one Negro a permanent employee became a hot debate. I was, of course, not a part of the arguments, but I heard about them from a few people who were on my side, so to speak.

MR. STEINER. In other words, people who were working there related to you that this kind of discussion was going on within the firm?

MR. ROBINSON. That is correct, and the only basis for this discussion was the fact I was Negro.

After much discussion the "good guys," from my viewpoint, won out. I was placed on regular, permanent status and remained there for two and a half years with no further trouble.

MR. STEINER. During your experiences in looking for employment at various times, have you ever made use of employment agencies?

MR. ROBINSON. Yes. In 1961, I was in the market for a job change. One of the people I contacted was an acquaintance who worked at an employment agency which serviced advertising agencies. I set up an appointment with this person and came to his employment agency to follow up a job opening for which he thought I was qualified, since he was already familiar with my background. I was sitting at his desk, on which there was a perfectly usable telephone, in the usual employment agency interview situation. After assuring me that I looked right for the opening, he excused himself, went into another office, made a phone call to the advertising agency which had the job opening and

returned to me blithely announcing, "Sorry, Manny, they don't hire Negroes."

I told him that the matter certainly would not rest there, and that I was filing a complaint with what was then known as SCAD, or State Commission Against Discrimination. It was at that point that my friend panicked, begged me not to make an issue of it, and when I persisted, he told me flatly that he would deny ever having made such a statement.

Obviously, the reason for his reaction was that he feared losing his job by becoming embroiled in such a contretemps. The point is that only a few years ago at least one advertising agency could feel perfectly free to make the flat statement, "We don't hire Negroes" in the face of all the equal job opportunity laws that were then on the books.

MR. STEINER. Have there been any other situations where you have applied for a job where you have felt there has been discrimination?

MR. ROBINSON. Yes. In 1965, I applied to one of the largest food manufacturers in the country, which is based near New York City, for a job in the area of research. It must be understood that there are three divisions which constitute the corporate structure of this company, and each division has its own research department.

The job opening was within one of the three separate research departments, each one of which was comprised of 10 to 15 professional staff people. I did not get the job, but what was interesting was why I didn't get the job. I heard later that the particular research department in which there was an opening already had one Negro on its staff. Therefore, the decision was made by the department head not to hire another Negro applicant for his department, lest two Negroes out of 10 or 15 be considered excessive by someone higher up in that division.

MR. STEINER. From whom did you hear this, Mr. Robinson?

MR. ROBINSON. Well, in fact, I heard this from the guy who actually interviewed me for that job.

MR. STEINER. He told you that?

MR. ROBINSON. He didn't tell me directly. He told somebody else who then repeated it to me.

MR. STEINER. An indirect story that you received?

MR. ROBINSON. Yes. Indirect, but accurate, I don't doubt. But if the opening had occurred in one of the other two divisions, where possibly there was no Negro on staff, my chances of being hired would have been at least equal to any other applicant's. Since there was already one Negro on the scene where the opening did occur, my chances flatly were nil. Again, I emphasize that this demonstrates that hiring of minority group members is nearly always color-conscious rather than color-blind.

MR. STEINER. Mr. Robinson, I've noticed, as you were testifying here, that you've been reading from some prepared notes. Who prepared those notes?

MR. ROBINSON. I prepared them myself in my own inimitable handwriting.

MR. STEINER. Right, thank you.

CHAIRMAN ALEXANDER. Mr. Robinson, in your experience and with your training, how do you feel we've progressed so far in this society, in New York City? Do you think you would run into the same kinds of problems that you mentioned if you went out to get a job today?

MR. ROBINSON. Well, may I just read something else that I wrote?

CHAIRMAN ALEXANDER. Either that, or just answer as you feel. What we want to know is what's on your mind.

MR. ROBINSON. Right.

CHAIRMAN ALEXANDER. As long as you wrote it, it's fine.

MR. ROBINSON. Right. I wish to point out that prior to about 1963 or 1964, only a few short years ago, the racial discrimination in white collar employment which has been described to you was rampant right here in New York City. Various euphemisms were used, but they added up to the same thing—few Negroes hired in any responsible positions. The story I used to get when I went for job interviews at advertising agencies or companies was, "What about client contacts," meaning that an agency's client would automatically take his business elsewhere if he had to deal with a Negro.

CHAIRMAN ALEXANDER. Let me stop you there for a minute. What did they mean about "client contact"?

MR. ROBINSON. Well, what they meant was that if I remained in a position where I had no contact with their clients, that everything was fine. However, if I had to go to a client in order to transact any kind of business, from their point of view the client would not like this.

CHAIRMAN ALEXANDER. And why wouldn't they like it?

MR. ROBINSON. Because I was black, and—

CHAIRMAN ALEXANDER. How many times did you run into this situation?

MR. ROBINSON. I ran into this situation at least five, six times, the business of "client contact" and of course that phrase "client contact" meant that I was automatically shut out from that job possibility.

CHAIRMAN ALEXANDER. And this is a kind of occupation that you want to pursue, and you felt you were prepared for it, is that correct?

MR. ROBINSON. Right, right.

CHAIRMAN ALEXANDER. And you kept trying, nevertheless, to seek opportunities, is that correct?

MR. ROBINSON. Yes, well, the thing is that there was never any discussion about my background or qualifications. The term "client contact" meant that it was all over, right then and there.

CHAIRMAN ALEXANDER. Do you have friends who are Negroes or who are Puerto Ricans who have similar backgrounds and who are interested in professional work with advertising agencies?

MR. ROBINSON. Yes.

CHAIRMAN ALEXANDER. And have they ever related any stories to you concerning problems they might have had?

MR. ROBINSON. Yes.

CHAIRMAN ALEXANDER. Without giving their names, could you give us an example of the kind of story a friend of yours with similar experience might run into?

MR. ROBINSON. Well, the experiences have been fairly similar to mine. I would rather not refer to them because I don't have the personal knowledge that I do of my own experiences. The only thing I can say is that my experiences are not very much different from those of a great many other people in my position.

CHAIRMAN ALEXANDER. What I really was wondering was whether the term "client contact" was used a good deal.

MR. ROBINSON. I don't know about that specific term, "client contact." Of course this turned out to be a myth, as was—actually, it's more of a reflection of the interviewer's bigotry than anything else. Now only three or four years ago, the climate in white collar employment changed to some degree, but not because of any new found social consciousness or social conscience toward Negroes. Rather, two factors prevail: one, the threat of boycott of products by Negroes; and two, the directive of the Federal Government requiring that there be no discrimination in businesses where government contracts exceed $50,000. I am saying, therefore, that the impetus towards placing Negroes on the payroll in white collar positions came from outside forces and pressures, and not from within the hearts of employers.

CHAIRMAN ALEXANDER. Now, you have this impression from your interviews, and also is it from knowledge of others who have talked to you about this, minority group individuals?

MR. ROBINSON. That's quite true. It meant that there has been somewhat of a scramble among agencies and companies that had not previously hired minority group members to get their token Negroes on staff. Some companies have reacted more enthusiastically than others once the breakthrough was made and they found that employing minority group members presented no special problems.

But what I am trying to emphasize here is the recency of minority group hiring efforts among advertising agencies and other companies.

CHAIRMAN ALEXANDER. So, once the myth's exploded that there isn't a client contact problem or that any minority group member, obviously, is capable of doing a job, then some progress has been seen.

MR. ROBINSON. Right. Yes, but the main—

CHAIRMAN ALEXANDER. From your observation.

MR. ROBINSON. Right, but to me in a token fashion rather than in an overall fashion. For example, when pressure was being brought to bear on the advertising agencies, I recall the president of an agency association piously making the statement that no discriminatory policies existed. Yet he was quoted as saying that he understood the civil rights organization which was applying this pressure was only interested in getting art directors hired. This to me showed how shallow any efforts at equal opportunity— equal employment opportunity were at that time and was illustrative of how employers gave themselves away by their own statements.

Now, during these hearings, it has been remarked that Negroes must in some way make their own efforts toward equal opportunity employment. This means that somehow the onus is placed upon the groups that have been effectively locked out of white collar employment. Such statements to me must be challenged in the light of reality, and the reality is that the blame for the low proportion of Negroes in white collar jobs lies in the history of conscious exclusion of Negroes from these jobs by employers and not in some fancied lack or deficiency or shortcoming among Negroes themselves.

CHAIRMAN ALEXANDER. Would you extend this generality to Puerto Ricans as well?

MR. ROBINSON. Yes, yes.

CHAIRMAN ALEXANDER. And so therefore, from your observations, and from observing the nation, when people are given an opportunity, when it's made realistic to them that in every kind of position they are welcome as long as they've got the talent—

MR. ROBINSON. Right.

CHAIRMAN ALEXANDER. It really isn't an answer to say people are going to have to work harder at it and show more determination. You're saying the determination has to be on both sides, I guess.

MR. ROBINSON. Well, I'm saying that the qualified people are there on the minority side, and that it's simply an evasion to place the onus on the minority group people who have—who don't or who haven't had the opportunity— they're not the ones who have had the power to discriminate.

CHAIRMAN ALEXANDER. And in fact, of all the people that have testified before us, from our facts, we haven't heard about a single Negro who has been a president of a corporation or on the board or vice president or a single Puerto Rican, so it would be a little difficult for the Negro to help the other Negro in that sense.

MR. ROBINSON. Right.

CHAIRMAN ALEXANDER. If that were possible.

MR. ROBINSON. Right.

CHAIRMAN ALEXANDER. And the major corporations, I think it's true of all those that our statistics reflect, none of them have Negro presidents.

MR. ROBINSON. Right. And I'm also saying

that this is not by accident, that it has been in the past quite conscious.

CHAIRMAN ALEXANDER. We appreciate very much your taking the time to give us your experiences and your views. Commissioner Jackson would like to ask some questions.

COMMISSIONER JACKSON. Mr. Robinson, I was very much impressed by that part of your statement which suggested that there was a direct relationship between the enforcement programs of the Federal Government, and the motivation of those businesses at which you have attempted to gain employment. Have you found that, without the external pressures, that there did not appear to be a willingness to bring about change in hiring patterns?

MR. ROBINSON. That's pretty much exactly what I'm saying, that without the external pressures, and I don't know—I posit this change at around the time, generally around the time of the march on Washington in 1963, that there was a change in hiring practices. But what I am saying is that no change would have—or hardly any change would have come about as a result of self-motivation on the part of employers.

COMMISSIONER JACKSON. Ha nessed the functioning of the vari programs that have been going on York and throughout the nation, a ﹍﹍, to what extent have these voluntary programs made any indentation upon the stimulation of change on the part of those who participate, those employers who participate, and to what extent is increased enforcement necessary in view of these voluntary programs, if any?

MR. ROBINSON. Well, my feeling is that the voluntary programs only go so far, that is, they go to the point of making the companies look good in terms of their representation, in terms of the minority groups' representation on their payroll, but that beyond that the question is quite doubtful. What I'm saying, again, is that there has to be a push from behind, rather than leaving the question completely to the hands of the employers.

COMMISSIONER JACKSON. Thank you.

CHAIRMAN ALEXANDER. Mr. Robinson, I want to thank you again. We appreciate your coming and talking with us. Thank you, sir.

SEX, STATUS, AND UNDEREMPLOYMENT OF THE NEGRO MALE

Kenneth B. Clark

The traditional status of the Negro in American life is determined by the work he has been permitted to perform. For the American Negro, occupational status and human status have been one from the time of slavery up to the most recent civil rights protest. The slogan of the March on Washington in August 1963, "Jobs and Freedom Now," was not only a demand for equal employment opportunities but an assertion of the Negro's desire for acceptance as a total human being. In demanding that the opportunities for mobility and free competition in the economic and job market be opened to him, the Negro is also demanding to be included in the American Protestant ethic that constructive work is the basis of human dignity and provides the basis for one's manhood. He is in fact demanding that that myth be discarded which was essential for the support of human slavery and its successor, racial discrimination— the myth that the Negro was less than human and that his subhumanity had to be dealt with by a castelike restriction to certain occupations.

But so far the Negro has not been successful; his demands have not been fulfilled. In an "affluent society" the Negro is still the victim of greater rate of unemployment than whites. What is even more significant in this whole area of occupational status is the fact that those Negroes who are employed are, for the most part, restricted to menial jobs which clearly limit dignity and self-fulfillment. In England the voluntary acceptance of the subservient role by the working-class Englishman gives the individ-

From *Employment, Race and Poverty* by Arthur M. Ross and Herbert Hill, copyright © 1967, by Harcourt Brace Jovanovich, Inc. and reprinted with their permission.

ual the power, or the illusion of power, to change; but inferiority of occupational role based on skin color reduces the actual and psychological chances of mobility or hope because skin color cannot be changed. In America the system tends to tie menial status to color, and escape seems futile.

The present bleak occupational predicament of the Negro will probably be reinforced in the future if present trends are not counteracted by massive and realistic corrective programs. Former Secretary of Commerce Luther H. Hodges stated in an address at the Equal Opportunity Day Dinner of the National Urban League on November 19, 1963:

In our total economy, white-collar jobs, which generally require more education, already outnumber our blue-collar jobs. This trend will continue. And, today, even our factory jobs are largely closed to applicants who lack a high school diploma....

Negroes, to a very large extent, have been excluded from the white-collar occupations which, since 1947, have accounted for 97 percent of the total increase in United States employment. Only one-sixth of all Negro workers are in white-collar jobs today, compared with nearly half of the white work force....

This is not only tragically unfair to Negroes, it is an intolerable loss of talent to our society and to our national economy.

Exclusion of Negroes from apprenticeship training programs conducted by the better-paying skilled craft unions is a well-known and documented method of relegating Negroes to unskilled and low-paying jobs. Roy Wilkins, executive secretary of the National Association for the Advancement of Colored People, stated in his introduction to *The Negro Wage-Earner and Apprenticeship Training Programs: A Critical Analysis with Recommendations:*

At present there is a broad exclusion of Negro youth from major apprenticeship training programs jointly conducted by industrial management and labor unions in the North as well as in the South. For many occupations the only way a worker can be recognized as qualified for employment is to complete the apprenticeship training program. This is true for the printing trades, among machinists and metal workers, the various crafts in the building and construction trades industry and many others. The role of the labor union in these occupations is decisive because the trade union usually determines who is admitted into the training program and, therefore, who is admitted into the union. This results in a loss to the entire economy when basic human resources are not utilized. This discrimination directly relates to the future status of Negro wage earners throughout the United States. Given a continuation of present rates of advance, it will take Negroes 138 years, or until the year 2094, to secure equal participation in skilled craft training and employment.[1]

If the Negro seeks economic mobility and human dignity through the path of education, the persistent problems of racial discrimination and exclusion continue to reduce his chances of success. A key factor in the restriction of the Negro to the status of an underemployed proletariat, whose lack of skills will soon result in his exclusion from an increasingly automated economy, is the pervasive inferiority of the education provided for Negro children and youth. The pattern of discrimination, exclusion, rejection, and humiliation that conspires to contain the masses of Negroes in their menial occupational roles is perpetuated by subjecting them to segregated and invariably inferior education. Substandard education makes it difficult, if not impossible, for Negroes to compete on equal terms with others for skilled or managerial jobs, even if discrimination were not a reality.

The economic value of education is quite different for Negroes than for whites in America. Those Negroes who manage to overcome the handicap of inferior elementary and secondary education and press on to higher education are by no means assured that this will result in equality of status or economic opportunity. While the picture of the Negro college graduate working as a porter might not be as true today as it was in the 1930's, it is still true, as Herman P. Miller points out, that,

The income gap between white and nonwhite *widens* as education increases. The lifetime earnings of nonwhite elementary school graduates are 64 percent of that received by the whites. At the high school level this ratio drops to 60 percent and among college graduates it is only 50 percent. *The fact is that in 1959, the average nonwhite with four years of college could expect to earn less over a lifetime than the white who did not go beyond the eighth grade.*[2]

This discrepancy is found not only in the South, but also in Northern, Midwestern, and Western states.

Constrictions on the occupational, educational, and economic status of Negroes become a powerful, damaging force that permeates almost every facet of life and becomes psychologically tied to intimate aspects of the self. The burden seems to fall with particular force upon the Negro male. He has little or no power to change his inferior status, and his entire life is dominated by the reality of his position. Not only does he have a menial job, but he becomes, therefore, a menial person. He sees himself as not quite human and is fixed in this role by his job and his skin.

Antidiscrimination and equal opportunities legislation have not alleviated the condition. Where legislation is in effect, job discrimination persists, only in a more subtle form. One must assume, therefore, that the manner in which covert discrimination operates makes it relatively immune to the laws that have abolished its cruder manifestations. In addition to rigorous enforcement of legislation, techniques must be used that are as subtle and as pervasive as the social evil they seek to overcome. One effective step would be to educate the public on the very real economic and human consequences of banishing the Negro male to the rigid status of an underemployed and explosive underclass. Although the human consequences of this problem are dealt with here, the economic and pragmatic effects are clear and inextricable.

While the Negro male is emasculated by educational and occupational discrimination, there is evidence that society as a whole is more willing to accept the Negro female. Approximately 55 percent of Negro college students are female in contrast to the nationwide pattern in which 60 percent of college students are male.[3] Dale L. Hiestand has pointed out that during the twentieth century, "the proportion of Negro women workers in semiskilled jobs and in the white collar fields has grown steadily and substantially."[4] His data also support the conclusion that proportionately more Negro women than Negro men have moved into the white-collar occupations.

These data are all the more devastating in a society such as ours where it is impossible for females to work in occupations of low status without a major loss in their general status. In our society, ordinarily, females are considered of lower rank than males. When the Negro male sees the Negro female in a relatively higher status, his loss of dignity is greatly intensified. He finds himself inferior not only to white males but to Negro females as well. He is in double jeopardy.

In every situation the Negro female appears to have priority of status. Consequently, any relationship between male and female is fraught with tension—in courtship, in domestic decisions, in discipline of children. Denials or attempts to obscure this condition merely highlight its pathos.

Theories to the effect that all American males are dominated by the female do not alter the basic predicament of the Negro male. The emasculation of the white male by his female generally involves her desire to have him attain status symbols in order to enhance her own status. When a woman insists that her husband ask for a raise, she operates, nevertheless, within the framework of male dominance. She accepts society's judgment that male status is superior. She believes, in effect, that she can attain status for herself only through her husband. Even the most emasculating females function in these terms, dominating males in order to have them compete more effectively for status. This can destroy the male, but it supports the prevailing principle of masculine social and economic superiority.

The pattern of relationship within the Negro family is deeply affected by this imbalance of relationship between the sexes. The Negro male often loses the ability to function as a father and a husband.

In our society, rightly or wrongly, the relationship between the male and female, even in the most intimate matters, is influenced by status. This is a truism often ignored. Males of high status are generally more desirable to females than males of lower status. Even the lower-class female gains psychologically if she is admired or possessed by a male of slightly higher status. On the other hand, lower-class females are fair game for all males. It is understood that the male will use his masculine superiority to gain higher economic status, higher occupational status, and sexual priorities. A male who seeks a better job, makes more money, and achieves a better education becomes more attractive to the female.

The Negro male is exposed to the values of white society, but he has not been permitted to function in terms of these values. He does not hold a status superior to the female, and neither can she, unless she is extraordinarily naive, hope to manipulate him in the status climbing accepted by white middle-class society. She is aware of the fact that moving upward is related to the color of skin, from which there can be no escape. She also knows that the male has little choice, but this does not prevent her from feeling some contempt for the male who cannot provide the protection and dignity which the white male appears to provide for his female. She, too, has accepted white middle-class values. For the male this acceptance leads to resentment, self-doubt, and self-hatred.

Related to this complex pattern is the number of successful Negro females, particularly in show business, who have married white males. They argue that they are required to do so because there are so few Negro males with whom they have anything in common. They imply that they have outgrown the Negro male. One can infer that they believe that no Negro male could bring them any additional status. Once having demonstrated a successful break through racial constraints, they reach a level of prominence which would be threatened by public association with a Negro male. Generally, Negro males do not have comparable status.

Even the successful Negro male may seek association with white females in quest for even higher status. But he has more barriers in his way than do Negro females who associate with and marry white males. He faces the open resentment of usually more powerful white males, the bigotry of the masses of whites, and the inability to counter this resentment either by superior power of his own, unless he be a wealthy professional or an extraordinarily talented entertainer or prize fighter. Negro females are considered the property of, and fair game for, "higher status" white males, while white males consider white females their exclusive property, not to be shared with "lower status" Negro males. This perspective is consistent with the general assumption that males have rights of possession of females and its specific application in the area of racial status.

Basically, the position of the Negro male makes it difficult for the Negro female to respect him in terms of the standards which this society considers important—material possessions, economic status, symbols of privilege, well-furnished homes in good neighborhoods, fashionable clothing, private schooling. Such things, obviously, are not available to unemployed or menially employed lower-class persons. If the Negro female is to respect the Negro male, she often has no choice but to respect him solely in terms of his qualities as an individual, without the support of material success. This is a difficult basis for interpersonal relations among the privileged individuals of our culture—and is not less difficult among the underprivileged.

The Negro female may ultimately learn to judge the value of her male almost solely in terms of his male prowess. One can surmise that such evaluation of a male by a female or vice versa must lead to an ephemeral relation. A relationship based primarily on sexual gratification cannot be enough; it is essentially an escape. Genuine relationships must be reinforced by other factors, such as the ability of the male to provide for and protect his female—to furnish the material basis for a stable and mutually gratifying life. But the Negro female has little choice but to be satisfied with transitory benefits. In the case of the most socially marginal Negroes, respect can be based on such resources as who is the most accomplished sexually, who is the toughest guy on the block,

who has the most explosive temper, who is the shrewdest slickster. These stereotypes are substitutes for real power, a pseudocompensatory power rooted in a precarious economic situation and reflecting tenuous personal relationships without reinforcement by society.

The Negro male is aware that he does not bring to the female the basis for respect that white males provide. Caught in this predicament, he can either submit to it and be totally menial in relation to the female, as well as on his job, or he can seek the escapes of the stereotyped, shiftless buffoon or the accommodating Negro, thereby intensifying the basic problem. He may seek escape through wine or narcotic addiction, removed from any direct exacerbating ego involvement with women or engage in spasmodic sexual exploration in which he seeks immediate gratification without sustained responsibility. For any sensitive man it would appear to be psychologically unbearable to remain in a situation with a female in which sexual gratification cannot be buttressed by symbols of status or power. Some Negroes may seek a resolution, or masking, of this predicament by exaggerated use of superficial masculine traits, such as a propensity for dalliance, taunting, hostility, and irritability and an adolescent preoccupation with the conquest of a number of females. Still others may seek satisfaction in exhibitionist displays of dress and flashy cars or in a flamboyant shrewdness in marginal or antisocial activities. The common denominator of these devices is the avoidance of situations in which he would expose himself to himself and to his female as the powerless individual that society has made him. He cannot bring evidence of real worth and substance to a relationship with a woman because of the reality of his inferior occupational and economic status. Insidiously his menial job status has produced the psychological reality. He has been taught effectively that he *is* inferior. He knows he is inferior and he knows that his woman knows it, and no matter how he tries to disguise it, he cannot help her compete for middle-class symbols of status.

The situation is even more threatening when it involves children. The Negro who cannot fulfill his responsibilities as a male, as defined by middle-class standards, cannot face his children without shame and humiliation. He feels required to escape from the family or to resort to one or many compensatory patterns. Under these conditions the child does not associate a masculine role with sustained responsibility. All too often escape from familial responsibility or promiscuity or hostility seems to be what is expected of the man and therefore of the boy who is to become the man. The child cannot be expected to understand the reasons, the dynamics, for the behavior of his father. To him it is merely the way of life. Rejection by his father becomes part of what is believed to be his role. Interestingly enough, many children with absent fathers idealize them in a kind of dreamlike image of their strength and prestige. These are the children society may refer to as illegitimate and consider a burden imposed on the welfare rolls by ignorant and immoral mothers. But very often the father stays away knowing that he can only bring poor wages to his family and shame to himself if he lives at home, but that his family will receive funds for dependent children if there is no father in the home. The economic rewards of broken family life match his own psychological needs for avoidance of a responsibility he cannot sustain.

One of the most devastating things a teacher can do to a lower-class child is to ask him: "What does your father do?" Such an inquiry, harmless enough in middle-class society, creates tremendous anxiety in the child. The child often responds with sheer fantasy, exaggerating his father's occupation, claiming that he is a policeman or a fireman or a clerk, or in another job that seems to the child to convey status. Almost never will he admit that his father is a porter or a dishwasher or an elevator operator. Rarely will he admit that his father does not live at home unless he disguises his absence by saying he is dead. The more intelligent the child, the more likely he is to use the defense of fantasy to cover his own humiliation.

The Negro male, therefore, is required to face the fact that he cannot protect his children or be the agent through which they will be adequately fed or clothed or educated. What appears to be irresponsibility or neglect by the absent fathers can be seen rather as the anguished escape of the Negro male from an impossible predicament.

He cannot function effectively as a husband and father, so he often does not function at all. Even his presence would not be significantly different from his absence. If he were present and unable to protect his wife and child, there would be psychological torment and the inevitable explosion into aggression. The additional tragic predicament of the Negro male is that his powerless status tends to be self-perpetuating. What the Negro boy learns first is that to be Negro and male is to be menial—and to be menial is to be defeated in the competition for socially desirable status and its constructive rewards. When these avenues are blocked, the individual must seek other avenues for attaining that minimal status essential for human life.

Programs designed to end poverty, no matter how enthusiastically generated, will fail unless they acknowledge the realities of the interrelationship between job discrimination and the psychological damage associated with the menial status of the Negro male, as well as the effects of these upon the stability of the Negro family. Unless these conditions are faced, understood, and remedied, one can expect nothing other than perpetuation and extension of the social and personal pathology associated with American racism. The emasculation of the Negro male is implicit in his exclusion from the opportunities to be a meaningful part of the American economy. It not only leads to waste and tragedy for him, his women, and his children, but remains a major threat to the apparent affluence and stability of the American society as a whole. By denying the Negro the right to share in its affluence, society not only condemns the Negro to tragedy but also nurtures the seeds of its own destruction.

NOTES

[1]Herbert Hill, *The Negro Wage-Earner and Apprenticeship Training Programs: A Critical Analysis with Recommendations* (New York: NAACP, 1960).

[2]Herman P. Miller, *Rich Man, Poor Man* (New York: Thomas Y. Crowell, 1964), p. 155 (Italics H.P.M.)

[3]Kenneth B. Clark and Lawrence Plotkin, *The Negro Student at Integrated Colleges* (New York: National Scholarship Service and Fund for Negro Students, 1963), p. 25, and R. E. Iffert, *Retention and Withdrawal of College Students*, United States Office of Education Bulletin, 1958, No. 1 (Washington: U.S. Government Printing Office, 1957), p. 8.

[4]Dale L. Hiestand, *Economic Growth and Employment Opportunities for Minorities* (New York: Columbia Univ. Press, 1964), p. 46.

ADDITIONAL READINGS FOR CHAPTER 4

Richard S. Barrett, "Gray Areas in Black and White Testing," *Harvard Business Review,* V. 46, N. 1 (January-February, 1968), pp. 92-95.

Gary S. Becker, *The Economics of Discrimination* (Chicago: The University of Chicago Press, 1957).

Eidson, Bettye K., "Major Employers and Their Manpower Policies," in "Between Black and White: The Faces of American Institutions in The Ghetto," Peter Rossi *et al., Supplemental Studies for the National Advisory Commission on Civil Disorders* (Washington, D.C.: U.S. Government Printing Office, July 1968) pp. 115-123.

St. Clair Drake and Horace R. Cayton, *Black Metropolis: A Study of Negro Life in a Northern City,* V. I, Rev. & enlarged ed. (New York: Harper & Row, Publishers, 1962), pp. 214-262.

Edmund K. Faltermayer, "More Dollars and More Diplomas," *Fortune,* V. LXXVII, N. 1 (January 1968), pp. 140-145, 222, 224, 229.

Louis A. Ferman, Joyce L. Kornbluh, and J. A. Miller, *The Negro and Employment Opportunity: Problems and Practices* (Ann Arbor: Bureau of Industrial Relations, University of Michigan, 1965.

——, *Negroes and Jobs: A Book of Readings* (Ann Arbor: The University of Michigan Press, 1968).

Eli Ginzberg and Dale L. Hiestand, "Employment Patterns of Negro Men and Women," in John P. Davis (ed.) *The Negro American Reference Book* (Englewood Cliffs, N.J.: Prentice-Hall, 1966), pp. 205-250.

Eli Ginzberg, with the assistance of James K. Anderson, Douglas W. Bray and Robert W. Smuts, *The Negro Potential* (New York: Columbia University Press, 1956).

Robert M. Guion, "Employment Tests and Discriminatory Hiring," *Industrial Relations,* V. 5, N. 2 (February 1966) pp. 20-37.

Nathan Hare, "Recent Trends in the Occupational Mobility of Negroes, 1930-1960: An Intracohort Analysis," *Social Forces,* V. 44 (December 1965), pp. 166-173.

Ulric Haynes, Sr., "Equal Job Opportunity: The Credibility Gap," *Harvard Business Review,* V. 35, N. 3 (May-June 1965), pp. 113-120.

Dale L. Hiestand, *Economic Growth and Employment Opportunities for Minorities* (New York: Columbia University Press, 1964).

Herbert Hill, "Racial Inequality in Employment: The Patterns of Discrimination," *The Annals of the American Academy of Political and Social Science,* V. 357 (January 1965), pp. 30-47.

Charles C. Killingworth, *Jobs and Income for Negroes* (Ann Arbor: Institute of Labor and Industrial Relations, University of Michigan, 1968).

Stanley Lieberson and Glenn V. Fugiutt, "Negro-White Occupational Differences in the Absence of Discrimination," *Sociological Inquiry,* V. 35, N. 1 (Winter 1965), pp. 188-200.

Elliot Liebow, Tally's Corner: A Study of Negro Streetcorner Men (Boston: Little, Brown and Company, 1967), pp. 29-71.

Ray Marshall, *The Negro and Organized Labor* (New York: John Wiley & Sons, 1965).

——, *The Negro Worker* (New York: Random House, 1967).

Herman P. Miller, *Rich Man/Poor Man* (New York: Signet Book, published by the New American Library of World Literature, 1965).

Daniel P. Moynihan, "Employment, Income and the Ordeal of the Negro Family," in Talcott Parsons and Kenneth B. Clark, *The Negro American* (Boston: Beacon Press, 1965), pp. 134-159.

National Industrial Conference Board, *Company Experience With Negro Employment,* Studies in Personnel Policy, No. 201 (New York: National Industrial Conference Board, Inc., 1966).

Paul H. Norgren and Samuel E. Hill, *Toward Fair Employment* (New York: Columbia University Press, 1964).

Herbert R. Northrup, *The Negro in the Automobile Industry* (Philadelphia: Industrial Relations Unit of the Wharton School of Finance and Commerce, University of Pennsylvania, 1968).

—— and Richard L. Rowan (eds.), *The Negro and Employment Opportunity: Problems and Practices* (Ann Arbor: Bureau of Industrial Relations, University of Michigan, 1965).

Theodore V. Purcell and Rosaland Webster, "Window on the Hard Core World," *Harvard Business Review,* V. 47, N. 4 (July-August 1969), pp. 118-129.

Arthur M. Ross and Herbert Hill (eds.), *Employment, Race and Poverty* (New York: Harcourt, Brace and World, 1967).

Rowan, Richard L., *The Negro in the Steel Industry* (Philadelphia: Industrial Relations Unit of the Wharton School of Finance and Commerce, University of Pennsylvania, 1968).

S. Prakash Sethi, *Business Corporations and the Black Man: An Analysis of Social Conflict: The Kodak-FIGHT Controversy* (Scranton, Penna.: Chandler Publishing Company, 1970).

James S. Spain, *et al.,* "Black Executives: The Darkies at the Bottom of the Stairs," *The MBA,* V. III, N. 7 (April 1969), pp. 35-37, 41, 45, 54, 68.

Lester C. Thurlow, *Poverty and Discrimination* (Washington, D.C.: The Brookings Institution, 1969).

U.S. Bureau of the Census, *Changing Characteristics of the Negro Population*, by Daniel O. Price, A 1960 Census Monograph (Washington, D.C.: U.S. Government Printing Office, 1969).

U.S. Department of Labor, *Manpower Report of the President: A Report on Manpower Requirements, Resources, Utilization and Training* (Washington, D.C.: U.S. Government Printing Office, March 1970).

U.S. Department of Labor (Bureau of Labor Statistics) and U.S. Department of Commerce (Bureau of the Census), *Social and Economic Conditions of Negroes in the United States*, B.L.S. Report No. 375 and Current Population Reports, Series P-23 No. 29

(Washington, D.C.: U.S. Government Printing Office, 1969).

5 *Housing*

Black Americans by the millions are locked in racial ghettos. Their segregation and confinement is a cycle of cause and consequence. Segregated housing brings segregated neighborhoods which, in turn, result in segregated schools, which, historically, has meant substandard education. Confinement in urban ghettos reduces the job opportunities of blacks as business and industry leave the city for suburban sites located, not infrequently, many miles removed from the centers of black population. Inadequate public transportation from inner-city neighborhoods to outlying areas accentuates the problem. Many ghetto residents either have no automobiles or else they have cars which are old and in poor running condition and, therefore, unsatisfactory for reliable transport for all but short distances. Accordingly, there is great need for low-cost, comprehensive mass transportation. Unfortunately, however, in some urban centers (such as Los Angeles, Detroit, and Boston), black neighborhoods have been virtually isolated from important job markets, shopping areas, and educational facilities because of the unavailability of viable (in terms of time and cost) public transportation to and from the ghetto. Thus, housing segregation affects not merely the quantity and quality of accommodations available to black Americans, but their entire life style.

Racial ghettos are made; they don't occur simply by accident. From the outset, many blacks find their freedom of choice in housing restricted by their depressed economic condition which automatically forecloses large areas of the city to them. Accordingly, rental housing in the oldest, most run down, highest density areas of core cities is frequently all that is available. Often these neighborhoods are those which were formerly inhabited by the ethnic group occupying the bottom position on the socioeconomic ladder. In addition to economic factors, well-documented techniques of real estate discrimination, rooted in prejudice, continue to build the walls of racial ghettos. Until recently, these discriminatory practices were, in many communities, reinforced by both legislative provision and judicial decisions which gave the imprimatur of the state to discrimination.

Once located in these neighborhoods, blacks usually have little option but to remain, a result both of economic factors and of "local custom" which effectively bars them from seeking housing elsewhere, assuming they can afford it. The only exceptions to this situation are the occasional wealthy black moving to a "liberal" locale or the geographical mobility afforded when whites move from a particular neighborhood into either a part of the city further removed from the center or to a suburb, thereby opening it up to blacks. The instances of stable, racially mixed neighborhoods are all too uncommon.

The problems which blacks encounter in obtaining housing result not simply from the existence of segregation but from the quantity and quality of housing which is available. In 1968, an estimated 25 percent of all nonwhites lived in severe overcrowding in "substandard," "deteriorating," or "dilapidated" structures which, however, are also often characterized by higher rents than those paid by whites for comparable or even better housing.[1] It is significant that blacks increasingly have resorted to rent strikes to apply pressure upon landlords to improve their dwellings.

Indeed, in the view of some blacks it is this aspect of the housing condition which is most acute since many blacks might prefer to live in predominantly black neighborhoods *if* they contained decent housing. These spokesmen are quick to point out, however, that choice of neighborhood must be left open to blacks and not imposed by whites.

The first selection in this chapter, excerpted from the testimony of Robert C. Weaver, then Secretary of Housing and Urban Development, before the U.S. Senate Subcommittee on Housing and Urban Affairs, describes the growing concentration of blacks in America's cities and advances the thesis that housing discrimination is at the root of many social problems. Next, he presents evidence that blacks pay more and obtain poorer housing than whites. Following Secretary Weaver is a series of letters exchanged between Captain Jack O. Lanier, U.S. Army, and the Resident Manager, Carriage Hill Apartments, which documents the sudden cooling of plans to rent an apartment following the revelation that Captain Lanier is black.

Roy Wilkins, Executive Director, National Association for the Advancement of Colored People, illustrates what the inability to purchase housing near suburban plants means for ghetto residents who might work in them. As one automobile worker whose factory had moved 22 miles outside of Detroit explained to Wilkins, "I am still working there because I have my seniority and everything, but I have 44 to 45 and 50 miles a day to commute, while the white boys are able to buy houses right there in the town and three or four blocks from the factory, and I have to drive 50 miles round trip."

"Patterns and Practices of Discrimination," excerpted from a report of the Massachusetts Advisory Committee to the U.S. Commission on Civil Rights, describes patterns and practices of discrimination employed by real estate brokers, developers, homeowners, and landlords. Though published in 1963, the report discusses discriminatory practices which, regrettably, exist today.

These selections present both quantitative and qualitative appraisals of the housing conditions faced by black Americans. More than that, they attempt to relate this information to the lives of the individuals who experience these conditions.

One further word is necessary. The preceding comments and the selections which follow have concentrated on urban housing. By every measure, the availability and quality of housing for blacks in semirural and rural areas is, according to the data available, *worse* than that in the cities. If anything, therefore, we have understated rather than exaggerated the severity of the difficulties encountered by blacks in their search for decent housing.[2]

NOTES

[1] See United States Department of Labor (Bureau of Labor Statistics) and United States Department of Commerce (Bureau of the Census) *Social and Economic Conditions of Negroes in the United States,* 1969, BLS Report No. 375 and Current Population Reports, series P-23, No. 29, (Washington, D.C.: Government Printing Office, 1969), pp. 55-61.
[2] *Ibid.*

RESULTS OF HOUSING DISCRIMINATION

Testimony of Robert C. Weaver, Secretary of Housing and Urban Development

SECRETARY WEAVER. For more than a quarter of a century Negroes living in rural areas have in large numbers moved into the cities. Much of this migration was out of the South and into the North and West. Within the South, too, Negroes have been drawn out of rural areas into the cities.

In 1960, nearly 10 million of the 19 million Negroes in the United States lived in the central cities of metropolitan areas. This is more than double the number prior to the outbreak of World War II. In the Nation's 25 largest cities, which include six in the South, only in Memphis did the population of nonwhites in the total population fail to rise between 1950 and 1960.

During this decade, in Los Angeles, the nonwhite population nearly doubled, while the white population rose only 17 percent. Chicago saw a 64-percent gain in its nonwhite population while facing a 13-percent loss in whites. New York experienced a 47-percent gain in nonwhites; Detroit 60 percent, Cleveland 69 percent, Baltimore 45 percent, Milwaukee 189 percent, and Buffalo 95 percent.

Millions of the Negroes who migrated from rural areas to central cities in recent decades are trapped in racial ghettos from which they cannot escape because housing is not freely available on equal terms to all Americans.

The housing of nonwhite families is consistently of poorer quality than that of white households in the same income levels. This is due, in large part, to the fact that the nonwhite

families do not have freedom of choice in the selection of their homes.

In 1960, 44 percent of all nonwhites lived in substandard housing as compared to 13 percent of the white families. Sixty-two percent of the nonwhite households rented as compared to 36 percent of the white households. Forty-eight percent of the nonwhite renters lived in substandard units as against 19 percent of the whites. Three times as large a proportion of nonwhite families, 28 percent, lived in overcrowded homes, as did white households, 10 percent; and this overcrowding was prevalent in all income classes.

For example, of nonwhite families with incomes of $6,000 or more, 25 percent lived in overcrowded conditions. This compares with only 9 percent for whites in the same income classes.

Discrimination in housing is at the root of many of the evils in today's racial ghettos. It chains almost all nonwhites to an environment which is not conducive to good health, educational advancement, cultural development or to improvement in their standard of living. It stands as an unprecedented impediment to the movement of nonwhites into the mainstream of American society.

The Civil Rights Commission in its recent report to the President on race and education established conclusively the relationship between poor housing in racial ghettos and the lack of educational opportunities.

The high rate of unemployment in racial ghettos, particularly in the case of nonwhites, also demonstrates the evils resulting from housing discrimination. Housing discrimination deprives hundreds of thousands of nonwhites of employment opportunities in suburban commu-

Reprinted from *Fair Housing Act of 1967*, Hearings Before the Subcommittee on Housing and Urban Affairs of the Committee on Banking and Currency, United States Senate, 90th Congress, First Session, on S1358, S2114, and S2280 Relating to Civil Rights and Housing, Aug. 21, 1967, pp. 35-37, 39-46; 86-89; 98-108; 120-126.

nities which are generally unavailable to them as residential areas. And in those cities which are extremely spread out, a similar deprivation occurs within the city limits when nonwhites are excluded from most residential areas.

Between 1960 and 1965 from one-half to two-thirds of all new factories, stores, and other mercantile buildings in all sections of the country, except in the South, were located outside the central cities of metrolitan areas. This indicates that expanding job opportunities are going to be in or near suburbia rather than in the core cities.

Since 80 percent of the nonwhite population in metropolitan areas in 1967 lives in central cities, the handicaps of nonwhite jobseekers are apparent. Unless nonwhites are able to move into suburban communities by the elimination of housing discrimination and the provision of low- and moderate-cost housing in these areas, they are going to be deprived of many jobs, because they will be unable to live in the central city and work in the suburbs because of the high cost of transportation.

The time has come when the Federal Government must establish a national policy against discrimination in housing as it has in other vital areas of American life. It should be enacted so that more than 20 million American Negroes and other minorities will attain the freedom to choose the homes in which they wish to live on the basis of what they can afford—just as all other Americans do....

These are arbitrary and artificial restraints that Americans would not tolerate if exercised against, say, the electrical appliance or the automobile industry. Yet they are directed against a housing industry that is already struggling with grave problems.

I believe the National Government has a responsibility to remove these purely artificial restrictions, instigated by prejudice, in order to permit the housing industry to achieve the full potential of a free market, along with all other industries.

THE URBAN CRISIS

The urban crisis before this Nation calls for action simultaneously on all fronts to alleviate poverty and to eliminate slums and racial ghettos. This country has an increasing awareness that the attack on our racial ghettos requires coordinated action by Federal, State, and local governments, private enterprise, management and labor, religious, and other private groups.

The success of our endeavors will depend to a large extent on the nation's ability to eliminate housing discrimination, proivde a substantial increase in or housing supply for low- and moderate-income families throughout the urban complex and revitalize the ghetto itself.

SENATOR [WALTER F.] MONDALE.... One of the old issues that always kicks around when we consider this proposal is whether property values decline if a Negro family moves into an all-white neighborhood. What is your impression of that?

SECRETARY WEAVER. I think we now have some fairly objective studies, particularly those made by the Commission on Race and Housing, which was financed by the Fund for the Republic under the leadership of Schwulst who was then chairman of the Bowery Savings Bank, which indicate there is no validity to the statement that the element of race alone and of itself and by itself inevitably brings a lowering of property values.

What we have is that a whole series of factors is involved.

If you have a limited access to nonwhites to housing at a given income level and as a result of that limited access you have a great concentration in one or two communities where the new element in the population may come in, and that engenders as it often does a psychological fear on the part of the former residents lest they would become the minority group numerically—you have panic selling, which is often typical and is done by the real estate pecple involved.

And you have blockbusting, where owners are told, "If you don't get out, Negroes will move in, and your property value will go down. Therefore I will give you about one-third of what it is worth because I am a great friend and will help you out," and then turn right around and sell it to nonwhites at a value of about one-third above what its value was before.

SENATOR MONDALE. The blockbuster strategy is basically an argument for the fact that Negroes do not drive down real estate values. Their strategy is to scare people on the basis of this myth, and then they will hold the property to make money. In other words, they don't believe what they are saying.

SECRETARY WEAVER. They state what is conventional wisdom, but then they operate on economics, which is that they get a much larger profit. They not only get the profit that would be involved in a commission for selling the property but they also get a profit due to the fact that they bought it under false pretenses as it were.

But, getting back to my analysis, it is those activities which are the result of residential segregation rather than the advent of the nonwhite buyer which cause the property values to decline.

That same study has a whole series of detailed research projects indicating, where nonwhites have moved into what was formerly an all-white neighborhood, more frequently—particularly if there is a shortage of housing—the values of the properties tend to go up because there is a greater market rather than decline.

So it is not race per se that causes this, but it is the whole sociological and economic situation as the result of residential segregation that may occasion it in some instances.

SENATOR MONDALE. Your testimony is that if we could remove on a national basis discrimination in housing the normal residential patterns would set in where people regardless of color could buy the housing they were able to buy on the basis of their income and that this would help break up the ghettos and would prevent the ghetto type of living, would help ease the pressure on ghetto type of living that we see today?

SECRETARY WEAVER. Yes. I think that what we have here really is two sides of the same coin. There is, unfortunately, a great deal of assertion today that you either do something about the ghetto or you don't do anything about it, that you either are concerned with open occupancy or you are concerned with fixing up the ghetto, and that these things are mutually inconsistent one with the other.

Nothing could be further from the truth.

Let us assume that we do have a program of trying to do something to wipe out our pockets of poverty, of which large numbers are now racial ghettos. If we are going to improve the quality and the standard of housing and the standard of living in these areas, the first problem we are going to run into is the problem of densities. And in order to restore these areas so they will no longer be ghettos but will be attractive places—because I might say in passing very often they are very valuable real estate—one of the things you are going to have to do is move some of the people in there out. And you certainly are not going to be able to take care of the natural increase of population that would occur if you are going to have any reasonable densities, not only from a point of view of housing but from a point of view of public facilities, schools and other services.

So that you cannot even talk about revitalizing the areas of nonwhite concentration now without envisioning an equal opportunity so that these people can move out into other places, as they will have to move if you are going to be successful in your attack on the ghetto.

SENATOR MONDALE. Do you have any way of estimating demand in nonghetto housing that would be opened up if an effective fair housing law was enacted? Or, to put it differently, how many Negro families capable of purchasing decent housing other than in the ghettos would be in the market elsewhere if it were not for the discrimination?

Do we have any way of knowing that?

SECRETARY WEAVER. I don't thing you can estimate that. You can estimate statistically the number of nonwhite families, as I have done some years ago in an article I wrote on this, in 1955 I think it was, in the Journal of Land Economics, where I pointed out the number of nonwhite families, say, with incomes of over $5,000 a year.

And you can also estimate the proportion of those that are now living in areas of nonwhite concentration.

But the next step, to assume that every one of them or what proportion of them would move into other areas were this available to them, is something that you cannot estimate accurately.

There are many who for political reasons, sometimes for business reasons, or for other reasons would elect to stay, even if they had the opportunity to move.

There are others who might not move today but might move 2 months from now or might move 3 or 4 years from now.

So that we do know that there is this limitation. I don't think we can quantify it. I have never seen any such study.

SENATOR MONDALE. Well, when you try to quantify such a fact, isn't it true that many Negro families with incomes adequate to permit them to purchase housing simply do not want to expose themselves to the humiliation of being turned down when they approach a home with a "For Sale" sign and then find they are turned away obviously because they are colored?

SECRETARY WEAVER. I don't think there is any question in our own experience in the enforcement of the Executive Order on equal opportunity in housing. We have found it is a great, great problem. Because the families will come in, and we will say that this is open occupancy, but they would have gone out the week before to a neighboring place and have had a very unfortunate and unhappy experience.

And they will say, "Well, it's the same old thing."

You know, after a man hits his head up against a brick wall time and time again, he then even doubts when he sees a little opening in that wall lest it be a snare and a delusion.

SENATOR MONDALE. This is an additional reason why we need a dramatic and fundamental declaration of national policy, it seems to me, to overcome this kind of most understandable reluctance on the part of the Negro community to seek to buy housing elsewhere outside of the ghetto even though they have the financial capacity to do so.

Has this unnatural crowding in the ghetto areas of our country artificially inflated real estate values and made it more costly in the ghetto?

SECRETARY WEAVER. There are a whole series of studies going back to the classical one made in the 1940's which indicate that the housing dollar in a black hand does not buy as much housing value as the same dollar in a white hand.

At practically every income level, practically every housing level, the nonwhite pays more for housing than does the white.

SENATOR MONDALE. Has that been quantified?

SECRETARY WEAVER. Yes, there have been studies of that.

SENATOR MONDALE. What do those studies indicate?

SECRETARY WEAVER. Those studies indicate that if you take the same type of housing in the same neighborhood and if you take the same quality of housing in comparable neighborhoods that invariably the nonwhite pays more for a lesser amount of housing value.

SENATOR MONDALE. Can you give the relationship there?

SECRETARY WEAVER. I can give you the references to the studies that are involved here.

SENATOR MONDALE. Could you give me the figures? Because I am sure I don't have the time to look at the studies.

SECRETARY WEAVER. I don't think that I can give you a figure as to how much less, because—

SENATOR MONDALE. Why don't you put in the record, if you can, the closest you can come to quantifying it? Because I noticed recently there was a study in New York City showing that the ghetto dwellers paid approximately 15 percent more for their normal consumer purchases than did the dwellers outside the ghetto of New York City.

Perhaps that same study included housing. I don't know.

SECRETARY WEAVER. I do not think it did.

SENATOR MONDALE. But if there have been studies of this kind dealing with housing, I think it would be helpful, to the extent it has been quantified, if we could have it.

SECRETARY WEAVER. I would be happy to submit for the record a summary of those studies. I could not give it off the top of my head.

(The information referred to follows:)

SUMMARY OF STUDIES THAT PROVIDE QUANTITATIVE FIGURES WHICH INDICATE THAT THE HOUSING DOLLAR OF THE NONWHITE BUYS LESS THAN THE HOUSING DOLLAR OF A WHITE

A primary source for data relating to nonwhite housing is the Report of the United States Commission on Civil Rights, which was published in 1959. Specifically, the Report contains illustrations of the findings from an extensive three-year research project of the Commission on Race and Housing.

The charts, and information provided by the Civil Rights Commission's State Advisory Committees, confirm the view expressed at the 1959 Civil Rights Commission's Washington hearing, by the Administrator of the Housing and Home Finance Agency. He stated that minorities are "generally able to buy less housing value and secure less home financing service on poorer terms per dollar than whites."

The following charts supplied by the Commission on Race and Housing in 1959 were based on census figures. They are discussed in the Civil Rights Commission's report at pages 344-347.

Charts 1 and 2 compare the percentage of rented dwellings classified by the Bureau of the Census as standard for whites and nonwhites by different rental brackets in four cities: Houston, New York, New Orleans, and Detroit. In each case, the whites are found to have a much higher proportion of standard dwellings in the same rental bracket. Although the differential is less in New York and Detroit than in the southern cities, the nonwhite in each case gets less for his rental dollar than the white.

Chart 3 shows that in eight major cities the nonwhite buyer of a house values at $6,000–$7,500 also gets less for his dollar than the white person who buys a house in the same category, although the percentage of nonwhite-owned dwellings in this

category that are standard is closer to the white percentage than in the case of rented units.

Chart 4 shows that in Birmingham, New Orleans, New York, and Los Angeles the nonwhite in every income group gets considerably less standard rental housing in relationship to his overall income position than does the white renter of similar income.

Chart 5 shows that in New Orleans the same is true of owned dwellings, while in New York the differential between whites and nonwhites in this situation is relatively small.

An indication that the situation as reported in 1959 in the U.S. Civil Rights Commission's Report of that year has continued to the present day is shown by more recent studies which have produced the identical conclusions. . . .

Chart 6 shows that in the above four cities there is substantially more overcrowding in rented dwellings of nonwhites than of whites in the same income category.

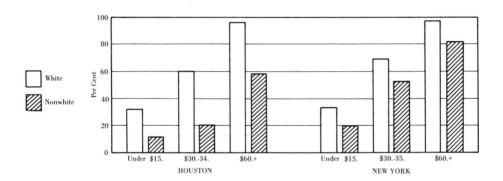

Chart 1. Rented Dwellings, Percent Standard by Gross Rent and Color (Houston and New York)

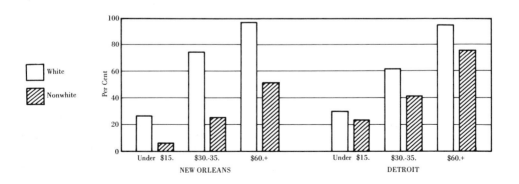

Chart 2. Rented Dwellings, Percent Standard by Gross Rent and Color (New Orleans and Detroit)

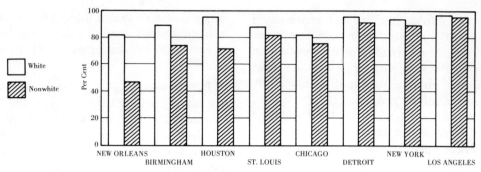

Chart 3. Owned Dwellings Valued at $6,000—$7,500
Percent Standard by Color

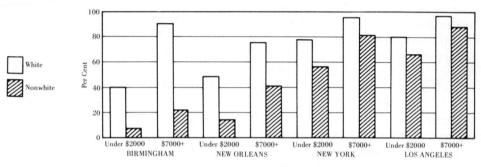

Chart 4. Rented Dwellings, Percent Standard by Income
and Color

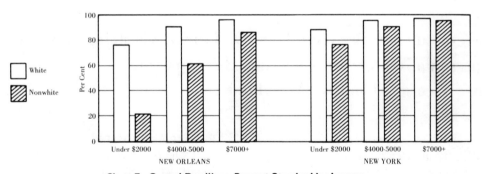

Chart 5. Owned Dwellings, Percent Standard by Income
and Color

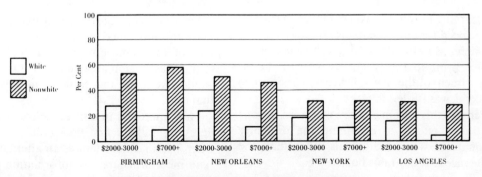

Chart 6. Rented Dwellings, Percent With 1.01 or More
Persons Per Room by Income and Color

SENATOR MONDALE. In your testimony I think one of your most impressive points was the relationship between forced housing in ghettos—and that is what it is—and the other factors that go into decent life, education, employment, and the rest.

You pointed out that there has been not only a flight of Negroes into the ghettos but a flight of employment opportunities out of the ghettos into the suburbs.

The cost of transportation and other difficulties are contributing to this rising rate of unemployment in the ghettos.

Do you see a continuation and an aggravation of these trends if fair housing is not adopted?

SECRETARY WEAVER. Yes, I do, And I must say I also see something more.

There has been a great deal of discussion recently about reversing this by bringing industry back into the ghettos and by getting employment opportunities adjacent to the ghettos in the central cities. I think that this, when proposed as a major program, defies all economic logic and I think that it is again a snare and a delusion.

It can be done in some instances—for example, in the Watts area—because of the large amount of land that is there. You can bring in some industrial employment. It happens, however, that Watts is adjacent to other industrial areas.

But the average ghetto area in the American city either does not have sufficient land space to accommodate both the people and industry or the land is so expensive that you cannot get industry, which is now being built horizontally rather than vertically. It used to be vertically that we built. Now we build a plant one or two stories over wide areas with great parking spaces.

SENATOR MONDALE. So that land costs become a critical factor?

SECRETARY WEAVER. So land costs become a critical factor. And if you were to attempt to do this on a large scale, then you would come right back to the problem I talked about earlier. You would have to find some place to put the people who are living on the land where you are going to put the industry, and you would have to have some form of breaking down the ghetto pattern and enforce segregation to do that, so that you are right back to where you started from. . . .

Correspondence Between Jack O. Lanier, Captain, U.S. Army, and Representatives of the Carriage Hill Apartments, Prince Georges County, Maryland

Washington, D.C., *August 22, 1966*
NAACP, *Washington Bureau,*
100 Massachusetts Avenue
NW., Washington, D.C.

Dear Sir: I submit to you evidence in support of the need for open occupancy in the Washington area. My attempt to obtain housing of my choice prior to my recent assignment to the Department of the Army, Office of The Surgeon General, was futile.

Perhaps this documentation will assist in your continued efforts to eliminate the difficulty encountered when individuals other than the white race seek desirable housing.

Sincerely yours,

JACK O. LANIER. *Captain, U.S. Army.*

BROOKE ARMY MEDICAL CENTER,
Fort Sam Houston, Tex., May 9, 1966.
RESIDENT MANAGER,
Carriage Hill Apartments,
Prince Georges County, Md.

Dear Sir: Your Carriage Hill apartments have been recommended to me as having just the kind of unit to meet my needs. I will be moving to the Washington area about 25 July 1966 and would like to be able to move into quarters at that time.

I am interested in a three bedroom unit with den, preferably a first floor unit. I would consider a second floor unit as an alternate. Please send me a brochure and information available concerning Carriage Hill. I am especially interested in the exact location and proximity to the downtown Washington area, bus service and elementary schools.

Thank you for your attention to my request. I look forward to your reply.

Very truly yours,
JACK O. LANIER, *Captain, U.S. Army*.

CARRIAGE HILL APARTMENTS,
Hillcrest Heights, Md., May 15, 1966.

Capt. JACK O. LANIER,
Brooke Army Medical Center,
Fort Sam Houston, Tex.

DEAR CAPTAIN LANIER: Thank you for your letter of May 9.

I regret very much not having a three bedroom and den apartment. Three bedrooms with a bath and one half is our largest unit. I enclose our brochure, rental schedule and floor plan which I hope will be helpful. We do have available three bedroom units and will be happy to reserve one for you. A deposit of $50.00 is required.

We are located approximately six miles from the downtown Washington area. During the rush hour it would be safe to allow at least forty minutes for travel by car and one hour by bus. At the moment we do not have bus service into our project; however, if all goes according to schedule, by the time you would be arriving here we will bus direct to downtown Washington from "Carriage Hill." Rush hour service is approximately five to eight minutes apart from 6:55 AM to 8:30 AM and during the non rush hour on a forty minute schedule.

Elementary, jr. high and high school students are bussed from the project by County bus. Churches and shopping are within a reasonable distance from our project.

If I can be of further help it will be my pleasure.

Cordially yours,
MARY M. MCLEAN, *Resident Manager.*

FORT SAM HOUSTON, TEX., *June 3, 1966.*

Mrs. MARY M. MCLEAN,
Resident Manager, Carriage Hill Apartments,
Hillcrest Heights, Md.

DEAR MRS. MCLEAN: Thank you for your letter of 9 May 1966 concerning the availability of apartments. I am interested in your units and have several questions before committing myself.

1. How far must children be bussed to the elementary school?

2. How near to your apartments is the closest bus stop for busses into downtown Washington?

3. Does each three-bedroom unit have adequate storage space for heavy items such as power mower, bicycles, washer and dryer, etc.?

4. Do you expect to have a three-bedroom, first or second floor, unit available on or about 25 July 1966?

5. Does each building have a laundry room with adequate machines?

I would appreciate an answer to the above questions as soon as possible. I would like to be able to move my family into quarters immediately upon my arrival to Washington about 25 July. Thank you very much for your kind assistance.

Very truly yours,
JACK O. LANIER,
Captain, U.S. Army.

CARRIAGE HILL APARTMENTS,
Hillcrest Heights, Md., June 6, 1966.

Capt. JACK O. LANIER,
1012 Scott Road,
Fort Sam Houston, Tex.

DEAR CAPTAIN LANIER: In reply to your letter of June 3.

1. Children are bussed approximately one mile from the project; if it were not for the foliage I expect we could see the building.

2. We have bus service thru the project now. When construction is completed it will traverse the area, at the present we have stops on the main street only.

3. There is not storage for heavy duty items such as you mention assigned to the apartments as such. However, we have areas where these items may be stored by you. We have storage areas for bicycles but not in each building.

4. It is quite possible we will have a three bedroom unit at the time you need one.

5. There are laundry facilities in each building, usually two washers and two dryers.

If I can assist you further it will be my pleasure.

Sincerely yours,
MARY M. MCLEAN.

June 13, 1966.

Mrs. Mary M. McLean,
Resident Manager, Carriage Hill Apartments,
Hillcrest Heights, Md.

DEAR MRS. MCLEAN: Thank you for your letter of 6 June 1966. Enclosed is my check for $50.00 as deposit for a three bedroom unit. I expect to arrive with my family on or about 20 July and will contact you upon arrival.

It would be helpful to know the address of the unit before leaving here so that the moving company can come directly to the apartments. However, my household goods will not arrive until after we do.

My first choice is one of your largest three bedroom, first floor units with the maximum amount of closet space.

In reply please let me know if there is a Nursery School in the general vicinity of the apartments.

Thank you for your assistance with our move to the area.

Very truly yours,
JACK O. LANIER, *Captain, U.S. Army.*

CARRIAGE HILL APARTMENTS,
Hillcrest Heights, Md., June 15, 1966.
Captain JACK O. LANIER,
1012 Scott Road,
Fort Sam Houston, Tex.

DEAR CAPTAIN LANIER: Thank you for your check. Receipt enclosed.

In order to consider an application I will need the following information:

Name:

Age:

Race:

Nature of employment and place of employment. (Washington area)

Name: of spouse

Name and ages of children (we do not accept more than three).

Present landlord and rental rate.

Apartment 103 3318 is on the first floor, seven steps down from the main entrance. There are three walk in closets and a good size closet in the smaller bedroom. Broom closet in kitchen and coat closet in foyer. The apartment is presently occupied, will be vacated July 3. We will redecorate. The building is just across the court from the bike room and not too far from a storage area where you may place your heavy equipment such as washer, drier, etc. The power mower cannot be stored if gas driven and not entirely empty of gas.

There are several nursery schools which call for and deliver children to this project. I really do not know just how close they are. I believe they may be within a fifteen minute drive from us.

I enclose a copy of our lease agreement for your information.

Sincerely yours,
MRS. MARY M. MCLEAN.

June 19, 1966.
Mrs. MARY M. MCLEAN,
Resident Manager,
Carriage Hill Apartments,
Hillcrest Heights, Md.

DEAR MRS. MCLEAN: As requested in your letter of 15 June 1966, I submit to you the following information:

1. Name: Captain Jack O. Lanier

2. Age: 34

3. Race: Negro

4. Nature of employment (Washington area): Army Medical Service Administrator (Army Officer)

5. Place of employment (Washington area): Office of the Surgeon General, Department of the Army

6. Name of spouse: Marion M. Lanier, School Teacher

7. Name and ages of children: Brian R., age 8½, Alison N., age 5

8. Current landlord: Ft. Sam Houston Family Housing Office (U.S. Government)

9. Present rental rate: $130 per month

Thank you very much for your very excellent assistance.

Very truly yours,
JACK O. LANIER.
Captain, U.S. Army.

COMMUNITY REALTY CO., INC.,
Washington, D.C., July 5, 1966.

Captain JACK O. LANIER,
1012 Scott Road,
Fort Sam Houston, Texas.

DEAR CAPTAIN LANIER: Enclosed herewith is a check for $50.00 for your security deposit which you furnished us on apartment 103, 3318 Curtis Drive, Hillcrest Heights, Maryland. I am sorry to inform you that your application for an apartment in this project has been disapproved.

Sincerely,

ROBERT B. ROBINSON, *Director,*
Property Management.

July 12, 1966.
Mr. ROBERT B. ROBINSON,
Director, Property Management,
Community Realty Co., Inc.,
Washington, D.C.

DEAR MR. ROBINSON: Your letter of 5 July 66 with a check for $50.00 has just reached me. I do not intend to cash this check and will take appropriate action concerning the apartment which had already been assigned me when I arrive. My house-hold goods are in the hands of a moving company this date based on arrangements made previously with Mrs. McLean, Resident Manager, Carriage Hill Apartments.

Very truly yours,

JACK O. LANIER, *Captain, U.S. Army.*

EDMUND W. DREYFUSS & ASSOCIATES,
Washington, D.C.

Hi Jack: I checked out the apartments over the weekend and found the following:

Keystone.—I haven't been able to contact the owner, but leasing personnel have indicated they have an open occupancy policy.

Crest View Terrace.—Located out Penn Ave. extended about 1 mile closer to D.C. than Keystone. About same physical layout as Keystone. *No open occupancy.*

Carriage Hill.—Located off Branch Ave. just south of Suitland Parkway. About same physical layouts as Keystone. I personally liked site layout better than Keystone. Leasing personnel indicated *"reluctantly"* that they had open occupancy. Development is new and many buildings were not completed. Therefore the chances of securing desired units about July 25 seem good.

I am not at all familiar with the development you asked about in your last letter. I will, however, keep my eyes and ears open for you.

Love to family,

Testimony of Roy Wilkins, Executive Director, National Association for the Advancement of Colored People and Chairman of the Leadership Conference on Civil Rights

MR. ROY WILKINS. It is impossible to offer testimony on any civil rights bill before Congress today without anticipating the question that is certain to be asked; What will this bill do toward ending city riots? . . .

One of the burning frustrations Negro residents carry with them in city ghettos is the knowledge that even if they want to and have the means to do so, very often they cannot get out. Certainly not without enormous effort and often not without humiliation. The white sections of the cities and the suburbs are, to a great extent, shut against them.

It is surely no surprise that in its recent report on six northern cities the Lemberg Center for the Study of Violence states that the sense of being forced to live in the ghetto and having few if any alternatives to it was one of the major causes of dissatisfaction, more widespread even than the discontent over the lack of jobs. While 60 percent of the Negroes in the six cities thought jobs opportunities were opening too slowly, the report says:

Impatience with the opening of housing opportunities is even closer to the boiling point; an average of 76 percent feel that efforts to provide opportunities for Negroes to live where they want are going too slowly.

The report observes that frustration in these two areas—jobs and housing—"are directly perceived by Negroes as being significant causes of riots."

We can all read the storm warnings here. S. 1358 can help avert that storm.

SENATOR [WALTER F.] MONDALE. Mr. Wilkins, I mentioned earlier, it is my belief that there is a profound debate going in the ghettos. One group argues that there is a lack of decency in America that destroys their confidence in moderate means and in rational appeals, that this country will not be fair and reasonable to all of our citizens. And thus the only alternative, if one is going to have any hope, is to resort to violence and rioting and other, what you might call irrational, methods of expressing one's resentment and hostility at these injustices. Hopefully from out of this will come some attention, if nothing else. Then, on the other hand, there are those who argue that our country is basically decent, if irresponsibly slow, and that if we mount the right kind of argument that this country will respond as it should, in this field of housing as well as others.

Do you agree that there is something of this nature, a debate of this nature that is underway now in America?

MR. WILKINS. Yes, sir; there is this kind of debate going on. Maybe not in those exact terms, but it is in the general area.

SENATOR MONDALE. And is it your impression that those who are making this pessimistic appraisal of American life are gaining a larger audience as we fail to respond to these minimum and obviously just appeals?

MR. WILKINS. I am absolutely certain of it, Senator, and I have to cite only an example from the newspapers of New York of the last 2 or 3 days, where two Negro sisters, one a welfare worker, and another a registered nurse, decided they wanted to buy a home together. One has children, the one does not. They found a home for $38,500, a new home, a two-family house that would satisfy their needs, and when they approached the owner he upped the price—first, he said the house was sold. Then he upped the price to $42,500. And they have been in litigation under the New York fair housing law since that time.

After 18 months they got a court order saying the price was excessive and ordering the sale to proceed.

Nothing has happened. The sisters have finally written to Mayor John B. Lindsay placing their predicament before him, and in that letter was the phrase outlining this debate to which you have referred. They said, "Our experience is being cited by those who want to damage the present system, being cited as an example of what we cannot do in the regular channels of our democracy."

Now, this is going on. I don't know how many recruits—part of your question was do I believe they are enlarging their recruitment?

I believe if they are not enlarging their recruitment, they are at least neutralizing those persons who normally would object to this, say, radical or extreme outline of the situation and subsequent procedure.

SENATOR MONDALE. The reason I asked this question is that I arranged for an off-the-record meeting a few weeks ago with some friends of mine in the ghetto of Minneapolis. First of all, I was surprised to see this extreme view expressed by some of them, and even more surprised and shocked to find out that they had lumped me right in with the worst white racists.

"We are all the same, it is all hopeless," they put it, "all you are talking about, Senator, is jazz." It is a whole new movement. It is a hostile movement. The violence is just under the surface. I think most of it is predicated on a sincere belief that nothing by way of a just response from this society is going to come about except through extreme means. The appeal for moderation to a person who believes that is a futile effort. I fear that we are developing, because of our inattentiveness to our profound social problems, a new generation of hostile and alienated youths that are going to be difficult to dislodge from their feelings of hatred, even when we do begin to act.

MR. WILKINS. That is right, Senator, and I might add that it is not only the youth that are being recruited to this point of view.

Today the New York Times had a story of a group of Negro elected school board officials from over the country who met with an official of the Department of Health, Education, and Welfare, to hear an all-day discussion on methods of what the Federal Department could do and what it couldn't do, and desegregation in schools, and improvement, quality, and so forth, and one of these men uttered perhaps the most tragic line we shall hear in this whole dialog. He said, "After listening to the Department spokesman, I now begin to understand a little bit of the phrase 'Burn, Baby, burn.'"

Now, for a man who is inclined toward the conservative, who believes in law and order, who thinks he can improve the school system, who has been elected to office, and who wants to carry out the oath of that office, for him to listen at the end of the day and come to the conclusion that the whole thing is so hopeless that he can understand anybody that wants to burn it down, this to me is a great tragedy of this whole farce that we are going through, this farce of ignoring the basic human desires of people. There has to be an element of sadness in this kind of development, and yet there is, I suppose, way down deep, an element of satisfaction—I don't want to call it pride—that others have come along who are not willing, not only not to use the channels established but not willing to listen to any of the palaver, so to speak, to the ritualistic reasons we give for failure to accomplish this. It is very sad.

We testify here today, sir, with the feeling that our appearance should not be necessary. The subject is one that could and should have been disposed of a year ago. For this bill in essence passed the House of Representatives last year as part of the proposed Civil Rights Act of 1966 and would have passed the Senate if it had been allowed to come to a vote. But a determined minority . . . initiated a talkathon that blocked consideration of fair housing on its merits.

SENATOR MONDALE. Why have we been so slow in this area?

MR. WILKINS. Senator, I have a theory which many of my associates are persuading me that is a little outdated and out, but I still think it has a little validity, that is, that housing enters into an area of emotion, family, home, mother, children. It represents—the purchase of a home, for example, perhaps the biggest investment a man will make in his life, the average man. If he spends $30,000 for a house, he will buy no bigger purchase than that in his lifetime. He wants it to be a home in a nice neighborhood where his children can grow up, where his neighbors, as much as he can control the situation, his neighbors will be the kind of people he wants to associate with, a neighborhood where his business will not be ashamed of its address, a neighborhood where his wife can go to her church or her club, and say I live on such and such a street or boulevard or avenue, and her associates will not turn up their noses. And a place where their children can play with other children, separating bad from the good, and it has been an axiom in American life that having Negroes in the neighborhood downgrades the neighborhood, hurts the investment, and derogates the importance and standing of your family and its association and political and economic standing.

Now I don't admit this, of course, but I only say it is there, and assisting this has been the—I say this with deliberation, the machinations of the organized real estate industry. They have encouraged this idea. It has meant money to them. They have been able to collect a bonus for all white neighborhoods or for a policy that guarantees that the Negroes will not move in here. As one man said to me this morning, "In our town," he said, "you could substitute Italian for Negro." He said, "We have a guarantee that the Italians will not move on this street rather than the Negroes."

So that all of these reasons they make sense for us having made such slow progress in this area.

SENATOR MONDALE. Could it also be that some of the earlier areas of injustice that we have acted on, such as voting rights, or discrimination in transportation, or public accommodations, have been largely confined to the South. They were residual problems in the North, and now for the first time we are coming to grips in a long overdue fashion with a problem that is found in virtually every large community in the country. It is not a southern problem alone, it is an American problem, and thus if nothing else the political burden is heavier than we had to bear in the early efforts.

MR. WILKINS. That is true, of course. It must be remembered that the northerns, the northern cities deliberately created the ghetto. They were the ones who met the influx of 1919, 1921, all the twenties, and all through the thirties, they met the Negro influx with a containment philosophy. They put them in the oldest sections of town, and drew a ring around the ghetto. The real estate dealers did it, and the banks, and mortgage and other lending institutions did it, and if you tried to borrow money to buy a home outside that district, you couldn't do it. And I might add, along came FHA [Federal Housing Administration] and for a 20-year period had a regulation that you could only move in—I forget their slick language, but what it meant was that a Negro could not buy in a neighborhood that was not compatible, or words to that effect.

SENATOR MONDALE. This Commission on Civil Rights testified today that up until 1947, the FHA required racial covenants to support a loan.

MR. WILKINS. This was a period before the so-called compatible neighborhood theory. It antedated that. It did actually require a covenant. It wasn't, of course, until 1949 that covenants were outlawed in the sense that it was ruled that courts no longer need enforce them.

Even in this period of activity, however, we got no housing legislation. We believe that sooner or later the country must come to grips with this problem, and the sooner the better....

We are pleased that the President again proposed a fair housing bill as a part of his program of civil rights legislation, despite the Senate's refusal to act on a similar bill last year. We are pleased too that he again suggested complete coverage of the housing market. For once the determination is made that discrimination in housing is a national problem and a national scandal—which it is—Congress should exert its full powers to prevent its continuance.

Exemption of any part of the housing market will only establish pockets of bias. This will permit certain interests to continue to appeal to the prejudice and fears that they help stimulate. A prime example of this is the Washington area. The District of Columbia has a fair housing regulation of extensive coverage; Maryland has a new law of limited coverage; Virginia has nothing. District of Columbia residents, including Negroes living in integrated sections, constantly receive through the mail material promoting allegedly desirable developments limited to "Caucasians only."

We have hoped in 1948, with the Supreme Court's decision rendering the racial covenant unenforceable, that practices such as these would cease. But nearly 20 years later those who profit from prejudice and discrimination are

still operating openly and without apology. Until we can end these practices, until the Negro, Puerto Rican, Latin American and other ethnic groups have access to the whole housing market, they will continue to be second-class buyers and lessees.

This second-class status is imposed upon them at first-class prices. For it is an established fact that the ghetto dweller pays more for what he gets in housing than his counterpart in physically more desirable areas. A recent item in the New York Times told of housing in Watts assessed as high as $20,000. One explanation of these high valuations was that the real estate companies and developers "have the residents over a barrel when it comes to rentals and sales." The residents are well aware of this, which may explain to a large degree their frustration and anger that sometimes erupt into violence.

As more and more rural-based people are displaced by the technological revolution in agriculture and move to the cities, the problem of adequate housing becomes greater, especially for the Negro, who is confined to the center-city by white suburbia and its environs.

The segregated housing pattern in turn creates or amplifies related problems. Thus we are being constantly reminded by various studies, both governmental and private, that school segregation is increasing both in the North and the South. In the North this is explained away by State and local officials as de facto segregation resulting from residential segregation. But the effect on the student differs little, if any, from de jure segregation.

The South, while professing "freedom of choice" where it will perpetuate segregation, is also promoting de facto segregation in many urban areas by the skillful use of urban redevelopment and other governmentally assisted programs.

Employment opportunities are also limited by lack of equal housing opportunity. Jobs follow the flight of industry and business from the city. The suburbs are often far removed from the residences of Negroes, who are unable to live near places of potential employment.

I might add here the Weston, Ill., atom smasher is a prime example of this, where the $275 million atom smasher was located in a little town of 600 population of Negroes, and the nearest Negro living 30 or 45 miles away.

SENATOR MONDALE. They had a survey that was presented during that debate showing that if the Negro could obtain a job there, his average commuting distance would be 74 miles.

MR. WILKINS. This is right.

SENATOR MONDALE. Which obviously means he has to commute to and from the Chicago ghetto.

MR. WILKINS. That is right, Senator, and not long ago I was in Detroit, being driven out from the city by an automobile employee, from one of the automobile factories, and he said to me, "My factory has now moved 22 miles outside of Detroit." He said, "I am still working there because I have my seniority and everything, but I have 44 to 45 and 50 miles a day to commute, while the white boys are able to buy houses right there in the town and three or four blocks from the factory, and I have to drive 50 miles round trip."

SENATOR MONDALE. Surveys have indicated that one of the important contributing factors to the explosion in Watts was that the construction of freeways had managed to isolate this community from jobs. The only way a person could get a job was to find some kind of transportation to get him there. Public transportation system was not adequate, and they were really left where they had no money to buy a car. This contributes to the frustration.

MR. WILKINS. That is true.

SENATOR [JOHN] TOWER. Mr. Wilkins, is there evidence that there has been a conscious and witting effort on the part of some business concerns to locate their plants in areas where Negroes would be denied access to jobs by virtue of the distance?

MR. WILKINS. No; I don't think so, Senator, not with that motivation. I think businesses have moved their plants outside of big cities for a variety of reasons, with no special knowledge of whether Negroes would or would not be able to. The fact of the matter is, however, that when such a condition is called to the proper officials of the State, that is where it belongs, they have been indifferent to this development. The companies, in some areas, have made efforts to try to do something about it, and some of them in their surveys of suburban locations have inquired, as you well know, and you must have heard in this committee, about everything, about churches, the accessibility to schools, about this, and that, and even the golf courses, how close they are, and they must have asked also about the housing policies and whether Negroes would or would not be accommodated.

At the risk of taking your time for 2 more minutes, I go back to an old story during World War II, and in Kansas City, Mo., it was announced that the North American Aviation Co. was going to locate a plant there, and the Kansas City Star, the daily newspaper, always curious about how much payroll money is going to be added to the purchasing power of the city, and therefore to the advertising columns of the paper, inquired over the telephone of the president of the company about his employment policies as far as Negroes were concerned, and he said, "Well, we don't intend to hire them with anything except maintenance jobs and janitorial work, maybe a truck driver or two."

They said, Well, we have 40,000 Negroes in Kansas City and they need income. And he said, "Well they will have to make it as janitors and maintenance men." This was the interview which he retracted 2 years later by employing Negro sheet metal workers and other workers in his plant, but there was a little reverse. There was an opportunity for housing there in Kansas City. The paper was simply looking for employment, and I give his reply to indicate, sir, that where the company may not be consciously seeking a site where Negroes would be excluded, it might be because the company had such a policy of exclusion in the first place that it didn't feel that site selection was a necessary concomitant.

SENATOR TOWER. Thus, you don't care where plants are located so long as housing is available.

MR. WILKINS. Precisely. It doesn't matter to me if a plant is in New York City or White Plains, if Negroes can rent and live close by every other employer, all right.

SENATOR MONDALE. Don't you also think—this is getting away from fair housing a bit—that in the future, whether we pass the strongest fair housing bill possible or not, there will be a large residue of ghetto dwellers who are simply going to be unable to afford to follow a plant out into the suburbs and buy decent housing, and for whom employment should be found, if at all possible, in the ghetto?

MR. WILKINS. By all means. There will be these people who can't follow, whose children go to school here, and maybe whose job in the plant does not allow for commuting expenses, extraordinary commuting expenses, let's say, and the necessary wear and tear on family ties back and forth. There will be a percentage of people in the ghetto, or even in the center cities, if they are not exactly ghettoes, who will not be able to follow the plant outside, but I submit, perhaps as you have indicated, Senator, this is a little separate problem.

The problem is, as I think Senator Tower has indicated, whether access to housing at the site of the factory is open equally to whites as well as Negro, as I assume, is the burden of your concern here in this legislation.

SENATOR MONDALE. Right.

MR. WILKINS. Once entrenched in the suburbs, firms often expand employment by local recruitment, further limiting minority opportunity. A recent study reported in the Washington Post stated that in a relatively short period of time, thousands of jobs will be lost by the District of Columbia to surrounding areas because of the Washington beltway.

The crowding and increased deterioration of the inner cities foster new slums and slum conditions. These slums breed many hazards such as depressed health conditions and lack of adequate health facilities, juvenile delinquency, soaring crime rates, fire losses, and other evils, including one recently dramatized by congressional inaction—an abundance of disease-carrying rats.

These conditions increase the cost of municipal services while at the same time decreasing the tax base from which the cost of the services is raised. . . .

There are others who say that this whole issue of discrimination in the sale or leasing of residential property is a private matter that is no business of the Federal Government. Such a position ignores reality. Suburbia as it now exists would not be possible without Federal assistance. It was built with FHA- and VA[Veterans' Administration]-insured financing to a large extent. Construction of its public facilities were helped by Federal assistance. Its inhabitants commute to work over highways built with Federal funds and are treated in hospitals built under the Hill-Burton Act. Their children attend schools receiving benefits of Federal programs. Within the last several weeks we have received in our office copies of a catalog published by the Department of Housing and Urban Development, 700 pages long, listing grant programs available through the Federal Government.

Unfortunately this Federal assistance in the past was often not only not on a nondiscriminatory basis, but actually promoted segregation. Thus for a long time, FHA policy was to condition approval of loans on adherence to neighborhood racial patterns. Local public housing authorities have built segregated public housing projects with the advice and consent of Federal authorities, and so on.

In the light of this massive assistance through which the Federal Government makes life as it is lived possible in so many communities throughout the land, it is ridiculous to say that there is no national interest in seeing that the benefits flowing from the Federal dollar should be shared by all.

Federal programs do not only assist communities, they create the necessity for new ones. A prime example is what will happen in Weston, Ill., in a few years if the atom reactor is erected there. A whole new residential complex will be necessary to accommodate the employees of this project and their families. As you are aware, NAACP and the Leadership Conference objected to the location of this project at the Weston site because of lack of any guarantee that Negroes will be able to live there. We shall continue to fight against this project and against the location of any federally financed project where discrimination in housing is permitted. But we would sincerely hope that passage of S. 1358 would make such fights unnecessary in the future.

And Mr. Chairman, I would like to interpolate here that one reason for the importance of S. 1358 in such a circumstance as Weston is the fact that the Legislature of Illinois has steadfastly refused to enact a State fair housing law. So that this bill, if passed, would be the only protection of Negro workers who ought to get employment at the Weston atom reactor plant.

SENATOR MONDALE. This was a case where the Atomic Energy Commission, I think, acted with some commendable degree of interest when they suggested they would refuse to locate the plant in a community where there was not fair housing legislation, meaningful housing legislation. We applauded them for that, and then they apparently went back on that original position, and are now willing to build it.

As you say, adoption of S. 1358 would help solve this problem by giving us a Federal law, and we all hope we can pass it, but I think we also ought to, at the same time, make it clear that we hope Federal agencies will do more than they have been doing to use the powers that they have of whatever sort to prod and urge and move along the progress of human rights, such as the Defense Department is beginning to do now in its housing surrounding Federal establishment.

I think if each agency would catalog the benefits that would flow from them, and act creatively to see that these benefits flow fairly, that a good deal could be accomplished as well.

MR. WILKINS. It would, sir; a great deal. I think the Atomic Energy Commission acted upon the gentleman's assurance from the State of Illinois that it would enact a fair housing law, and of course Illinois reneged. They didn't enact it. Even after they got the atom smasher, which is $275 million and a $60 million a year maintenance cost, 2,000 employment, and all that payroll falling right into the laps of Illinois, they simply forgot all about their promise.

SENATOR MONDALE. I offer to settle that. Just tell them to erect it in Minnesota.

MR. WILKINS. I wish you had been successful, sir.

In the meantime we urge the executive branch of government to adopt a national policy, binding on all Federal agencies, that would require as a conditional precedent to the erection of any major facility, legally binding assurances that the community in which the project is located has housing available to all potential residents on a nondiscriminatory basis.

Perhaps the most shameful aspect of housing discrimination is the situation that confronts thousands of Negro servicemen who are being trained to defend their country and may even die for it and yet are denied the right to a decent place to live.

We have brought our protests to the Defense Department and it is gratifying to find Secretary Robert McNamara and his staff sympathetic to the problem. The Secretary has even taken a step toward doing something about it. He has or-

dered a survey of the situation and has already declared segregated housing off limits at about a half dozen bases in Maryland. While this is a beginning, it is no more than that. The Secretary has almost 300 bases under survey.

The Leadership Conference and its participating organizations have repeatedly urged the Department to extend the off-limits sanction against all housing that discriminates against servicemen. Obviously, the passage of S. 1358 would go far toward putting an end to this injustice by outlawing such discrimination everywhere.

But as you pointed out, Senator, the Defense Department is beginning to do something about it, although we point out while this is an excellent project, and has worked well in the areas where it has been tried, it ought to be extended throughout the United States.

I had, sir, the dubious pleasure of going to the State of Maine in the month of February. I don't know why anyone would pick out February to go to Maine, but I had to go there, and at Bangor they met me, and on the inquiry about what kind of problems you have here in Bangor, you couldn't have any problems except this below zero water and this 10 feet of snow, they said well, we do have a problem. At the Air Force base our men can't get housing.

Now, way up there in Maine, at Dow Air Force Base, Negro families of servicemen in the service of their country were not able to rent decent housing. One woman said, "The only place for my child to play is in the automobile tracks made from the curb to the garage, and I want a place"—another woman explained she didn't have up-to-date heating, and so on. So Maine, we customarily use Mississippi as a whipping boy, I do, but Maine we have.

SENATOR MONDALE. The Assistant Secretary of Defense, Mr. Morris, testified on their survey of housing integration policies. While these tend to be less encouraging in the South than in the North, the patterns aren't too encouraging in the North either. Nebraska is only 48 percent satisfactory. Maryland, up until the fair housing was 24 percent, the worst in the country. Illinois, 5 percent, and so on. I think this is one of the major aspects of this problem. It is no longer just a southern problem, it is a national problem, and you will find it almost anywhere, which is the reason for a national law.

SENATOR TOWER. I will hasten to concur with that.

SENATOR MONDALE. Those in the North have had a good time criticizing the South, but we have had it coming, too. We should have been working on this years and years ago. It is a disgrace, and maybe the invention is returning to plague the inventor, but thankfully it has. We are all guilty.

MR. WILKINS. Senator, your phrase recalls that of another distinguished southerner so characterized by others, Gov. James Burns, of South Carolina, who was asked in 1953 what was the reason for all the building of Negro schools. And weren't they trying to stave off a Supreme Court decision outlawing segregation? And he said, "Well," he said, "I will tell you, we are trying to do in 2 years what we should have been doing for the last 50 years." And of course what you have said just now, the Defense Department should have tackled this a long time ago. It is an absolute and utterly inexcusable disgrace that a man who puts himself in the uniform of his country and offers all he has, his life, in defense of his country, that he should not be able to find a decent home where he can live while he is in the service of his country.

It is bad enough after he gets out of that service but to say that while he has the uniform on his wife and children can't get a place to stay, and the Defense Department and his Government will not move to help him. I hope that S. 1358 will help to accelerate this move; so far it has done very well by Secretary McNamara.

The bill, as I have previously noted, would cover all aspects of housing sale, rental, financing, and would be applicable to the entire housing market, with a minor exception for religiously sponsored institutions. This full coverage is as it should be, and we support it wholeheartedly.

Another aspect of the bill, which is an improvement over the one introduced last year, is the provision for administrative enforcement. This has many advantages. It lifts the burden of enforcement from the aggrieved party, who often lacks the time and resources to protect his rights. It generally is less drawn out and less complicated than litigation. It provides expert treatment of complaints in assembling and assessing the facts and in fashioning remedies. By providing within the administrative procedures a requirement for conciliation, it affords an opportunity for the parties to reach together a reasonable settlement that might not be possible once adversary proceedings have begun.

Having noted these positive aspects of the bill, we would ask for one major revision—a return to immediate coverage upon passage of the bill—as was provided in the 1966 bill—rather than gradual implementation in three steps. We understand and sympathize with the President in his suggestion of the graduated approach. But we believe developments since the bill was introduced have created a crisis situation that demands immediate action.

I have previously said that we do not look to this bill to cure all the ills of the ghetto, even those associated with housing. Were it law today, millions of Negroes and other ghetto residents would be unable to move because of financial limitations and the lack of available housing to accommodate all who need it. But there is much more at stake here than immediate results. This bill raises the basic question of the good faith of America. Will it continue to allow second-class status to be imposed upon millions of its citizens by refusing to provide a legal means of escape from residential segregation? Or will it provide a method under the Constitution for those entrapped in the ghetto to move out when conditions make it possible and they desire to do so? The answer to these questions is for Congress to give, and which answers it gives can have much to do with shaping America's future.

We urge the passage of S. 1358 with an amendment putting total coverage in effect upon passage of the bill. . . .

PATTERNS AND PRACTICES OF DISCRIMINATION

Massachusetts Advisory Committee to the U.S. Commission on Civil Rights

Complaints filed with the Massachusetts Commission Against Discrimination, the files of the Fair Housing Federation, and the testimony given at the Open Meeting of the Advisory Committee clearly reveal the patterns of discrimination that have impeded integration and frustrated and humiliated Negroes in their attempts to find decent housing.

REAL ESTATE BROKERS, DEVELOPERS, LANDLORDS, AND HOME OWNERS

The techniques of discrimination employed by real estate brokers, developers, home owners, and landlords are varied, sometimes blunt, sometimes subtle.

OUTRIGHT REFUSAL

Negroes have been brusquely informed that they were unacceptable as tenants or clients solely because of their race. One Negro, relating his experience to the Advisory Committee, quoted a landlord as saying, "We have come to an agreement that we will not rent to Negroes on this street." In another case, which came before the Massachusetts Commission Against Discrimination, (hereinafter referred to as "MCAD") the Negro complainant was told that Negro tenants were unacceptable and then was abruptly invited to seek housing in Roxbury, i.e., in the "black boomerang" area.

Reprinted from *Report on Massachusetts: Housing in Boston*; Massachusetts Advisory Committee to the U.S. Commission on Civil Rights (Boston, Mass: December, 1963), pp. 20-26. Footnotes omitted.

CONVENIENT RENTALS AND SALES

Probably the excuse resorted to most often for refusing housing to Negroes is that the house or apartment in question has been sold or rented. Thus when a Negro applicant met the owner at the appointed apartment, she was told that all the apartments had been rented; this statement was later shown to be untrue. Mrs. Gerald McLeod, testifying before the Advisory Committee, recounted one of her experiences as follows:

. . . I saw an advertisement in the newspaper and I called up [the real estate broker] and asked for more information about this particular house. It was not what we wanted . . . She assured me that she had a lot of houses to show us. We made an appointment to meet the next day. Then I thought that perhaps I should have told her at the beginning that we were Negroes and saved myself an embarrassing trip. I said [to myself], I will call back and explain that I am a Negro. When I called back I didn't talk to the real estate agent. I spoke to the secretary. She was very upset about this and said that she would call back. She did call back in a short time and said that she was very sorry but that the houses that she was going to show me were suddenly not available; *that either they had been taken off the market or they were sold.*

THE OSTENSIBLY NONDISCRIMINATORY REJECTION

A more refined method of discriminating is the attempt by landlords and owners to raise an ostensibly nondiscriminatory objection to the acceptance of an otherwise qualified Negro applicant. A case which came before the MCAD in 1961 is illustrative.

A "tester" first inquired about the 6-room apartment in question and was told that children were acceptable. When the Negro complainant applied for the apartment, however, the landlord said the first floor tenants would object to children. When the first floor tenants said they did not object, the landlord stated the third floor tenants would object. When the third floor tenants stated they did not object, the landlord said that she objected to children, assertedly because children were destructive and the apartment had recently been renovated.

In another case of the same type, the landlord, having asked the Negro applicant the size of his family and his financial condition, informed him that his family was too large for the apartment and that his income was insufficient. Yet, the following day, a white member of CORE, using the same family circumstances, applied for the apartment and it was offered to him. He was not asked about his salary.

DELAYING AND DISCOURAGING AN APPLICANT

Sometimes, instead of rejecting a Negro's application outright, there will be attempts to dissuade and discourage the applicant by stalling or avoiding him, by delaying the processing of his application or by showing him undesirable homes. Testimony concerning these attempts was contained in statements submitted to the Advisory Committee, such as "then [the] delaying tactics began"; "we were shown two very rundown houses"; we were told "we would not be happy out there." Mrs. Merlin Reid described her experiences as follows:

The first agency we approached was a very large concern. We were asked what price range we were interested in, and were then shown the catalog of homes which were priced considerably beyond our reach. After having graciously shown us the catalog and giving us some mortgage information, the agent then said, "Now your trip wasn't a total waste, was it?" We then completed our business and said that we hoped to hear from him soon. We never heard from him again.

We then approached another agent, in the same town, in reference to houses advertised in the daily newspapers. We were politely shown those houses which were in poor condition, or by some coincidence were already sold. The agent said that we could

expect to hear from him soon. We never did. These same events took place at three or four agencies, and we soon began to become discouraged.

We finally decided to try another town. The agents, it seemed, were waiting for us at the door. We received the same polite treatment and we departed with the same feeling of degradation and loss.

Sometimes it becomes difficult to locate the people who have the authority to rent or sell, or appointments are not kept and promised phone calls are not made, or a prolonged credit check is required. In one case a broker couldn't find time to accept a deposit check!

THE NEIGHBORS

Some brokers, developers, landlords, and owners, while admitting their disinterest in the Negro home seeker, disclaim responsibility for the situation. Brokers contend they are merely obeying their principals' orders; landlords foresee an exodus by their present tenants; owners and developers succumb to the objections of neighbors. As one witness described her experiences, "Regardless of the fact that my husband is a physician, it simply did not matter. Most of the people used the excuse that 'We are afraid of what our neighbors would think.'" After having found an agreeable owner and real estate agent and after putting down a deposit, another Negro buyer failed to secure the house, because "then the neighbors began to threaten both the owner and the agent. Almost immediately our check was returned and another of our dreams shattered." In the words of another Negro homeseeker:

. . . She [the owner] told us that no one else seemed interested in the house and, as far as she was concerned, we could buy it. Before we got home the lady called up and left word that the house had been sold. Later on we found out that the house had not actually been sold. A neighbor had seen us there and become upset and disturbed and she talked the owner out of selling the house to us. She actually had to leave town without selling the house because of the objection of the neighbors.

If the owner refuses to accede to the initial neighborhood pressure, he may be exposing himself to outright abuse, as Mr. and Mrs. Dover Wooten learned when they rented an apartment to a Negro family in a three-family dwelling adjacent to their home.

. . . The neighbors got a petition up and threatened the Wootens and their children with all sorts of abuse, for "degrading the neighborhood," and attempting to make a "ghetto" out of the street.

They had raw eggs thrown all over the front of their new house, along with many other unpleasant happenings. Several neighbors said that they would sell their property—and in course of time they did, but not before a "hate" campaign had been thoroughly indoctrinated [sic] in the neighborhood.

The Wooten incident also involves the problem of panic selling. After a few homes in an all-white area have been sold to Negroes, other residents may panic and sell their homes. Panic selling may be stimulated and intensified by "blockbusting." The "blockbuster," preying upon underlying racial prejudice, inspires panic sales by urging white residents to sell their property on the ground that it will drop in value because Negroes are moving into the area.

"Panic selling" and "blockbusting" sometimes have been forestalled by prompt countermeasures. In the spring of 1962 a home in a sizeable development (110 houses) in a Boston suburb was sold to a Negro family. Upset by this, a family living nearby quickly sold their home, through a realtor, to another Negro family. The second sale generated a significant amount of apprehension in the area. A white family directly across the street, contending that property values would drop, threatened to sell [its home] to another Negro family. At this point, the local Fair Housing Practices Committee sent a letter to all the homeowners in the development explaining the problem, pointing out the moral issues involved, and imparting information concerning property values. The Committee also arranged to meet with realtors to lay the groundwork for a cooperative effort to prevent panic selling to Negro families in the future. The panic lessened, and the realtors agreed to cooperate in the future by refraining from promoting the sale of additional houses in the area to Negroes.

MULTIPLE LISTING

Some real estate brokers in Boston participate in the Multiple Listing Service which provides widespread listings. It is directed by the Multi-

ple Listing Board, "a Board within the Boston Real Estate Board." Its operation can perhaps best be described by an example. If a homeowner in one of Boston's suburbs experiences difficulty disposing of his home, he may ask, or his real estate broker may suggest, that the home be listed with the Multiple Listing Service. The current listings of the Multiple Listing Service are periodically transmitted to member brokers in the area. Each member in the Greater Boston area may then attempt to sell that particular house to one of his clients. If a member broker sells the house, he divides his commission with the original broker.

One of the advantages of the Multiple Listing Service is that it would permit, for example, a Boston broker to sell his client's home in Boston and then sell his client a home in the suburbs— two sales instead of one.

Only members of the Multiple Listing Board may take advantage of this service. Samuel McCoy, a Negro real estate broker from Roxbury, testified before the Advisory Committee that his application for membership had been denied by the Multiple Listing Board. Mr. McCoy indicated that the ostensible reason for the denial was his inability to "reciprocate." (The reasoning appears to be that when brokers in certain locations cannot contribute listings of comparable value to the other brokers in the area, they should not be permitted to take advantage of the listings of such other brokers. The implication is that since a broker in the "black boomerang" area cannot provide listings of any value to, say, a . . . [surban] . . . realtor, he should not be allowed to benefit from the . . . [surburban] . . . realtor's listings.) Mr. McCoy expressed the opinion that "the reason there is such a concentration of Negroes within the 'black boomerang' area, as it was identified, is because no one is in a position to offer them the listings which are available in Multiple Listings."

ADDITIONAL READINGS FOR CHAPTER 5

Charles Abrams, *Forbidden Neighbors—A Study of Prejudice in Housing,* (New York: Harper & Row, Publishers, 1955).

———, "The Housing Problem and the Negro," in Talcott Parsons and Kenneth B. Clark (eds.), *The*

Negro American (Boston, Mass: Beacon Press, 1965) pp. 512-524.

Fred E. Case, *Minority Families in the Metropolis,* Research Report No. 8 (Los Angeles: Real Estate Research Program, Graduate School of Business Administration, University of California, Los Angeles, 1966).

Dennis Clark, *The Ghetto Game: Racial Conflicts in the City* (New York: Sheed and Ward, 1962).

John H. Denton (ed.), *Race and Poverty* (Berkeley, Calif.: Diablo Press, 1964).

——, *Apartheid American Style* (Berkeley, Calif.: Diablo Press, 1967).

Lynn W. Eley and Thomas W. Casstevens (eds.) *The Politics of Fair Housing Legislation* (San Francisco: Chandler Publishing Co., 1968).

Linton Freeman and Morris Sunshine, *Patterns of Residential Segregation* (Cambridge, Mass.: Schenkman Publishing Co., 1970).

Nathan Glazer and Davis McEntire (eds.) *Studies in Housing and Minority Groups* (Berkeley, Calif.: University of California Press, 1960).

George and Eunice Grier, *Equality and Beyond: Housing Segregation and the Goals of the Great Society* (Chicago: Quadrangle Books, 1966).

Morton Grodzins, *The Metropolitan Area as a Racial Problem* (Pittsburgh: University of Pittsburgh Press, 1958).

Rose Helper, *Racial Policies and Practices of Real Estate Brokers,* (Minneapolis: University of Minnesota Press, 1969).

Herbert Hill, "Demographic Change and Racial Ghettos: The Crisis of American Cities," *Journal of Urban Law,* V. 44 (Winter 1966), pp. 231-285.

John F. Kain and John R. Meyer, "Transportation and Poverty," *The Public Interest,* N. 18 (Winter 1970) pp. 75-87.

William M. Ladd, "The Effect of Integration on Property Values," *American Economic Review,* V. 52 (September 1962), pp. 801-808.

Luigi Laurenti, *Property Values and Race: Studies in Seven Cities* (Berkeley and Los Angeles: University of California Press, 1960).

Davis McEntire, *Residence and Race* (Berkeley: University of California Press, 1960).

J. R. Meyer, J. F. Kain, M. Wohl, *The Urban Transportation Problem* (Cambridge, Mass.: Harvard University Press, 1965), esp. pp. 144-167.

The National Commission on Urban Problems, Paul H. Douglas, Chairman, *Building the American City* (Washington, D.C.; U.S. Government Printing Office, 1969.)

The President's Commission on Urban Housing, Edgar F. Kaiser, Chairman, *A Decent Home* (Washington, D.C.: U.S. Government Printing Office, 1969).

Chester Rapkin, "Price Discrimination Against Negroes in the Rental Housing Market," in *Essays in Urban Land Economic* (Los Angeles: Real Estate Research Program, University of California, 1966).

Sandi Rosenbloom, "Taxis, Jitneys and Poverty," *Trans-action* V. 7, N. 4 (February 1970), pp. 47-54.

Morton J. Schussheim, "Housing in Perspective," *The Public Interest,* N. 19 (Spring 1970), pp. 18-30.

George Sternlieb, *The Tenement Landlord* (New Brunswick, New Jersey: Rutgers University Press, 1969).

Karl E. Taueber and Alma F. Taueber, *Negroes in Cities: Residential Segregation and Neighborhood Changes* (Chicago: Aldine Publishing Co., 1965).

United States Housing and Home Finance Agency, *Our Nonwhite Population and Its Housing: Changes Between 1950 and 1960,* (Washington, D.C.: U.S. Government Printing Office, July, 1963).

6 *Retail Merchandising*

R etail merchandising, like housing and employment markets, is an important and continuously functioning business institution linking black Americans to the white business community. Like other interfaces of the black community and the American economy, retail merchandising has not functioned equitably for the former. With regard to the availability, quantity, quality, and prices of goods and services, black consumers have generally been in a less favorable condition than their white counterparts. This condition of inequity is not a consequence simply of racial discrimination. For a variety of reasons—including taxes, pilferage, insurance (or lack of same), higher rentals, and the generally smaller size of ghetto enterprises—it frequently costs more to do business in the ghetto. Accordingly, it costs the consumer more to shop in the ghetto. There is little question, however, that in addition to these structural factors, outright discrimination has worsened the lot of the black consumer.

Coupled with the economic problems are the important social implications of white ownership. White-controlled retail stores stand in the ghetto, in the minds of blacks, as salient, concrete evidence of external controls. While in most communities members of the dominant ethnic group own the bulk of the retail businesses, in black neighborhoods, most businesses are controlled by whites. By way of example, in Harlem, a community which is 80% nonwhite, in mid-1960 nearly two-thirds of the commercial establishments were owned by whites. In Washington, D.C., where blacks comprise two-thirds of the total population, the percentage of black business ownership in late-1960 was less than 10 percent.[1] Because of the related factors of economic inequity and community hostility to these local representatives of white commercial control, white-owned retail stores have borne the brunt of physical damage and looting during recent civil disorders in urban ghettos.

The first selection in this chapter, "Exploitation of Disadvantaged Consumers by Retail Merchants," excerpted from the Kerner Commission Report, discusses the two-sided problem of the merchant-consumer relationship in the ghetto. There are differences in price and credit practices between white middle-income areas and black low-income areas. But these differences seem to have two origins: one, real extra costs-of-doing-business in the ghetto arising from factors mentioned above (and others), and two, exploitation by the merchant of the ghetto consumer's lack of alternatives and information.

"Consumer Problems: Shady Sales Practices," by sociologist David Caplovitz, documents the latter problem: the systematic duping of consumers through the use of deceptive selling techniques. An interesting, but unexplained, finding by Caplovitz, is that 68 percent of the black, and 65 percent of the Puerto Rican families examined in his study reported consumer problems with retail merchants. By way of comparison, only 42 percent (still a substantial amount) of the white respondents reported these difficulties. The selection from *Consumer Credit and the Poor*, a Hearing before the Subcommittee on Financial Institutions of the Committee on Banking and Currency, U.S. Senate, compares low-income market retail operations with general market retail practices. The study compares the use of installment credit, gross margins, prices, and profits for the two types of retailers and concludes that, to a large extent, the apparent price discrepancies between the two are a consequence of disparate costs. The final reading, excerpted from the summary of a Federal Trade Commission study, "Economic Report on Food Chain Selling Practices in the District of Columbia and San Francisco," compares the operation of the retail food distribution system in ghetto neighborhoods and suburban areas. It concludes that the system performs "less satisfactorily" in the former, although not as a result of deliberate discrimination.

The materials in this chapter cover a range of economic problems confronting black Americans and white ghetto merchants. Part of the resolution of social and economic inequity lies in having blacks assume the ownership and management of the businesses providing vital goods and services to the community. (See Chapters 8 and 12 for a discussion of black business.) The diseconomies inherent in operating retail businesses in low-income areas will require other, more dramatic solutions. For this aspect of the discussion, we refer the reader to a compilation of readings, Frederick D. Sturdivant (ed.), *The Ghetto Marketplace* (New York: The Free Press, 1969), which provides an excellent coverage of the subject.

NOTES

[1]See *Hearings* before the Select Community on Small Business, U.S. Senate, 90th Cong., 2nd Session, on *The Role of the Federal Government in the Development of Small Business Enterprises in the Urban Ghetto* (Newark, N.J.–May 24, 1968; New York, N.Y.–June 17, 1968) (Washington, D.C.: Government Printing Office, 1968), pp. 409-417; and Urban America Inc. and The Urban Coalition, *One Year Later: An Assessment of the Nation's Response to the Crisis Described by the National Advisory Commission on Civil Disorders* (Washington, D.C.: Urban America, Inc. and The Urban Coalition, 1969), pp. 17-19.

EXPLOITATION OF DISADVANTAGED CONSUMERS BY RETAIL MERCHANTS

National Advisory Commission on Civil Disorders

Much of the violence in recent disorders has been directed at stores and other commercial establishments in disadvantaged Negro areas. In some cases, rioters focused on stores operated by white merchants who, they apparently believed, had been charging exorbitant prices or selling inferior goods. Not all the violence against these stores can be attributed to "revenge" for such practices. Yet it is clear that many residents of disadvantaged Negro neighborhoods believe they suffer constant abuses by local merchants.

Significant grievances concerning unfair commercial practices affecting Negro consumers were found in 11 of the 20 cities studied by the Commission. The fact that most of the merchants who operate stores in almost every Negro area are white undoubtedly contributes to the conclusion among Negroes that they are exploited by white society.

It is difficult to assess the precise degree and extent of exploitation. No systematic and reliable survey comparing consumer pricing and credit practices in all-Negro and other neighborhoods has ever been conducted on a nationwide basis. Differences in prices and credit practices between white middle-income areas and Negro low-income areas to some extent reflect differences in the real costs of serving these two markets (such as differential losses from pilferage in supermarkets), but the exact extent of these differential real costs has never been estimated accurately. Finally, an examination of exploitative consumer practices must

Reprinted from *Reports of the National Advisory Commission on Civil Disorders* (Washington, D.C.: U.S. Government Printing Office, 1968), pp. 139-141.

consider the particular structure and functions of the low-income consumer durables market.

INSTALLMENT BUYING

This complex situation can best be understood by first considering certain basic facts: ● Various cultural factors generate constant pressure on low income families to buy many relatively expensive durable goods and display them in their homes. This pressure comes in part from continuous exposure to commercial advertising, especially on television. In January 1967, over 88 percent of all Negro households had TV sets. A 1961 study of 464 low-income families in New York City showed that 95 percent of these relatively poor families had TV sets.

● Many poor families have extremely low incomes, bad previous credit records, unstable sources of income, or other attributes which make it virtually impossible for them to buy merchandise from established large national or local retail firms. These families lack enough savings to pay cash, and they cannot meet the standard credit requirements of established general merchants because they are too likely to fall behind in their payments.

● Poor families in urban areas are far less mobile than others. A 1967 Chicago study of low-income Negro households indicated their low automobile ownership compelled them to patronize primarily local neighborhood merchants. These merchants typically provided smaller selection, poorer services, and higher prices than big national outlets. The 1961 New York study also indicated that families who shopped outside their own neighborhoods were far less likely to pay exorbitant prices.

• Most low-income families are uneducated concerning the nature of credit purchase contracts, the legal rights and obligations of both buyers and sellers, sources of advice for consumers who are having difficulties with merchants, and the operation of the courts concerned with these matters. In contrast, merchants engaged in selling goods to them are very well informed.

• In most states, the laws governing relations between consumers and merchants in effect offer protection only to informed, sophisticated parties with understanding of each other's rights and obligations. Consequently, these laws are little suited to protect the rights of most low-income consumers.

In this situation, exploitative practices flourish. Ghetto residents who want to buy relatively expensive goods cannot do so from standard retail outlets and are thus restricted to local stores. Forced to use credit, they have little understanding of the pitfalls of credit buying. But because they have unstable incomes and frequently fail to make payments, the cost to the merchants of serving them is significantly above that of serving middle-income consumers. Consequently, a special kind of merchant appears to sell them goods on terms designed to cover the high cost of doing business in ghetto neighborhoods.

Whether they actually gain higher profits, these merchants charge higher prices than those in other parts of the city to cover the greater credit risks and other higher operating costs inherent in neighborhood outlets. A recent study conducted by the Federal Trade Commission in Washington, D.C., illustrates this conclusion dramatically. The FTC identified a number of stores specializing in selling furniture and appliances to low-income households. About 92 percent of the sales of these stores were credit sales involving installment purchases, as compared to 27 percent of the sales in general retail outlets handling the same merchandise.

The median income annually of a sample of 486 customers of these stores was about $4,200, but one-third had annual incomes below $3,600, about 6 percent were receiving welfare payments, and another 76 percent were employed in the lowest paying occupations (service workers, operatives, laborers, and domestics)—as compared to 36 percent of the total labor force in Washington in those occupations.

Definitely catering to a low-income group, these stores charged significantly higher prices than general merchandise outlets in the Washington area. According to testimony by Paul Rand Dixon, Chairman of the FTC, an item selling wholesale at $100 would retail on the average for $165 in a general merchandise store, and for $250 in a low-income specialty store. Thus, the customers of these outlets were paying an average price premium of about 52 percent.

While higher prices are not necessarily exploitative in themselves, many merchants in ghetto neighborhoods take advantage of their superior knowledge of credit buying by engaging in various exploitative tactics—high-pressure salesmanship, bait advertising, misrepresentation of prices, substitution of used goods for promised new ones, failure to notify consumers of legal actions against them, refusal to repair or replace sub-standard goods, exorbitant prices or credit charges, and use of shoddy merchandise. Such tactics affect a great many low-income consumers. In the New York study, 60 percent of all households had suffered from consumer problems (some of which were purely their own fault), about 43 percent had experienced serious exploitation, and 20 percent had experienced repossession, garnishment, or threat of garnishment.

GARNISHMENT

Garnishment practices in many states allow creditors to deprive individuals of their wages through court action without hearing or trial. In about 20 states, the wages of an employee can be diverted to a creditor merely upon the latter's deposition, with no advance hearing where the employee can defend himself. He often receives no prior notice of such action and is usually unaware of the law's operation and too poor to hire legal defense. Moreover, consumers may find themselves still owing money on a sales contract even after the creditor has repossessed the goods. The New York study cited earlier in this chapter indicated that 20 percent of a sample of low-income families had been subject to legal action regarding consumer purchases. And the Federal Trade Commission study in Washington, D.C., showed that retailers specializing in credit sales of furniture and appliances to low-income consumers resorted to court action on the average for every $2,200 of sales. Since their average sale was for $207, this amounted to using the courts to collect from one of every 11 customers. In contrast, department stores in the same area used court action against approximately one of every 14,500 customers (assuming their sales also averaged $207 per customer).

VARIATIONS IN FOOD PRICES

Residents of low-income Negro neighborhoods frequently claim that they pay higher prices for food in local markets than wealthier white suburbanites and receive inferior quality meat and produce. Statistically reliable information comparing prices and quality in these two kinds of areas is generally unavailable. The U.S. Bureau of Labor Statistics, studying food prices in six cities in 1966, compared prices of a standard list of 18 items in low-income areas and higher-income areas in each city. In a total of 180 stores, including independent and chain stores, and for items of the same type sold in the same types of stores, there were no significant differences in prices between low-income and high-income areas. However, stores in low-income areas were more likely to be small independents (which had somewhat higher prices), to sell low-quality produce and meat at any given price, and to be patronized by people who typically bought smaller-sized packages which are more expensive per unit of measure. In other words, many low-income consumers in fact pay higher prices, although the situation varies greatly from place to place.

Although these findings must be considered inconclusive, there are significant reasons to believe that poor households generally pay higher prices for the food they buy and receive lower quality food. Low-income consumers buy more food at local groceries because they are less mobile. Prices in these small stores are significantly higher than in major supermarkets because they cannot achieve economies of scale, and because real operating costs are higher in low-income Negro areas than in outlying suburbs. For instance, inventory "shrinkage" from pilfering and other causes is normally under 2 percent of sales, but can run twice as much in high-crime areas. Managers seek to make up for these added costs by charging higher prices for good quality food, or by substituting lower grades.

These practices do not necessarily involve "exploitation," but they are often perceived as exploitative and unfair by those who are aware of the price and quality differences involved, but unaware of operating costs. In addition it is probable that genuinely exploitative pricing practices exist in some areas. In either case, differential food prices constitute another factor convincing urban Negroes in low-income neighborhoods that whites discriminate against them.

CONSUMER PROBLEMS: SHADY SALES PRACTICES

David Caplovitz

On several occasions during the interview, families were given the opportunity to report whatever consumer problems they may have had, and how they felt about certain purchases they had made. These materials tellingly portray the difficulties encountered by low-income consumers. The main task of this and the following chapters will be to describe and illustrate the various troubles these consumers have—the kinds of exploitative schemes they encounter and the strains they experience as a result of their credit obligations. As a prelude to this, we first present statistical data showing the frequency of these problems and the kinds of families who are apt to have them.

FREQUENCY OF CONSUMER COMPLAINTS AND DIFFICULTIES

In response to a question about whether they were ever cheated by a merchant, more than two in every five answered that they had been. Some complained about the poor quality of the merchandise or its high price without further elaboration. However, many—about a third of the entire sample—described in detail some incident in which they felt they had been cheated. In response to another question asking about difficulties with storekeepers, some 12 percent cited additional incidents.

Furniture purchased at the time of the move to public housing was a source of dissatisfaction for a number of families. About one in five

Reprinted from *The Poor Pay More: Consumer Practices of Low Income Families* by David Caplovitz (New York: The Free Press, 1963), pp. 137-154, by permission of the author and the publisher.

complained about the quality of the furniture they had bought.

Still another statistic bearing on the consumer complaints of these families concerns their opinion of their most recently purchased appliance. More than a third of the families had some regrets. Significantly, the most frequent complaint had to do with buying on credit. More than half of those who regretted the purchase said they would not buy it on credit if they had it to do over again. As this indicates, and as their reports will bear out, most of the consumer problems of these families stem from buying on credit. Either the families did not anticipate the difficulty of keeping up payments, or else they discovered that the merchandise sold under "easy-payment" plans was of extremely poor quality.

In view of the high level of credit buying among these families, we might expect that many have experienced the legal sanctions of repossession and garnishment. But, it will be remembered, the local merchants told us that they were reluctant to apply legal sanctions and did so only when more personal efforts at control had failed. The statistical data bear this out. Only twenty-seven families (6 percent of the sample) had something bought on credit repossessed. Somewhat more (8 percent) had been garnisheed. The use of persuasion and threats rather than legal controls is illustrated by the fact that another 10 percent had been threatened with garnishment although it was not actually carried out. In all, one in every five families had encountered the penalties of repossession, garnishment, and threat of garnishment.

The items dealing with cheating, complaints about purchases, and legal difficulties have been combined into a single tabulation of consumer problems and difficulties. The idea of "consumer problems," as summed up here, consists of two aspects: instances in which merchants failed to live up to their obligations and those in which consumers failed to live up to theirs. The former refers to high-pressure tactics, overcharging, fraud, and misrepresentation; the latter to the legal difficulties and threats resulting from missed payments.[1] The distribution of families according to this measure is shown in Table 1.

Forty percent of the 464 families did not report any difficulties as consumers. They were satisfied with their recent purchases, they did not feel that merchants had cheated them, and they never had goods repossessed nor were they ever garnisheed. Another 17 percent complained about the price or quality of some purchases without furnishing any details. These are rather ambiguous cases. Some in this group may have been merely voicing a general suspicion of merchants. Others may have experienced as much exploitation as those in the next group but were less articulate in communicating their problem. Because of this ambiguity we have not grouped them with the families who were more explicit in detailing their complaints of exploitation (almost a fourth of the sample). And finally, 20 percent had such severe difficulties that they encountered legal pressures. These were not only cases of consumers defaulting on payments; for as we shall see, many in this group were also exploited. If we make the conservative assumption that only the last two categories refer to serious consumer problems, we find that this description applies to more than two in every five families.

Table 1. *Distribution of Families According to Severity of Consumer Problems*

	Cases	Per Cent
No apparent difficulties	186	40
Complaint about price or quality only — no details	79	17
Accounts of exploitation not involving legal controls	105	23
Complications resulting in repossession, garnishment, or threat of garnishment	94	20
Totals	464	100

TROUBLE-PRONE CONSUMERS

Accounts of consumer difficulties were much more frequent among the families who had bought on credit. Only 34 percent of those who always paid cash for their major purchases had consumer complaints, compared with 70 percent of those who always or sometimes used credit. And of those who had bought from peddlers, 75 percent reported some consumer difficulty, compared with 44 percent of the families who never bought from them.

It is of course not surprising that the insolvent families reported such problems much more frequently than the others. This can be seen from Table 2. The third row shows that the solvent families were somewhat more successful in avoiding serious exploitation. The more significant pattern, however, appears in the fourth row. Insolvent families were much more prone than the others to troubles stemming from missed payments.

In view of these relationships, we already know a good deal about the families who had consumer problems. Like the credit users and the insolvent families, they tend to be young, large, and nonwhite. The relationship with age is particularly striking. Eighty-five percent of the youngest families reported consumer problems, compared with 37 percent of the oldest. Such troubles were reported by 68 percent of the Negroes, 65 percent of the Puerto Ricans, and 42 percent of the whites.

We now turn to a closer examination of the problems themselves. It should be kept in mind that the difficulties to be described were experienced by less than half of the families we interviewed. Moreover, we have deliberately selected the more detailed and complicated incidents for illustrative purposes.

TYPES OF EXPLOITATION

The numerous accounts of exploitation fall under several general headings. Some reveal the high-pressure sales techniques to which these families are subjected. Others relate to the misrepresentation of the price of goods. And still others refer to the substitution of inferior goods for those ordered. Included here are accounts of the sale of reconditioned goods as new.

Table 2. *Consumer Difficulties According to Family Solvency*

[In Per Cent]

Difficulties	Relatively Solvent	Somewhat Solvent	Relatively Insolvent
None	53	43	23
Price or quality complaints—			
no details	19	16	15
Accounts of exploitation	17	26	26
Legal complications	11	15	36
Total per cent	100	100	100
Total cases	(171)	(144)	(149)

The repetitiveness of the incidents is quite striking. Some families were victimized by unethical television repairmen, a few by the same company. Another group were victims of the pots-and-pans salesmen; encyclopedia salesmen show up in several of the accounts, as do the peddlers selling sink attachments.

As we shall see, the incidents touch upon a number of themes. These include the role of the mass media in setting off the chain of events with alluring ads; the anonymity of many of the credit transactions to the point where the consumer is not sure who the merchant is; the bewilderment of the consumer in the face of powerful forces brought into play by the merchant; and the hopelessness, frustration, and resignation of many in the face of exploitation.

BAIT ADVERTISING AND THE SWITCH SALE

A sizable number of the families had been victimized by "bait" advertising. Responding to advertisements for sewing machines, phonographs, washing machines, and other items offered at unusually low prices, they succumbed to the salesmen's "switch-sale" technique by buying a much more expensive model.

The technique is illustrated by the story of a 26-year-old Negro housewife:

I saw a TV ad for a $29 sewing machine, so I wrote to the company and they sent down a salesman who demonstrated it for me. It shook the whole house, but I wanted to buy it anyway. But he kept saying it would disturb all the neighbors by being so noisy, and *went out to the hall and brought in another model costing $185.* . . .

I actually had to pay $220. He promised if I paid within a certain amount of time I would get $35 back. *But since my husband was out of work, we couldn't pay within the time period,* so I didn't get the refund. . . . *I was taken in by the high-pressure sales talk.*

A middle-aged Puerto Rican husband was victimized by a variant of this racket. Instead of responding to an ad, he received a call from a salesman saying that his wife had won a sewing machine:

He brought the machine to the house. It was worth $25, and we ended up buying another one for $186. A friend of mine bought a similar machine maybe better than mine, for $90. *They tricked me into buying the machine for $186 on credit.*

In these cases, the reactions are much the same, the feeling of being tricked by a high-pressure salesman. In each instance, a purchase was made at a price higher than the anticipated one.

The "switch sale" is by no means limited to sewing machines. A 28-year-old Negro housewife told the following story about a phonograph sale:

I saw an advertisement in the paper *for a $49 Hi-Fi set.* The ad said: "Phone for free demonstration," so I did. The salesman came a few days later, bringing a set that was different from the one I saw advertised. I told him it wasn't the set I saw in the paper, but he said it was, so we hassled for a while. He kept high-pressuring me, saying he had one in the car he knew I would like. So finally, I told him to bring it up. He did, and played it for me.

I asked him to leave it so my husband could hear it, but he said "no." Then I asked him to come back later when my husband would be home and he said "no" again. Well, I decided to gamble and signed the papers. [Later they mailed a coupon book. The set came to $175.]

He asked me for a down-payment, so I gave him my old radio and got $10 off. *And right after that, my husband came in. He didn't want the set, but the salesman told him we couldn't return it.* Later my husband examined the set. The salesman had said it contained four woofers and two tweeters, but my husband found out they didn't exist. We called the store, but they said we couldn't change it, so we had to pay the full amount.

Once the set stopped working. We phoned the store and got free repairs. *But the second time the set broke down, we called the store and were told that the company no longer dealt in Hi-Fi sets, only in sewing machines.*

One law of the commercial jungle facing the low-income consumer is vividly dramatized in this irreversibility of the credit transaction. Tacit in all dealings with ethical merchants is the right to exchange merchandise if the customer is not satisfied. Not so in the low-income market. Once the signature is obtained on the contract, the sale is consummated. It should be noted that the husband returned in time to register his displeasure to the salesman. But the concept of the satisfied customer is foreign to such hit-and-run transactions. Even when the couple discovered that the phonograph did not measure up to the salesman's claims, they were still unable to exchange it. As we shall see, this is not an isolated occurrence. Other families also discovered that the principle of exchange does not apply to them. The "run-around" this couple received when seeking service is also fairly typical. The explanation given seems quite thin, and yet it was apparently enough to free the store from the complaining customer. The incident also illustrates the way "easy credit" breaks through traditional constraints upon consumption. However reluctant at first, this housewife was still able to indulge her impulse to buy without consulting her husband.

Bait advertising was reported by a 37-year-old Negro mother living on welfare. She had seen a newspaper ad, placed by a 125th Street furniture store, announcing the reupholstering of couches with good material for $49.95:

I phoned them and they sent out a salesman. I told him I saw the ad and wanted my couch covered for $49.95. I asked him to show me the material. He pulled out some patterns and looked at them and said, "These aren't so hot. I really want to give customers something they'll be satisfied with." Then

he flipped to the higher-priced patterns—*but I didn't know they were higher-priced then*. I picked out a pattern and asked him how much. He told me $149. *But I only had $49 in cash and wanted to pay only in cash, so I told him that this was too high. He praised the material so much, talking about its quality and durability, that I finally told him that if I could get an account I'd take it. He gave me a contract. I just took a quick look and signed it.* They sent for the couch and returned it two weeks later. The work on the seams of the pillows was awful. . . . Six months later, the wire in the spring popped out the side and the other side had a pointed end on it.

By now the elements of the process are familiar: the "bait ad," the high-pressure salesman, the purchase of a much more expensive item, and, as often happens, dissatisfaction with the merchandise. Of particular interest in this case is the fact that the woman had every intention of paying cash when she responded to the ad but was converted into a credit buyer in spite of her intent.

A 45-year-old white housewife reported the "switch sale" in connection with encyclopedias:

About four years ago I saw an encyclopedia advertised on TV. I called for a salesman and he showed me a set, but it wasn't worth the money. He then talked me into buying a more expensive set.

Like other victims of bait advertising, this woman encountered further difficulties. Although promised an annual yearbook for $3.00, she never received it or recovered her money.

The idea of the unusual bargain takes other forms besides bait advertising. Sometimes the consumer is "hooked" by the promise of free merchandise. A 30-year-old Puerto Rican husband told us that he had once received a phone call from someone who promised him a present:

The man brought a wastepaper basket as the present and he also had with him a vacuum cleaner which he demonstrated. *He talked me into buying the vacuum cleaner even though I thought the price was too high.* I felt "high-pressured."

Another variant of the "something for nothing" appeal is based on the principle of the "pyramid club." Consumers are promised a refund if they help the salesman find a certain number of customers. One instance, reported by an 18-year-old Negro housewife, involved the added inducement of an outright monetary gift:

My mother sent the vacuum cleaner salesman here. He said that he would give me $5 just to talk to me. Then he said that if I got him nine more sales I could have the vacuum cleaner free. I wasn't able to find any customers and I can't work the vacuum cleaner with all its attachments. I don't want it and I've stopped making the payments on it.

Here we see an example of the great disparity between the more traditional logic of these consumers and the law of installment buying. Whether or not the consumer wants the merchandise has no bearing on the merchant's right to payment once the contract is signed.

The "contest" theme is a popular one in the exploitation of consumers. A 32-year-old Negro housewife told us that she entered a contest by filling out a coupon in a Third Avenue store:

Later I was told I won first prize—$30 off on a set of silverware. A man came four different times with different silverware—some used, some with pieces missing. He told us to keep the set for the time being, and that he would return with the set we wanted. Before we ever received the set we ordered, they sent a final notice to pay or my husband's salary would be garnisheed. My husband told his boss who told him to take the silver back to the place and leave it. My husband did take it back, but the man refused to give him a receipt.

Another Negro housewife told of a puzzle contest tied in with the purchase of encyclopedias:

In different comic books my husband found puzzle contest ads. The prizes were for $10,000, $5,000, and $1,000, plus a lot of other prizes. Over a period of about two years, while he was solving different puzzles, he was required to buy a book a month for $1.98 each. My husband bought twenty of these books. After he got the whole set, he wrote to find out about his position in the puzzle contest. In return he received more puzzles to solve. This went on for some time. Then the firm stopped sending puzzles. And they never did answer any of his letters asking about the contest.

It is apparent that these schemes are able to work because of the naiveté of the consumers. This reader of comic books undoubtedly worked on the additional puzzles in good faith.

Some salesmen misrepresent themselves as officials of the Housing Authority. As we noted earlier, some families found themselves buying sink panels from men they thought were Housing-Authority employees. The 18-year-old housewife victimized by the vacuum-cleaner salesman was also a victim of this practice:

Soon after we moved in, a man came saying he was part of the housing management. He installed the cabinets under the kitchen and bathroom sink. Then he told me they cost $19. I thought he meant *both* cost $19, but I found out that they were $19 each. They're not worth it. But I didn't do anything about it.

Another woman, a 37-year-old Puerto Rican, signed a contract for a set of encyclopedias thinking that she was filling out Housing-Authority forms:

When I first moved, a man who said he was the manager asked me to sign some papers. *It turned out I signed for encyclopedias thinking I was signing some housing authority forms* as a new tenant. I went to the Legal Aid Society to complain. The case is still in court. My husband was threatened with a garnishee by the encyclopedia company. [*She said the company went out of business. The account has been taken over by KIP, Inc., and they are the firm suing the family for $96.*]

This incident points up more than the practices of unscrupulous salesmen. It also shows the complex web of business institutions involved in credit transactions which the traditional consumer finds so difficult to understand. As we shall see, other interviewees also had the notion that the firm they were dealing with had gone out of business and that some other party had taken over the account. More likely, the original firm sold the contract at a discount to a credit agency, a practice of which many low-income consumers are only dimly aware.

MISREPRESENTATION OF PRICES

The preceding incidents illustrate various schemes through which low-income families are pressured into buying. Other incidents exhibit another fairly common form of duplicity: the misrepresentation of price, particularly in credit transactions. Although the merchant is required by law in New York State to enter both the cash price and the finance charges on the installment contract, some circumvent this law either by not explaining the terms of the contract or by not sending the customer his copy of the contract until sometime after the sale is consummated. In several instances we found that the consumer did not learn the full cost of his merchandise until he received the payment coupons some time after the sale. This practice is illustrated by the following typical episodes:

[41-year-old Puerto Rican husband, welfare family] I was cheated on a TV set I bought. At first the price was supposed to be $220. After I signed the contract I found out that it was really $300. *But then it was too late.*

[34-year-old Puerto Rican housewife] I was told by the salesman that the credit price for the Hi-Fi set was $299. *When I got the payment book, I found out that I had to pay them $347.*

[28-year-old Negro housewife] I heard an ad on the radio about a special bargain on washing machines for only $100. After I ordered it and had it installed, I got a bill for $200. I said I wouldn't pay it and they took it away. *I paid a $50 down-payment, and they never gave it back to me. I'm just glad I did not have to pay the balance.*

In the last case, we see that the misleading price appeared in an ad. The consumer made the purchase over the telephone, and therefore the true cost was not revealed until after the installation. It should also be noted that the misleading advertisement led to the loss of a $50 down-payment. The vulnerable position of many low-income consumers is suggested by this woman's feeling of relief that she did not lose even more money.

The manner in which salesmen lie to families about the cost of goods is revealed by another incident involving a door-to-door salesman selling washing machines:

[Husband and wife, aged 33 and 27, Puerto Rican] A salesman came to the door about three months ago and showed us a pamphlet with pictures of washing machines. He said it would be simple to buy it on credit. We met him at the furniture company, *where he showed us the machine and said it would not cost more than $290. So we signed the papers and didn't have to pay any cash.* When the machine was installed it didn't work.

We called the store three times and were promised a mechanic, but he never came. *And we got a credit-payment book in the mail for $462.66,* saying we were supposed to pay $18 a month. [*They also received a sales slip, and on this bill there is a typed statement to the effect that a down-payment of $29.30 was made by Mr. R. Both Mr. and Mrs. R. deny any cash payments.*] A month later we got a statement saying that payments were overdue and we would have to pay 93 cents more. We don't want this machine and they're going to sue us.

In this incident the true price was almost 60 percent more than the one quoted by the salesman. Perhaps the mysterious down-payment credited to this family was made by the peddler-intermediary in order to reassure the merchant.

A number of families told us that peddlers frequently misrepresented the price of their merchandise, quoting lower prices initially and then demanding higher ones on later visits. Typical of these accounts is the story of a 36-year-old Puerto Rican mother on welfare:

In March, 1960 a peddler knocked at my door and *insisted so much that I said I'd take a lamp for $29.* I gave him a $3 deposit. When he came back with the account book the next week, *the price had gone up to $42.* I said I wouldn't pay it. *So he took away the lamp, but he never gave me back the $3.*

Again we see the loss of a down payment as the outcome of this practice.

In the following case, a peddler's effort to mislead the customer about the price of a wrist watch was less successful:

[26-year-old Negro husband] I bought a wrist watch from a salesman who came around to the place where I work. He said it cost $45. I signed a little slip of paper . . . didn't even read it. A few weeks later I got a payment book through the mail saying I owed $73, even though I had made a $15 down-payment. I sent the $30 I still owed with a letter explaining that that was all I owed on the $45 watch—not the $73 listed in the book. I never heard from them again. The watch was no good. It lasted only a few months. I had it fixed and it still didn't work right. After that, I never buy from those guys again.

The following incident reveals several forms of exploitation on the part of a furniture store dealing with a Puerto Rican woman who had just come to this country:

This happened when I came to this country eight years ago. I went to a furniture store. They were offering two tables as a gift for people who would buy furniture. *I bought $500 worth and two tables were given to me. When the bill came, it was from a finance company, not the store; and it was for $900, not the $500 price they told me at first.* I went to the store and they told me that I was paying a service charge, credit charge, transportation and so forth, *plus the cost of the two tables. I told them that they were a gift. They said they were worth $75 and the tables offered as a gift were another kind. I asked them to let me see them but they told me they ran out of them.* The Welfare took over here and told me not to pay them anything. They should contact the Welfare Office. I do not know what happened. The store never called me again. I guess the Welfare paid them.

Perhaps misrepresentation of cost to this degree no longer happens. Certainly this practice was made illegal by the passage of the "all goods bill" by the New York State legislature in 1957.[2] Yet merchants seem to have ways of getting around the law.

As several cases have shown, misrepresentation of price can lead to the loss of down-payments when the families refuse the merchandise. But this is not the only way in which consumers can lose money in the low-income market. In one incident, a young Puerto Rican couple lost what they had paid on their furniture when the store with which they were dealing sold out to another one:

My wife and I bought some furniture and for the first few months we paid our money to the store. Then the store sold out, so we had to start paying the second store. [The second store noted what they had already paid in their payment book, but it did not appear in the store's own records.] *The store told us they were going to take us to court if we didn't pay $150 more. But I'd rather pay the extra money than go to court and lose any days of work, because I just got my job and don't want to risk it.*

It is difficult to tell from this account whether the original furniture store did in fact go out of business or whether this transaction also involved the sale of the contract to a credit firm. The attitudes of this couple are not atypical. Fear of losing a job often lies behind the apparent apathy and resignation of these consumers when they encounter difficulties.

SUBSTITUTION OF GOODS

Not only are prices misrepresented in the low-income market, but so is quality. Some families were sold reconditioned merchandise that had been represented as new, and others received merchandise inferior to that ordered.

The sale of used merchandise as new is of course illegal. Yet, as we noted in . . . [an earlier chapter] . . ., some merchants hinted that their competitors engaged in this practice. The following reports indicate that this does indeed happen. A 36-year-old Puerto Rican mother on welfare gave this account:

I bought a TV set from a First Avenue store. *It was a used set which was sold as new.* After seven days it broke down. The store took it back and returned it in two weeks. It broke down again and they took it for thirty days. They brought it back and it broke down one week later. They took it away again and I *asked for a refund because there was a guarantee of ninety days which had not run out. But they wouldn't give me back my $100 or bring me another TV.* I went to the store several times but with no results.

A basic inequality in the merchant-consumer relationship is pointed up by this incident. When the low-income consumer fails to live up to his obligations of payment, the merchant is able to utilize the law to protect his rights. When the merchant fails to respect a guarantee, however, the consumer is more likely to lose his initial investment than to obtain justice. In part, this is due to his ignorance of the laws which protect him and the agencies which can help him. But this inequality also partly stems from the merchant's superior resources. He can turn the job of collecting over to lawyers, collection agencies, and the courts. The consumer, on the other hand, must invest his own time in at least initiating legal action, time which, as we have seen, he cannot easily take from his job.

In another incident the sale of a used TV set as new was confirmed by a repairman. A 39-year-old Puerto Rican mother living on welfare had this experience:

I got a new TV set and some beds for $452.67. The TV alone was $280. It broke down after two years, and I paid $30 for repairs. *The TV repairman said that the set was a reconditioned one in a new cabinet.*

The substitution of merchandise is illustrated by an incident told by a 26-year-old Negro husband:

We've spent more money repairing the TV than it cost. *The store sent a different one than we asked for and it didn't look new.* We complained to the store and they offered a trade for $25 on another one.

Another example of delivering the "wrong" item was provided by a 53-year-old white mother. In this case only a part of the equipment was delivered.

A peddler high-pressured my daughter into ordering a Hi-Fi from the catalogue he had. He then delivered a pick-up instead of a phonograph. He kept insisting that my daughter had marked a pick-up, and he wouldn't exchange it. [She has already paid $167 which is twice the current market price for this item.]

Substitution of merchandise frequently happens in furniture purchases. A 39-year-old Puerto Rican husband reported:

I ordered furniture in November, 1959. It was supposed to be delivered in December, but it didn't come until January, 1960. *Then they sent furniture that I hadn't selected. I tried to get the store to take it back but they wouldn't do it.* I had to keep the furniture. Then in February I got a letter from a credit corporation in Valley Stream, N.Y., saying that all payments had to be made to them and not to the store. *The store was closed.*

It should be noted that this man, like many others, interpreted the sale of his contract to mean that the store was no longer in business. This misunderstanding of the merchant's credit arrangements contributes to the consumer's belief that there is nothing he can do about his problem. In other words, the sale of contracts by the merchant results in absolving him of his responsibility toward the consumer even though under the law he is still responsible for the terms of the transaction.

A 29-year-old white housewife had a similar experience:

The bureau was supposed to be new. I raised hell with him. He gave me a different one from the one I saw in the store. *I went back the same day. But he wouldn't take a thing back.*

The delivery of goods inferior to those contracted for is illustrated by other incidents involving furniture:

[Young Puerto Rican couple] We were cheated on the bunk beds and youth bed we bought from a store on Third Avenue. We paid $200. *They offered spring mattresses, but they sent cotton mattresses. We complained, but the store insisted, and we had to accept their story.*

[34-year-old Puerto Rican housewife] I paid $44 for linoleum I bought from a peddler. *He showed me a sample, but the linoleum he brought was of a poorer quality.* I told him what I wanted, but he gave me something else. I complained, but he wouldn't do anything about it.

Some families were victims of the TV repair racket which received much publicity several years ago. Repairs made with used components involve extraordinary expenses as can be seen from the stories of two victims who happened to deal with the same company. A 42-year-old white housewife, who produced the bills for her repairs, gave this account:

We got a circular for TV repairs that was dropped in our mailbox. Since our TV set broke down about then, my husband phoned the TV repair service. The circular said that the first visit was free. The first time the repairman came he said a small tube had burned out, so he put in a new one and *charged for it*. We paid cash and were given a receipt with a 90-day guarantee on the tube. A few days later the set broke down again. We called the repair service again, and this time he said we needed a new picture tube. He put one in, but after a few days the new tube went dark. When the repairman came back the third time he took the chassis to the shop and left the picture tube on the floor. He brought the set back again, put in a new tube, and then we paid the second bill. The first bill was $32.58; the second was $54.81. The set worked for a few days and then it went dark again. We were so disgusted we called another man. *This one told us that it wasn't a new tube and it wasn't the RCA tube the bill said it was.* This man charged only $3.00 and told my husband to get in touch with the District Attorney's office. We went there but they told us that if the receipt didn't say it was a new tube, they couldn't help us.

A 40-year-old Puerto Rican mother living on welfare also dealt with this company and showed the interviewer her bills:

I received this circular and called the —— TV Repair Service. They picked up the set, fixed it, and charged $77.68. *They did not put in a new tube* and I had to have it repaired at another store for $60, at still another store for $40, at another for $18, and finally another man who charged $7. I spent $203 for repairs on my set. A loan from a finance company for the $78 repair came to $105. *The total cost to repair the TV was $230.*

It is difficult to believe that the repairs were made in as rapid succession as her story implies, but even if spread over several years, the costs are exceptionally high.

THE ANONYMITY OF CREDIT TRANSACTIONS

Several families responded to the question about cheating by describing pots-and-pans salesmen who sold them poor-quality merchandise at exorbitant prices. The details of these stories are similar. The salesman shows up either with the goods or with a catalogue. He stresses the unusually low payments, gets the housewife to sign a contract, extracts a small down-payment, and then disappears. Sometime later the family receives a payment book from a finance company and frequently learns only then that the set of pots and pans will cost as much as $60. What is striking about these accounts is the anonymity of the transaction. Several interviewees reported that they tried unsuccessfully to find out the name of the store from which they had bought the merchandise. The high-pressure techniques of these salesmen as well as the theme of anonymity are illustrated in this report by a 30-year-old Puerto Rican husband:

This happened about four or five days after we moved in. My wife was home and a man knocked at the door. He was selling pots and he pressured my wife to look at them. He said that they would cost only $5 a month and that he would leave her a piggy bank so she could save for other things. Then he told her to "sign here," and when all the payments were made she's get a present. He then asked her if he could just leave the pots for a second while he went downstairs. But since she was signed up he never came back. We got a coupon book and mailed $5 each month to a bank in New Jersey. . . . *I don't know the name of the store but I guess it's somewhere in Fenway, New Jersey. I have no records of it.*

[Another young Puerto Rican husband gave a similar account:] A salesman came around selling aluminum pots and pans. They're not worth a damn. I gave him a dollar down and then the bank sent me a book and I had to send in payments. *Some bank in New Jersey. I tried to find out the store's name, but I couldn't.* The set cost $60—$5 a month for twelve months.

These incidents illustrate the various ways in which merchants take advantage of low-income consumers. They show the high pressure tactics, the substitution of goods, the exorbitant prices and the shoddy merchandise that are commonplace in the low-income market. In the next chapter, we will consider one further consequence of this system; the pressures and legal entanglements that face the consumer when he fails to maintain payments.

NOTES

[1] These dimensions are not wholly independent of each other. As we shall see, some families stop payments when they discover they have been cheated.

[2] Among other provisions, this law places a limit on credit charges, requires that the cost of credit as well as the cash price be entered on the contract, and that a copy of the contract be given to the consumer at the time of the sale. Dr. Persia Campbell, State Consumer Counsel during Governor Harriman's administration, was largely responsible for drafting this widely hailed progressive measure. [Ed. note: Similar provisions are found in the federal "Truth-in-Lending" Act which went into effect in 1969.]

CONSUMER CREDIT AND THE POOR

Federal Trade Commission Staff

INSTALLMENT CREDIT AND THE LOW-INCOME MARKET RETAILER

INTRODUCTION

The Federal Trade Commission has undertaken a broad program to eliminate deception in the sale of goods and services through installment credit. Such deception can be a serious problem for consumers from all income groups. Abuses in the use of installment credit may fall most heavily, however, on the poor and disadvantaged. . . .

This study is intended to provide objective information about installment credit practices, good and bad, as they affect consumers in the District of Columbia. A specific purpose is to compare the practices of retailers of furniture and appliances who sell primarily to a low-income market with those who sell to a more general market.

It should be made clear that the study is limited in scope. It does not attempt to provide information about all aspects of the operations of low-income market retailers. . . .

TYPES OF RETAILERS AND MERCHANDISE INCLUDED IN THIS STUDY

All retailers in the District of Columbia with estimated sales of over $100,000 per year who sold furniture and appliances were surveyed by the Federal Trade Commission. . . .

The survey included 96 retailers with combined sales of $226 million. This approximates

Reprinted from *Consumer Credit and the Poor,* Hearing Before the Subcommittee on Financial Institutions of the Committee on Banking and Currency, U.S. Senate, 90th Congress, Second Session, April 19, 1968, pp. 43-63. Footnotes omitted.

85 percent of the 1963 Census total sales of appliance, furniture, and department store retailers in the District of Columbia. Sixty-five retailers with combined sales of $151 million reported that they regularly used installment sales contracts. The remaining stores used revolving credit plans, charge accounts, or sold their merchandise only for cash. Of the $75 million in sales by this group, three large department stores accounted for $54 million. These department stores sold furniture and appliances through revolving credit arrangements.

Although revolving credit is a significant element in the retail credit market, to simplify data collection and analysis this study focuses primarily on installment credit contracts. It is difficult to collect data on revolving credit because such accounts are usually continuing arrangements. Balances may be carried for years, with regular payments offset by periodic purchases. Also, a variety of goods in addition to furniture and appliances are financed by department stores under revolving credit arrangements. The exclusion of revolving credit greatly simplifies the analysis in this report and there is little reason to believe that it creates any substantial bias in the results.

Further tabulations included in this report are based on returns of retailers who used installment contracts. Appropriate mention will be made whenever applicable of the practices of other retailers not using such contracts.

The survey revealed considerable variation among stores with respect to the percentage of sales made on installment credit. Some discount appliance stores made very few sales on installment credit or none at all. At the other extreme, a number of retailers sold almost entirely on

Table 1. *Comparison of 1966 Sales of Survey Retailers with Sales Reported in 1963 Census of Business for the District of Columbia*

Type of retail store	U.S. Census total sales, 1963 ($000)	Survey retailers, 1966:					
		Number of retailers	Total sales, all retailers ($000)	Number of retailers	Total sales, retailers offering installment credit ($000)	Number of retailers	Total sales, retailers not offering installment credit[1] ($000)
Department stores (SIC 531)	$186,439	6	$144,864	3	$ 91,361	3	$53,500
Furniture and other home-furnishings stores (SIC 571)	50,442	59	51,255	38	33,929	21	17,326
Appliance stores (SIC 572,573)	29,912	31	29,693	24	25,677	7	4,016
Total	266,793	96	225,812	65	150,970	31	74,842

[1]Includes stores using revolving credit arrangements: 30 -, 60-, 90-day credit arrangements; and stores operating on a cash basis.

Source: FTC Survey; 1963 Census of Business, vol. III, pt. 2, pp. 110-5.

installment credit. In addition, other factors such as gross margins or "markups" varied widely among stores. To analyze differences in credit practices, retailers surveyed were classified in various groups.

One means of classification was by type of establishment, i.e., department store, appliance store, or furniture store. Type of store did not, however, appear to be the most crucial element in determining credit practices. A second method of classification was by income of customer, i.e., low-income market retailers versus general market retailers. Since direct data were not available on income of customers served by various stores, two criteria were used to identify retailers serving low-income customers: (1) location of store and (2) advertising practices. As a first approximation, retailers located in or adjacent to low-income residential areas were considered to serve low-income customers primarily. Identification of low-income residential areas was done on the basis of 1960 Census data. In general, it was relatively easy to identify whether or not stores were located in low-income areas.

The District of Columbia is characterized by a wide variation in family income. Additionally, there is a close relationship between geographic sections within the city and the income level. . . .

Low-income market retailers were, for the most part, located in what could be described as neighborhood shopping areas in or adjacent to low-income areas. A characteristic of low-income market stores is that they are unlikely to draw any substantial volume of business from the more affluent sections of the city or from the suburbs.

The classification of stores as low-income market retailers was established not only by location but also on the basis of advertising practices. It is possible that a store could be located in a low-income area yet sell to a more general market through citywide advertising. Leading Washington newspapers and radio stations which appeal to all income levels, rather than specifically to low-income groups, were checked and no retailers engaged in extensive advertising to the general market were included in the low-income market group.

Thus, stores finally classified as low-income market retailers had to meet two qualifications: location in a low-income area and absence of significant citywide advertising directed to a general market. Eighteen retailers met these criteria. While classification of stores into the two groups, low-income market retailers and general market retailers, involved some arbitrary decisions, the basic differences between practices of the two groups are quite clearcut.

Of the 18 low-income market retailers, 14 could be described as furniture stores; 2 as appliance stores; and 2 as miscellaneous merchandise stores. These distinctions did not appear particularly important for purposes of analysis, however, and the low-income market retailers were treated as a combined group.

VARIATIONS IN INSTALLMENT CREDIT SALES

A striking characteristic of low-income market retailers is the high proportion of their total sales accounted for by installment contract transactions. Table 2 indicates that installment credit transactions accounted for 92.7 percent of the total sales of the 18 low-income market retailers. In contrast, installment credit accounted for only 26.5 percent of total sales of general market retailers. Most of the low-income market retailers made more than 90 percent of their sales through credit; none of the general market retailers had such a high proportion of installment credit sales. Many of the general market retailers in fact had the bulk of their sales accounted for by cash transactions or by noninstallment credit.

While extent of installment credit sales is the primary factor distinguishing low-income market retailers, there are also significant differences in the general business methods employed by this group. Prices and gross margins tend to be substantially higher for low-income market retailers. Bad-debt expenses are also considerably higher. Extensive use of credit together with higher prices and gross margins form a distinctive pattern for low-income market retailers. However, before discussing the findings concerning these differences, it is useful to place low-income market retailers in proper perspective with respect to the total market for appliances and home furnishings in the District of Columbia.

A PERSPECTIVE ON THE IMPORTANCE OF LOW-INCOME MARKET RETAILERS

The 18 low-income market retailers had net sales for 1966 of $7.9 million (table 2). This amounts to only 5.2 percent of sales of all retailers surveyed. Nevertheless, it is a substantial amount when compared to total expenditures by low-income consumers on furniture and appliances. Low-income consumers within the District of Columbia accounted for only a fraction of total expenditures on furniture and appliances. The low-income market for such goods is considerably smaller than the total consumer market. No statistics are available on total expenditures for furniture and appliances by low-income consumers, but it is possible to make reasonable estimates. We estimate that District of Columbia households with an annual income under $5,000 in 1966 had total income of about $260 million. Additionally, we estimate that in 1966 these households spent about $18 million on furniture and appliances....

Low-income market retailers surveyed had total sales in 1966 of $7.9 million, about 44 percent of our estimated total expenditures by low-income households for furniture and appliances. This suggests that the low-income market retailers surveyed are definitely an important factor in the low-income marketplace, even though they did not account for a major portion of total retail sales of furniture and appliances in the District.

GENERAL MARKET RETAILERS

Forty-seven of the stores surveyed were classified as general market retailers, appealing either

Table 2. *Value of Installment Contracts as a Percent of Sales, District of Columbia Retailers, 1966*

Type of retailer	Number of companies	Net sales ($000)	Installment contracts:		
			Value ($000)	Percent of total	As percent of net sales
Total	65	$150,970	$45,251	100.0	30.0
Low-income market retailers	18	7,874	7,296	16.1	92.7
General market retailers	47	143,096	37,955	83.9	26.5
Appliance, radio, and television	22	25,089	8,466	18.7	33.7
Furniture and home-furnishings	22	26,643	10,608	23.5	39.8
Department stores	3	91,364	18,881	41.7	20.6

Source: FTC Survey.

to a broad consumer market or primarily to middle and high-income groups. General market retailers were further classified into the following subcategories: furniture stores, appliance stores, and department stores. This was necessary for comparative and analytical purposes because, unlike the relatively homogeneous low-income market retailers, there were some differences in pricing and credit policies of the various types of general market retailers.

Appliance, radio, and television. There are two types of merchandise that are customarily sold and serviced by appliance, radio, and television retailers—brown goods and white goods. Television sets, radios, and stereo-phonographs are electronic home entertainment merchandise, collectively referred to among retailers as "brown goods." Washing machines, dryers, refrigerators, and freezers are collectively called "white goods." Sewing machines and vacuum cleaners are other household appliances customarily sold by brown and white goods retailers. The general market classification of appliance, radio, and television retailers included 22 companies operating stores primarily selling these types of merchandise. These retailers sometimes sell furniture and floor coverings, but only as secondary merchandise lines. Discount stores and full-service retailers are included in this retailer classification.

Furniture and home furnishings. Those retailers that specialize in the selling of furniture and home furnishings to a *broad* consumer market— a total of 22—have been grouped together for analysis. Retailers selling furniture primarily to low-income consumers are included in the low-income market retailer classification. Among furniture and home furnishings retailers are those that carry a wide line of furniture, as well as a secondary line of appliances, and those that specialize in particular home furnishings items, such as rugs and carpeting.

Department stores. The category of department stores, of which three included in this study sold goods on installment credit, includes large stores selling apparel in several merchandise departments, but also having departments engaged in selling furniture, home furnishings, appliances, radios, and television sets. Such stores are an important outlet for furniture and appliances. To qualify as a department store, a retail establishment must employ 25 people or more. Some smaller stores, classified in this study as low-income market retailers, also carry apparel and soft lines of home furnishings, as well as appliances and furniture. . . .

GROSS MARGINS, PRICES, AND PROFITS

In addition to obtaining information on the use of installment credit, the Commission survey requested financial statement data as well as wholesale and retail prices on popular appliance and furniture items. This information was classified by type of retailer and indicated that operating results for low-income market retailers differed significantly from general market retailers in a number of important respects.

GROSS MARGINS

Gross margins represent the difference between the wholesale cost of goods and total revenue derived from their sale at retail as a percent of selling price. Gross margin is the amount remaining to the retailer to cover operating expenses, including salaries, commissions, rent, equipment, other overhead expenses, and net profit.

Though gross margins for different types of retailers in the survey sample varied, the most significant variation was found when margins of low-income market retailers were compared with those of general market retailers (table 3). The 18 low-income market retailers had an average gross margin of 60.8 percent. The average for general market retailers was 37 percent, ranging from a low of 30 percent for appliance, radio, and TV stores to a high of 41 percent for furniture and home-furnishings stores.

Obviously, the higher the gross margin on a particular product, the higher will be its retail price. On the average, goods purchased for $100 at wholesale sold for $255 in low-income market stores, whereas the retail price was $159 in general market stores. . . . (These are cash prices and do not include separately imposed finance charges.) Thus, low-income market retailers marked up their cost 2½ times to determine

Table 3. *Net Sales and Gross Margins of District of Columbia Retailers, 1966*

Type of retailer	Number of companies	Net sales		Gross margin	
		Value ($000)	Percent of total	Value ($000)	As percent of sales
Low-income market retailers	18	$ 7,874	5.2	$ 4,790	60.8
General market retailers	47	143,096	94.8	52,988	37.0
Appliance, radio and television	22	25,089	16.6	7,586	30.2
Furniture and home-furnishings	22	26,643	17.7	10,979	41.2
Department Stores	3	91,364	60.5	34,423	37.7
Total, retailers using installment contracts. .	65	150,970	100.0	57.778	38.3
Retailers not using installment contracts . .	31	74,842		26,902	35.9
Total, all retailers surveyed	96	225,812		84,680	37.5

their selling price. This was the average for the market retailers in the sample. The retailer with the largest volume of sales in this group had a gross margin of 67.9 percent of selling price, which means that he marked up his merchandise on the average to more than three times its cost.

General market retailers that used no installment contracts were also contacted in the survey and their gross margins, as indicated in table 3, did not differ significantly from the average for general market retailers as a whole. One appliance, radio, and TV dealer, who sold on a strictly cash basis, reported a gross margin of 7.2 percent. This meant that any appliance selling at wholesale for $100 was resold at retail for only $107. This case is very exceptional, of course.

A number of substantial general market furniture stores reported that they relied on revolving credit accounts and used no installment contracts. The gross margins of these retailers were somewhat higher than those that used installment contracts, averaging 46.6 percent of sales. Likewise, there were three department store companies that reported no installment contract sales, employing instead revolving charge account plans. Their average gross margin of 34.9 percent of sales was somewhat lower than the average gross margin of 37.7 percent shown in table 3 for those department stores using installment contracts.

GROSS MARGINS ON SPECIFIC MERCHANDISE

Retailers surveyed were asked to select two "best-selling" items in each appliance and furniture line of merchandise and report their wholesale costs and selling prices. The difference between these figures (selling price minus cost of goods) represented the gross margin, which was expressed as a percent of selling price. Table 4 gives the average gross margins on each merchandise item for each type of retailer surveyed. In some instances the gross margins given were for items especially reduced in price for volume sales. Consequently, the averages of these gross margins are somewhat lower than the average gross margins shown for each type of retailer in table 3.

For every merchandise item specified, low-income market retailers had the highest average gross margins reported—ranging from 66.3 percent on sewing machines, to 51 percent on washing machines, and down to 46.4 percent on television sets. General market appliance retailers had the lowest gross margins for 9 of the 11 merchandise items.

Certain merchandise items showed some consistency as to the market level of gross margins. Television sets were sold by all three types of general market retailers at gross margins below 29 percent, and this item sold at the lowest (46.4 percent) average gross margin reported by low-income market retailers. Furniture had relatively high gross margins for all types of retailers. There were some items, however, on which there was no consistency between types of retailers. For instance, radios were the second highest gross margin item (60 percent) for low-income market retailers and the lowest gross margin item (23.4 percent) for general market appliance retailers. Thus, a consumer who would have paid $250 for a radio from a low-

Table 4. *Average Gross Margins of District of Columbia Retailers on Best-Selling Items of Appliances and Furniture, 1966*

Merchandise items	Average percent gross margin of:			
	Low-income market retailers	General market retailers		
		Appliance stores	Furniture stores	Department stores
Television sets	46.4	23.7	28.4	25.2
Carpets	50.0	....	37.5	33.2
Refrigerators	50.6	24.5	24.9	34.6
Washing machines	51.0	25.0	32.3	35.3
Stereo-phonographs	52.7	33.0	36.5	34.7
Freezers	53.7	24.8		33.7
Dryers	53.9	25.7	28.4	37.7
Furniture	56.2	....	47.5	50.4
Vacuum cleaners	57.9	26.3	30.2	36.4
Radios	60.0	23.4	38.0	27.9
Sewing machines	66.3	49.0		42.7

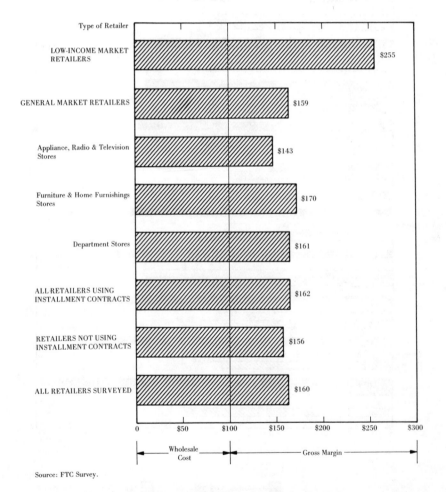

Source: FTC Survey.

Figure 1. Average Selling Price, Assuming $100 Wholesale Cost, by Type of Retailer.

income market retailer could have purchased a radio of comparable wholesale value at a general market appliance store for $130.

Table 5 converts these gross margins to a

comparative price basis. Since the cost of the merchandise has been arbitrarily held constant, the "retail prices" shown in table 5 directly reflect absolute differences in average gross margins by the type of store and make it possible to compare relative prices on each best-selling item when purchased from low-income market retailers of general market appliance, furniture or department store retailers. As shown in table 5 and figure 2, a television set that cost retailers $100 could have been bought for $131 in a general market appliance store, but would have been priced at retail to the low-income consumer at $187 by the average low-income market retailer. A washing machine with the same wholesale cost sold on the average in general market appliance stores for $133, in furniture stores for $148, in department stores for $155, and in low-income market stores for $204. The other merchandise items in table 5

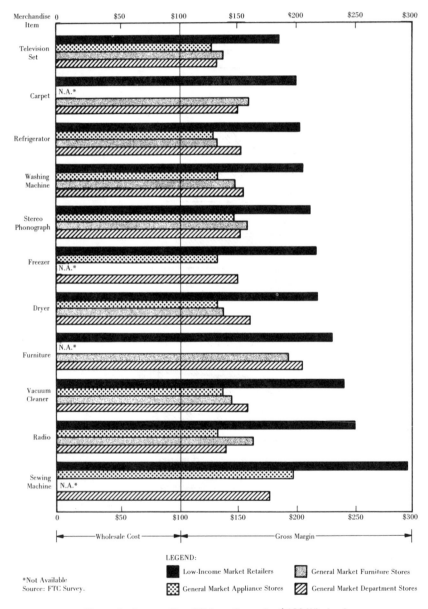

Figure 2. Average Retail Prices, Assuming $100 Wholesale Cost, of Comparable Merchandise Items Purchased From Low-Income Market and General Market Retailers.

Table 5. *Average "Retail Prices" of District of Columbia Retailers on Best-Selling Items of Appliances and Furniture in 1966, Assuming Wholesale Cost of $100 for Each Item***

| | Average "retail price" assuming $100 wholesale cost of: | | | |
| | Low-income market retailers | General market retailers: | | |
Merchandise item		Appliance stores	Furniture stores	Department stores
Television set	$187	$131	$140	$134
Carpet	200		160	150
Refrigerator	202	132	133	153
Washing machine	204	133	148	155
Stereo-phonograph	211	149	157	153
Freezer	216	133		151
Dryer	217	135	138	160
Furniture	228		190	202
Vacuum cleaner	237	136	143	157
Radio	250	130	161	139
Sewing machine	297	196		174

*These are cash prices and do not reflect separately imposed finance charges.

and figure 2 provide similar comparisons. In each instance the "retail price" projected for the low-income market retailers is the highest because reported average gross margins were highest, but the amount of the differential varies by merchandise items.

DIRECT PRICE COMPARISONS

Hypothetical price comparisons are useful for purposes of generalization, but we need not depend on just such comparisons. The striking differences between the low-income market and the general market perhaps may best be illustrated by a comparison of prices for similar (in some cases identical) products. Table 6 matches similar makes and models of appliances sold by low-income market retailers as well as general market retailers. Not all of the products shown are identical models, but the similarity in wholesale costs suggests that the comparisons are valid. It should be pointed out that in a great many cases low-income market retailers simply did not carry the same lines of products as general market retailers. As a result, in most instances price comparisons could not be made. While table 6 illustrates extreme differences, it should be remembered that the retailers themselves reported prices for their two *best-selling* models in each product category. These comparisons were not made by researchers poking around in dusty corners of stores looking for grossly overpriced or mismarked items rarely sold. They are based on the retailers' own reported prices.

The general conclusion that emerges from data contained in table 6 is that the low-income market is a very expensive place to buy durable goods. On television sets (most of which are the popular 19-inch black and white portables) the general market retailer price is about $130. In the low-income market a customer can pay up to $250 for similar sets. Other comparisons include a dryer selling for $149.95 from a general market retailer and for $299.95 from a low-income market retailer; and a vacuum cleaner selling for $59.95 in the general market and $79.95 in the low-income market.

These comparisons indicate that the poor often do pay more when they buy durable goods from retailers catering to the low-income market. Why would anyone pay such high prices? The most probable reason is that the poor often cannot pay cash for such items and are attracted by the more liberal credit policies. General market retailers offering low prices have tighter credit policies. Low-income market retailers, on the other hand, feature "easy credit," but the customer pays a great deal for this privilege in the form of grossly higher prices. Table 6 does not take into consideration the finance charges. (Finance charges refer to any extra charges imposed by the retailer when merchandise is sold under installment contract. These charges do not necessarily reflect the true cost to the retailer of granting credit.) As shown [earlier], finance charges of low-income market retailers are generally somewhat higher than those of general market retailers.

Table 6. *Comparison of Reported Wholesale and Retail Prices for Best-Selling Products, Low-Income Market and General Market Retailers*

Products	Wholesale cost		Retail price[1]	
	Low-income market retailer	General market retailer	Low-income market retailer	General market retailer
Television sets				
Motorola portable	$109.00	$109.50	$219.95	$129.95
Philco portable	108.75	106.32	199.95	129.95
Olympic portable	[2]90.00	85.00	249.95	129.95
Admiral portable	94.00	91.77	249.95	129.99
Radio: Emerson	16.50	16.74	39.95	25.00
Stereo: Zenith	32.99	32.99	99.95	36.99
Automatic washers:				
Norge	144.95	140.00	299.95	155.00
General Electric	183.50	160.40	339.95	219.95
Dryers:				
Norge	80.00	87.00	249.95	102.45
General Electric	206.90	205.00	369.95	237.76
Admiral	112.00	115.97	299.95	149.95
Vacuum cleaners:				
Hoover upright	39.95	39.95	79.95	59.95
Hoover canister	26.25	24.55	49.95	28.79

[1]Retail prices are cash and do not include separately imposed finance charges.
[2]Reported as approximate wholesale cost.

Source: FTC Survey.

Low-income market retailers often can recover the wholesale costs of merchandise when less than half the payments have been made. For example, suppose a customer buys the Motorola television listed in table 6 from a low-income market retailer. He pays $219.95 plus finance charges. Assume the customer pays one-tenth or $22 down. This leaves a balance of $197.95. At a 13.5 percent add-on rate, (equivalent to an effective annual rate of finance charges of 25 percent, calculated by the actuarial method—United States Rule), his finance charges would be $26.72 for 1 year. The total amount owed would be $197.95 + $26.72 or $224.67. If the customer makes 12 monthly payments, the amount of each payment would be $18.72.

In this circumstance, were the customer to default after making only 6 of his scheduled 12 payments, the low-income market retailer would already have recovered more than his wholesale cost. The six payments plus the original amount down equals $134.32—compared to the wholesale cost of $109 for the TV. Even if the low-income market retailer were to make no additional charges for financing, 6 months of payments would be more than sufficient to cover the original wholesale cost. (If no additional charges were made for financing, payments would be $16.50 per month. The six payments plus the original amount down equals $111— compared to the wholesale cost of $109.)

A general market retailer would be in a much different position if a customer defaulted after making only half his payments. Assume that he sold the same TV set for $129.95, also with one-tenth, or $13 down. Using the 12 percent add-on rate, (equivalent to an effective annual finance charge of 22 percent), the balance including finance charges would be $130.98. Monthly payments would be $10.92 for 12 months. If the customer defaulted after six payments, the general market retailer would have received only $78.52—compared to the wholesale cost of $109.50. Thus, he (or the finance company that held the contract) would suffer a substantial loss.

OPERATING EXPENSES AND NET PROFITS

Not all of the low-income market retailers covered in this survey maintained and submitted financial statements adequate for detailed analysis of expenses and net profit. Likewise, most of the small-volume general market retailers did not submit detailed financial statements. Of the 18 low-income market retailers, however, 10 submitted statements permitting some analysis of specific expense items. These 10 low-income market retailers were matched with 10 general market retailers of comparable size and mix of merchandise who submitted statements permitting a comparative analysis of expenses and profits.

A comparison of expenses and profits as a percent of sales for the matched samples of 10 low-income market retailers and 10 general market retailers of furniture and appliances is shown in table 7. The 10 low-income market retailers paid only 37.8 percent of their sales revenue for the merchandise they sold, while the cost of goods sold by the general market retailers was 64.5 percent of their sales revenue. As previously noted, low-income market retailers sell comparable merchandise at much higher retail prices, which accounts for this wide difference in cost of merchandise as a percentage of sales. The remaining gross margin for the 10 low-income market retailers was 62.2 percent and for the 10 general market retailers, 35.5 percent of sales. The gross margin to cover expenses and net profit was 26.7 percentage points higher for the low-income market retailers.

Practically all of the substantially higher gross margin of the 10 low-income market retailers was offset by higher expenses and did not result in markedly higher net profit as a percentage of sales. As shown in the right-hand columns of table 7, of the total difference in gross margin of 26.7 percentage points, 94 percent of the difference (25.1 percentage points) was accounted for by higher expenses and 6 percent of the difference (1.6 percentage points) was accounted for by higher net profits on sales of low-income market retailers.

More than one-third (38.9 percent) of the higher gross margin of the 10 low-income market retailers was spent on salary and commission expense. This expense item included all employees' compensation and officers' salaries and was 28.2 percent of sales for low-income market retailers, compared to 17.8 percent of sales for general market retailers. A major reason for low-income market retailers' higher personnel expense is believed to be their use of outside salesmen who canvass house-to-house or follow-up requests for home demonstrations and often make collections of installment payments at the home of the customer. Several of the 10 low-income market retailers pay their outside salesmen-collectors commissions on both sales and collections. Other reasons for higher personnel costs of low-income market retailers could be that they have more sales personnel and pay higher rates of compensation compared to small-volume general market retailers; and since they finance all or a larger proportion of their own installment contracts,

Table 7. *Comparison of Expenses and Profits as Percent of Sales for 10 Low-Income Market Retailers and 10 General Market Retailers of Furniture and Appliances in the District of Columbia, 1966*

Revenue component	10 low-income market retailers	10 general market retailers	Difference in margins and ratios	
			Percentage points	Percent of total
1966 net sales	$5,146,395	$5,405,221	....	
	Percent	Percent		
Operating ratios as percent of sales	100.0	100.0	....	
Cost of goods sold	37.8	64.5	....	
Gross profit margin	62.2	35.5	+26.7	100.0
Salary and commission expense[1]	28.2	17.8	+10.4	38.9
Advertising expense	2.1	3.9	-1.8	-3.7
Bad debt losses[2]	6.7	.3	+6.4	24.0
Other expenses[3]	21.3	11.2	+10.1	37.8
Total expenses	58.3	33.2	+25.1	94.0
Net profit return on sales	3.9	2.3	+1.6	6.0

[1]Includes officer's salaries.
[2]Includes amounts held back by finance companies to cover bad-debt losses.
[3]Other expenses, including taxes, after deduction of other income.

Source: FTC Survey.

they require more employees to keep records of small payments on installment credit accounts.

The proportion of sales revenue spent on advertising was higher for the 10 general market retailers than for the 10 low-income market retailers. This is consistent with the lack of extensive citywide advertising among the low-income market retailers in the total sample. The difference in advertising ratios was 1.8 percentage points. The 10 general market retailers spent 3.9 percent of their sales revenue on advertising, while the advertising by the 10 low-income market retailers amounted to 2.1 percent of their sales revenue.

Higher bad-debt losses of low-income market retailers accounted for about one-fourth (24 percent) of the total difference in gross margins. It was evident from analysis of financial statements, finance charges, and retail prices of low-income market retailers that they often charge higher prices anticipating that part of the increased revenue will cover higher collection expenses of their method of doing business. For the group of 10 low-income market retailers, bad-debt loss was 6.7 percent of sales, while comparable size general market retailers had bad-debt losses of less than 1 percent of sales.

Other expenses accounted for more than one-third (37.8 percent) of the higher gross margin of low-income market retailers. The remaining items of expense amounted to 21.3 percent of sales for the 10 low-income market retailers and to 11.2 percent of sales for the 10 general market retailers. Items of occupancy, delivery, and administrative expense were included among the other expenses, but a comparative analysis of these items could not be made because of inconsistency in expense account classifications and accounting methods. Nevertheless, there were certain items of expense that appeared more often and in larger proportionate amounts on the low-income market retailers' statements, which account for part of their higher ratio of other expenses to sales. Since most of the low-income market retailers financed their own installment sales, the expense of processing this credit and interest on borrowed funds appeared as substantial items on their statements. Legal and professional fees were larger items of expense among low-income market retailers, reflecting cost of suits filed for the collection of delinquent accounts. Insurance costs were generally higher as a percentage of sales for these retailers.

Net profit as a percentage of sales for the 10 low-income market retailers was 3.9 percent, as compared to 2.3 percent for the 10 general market retailers. This difference of 1.6 percentage points in higher net profit for the low-income market retailers amounted to less than one-tenth (6 percent) of the total difference in gross margins. The business methods employed by low-income market retailers involved substantially higher costs which offset the higher prices charged, leaving no markedly higher net profit as a percentage of sales.

Net profit after taxes as a percent of owner equity was also determined for these two groups of retailers. This average net profit was 12.7 percent for the 10 low-income market retailers and 8.1 percent for 9 out of the 10 general market retailers. The variation in rates of return on owner's equity within each group of retailers was so great as not to warrant a conclusion that rates for one group were different from those of the other.

OVERALL NET PROFIT COMPARISONS

The previous section compared profits for a selected sample of 10 low-income market and 10 general market retailers. Less extensive data on income and profits were obtained from other retailers. Almost half the retailers surveyed submitted profit and loss statements and balance sheets. The companies included corporations, partnerships, and proprietorships. There was a considerable amount of variation in the accounting methods used and in individual firm returns. Nevertheless, it is possible to make some overall comparisons of net profits for each group of retailers. Low income market retailers reported the highest net profit after taxes on net sales, 4.7 percent (table 8). Among the general market retailers, department stores were highest with 4.6 percent. Furniture and home-furnishings stores earned a net profit after taxes of 3.9 percent; and appliance, radio, and television retailers were last in order of profitability with 2.1 percent after taxes on sales.

Low-income market retailers reported an average rate of return after taxes on net worth of 10.1 percent. Rates of return on net worth

Table 8. *Net Profit After Taxes as a Percent of Sales and Rates of Return After Taxes for District of Columbia Retailers Surveyed, 1966*

Type of retailers	Net profit after taxes as a percent of sales	Percent rate of return after taxes on stockholders' equity
Low-income market retailers	4.7	10.1
General market retailers:		
Appliance, radio, and television stores	2.1	20.3
Furniture and home-furnishings stores	3.9	17.6
Department stores	4.6	13.0

Source: FTC Survey.

varied considerably among general market retailers. Appliance, radio, and television retailers reported the highest rate of return after taxes, 20.3 percent of net worth. Next in order were furniture and home-furnishings retailers with 17.6 percent, and department stores with 13 percent return on net worth.

Data on profits reported above are limited and to some extent inconclusive. It does not appear, however, that low-income market retailers made profits which were substantially higher on the average than general market retailers. The high prices charged by low-income market retailers must have been accompanied in many instances by substantially higher costs arising from their method of doing business. Some of these costs probably arose from greater losses on credit sales. To some extent, costs may have been higher because of smaller volume and generally more costly and less efficient store operation.

FOOD CHAIN SELLING PRACTICES IN THE DISTRICT OF COLUMBIA AND SAN FRANCISCO

Federal Trade Commission Staff

SUMMARY

This study confirms previous Government findings that the distribution system performs less satisfactorily in low-income areas of our inner cities than in suburban areas. Many foodstores serving low-income, inner-city areas are small, less efficient, and have higher prices. Consumers in these areas are frequently sold lower quality merchandise and are provided fewer services than in other areas. Moreover, the retail facilities of low-income areas are often old and in a shabby state of upkeep.

On the basis of special investigational surveys and hearings the staff found no evidence that leading chainstore operators in the District of Columbia and San Francisco employ discriminatory policies designed to exploit low-income customers. Each of the largest food chain operators had an official policy of price and quality uniformity. To a significant degree, systematic departures from store-to-store price uniformity were discovered. However, for the most part, these involved responses to special competitive situations and could not be interpreted as reflecting an effort to discriminate against low-income customers although that was generally the result.

These findings, however, should not lead one to conclude that food distribution in low-income areas is free of problems, or that the low-income customer does not pay more for food.

Reprinted from *Economic Report on Food Chain Selling Practices in the District of Columbia and San Francisco*, Staff Report to the Federal Trade Commission, (Washington, D.C.: U.S. Government Printing Office, July 9, 1969), pp. 3-9. Footnotes omitted.

On the contrary, the reverse is quite likely to be true. Food marketing is not as well organized in low-income areas as in newly developed suburban areas. There simply are not as many modern, efficient supermarkets in low-income areas as there are elsewhere. Thus, the low-income consumer is more likely to do his shopping at a small, independent mom-and-pop store. Such stores generally charge higher prices, whether located in low- or high-income areas. At the same time those supermarkets which are operating in low-income areas generally face less intense competition than they would elsewhere. The lack of competition means there is less pressure to maintain tight managerial control, to improve quality and service, or to lower prices.

Although departures from official company price lists are occasionally authorized to dispose of distressed perishable merchandise, differences in competitive conditions clearly outweigh this as a reason for deviations from official areawide prices. Deviations from areawide prices of chain organizations most frequently occur where stores of one chain meet those of other chains in strong "head-to-head" competition. In these areas special price reductions are frequently authorized, more concern is shown for the appearance of physical facilities and the quality of services provided, and there are more extensive promotional efforts, including the giving away of things of value, such as prizes in promotional games. In many instances authorized price reductions amount to several cents per dollar of total store sales. It is highly significant that not once during the period investigated in this study did a "special competitive situation" occur in an inner-city poverty area in either of the two cities studied.

The structural characteristic that is primarily responsible for ineffective competition in low-income inner-city areas is an inadequate number of supermarket competitors. To a great extent, the condition of entry into the low-income central city is related to entry conditions and the degree of competition in the metropolitan area as a whole. In these aspects of competitive structure there are important differences between the two cities studied—Washington, D.C., and San Francisco—that may in part explain the performance differences found between the two cities. Concentration of grocery store sales is very high in the Washington, D.C., metropolitan area—the highest of all major U.S. cities. The four largest chains in the Washington metropolitan area accounted for 67 percent of total grocery store sales. This percentage was half again higher than the average for other cities ranking among the 20 largest. San Francisco, on the other hand, ranked low in sales concentration among major cities. The four largest chains in the San Francisco metropolitan area accounted for only 33 percent of total grocery store sales. Concentration of supermarket sales in the inner city is much higher. In the District of Columbia, which is somewhat larger than the "inner city" of the metropolitan area, the four largest food chains accounted for 83 percent of supermarket sales.

Entry barriers into the Washington market also appear to be high. Within the last decade two chains have attempted to break into the Washington market. One of these has abandoned its attempt and the other has achieved only marginal success. The Kroger Co., the nation's third largest grocery chain, entered the market in 1960 with the purchase of a small local chain. After making a substantial effort to expand its market share, Kroger sold its Washington area stores in 1966 to another grocery chain operating in the area.

The second chain that attempted to enter was an aggressive low-margin food retailer from the New Jersey area, which had a history of successful entry into several markets before attempting to enter the Washington market. This chain came into the Washington market by opening three stores. It has since closed two of them. Just prior to this chain's entry into the Washington

market, the stores of two leading Washington area chains located near the stores of the new entrant cut their prices substantially below those charged in the rest of the metropolitan area. In doing so, these stores operated on abnormally low margins and—for those stores for which data were available—sustained substantial losses.

Special competitive pricing situations were not the only variations in food chain conduct due to competition. Pricing surveys conducted by the Federal Trade Commission staff revealed that food chain promotional activities also varied according to the competitive setting of the store. Specifically, advertised special items were more frequently unavailable in less competitive, low-income area stores than in more competitive, higher income area and suburban stores.

Prices of advertised special items present substantial savings to purchasers. Sales of advertised special items during a typical week commonly reduce the average price level of a store by 5 percent. Those customers that take full advantage of the specials can save 10 percent or more on their weekly food bills. The availability or unavailability of specials therefore is an important aspect of pricing conduct. Federal Trade Commission price surveys of stores of Washington area chains found that 23 percent of advertised special items were not available in low-income area stores as compared to only 11 percent not available in higher income area stores. In San Francisco the percentages were 7 and 5 percent, respectively. In addition to unavailability, advertised special items were also frequently found to be mispriced. For both cities, an average of 7 to 8 percent of advertised special items available in stores was found to be mispriced. There were three chances in four that the incorrect price was higher than the advertised price.

In addition to advertised specials, variations in many nonprice dimensions of chainstore conduct affecting the values received by customers were also related to competitive conditions. Although the FTC price surveys were primarily designed to record price and availability information, the checkers also observed various quality characteristics. An analysis of these reveals substantial differences in the appearance of perishable products such as produce and meat items packaged in the store.

The policy of the largest chain in the Washington, D.C., metropolitan area in distributing $1,000 winners of its games-of-chance promotion further illustrates the manner in which merchandising and promotion policies may be varied depending upon competitive conditions. During 1966, this chain awarded 48 $1,000 winners in the area served by its Washington division. Yet, whereas the central city represented by the District of Columbia contained 30 percent of the division's stores, only two of the 48 $1,000 winners were awarded at stores located in the District. Both prizes were awarded by stores in upper-income areas located at the far Northwest fringe of the District. The winners themselves lived in suburban Maryland. Available information indicates that the distribution of the balance of prize money—85 percent of the total—approximated the distribution of store locations. Some other leading chains in the Washington area also systematically allocated their major winners to certain stores; however, data were not available to determine how this allocation affected different areas.

During investigational hearings conducted over a 9-month period, the major food chains in the Washington, D.C., and San Francisco metropolitan areas explained their pricing systems and submitted various documents relevant to understanding them. Hundreds of pages of testimony were taken. Although some conflicting evidence was presented, none of the testimony indicated that any of the chains engaged in discrimination aimed specifically at low-income areas. The price and nonprice policies of chains appeared to be attuned to the competitive circumstances in which individual stores operated.

Finally, the evidence indicated that most chains had insufficient central office control over the operations of individual stores to prevent extensive mispricing of individual items. Price surveys indicated that between 5 and 10 percent of the prices found in the stores of a chain differed from those officially authorized by the chain for the dates of the surveys. For items not offered as "specials," there appeared to be a near equal likelihood that the unauthorized prices would be either high or low.

POLICY ALTERNATIVES

There are two general approaches to improving the quality of low-income area food retailing. One focuses on conduct, with a view to preventing excessive mispricing and unavailability of advertised items. The other focuses on changing the structure of the market to make it more competitive. Performance of low-income area supermarkets would likely improve if more supermarket competitors entered the low-income area market.

Before turning to policy alternatives, a word of caution should be raised concerning oversimplified solutions to complicated problems. A frequently proposed reform for lowering food costs to low-income area residents would require food chains to charge the same prices and provide the same product quality and arrays of services in their low-income area stores as in their suburban area stores. This is a simple approach, but like so many simple approaches it may overlook essential facts. The primary reason low-income inner-city residents pay more for food is that there are too few supermarkets in these areas. Most chains serving our major cities avoid operating in the low-income inner city and many chains that once operated in those areas withdrew to the suburbs as the inner city became a less desirable place to operate. Were it not for the few chain and independent supermarkets remaining in the low-income inner-city areas, food prices to the poor would be higher. Therefore ill-founded price regulations could hasten the day when many of the remaining supermarket companies will have abandoned the inner city. In situations where costs are higher in the inner city they must be covered. Short of a Government subsidy of some sort, such higher costs must ultimately be reflected in prices charged and services offered. This fact must be recognized in efforts to increase the availability of supermarkets in the inner city.

REGULATION OF CONDUCT

This study found that in a great many instances advertised items were out of stock or that prices had not been marked down in accordance with the advertisements. For all chainstores surveyed in Washington, 14 percent of items advertised were unavailable; in San Francisco, 6 percent of items advertised could not be found on the shelves. In both cities unavailability rates were substantially higher in low-income areas.

The use of advertised "specials" is a key element in the competitive strategy of supermarkets. While many consumers trade at the same supermarket week after week, others comparison shop or can be persuaded by lower advertised prices to switch their loyalties to another store in order to save money. Since consumers cannot make price comparisons for the thousands of items in a supermarket, their attention is most likely to be drawn by specials advertised in newspapers or featured through displays within the store. A study of food store pricing states:

There are a few items such as coffee, flour, sugar, soap powders, and the like which each store feels must be in a majority of its "ads," since consumers are generally well informed concerning their prices and some will transfer their patronage from one store to another if a substantial price difference on these items are noted.

While such items may be sold at or near cost, the store will profit if additional customers are attracted, as they usually will also buy many other items at regular prices. Even so, customers benefit substantially from low-priced specials. It has been estimated that consumers can save 10 percent or more on their total food bills by taking full advantage of such specials.

To the consumer who is drawn to a store by advertised specials, their unavailability represents both inconvenience and higher costs. Supermarkets, of course, will occasionally run out of an advertised item because of an unexpected heavy demand. However, if a retailer habitually advertises items when quantity is insufficient to meet demand, this constitutes a form of deceptive advertising.

The need for a seller to maintain adequate stocks of advertised items has previously been emphasized in the Federal Trade Commission's *Guides Against Bait Advertising*. These guides define bait advertising as "an alluring but insincere offer to sell a product or service which the advertiser in truth does not intend or want to sell. Its purpose is to switch consumers from buying the advertised merchandise, in order to sell something else, usually at a higher price." The offer that food chains make in their advertisements to sell at stated prices is, of course, not completely insincere, but will still tend to be misleading if adequate stocks of the advertised items are not maintained. Section 3(c) of the guides goes on to point out that one of the factors to be considered in determining if an advertisement is a bona fide offer is:

* * * the failure to have available at all outlets listed in the advertisement a sufficient quantity of the advertised product to meet reasonably anticipated demands, unless the advertisement clearly and adequately discloses that supply is limited and/or the merchandise is available only at designated outlets.

Section 5 of the Federal Trade Commission Act, in a broader sense, declares unlawful "unfair methods of competition in commerce, and unfair or deceptive acts or practices in commerce." The Commission can take a variety of steps to combat such practices, including issuance of further guides or the filing of complaints.

It would appear that the simplest and most effective remedy is for food chains themselves to make sure that adequate stocks of advertised items are available. Beyond this, policies can be adopted to deal with infrequent cases where items would be out of stock. At present, some chains have "raincheck" policies that permit the customer to obtain the advertised item for the same price at a later date if it is out of stock. These policies are not an adequate remedy. They impose no real penalty on the store and, thus, no incentive to maintain sufficient stocks. Since many customers will not bother to obtain "rainchecks," the store may still find it advantageous to run out of low-price special items. Also, there is no compensation to the customer for the inconvenience incurred. He may want or need an item now, rather than next week; or he may not want to take the time necessary to obtain a "raincheck." One possible alternative would be to offer the customer an item of like or higher quality if stocks of the advertised item are depleted. Thus, if a store is out of hamburger at a "special" price, it would provide the customer with ground round at the same price. Another alternative would be to permit the customer the same discount on another item if the advertised item is unavailable. Thus, if hamburger is reduced in price 10 percent per pound, the customer would be permitted at least a 10-percent reduction on a substitute cut of meat.

In addition to the maintenance of adequate stocks of advertised items, food chains should also conspicuously post prices of such items in all stores. The price of each advertised item should be clearly indicated on the item and at its position on the shelf. Shelf markers should remain in place during those infrequent instances when the store runs out of stock and a notice could be added indicating an item that could be purchased at the same or greater discount than the advertised item. A list of advertised items should be posted at all checkout counters and at other strategic spots throughout the store, such as near the meat counter and on bulletin boards. This will assist consumers in taking maximum advantage of advertised specials, without the necessity of referring to sometimes confusing newspaper advertisements.

Many of the problems of mispricing and unavailability of items appear to occur at the individual store level. There was a great deal of variation from store to store within a given chain, and generally those stores with the highest out-of-stock rates were located in low-income areas. Stores in these areas faced considerably less competition than those in higher income areas. The pressure of competition undoubtedly forces stores in higher income areas to keep advertised items available, because if customers became dissatisfied they would have the alternative of going to another store. In low-income areas the lack of competition allows store managers to become quite careless in maintaining stocks. If the customers are dissatisfied, there is little they can do, as they cannot conveniently shift their patronage to another store. Given this lack of competition, it is the responsibility of the chainstore management to exercise closer supervision over stores in low-income areas. The corporate management of food chains may find it necessary to adopt additional controls over low-income area stores, including more frequent price and inventory checks, stronger supervision at the district level, and changes in the manner in which store managers are assigned and compensated. At present, it appears that the least efficient managers often are assigned to low-income area stores. These managers may be tempted to cut corners to improve their stores' performance. It would be desirable to organize manager compensation plans so that better quality store managers would be attracted to low-income area stores.

Beyond the question of discrimination against low-income consumers, this study has found that several aspects of food chain behavior in general leave a great deal to be desired. In both low- and high-income areas, items on grocery shelves are mispriced or incorrectly marked far too often. Food chains claimed that a certain amount of mismarking is an inevitable result of human error. Mispricing rates found in our surveys, however, far exceeded those considered tolerable even by the management of some food chains. In both Washington, D.C., and San Francisco, 7 percent of the marketbasket items surveyed were mispriced. Several chains had 10 percent or more items mispriced. These error rates indicate a degree of carelessness and laxity which should not be tolerated in the supervision over prices. It is the responsibility of food chain management not just to issue general policy directives on pricing but also to see that these policies are implemented in full at the individual store level. Such errors in marking of prices add an element of confusion and make the task of intelligent choice more difficult for shoppers. As an additional means for reducing the frequency of deviations from authorized prices, food chain management might require each store manager to post a list of currently authorized prices at a convenient location in his store.

ADDITIONAL READINGS FOR CHAPTER 6

Marcus Alexis, Some Negro-White Differences in Consumption, *The American Journal of Economics and Sociology*, V. 21 (January 1962), pp. 11-28.

Alan B. Batchelder, *The Economics of Poverty* (New York: John Wiley & Sons, 1966).

Raymond A. Bauer, Scott M. Cunningham, and Lawrence H. Wortzel, "The Marketing Dilemma of Negroes," *Journal of Marketing*, V. 90, (July 1965), pp. 1-6.

—— and ——, "The Negro Market," *Journal of Advertising Research*, V. 10, N. 2 (April 1970), pp. 3-13.

Henry Allen Bullock, "Consumer Motivation in Black and White," *Harvard Business Review*, V. 39, N. 3 (May-June 1961), Part 1, pp. 89-104; N. 4 (July-August 1961), Part 2, pp. 110-123.

David Caplovitz, "The Other Side of the Poverty Problem," *Challenge Magazine*, V. 14, N. 1 (September-October 1965), pp. 12-15.

William E. Cox, *The Commercial Structure of Depressed Neighborhoods* (Cleveland, Ohio: Bureau of Business Research, Case Western Reserve University, 1968).

Donald F. Dixon and Daniel J. McLaughlin, Jr., "Do the Inner City Poor Pay More for Food?," *The Economic and Business Bulletin*, V. 20 (Spring 1968), pp. 6-12.

D. Parke Gibson, *The $30 Billion Negro* (New York: The Macmillan Company, 1969).

Phyllis Groom, "Prices in Poor Neighborhoods," *Monthly Labor Review*, V. 89, N. 10 (October 1966), pp. 1085-1090.

Robert J. Holloway and Richard N. Cardoza (with the assistance of Richard Allendorf, Robert Finke, and Stephen Margrett), *The Low Income Consumer: An Exploratory Study* (Minneapolis: School of Business Administration, University of Minnesota, February, 1969).

Lola M. Irelan (ed.) *Low Income Life Styles* (Washington, D.C.: U.S. Department of Health, Education and Welfare, Welfare Administration, Division of Research, publication #14, N.D., 1966).

President's Committee on Consumer Interest, *The Most for Their Money*, A Report of the Panel on Consumer Education for Persons with Limited Incomes (Washington D.C.: U.S. Government Printing Office, 1965).

Louis G. Richards, "Consumer Practices of the Poor," in Lola M. Irelan (ed.), *Low Income Life Styles* (Washington D.C.: U.S. Department of Health, Education and Welfare, Welfare Administration, Division of Research, publication #14, N.D., 1966), pp. 67-86.

Frederick D. Sturdivant (ed.), *The Ghetto Marketplace* (New York: The Free Press, 1969).

"Special Issue: Research on Negroes," *Journal of Advertising Research*, V. 10, N. 2 (April 1970).

U.S. Department of Agriculture, *Comparison of Prices Paid for Selected Foods in Chainstores in High and Low Income Areas of Six Cities* (Washington D.C.: U.S. Government Printing Office, June 1968).

U.S. Department of Labor (Bureau of Labor Statistics) *A Study of Prices Charged in Food Stores Located in Low and Higher Income Areas of Six Large Cities* (Washington D.C.: U.S. Government Printing Office, June 1968).

U.S. Department of Labor (Bureau of Labor Statistics), *A Study of Prices Charged in Food Stores Located in Low and High Income Areas of Six Large Cities for Non-Food Items* (Washington D.C.: U.S. Government Printing Office, February 1968).

U.S. Federal Trade Commission, *Economic Report on Installment Credit and Retail Sales Practices of District of Columbia Retailers* (Washington D.C.: U.S. Government Printing Office, March 1968).

It is a political truism that "money is the mother's milk of politics," referring to the critical importance of funds to the successful conduct of political campaigns. This maxim requires only slight change to reveal a like truth pertinent to the problems about ghetto business: credit is the mother's milk of business entrepreneurship.

Credit, needed by both the black businessman and the black consumer, does not flow through the ghetto to the extent that it does in other sectors of the economy. Bank loans, installment contract financing, construction mortgage moneys, insurance, and other sources of financial liquidity, leverage, and security are either unavailable, or available at greater cost to the ghetto enterprise and inhabitant than to his white counterpart.

A recent publication by the Federal Reserve Bank of San Francisco summarized the problems confronting various categories of ghetto credit seekers in the following terms:

> The difficulty which ghetto residents have experienced in obtaining credit from institutional lenders obviously reflects the low and unstable levels of their incomes, and thus the difficulty they encounter in repaying debts. And when high levels of debt interact with low (and unstable) levels of income, the risk of delinquency naturally increases. . . .
>
> Consumer lending in the ghetto involves high risks. From the lender's viewpoint, consumer loans are costly, partly because of their small size and partly because of the bank's heavy loan-loss experience with such loans. . . .
>
> For much the same reasons, ghetto residents have found it difficult to obtain mortgage loans to purchase homes. . . .
>
> [M]inority businessmen typically have found it difficult to obtain financing for new businesses from commercial lenders. The minority owned firm typically lacks sufficient collateral and sufficient experience in handling business loan applications, and, with all that, must deal with the difficult problem of operating in a small, uneconomic market. . . .
>
> The apparent outflow of capital from the central city may be explained by the opportunity which lenders have of making less risky and more profitable investments elsewhere. . . . (Verle Johnston, "Financing the Inner City," in Federal Reserve Bank of San Francisco, [*Monthly Review*] (October, 1969), p. 201.)

Thus, potential lenders do, indeed, face problems and risk in providing credit within the black (and other poverty) communities. An aggravating factor has been the inflationary pattern of the economy which has pushed interest rates ever upward to the highest levels in recent history. Accordingly, financial institutions have sought to maximize their investment income by making only high yield, high quality loans, which are rarely to be found in the ghetto.

The general unavailability of credit has had a stultifying effect upon the economic aspirations of the black community. Again, the pattern is circular. On the one hand, the dearth of credit is a consequence of the ghetto's inherent lack of a sound economic base; on the other hand, however, it reinforces and perpetuates the lack of economic vitality characteristic of most black communities. Additionally, the failure of established financial institutions to extend credit has often placed ghetto residents at the mercy of "loan sharks" and gougers.

To husband a business firm, the entrepreneur or manager needs a benign climate. In the first selection of this chapter, "The Present Condition of Banking in the Ghetto," Theodore L. Cross describes the credit environment of the black American as follows: "The Negro . . . operates in a credit-isolated economy. . . . There is no free market bargaining for a loan. The banker 'grants' a loan to a Negro businessman. The bank or insurance company 'pledges' loans for slum housing."

The second reading, "Characteristics of Installment Contract Arrangements," excerpted from a study by the Federal Trade Commission, provides a revealing look at the installment contract financing process which plays a prominent role in the retailing of appliances and furniture within the black community. According to the FTC study, in 1966, for nearly half of the retailers surveyed who were located in low-income (mainly black) areas, installment credit sales were at effective annual financing rates ranging from 26 to 33 percent. By way of comparison less than 1 percent of installment contracts entered into by "general market" retailers had finance charges exceeding 24 percent. The reader will better understand the origins of this disparity after he studies the comparative data on judgments, garnishments, and repossessions by low-income market and by general market retailers which are presented in the excerpt.

Another vital ingredient for the creation of a favorable economic climate for ghetto business enterprise is the availability of insurance protection against the risks normally attendant to conducting business anywhere: fire, property damage, public liability, and burglary. As a consequence of the generally deteriorated conditions of black communities and the greater frequency of civil disturbances (and resulting claims) during the past few years in the aftermath of Watts, Detroit, and Washington, D.C., insurance for property owners in ghettos often has become unavailable or prohibitively expensive. Entire areas of some of the largest cities in the nation have been "red-lined" (excluded) from insurance coverage. Similarly, insurance companies, an important source of mortgage capital, avoided investment in ghetto areas until a federally backed guaranty program made the risk somewhat more attractive. The final selection in this chapter, "The Insurance Problem: Basic Findings" is drawn from a report by a presidential panel convened to examine the insurance crisis in our cities.

The selections which follow present a picture of the problems confronted by the black community vis-à-vis the financial institutions whose operations are so critical to the American economy. Similarly, they offer some insight into the difficulties that lenders and insurers face in meeting the needs and expectations of an economically depressed segment of the population.

THE PRESENT CONDITION OF BANKING IN THE GHETTO

Theodore L. Cross

A Harlem civic leader used to say to his New York City radio audience: "I remember listening to a white bank president in Hartford who said in my presence that he had never known a Negro in whom he had confidence for more than a $300 loan. He's dead now; God rest his soul."

This statement cannot be dismissed as simply bigotry of a white banker. Today, three hundred dollars has much less value than when the statement was made; yet the Negro credit profile has not changed.[1] If you run a routine bank credit check on a ghetto borrower, you still find nothing—not bad credit, but simply no credit. Of the 23½ million Negroes and Puerto Ricans in the United States today, only a minuscule percentage can execute an unsecured note for three hundred dollars which is bankable at even an *interracial lending institution*. Moreover, when measured by credit risks in the "safe" economy downtown, there is virtually no interest rate high enough to compensate a lender for the average unsecured or commercial credit risk in the ghetto. The president of a large New York City life insurance company assigns a theoretical free market interest rate to a non FHA mortgage in the Bedford-Stuyvesant ghetto to be as high as 25 percent per year.

For bankers with a sincere desire to face up to the chronic dilemma which is seemingly as insuperable as the cycle of poverty itself, the plain and simple fact is that, even when patterns of discrimination and unequal opportunity are put aside, *the Negro businessman is not credit worthy because of the inherent weakness of his business and his production and marketing skills. At the same time, he is unable to establish a strong business tradition because of his inability to attract credit. Herein lies the cycle of total entrepreneurial failure.*

In the normal, free-market credit economy, every credit risk commands a compensating interest. The normal credit market is so fluid and so precise that the rate can be found in a banker's manual. For example, automobile purchase loans command a pegged rate of six percent in advance (about 12 percent per annum). This rate is generous enough to allow banks a profit—with good and bad credit risks averaging out. Banks have long ago learned: "You take 'em or you turn 'em down." There are no first, second, or third class private-citizen-borrowers. But the ghetto borrower is excluded from the credit man's actuarial calculations.

The Negro, moreover, operates in a credit-isolated economy. Loans are always impossibly expensive, but more importantly, funds are frozen and completely unresponsive to credit risk.

However unjust, the "color tax" on ghetto loans is only a symptom of a fundamental problem that goes beyond discrimination in lending institutions. Ghetto credit is isolated,[2] it is frozen, it does not flow, it does not respond in rate to individual differences of credit risk. The magic of credit liquidity is absolutely missing.

In the ghetto economy, there are no free credit markets. In the banker's lexicon, all loans and

Reprinted from *Financial Institutions and the Urban Crisis*, Hearings Before the Subcommittee on Financial Institutions of the Committee on Banking and Currency, U.S. Senate, 90th Congress, Second Session, on Private Investment in the Inner City, September 30 and October 1-4, 1968 (Washington, D.C., U.S. Government Printing Office, 1963) pp. 396-401.

credits are "soft." There is no free market bargaining for a loan. The banker "grants" a loan to a Negro businessman. The bank or insurance company "pledges" loans for slum housing.

Because the ghetto commercial loan is "soft" and does not originate from an arms-length bargaining credit transaction, a credit to a Hough businessman (without a Small Business Administration guarantee of repayment), or a conventional home mortgage in Bedford-Stuyvesant is basically unsaleable by the lender except at a sacrifice. The institution lending in the ghetto is "locked in" to its loans. This is true even if the borrower is sound and real estate collateral is good.

Credit is not exported to the ghetto because the ghetto borrower is inherently risky, unpredictable and unreliable. The downtown banker's aversion to getting stuck with a "soft loan" is reinforced when the aspiring Negro businessman enters a branch to apply for a business loan—in itself an unlikely act of bravery. Many of the most able and intelligent young men in the ghetto economy dress in the African style and have a "cool" manner of speech—an approach which is hardly likely to inspire the confidence of the lending officer. Moreover, the downtown banker often avoids taking the note of a Negro businessman, because the banker doesn't want the potentially bad publicity that may ensue "pulling the strings" on a minority borrower. A responsible banker today would no more foreclose on a struggling Negro entrepreneur than he would foreclose on the homestead of an impoverished widow, or on a church. National concern for the Negro's plight, and strong national commitments to equal rights and opportunities have therefore further restricted the flow of credit to the ghetto.

Political equality has actually aggravated the Negro's credit plight.

The flow of normal credit is further constrained by new credit risks born of rioting and curfews. All these new credit-freezing forces are superimposed upon historic and basic Negro credit weaknesses, fostered by unemployment, a welfare economy, the lack of Negro entrepreneurial experience and still persisting patterns of bank lending discrimination.

The weakness of credit in the ghetto is paralleled by heroic but almost hopeless efforts to establish indigenous locally-owned banks in the black slums. In the latter part of the nineteenth century, a vigorous Negro banking movement existed in this country. Following the Civil War, the black owned and controlled Freedmen's Banks were established to encourage thrift among newly emancipated slaves. At one time the Freedmen's Bank had thirty or more branches, with offices in Washington, Philadelphia and New York City, exclusively servicing Negro depositors and businessmen.

The Negro banks were particularly strong in the South where economic segregation gave them an umbrella of protection from the competition of white-owned banks. But, in the North, the Negro was always permitted to trade at white banks. Ironically, this competitive sharing of the Negro customer's deposit, loan and thrift business weakened Negro banks in Northern cities.

Most of these Negro banks failed along with thousands of the nation's banks in the panics and the depressions of the past 75 years. One contributing factor to their failure was the fact that they were not sustained by low cost commercial loan portfolios which are the backbone of American banking. The Negro economy of small shops, service establishments and funeral parlors did not require commercial credit. And when the great commercial banks moved into the field of retail and personal credit in the 1930's, they naturally avoided high-risk ghetto areas.

In the past there have been occasional experiments with so-called "interracial" banks. In 1928, John D. Rockefeller opened the interracial Dunbar National Bank at West 150th Street and Eighth Avenue in Harlem. While Rockefeller retained ownership, his objective was the operation of a bank that both employed Negroes and accepted their deposits. Two years later, *The Pittsburgh Courier* noted only Rockefeller's courage: "The only whites are the two executives, the President and cashier." The bank was liquidated in 1938.

Today the sources of Negro-operated and controlled bank credit is severely restricted. There are 49 Negro-owned and operated banks and savings and loan associations in the country. Their total assets are in the hundreds of millions of dollars, compared with $334 billions for all banks in the nation.

The strongest and most aggressive credit institution operating in the American ghetto today, an outstanding monument to black credit power, is Harlem's Freedom National Bank, with a branch in Brooklyn's Bedford-Stuyvesant which represents 20 percent of the bank's total business. Freedom National claims to have made more Small Business Administration insured loans to Negro businesses than any other bank in the country. A national television program, broadcast immediately following the assassination of Martin Luther King, Jr. in 1968, reported dozens of commercial loans made by Freedom National Bank to Negro hardware stores, druggists, and restaurants—all had previously been declined by the large metropolitan banks of New York City.

The American Bankers Association can take little comfort in the bold efforts of Freedom National Bank to move commercial business credit into the slum. There are three hundred banks in the United States with deposits exceeding 160 million dollars. Freedom National, the largest Negro-owned bank in the country, has deposits of only $30 million; it currently ranks 1,733. As F. Scott Fitzgerald once said: "Large banks are very different fromsmall banks . . . they have more money"; the money in the large banks is barely trickling into the slum economy.

Downtown banks labor under a special disability in the bad press they command in the slum areas. To a deep extent, Negroes are distrustful and suspicious of the money society.

My surveys indicate that only about ten percent of Puerto Rican-American businesses (usually food retail outlets—"bodegas") have a bank account; only five percent use any type of bank credit. A large number of them initially started in business with the financial help of loan sharks.

David Rockefeller, [former] President of the Chase Manhattan Bank, tells of the experience of one of his credit men who visited 300 retail establishments in Harlem to find out what additional business services the bank could supply to ghetto businesses: "Almost everywhere he went, he was viewed with suspicion and felt hard pressed to find ways of counteracting it. He took to keeping the flaps of his coat open to indicate that he was not carrying a gun. Frequently, he had to begin his visit by explaining that he was not a policeman, a tax collector, a social worker, or a holdup man."

Negroes are timid about even walking into a bank. To compound the problem, black nationalists teach that the large metropolitan banks are financing the slum lords, the gouging credit merchants, the loan sharks. The banks have not successfully refuted these charges. The Chemical Bank New York Trust Company in New York City has been financing "open housing" for ten years, but few people have heard of this splendid program.

The hostility of many Negroes to the banking community is illustrated by the organized efforts now being carried out to encourage mass voluntary bankruptcies as a means of punishing local merchant banks and finance companies. Extremist groups are conducting courses on the advantages and techniques of bankruptcy; lawyers have been enlisted to handle Negro insolvency cases. This type of activity continues to shut off all respectable credit, and put all business in the ghetto on a cash and carry basis. Only the loan shark survives since the legal umbrella of personal bankruptcy does not bar his strong-armed methods for collecting debts.

The dearth of ghetto bank credit does not mean that Wall Street and other metropolitan banks do not have branches in slum areas though they are extremely rare. In Manhattan, as a whole, the ratio of commercial banks is about one for every *five thousand* residents of the city. In Harlem the ratio is one commercial bank for every *thirty thousand* residents. In Los Angeles, in the Fall of 1967, I was unable to identify one commercial bank in the Watts area of Southwest Los Angeles. The Brooklyn Bedford-Stuyvesant ghetto of 400,000 inhabitants, the country's most pernicious (slightly smaller in population than the entire city of Cincinnati, and all black), has one commercial bank. While modern and attractive branches of Chase Manhattan, Bankers Trust, Manufacturers Hanover and many others are visible on Harlem street corners, and some of these branches are reasonably successful, branch banks in slum areas are usually not economically viable.

The high cost of doing a banking business in the ghetto is due primarily to the *bad debt loss*. At an interracial bank in the Brownsville ghetto of Brooklyn the bad debt loss on consumer loans is almost three times as high as the average for all banks in New York City.[3]

The high cost of banking in the ghetto is also due to the fact that the slum area bank must service a very large number of customers who have very small and active savings accounts. These banks invariably have a very low ratio of "low cost" demand deposits or checking accounts to "high cost" time deposits or savings accounts. At the three New York City ghetto branches of Puerto Rico's Banco de Ponce, pass book savings deposits account for 87 percent of total deposits.

In the downtown economy banks accept and absorb the cost of heavy activity on special checking accounts because (1) the bank charges for each check drawn on the account and (2) the banks have successfully guarded their legal privilege not to pay interest on checking accounts. But in the ghetto economy, even the small businessman maintains a savings account instead of a special checking account. The ghetto bank must therefore absorb, without compensating fee, all the extra-activity costs of withdrawal and deposits in savings accounts. In addition, the ghetto branch bank pays interest to its depositor who keeps a saving account but uses them like a checking account.

As an example of the punishing extra costs of banking in the ghetto, consider the situation at Harlem's Freedom National Bank. The bank's $30 million in deposits requires 85 employees. A typical $30 million bank operating in the normal economy would have half that number on its payroll.

In the normal economy, a commercial loan to a small businessman may be simplicity itself: an unsecured note or a note secured by a pledge of securities, inventory or accounts receivable. A one million dollar commercial loan made to a prime borrower is committed on the telephone without the cost of any credit check whatsoever. In the ghetto economy the making of each commercial loan is a struggle. Collateralization of the loan is usually a mixed bag of basically unmarketable and unbankable items: a second mortgage on the borrower's home and car, a wage assignment from his wife if she works, a pledge of accounts receivable owed by customers who are inherently slow payers. If the loan is to be guaranteed by the Small Business Administration, the delays are usually intolerable.

The cost burden of banking in the ghetto is greatly increased by the fact that the commercial borrower has no financial experience or training. The President of Freedom National Bank has stated that one of the major problems of the commercial banker in the ghetto is to determine exactly how much the borrower needs to borrow in order to save his business. The ghetto bank is ineffective unless it can render or call in management consulting services not usually required in the normal economy.

The same extra cost patterns also exist for consumer loans in the ghetto. In Harlem, the average installment loan is very small; the collateral is secondhand and unmarketable. The borrower's "credit profile" is inevitably held unbankable by downtown standards. The ghetto borrower's bad-debt-loss is inevitably much higher.

In our urban economy the downtown branches skim off the cream of the desirable consumer loans. The marginal and submarginal loans are left for the financial institutions of the ghetto.

Nick Ortiz, Manager of the Banco Popular de Puerto Rico branch in New York City, cites the basic problems and costs in lending in the ghetto:

(1) High Promotional costs—seventy five percent (75%) of their customers never had any banking experience (a checking or savings account, or even a loan).

(2) About 50% of their personal loans (largest income producing areas to these banks) are for $600 or less. A bank loses money on any loans for less than $300.

(3) Income from commercial loans is very limited.

(4) A lot of their energy is channeled into social activities, civic and general guidance as part of their effort to uplift the community.

(5) Highly competitive salaries must be paid in order to maintain a civic-oriented, business-minded, bilingual staff.

(6) By serving small businessmen and marginal clients in our ghetto areas they face alone the consequence of greater credit risks.

Banks do not talk much about their profits or losses in slum area branches. We do know that in 1968 Freedom National in Harlem earned about two hundred thousand dollars on total assets of thirty million dollars. Although inherently marginal, most ghetto branches of downtown banks are wisely sustained as "demonstration projects." Their continued existence often reflects home office bank management policy of never terminating a branch operation except under the most trying conditions.

Burdened with the extra costs of extending credit in the ghetto economy, the downtown banker faces the identical dilemma of the department store chain or the manufacturer who seeks to sell in or manufacture in the slum economy. To manufacture or market in the ghetto economy on even a break-even basis would require a massive, compensating retail or wholesale markup. A national corporation will avoid all business activities in the black poverty areas rather than impose such an extra tax on the black purchaser.

Indeed, ghetto interracial banks charge a higher interest rate on ghetto consumer loans than prevails in the normal economy. For example, the effective interest rate on consumer loans at the New York City ghetto branches of Banco de Ponce is about 1 percent higher than the prevailing rate downtown. These minority-group-controlled banks are not vulnerable to charges of racial discrimination. Therefore, they may compensate themselves in part for the higher costs of extending credit in the ghetto economy.

However, there is no possible way that Chase Manhattan Bank can establish at its ghetto branches a higher rate on consumer loans, or an extra penalty charge for unusual activity in deposit accounts than prevails at downtown branches in the normal economy.

Bank loans to International Business Machines are made at six percent, the prime rate, and to a fledgling business borrower at seven and one-half to eight percent. The customer recognizes and accepts the different rate as being based on lower costs and credit risks. No such reasons or "excuses" are acceptable in the ghetto economy. In a nation where credit differences and discrimination are synonymous the ghetto rate must be the same as the downtown rate. Until the differences in cost are adjusted or compensated in a manner which is just and ethically acceptable to the nation, the ghetto economy will continue to be ruled by the high interest rate credit merchants who prevent the formation of normal patterns of credit.

Federal and state laws in the United States now prohibit the refusal to deny credit on account of race or color. But these laws cannot legislate credit into the ghetto; they cannot restore credit to an economy whose tariffs of risk and unprofitability have resolutely banished all forms of reasonably priced credit. Twelve thousand commercial banks have no functional need to extend credit in the slums. Under present conditions, there is absolutely no basis on which loans can be exported to black areas on a basis both fair to the stockholders of the lender and his ghetto borrower.

The ghetto's need for loans at reasonable rates is urgent. The need will not be supplied until laws against credit discrimination are supplemented by a system of federal credit incentives which also abolish the resolute determination of the ghetto economy to remain credit poor.

NOTES

[1] Perhaps it has been modified. Most installment credit officers used to consider only the income of the head of the household, ignoring the income of working spouses. This rule excluded hundreds of thousands of Negro families from credit since two working parents is even more common in the ghetto economy. Some banks are now revising their lending manuals.

[2] The ghetto credit economy has been compared to the credit starved undeveloped nations in Latin America and Africa. In these countries long-term mortgages are either not available or are written for at most five years. The latter commands a 20 percent interest rate. The reasons, here, are that lenders have confidence in their nation's currency and are therefore unwilling to risk repayment in a devalued currency. The problem of opening up the credit arteries to the ghetto has far greater dimensions since the dollar is as sound in Bedford-Stuyvesant as it is in Beverly Hills.

[3] The bad debt loss experience at the Banco de Ponce branch is ¾ percent in Brownsville. The New York City average as a whole is 0.3 percent.

Banks, like supermarkets, operate on a very narrow margin. The added loss on bad debts is in itself sufficient to make the difference between opening and not opening a ghetto branch bank.

CHARACTERISTICS OF INSTALLMENT CONTRACT ARRANGEMENTS

Federal Trade Commission Staff

Sixty-five furniture, appliance, and department store retailers surveyed indicated significant use of installment contracts in financing customer purchases. In 1966, a total value of $45.3 million in contracts were entered into by this group, equivalent to 30 percent of their total sales. The average value per contract was $146. The average value for general market department stores was only $100, while for general market appliance and furniture stores it was $210 and $359, respectively. The average value of contracts for low-income market retailers was $140 (table 1).

To understand better the current business practices with respect to the use of installment credit instruments, information was sought regarding contract assignment practices, rates of finance charges, and problems of default. Our findings on these subjects are summarized in this chapter.

INSTALLMENT CONTRACT ASSIGNMENT

As a matter of practice, much installment credit is supplied indirectly by finance companies or banks rather than by the retailers directly involved in making purchase-loan transactions. Retailers have arrangements with one or more finance companies or banks to which, after credit approval, the conditional sales contracts or notes are assigned or discounted. The assign-

Reprinted from Consumer Credit and the Poor, Hearing Before the Subcommittee on Financial Institutions of the Committee on Banking and Currency, U.S. Senate, 90th Congress, Second Session, on The Federal Trade Commission Report on Credit Practices (Washington: U.S. Government Printing Office, 1968), pp. 64-76. Some footnotes omitted.

ment may be coordinated with the purchase and delivery of the merchandise, or it may be made after the sale but before the first payment is due. In rare cases assignment may be made later.

When a contract is assigned by the retailer, the customer's financial obligation is shifted to the "holder in due course" and, under the law, the customer's legal obligation for payment is not to the retailer but to a financial intermediary. (This is true when contracts are assigned *without* recourse. If contracts are assigned *with* recourse, they are returned to the retailer in case of default and he, rather than the assignee, bears the risk.) This is true regardless of any subsequent dispute that may arise between customer and retailer involving the quality of the product.

Of the $45.2 million in installment contracts reported for 1966 in the Commission's survey, $15.8 million or 35 percent was assigned to finance companies and banks (table 2). Among all retailers reporting installment credit sales, department stores alone assigned no contracts. General market appliance and furniture stores were most dependent on assignment and together accounted for 91 percent of all reported assignments. For appliance stores almost all (98 percent) installment credit contracts were assigned; for furniture stores, 57 percent. Finance companies held virtually all of the appliance retailer assigned paper, but only one-third (36 percent) of the furniture retailer paper. Banks held the balance (64 percent) of assigned contracts involving purchases from furniture stores.

Despite the fact that more than 90 percent of sales by low-income market retailers was on an installment basis, this group assigned only 20 percent of their contracts. These typically were the largest contracts. Whereas the average value

Table 1. *Average Value of Installment Contracts of 65 District of Columbia Retailers, 1966*

Type of Retailers	All Contracts	Assigned Contracts	Unassigned Contracts
All retailers	$146	$264	$117
Low-income market retailers	140	298	124
General market retailers	147	261	116
Appliance, radio, and TV	210	212	141
Furniture and home-furnishings	359	383	332
Department stores	100		100

Source: FTC Survey.

Table 2. *Number and Value of Installment Contracts Assigned and Unassigned by District of Columbia Retailers, 1966*

Type of Retailers	Number of Companies	Net Sales ($000)	Total Installment Contracts		Contracts Assigned		Contracts Unassigned — Held by Retailers	
			Value ($000)	Value as Percent of Net Sales	Value ($000)	Percent of Total Value of Contracts	Value ($000)	Percent of Total Value of Contracts
Total	65	$150,970	$45,251	30.0	$15,818	35.0	$29,433	65.0
Low-income market retailers	18	7,874	7,296	92.7	1,441	19.8	5,855	80.2
General market retailers	47	143,096	37,955	26.5	14,377	37.9	23,578	62.1
Appliance, radio, and television	22	25,089	8,466	33.7	8,323	98.3	143	1.7
Furniture and home-furnishings	22	26,643	10,608	39.8	6,054	57.1	4,554	42.9
Department stores	3	91,364	18,881	20.6	none	none	18,881	100.0

Source: FTC Survey.

of unassigned contracts was $124 in 1966, the average for contracts assigned was $298 (table 1).

In all, of the 65 retailers reporting sales on an installment contract basis, 49 assigned all or part of these contracts to finance companies or banks (table 7). Twenty-one of 22 appliance retailers and 18 of 22 furniture retailers assigned contracts. Four low-income market retailers assigned all and six others assigned some of their installment contracts to finance companies. Only department stores assigned no contracts arising from installment sales.

Finance companies are most actively engaged in the purchase of installment contracts arising from retail sales transactions (table 3). Seventy-five percent of the total value of contracts assigned was assigned to finance companies, principally by general market appliance stores and low-income market retailers. Banks supplied 25 percent of all installment contract assignment financing, principally for general market furniture retailers. Nearly all of this business was done by four banks. For other retailers, most contracts were assigned to finance companies, four of which supplied 77 percent of the funding. General market appliance stores assigned virtually all of their contracts. Four finance companies took 90 percent of this paper. The pattern of assignments by low-income market retailers (who assigned only one-fifth of their paper) was less concentrated, with the top four finance companies accounting for only 65 percent of reported assignments.

Table 3. *Distribution of Total Installment Contracts Assigned to Finance Companies and Banks*

Contract Assignment	Value ($000)	Percent of Total	Number	Percent of Total
Total of all assigned installment contracts	$15,818	100.0	59,934	100.0
Contracts assigned to finance companies	11,917	75.3	50,845	84.8
Contracts assigned to banks	3,901	24.7	9,089	15.2
Total contracts assigned to finance companies[1]	11,917	100.0	50,845	100.0
Leading 4 finance companies[1]	9,215	77.3	40,786	80.2
Total contracts assigned to banks[2]	3,901	100.0	9,089	100.0
Leading 4 banks[2]	3,782	96.9	8,860	97.5

[1] The total number of finance companies to which contracts were assigned by retailers surveyed was 21.
[2] The total number of banks to which contracts were assigned by retailers surveyed was 10.

Source: FTC Survey

INSTALLMENT CONTRACTS UNASSIGNED

Of the $45.3 million in installment contracts reported for 1966 in the Commissions's survey, $29.4 million or 65 percent was unassigned—held by the retailers themselves. The extent to which contracts were unassigned varied considerably by type of retailer. Department stores surveyed held all of their contracts; low-income market retailers held four-fifths (80 percent); and general market furniture stores held over two-fifths (43 percent) of the total value of their installment contracts. General market appliance retailers, however, held practically none (2 percent) of their installment paper (table 2). In total, of 65 retailers reporting installment sales, 16 held all of their own contracts. They included 3 department stores, 8 of the 18 low-income market retailers, and only 5 of the 44 appliance and furniture stores.

FINANCE CHARGES ON INSTALLMENT CONTRACTS

With one exception, the stated finance charges were calculated on an "add-on" basis by both low-income and general market retailers. This exception was a low-income market retailer who made no separate finance charges in calculating payments due on installment contracts. All of its sales were on a time basis and the price for these goods on the average was three times the cost of goods sold. This markup was somewhat higher than the average for low-income market retailers as a group, who, as a matter of course, added to their selling price additional charges for installment credit.

Other retailers used "add-on" rate charts to determine customers' monthly payments. No account is taken of diminishing balances over the period and, consequently, the "add-on" is not a true or effective annual rate. Table 4 indicates that the average add-on rate for contracts assigned to finance companies and banks was 11.7 percent of the initial balance, and the average add-on rate for unassigned contracts was 10.7 percent of the initial unpaid balance.

The true or effective annual rate that consumers were paying on these installment contracts was approximately twice the add-on rate. This is because with each payment the amount borrowed was reduced, making the average balance borrowed about half the original unpaid balance. If it is assumed that equal payments are made at equal times (usually monthly) throughout the total period of the contract, the true or effective annual rate can be calculated by a relatively simple formula called the constant ratio method. This formula was applied and checked with actuarial rate tables to obtain the equivalent effective annual rates shown in table 4 and subsequent figure and tables. For installment contracts entered into by the retailers surveyed, in 1966 the average effective annual rate of finance charges was 21 percent on those

Table 4. *Finance Charges on Installment Contracts Assigned and Unassigned by District of Columbia Retailers, 1966*

Type of Retailers	Assigned Contracts		Finance Charges on Contracts Assigned to Finance Companies and Banks		Unassigned Contracts		Finance Charges on Unassigned Contracts	
	Value ($000)	Percent of Total	Percent Add-on	Effective Annual Rate (Percent)	Value ($000)	Percent of Total	Percent Add-on	Effective Annual Rate (Percent)
Total[1]	$15,818	100.0	[2]11.7	[2]21	[1]$27,174	100.0	[2]10.7	[2]20
Low-income market retailers[1]	1,441	9.1	13.4	25	[1]3,596	13.2	[1]12.5	[1]23
General market retailers	14,377	90.9	[2]11.5	[2]21	23,578	86.8	[2]10.4	[2]19
Appliance, radio, and television retailers	8,323	52.6	12.9	24	143	0.5	10.1	18
Furniture and home-furnishings retailers	6,054	38.3	9.8	18	4,554	16.8	9.2	16
Department stores . . .	none	none	. . . .		18,881	69.5	10.7	20

[1] One low-income market retailer has been omitted, because it made no separate charges for installment financing.
[2] Weighted averages.

Source: FTC Survey.

assigned to finance companies and banks and 20 percent on those held by the retailers themselves.

Table 5 shows the distribution of all installment contracts by effective annual rate of finance charge for those retailers reporting charges on installment credit sales. The bulk of installment credit sales by low-income market retailers were at effective annual financing rates of 22 percent or more. Nearly half (47.9 percent) was at rates ranging from 26 to 33 percent.

Contracts arising from sales by general market retailers rarely entailed such high charges. Three-fourths were at finance rates of 20 percent or less. This figure is heavily weighted by department store installment credit sales. Less than one percent of general market retailer contracts had finance charges exceeding 24 percent.

Among general market retailers, only appliance stores had rates consistently exceeding 20 percent. These retailers assigned most of their contracts at effective annual rates of 23 to 24 percent. Thus, virtually all of the contracts involving rates exceeding 24 percent were written by low-income market retailers.

Figure 1 summarizes the distribution of effective annual rates of finance charges on installment contracts of low-income market and general market retailers for all installment contracts, as well as for assigned and unassigned contracts.

CONTRACTUAL ARRANGEMENTS FOR ASSIGNMENT OF INSTALLMENT CREDIT

To better understand the factors determining finance charges, contracts were analyzed on the basis of whether they were assigned to finance companies and banks or held by the retailers themselves. Assignment of contracts is a method of transferring the costs and, in many cases, the risk of handling installment contracts from the retailer to the finance company. There is a

Table 5. *Installment Contracts Distributed by Effective Annual Rate of Finance Charge (Assigned and Unassigned)*[1]

Effective Annual Rate of Finance Charge	Value of Contracts at Each Effective Annual Rate for:					
	Low-income Market Retailers		General Market Retailers		All Retailers Combined	
	Value of Contracts ($000)	Percent of Total	Value of Contracts ($000)	Percent of Total	Value of Contracts ($000)	Percent of Total
33 percent	$ 360	7.1	. . . .		$ 360	0.8
29 percent	283	5.6	$ 99	0.3	382	0.9
27 percent	1,087	21.6	. . . .		1,087	2.5
26 percent	685	13.6	. . . .		685	1.6
24 percent			3,541	9.3	3,541	8.2
23 percent			4,576	12.1	4,576	10.6
22 percent	871	17.3	1,173	3.1	2,044	4.8
20 percent			16,872	44.4	16,872	39.2
18 percent	1,550	30.8	173	0.5	1,723	4.0
17 percent . . . . :			6,311	16.6	6,311	14.7
16 percent			77	0.2	77	0.2
15 percent . . . . : . . .	187	3.7	3,210	8.5	3,397	7.9
14 percent			460	1.2	460	1.1
13 percent			115	0.3	115	0.3
11 percent	14	0.3	635	1.7	649	1.5
Rate not available			713	1.8	713	1.7
Total	5,037	100.0	37,955	100.0	42,992	100.0

[1] Includes all installment contracts for which separate finance charges were specified.

Source: FTC Survey.

variety of contractual arrangements between retailers and finance companies or banks for the assignment of contracts. The nature of these arrangements is an important factor in determining finance charges. Contracts that are unassigned often have different risk characteristics than those that are assigned. Thus, finance charges may vary depending on whether or not retailers assign their contracts.

Finance charges on assigned installment credit contracts. Sixty-eight percent of the value of all assigned contracts carried finance charges yielding an effective annual rate of 22 percent or more. For low-income market retailers this proportion was 98 percent. Sixty-two percent of all assigned contracts had rates ranging between 22 and 24 percent (table 6 and figure 1). Contracts assigned at these rates were, for the most part, entered into by general market appliance retailers. Practically all of the assignments at 17 percent or less were by general market furniture stores and, as noted below,

usually involved recourse arrangements with banks.

Recourse arrangements on assigned contracts. Most commonly, finance companies, in accepting assignment of installment credit contracts from retailers, reimburse the retailer for an amount equivalent to the unpaid cash balance indicated on the contract. In the simplest type of transaction, the finance company's income from providing credit is equivalent to the stated financing charge and is designed to cover all costs of credit, collection, and risks of default.

In fact, however, there are many possible variations on this type of transaction. A number of these variations were uncovered in the course of our survey. The first and simplest relates to the question of recourse. Typically, contracts assigned to finance companies are on a nonrecourse basis. In such circumstances the finance company assumes all risks associated with default and is solely responsible for any proceedings to enforce satisfaction of the debt.

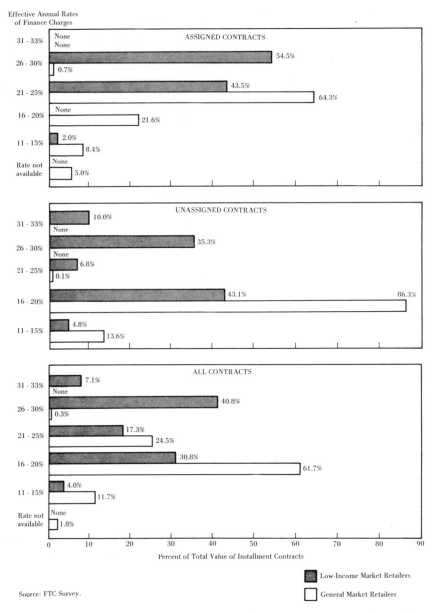

Figure 1. Distribution of Effective Annual Rates of Finance Charges on Installment Contracts of Low-Income and General Market Retailers, 1966.

Assignment, however, may be on a recourse basis, in which case the retailer assigning the contract in effect guarantees it in the event of customer default. In terms of total value, almost all contracts on a recourse basis involved banks serving general market furniture retailers. (There were instances, however, when finance companies took assigned installment contracts only on a recourse basis. These were usually on contracts assigned by low-income market retailers.)

More than 50 percent of total assignments [and 73 percent of assignments to finance companies] were at rates yielding effective annual finance charges of 23 to 24 percent (table 6 and appendix table A). The highest yielding nonrecourse assignments to finance companies were by low-income market retailers. Fifty-five percent of such assignments yielded 26 to 29 percent. Assignments with the lowest finance charges (17 percent or less) involved, for the most part, banks who took paper on a recourse

Table 6. *Assigned Installment Contracts Distributed by Effective Annual Rate of Finance Charge*

Effective Annual Rate of Finance Charge	Value of Contracts at Each Effective Annual Rate for:					
	Low-income Market Retailers		General Market Retailers		All Retailers Combined	
	Value of Contracts ($000)	Percent of Total	Value of Contracts ($000)	Percent of Total	Value of Contracts ($000)	Percent of Total
29 percent	$ 283	19.6	$ 90	0.7	$ 382	2.4
27 percent	23	1.6	....		23	0.2
26 percent	480	33.3	....		480	3.0
24 percent	....		3,535	24.6	3,535	22.3
23 percent	....		4,576	31.8	4,576	28.9
22 percent	627	43.5	1,137	7.9	1,764	11.2
17 percent			3,105	21.6	3,105	19.6
15 percent	14	1.0	2	(1)	16	0.1
14 percent			460	3.2	460	2.9
13 percent			115	0.8	115	0.8
11 percent	14	1.0	635	4.4	649	4.1
Rate not available			713	5.0	713	4.5
Total	1,441	100.0	14,377	100.0	15,818	100.0

[1] Less than 0.1 percent

Source: FTC Survey.

basis (appendix table A). The latter's activity, however, was limited almost entirely to contracts involving sales by general market furniture retailers.

Participation and holdback arrangements. In addition to recourse considerations. agreements between finance companies and retailers may specify participation or holdback fees. A participation arrangement, frequently referred to as a kickback, is a bonus given by a finance company to a retailer assigning a contract. This bonus involves some percentage return over and above the initial unpaid balance of the contract. It is the equivalent of the retailer and finance company splitting finance charges. Twenty-nine of the forty-nine retailers in our sample reporting installment contract assignments had a participation arrangement with one or more finance companies (table 7). These returns to the retailer ranged between 0.5 and 5 percent of the amount of the unpaid cash balance.

Holdback arrangements may be viewed as the reverse of kickbacks. There were nine retailers who reported a holdback requirement by fi-

nance companies. This is a restrictive provision assessed upon retailers who are in a poor bargaining position and have generally poor-risk paper that they want to assign. Finance companies and banks in these cases are reluctant to take the contracts unless the retailer is willing to take less than the full amount of the initial unpaid cash balance. In other words, the retailer must literally "pay" the finance company or bank to take the assignment. This is a payment over and above the finance charges paid by the customer originally signing the contract. Holdbacks, which ranged from 3 to 30 percent, were reported primarily by low-income market retailers. These payments are held in reserve by the financer until all contracts are liquidated. Losses are charged against this reserve and holdback payments are returned to the retailer only if the losses do not exceed the amount held back. Low-income market retailers were unable to assign a significant volume of installment contracts at less than 26 percent (effective annual rate) without some form of holdback arrangement. Other retailers assigning large quantities of paper, usually at 23 to 24 percent, for the most part had no holdbacks charged against them.

Table 7. *Special Provisions Included in Contractual Arrangements Between Retailers and Finance Companies or Banks*

Type of Retailers	Number of Retailers Assigning Contracts	Number of Retailers Reporting:				
		Participation Arrangements			Holdback Requirements	
		Participation (Kickback)	Range of Participation	No Participation	Holdback by Financer	Range of Holdbacks
		(percent)				(percent)
Low-income market retailers	10	4	1.2–2.0	6	5	5–30
General market retailers:						
Appliance, radio, and television retailers	21	17	1.0–4.0	4	1	3–5
Furniture and home-furnishing retailers	18	8	0.5–5.0	10	3	3–5
Department stores	None	. . . .				
Total	49	29	0.5–5.0	20	9	3–30

Source: FTC Survey.

FINANCE CHARGES ON UNASSIGNED CONTRACTS

Sixty-five percent of reported installment credit was unassigned (table 2). The volume of unassigned contracts on which finance charges were made ($27.2 million) was heavily weighted by department stores who accounted for $18.9 million or over two-thirds of the total (table 4). Department stores were alone among retailers assigning no contracts. Installment sales amounted to 20 percent of their total sales.

Other unassigned installment credit was supplied by general market furniture stores and low-income market retailers. General market furniture retailers held $4.6 million in contracts, equal to 43 percent of their credit sales and about 17 percent of total sales. Low-income market retailers held unassigned contracts of $5.9 million, equivalent to 80 percent of all their credit sales and nearly the same percent of their total sales. For those low-income market retailers imposing separate finance charges on installment credit, the value of unassigned contracts was $3.6 million, equal to 64 percent of this group's total sales, virtually all of which were on an installment credit basis.

Ninety-three percent of the total value of *unassigned* installment contracts carried finance charges yielding an effective annual rate of 20 percent or less (table 8 and figure 1). This was heavily affected by the relatively low rates on unassigned contracts financed by general market department stores and furniture stores.

Finance charges on unassigned contracts of department stores ranged from 17 to 20 percent. Our survey indicated that most contracts (89 percent) were at the 20 percent rate (appendix table B). Finance charges by general market furniture stores for the most part (98 percent) ranged between 15 and 17 percent.

Finance charges by low-income market retailers were more variable. Among this group of retailers one large company, which sold entirely on installment credit, made no finance charges on its unassigned installment contracts, preferring instead to price its merchandise to cover installment costs. Other low-income market retailers charged an average effective annual rate of 23 percent on unassigned installment contracts. The highest effective annual rates of finance charges made were 33 percent and 27 percent. Total contracts at these rates accounted for about 40 percent of the total value of contracts held by those low-income market retailers making finance charges. The other predominant effective annual rate was 18 percent and accounted for 43 percent of the total value of contracts (table 8 and figure 1).

Table 8. *Unassigned Installment Contracts Distributed by Effective Annual Rate of Finance Charge[1]*

Effective Annual Rate of Finance Charge	Low-income Market Retailers		General Market Retailers		All Retailers Combined	
	Value of Contracts ($000)	Percent of Total	Value of Contracts ($000)	Percent of Total	Value of Contracts ($000)	Percent of Total
33 percent	$ 360	10.0			$ 360	1.3
27 percent	1,064	29.6			1,064	3.9
26 percent	205	5.7			205	0.8
24 percent			$ 6	(2)	6	(2)
22 percent	244	6.8	36	0.1	280	1.0
20 percent			16,872	71.6	16,872	62.1
18 percent	1,550	43.1	173	0.7	1,723	6.3
17 percent			3,206	13.6	3,206	11.8
16 percent			77	0.4	77	0.8
15 percent	173	4.8	3,208	13.6	3,381	12.5
Total	3,596	100.0	23,578	100.0	27,174	100.0

[1] Includes all installment contracts for which separate finance charges were specified.
[2] Less than 0.1 percent.

Source: FTC Survey.

JUDGMENTS, GARNISHMENTS, AND REPOSSESSIONS BY RETAILERS

When an account under an installment sales contract becomes delinquent, the holder of that contract can proceed to collect by several legal means. A judgment can be obtained that will permit repossession of the merchandise or garnishment of the wages of the purchaser. (Repossession can be accomplished without court action by the holder of the installment conditional sales contract. In such instances, if the proceeds of a public sale of the repossessed item does not cover the unpaid balance plus fees, the holder can still sue on the contract *and* get a judgment for the deficiency.)

If the retailer has assigned the contract *without* recourse, the finance company or bank takes the risk of loss and proceeds to exercise its legal rights. Consequently, retailers are not involved in the collection process if they assign without recourse. If a delinquent account comes back to the retailer who has assigned *with* recourse or if an account originally financed by the retailer himself becomes delinquent, the retailer does not become involved in legal processes if he turns the account over to a collection agency.

For these reasons, many retailers in this survey had no records on this volume of judgments, garnishments, or repossessions.

Eleven low-income market retailers obtained 2,690 judgments in 1966. Their legal actions resulted in 1,568 garnishments and 306 repossessions (table 9). In contrast, general market retailers reported very few judgments. The 8 furniture and home-furnishings stores providing such data reported only 70 judgments for the year 1966. Low-income market retailers obtained almost that number of judgments in an average *week*. One large department store, whose 1966 sales far exceeded the total for the entire low-income market group, reported only 29 judgments.

To gain additional perspective on the extent to which the courts are being used as a collection agency, the number of suits filed in 1966 by the surveyed retailers in their own names was determined from the records of the District of Columbia Court of General Sessions. These suits included actions for collection of 30-day, revolving credit, and installment contract accounts. They did *not* include suits filed by collection agencies as assignees of retailers' accounts. During 1966, the 18 low-income

Table 9. *Judgments, Garnishments, and Repossessions on Delinquent Installment Contracts Reported by District of Columbia Retailers, 1966*

Type of Retailers	Number of Retailers Reporting	Total Judgments	Judgments Resulting in:	
			Garnishments	Repossessions
Low-income market retailers	11	2,690	1,568	306
General market retailers:				
Appliance, radio, and television retailers	3	....		3
Furniture and home-furnishings retailers	8	70	26	13
Department stores	1	29	9..........	
Total	23	2,789	1 2,603	322

Source: FTC Survey.

Table 10. *Debt Suits Filed in the District of Columbia by Low-Income Market
and General Market Retailers, 1966*

Type of Retailers	Number of Suits Filed	Number of Retailers	Net Sales 1966 ($000)	Net Sales per Debt Suit
Total sample of low-income market and general market retailers	3,646	65	$150,970	$41,406
Low-income market retailers	3,030	18	7,874	2,406
General market retailers:	616	47	143,096	232,299
Appliance, radio, and television	53	22	25,089	473,377
Furniture and home-furnishings	207	22	26,643	128,710
Department stores........................	356	3	91,364	256,640

Source: District of Columbia Court of General Sessions, Debt Suit Files; FTC Survey.

market retailers in this study filed 3,030 suits, the equivalent of one suit for every $2,599 of their net sales. Among the general market retailers in the sample, 22 appliance stores filed 53 suits; 22 furniture stores, 207; and 3 department stores, 356 (table 10). All together, there were only 616 suits filed by the 47 general market retailers, which averaged one suit for every $232,299 of their net sales.

An additional unknown number of suits involving default on merchandise credit sales was filed by collection agencies. Various retailers may prefer to assign delinquent paper to a collection agency. This shifts the responsibility for obtaining legal assistance and minimizes whatever risk of bad publicity credit suits might incur.

Nevertheless, it is clear that general market retailers resort to the courts, either directly or indirectly, much less frequently than do low-income market retailers. If the 47 general market retailers had obtained judgments at the same rate as did the low-income market retailers, a very large number of court cases would have occurred. Instead of the 616 judgments which they actually obtained, general market retailers would have had a total of 55,000 judgments if they had filed one suit for every $2,599 in sales, as did the low-income market retailers (table 10). In fact, the total number of suits in 1966 involving claims of $10,000 or less was 49,000, only a part of which were claims for payment for merchandise purchases. The latter figure involved claims for a multitude of causes: auto accidents, small loan defaults, failure to pay utility bills and the like. Clearly, a number of low-income market retailers have come to view the courts as an integral part of their credit-collection system and in so doing have put a heavy burden on our legal system.

THE INSURANCE PROBLEM: BASIC FINDINGS

President's National Advisory Panel on Insurance in Riot-Affected Areas

There is a serious lack of property insurance in the core areas of our nation's cities. For a number of years, many urban residents and businessmen have been unable to purchase the insurance protection they need. Now, riots and the threat of riots are aggravating the problem to an intolerable degree. Immediate steps must be taken to make insurance available to responsible persons in all areas of our cities.

INSURANCE: A NECESSITY FOR HOMEOWNERS AND BUSINESSMEN

Insurance is a basic necessity for a property owner. By paying a premium that represents a relatively small amount compared to the value of his home or business, an owner acquires protection against the possibility that his property may be damaged or destroyed. The opportunity for every responsible individual to obtain security for his savings and investments is vital in a free society. This requires fair access to insurance.

Without insurance, the savings of millions of individual citizens are exposed to the risk of loss from natural and manmade hazards they cannot control.

Society cannot erase the suffering of the innocent victims of fire, windstorm, theft, or riot. But it can at least provide the opportunity to obtain insurance to safeguard their capital, and thereby prevent a disastrous occurrence from becoming a permanent tragedy.

Reprinted from *Meeting the Insurance Crisis of Our Cities*, A Report by the President's National Advisory Panel on Insurance in Riot-Affected Areas (Washington: U.S. Government Printing Office, January, 1968), pp. 1-8. Footnotes omitted.

INSURANCE: AN ESSENTIAL FORCE IN REVITALIZING OUR CITIES

Insurance is essential to revitalize our cities. It is a cornerstone of credit. Without insurance, banks and other financial institutions will not—and cannot—make loans. New housing cannot be constructed, and existing housing cannot be repaired. New businesses cannot be opened, and existing businesses cannot expand, or even survive.

Without insurance, buildings are left to deteriorate; services, goods, and jobs diminish. Efforts to rebuild our nation's inner cities cannot move forward. Communities without insurance are communities without hope.

THE URBAN CORE INSURANCE CRISIS

Unavailability and high cost. A great deal of evidence confirms that there is a serious lack of property insurance in our nation's inner cities. Residents and businessmen from urban core areas throughout the nation have stated that they cannot purchase the property insurance they need. Some say they cannot find insurance at all. Others say that they cannot obtain insurance at prices they are able to afford. Some who now have insurance are afraid that their insurance will be cancelled in the near future or not renewed. Many do not make legitimate claims for fear of losing the insurance they have.

In Newark, New Jersey, when a butcher was asked whether he had any insurance, he answered: "No, sir. Nobody wants to insure us. No insurance—everyone I see. I [would] give my right hand [for it]."

A Detroit, Michigan, homeowner told us:

I was paying $85 previously for three years' coverage, and now they told me [it would cost] the same amount of money for one year.

The owner of a shoe repair store in Omaha, Nebraska, was asked whether he had insurance on his merchandise, and responded:

No sir, not a penny. . . . [T]en days after the riot, automatically all insurance was dropped out.

These are not isolated voices. Insurance problems have affected whole communities. At our hearings, the president of a leading savings and loan association in the Watts area of Los Angeles testified:

Real estate activity is practically at a standstill. Residents in this curfew area, wanting to purchase property outside the area, find it almost impossible because of their inability to sell the property they presently occupy. The sale of these properties is dependent upon financing through reputable financial institutions, which are reluctant to do so because adequate fire insurance coverage is not available. . . .

The problems now being faced by residents of ghettos in this country are the result of long periods of discrimination, and we should not permit the results of discrimination to be used as an excuse for doing nothing. The problems of the ghetto must be solved, and we submit that a lack of adequate insurance coverage adversely affects the economy of a community.

Adequate insurance is unavailable not only in our major cities but in other areas as well. One insurance company executive said:

[W]e emphasize that the problem is not alone that of the core areas of a limited number of metropolitan centers, but also that of hundreds of towns and cities of every size throughout America.

In order to determine the intensity of the problem, we conducted a systematic survey including personal interviews of approximately 1,500 homeowners and 1,500 businessmen in poverty areas of Boston, Cleveland, Detroit, Newark, Oakland, and St. Louis.

The survey disclosed that over 40 percent of businessmen and close to 30 percent of homeowners had serious property insurance problems.

Over 20 percent of the businessmen and 6 percent of the homeowners surveyed did not have basic fire insurance coverage. In Boston, over 35 percent of the businessmen surveyed had no fire insurance, and in Detroit over 12 percent of the homeowners were without it.

Of those who were uninsured, 35 percent of the businessmen and over 50 percent of the homeowners said that insurance was unavailable. Close to 30 percent of the uninsured businessmen and homeowners said that insurance cost too much.

Nearly 50 percent of the businessmen surveyed had no burglary and theft insurance. In Boston the figure was 74 percent.

Of those businessmen without burglary and theft insurance, nearly 30 percent said they wanted it but it cost too much; nearly 25 percent said they wanted it but could not get it at any price.

Impact of the riot peril. Recent riot losses have further constricted the supply of insurance in our inner cities. Regardless of whether the management of the insurance industry anticipates rioting in the future, it feels that it must—in the interest of its policyholders and stockholders—prepare for even the remote possibility of extraordinary losses from civil disorders.

This theme has been repeatedly emphasized by a broad spectrum of insurance company spokesmen. The president of the American Insurance Association, an organization representing 170 companies, testified at our hearings:

It is not enough merely to hope that riots will not recur and that, if they do, the damage will not be beyond the capacity of insurers to absorb in their normal operations. Watts served notice on all of us, and still the public and insurers were largely unprepared for what happened in 1967. The lesson is all too clear. I hope that we will profit by this costly experience and not be lulled into complacency and nonaction by wishful thinking that losses cannot reach catastrophic proportions.

The general manager of the American Mutual Insurance Alliance, an organization of 122 companies, told the Panel:

Some companies are especially concerned over their exposure to the continuing threat of sporadic civil disorders. These companies are being asked to maintain existing insurance in urban areas, and so far they are doing so. But they may not be able to continue doing so, out of concern for their solvency, unless some method can be found to neutralize this excessive riot exposure....

[W]e have to recognize the possibility, however remote, that future disorders could develop large enough dimensions to threaten the future ability of insurers to meet their obligations to policyholders.

The president of the National Association of Independent Insurers, an organization representing 350 companies, testified:

[O]ur industry does not possess either the power to forestall future riots or the ability to predict the scope and severity of any which may occur. We must therefore reckon with the possibility—whether imminent or remote—that more riots may occur, and that they might conceivably produce insurance losses far surpassing the financial capacity of the companies involved to absorb.

The industry is not the only knowledgeable group that sees in recent riots a formidable threat to the supply of insurance and the solvency of the insurance business. Thus, the National Association of Insurance Commissioners—an organization of the insurance commissioners of the 50 states—on the basis of the studies of a select committee on the insurance problems of civil disorders has recently reported:

The hazard of loss from riot or civil disorders viewed in the context of recent events poses grave underwriting, rating and capacity problems for the private property and casualty insurance industry. Civil unrest has manifested itself throughout many parts of our nation. Its future course is uncertain. This fact has apparently led major insurer managements and underwriters to conclude that they must either be individually relieved, in whole or in part, from exposure to these perils or guard themselves by careful control on writings in areas regarded as vulnerable. These conditions and attitudes constitute not only a deterrent to the development of programs designed to expand the availability of fire and extended coverage insurance in most cities, but threaten to result in even more serious constriction of such markets.

Insured property losses from riots in the summer of 1967 were under $75 million, far less than the $715 million loss caused by Hurricane "Betsy" in 1965 and less than 3 percent of the total property losses that will be paid for 1967. Nevertheless, the sum approximated 13 percent of the entire underwriting profit of the insurance industry in 1966.

Riot losses have further burdened those lines of insurance already relatively unprofitable and those segments of the industry already the most heavily committed to writing urban core business. Thus, even though the Panel has no doubt that the insurance industry has the financial strength to absorb losses even greater than those sustained in the summer of 1967, we believe that the industry is justifiably concerned about the threat—no matter how unlikely—of future riot losses.

Another aspect of the industry's concern, in view of the civil disorders, is uncertainty about whether it can obtain enough reinsurance—insurance purchased by insurance companies to protect themselves against excessive loss. One of the largest reinsurers in the world has informed the Panel that reinsurance will continue to be available, but at higher rates and on more restrictive terms. The insurance executive wants security against catastrophic loss just like any other businessman. As one insurance executive described the situation at our hearings:

Still another threat to the solvency of our companies is the probability . . . that reinsurers in our country and other countries—particularly in England and the Continent—will restrict or withdraw their riot coverage. If this happens, it will mean that primary underwriters will not be able to spread their catastrophic losses for the riot peril. Such an event is in contradiction to our basic operating procedures and would further expose the solvency of the primary insurers. . . .

It is an inescapable fact, gentlemen, that a direct relationship exists between insurance market inadequacies and the financial capacities of our insurance companies. Our industry just does not have, nor can it be expected to have, the financial structure to cope with widespread civil disorder. It cannot continue to expose its very solvency no matter how remote the recurrence of widespread rioting may be.

Executives of our nation's most respected insurance companies have stated that without some financial assistance from government to protect them against catastrophic riot losses, they will be unable to continue offering property insurance in the center city. They stress that this is a matter of urgency. As one said at our hearings:

[W]e believe that the best and only way to induce insurance companies to provide coverage on all otherwise insurable risks is to relieve them of the exposure to catastrophic riot loss. . . . In other words, in the absence of such governmental backup, the Urban Areas Plan could result in risks which are found on inspection to be "insurable" still not finding a market because of the magnitude of the riot exposure alone.

The insurance problems created by riots cannot be allowed to jeopardize the availability of property insurance in center city areas. But the problem of providing adequate and reasonable insurance in the urban core cannot be solved merely by supplying financial assistance to protect insurance companies against catastrophic riot losses. It is clear that adequate insurance was unavailable in the urban core even before the riots. Our survey indicates that property insurance problems are severe in St. Louis—where there were no riots—as well as in Detroit; in Oakland—where riots were minor— as well as in Newark. We are dealing with an inner city insurance problem that is broad in scope and complicated in origin, and riots are only one aspect of it.

Factors underlying the crisis. For a variety of reasons explained in detail in Chapter II, the insurance industry believes that providing insurance to homeowners and businessmen in the urban core is generally unprofitable. As a result, the insurance enterprise does not function well to meet insurance needs in these areas.

The number of insurance agents and brokers selling insurance to residents and businessmen in urban core areas is relatively small. The effort to place the business may be more time-consuming and the results less lucrative than with business from other city areas and the suburbs. Agents and brokers who seek business in urban core areas find that their applications for insurance are screened carefully by the insurance companies with which they deal. An agent who submits too many applications that a company considers too risky may have his agency contract terminated.

Many agents simply avoid urban core business. An agent in Kansas City, Missouri, told the Panel:

Probably less than 1 percent of our premium volume comes from the areas which are generally thought to be trouble spots or potential trouble spots. One reason for this truthfully is probably that I know it is hard to place this business and not only do not solicit it but actually discourage it.

An agent in Washington, D.C., said:

We don't have any trouble with business in blighted areas because we stay away from it. It's bad business.

The basic factor underlying the shortage of insurance in urban core areas is that insurance companies generally regard any business in those areas as relatively unprofitable. Instead of basing their decisions to insure solely on the merits of individual properties, many companies consider the application of an inner city homeowner or businessman on the basis of the neighborhood where his property is located.

Underwriting materials sent to the Panel in response to requests for information reveal clearly that business in certain geographic territories is restricted. For example, one underwriting guide states:

An underwriter should be aware of the following situations in his territory:
  1. The blighted areas.
  2. The redevelopment operations.
  3. Peculiar weather conditions which might make for a concentration of windstorm or hail losses.
  4. The economic makeup of the area.
  5. The nature of the industries in the area, etc.
This knowledge can be gathered by drives through the area, by talking to and visiting agents, and by following local newspapers as to incidents of crimes and fires. A good way to keep this information available and up to date is by *the use of a red line* around the questionable areas on territorial maps centrally located in the Underwriting Division for ease of reference by all Underwriting personnel. (Italics added.)

A New York City insurance agent at our hearings put it more pointedly:

[M]ost companies mark off certain areas . . . to denote a lack of interest in business arising in these areas. In New York these are called K.O. areas—meaning knock-out areas; in Boston they are called redline districts. Same thing—don't write the business.

The companies' motives for restricting the supply of insurance in urban core areas are not hard to find. Every company has a limited capacity to accept risks, and every company legitimately seeks to maximize profits on the insurance it writes. In doing so, company underwriters are given incentives for choosing the least hazardous risks in relation to the amount of premium charged. Thus, in attempting to select only better risks, they find it easier to block out areas considered to be blighted than to evaluate properties individually.

In considering center city properties to be relatively poor risks, insurance companies may have in mind that buildings in these areas may be older and less fire resistant than new buildings in other areas or the suburbs. They may have defective heating and electrical systems. Narrow and congested streets may hamper firemen. The density of construction and the closeness of properties may invite the spread of individual fires into conflagrations. Damage from heat, smoke, and water may be widespread.

Companies may also feel that environmental hazards generally exist. Property in excellent condition may be exposed to nearby fire risks. It may be vulnerable to unusual crime hazards. Newly-arrived residents from rural areas may be unaccustomed to the requirements of urban living. Overcrowding increases tension and antisocial behavior.

The added risk of riots, even though regarded as a remote possibility, has now prompted some companies to state that continued deterioration of the present situation would make them positively unwilling to provide any insurance in urban core areas.

Yet none of these factors may be of significance with respect to any individual property. What could be regarded as generally reasonable procedures may be arbitrary and discriminatory when applied in any particular case. Applications for insurance must be considered on their individual merits if everyone is to have fair access to insurance.

STOP-GAP MEASURES

In response to the urgency of the center city insurance problem, this Panel, on September 15, 1967, called for state regulators and the insurance industry to prevent mass cancellations and nonrenewals and to halt a further constriction of the market. As a first step toward increasing the availability of insurance in center cities, we also urged the adoption and expansion of "Urban Area Plans." Under these plans, individual properties are insured unless a physical inspection discloses demonstrable reasons why the property itself cannot be insured.

Encouraging developments are taking place. State insurance commissioners, in consultation with the industry, have taken actions to maintain existing insurance coverage. Thus, in Michigan and New Jersey, for example, commissioners have extended a moratorium against cancellations and nonrenewals and have begun to work with the industry on steps to enlarge the supply of insurance in urban core areas. Some states—for example, Illinois and Kansas—have adopted Urban Area Plans; others, such as New Jersey and Connecticut, are working to develop these and similar methods to overcome the insurance crisis. The National Association of Insurance Commissioners has made its concern a matter of record and has encouraged action to meet the problems.

Insurance companies have generally acted responsibly while awaiting the development of a more basic solution to the problem. They have not engaged in mass cancellations or nonrenewals. They have endeavored to maintain existing markets.

Despite these constructive efforts, there is great uncertainty over the future of the inner city insurance market. In some cases, the moratoria on cancellations and nonrenewals imposed by state insurance departments in the wake of the summer's riots are by their terms limited in time. Clearly, critical problems remain to be solved.

THE URGENT NEED FOR A COMPREHENSIVE PROGRAM

We believe that further steps must be taken immediately. We recommend that a comprehensive and affirmative program be placed into operation at once. The resources and talents of the insurance industry and of local, state and federal governments must be marshalled to assure property owners everywhere fair access to insurance.

Unless bold and cooperative action is taken without delay, the problems of insurance availability will only become more serious, and solutions will be even more difficult to achieve.

Some representatives of insurance companies have said that if the underlying problems of urban blight were corrected, insurance would be readily available. But if insurance were more readily available for property that is adequately maintained, the underlying problems of urban blight would be more readily corrected.

Owners of well-maintained homes and businesses in urban core areas should not be asked to wait for better days to come. Indeed, they will not wait—those who can will move out at the first opportunity. Those who do not move will have less incentive to keep up their properties. Insurance must be made available now.

Yet any workable program must take other realities into account. Insurance companies are legitimately interested in profits and in maintaining their financial safety and stability. They therefore seek to avoid high risks. The states are already burdened with urgent demands on their resources. The federal government's responsibilities already more than match its tax revenues.

We believe that a successful program can be designed to operate within the context of the existing structure of the insurance industry and the existing pattern of state regulation and taxation of the insurance industry.

We believe also that federal measures should support rather than supplant local efforts. Action by the federal government should encourage and assist those with front-line responsibilities.

We are convinced that the solution of the insurance problem of the center cities lies in the cooperative efforts of all who are involved. No single interested segment—the insurance industry, local, state and federal governments, or the residents and businessmen of the urban core—can, acting alone, ameliorate the complex and interdependent conditions that cause this problem.

All must accept a measure of responsibility. By doing so, the insurance crisis can be met.

The principal alternative to this approach is for government itself to provide insurance directly. We believe that so marked a departure from the free enterprise insurance system is unjustified at this time. We have confidence in the strength of the insurance industry and the abilities of the state insurance departments. We feel that they can, with limited federal assistance, meet the challenge posed by the critical insurance needs of our center cities.

ADDITIONAL READINGS FOR CHAPTER 7

"Business in the Ghetto," Proceedings, American Bar Association National Institute, April 11 and 12, 1969, *The Business Lawyer,* V. 25, Special Issue (September 1969).

David Caplovitz, *The Poor Pay More: Consumer Practices of Low Income Families* (New York: The Free Press, 1963).

Theodore L. Cross, *Black Capitalism: Strategy for Business in the Ghetto* (New York: Atheneum, 1969).

Economic Development Opportunity, Hearings before the Select Committee on Small Business, U.S. Senate, 90th Congress, 2nd Session, on the Role of the Federal Government in the Development of Small Business Enterprises in the Urban Ghetto, May 24, 1968 and June 17, 1968 (Washington, D.C.: U.S. Government Printing Office, 1968).

Fair Credit Reporting, Hearings before the Subcommittee on Financial Institutions of the Committee on Banking and Currency, U.S. Senate, 91st Congress, 1st Session, on S. 823, A Bill to Enable Consumers to Protect Themselves Against Arbitrary, Erroneous, and Malicious Credit Information, May, 19, 20, 21, 22 and 23, 1969 (Washington, D.C.: U.S. Government Printing Office, 1969).

Federal Trade Commission Bureau of Economics, *Economic Report on Installment Credit and Retail Sales Practices of District of Columbia Retailers* (Washington, D.C.: U.S. Government Printing Office, May, 1968).

Eugene P. Foley, "The Negro Businessman: In Search of a Tradition" in Talcott Parsons and Kenneth B. Clark (eds.), *The Negro American* (Boston: Beacon Press, 1965, 1966), pp. 555-592.

William F. Haddad and G. Douglas Pugh (eds.), *Black Economic Development* (Englewood Cliffs, N.J.: Prentice-Hall, 1969).

Verle Johnston, "Financing the Inner City," in *Monthly Review* (Federal Reserve Bank of San Francisco, October 1969), pp. 199-210.

Mary Gardner Jones, "The Kerner Report and the Federal Trade Commission," Federal Trade Commission, Legal and Publications Office, April 26, 1968.

Walter McQuade, "Mortgages for the Slums," *Fortune,* V. LXXVII, N. 1 (January 1, 1968), pp. 162-163.

President's Commission on Consumer Interest, *The Most for Their Money,* A Report of the Panel on Consumer Education for Persons with Limited Incomes (Washington, D.C.: U.S. Government Printing Office, 1965).

Private Investment in the Inner City, Hearings before the Subcommittee on Financial Institutions of the Committee on Banking and Currency, U.S. Senate, 90th Congress, 2nd Session, on Private Investment in the Inner City, in the Fall of 1968 (Washington, D.C.: U.S. Government Printing Office, 1968).

"Putting the Poor Out of Business: Unhappy Career of the Economic Opportunity Loan Program (SBA)," *The Nation* (June 12, 1967), pp. 750-753.

George F. Reed, "The Question of Insurance," *The Business Lawyer,* V. 25, Special Issue (September 1969), pp. 165-172.

Review of Small Business Administration's Programs and Policies—1969, Hearings before the Select Committee on Small Business, U.S. Senate, 91st Congress, 1st Session, on Review of Small Business Administration Financial Assistance Programs and Policies, June, July, and October 1969 (Washington, D.C.: U.S. Government Printing Office, 1969).

The Urban Coalition, *Consumer Credit and the Low Income Consumer,* Preliminary Report (Researched and Written by William G. Kaye and Associates, Rockville, Md., for the Urban Coalition, November 1969).

8 *Black Enterprise*

In the preceding chapters, we have examined the relationship of black Americans to what are essentially white economic institutions—a relationship in which blacks historically have played a primarily passive role, being acted upon or affected by these institutions, but exercising little impact upon or control over their operations. The purpose of this chapter is to examine a uniquely black phenomenon, business institutions which have been owned and managed by blacks and whose primary, if not exclusive, reason for existence has been to service the black community.

Black business since the end of the nineteenth century has been largely an all-black affair. For a period of approximately twenty-five years following the Civil War, a number of black-owned businesses catering to white trade flourished in northern cities such as Chicago and Philadelphia—particularly in services such as food catering, tailoring, barbering, and delivery. By the turn of the century however, most of these firms were on the decline, many of them the victims of competition from recently arrived European immigrants who preempted their white patrons.[1] Those black businesses which survived and those which were established henceforth oriented their activities to fellow blacks who were beginning to concentrate in urban centers. In the South, those black enterprises which have existed since the end of the Civil War have had (with rare exceptions) an exclusively black clientele.

Whites have played virtually no direct role in black enterprises, although the white community has been an important indirect influence as the controller of business institutions whose unwillingness and inability to fulfill the multiple economic needs of the black community contributed to the creation of black businesses. Black banks, insurance companies, publications, and a variety of specialized service establishments have been developed to meet these needs.[2] However, white America has also arrested the development of these black enterprises by effectively limiting the financing, managerial development, sources of supply, geographical expansion, and markets available to the black entrepreneur. All too rarely have black businesses participated in the mainstream economy, but have functioned virtually exclusively in those areas where economic segregation (or failure to provide goods and services) by white business acted as a type of "protective tariff" for the black businessman.

The subject of black business has assumed renewed significance during the past few years with the publicity accorded "Black Capitalism" during the late 1960s. Champions of the cause of black economic development have appeared within divergent sectors of American society—ranging from militant black organizations such as the Nation of Islam (Black Muslims) to the bastions of the Establishment, including the American Presidency. Accordingly, it is important to look at the past and present of black business in the United States, and to assess its potential for the economic uplift of the black community in the years ahead.

Although economic factors (discussed in this chapter) are primarily responsible for the failure of blacks to develop a strong entrepreneurial class, we can fruitfully speculate that at least two other elements may have been present. The first (and clearly the more important) relates to the devastating psychological impact of slavery and its repressive aftermath upon the psyche of the black American. The second factor is the possible effect of the particular variety of Protestantism practiced by many blacks, particularly in the South.

Although the origins of successful entrepreneurship have long puzzled scholars, there is respectable opinion that sociological and psychological ingredients are of great importance to economic development.[3] At the turn of the century, Max Weber hypothesized that certain aspects of the theology of ascetic Protestantism contributed indirectly to the development of particular attitudes and behavioral patterns among believers that were conducive to economic growth. Among these were the restriction of consumption and an emphasis upon productive activities, personal independence, intensive goal orientation, and the rationalization of one's daily activities.[4]

Weber's thesis has been a subject of vigorous debate since it was first presented, but his basic proposition concerning the importance of a particular mental set or psychological apparatus to economic development has received wide acceptance. Generalizing from Weber's analysis, social psychologist David C. McClelland has emphasized a "need for achievement" *(n Achievement)* as essential to economic development, and economist Everett E. Hagen stresses the critical role of a "need for autonomy" *(n Autonomy)* on the part of the economic innovator. Both scholars agree that economic avenues must be available in which the entrepreneur can, to use the vernacular of the day, "do his own thing." This point is particularly important when one considers the historical situation of the black American.

The black experience within America was one designed to thwart high *n Achievement* and *n Autonomy* on the part of black Americans. Independence and individuality were totally antithetical to both a system of slavery and a social order which viewed blacks as fit for only the most menial and subservient positions within the society. Indeed, for blacks, self assertion and personal achievement, especially on the part of males, frequently exposed the individual to physical and psychological risk. Knowing and keeping one's "place" is incompatible with making strides in any field of social or economic endeavor. Rather, the ethos of American society has inculcated a sense of impotence and inferiority within the black population, traits hardly conducive to the development of an aggressive entrepreneurial class. It is not surprising that McClelland found that, as a group, blacks scored significantly lower than practically all other groups tested with regard to *n Achievement*. Significantly, however, middle and upper class blacks were "conspicuously high" in *n Achievement* level, giving rise to the hope that entrepreneurial development by blacks will increase in the future as more and more blacks overcome existing societal constraints and develop a positive black self-identity.[5]

Let us turn now briefly to the question of the impact of religion upon black economic development.[6] It is plausible that the Southern Baptist variety of Protestantism, emphasizing as it does acquiescence to the will of the Lord and the existence of an afterlife for true believers significantly better than that experienced on earth, and pervaded by a heightened emotional fervor, prevented the emergence

'disciplined, methodical, rational way of life,"[6] which is so important to the
)pment of capitalistic business enterprise. Significantly, until very recently
nic activity has been of little interest to the black clergy except in the constant
ations to the faithful to avoid the paths of sin which abound in the world of
rce.[7] This religious indifference—or even hostility—to business involvement
inished considerably of late, and a number of ministers, most notably the
Revs. Leon Sullivan and Jesse Jackson, have been leaders in community economic
development.

Of all contemporary black religious groups, it is the Black Muslims
which has developed most fully the "spirit of capitalism" (or at least of entrepreneurial endeavor) which Weber associated with Protestantism. The theology of the Black
Muslims emphasizes many of the behavioral traits—frugality, intensive productive
activity, a merging of the secular and religious life, and an emphasis upon
education—Weber found among the Calvinists of Geneva.[8] It is noteworthy that in
1968 alone, the Muslims invested an estimated $6 million (drawn strictly from
Muslim resources) in business ventures and real estate.[9] We are aware that the
economic experience of the Black Muslims provides only indirect evidence
concerning the historical role of religion in black economic development, especially
since many black males have not been affiliated regularly with any church group and
thereby subject, for better or worse, to religious influence. However, the Muslim
experience does raise the interesting question whether and how black churches can
become influences in furthering black enterprise.

We have raised the two socio-psychological factors discussed in the preceding
paragraphs not to suggest they are more important than the structural economic
constraints which have existed within America and have blocked the development of
black business. It appears to us, however, that, as a preamble to an analysis of the
future potential of black business the reader should consider the possibility that
noneconomic variables may have had some significance in the retardation of black
economic development in the past.

Turning now to the readings, E. Franklin Frazier's "Negro Business: A Social
Myth" is drawn from his *Black Bourgeoisie,* a classic examination of the black middle
class. In this essay, sociologist Frazier critically examines the importance of black
enterprise to the life of black communities within the United States and comes to the
conclusion that the "myth" of the economic importance of black business has had a
negative impact upon black people. Although his criticism of the role of the black
middle class is somewhat dated,[10] his overall discussion of the social and economic
significance of black business is still pertinent today. The essay by Harding B. Young
and James M. Hund, "Negro Entrepreneurship in Southern Economic Development,"
looks at black business experience in the South, which, as a consequence of
segregation, provided a relatively fertile environment for black entrepreneurship.
The authors examine the characteristics of entrepreneurship, assess the southern
black experience in business activity, and project the likely course of black economic
development during the years ahead. Many of their observations are equally relevant
to black business in the North. The final selection, consisting of a statement and
testimony by Andrew F. Brimmer, the first black Governor of the Federal Reserve
System, sets forth a number of the important economic factors which are, have been,
and are likely to continue to be, critical to the development of black business within
this country. As a result of his analysis, Brimmer, a professional economist, sounds a
note of caution concerning the prudence of establishing a substantial number of
small-scale black enterprises serving diverse sectors of the American economy.

It is of interest to note that black business in the past has always operated in the
context of a capitalistic economic system. As will be explored in the material in

Chapter 12, a number of recent proposals for black economic development have stressed the necessity of alternative forms of business activity in which the ownership, control, and ultimate benefit of the operations of black businesses will reside within the black community.

NOTES

[1] Implicit recognition of the dire straits into which black business had fallen came in 1900 with the formation of the National Negro Business League by Booker T. Washington. Washington viewed business success as a prime vehicle by which the black man could wipe out racial prejudice and achieve social mobility. The express purpose of the League was to stimulate flagging efforts by blacks in the area of industry and commerce. While the overall impact of the League on black business development during the more than seventy years of its existence is difficult to assess, it has been a continuous rallying point for black entrepreneurial efforts throughout the nation.

[2] For historical accounts of black business, see, e.g., W. E. B. DuBois, *The Philadelphia Negro: A Social Study* (New York: Schocken Books, 1967), esp. pp. 115-126; St. Clair Drake and Horace R. Cayton, *Black Metropolis: A Study of Negro Life in a Northern City,* V. II, rev. enlarged ed. (New York: Harper & Row, Publishers, 1962), esp. 430-469; Abram L. Harris, *The Negro as Capitalist: A Study of Banking and Business Among American Negroes* (Philadelphia: American Academy of Political and Social Science, 1936); Robert H. Kinzer and Edward Sagarin, *The Negro in American Business* (New York: Greenberg, 1950); V. V. Oak, *The Negro's Adventure in General Business* (Yellow Springs, Ohio: The Antioch Press, 1949); Allan H. Spear, *Black Chicago: The Making of a Negro Ghetto, 1890-1920* (Chicago: The University of Chicago Press, 1967); and the works from which the selections in this chapter are drawn.

[3] See especially David C. McClelland, *The Achieving Society* (Princeton, N.J.: D. Van Nostrand Company, Inc., 1961); —— and David G. Winter, *Motivating Economic Achievement* (New York: The Free Press, 1969), and Everett E. Hagen, *On the Theory of Social Change* (Homewood, Ill.: The Dorsey Press, Inc., 1962). Cf. Gustav F. Papanek, "The Development of Entrepreneurship," *American Economic Review,* V. LII, N. 2 (May 1962), pp. 46-58. William Caudill and George De Vos, "Achievement, Culture and Personality: The Case of the Japanese Americans," *American Anthropologist,* V. 58, N. 6 (December, 1956), pp. 1102-1126.

[4] *The Protestant Ethic and the Spirit of Capitalism,* translated by Talcott Parson, (New York: Charles Scribner and Sons, 1958).

[5] McClelland, *The Achieving Society,* pp. 376-377. As a more general conclusion, he found that slavery lowers *n Achievement* on the part of both the slave and slaveholder.

[6] The comments which appear in this section of the chapter benefited greatly from an excellent unpublished paper, "An Analysis of the Adoption of the Protestant Ethic by the Black Muslims and the Lower Class Black Baptist" (March 1970), by John P. Fernandez, a Ph.D. candidate in sociology at the University of California, Berkeley and a student of the Berkeley author. We express our appreciation to Mr. Fernandez for permitting us to draw upon his research and thinking. The above-quoted phrase appears in Mr. Fernandez's paper.
For general discussions of the role and influence of religion upon the life of black Americans, see E. Franklin Frazier, *The Negro Church in America* (New York: Schocken Books, 1966) and Joseph R. Washington, *Black Religion: The Negro and Christianity in the U.S.* (Boston: Beacon Press, 1964), and ——, *The Politics of God: The Future of the Black Churches* (Boston: Beacon Press, 1967).

[7] Cf. Gerhard Lenski, *The Religious Factor: A Sociological Study of Religion's Impact on Politics, Economics and Family Life,* rev. ed. (Garden City, N. Y.: Anchor Books, Doubleday and Company, Inc., 1963), pp. 82-133.

[8] See E. U. Essien-Udom, *Black Nationalism: A Search for an Identity in America* (New York: Dell Publishing Co., Inc.), and C. Eric Lincoln, *The Black Muslims in America* (Boston: Beacon Press, 1961).

[9] Time (March 7, 1969), p. 26.

[10] See, e.g., Ernest Holsendolph, "Middle Class Blacks are Moving off the Middle," *Fortune,* V. LXXX, N. 7 (December, 1969), pp. 90-95, 151, 154, 156.

NEGRO BUSINESS: A SOCIAL MYTH

E. Franklin Frazier

[W]e saw that the capital investment represented by Negro business was insignificant from
the standpoint of the American economy and
that it provided an exceedingly small amount of
employment and income for Negro workers.
Here our purpose is to show how false ideas
concerning the importance of Negro business
have become a social myth and how this myth
has been propagated among Negroes. This
social myth has been one of the main elements
in the world of "make-believe" which the black
bourgeoisie has created to compensate for its
feeling of inferiority in a white world dominated by business enterprise.

ORIGIN OF THE MYTH

When did this myth first take form? It was
formulated, it should be noted, during the last
decade of the nineteenth century when a legal
system of racial separation and subordination
was inaugurated and the hope of Negroes to
attain equality in American life was crushed.
The myth was created by a small group of Negro
intellectuals and Negro leaders who accepted
racial separation as the inevitable solution of the
race problem. From the 1880's on, as Professor
[Abram L.] Harris has pointed out in his *The
Negro as Capitalist:*

. . . the Negro masses, urged by their leaders, were
led to place increasing faith in business and property
as a means of escaping poverty and achieving

economic independence. Although ostensibly sponsored as the means of self-help or racial cooperation,
as it was sometimes called, through which the masses
were to be economically emancipated, Negro business enterprise was motivated primarily by the desire
for private profit and looked toward the establishment of a Negro capitalist employer class. One of the
clearest expressions of the growing tendency to look
upon the development of Negro capitalists and
business enterprise as the basis of racial economic
advancement is to be found in the proceedings of the
Fourth Atlanta University Conference (1898) on
"The Negro in Business."

At this conference, the best formulation of the
myth of the economic salvation of the Negro
through Negro business was presented by the
late John Hope, who later on, after becoming
president of the Atlanta University system
(exclusively for Negroes), hoped to train the
future leaders of "Negro business." He stated:

Industrial education and labor unions for Negroes
will not change this condition [displacement of Negro
workers by white workers]. They may modify it, but
the condition will not be very materially changed.
The white man will meet the Negro on the same
ground and work for the same wages. That much we
may as well take for granted, calculate the consequences of, and strive by every means to overcome
this falling off in our old-time advantages. . . . We
must take in some, if not all, of the wages, turn it into
capital, hold it, increase it. This must be done as a
means of employment for the thousands who cannot
get work from old sources. Employment must be had,
and this employment will have to come to Negroes
from Negro sources. This phase of the Negro's
condition is so easily seen that it needs no further
consideration. Negro capital will have to give an
opportunity to Negro workmen who will be crowded
out by white competition; and when I say Negro

workmen I would include both sexes.... Employment for colored men and women, colored boys and girls must be supplied by colored people....

We are living among the so-called Anglo-Saxons and dealing with them. They are a conquering people who turn their conquests into their pockets. . . . Business seems to be not simply the raw material of Anglo-Saxon civilization—and by business I mean those efforts directly or indirectly concerned with a purposive tendency to material development and progress, with the point in view of the effort bringing material profit or advantage to the one making the effort; and I would include all such efforts whether made in peace or war. I was saying, business seems to be not only simply the raw material of Anglo-Saxon civilization, but almost the civilization itself. It is at least its mainspring to action. Living among such a people is it not obvious that we cannot escape its most powerful motive and survive? To the finite vision, to say the least, the policy of avoiding entrance in the world's business would be suicide to the Negro. Yet as a matter of great account, we ought to note that as good a showing as we have made, that showing is but as pebbles on the shore of business enterprise....

Among the resolutions adopted at the conference was the following:

The mass of the Negroes must learn to patronize business enterprises conducted by their own race, even at some slight disadvantage. We must co-operate or we are lost. Ten million people who join in intelligent self-help can never be long ignored or mistreated.

THE MYTH BECOMES INSTITUTIONALIZED

Two years after the Atlanta Conference on the Negro in business, Booker T. Washington took the initiative in organizing the National Negro Business League, which held its first meeting in Boston, Massachusetts. At this meeting, attended by 115 delegates from 20 states (mostly southern) and the District of Columbia, Washington was elected president of the permanent organization. The four sessions of the two-day meeting were characterized by much oratory and enthusiasm. In his opening address, Washington made the highly dubious generalization that wherever he had "seen a black man who was succeeding in business, who was a taxpayer, and who possessed intelligence and

high character, that individual was treated with the highest respect by the members of the white race." Faith in the power of business enterprise and money to wipe out racial prejudice was repeatedly echoed by the delegates, one of whom stated, "Fortunately human selfishness, the desire of every man to get all he can with least effort or money, has banished all prejudice." These sentiments, it might be noted, won the approval of the leading Boston (white) daily paper.

By far, most of the oratory at this meeting was devoted to the achievements of the Negro in business and the bright future for the Negro in the field of business enterprise. At one point during the meeting, the compiler or statistician interrupted the oratory to announce that according to information provided by the delegates they owned personal and real property amounting to $781,900. In the enthusiasm of the meeting, it appears that no one stopped to realize that even if the figures were true, they represented a very small amount of wealth for 115 businessmen. Nor does it seem that anyone gave sober thought to the report which was presented on the character of Negro business and the amount of capital which it represented.

The report included the study presented at the Atlanta Conference according to which 432 of the 1906 Negro businessmen who sent in reports had small grocery stores; 166 were general merchandise dealers; 162 barbers with $500.00 or more invested in their businesses; 80 undertakers; 68 owners of saloons; 64 had drugstores; and 61 restaurants. The study presented a fair idea of the character of Negro business, since the figures from the United States Census gave a similar picture. These 1906 Negro businessmen represented about a tenth of all persons reported in the Census who, by the broad definition given to "business" by the National Negro Business League, were regarded as engaged in business. For example, the League counted as Negro businessmen the "boarding and lodging house keepers," "hucksters and peddlers," and "newsboys" reported in the Census.

But what else could be expected in a meeting which was designed to bolster faith in a myth? The delegates were urged to spread the faith in this myth in organizing local business leagues throughout the country.

PROPAGATION OF THE MYTH

The success of the exhortation to spread the faith in salvation by business is indicated by the fact that within five years more than 300 local business leagues were organized. Then in 1907 there appeared a book on Negro business by Booker T. Washington, who was elected year after year president of the National Business League. This book, which according to the author was written to "take note of the undoubted business awakening among the Negro people of the United States," contained a series of success stories concerning Negroes in various enterprises. The series begins with stories showing how "the Negro farmer often passes from agriculture into business." Outstanding among these farmers who had become businessmen was a Negro farmer from Kansas who became known as "the Negro Potato King." There followed stories of Negroes who had succeeded as caterers, hotel keepers, undertakers, publishers and bankers. One of the leading bankers was a minister whose success, according to Washington, showed "how closely the moral and spiritual interests of our people are interwoven with their material and economical welfare."

It was not strange that a minister was named among the successful Negro businessmen, since the membership of the League was composed largely of professional Negroes, many of whom could hardly have been regarded as businessmen. If one examines the list of members of the League, especially those holding the offices, it will be found that they represent the leadership of the Negroes without respect to their relation to business enterprise. In fact, the report of the Eleventh Annual Conference of the League, which was held in New York City in 1910, stated as one of the notable features of this convention that a "diversity of interests" was represented. Stated otherwise, it was notable in the sense that the crusade to gain supporters for the faith in business enterprise as the salvation of the Negro was gaining adherents among Negroes in all walks of life. The religious nature of this crusade was indicated in the annual address by Booker T. Washington which was delivered in the form of a "Business Sermon" based upon the Biblical text, "To him that hath shall be given." According to Washington, "these lines spoken by the Master strike the keynote for individual success and equally so for racial success." He exhorted his hearers to go out from the meeting "determined that each individual shall be a missionary in his community— a missionary in teaching the masses to get property, to be more thrifty, more economical, and resolve to establish an industrial enterprise wherever a possibility presents itself."

In this same annual address, Washington also stated that "before the starting of the Business League, there was not a single Negro bank in the State of Mississippi. At the present time, Mississippi has eleven Negro banks. When this Business League was organized in Boston ten years ago there were only four Negro banks in the United States; at the present time there are fifty-six Negro banks." If Washington were living today he would probably be saddened by the fact that there are no Negro banks in the State of Mississippi and that there are only eleven Negro banks in the United States, with total assets amounting to less than a single white bank in many small cities. But at the time that the myth of Negro business was being propagated, little concern was shown for the real economic position of the Negro and his experience in business. At each annual meeting of the League, the delegates were exhorted to spread the faith in business enterprise and were told of the golden opportunities to reap wealth by supplying the needs of the Negro masses. At the thirteenth annual convention in Chicago in 1912, Washington asked in his annual address, "If the white man can secure wealth and happiness by owning and operating a coal mine, brick yard, or lime kiln, why can not more Negroes do the same thing? If other races can attain prosperity by securing riches on a large scale from our seas, lakes and rivers in the form of fish and other sea foods, thousands of Negroes can do the same thing. Activity in all these directions finds no races or color line."

Two years later, when the League met in Muskogee, Oklahoma, Washington stated that "when the 2,000,000 Negroes in the Southwest have made the most of their opportunities . . . and brought up the riches contained in the earth they will be able to support . . . 1,000 more grocery stores owned by Negroes, 500 additional dry goods stores, 300 more shoe stores, 200 more good restaurants and hotels, 300 additional millinery stores,

200 additional drug stores and 40 more banks." These fantastic dreams of business enterprise were applauded by the delegates who attended the annual meetings. Moreover, the delegates themselves engaged in oratory about the progress of the black bourgeoisie in obtaining wealth. They related stories of the acquisition of wealth in business enterprises which, when coldly studied, were really of little significance. Nevertheless, the crusade to win believers in the myth of Negro business continued after these conventions closed. It was preached during the pilgrimages which Washington made through the South. During these pilgrimages he constantly pointed out to the Negroes the opportunities which they were overlooking for gaining wealth through business enterprises and he invited Negro businessmen to give testimonies of their achievements in gaining wealth.

After the death of Washington the League continued to carry on the crusade to instill in Negroes faith in business enterprise as the way to economic salvation. Under the influence of the enthusiasm and oratory which characterized these meetings, the participants continued to relate all sorts of fanciful stories concerning their wealth. Myths grew up concerning Negro millionaires that had no basis in fact. The participants, who were drawn from many fields of professional activities, were often led to describe their activities as being inspired by the spirit of business enterprise. For example, at the meeting in Chattanooga, Tennessee, in 1917, Eugene K. Jones, the executive secretary of the National League on Urban Conditions of Negroes, a social work agency, declared that his organization was "a business organization" which made "a business of social welfare work."

While the myth of Negro business was being propagated, the hard realities of the Negro's insignificant achievements in business were apparent to anyone who was not under the spell of the oratory of the conventions of the League. In order to create a substantial basis for the myth, the National Negro Business League undertook to establish the Colored Merchants Association (CMA) grocery stores throughout the country. According to the CMA plan ten or more Negro retail stores in any city were to buy a share of stock in the CMA in which they paid weekly dues and buy from a wholesale dealer selected by the League. The first CMA organization was established in Montgomery, Alabama, in 1928, and soon thereafter organizations were set up in about eighteen other cities. The organization of the CMA was hailed as a new and realistic approach of the League to the promotion of business enterprise among Negroes. *The Chicago Whip,* a Negro newspaper, stated that the establishment of the CMA stores marked the end of the period of oratory and added, "It is well known now that flamboyant oratory makes no lasting impression, gives no deep insight into the manner in which things are done, nor does it convey the information that the untrained business man is so sadly in need of." The establishment of the CMA stores was marked by much fanfare. In Harlem, in New York City, the opening of the CMA stores was celebrated by a parade which included men and women from business, fraternal and church circles. Despite the fanfare and hopes of the bourgeoisie, the CMA movement failed after a few years. Those who had bought stock in the CMA lost their money, if not their faith in Negro business enterprise. Those who maintained their faith are still not sure whether the failure was due to the lack of support by Negro retailers or that Negro consumers preferred nationally advertised products.

The failure of the CMA adventure did not affect the faith of the black bourgeoisie in the myth of Negro business, since the faith was constantly being strengthened by the expansion of business education among Negro colleges. The number of Negro colleges giving business education grew from six in 1900 to more than twenty in 1940. The majority of the students pursuing courses in business receive a technical education in such subjects as typewriting, bookkeeping, and shorthand. In five of the Negro colleges the students are given professional courses in management and other functions exercised by the owners and officials in business enterprises. A small number are prepared to teach the business courses which they have studied. Of the thirty-five graduates of Atlanta University who received the master's degree in business, five were teaching business and eight were employed in Negro colleges as treasurers, business managers, bursars, and one as a registrar. Although twenty-nine of the thirty-five were employed in fields related to the business courses which they had taken, it does not appear that business education had enabled them to become entrepreneurs. The vast majority of students who take technical and business courses in Negro colleges could acquire the same technical competence in some commercial business school. But in the Negro college, business education is given professional status and is glorified because of the myth of Negro business as a way to economic salvation for the Negro in American society.

Beliefs in regard to the myths surrounding Negro business are not affected by the facts presented in . . . [an earlier chapter]. For example, it has always been claimed that despite the oppression of the Negro in the South, there was a compensatory fact, namely, that the South offered an opportunity for the development of Negro business. This claim is still made today by those who believe in the myth despite the fact that in proportion to population there are more retail stores in the North than in the South, and that the stores in the North have a larger number of full-time employees and a greater volume of sales. Moreover, despite the fact that there are less than half as many stores in the North as in the South, the total payroll in the North is greater than in the South and the sales three-fourths as great as in the South. Nor has the belief in the myth been affected by the fact that the attempts of Negro businessmen to establish industrial undertakings have constantly resulted in failures. Even when they have had the support of northern white philanthropists, Negroes have failed to establish industries of any importance. For example, during the first decade of the present century, Julius Rosenwald was persuaded by Booker T. Washington to invest $30,000 in a cotton oil mill in Mound Bayou, an all-Negro town in Mississippi. This venture failed, as other such business ventures, and the oil mill was converted into a dance hall. Negroes appealed again to Julius Rosenwald in the 1920's to salvage the wreckage of the manifold undertakings of a Negro banker in Atlanta who attempted to build up a large financial empire on the basis of stores and real estate holdings. But on this occasion, Rosenwald evidently did not think that his philanthropic contributions to Negroes should include the salvaging of their unsound business undertakings.

Nevertheless, northern philanthropy has been sympathetic to the efforts of Negroes to create business enterprises. This has been manifested especially in their financial support of the study of Negro business. Despite the myths surrounding the importance of Negro business, the obvious fact that Negro businesses have failed to become important has continually haunted the minds of the most ardent believers in Negro business as a solution of the Negro's problems. Hence, there has been a constant interest in discovering why Negro businesses have failed so often or have not become important in the economic life of the Negro. A quarter of a century ago, the Spelman Fund, established through Rockefeller contributions to social research, made an initial grant of $15,000, which was supplemented by $5,000, for the study of Negro business. The chief results of this study, which comprised less than fifty pages, were to show that almost all Negro businesses were small retail businesses and undertaking establishments serving Negroes, that they were conducted by their owners, and that they were in Negro neighborhoods. Once again, in 1943, the General Education Board was requested by Atlanta University and the National Urban League to contribute $25,000 to a study of Negro business. The co-operation of the National Urban League was sought by Atlanta University because the League had "become convinced that Negroes might help themselves by improving and expanding the business enterprises which they control."

Neither of these studies revealed the fundamental causes of the failure of Negroes to carry on successful business enterprises either on a small or large scale. They did not deal with the simple but fundamental sociological fact that the Negro lacks a business tradition or the experience of people who, over generations, have engaged in buying and selling. Neither the tradition of the gentleman nor his peasant heritage had provided the Negro with this outlook on the world. Nor did these studies deal with the relation of the efforts of Negroes to establish factories and business enterprises to the structure of the American economy. To have presented such facts these studies would have tended to destroy the Negro's faith in the myth. I have heard Professor Harris criticized by the president of a Negro college because in his book, *The Negro as Capitalist,* he showed that one of the fundamental causes of the failure of Negro banks was the impossibility of the Negro banks to function in a segregated Negro economy which lacked sound businesses requiring credit. The college president's criticism was not directed against the facts presented in this study but against its effect upon the Negro's faith in business enterprise as a solution to his economic problems. The myth concerning Negro business, from the standpoint of many Negro leaders, is more important than the facts of American economic life which determine the fate of Negro business enterprises.

The myth of Negro business is tied up with the belief in the possibility of a separate Negro economy. It has constantly been proposed by those who believe in a separate Negro economy that the Negro can build his own manufacturing plants, stores, and banks with the earnings of Negro workers who, by patronizing these Negro enterprises would create more capital and give employment to Negroes. Of course, behind the idea of the separate Negro economy is the hope of the black bourgeoisie that they will have the monopoly of the Negro market. They state that it is a sacred obligation of Negroes to patronize Negro business and that they should not complain if they pay higher prices for goods and can not buy exactly what they want so long as they buy from Negroes. During the Depression years, the black bourgeoisie in northern cities began to sponsor a campaign with the slogan, "Don't Buy Where You Can't Work." The result of this campaign was the growth of anti-Semitism which expressed itself during race riots when Jewish businessmen in Negro neighborhoods became the targets of Negro mobs.

The idea of a separate Negro economy was given an odd turn by a Negro college professor who taught and popularized the theory of the "double duty" dollar. According to this theory, the Negro worker would not only purchase with his dollar the necessities of life, but he would provide with the dollar he spent the wages for Negro workers. Anyone who opposed this fanciful economic theory was called an enemy of Negroes. As the result of the faith in the myth of Negro business there have sprung up all over the country fanciful schemes, such as one recently started in the national capital which proposed that each Negro man, woman and child contribute one dollar to a fund to establish manufactur-ing plants which would make shoes and clothes for the Negro market.

THE MYTH AND THE CHANGING STATUS OF THE NEGRO

The changing status of the Negro in the United States, which has resulted from World War II and the world crisis, has not failed to influence the myth of Negro business. Paradoxically, on the surface at least, the increasing employment of Negroes desiring business careers by white business enterprises has not shaken faith in the myth of Negro business. The reason for this becomes apparent when one considers the relation of the myth to the world of make-believe which the black bourgeoisie has created.

As we have seen, the black bourgeoisie derives its income almost entirely from white-collar and professional occupations which give it a privileged status within the isolated Negro community. Since the black bourgeoisie has rejected identification with the masses, its isolation has been further intensified. In escaping from identification with the masses, the black bourgeoisie has attempted to identify with the white propertied classes. Since this has been impossible, except in their minds, because of the racial barriers those identified with this class have attempted to act out their role in a world of make-believe. In the world of make-believe they have not taken over the patterns of behavior of the white-collar and professional white workers, but the values and as far as possible the patterns of behavior of wealthy whites. With their small earnings, their attempt to maintain the style of living of the white propertied classes has only emphasized the unreality of their way of life. Faith in the myth of Negro business, which symbolizes the power and status of white America, has been the main element in the world of make-believe that the black bourgeoisie has created.

The prosperity which the United States enjoyed as the result of World War II and the war economy during the Cold War has trickled down to the Negroes, especially since some of the barriers to the employment of Negroes have been lowered. The increase in the earnings of Negro workers has brought increased prosperity to Negro businesses, especially to Negro insurance companies and the Negro publishers of newspapers and magazines. Also, the lowering of barriers to the employment of Negroes in white-collar occupations has increased the proportion of Negroes able to maintain a middle-class standard of life. Despite these improvements in the position of the black bourgeoisie, there were some misgivings about the continuance of their properous condition after the War. The feeling that it was necessary to assess the economic improvement in the condition of Negroes in white-collar and professional occupations was the chief motivation for calling a conference at Howard University in 1946.

At the opening session of this conference, the president of Howard University declared that,

The Negro people, just a bit over eighty years from slavery, are a child people in their ability to organize the ordinary things that have to do with effective existence. Take the simple things that engage the attention of a community and involve the major activities of human beings in a small town—the gathering together and the distribution of food in a grocery store, a butcher shop, or a restaurant. In the little one-horse town or your Harlem or your Los Angeles, you miss Negro faces in this fundamental business of assembling and distributing food products. We have a handful of men engaged in the grocery business, a handful in the butcher business, and a handful in the bakery business—although we have some of the best bread bakers in the world. We have nobody in the pastry business. There is also the question of clothing. Any group of 10,000 human beings will naturally require a certain amount of clothing of all kinds. Go into the communities where we live. Enterprises and persons engaged in the effective distribution of these things—to say nothing of their production—are practically missing among us. Then there are some of the service activities connected with clothing—for example, the laundry business. There are practically no Negro-operated laundries, even in the Southern area, where we used to monopolize the washing of clothes. We have so few tailor shops or millinery shops. Yet none of these things are beyond our power. We just simply have not focused our attention upon them.

Much of the discussion at this conference was of the same nature, dealing with the failure of the Negro to seize the opportunity to organize businesses which would thrive on the Negro market. Scarcely any attention was given to the organization of American economic life and how this fact affected the prospects of Negro business. Nor was any discussion directed to the fact that Negro white-collar and professional workers could not assemble the capital and organize the managerial ability necessary for large-scale production and distribution. There was in this conference, as in the conferences of the National Negro Business League, much exhortation to Negroes to engage in business, which revealed a continued faith in the myth of Negro business as providing a solution to the economic problems of the Negro.

When the National Business League celebrated its fiftieth anniversary in 1950 at Tuskegee Institute, the League rededicated itself to the achievement of the aims of the founder, Booker T. Washington. The president of the League announced that the philosophy upon which the League was founded was "as potent today as it was when it was first given. From the very beginning of the League," he added, "its preachments, propaganda and programs have been directed towards alerting our minds to the importance of entering into and building business of all kinds and to the necessity of becoming business minded on a national scale." However, only two years later, when the president of the League reported on the results of his attempt, during his travels amounting to 172,000 miles, to develop faith in the importance and future of Negro business, he had to meet the objection that the League's program really provided for a separate economy. The president said that it did not take him long to convince the person who raised the objection "that a separate economy was a myth." Then he explained, "The customer of the Negro-owned grocery may work for and get his money from employment at General Motors—or General Electric, or at the Ford Automobile Plant, or in department stores owned by other groups—that fact alone eliminates the possibility of a separate economy." Then the president attempted to show how other minority groups, especially the Jews, had become important in the economic life of various countries through their separate business operations.

That the president of the National Negro Business League felt that it was necessary to repudiate the myth of a separate economy, while defending the myth of Negro business, was due to the fact that Negroes were beginning to secure employment on an unprecedented scale in the marketing branches of white businesses. White firms have found it extremely profitable to employ Negroes in advertising products for Negro consumers, in establishing public relations with the Negro community, and as salesmen. Negroes have been employed on a large scale by the distributors of liquors, beers and non-alcoholic beverages, cigarettes, gasoline, and automobiles. The employment of Negroes by large corporations has overshadowed even the exaggerated achievements of Negro businessmen. The importance of the employment of aspiring Negro businessmen in white enterprises stimulated the department of Business Administration at Howard University to hold a "Career Conference in Marketing" in February, 1954. At this conference, the new careers which were opening up to Negroes were discussed and the successful examples of Negroes in these new occupations were presented to students who wanted to become businessmen.

The employment of Negroes in the field of marketing or distribution by large American corporations is a phase of the integration of the Negro into American life. The National Negro Business League, which has proclaimed since its establishment that business success would break down racial barriers, has been compelled to go along with this new development. In fact, some of the younger members of the National Business League, many of whom are not really engaged in *Negro* business, have proposed to delete "Negro" from the name of the League.[1] But this has not met with general acceptance because the leaders recognize that "integration" means the ultimate disappearance of *Negro* business. Some Negro businessmen have pointed to cities where Negroes have recently been accepted into "white" restaurants, theaters, and cinemas to show how integration has meant the decline in *Negro* business. Moreover, as the increasing economic welfare of the Negro has produced all sorts of extravagant claims about the purchasing power of Negroes, Negro businessmen have sought a share in this market.

The myth of Negro business has also been strengthened by the encouragement which the white community has given to the belief of Negroes that the accumulation of wealth through business will solve their problems. Negro salesmen, who are employed by white business and are only sentimentally attached to *Negro* business, are meeting at luncheons with white salesmen; and Negro salesmen are being featured in the public relations literature sent out by corporations. Yet no Negro businessmen are taken into the white business groups which own and control the life of the American community. The white community is assured, nevertheless, that the Negro leaders who propagate the myth of Negro business are uncompromising enemies of any radical doctrines. The myth that Negroes were spending 15 billion dollars in 1951[2] was widely circulated by whites as well as Negroes since it served to exaggerate the economic well-being of Negroes in the United States and to whet the appetites of the black bourgeoisie, both *Negro* businessmen and Negroes employed by American corporations, in their efforts to reap benefits from the increased earnings of Negroes.

The myth of Negro business thrives despite the fact that Negro businessmen can best be described as a "lumpen-bourgeoisie." The myth of Negro business is fed by the false notions and values that are current in the isolated social world of the Negro, a world dominated by the views and mental outlook of the black bourgeoisie. The extent to which these false notions influence the outlook of Negroes cannot better be illustrated than by the case of the Negro Pullman porter who owned his home and four shares of stock, valued at about eighty dollars, in a large American corporation. He declared that he was against the policies of Franklin D. Roosevelt and the New Deal because they taxed men of property like himself in order to assist lazy working men. Such delusions are created largely, as we shall see . . . by the Negro press.

NOTES

[1] Ed. Note: In 1970, the name of the organization is listed officially as the National Business League.

[2] Ed. Note: Now estimated to be in excess of $30 billion. See E. Parke Gibson, *The $30 Billion Negro* (N.Y.: The Macmillan Company, 1969).

NEGRO ENTREPRENEURSHIP IN SOUTHERN ECONOMIC DEVELOPMENT

Harding B. Young and James M. Hund

Ten years after the end of World War II and ninety years after the end of the War Between the States, Negroes could not be found in the upper levels of the nation's business leadership. In any comparison of North and South in terms of contribution to such leadership, it was recommended that the Negro population be excluded. Yet various segments of the public press have recently commented, often flamboyantly, on the aggregations of Negro wealth, Negro society, and the accomplishments of individual Negroes in many endeavors. The easy assumption is that any marked accomplishments must have occurred in the North, because the stifling effects of segregation would certainly have prevented such from being realized in the South. Most of the scholarly studies of Negroes in business appeared a decade ago or more.

It is appropriate, then, to review from several aspects the status of Negro entrepreneurship and to hazard some predictions for the future. Accordingly, in what follows there are offered first some notions on the dimensions of this phenomenon and the past and present barriers to its development. A description of the fields of Negro entrepreneurship in the South is then presented. Finally, in the light of the changes which have occurred, some conclusions will be drawn about the form and future course of Southern Negro entrepreneurship. In carrying out this effort there has been an attempt "to grasp the economic significance of certain aspects . . . of business enterprise conceived as

Reprinted from *Essays in Southern Economic Development,* M. L. Greenhart and W. T. Whitman, eds. (Chapel Hill, N.C.: University of North Carolina Press, 1964), pp. 112–157, by permission of the authors and the publisher. Some footnotes omitted.

social phenomena, and . . . to view these elements as in a state of constant change." In other words, emphasis is on merging "some aspects of the supposedly distinct disciplines of business administration, economics, sociology, and history."

"From the very moment of emancipation, Negro leaders urged the free men to have faith in business and property as an escape from poverty and as the road to the achievement of economic independence." To a great extent this has been a will-o'-the-wisp because of the barriers which have prevented achieving the objectives of such exhortation. In a bitter, though realistic, vein, Franklin Frazier has dubbed this "Negro Business: A Social Myth." He notes that "it has always been claimed that despite the oppression of the Negro in the South, there was a compensatory fact, namely, that the South offered an opportunity for the development of Negro business. Nor has the belief in the myth been affected by the fact that the attempts of Negro businessmen to establish industrial undertakings have constantly resulted in failures." If one defines "industrial undertakings" as manufacturing, mining, or large-scale distribution, one can find but few outstanding successes, but not so much on account of failure as for lack of enterprises in these fields. A broader definition will find notable exceptions to Frazier's sweeping generalizations, and it is these which are the principal concern of this paper.

Even though many of the problems associated with Negro entrepreneurship are matters of slow change and are intimately entwined with the social progress of the Negro in the United States, it is not possible here to recapitulate a century or more of this progress. Yet the conditions under which Northern white entrepreneurship and its counterpart in the South have arisen are quite different, though undoubtedly some close parallels might be found historically in first- and second-generation national and ethnic groups. [Arthur H.] Cole has, for example, noted the importance of non-economic stimuli and motivations among businessmen as being universal in character. Achievement "can be regarded as an expression of the almost universal human desire for prestige." "Whatever the immediate motivations, those potent in business seem related to one or another of the psychological incentives of search for security, prestige, power, and social service." In spite of this emphasis on prestige as a universal, it will be pointed out in some detail below that the relative importance of this motivation in the Negro community is quite different from what it is in the white. Exceptions of this kind call for some historical perspective on, and a current evaluation of, the factors which have both encouraged and retarded the growth and development of Southern Negro entrepreneurship. This is the task of the next section.

ENTREPRENEURSHIP: REQUIREMENTS AND BARRIERS

Entrepreneurship is not an economic phenomenon which autonomously springs into being like Minerva from the head of Zeus. Its seeds may exist in dormant condition, but require a beneficent climate for germination and development to full flower. In his excellent introduction and background to Southern entrepreneurship, Professor [C. A.] Hickman notes the degree to which environment will appreciably affect the supply of entrepreneurship. Some relevant factors are: "the degree of urbanization, the mobility of the population, the extent and quality of education, family attitudes, political patterns and social mores and values. . . ." It is because of, or in spite of, such factors that entrepreneurship occurs. These factors, and others such as markets, financing, experience, and communication, are examined in this section as contributing to or retarding the development of Negro entrepreneurship in the South. The following section presents examples

of the kinds of Negro business enterprises which have arisen in response to the combination of forces stemming from the several conditioning factors.

For purposes of this discussion, a relevant definition of entrepreneurship must be chosen from the many which have been suggested in the literature. Just as in defining leadership, a choice must be made between a reliance on personal effectiveness or organizational behavior. One is tempted to choose the former and mold a definition around those who have demonstrated the strength of character and ability to pierce through the several barriers to be discussed rather than around those who might be deemed "peak coordinators" or maintainers of efficient decision-making systems. Yet [Clarence] Danhof, concentrating on personal effectiveness, claims that "an individual may be characterized by entrepreneurial activity only if he is primarily concerned with changes in the formula of production of an enterprise over which he has full control." This is too restrictive for a discussion of Negro entrepreneurship. Cole, focusing on organizational behavior, offers an all-encompassing definition: "purposeful activity of an individual or group of associated individuals, undertaken to initiate, maintain, or aggrandize a profit-oriented business unit for the production or distribution of economic goods and services." One of Cole's reviewers agrees that "It may be well to drop the figure of the 'heroic' entrepreneur, but there is much to be said for limiting the function to its creative, shaping aspects, less in terms of major achievements or acts of synthesis than in the constant modification of structures, situations or ideas in a continuing process of interaction." It will be seen that these suggestions have particular applicability to Negro entrepreneurship where neither the qualities and functions of a Thomas A. Edison nor an Alfred P. Sloan are to be found. For the South as a whole, Hickman found the entrepreneurial function less complex. He points out that coordination, balance, and unification have been needed only recently, entrepreneurship being more nearly in one set of hands, undiffused, than would be the case in a very large firm. This is true of most Negro enterprises, yet the situation is often more complex because of the combination of social and economic motives behind Negro entrepreneurship. It is perhaps time to note just how the several factors presented above have shaped this phenomenon, viewed first in some historical perspective and then in the forms they assume today.

"KNOW-HOW"

Entrepreneurship and craftsmanship are certainly not coextensive, but many craftsmen have been found in the entrepreneurial ranks, particularly if craftsmanship is broadened to include invention. Where a Lee deForest and a Preston Tucker could fail, a Thomas Edison and a Henry Ford could succeed brilliantly. Immediately after the Civil War, the Negro had a virtual monopoly on labor in the Southern plantation economy because white people had generally eschewed it. "Negroes were to a large extent the craftsmen and the mechanics . . . for even skilled labor was degraded. The whites had often been denied the opportunity of acquiring training since so many masters had preferred to work with slaves." It is true that these skills were employed in plantation work in an agricultural economy, but in terms of being equipped for the coming transition to a more urbanized and industrialized economy and culture, the Negro had an edge. Of course, the things which he sorely lacked were the other two of the triad of economic factors, land and capital. In the shrinkage of economic values which accompanied the collapse of the Confederacy, his white brother was not much better off in terms of capital accumulation. Even though the Negro possessed the rudiments of industrial skills on the eve of expansion of the non-agricultural economy, existing cultural mores and values did not point to business as the place for the Negro to seek fulfillment. "In these men just released from slavery three ambitions seemed to dominate: a desire to learn Greek and Latin; to hold public office; to become preachers." During Reconstruction the second of these was possible in the South, and is becoming possible again today. The first was sublimated into general academic work, and the third persists. Several other professions have over the years been added to the list.

If economic inflation rather than deflation had followed in the years after the Civil War,

the lot of the Negro might have been somewhat easier, but as the agricultural economy became less able to support both Negroes and whites, prompting migration to the cities, economic competition for jobs became severe. Even though the Negro had the skills, he was also a minority group which could be easily distinguished. Not only were Negroes driven out of old jobs, but they were not given the opportunity to try for the new ones opening up. Jim Crow legislation came during the 1890's, the pressures of deflation continued, and political representation for the Southern Negro became a thing of the past. "During this development, defensive beliefs were constantly growing among whites in the South that the Negro was inefficient, unreliable, and incompetent to work with machines. It was true that fewer and fewer young Negroes could keep up with skills when they were not allowed to experience the better working conditions and the new techniques or get training."

This legacy of these attitudes and practices lingers today in the difficulty Negroes with basic abilities and some financial resources have in securing experience which can serve as a firm basis for entrepreneurship. One Negro banker remarked in an interview that mastery over the separate business functions at both the operating and managerial levels calls for a balanced combination of formal education and on-the-job training which is seldom found among Negro businessmen. Far too often Negroes who wish to engage in given business enterprises can cite no prior experience in the line of business they plan to enter. They do not seem to realize the importance of knowhow. Aside from the larger amount of capital needed to enter manufacturing, and the requisite access to markets, there was the feeling expressed by many who were interviewed that the Negro will enter manufacturing only after he better understands the corporate form of enterprise and has had more training in management.

Herein lies one of the central problems of the Negro businessman. First, he has had no tradition in business. Only in a few instances has he had the opportunity to learn from his father, or has taken the opportunity when presented. Until very recently he has been denied the opportunity to work at the managerial level in a white enterprise in the North or South to gain the necessary on-the-job experience. Education can sometimes be a partial substitute for experience. How has the Negro fared in this regard?

EDUCATION

Some Negroes have managed to gain experience or know-how in a particular chosen field and have been motivated to enterpreneurship. For them one barrier has been the lack of other qualified personnel with which to staff an expanding enterprise. It is true that many business ventures have been initiated by Negroes with the hope of offering, as an important ancillary benefit, other than menial employment to members of the race. Yet a nucleus of qualified people is essential. The fact is that the image of business in the minds of those fortunate enough to pursue college work has held little attraction. Forty-five years ago Thomas I. Brown noted that "but a small percentage of college-bred Negroes seem to enter business." This continues to be true today, as corroborated by those interviewed. The view was expressed that far too few Negro college graduates enter business; even where available, business education has not been in great demand. It has only been in the past ten to fifteen years that departments of business administration have been added to Negro colleges and universities. Where they exist, many suffer from lack of teachers qualified in both training and experience, though there are some notable exceptions. It has therefore been difficult to provide a flow of appropriately educated people for the would-be entrepreneurs to hire. The training programs of the insurance companies mentioned below are evidence of this.

Several reasons for the reluctance to enter business were offered. Most important was the belief that the professions have been more attractive because of the economic security and prestige afforded. The average Negro would rather risk his nest egg or line of credit on dental equipment than on a business venture. Since he is at the bottom of the economic ladder, his chances of making a comeback from failure are not considered good. The prestige accorded the image of the successful Negro in legitimate business is hardly worth the risks. Of those college-trained Negroes who have entered business in any substantial way, the highest percent-

age have been in the general area of finance—banks, insurance companies, mortgage companies, and savings and loan associations. This probably accounts for the large measure of success which has been achieved in these fields of enterprise. The authors' research confirmed [Joseph A.] Pierce's observation that "on the average, the enterprises operated by persons who took business education in college have been established longer, employ more persons, and have larger volumes of business than those operated by persons with no business education."

Even in the general area of finance, respondents reported their inability to recruit and retain persons adequately prepared for the highly complex business structure. This problem is further magnified by the fact that Negro business firms find themselves in competition with white firms which are increasingly employing top-quality Negro help. One man stated that part of the solution here is for Negroes to hire whites (or reverse integration, one might call it). Some evidence of this approach is appearing, although it involves some readjustment in attitudes toward one of the basic purposes for Negro business, the provision of jobs for Negroes above the unskilled and semi-skilled levels.

Finally, it must be assumed that in the large migrations of Negroes to the North, beginning in 1900, but particularly in the past twenty years, much of the South's potential Negro entrepreneurship has been lost. Any numerical estimate is of course impossible, but it is not hard to imagine that those Negroes with ambition for business success who did not have the advantage of higher education would move. One could add to this group those who had no available access to business opportunity through marriage or family connections. The calculated chance for success has been important, and receptive markets have raised appreciably the chance.

RESTRICTED MARKETS AND THE CHANCE FOR SUCCESS

Trying to make a virtue out of a necessity, leaders like Marcus Garvey declared that Negroes must become independent of white capital and white employers. Booker T. Washington also encouraged the development of Negro business, bringing about the National Negro Business League in 1900 to encourage such activity. "The dominant direction of this interest has been more racial than economic. Attention has been centered more upon Negro business for Negro patronage than upon this business as a purely economic venture for profit." This was necessarily so, since it is hard to conceive of building an enterprise devoted to the production of goods and services which could survive catering to the Negro ten percent of the population unevenly scattered over the land. Business had to be local in nature, serving concentrated centers of Negro population. The market was and is restricted in two ways. First, it is racially restricted; second, it is restricted as to income.

Negro customers, who constitute the great bulk of the patronage of Negro businesses, are members of the poorest racial group in America. Although there has been a marked increase in the level of Negro income, there is still a sizable gap, in figures for the nation, of over two thousand dollars between white and Negro median wage incomes. In the South this disparity is even greater. For example, in the state of Georgia the median white family income in 1960 was $5,027 as compared to $2,188 for the non-white family. Interviews revealed that while Negro businesses in the South depend mainly upon Negro patronage, such establishments are not sharing significantly in the increases in Negro purchasing power which have occurred except in areas left to Negro businessmen by patterns of segregation, law, and custom. These patterns affect both sides of the market, buying and selling. Negro businesses not dependent on segregation find they are in keen competition with those of whites in many lines. Retail trade has been the prime example, but now one or more white insurance companies in the South are considering employing Negro salesmen to work the Negro market. This looms in special significance when it is recalled that at one time white companies would not insure the lives of Negroes at all. Such competition has been increasing as attention is called more and more to the growth of Negro purchasing power. A counter-penetration on a national scale has not been accomplished by Negro firms, though cosmetics seems to offer a possible exception.

The president of one Negro insurance company related that because of custom, Negro firms do not insure lives of whites, and employment is restricted to Negroes. Such organizations are caught in this situation and therefore give white companies an advantage. It has been pointed out that this is changing, but with few exceptions the market for Negro business firms has been limited to less than ten percent of the population and about five percent of the income. Job discrimination together with a lower level of training and skill have kept the Negro's income low.

At low-income levels one customarily finds little or no accumulated savings and a high propensity to consume. Of necessity, purchasers at these levels avail themselves of credit when it is extended. Negro businesses as a whole are under-capitalized and therefore unable to grant credit and at the same time try to carry a wide variety of goods to meet competition of white firms. As a result the Negro housewife avoids the colored grocer as well as the chain store. Often the Negro family goes to a cheap clothing store to purchase on credit rather than to get good values. When the Negro furniture dealer is unable to extend credit, he finds it difficult to compete with the white retailer who experiences no trouble in having his paper picked up by the local bank.

Even in those cases where some business success was realized, it was not always tolerated by the surrounding community. It is reported, for example, that "in many towns any sign of marked progress by a Negro business house [was] taken as a notice that that business should be crippled or destroyed. Hence, in a certain town . . . it is said to [have been] customary for the white city fathers to revoke the license or charter of any Negro business which does well. . . . If the Negro proprietor is making money, he dare not let it appear so."

This necessity to operate in a somewhat furtive manner has carried over today and is at least partly accountable for the unattractiveness of so many Negro places of business and for the lack of adequate business records. The latter also stems, of course, from lack of training in business procedures and a desire to avoid the scrutiny of the tax collector, who will most certainly be white and a possible source of information which could lead to retaliation. This is probably unwarranted today.

E. E. Hagen has pointed to the rise of business leaders from among disadvantaged groups at various times and places under conditions where success in business could compensate for discrimination against entering the high-prestige professions. Elaborating on this theme, [David C.] McClelland injects the provisos that the minority group be predominantly middle class and reasonably high in his dimension of "n Achievement" [Need for Achievement]. These conditions have not generally existed for American Negroes. The high-prestige professions have been open, though often only in terms of service to the race, while only a small segment of the minority group has attained middle class status. It is success in business which has been most difficult to attain.

Given a background of slavery, rejection, and segregation, it is surprising that any seeds of entrepreneurship could find soil suitable for germination, particularly in the South. Much of Negro business supports the hypothesis that innovation will be slow or non-existent when stress on the organization, or the difference between the level of aspiration and the level of achievement, is great. Frustration or desperation have often been the result where aspirations have far exceeded achievements, personal or organizational. Such outcomes of entrepreneurial efforts have hardly served to enhance the image of Negro business.

FINANCING

Even for those Negroes who have succeeded in meeting the requirements of education and/or experience, and who feel they can make money in a restricted market, the problem of financing remains if anything but the smallest of enterprises is to be undertaken. There is probably more wealth in the Negro community than is commonly assumed, but it is not often concentrated in what one views as the usual channels to be tapped for equity money or loans. This may be due to the historical fact of Negro bank failures and a consequent unwillingness to entrust one's funds to a Negro financial institution. The failure of the much-heralded Freedmens Bank after the Civil War, and the other failures of Negro financial institutions, have dimmed the faith of Negroes in economic units the white economy regards as essential to the growth of business enterprise.

As might be expected, those interviewed in the study reported financing as their most serious obstacle to business growth and expansion. It would seem that there has been little change in this regard during the last twenty years. Pierce noted this in his work as he attributed the chief difficulties in organizing a Negro business or in promoting its expansion and growth to the lack of adequate capital and hard-to-get or inaccessible credit.

The difficulties faced by Negro businessmen seeking bank credit stem from several factors: prejudice of the white bank officials; the lines of business in which Negroes engage; the adequacy of records kept in a large percentage of businesses; lack of financial sophistication by many Negro businessmen; and finally, the marginal position of many businesses.

Evidence of the first factor was often found during the course of the study, though it was impossible to validate by actual check. For example, in one large city a distributor of consumer products said that he has found it extremely difficult to get a business loan from a white institution and so has worked to get a Negro-sponsored commercial bank in that city. In his words, "Banks do the bulk of lending on financial statements and on character. Negroes have no character so far as white banks are concerned. The more collateral over the loan, the better." He cited an attempt to borrow $2,000 with good financial statements. The borrower had to pledge $3,000 in gilt-edged securities. At the same time another bank over eight hundred miles away was willing to make the loan on the strength of the same financial statements.

In another Southern city a Negro bank official said that prior to 1949 a Negro could hardly get a legitimate business loan, usurious rates being the rule for Negroes. If one were obtained, it carried balloon payment provisions rendering it almost impossible to repay. Banks have been more interested in guarantees by whites than in the applicant's business ability, according to some of those interviewed. This would seem to confirm what Pierce found in his study: "Southern mores, generally, require endorsement by whites as a definition of the character of

Negroes. . . . Frequently this means that Negroes are not investigated for their business competence as whites might be."

The president of one of the larger Negro-sponsored banks related another side of this story. He said that very often unsuccessful business operators attribute their poor showing to a lack of sufficient capital and the inability to obtain a bank loan when these may not be the real causes of their difficulty. To use his words: "We might as well observe that the charge of discrimination because of race is often incorrectly raised when some Negroes are unable to obtain desired credit assistance for their business operations. Actually, the credit may be denied for perfectly sound reasons which have no immediate relation to the applicant's racial identity." Capital, he maintained, is constantly looking for profitable avenues of use in both large and small business. It is the responsibility of the borrower to demonstrate his capacity to make profitable use of capital. In the opinion of this bank official, a firm intention to liquidate indebtedness on schedule coupled with the preparation of regular, accurate financial statements is the best approach to securing financial assistance.

In this connection the proprietors of a large restaurant and lounge said that they have never experienced difficulty in securing money, and that long ago they learned the importance of good record-keeping. A Negro educator, also a businessman of some note, told the authors that many businessmen keep records sufficient for tax purposes, but that these are often not adequate to make business decisions or serve as means of control. Accordingly, they will then be wanting as support for a loan application. This partially explains the reticence of white banking institutions to make loans to Negro businesses. The Negro institutions, on the other hand, are often more conservative in their loan policies, but at the same time have been willing to work with selected businesses so that the necessary records could be developed to present a clear financial picture.

Another bank president emphasized the average Negro businessman's unwillingness to put all his effort and capital into his business. He may invest instead in some "broken down real estate," hoping thus to be a landlord rather than ploughing back earnings into the business.

There is also the natural inclination to expand personal consumption at the expense of reasonable retention of earnings. "The rule is sacrifice" to get capital formation, and this conservative, self-reliant attitude does not enjoy high popularity, according to this banker.

An additional aspect of the problem of financing, according to some respondents, is the information held by credit agencies about Negroes. This is, they contend, often incomplete and inaccurate. Because of the lack of communication, for example, of the kind afforded by Chambers of Commerce, Rotary Clubs, and other civic and business groups, credit agencies rely on figures only when white references are not presented. It is felt that the merchants' bureaus rate all Negro customers as sub-standard and therefore charge higher rates—15 percent instead of 8 percent.

The greatest barrier is the need for equity capital, a problem of all business, and particularly small business. Here the Negro businessman faces a dilemma. The small Negro banks, just like other banks, cannot supply venture capital which is sorely needed to enable the Negro businessman to break out of the service type of establishments into manufacturing, which contributes so much more in terms of value added and employment. On the other hand, Negroes, because of the low level of incomes and consequent inability to save large amounts of capital to build up their enterprises, have been unable (and, as has been pointed out, unwilling) to rely on internal financing. It seemed to the authors that there exists in some quarters an unawareness of sources of capital which might be tapped, such as the Small Business Administration, to which some have successfully applied. There was also some lack of sophistication concerning the proper balance in a capital structure for different kinds of business.

Since the urgent need is for equity financing which banks cannot provide, the Negro businessman may well turn to greater use of the corporate form of business. Many corporations which do exist are closed and in some instances are still family organizations. There is some evidence that cooperation and a pooling of equity funds is taking place. Possessing but little capital as individuals, it is incumbent for those with entrepreneurial instincts to get these individuals to pool their resources. As can be seen, a requisite for such pooling is the existence of a spirit of mutual trust.

MUTUAL TRUST

If wider use of the corporate form of business is to serve the potential Negro entrepreneur by providing a pooling of capital funds, it must be preceded by growing willingness to participate in risky ventures. Because of their disadvantaged position, Negroes have often been relieved of what they had by members of both races. The stereotypes of Amos and Andy and the Kingfish, though repugnant to a race trying to better itself, are nonetheless easy to identify today. This lack of mutual trust, coupled with wariness in dealings with whites, has been a serious obstacle to the development of Negro enterprise.

In a biting commentary the Reverend [Edward] Gholson has declared that "much of the wealth which he [the Negro] has acquired has been literally stolen from him by unscrupulous and designing individuals who felt a kind of divine mandate to live by the sweat of another's brow. Having a better knowledge of economic trends, and enjoying a better economic position, they could do this not only with impunity but with public approval." Such experience stirred in the Negro a deep distrust of the white man in business. This was added to the psychological set carried forward from the days of slavery when Negroes were divided into "house" and "field." The former usually had more privileges and more education and were naturally exposed to the culture of the day. They also gained favors by acting as a sort of spy system on their less fortunate fellows, so that even within the Negro race in the South there was no natural development of solidarity and mutual trust.[1] Centers of Negro business in the South visited by the authors exhibited both extremes of this dimension, which helps historically to account in a major way for the success or lack of success of Negro entrepreneurship.

The extreme of distrust or individualism was found in New Orleans. "Coming down through the years since slavery Negroes have been successfully brainwashed not to trust each other" is the way it was expressed by a long-time resident of that city. He listed different racial backgrounds and cultures which characterize New Orleans and an absence of leadership as reasons for the lack of real entrepreneurship among Negroes there. With a Negro population of a quarter million, New Orleans has no Negro savings and loan association or commercial bank. Three attempts have been made to organize a commercial bank. Once, the state banking commission would not grant approval; and since then it has been impossible to raise the $300,000 necessary for a federal charter. At the same time there are some eighteen small industrial-type insurance companies in the one city, each with its own family interest. According to one respondent, this variety of backgrounds will make it extremely difficult to effect mergers necessary to avert failures which must certainly occur attendant on the swing away from industrial to ordinary insurance.

COMMUNICATION

Granted the ingredients of education and know-how joined to adequate financing, directed toward viable market objectives, and reinforced with a spirit of mutual trust, successful entrepreneurship outside "the rackets" still requires what Cole had called "a beneficent climate of social opinion, a changing climate, to be sure, but one that does not discourage the flotation of new enterprises." Relegation of Negro business to a position out of the mainstream serving only in those areas where white businessmen did not choose to serve could hardly be regarded as a climate favorable to entrepreneurship. With the focus of business in general changing from community, to industry, and then to nation, most Negroes were perforce limited to community, though exceptions to this can be found.

The beginning of modern economics as we know them today was tied to the emergence of markets and trade following the feudal period. The years following the Civil War are comparable for the South. The general trend to commercial development and the spread of communication media and the lifeblood they gave to commerce were largely missing for the Negro. He could not join trade associations or local Chambers of Commerce where information of the market-place was exchanged, and trade publications seldom were directed to his problems in business. This is the rule even now. Various professional organizations pertaining to one of the functional fields of business are generally closed to his membership.

One businessman who engages in manufacturing said that the lack of communication constitutes a part of his trouble in obtaining financing and access to markets. He maintained that the Negro bank is not familiar with his kind of manufacturing business and the white bankers do not know him. "One way to open up the channel of communication and thereby permit the Negro to learn some know-how of business would be to integrate the Chamber of Commerce," says this manufacturer. Thompson has described this situation with particular reference to New Orleans: "There is no Negro member of the New Orleans Chamber of Commerce, the powerful Young Men's Business Club, Rotary, or any other organization where economic trends, opportunities, and planning are discussed by experts. This, coupled with the fact that the Negro Business League in New Orleans has always been anemic, means that the individual Negro businessman has few, if any, opportunities to benefit from the thinking and experience of other businessmen."

Of course it would be ridiculous to contend that there are no points of contact between the white and Negro business communities in any given situation. But on the Negro side they are often limited to a few persons of prominence such as the barbers who were the founders of the two large life insurance companies or the president of the multiple-line casualty company who gained his experience working with whites. There have been others who for one reason or another served as communication links between the two communities and were sometimes dubbed "Uncle Toms" for their efforts. In failing to wave the black flag and thus destroy his effectiveness, Dixie's only Negro legislator in a century, Senator Johnson of Atlanta, is beginning to have this reputation.

One can see, then, that for the Southern Negro the usually assumed requirements for the rise of entrepreneurship have often been lacking or present only in diluted form. Some of these, it might be added, were missing for the white man too, notably tolerance for any breakdown in the social structure or acceptance of change. The combination of a rural economy and an orientation to European customs and values when considering a career left but little acceptance for money-making or a social structure built on obvious accumulation of property and conspicuous consumption rather than on land. Incentives for white men to engage in entrepreneurship in the South were weaker than in the North, and artificial barriers have made entrepreneurship appear even less appealing to the Negro.

Yet in spite of the difficulties, past and present, recited in this section, Negro entrepreneurship has occurred in the South. It has performed several important functions beyond the merely economic, though in terms of employment offered and markets served it has not made important contributions. It is the task of the following section to describe specific enterprises in a cross section of Negro business.

SOUTHERN NEGRO ENTREPRENEURSHIP TODAY

FINANCIAL INSTITUTIONS

The greatest entrepreneurial activity demonstrated by Negro businessmen has been in the area of financial institutions. Here the authors noted the most complete preparation for the entrepreneurial role and the most astute leadership. These institutions include insurance companies, banks, and savings and loan associations.

Insurance companies. Negro insurance companies visited by the authors ranged from the special assessment type with assets of $1,500,-000 to the largest life company with present assets close to $77,000,000 and $337,000,000 insurance in force. A composite statement of member firms of the National Insurance Association, Inc., based on forty-one companies submitting the full statistical report as of September 1, 1961, shows total assets of over $300,-000,000. At present it is estimated that the fifty-one N.I.A. companies have total admitted assets of close to $320,000,000 and total insurance in force of $1,900,000,000. Three major Southern institutions included in this association were visited—North Carolina Mutual, Durham, North Carolina; Atlanta Life, Atlanta, Georgia; and Universal Life, Memphis, Tennessee. Fig-

Assets and Insurance in Force of Three Southern Life
Insurance Companies Visited[2]

| Name of Company | ASSETS | | | |
	Dec. 31, 1960	Dec. 31, 1951	Increase	Percent
North Carolina Mututal	$67,600,990	$33,558,781	$34,042,209	101.44
Atlanta Life	53,663,900	26,622,571	27,011,329	101.46
Universal Life	18,749,310	9,284,149	9,465,161	101.94
	LIFE INSURANCE IN FORCE			
North Carolina Mutual	$277,186,658	$164,540,211	$112,646,447	68.46
Atlanta Life	176,192,665	145,721,897	30,470,768	20,91
Universal Life	116,220,219	73,594,999	42,625,220	57.91

ures from company records indicate changes in assets and life insurance in force as follows:

These statistics indicate the growth of these life companies over a decade. However, the figures should be interpreted in the light of changes which have taken place in the Negro market over the last twenty years. Population has doubled since World War II, and income has increased more than 50 percent since 1950 and has more than tripled since 1940. There are more and more Negroes moving from lower to upper levels of income. At the same time their life expectancy is sixty-four years, over 40 percent greater than twenty years ago.

The most notable example of entrepreneurship in life insurance is that of North Carolina Mutual. The Penrose definition of enterprise ". . . as a psychological predisposition on the part of individuals to take a chance in the hope of gain, and in particular, to commit effort and resources to speculative activity," does not characterize the motivation of the founders of this company. A definite need existed, as most white companies simply refused to insure the lives of Negroes. Those which did offer insurance would not consider individual applications and considered all Negroes as substandard risks justifying higher premiums. With the expenses of final illness and burial sapping small financial resources, the hat was often passed at the cemetery. Two persons in the city of Durham who were always called on for assistance were John Merrick, who operated a barber shop for whites, and a young Negro physician. To provide a systematic and organized approach to aid, they set out to organize

an insurance company. These men had no knowledge of, or experience in, life insurance, although they did have some familiarity with fraternal organizations. Joining the two was C. C. Spaulding, bringing to the position of general manager his experience as a grocer.

During the company's early years trained personnel were not available, and trial and error was often the method. Establishing confidence in a financial institution owned, managed, and staffed by Negroes was a pioneering job. But the regulatory authorities approved the operation and claims were paid. Word of this spread, and the company was on its way to becoming the 185th largest among more than 1,400 in the United States. Employment is offered currently to 1,200 Negroes in more than 50 job categories such as those of executive, technician, lawyer, investment specialist, manager, programmer, and salesman. Equipment and other facilities are all modern, including the latest in electronic data processing. The firm is at present engaged in building a new home office on the famous Duke four acres in Durham.

One of the major problems faced by the company through the years has been obtaining and retaining qualified personnel. One response has been home-office and regional schools in agency management and life-insurance selling. In addition, office personnel have been given special courses, and appropriate persons have been enrolled in leading schools in insurance.

Growth of the company can be attributed to various factors: improved training of the home office and field staff; new lines of insurance coverage; improved economic status of the

Negro stemming from improved job opportunities for him; and merger with other companies. The company's image has continually strengthened, and as income and life expectancy of the Negro have increased, so has his demand for ordinary insurance to replace the weekly premium type.

The second largest Negro-owned life insurance company is located in Atlanta. It is a stock company, founded by another barber who catered to the white trade. Professor Hickman in his descriptions of entrepreneurship spoke of the eclectic concept of Gambs and Wertheimer, which includes ". . . good contacts with persons informed on business and political matters; discretion . . . ability to pick good lieutenants . . ." as characteristics of the true entrepreneur. Such a description fits the founder of this company. It was in barbering that Mr. Herndon made many acquaintances with people of influence in the community who helped him. He was approached by a group of Negro ministers who had been administering a benevolent society which they wished him to take over. In 1905 the Atlanta Mutual Benefit Association was formed. It was a weekly premium operation, but by 1927 it was writing ordinary insurance too.

Influenced by the failure of Standard Life in Atlanta, Atlanta Life has striven to make safety its prime objective. Operating through sixty offices in eleven states, it employs close to 1,700 people in the field; and a career training course is now peopled almost entirely by college graduates. The administrative officers are highly competent in their specialties.

In Memphis, Tennessee, is another example of entrepreneurship in life insurance, headed by a man holding degrees from Fisk, the University of Michigan, and New York University. He is also president of the Tri-State Bank of that city. Unlike other Negro entrepreneurs, he has a business background furnished by his father, who was the founder. The latter had been active in business in Mississippi and moved to Memphis to form Universal Life. In 1958 the company purchased Excelsior Life of Dallas, and in 1961, it took up 83 percent of the stock of Louisiana Life of New Orleans. The company employs 122 persons in its home office and 650 in the field. Supplying money for mortgages on Negro housing projects, it has serviced hundreds of borrowers and lent millions of dollars, two-thirds of it federally insured.

As with other life companies, the major problem is finding the qualified personnel so essential to efficient operations. The president's approach is to locate young men with potential within his organization and to pay for their training in a leading institution such as Harvard or the University of Michigan. Life Office Management Training Programs are also used. Of note was this man's comment that Negro businesses suffer from trying to operate exclusively with Negro personnel.

Although these three enterprises are soundly managed and make profits, one can easily detect the persistence of uplift motives. Each company takes pride in the fact that it has contributed to better housing. "Because of the Negro financial institutions," the president of one company said, "you will find that Negroes are better housed in Durham, Atlanta, and Memphis than anywhere in the world." Not only does the Negro financial institution make mortgage loans, it calls to the attention of the white community the fact that the Negro is a good risk for a home mortgage. In addition to home development, one executive reported certain funds allocated for small churches, widows, or young men just starting careers. An example was cited of a young mechanic who had made application for a five year $18,000 loan to finance a truck service station and small restaurant. Although the amount requested was larger than the company usually lends to an individual, it was approved because the officers felt this young man was deserving of help he might not otherwise be able to obtain.

In contrast to the vigorous life companies just described, the authors found in New Orleans eighteen small family-owned companies selling industrial insurance. One company executive talked at length about the problems of entrepreneurship in that city and about the insurance business in particular. With the trend to ordinary life one would wonder whether such companies can continue to survive, much less grow.

An interesting example of fraternal insurance is in a Southwestern city where a small burial society has grown to a membership of 25,000 and assets of $1.5 million. Insurance in force amounts to $20 million and over $100,000 in claims is paid yearly. Since this city has not had until recently a commercial bank, and only a small savings and loan, sources of funds such as this have played an important role in financing some Negro enterprises at reasonable rates of interest.

Negroes have also entered the casualty, fire, and fidelity insurance fields. Two examples will be offered. The entrepreneur behind the growth of the first company is a graduate of Morehouse College who started as an insurance agent. When his company was sold to a white firm, he developed some of his own brokerage connections and was later able to establish his own company. Deciding to try for some large accounts, he formed an alliance with the oldest established firm in the city. By serving as a subagent for them, he was able to learn the techniques and practices of the industry. By 1947, premium volume was over $300,000, and was thought to be sufficient to start the company referred to above. The president of the local commercial bank was consulted, along with other Negroes in the professions and business. Capital of $200,000 was raised in thirty days to meet the state requirement. Here is an example of the importance of mutual trust.

By 1958, the executives of the company saw that they should follow the trend to become a multiple-line firm. The public took up a stock issue of $300,000 rather quickly, and they are now the only multiple-line Negro company operating in the United States. Operations are carried on in four states, and resources are $1 million with an annual policy volume of over $800,000.

The president attributes his success to a number of factors. First, the support and cooperation received from the local bank aided immeasurably. This support went beyond providing financial entrepreneurship; it served to provide customers through its contacts in the business community. Because these people are in the service business, any prosperous Negro businessman is a potential customer for them all. Second, nearby Negro educational institutions were of indirect and direct benefit. Some of their professors have business interests and have brought their students into the businesses with them. The institutions have also provided a flow of educated trainees. Finally, the business climate, while not frankly encouraging to the growth of Negro enterprise, has not been repressive. There has even been the desire to have some Negro business succeed to prove lack of repression.

The rise of fraternal orders among Negroes created the need to provide bonding for those who were handling funds and who could not get coverage from existing companies. The firm visited in the fidelity insurance field was organized with the assistance of Negroes in the life insurance field. A stock company with $50,000 capital and $25,000 surplus was formed. The stock was distributed locally to organizations and individuals. The major problems have centered around this undercapitalization. By requirement, not more than ten percent could be committed to any one risk, which created a limit of about $7,000. As economic growth required larger amounts of insurance, the limitation kept the firm's volume low. While the firm can now write up to $27,000 on one risk, it cannot do business in other states because of limited capital. In fact, it had to withdraw from one state where it had been operating.

The president feels that the prospect of increasing capital is almost nil, since profits are restricted by insurance rates and most of the income is from premiums and not investments. With the trend away from fidelity into multiple-line firms, this company is now in the process of merging with a fire insurance firm in the city to make a multiple-line company with a minimum capital of $750,000. It will, in time, become a subsidiary of a Negro life insurance company. With consummation of the merger the president believes the company will be better able to compete in the developing situation where patronage will be on the basis of service and not on race.

Commercial banks. "The Negro banking industry has long been a source both of race pride and race difficulty. The banker . . . symbolizes the successful businessman of the community, and the race, anxious to demonstrate the extent of its success in the business world, has looked hopefully upon its banking efforts." While there have been failures, beginning with the famous Freedmen's Savings Bank, a bank for Negroes managed by whites, the experience has not been unlike that of white banks. Reasons for these failures are those common to all types of banks: speculation, over-capitalization, stock manipulation, mismanagement, and misappropriation.

According to what the authors found in three commercial banks visited, such reasons for failure are not likely to characterize them. The president of each is well educated, knowledgable in financial matters, and surrounded with competent executives. Generally conservative practices seem to prevail.

As in the case of insurance, Negro banking has aimed at satisfying a definite need—to provide a range of credit assistance to Negroes. An important side effect has been to force a reconsideration of loan policies in white banks which welcome Negro depositors but are generally not interested in extending loan services. There has been no real competition from white banks for Negro business loans; a survey of major Atlanta banks revealed but few Negro business loans on their books.

In most instances the same people who were founders of the insurance companies were also instrumental in starting the banks. In some cases the banks were created as depositories for the insurance companies. This connection helped to win public confidence, lack of which was a problem inherited from early failures.

Despite marked progress and growth, the fact is that Negro banking today is still an extremely small part of the American banking industry and can service only a small proportion of American Negroes. For example, the ten Negro banks in 1960 had combined resources of $53 million, which is about the size of the Bank of Georgia alone, and only one thirty-third of one percent of total assets of all banks in the United States. But an individual bank such as Citizens Trust in Atlanta today has more assets than all Negro banks combined had in 1933. The past twenty years have seen extraordinary growth. In 1940, the eight commercial banks owned and operated by Negroes had total assets of only $5 million. Over the same twenty-year period, the total assets of all U.S. commercial banks went from $68 billion to almost $200 billion. The problem has been in founding new institutions. If the premise is accepted that no business community can achieve its full business potential without adequate banking facilities, it is

easily seen that the Negro business community has suffered from this situation. On the other hand, bank growth is based on the number and strength of business customers. One might ask which will come first in the Negro community.

The newest entrepreneurial attempt in banking was found in Houston, Texas. There a young Harvard Business School graduate and professor at Texas Southern University has sparked the organization of a commercial bank. Local Negroes of means, and a number of persons from the white educational community, have assisted. With a broad base of community support, the $500,000 initial capital was quickly oversubscribed. The building is almost finished, and even those who had opposed the idea have bought stock.

Houston had no Negro commercial bank, and Negroes found it difficult to obtain financing. One aspect of the problem as expressed by the new bank's president is a lack of communication between the white and Negro business communities. He recognized that while race is a factor, large banks deal with large customers, and it happens that most Negro business is small. In his opinion, the business interests of Houston's 250,000 Negroes cannot reach their full potential without adequate banking facilities, which until recently have been lacking. Although the primary motivation behind establishing the bank was to provide working capital financing, it is not intended to serve Negroes alone. Rather, it will cater to the total financial needs of the racially mixed area where it is located. Many of the local businessmen are stockholders and will naturally take their business to the new bank.

Again, the barrier to organization of the enterprise has been locating persons with training and experience in banking. Negro banks in other cities can ill afford to release some of their trained employees in whom they have made a heavy investment. The problem is made all the more acute by the fact that Negroes have not been in responsible managerial positions in banks other than those operated by Negroes. The number of Negro savings and loan associations has grown faster than the number of commercial banks, and some people might be recruited from them.

Savings and loan associations. The increasing significance of the savings and loan association in Negro financial circles is fairly apparent because of the enormity of the Negro housing problem. There are approximately forty-five savings and loan associations in the United States with assets totaling about $300 million. According to the Department of Commerce, in 1947 there were only twenty-five with combined assets of $9-$10 million. Besides demonstrable need, there are other reasons accounting for this growth. First, the recent success of Negro-managed financial institutions has led to increased confidence in them, and good management has justified this confidence. The increase in the level of Negro income generally has made home ownership a more feasible solution to housing pressures. Regulation has contributed to success. Being federally chartered, these associations are required to hold membership in, and are supervised by, the Federal Home Loan Bank System and the Federal Savings and Loan Insurance Corporation. Furthermore, since charters are from the federal level, possible discrimination at the state level is by-passed. Federal examinations have been welcomed by the Negro savings and loan executives as instilling confidence and assuring proper operation.

Three associations were visited. An outstanding example is an association which began operating with $1,500 of the original $15,000 permanent capital subscribed by the board of directors, composed of fifteen of the city's leading Negro business and professional men. Since the granting of a federal charter a decade ago, shareholders have received $700,000 in dividends; and loans have been made in the metropolitan area of over $12 million. Many whites are counted among the 5,000 shareholders, indicating public confidence. In 1963, a branch office was opened in another part of the city, and by the end of that year assets amounted to over $10 million. Loans of $8.6 million were distributed as follows: 39.4 percent for home purchases, 29.2 percent for refinancing, 26.8 percent for home construction, and the remaining 4.6 percent for other purposes.

Another example is an association located in a smaller city, but with equivalent resources and 30 percent of deposits coming from whites in the area. The president of the company, a native of Atlanta and a graduate of Atlanta University, started work as an agent for an insurance company in his home city. He moved to take over management of the association in 1935, and attributes much of its success to the coordination and cooperation between the local bank and insurance company. There is some competition from white banks and savings and loan associations in this city, but it is not bitter because the profit potential is not great. They do not take up each other's paper. He noted, however, that the white banks' reaction to the Negro-managed savings and loan company has progressed from curiosity to concern to competition.

One of the most remarkable examples of entrepreneurship was found in a large Southern city where Negro business revolves around one family. Interests include: a life insurance company with over $50 million of insurance in force; a federal savings and loan association with assets of $5 million accumulated in three and one-half years; a chain of funeral homes throughout the state valued at $250,000; a cemetery worth $200,000; apartment houses containing more than seventy units; a realty and investment company with assets over $300,000; a business college which trains personnel to run these far-flung enterprises; and a modern motel and restaurant. Recently completed is a million-dollar building which houses some of these enterprises. Employment is afforded over 360 persons with an annual payroll of close to $800,000. These business interests are reputed to serve over two-thirds of the Negro population of the state.

In contrast to many of the examples cited so far, the president and founder of this "empire" had little formal education. Furthermore, he has catered to a totally segregated clientele. His accomplishments could not be duplicated today. For him a strong motivating force has been a fervent desire to provide employment for Negroes, seeing economic strength as one avenue to improve the Negro's position in the South.

NON-FINANCIAL ENTERPRISES

The preceding section attests to the success of Negro entrepreneurship in banking and insurance, where Negroes have moved to fill the needs created by the general unwillingness of white institutions to trust Negroes in financial matters. Any Negro-business census performed today in selected Southern cities along the lines of Pierce's study of twenty years ago would still reveal the great bulk of such business to encompass very small concerns in retail trade and services, employing from two to ten people, with assets and gross annual sales of less than $20,-000. Such establishments, located mostly in neighborhood areas, make up about 94 percent of total Negro businesses, with financial institutions comprising another 4 percent. Only 2 percent of total establishments thus remain to include such activities as printing and publishing, manufacturing and distribution, or construction and real estate. It is in these areas where evidence of entrepreneurship can be found.

One might at once ask why there is so little business success outside the general area of finance. In 1917, Brown noted that "corporate business success of any appreciable proportions calls for individuals with liberal intellectual culture, efficient business training, and keen business sense." These he found lacking among Negroes, a situation which has not changed greatly in the intervening forty-five years. Frazier has complained that in past studies of Negro business there has been failure to state the basic reason for the lack of business success. In his view, it is the "fundamental sociological fact that the Negro lacks a business tradition. . . . Neither the tradition of the gentleman nor his peasant heritage had provided the Negro with this outlook on the world." Even if a tradition and training roughly comparable to that possessed by whites be assumed, the size and distribution of the market served would remain a problem. The patterns of segregation, in both the North and the South, would still preclude a market penetration sufficient to support businesses which could make important contributions to economic development in terms of value added, sales, or any other measure which might be chosen. White firms are paying increased attention to the so-called Negro market. There is a definite disadvantage in dealing with a theoretical ten percent of the population which is in the lower-income brackets. It is not so apparent in the retail and service industries where patrons are concentrated. It would be immediately encountered in manufacturing for a racial segment of the national market. "Where Negro business cannot base its appeal on convenience of locality, or on custom and law, but on competition, the Negro-owned store obtains practically none of the white trade, but also obtains only a fraction of the available Negro trade.[4] Nationwide competition in the general market is even more difficult.

Manufacturing and distribution. In spite of the barriers to success just recounted, examples of Negro entrepreneurship in manufacturing and distribution were found by the researchers. Probably one of the most interesting demonstrations of self-help can be found in Clinton, N.C., an area seriously affected by the unemployment or underemployment typical of so many Southern towns in agricultural areas. A sewing company was organized in 1961 and is operating in two modern plants turning out children's clothing. A Negro physician and other leading Negroes of the town were the organizers, abetted by local support of a stock issue now held 60 percent by whites and 40 percent by Negroes. Over one hundred girls are employed in the production work, and active day-to-day management is in the hands of a Northern white man familiar with the business. Money has been borrowed from the local white savings and loan association, and the employees have a stock purchase plan. The marketing problem is minimized, since the firm acts as a subcontractor and does not have to compete in the primary market.

Some Negro manufacturing has been centered around the so-called Negro market. The best-known example is cosmetics, particularly hair preparations. Two firms were visited which differed in some respects. The owner of one came out of the rice paddies of Louisiana and managed to secure an education as a pharmacist. On weekends, he packed his mixtures in a car and sold them house-to-house on plantations. His next step was to attract agents to sell the products while he devoted his time to manufacturing. The operation at present is relatively small, carried on in outdated premises. The machinery seems modern, but the packaging is not. Most of the quarter-million in annual sales goes to Louisiana, Texas, and Mississippi, though there are active accounts in Cleveland, St. Louis, and Chicago, and on the West Coast. Distribution is principally through chain stores. Though some of the products would likely be used only by Negroes, a major portion of the line is in general use, and the owner estimates that 40 percent of his sales go to whites.

The other firm is thirty-five years old, but much more modern in appearances, in terms of both product line and place of business. The present owner is a son of the founder, who had also invested in a newspaper, an insurance company, and a construction firm. This man had gone to Fisk and then to Columbia University, where he had learned about preparing mixtures basic to cosmetics. His son, the present owner, had also gone to college, but was not prepared for business management. He admitted to the authors that he had made mistakes and thus was learning the hard way—through experience. He made an interesting comment to the effect that the average white man has seen and known a businessman; the average Negro has not. In locating his new factory and office out of the Negro business district, and in hiring white salesmen, he has tried to break out of the category of "Negro businessman," which for him implies severe limitations.

The two principal problems faced by this young entrepreneur are staffing and finance. He admits that he is a one-man organization with no depth in the executive ranks. The ready-made Negro executive is just not available for hire, some of the best having already been hired by white firms trying to exploit the Negro market. Even he had been offered the job of sales manager for the Negro market for a large Northern cosmetics firm. He refused the offer, not wishing to have his activities circumscribed in this way. As he now operates, he competes on a national basis with the giants of the industry. In many places where his products are sold, however, it is not known by the dealers and their clientele that they come from a Negro firm.

To compete on a national basis requires substantial capital, not only for manufacturing facilities extensive enough to handle volume orders at low cost, but for money to carry a large inventory of raw materials and shipments in transit. The short-term commercial loans needed to carry the latter two items would not be difficult for a white firm with similar markets to secure. Two things make it difficult for a Negro firm, First, white institutions in the South have not been interested in Negro loans, even though they are familiar with the financing of enterprises engaged in manufacturing and wholesale distribution. Second, the Negro institutions are, on the other hand, often unfamiliar with these lines of business and are accordingly cautious about accepting such risks. This cosmetics firm has therefore been financed in a piecemeal fashion, borrowing from banks, friends, family, or the Small Business Administration. Here is a business, then, suffering from certain handicaps while trying to clear the barriers of segregation and to meet the full force of competition from established white businesses.

The researchers also visited firms engaged in the distribution of cosmetic products. Though originally designed for a racial market, the product lines now have general appeal, as pointed out above. In one city, this type of business is carried on by a college graduate who has also earned a degree at Oxford University and taught at Fisk University. His time has been divided between his business and civic activities. While serving as president of the Negro business association, he was active in organizing the first Negro commercial bank in his city. The distributorship now has eight offices, fifteen salaried people, and about three hundred commission salesmen are employed.

A strong motivating force behind the entrepreneurial activities of this man has been the desire to create jobs for Negro students coming out of college. While a professor, he wanted to prove to himself that this could be done. Many students are currently employed, and one college graduate earns $12,000 per year with the organization. In turning from the teaching profession, this man started working as a "troubleshooter" for the manufacturer of his present line of products. He wanted to learn the business from the ground up—not only sales but also administration. In time, he asked for a distributorship, managed to borrow some money, and settled in a growing Southern city. The eight offices were opened in eight years. Capital has been a perennial problem in spite of the demonstrable success of the business. Lack of Negro-operated banking facilities has been a factor, and was a spur to this entrepreneur's activity in bringing these into being.

This enterprise does not cater exclusively to the Negro market; two white salesmen are employed to sell to the white dealers. Integration can only help this business, as even more of the general market can then be tapped. There are still potential customers of both manufacturers and distributors of these products who will not purchase from a Negro firm, and various measures are taken to hide this identity. Employing white salesmen to call on white accounts is one. "Forced identity" is also avoided by using a "blind" Fifth Avenue address on advertising and promotional literature.

Another firm in cosmetics distribution has from 1,500 to 2,000 retail stores as customers in a three-state area in the Deep South. It is in the form of a partnership. One man has supplied most of the money, the other the know-how gained from experience as a pharmacist in a Northern city. The latter started out in sheet-metal work and drafting, but found discrimination in the North in that line. He turned to pharmacy school and with this education was able to secure employment, first with a small drug chain and then with a very large one. Moving back to the South in 1961, he rejoined the firm and has been responsible for a major increase in the volume of business done. Experience with the large drug chain equipped him to activate and then enlarge a training program for the commission salesmen, who now number about twenty.

Operations differ from the firm described above in that retail drug stores and beauty shops are an important part of the business in the large city where the firm is located. Another important difference lies in the attitude toward dependence on a racial market. The retail and service activities located in the Negro neighborhoods obviously focus attention on the racial aspects of the business, but racial loyalty is also viewed as some insulation from the full force of competition. Added to this is the greater availability of educated employees. All are high school graduates, and a few have had some higher education. To a degree, this may represent underemployment of certain talents, but with other avenues of employment closed to those who do not prepare for the professions within the segregated community, these opportunities appear attractive and can be financially reward-

ing. In sum, the present orientation of both the firms in cosmetics distribution is toward the Negro customer, but, in the case of the first, integration is welcomed as an opportunity for business expansion rather than as a precursor of stiff competition.

In the general area of distribution, another example is a firm which holds a franchise from one of the large tire manufacturers. The principal in this firm is a college graduate possessing a master's degree who had at one time been the principal of a school. His firm is now enjoying gross sales of nearly a quarter-million dollars per year and is about to undergo expansion into another district. When he asked for his own franchise in the upper-class Negro district, know-how had to be joined to capital. The latter was obtained by privately selling an issue of stock which brought in $26,000. The business was started on a cash basis, but as it grew, credit was extended. This required more capital, and bonds bearing a six-percent coupon were sold and later converted into others bearing seven percent when some difficulty was encountered meeting interest payments. The tire manufacturer extended a line of credit, and friends of the owner granted further loans. Recently the company has been approved for a SBA loan. Almost all avenues of finance have thus been exploited.

On the strength of the franchise with the national tire firm, even local white banks have extended credit; so this entrepreneur does not now regard financing as a major problem. He admitted to paying some very high interest rates at certain junctures in the history of the business, but was inclined to regard this as a problem of all small business. Perhaps this opinion is colored by the fact that his franchise lends his business an image of legitmacy in the eyes of the white business community not enjoyed by other Negro businesses of equal stature. For him, the major problems seem to be getting and retaining competent personnel and the development of an understanding by the community in general that a Negro business can be successful, well-run, dependable in its dealings with the public, and a contributor to the welfare of the community.

This section can be concluded by briefly mentioning some occupations in which success has been almost wholly dependent on the maintenance of segregation. These are undertaking, food service, and innkeeping. The first has undoubtedly been the most profitable. This is because of the heavy emphasis placed on a decent burial, one often far beyond what the deceased's income level would warrant. However, the many burial societies, often originally connected with fraternal orders, and other forms of insurance provides a firm base on which this industry can operate. The authors found in several instances that operation of a funeral parlor or a casket business was the first in a series of business enterprises, and that the owners of such establishments serve as private sources of capital for other would-be entrepreneurs in the community.

Eating and drinking places, along with cleaning-and-pressing "clubs," have long been the most numerous of small businesses operated by Negroes. The great majority of the former are uninviting. However, two places visited in the research rival comparable white establishments. One was started by two brothers, one of whom had had relevant experience. Together they had two-thirds of the money needed to get into business, and were able to borrow the remainder from the local Negro bank. In 1959 new modern premises were occupied. When a white bank proved "slow" to provide financing, a Negro bank made 67 percent of the construction costs available. Expansion has followed, and plans have been made to go into innkeeping and possibly other businesses.

Construction and real estate. Nowhere is the Negro's need more desperate than in the field of housing. Expansion in the South, as in the North, has been directly tied to patterns of segregation in many ways which will not be enlarged upon here. Suffice it to say that "segregated money" for home mortgages and the opportunities for profit from real estate speculation have made home ownership for the Negro a much more expensive item in his market basket than it is for whites similarly situated. The growth of Negro financial institutions gives promise of substantial improvement over abuses of the past. Even large white insurance companies are beginning to remove racial restrictions on the mortgages they will buy. Added to this is the executive order on discrimination

in housing. The president of an Atlanta savings and loan company stated that "for both economic and social reasons, we don't make loans to colored people moving into all-white or transitional neighborhoods. We owe it to our stockholders not to risk their money on such properties. We also have to consider impairment of the value of the mortgages we already hold in those areas." If existing white institutions will not finance the expansion of available housing for Negroes, then Negro institutions must do it or new housing must be built.

The effective approach to desegregating money seems to be through competition. Wherever one finds a Negro financial complex, one finds comparable white institutions making loans to Negroes. Upon the organization of a Negro commercial bank in Houston, white lenders in that city conceded that the bank would affect them. "We're not admitting it publicly, but we're beginning to make an effort to show our Negro customers that we're interested in lending to them," said the vice president of a white savings and loan association. "In the past we haven't been interested in making mortgage loans to Negroes."

Adequate financing is the essential prerequisite of construction activity. Some has been accomplished by Negroes in selected Southern cities, though all the concerns visited will not be discussed. One gentleman, now retired, produced $4–$5 million in construction in one city, and had at one time a payroll of $1,500 per week. His parents were born slaves but had college educations, and he went to Hampton Institute, where he came under the influence of Booker T. Washington. After World War I, he worked in Philadelphia as a laborer and later as a construction superintendent, and thus acquired experience. Returning to the South in 1921, he worked hard and received financing from a Northern life insurance company. He stated that, during the Depression in his city, no Negroes who owned homes lost them. Even granting the qualifying assumption that Negro home-ownership was limited at that time to the relatively well-to-do, it is still a notable record. It is evidence of the place which Negroes accord home-ownership in their scale of values, and the consequent strength of the desire to repay, one of the principal factors upon which a lender depends.

One active construction firm is operated by two men both of whom have college educations. One graduated from Tuskegee Institute, the other from the University of Chicago. They formed a partnership in order to be able to bid on large contracts such as college buildings and housing projects. The Tuskegee graduate gained his experience with a New York firm following World War II and then returned South to go into business for himself. After ten years, he joined the Chicago graduate, who had been teaching mechanical drawing in high school.

For this firm, the major problems are again the familiar ones of financing and staffing. The former is minimized in the financial climate in which they operate; the local Negro financial institutions have taken $25 million in mortgages over the past ten years. Insurance companies will not lend on unimproved property, and so obtaining construction loans and making the required bonds are the financial hurdles. The greatest need is for qualified employees. There are reportedly fewer skilled Negro carpenters, cement finishers, and brick masons than there were some years ago. One contributing factor is the progress of unionization in the South. Many unions have been segregation-minded, and one author writing a decade ago stated that "a really successful organizational drive would write finis to Negro prospects in southern manufacturing for many years to come." The partners feel that insufficient emphasis is placed on vocational education in the Negro high schools. Only two schools in their city offer mechanical training. However, as Dewey pointed out: "So long as individual Negroes cannot gain admission into white work groups, vocational training is both wasteful and a cruel hoax, unless it takes the form of providing Negro work groups to particular employers." The firm under discussion is encouraging the first Negroes to enter the state technical institute and offers them jobs during the vacation periods. There are only two or three registered Negro architects in this same city, but the company was hoping to hire one, in addition to a structural engineer and an estimator. With the addition of these skills, they will be fully qualified to bid on city jobs. Recently a large multiple-housing project, a part of urban renewal, was awarded to the firm in competitive bidding.

More in real estate management than in construction are two other firms visited. One has entrepreneured a development of thirty-two individual homes built mostly with Negro labor by Negro contractors. It has also purchased, and is providing the management for, a housing project of 267 units valued at $1,250,000 in a neighboring city. The other firm is active in developing a shopping center and building residences. With favorable Negro financing as a start, the single-unit development was financed by working through the FHA and local institutions. The other project was handled by borrowing enough to purchase the equity with the property as security for a mortgage on the remainder. Both firms are, however, one-man shows, though some younger help is being developed.

In one city, the problem is not so much availability of money as it is a flow of qualified borrowers. The people have low salaries and wages, and the relative certainty of continuous employment must stand behind home purchase. Urban renewal is currently underway in many places in the South, particularly where slum conditions have existed in Negro areas. It will have both favorable and unfavorable results as far as individual businesses are concerned. Some small, underfinanced units will probably not reopen, while other new ones will emerge. In any event, it is an opportunity for local Negro finance and know-how to demonstrate their capabilities and resourcefulness.

The developer in the other city who was interviewed reported less favorable financing for real estate development. A native of New York who attended two institutions of higher learning, he has succeeded in borrowing a substantial sum from a local white bank, a success attributable partly to his political connections. He reports the local Negro bank as too conservative. There is a ready market for homes in the $9,000 to $10,000 price range. Whites are not particularly interested in Negro risks, often preferring to have Negroes continue renting from them. In an attempt to counter these rather typical attitudes, this developer worked with Negroes to point up the necessity of meeting obligations on time, since many delinquencies were for lateness rather than failure to pay. He also investigated the credit of many with the intention of helping them qualify for VA and FHA loans. He talked with the local FHA representative and managed to prove that Negroes could qualify, and will pay on their homes. One of the local savings and loan associations was requested to check its Negro contracts, and a low percentage of foreclosures was found.

In spite of this progress, the interviewee was not very optimistic about the future of purely Negro entrepreneurship in his city. There is not enough cooperative spirit among local Negroes, perhaps because of the failure of some fraternal orders and poor leadership in the past. Integration of Negroes into white firms was seen as a more likely method of "hatching" men with entrepreneurial instincts than a strictly Negro business structure.

Newspapers and printing. The service trades of printing and publishing have afforded the last area of entrepreneurial activity to be discussed. Principals or employees in five newspapers in four cities were interviewed, as were owners of two printing establishments in two cities. These establishments are small, but one of them, doing an annual volume of $100,000, is the third largest of the fifteen print shops in the city where it is located. It was started by two men who had studied at Hampton Institute and another who had been a journeyman printer for a newspaper in a neighboring city where all three had once been employed. Printing was begun to supplement a newspaper business which was failing because the children of the former owner had no experience or taste for the business. They wished to sell and were willing to be paid from the receipts of the new owners as they came in. The newspaper ceased publication and the printing business was expanded.

Again, financing was the initial problem. The three had no collateral, the business was at low ebb, and only small sums from individuals could be obtained. Hiring has been selective, three people have been trained, and eleven qualified people are now employed. Expansion of the business into other commercial lines is under way, and there is no dependence on a single customer or type of work. The owners view progressing integration not as a threat, but as a help, since a larger market would be opened to them.

The other printing concern was started in 1921. The present owner, a graduate of Bishop College, taught at the local Negro university and operated a print shop to do the university's work. By 1953, with the help of an RFC loan after World War II, the firm had expanded its operations so as to require his full attention. There has been constant reinvestment of earnings. The Negro community provides only about 25 percent of the business volume, mostly church bulletins, an undependable source of business. With sales volume running at less than $40,000 per year, and with the obvious requirement of competition with better-established white firms, growth of this enterprise seems limited. At one time the owner considered a stock issue, to be sold principally to customers, but the idea was abandoned.

One of the most interesting people interviewed was the retired owner of a weekly paper in a large Southern city. He started out in an insurance company and put out a house organ which became a weekly paper when he left the insurance business. Thus in 1924 a Negro paper made its first appearance since Reconstruction. The white papers would not carry news about Negroes except that concerned with their crimes. There was, and is, a need for a place where Negro social, fraternal, school, church, and athletic news can be adequately covered, and not just in the sensational way it is often handled in both the Negro and white press. Only recently have white papers in the South begun to devote any space to such news.

A recognized *raison d'etre* of the Negro press is protest. This was the theme of the publisher of another paper begun in 1924 as a partnership and later purchased by one of the partners for less than $500. Having hired the printers and trained the office staff, he now employs twelve people. With circulation running about 23,000, it is estimated that 100,000 people see the paper. It perhaps wields more influence than any other Negro paper in the state.

Competition from Negro counterparts has been the spur even in newspaper publishing. Some white papers are now printing Negro news, particularly sports, though they have not yet gone to protest editorials nor to publishing pictures of Negro "society" figures. In one city, there are two Negro papers, one of quite recent origin, the other dating back to before the Depression, when it was founded by a graduate of the Harvard Law School. With money built up from his law practice, he established a chain of six papers in the state. Currently, sixty-five people in two cities are employed to contribute to issuing the paper twice a week for statewide distribution.

The other paper in this same city is owned by a former employee of the first paper who built up some capital and decided to reenter the business. The decision was based on two factors. He felt, first, that there was need for a fresh editorial policy, and, second, he proposed to use a less expensive printing process. Unable to obtain backing from white financial sources, he turned to individual Negroes of wealth in the community, who helped him launch the new enterprise. It will be interesting to see if both papers can survive the competition.

In this section, the objective has been to fill in with some richness of detail and illustrations of entrepreneurship the discussion on requirements and barriers presented earlier. It is to be hoped that now the motives, beginnings, and sometimes tortuous paths which have led to success in various industries in several locations can be appreciated. Evidence of the competitive struggle for industrial development is constantly before us. One could hardly have expected the Negro to keep pace, and his accomplishments are therefore all the more remarkable. In the concluding section, there will be an opportunity to point out some recent developments, to appraise Negro entrepreneurship in the South, and to make some predictions of its future course.

NEGRO ENTREPRENEURSHIP IN THE SOUTH: RETROSPECT AND PROSPECT

Race and segregation have created a sharp cleavage between white and Negro business communities. However, Southern Negro entrepreneurship cannot be regarded as an independent phenomenon. Both communities have been handicapped by the dislocations associated with the imperative transition from an impoverished agricultural economy to the increased income levels promised by industrialization. Almost all research on the Southern economy emphasizes the many areas in which the South lags behind the national average, particularly when the measures are on a per capita basis. It can be no secret that the present pattern of industrialization is not calculated to remedy these disparities, since the nation's future is on the technological frontiers, and these are only beginning to appear in the South. Manufacturing in the South is mostly in non-durables such as textiles, lumber, food, and apparel; the demand for these products is comparatively income-inelastic. These are the fields in which local firms have engaged. The measurements of the Southern economy are further depressed by the inclusion of large numbers of educationally and economically depressed Negroes. Southern Negro entrepreneurship is certainly unequal to the task of greatly improving the economic status of any significant percentage of these people, but the preceding sections have pointed to the contributions made.

In spite of attempts to prove otherwise, the fact remains that the Negro is largely imitative of the community in which he lives, in terms of both culture and economic activity. Considering the traditional attitudes towards business careers in the South, in both white and Negro communities, it is not surprising that Negroes with sufficient background and education have not been attracted to business in large numbers. Hickman surmised that the entrepreneurial function carried on by whites might be different in the Southern setting "if only because a different set of alternatives, constraints, and pressures confront the entrepreneur. It is perhaps even more evident that this existence of a dual society drastically constricts opportunities for entrepreneurship on the part of Negroes in the South. To be sure, entrepreneurship is possible within the separated Negro business community and Negro market . . . [but] entrepreneurship in the broader economic community of the South is blocked for the Negro." One of the tasks of this paper has been to examine these statements.

On the surface they seem to be justifiable generalizations, and space has been devoted to elaborating on the latter one. At the same time, the burden of the research was to seek out and investigate not only those examples which indicate that entrepreneurship has been successful "in the separate community and market," but those which serve to break down the notion that "entrepreneurship in the broader economic community is blocked." True it is that many barriers remain, but a breakdown is occurring. The summer of 1963 witnessed some swift moves in this direction.

At this point one may well ask the question: What has been the contribution of Southern Negro entrepreneurship, and in what directions do further developments lie? Certainly the greatest contribution has been the amelioration of some of the conditions under which the Negro people have lived over the years. The "social service" motive has been strongly behind the financial enterprises, for example. It is true that these avenues of opportunity were open because comparable white institutions generally refused to offer such services to Negroes. Yet the availability of financing, corporate or personal, for reasonable risks at reasonable rates has been a major factor in permitting segments of the Negro community to progress in accord with their capabilities. Insurance has not only removed the fear of being buried in a potter's field, but has made possible investment in projects calculated to add to the betterment of widely scattered Negro communities. Thrift has been encouraged in a people whose natural propensity to consume is very high, and has made available funds for housing, churches, private recreational facilities, and the setting-up in practice of the various kinds of young Negro professionals so badly needed.

For budding and growing business enterprises, good, sound advice has often accompanied the lending of funds, though in certain areas, such as manufacturing, the Negro financial institutions are less well prepared. One banker told the authors that often the notion held by the prospective borrower of what comprises a reasonable business opportunity is naive. To put it simply: "Everyone's got to eat" does not automatically mean that a restaurant in a given location will succeed. The bankers have impressed on their clients the need for reinvestment and for resisting the natural urge to make a little money, put it in a piece of property, and become a landlord. With housing pressures for both businesses and families severe, owning property seems like the royal road to economic independence. Almost without exception, the Negro businesses of any substance visited by the researchers were the result of heavy reinvestment and other conservative financial policies, usually coupled with abstemious habits on the part of the entrepreneurs themselves.

One of the most direct contributions of the financial institutions has been to afford employment opportunities to well-educated men and women who would otherwise have added to the substantial amount of underemployment which exists in this racial group, not only in the South, but in the nation as a whole. Not only is employment offered, but the young Negro is given an image of what it means to succeed in business and is thereby encouraged to go into it instead of one of the professions. This is not to imply that the professions are overcrowded. Quite the contrary. Not only are more doctors and dentists needed, but, for business to flourish, lawyers and certified public accountants are prime requisites. The point is that Negro businessmen can provide employment opportunities pending integration and the gradual elimination of discrimination in employment. This asset will assist in halting the migration of the better qualified from the South and thus build up a large cadre of modestly trained people who can serve as a way of moving the Negro into the mainstream. This was one of the themes of the National Conference on Small Business sponsored in Washington in 1961 by the U.S. Department of Commerce.

The once-held position that the economic salvation of the Negro lay in the development of his own business empire was either naive or deliberately misleading, though the Black Muslims seem entirely willing to go that way. Small business of the personal service types can prosper, as has been depicted above, and add a good deal to the communities touched by its payrolls and employment. Occasionally, as in cosmetics, Negro business can deal with the national market with marked success while not depending wholly on its racial components. Yet the stock of capital, in the wider sense of the term, is insufficient to warrant prediction of rapid acceleration in the growth of Negro business. On the other hand, there may be a sizable expansion in the number of Negro entrepreneurs. Is this a paradox?

The "stock of capital" referred to includes not only financial resources, but also such things as appropriately educated graduates of both colleges and secondary schools, a fund of generally held know-how in the skilled trades, ancillary services connected with law and accountancy, and more widely distributed abilities in the field of sales. To this must be added sufficient mutual trust to permit larger aggregations of capital and the corporate form of business, and a culture which recognizes, respects, and rewards legitimate business success. Recent evidence of progress is seen in Washington, D.C., where the city's wealthier Negroes are being pressed by leaders "to invest in Negro businesses and back what would be the first Negro-owned savings and loan association there." In Detroit the Group on Advanced Leadership requires members to put up ten dollars each for a "redevelopment corporation" to spur "capital formation among Negroes." Too many enterprises have been family affairs in the Negro community, and management has often deteriorated when passed to the second or third generation. Cole notes that "biological and social forces are antagonistic to the family enterprise." In Europe, the family buys out the disgruntled and the spendthrift; and management is not allowed to deteriorate. Closely held family business has, for example, been common in New Orleans, and nothing very remarkable has developed there in terms of either business enterprise or leadership.

Granted that the total amount of capital, so defined, is lacking, it does not follow that it may not be sufficiently concentrated in some persons or places to encourage the rise of entrepreneurs. After all, they have emerged in the past under less favorable circumstances generally than exist today. The word "generally" is important, as the one major circumstance which is for many kinds of businesses less favorable today is the breakdown of segregation and discrimination, both of which have individual applicability. Integration in today's context means that publicly available facilities will be open to all who can pay the price or qualify as citizens. The Negro has been barred from patronizing many kinds of businesses by his color rather than his income level, and has thus been forced to take his trade to comparable establishments in the segregated community. Since many of these businesses do not hold to the standards of like enterprises in the white community, they are in truth supported by segregation, since many of their customers would gladly trade elsewhere. These units will be forced to upgrade or fail. Were integration an accomplished fact today, it would be easier to predict the latter.

Discrimination has in most respects been an unfortunate burden for the Negro. However several interviewees presented a new facet of this practice. It often handily serves as the universal justification for failure. Though many times it accounts for lack of training and thus indirectly for failure, it is used to cover other sins, usually of omission. For many it is a justification for never making the effort, since, it is argued, potential success would be thwarted by discrimination. As this barrier is removed, the Negro will have to stand up to the general level of competition in the marketplace, though current demands by some activist organizations are hardly in this spirit. If his opportunities for education and then for jobs are unhampered by artificial barriers, he will then have to face the truth of his capabilities and accomplishments. Speaking to the graduating class at Morris Brown College in Atlanta in June 1963, Harry Golden reminded his hearers that "the ghetto is a fortress as much as it was a prison." When all people are dealt with by universalistic criteria, a Negro can be denied a job or fired from one if he does not measure up to these criteria. Integration will also muffle criticism of Negro businesses which hire whites and thus depart from a strict policy of racial loyalty. Unfortunately this day is hardly on the horizon, but the march towards it is accelerating. Removal of the psychological "protection" of both segregation and discrimination will not be a completely unmixed blessing, particularly during the period of transition.

Yet this is a situation in which increasing numbers of Negro entrepreneurs can emerge. One has only to look back to the specific examples detailed above. The great majority of the successful men there depicted had either or both of the two important ingredients for entrepreneurship: advanced education and experience in the chosen field. Some have themselves been educators or professionally trained men. Much of the strength of the business community in Atlanta, for example, is attributable over the years to the existence of the Atlanta University complex, with its several undergraduate colleges and professional schools. In many instances, the acquisition of know-how has occurred in the North. This is particularly true in construction, since the chance for the Negro to work at skilled trades in this industry has been almost non-existent in the South. With technical schools such as Georgia Institute of Technology opening its doors to Negroes, and with the increased opportunity to receive training in white businesses, Negroes in the South will more easily lay claim to the requisites of entrepreneurship. If Negroes have under former conditions succeeded as entrepreneurs in markets not wholly protected by segregation, improved conditions should presage a marked growth in their numbers.

This bright day is at present only a hoped-for goal, and many things must be done before it becomes a reality. High on such a list are improvements in the education available to Negroes. Certainly progressing integration will not mean the end of the Negro colleges and institutes of the South. In the past, with certain exceptions such as Hampton and Tuskegee, or programs of business education at places such as North Carolina College or Atlanta University, Negro higher education has been heavy on either the academic or pre-professional program. Since but few Negroes were encouraged to go into business, preparation typically offered has been for occupations of high status, such as public-school teaching, medicine, dentistry, or the ministry. [Lloyd] Saville expresses the opinion that "education . . . offers the promise of facilitating the troublesome transition from an agricultural society to an industrial . . . only by enabling the individual to produce more by the efficient utilization of individual initiative, . . . [and] to realize for himself the economic alternatives available to him in an industrial society." This will require a reorientation and reorganization of the curricula of many Negro educational institutions.

At the small business conference referred to above, the opinion was voiced that business and education may be growing further apart. With the mass of the teachers coming from the academically oriented programs of the Negro colleges, it is understandable that the average Negro high school student knows very little about what business is like. Many substantial Negro concerns are now offering scholarship aid to encourage young people of promise to enter upon business careers, and they must receive proper counseling in the high schools.

Beyond the level of formal education and specific training or experience in a chosen field lie the many "extra-curricular" contacts so necessary to becoming part of the business community. Most local Chambers of Commerce do not welcome Negro members, and Southern regional associations within a specialty such as banking or accountancy have the same policies. The substitute Negro groups are out of the mainstream, their educational value is meager, and valuable business contacts are necessarily foregone.

Harry Golden, in the same context alluded to above, remarked that the free exchange of ideas in an open society has been the foundation of all civilized progress. In a more practical vein, contracts are often closed verbally at luncheon in private clubs, and business opportunities and deals discussed on the golf course. Acquisition of civil rights will not secure admittance to these business scenes. Southern Negro businessmen often do participate in national conventions, but this is no substitute for contact with local figures. Yet there are hopeful signs that even some of these barriers are being softened, if not broken. This is at least a move toward the "beneficent climate of social opinion" so strongly emphasized by Cole.

Most of the emphasis has been on the more noble motives behind Negro entrepreneurship, but the scarcity of contacts between the two communities, combined with the lack of mutual trust, has the potential of putting power in the hands of relatively few in any given Negro community. If these few are possessed of more pedestrian motives, exploitation can be the result. If, for example, regular channels are not open to secure funds, those few Negroes of wealth can exact a high toll for their assistance, particularly if the borrower, perhaps through lack of trust, wishes to retain full control of his enterprise. More contacts with the total business community fostering a high level of sophistication in business, coupled with the development of mutual trust, would reduce dependence on these few persons and in so doing, dilute the possibilities for exploitation where they exist.

The removal of "reverse discrimination," or a "Negroes only" policy, in Negro businesses will be an additional avenue of contact with the total business community. If the Negro entrepreneur is to cease being identified by his color, he must integrate his enterprises and become just another businessman. Many already recognize this. Mr. L. D. Milton, president of Citizens Trust of Atlanta, has observed that "the more successful Negroes become in the operation of businesses, the stiffer becomes the competition which they must face from other firms—competition for both customers and employees." The Negro must thus become as universalistic in his approach to economic resources as the white man tackling the same business.

Finally, then, one finds the present generation of Negro entrepreneurs fairly well characterized by the definition chosen earlier. They have not been heroic innovators, effecting major changes in the formulae of production. They are even accused by some of their younger colleagues of having stood still and "locked up security." Yet they have been agents of change in a period of transition, a period of social and economic change in the South. Increasing numbers will make contributions in the future. The burden will be great, but past performance gives promise of success.

NOTES

[1] The failure of Negroes to develop cooperatives was attributed to the fact that "envy and jealousy continue to work mightily against coordination of effort among colored people."

[3] This is pointed up in the effects of the boycott of white establishments during desegregation campaigns. Some store owners in downtown Albany, Ga., reported a 40 percent decline in sales, some of this undoubtedly due to whites avoiding areas of racial disturbance. The same report also noted an increase in business in Negro stores to such an extent as to encourage further investment by Negroes in these businesses. Wall Street Journal, Sept. 6, 1962, p. 1.

SMALL BUSINESS AND ECONOMIC DEVELOPMENT IN THE NEGRO COMMUNITY

Andrew F. Brimmer

STATEMENT

I greatly appreciate the opportunity to share with the Select Committee on Small Business my views on the "role of small business in minority economic development." In responding to the invitation to testify, it occurred to me that I might be able to make a modest contribution to these hearings through an appraisal of the prospects for minority groups in business, based on an economic analysis of the market in which Negro businessmen are attempting to operate profit-making enterprises in the United States today. Thus, my efforts consist of an objective examination in which I set aside questions relating to noneconomic goals (such as enhancing pride of ownership) which other observers may find it worthwhile to pursue.

On the basis of my analysis of the economic evidence, I have concluded that we should be extremely cautious in encouraging Negroes to seek careers as self-employed, small business-men. This is expecially true if the expectation of success is based on the assumption that such a business can be conducted in a separate, all-black environment, protected from the competition of firms doing business in a nationwide market. In general, if one wishes to restrict his efforts to small-scale neighborhood retailing and the provision of relatively simple personal

Reprinted from *Organization and Operation of the Small Business Administration,* Hearings Before the Select Committee on Small Business, House of Representatives, 91st Congress, 1st Session, pursuant to H. Res. 66, a Resolution Creating a Select Committee to Conduct Studies and Investigations of the Problems of Small Business, Washington D.C., July 22, 23, 24, and 25, 1969 (Washington, D.C., U.S. Government Printing Office, 1969), pp. 422-437. Footnotes omitted.

services, it is quite possible that he can earn a living—although it is likely to be a modest one. However, if the desire is to engage in manufacturing, construction, transportation or wholesale trade, the prospects of success appear to be extremely dim—if the firm's output is to be sold mainly in the limited market provided by the Negro community, Between these extremes, the outlook for successful operation becomes less-and-less promising as the scale and technical sophistication of the enterprise increase.

ECONOMIC IMPACT OF SEGREGATION AND DESEGREGATION

Before proceeding further with this assessment of the prospects for Negroes in small business, we should pause briefly to review the consequences of economic separatism which resulted as an historical legacy of racial discrimination and segregation and the later consequences when some of these barriers were removed. In general, the effects were similar to those produced in international trade when a high tariff wall is erected between two countries. Separate markets prevail in the two areas for items subject to tariff control. For the Negro community in the United States, the greatest barrier imposed by segregation was not in the market for goods—to which they generally had relatively open access—but in the market for personal services, such as barber and beauty shops and funeral services. Consequently, a protected market evolved for the provision of these services within the Negro community.

Moreover, as one would expect, this wall of protection provided incentives for Negro professionals and entrepreneurs who began to specialize in activities servicing the Negro community. Negro professionals were highly concentrated in fields such as medicine, education, and religion—all hampered by segregation—but all of which also provided a protected market. In occupations which were dependent upon unprotected national markets, Negroes were conspicuously absent. For example, in 1960 (the last year for which we have detailed information) engineers, scientists, and technicians comprised only 3.8 per cent of all Negroes classified as professional, technical, and managerial; the corresponding figure for whites was 10.5 per cent. The fraction of Negro professionals who were architects was less than one-fifth the fraction for whites. Clearly Negro professionals were concentrating on servicing the Negro community.

In business the same pattern prevailed. Negroes were concentrated in enterprises servicing the protected Negro market. Life insurance provides probably the best example. For years, the major life insurance companies either did not sell policies to Negroes or did so on the basis of different actuarial tables which greatly increased the cost of protection to Negroes. The result was the creation of an environment where Negro life insurance companies were able to grow and prosper. In enterprises that sold to a more general public, such as hardware and department stores, Negroes have not made much headway.

The recent progress toward desegregation in the United States (symbolized by the opening of public accommodations) has eroded the position of many Negro businessmen who were dependent upon segregation to protect their markets. For instance, in many large cities in the East and Midwest, most of the hotels and restaurants which previously catered to Negroes have encountered hard times, and a few have actually closed their doors.

The trend towards desegregation in American life has influenced the Negro businessman in another important manner. Not only have many of his traditional customers deserted him to shop in the more diverse stores serving national markets but he has also encountered an increasing competition for his traditional supply of labor. Large national corporations for some time have been actively recruiting Negro personnel. Initially the aim was to help market their products in Negro areas, but more recently they have also been seeking manpower for their overall operations. Negro businessmen operating from much smaller economic bases are unable to offer competitive salaries or commensurate opportunities and are thus having a great deal of difficulty retaining qualified employees.

The adverse effects of these changes on Negro businessmen concentrating in those activities formerly protected by segregation is quite striking. This can be seen most clearly in the income trends among nonwhite men during the 1960's. For example, between 1959 and 1967, mean income of all self-employed nonwhite males rose by roughly 114 percent to about $7,200; among all self-employed white men, the rise was only 44 percent to approximately $8,500. In sharp contrast, income gains for self-employed retail merchants were much smaller for both groups (39 percent to about $7,400 for whites and 28 percent to about $4,500 for nonwhites).

Expressed differently, in 1959, average incomes of both white and nonwhite retail merchants were well above the average incomes of all employed men (13 percent above all whites for white retailers and 28 percent above all nonwhites for nonwhite retailers). By 1967, however, the averages for self-employed retail merchants showed smaller rises and were below the average for all employed men—9 percent below all whites for white retailers and 12 percent below all nonwhites for nonwhite retailers.

ECONOMIC ENVIRONMENT OF NEGRO BUSINESS

The legacy of racial segregation is important because it has shaped the economic environment in which Negro businessmen are currently operating—and in which they are likely to operate for some time. The main economic characteristics of the Negro community are widely known and need not be reviewed in detail here. For example, in 1967, Negroes had a median family income of $4939 which was only 59 percent of that of white families. These income figures are important because they clearly point up the differences in purchasing power in the two communities—a matter of fundamental importance to businessmen. However, when we examine the financial assets and liabilities of Negroes compared with other families, the differences in market potential are thrown into even sharper focus.

These differences are clearly marked in tables 1 and 2 (attached), which summarize data on assets and liabilities from the Survey of Consumer Finances conducted by the Survey Research Center at the University of Michigan. The ownership of financial assets is presented in table 1. As mentioned earlier, Negro life insurance companies emerged as a response to the failure of white life insurance companies to serve the Negro market. The result of this segregated market is that Negroes at all levels of income appear to have a slightly higher probability of holding life insurance than whites. The picture on other financial assets is quite different. Negroes at virtually all levels of income are less likely to have savings accounts or stocks. The lone exception appears in the over $10,000 income class where Negroes rely heavily on savings accounts but invest far less frequently in stocks. In fact, although not shown in Table 1, the Michigan Survey reported that in 1966 Negro families obtained only 2 percent (versus 6 percent for non-Negro families) of their total money income from dividends, rent, interest and trust funds.

The most important data in table 1 are for the income categories between $5,000 and $10,000. These two categories contain roughly 40 percent of all Negro families, and it is this range of income which provides the broadest foundations of the Negro market. The asset data for families within this critical income range show that Negroes have considerably less financial accumulation than white families. This finding implies that these Negro families would not be as good potential consumers as the income figures might suggest.

The other side of the financial picture is liabilities. (See table 2, attached.) One is immediately struck by the fact that Negroes at all levels of income are much more heavily burdened with installment debt. The repayment of this debt represents a sizable claim on disposable income and thus makes a Negro family a poorer potential consumer for additional goods and services than a family of similar income who is less encumbered by installment debt payments. The case of mortgage debt is a bit more difficult to analyze. The probability of home ownership rises substantially with income and is higher at all levels of income for whites than for Negroes. A single (not fully explained) exception to this general trend is the high tendency for Negro families in the lowest income category to own homes. In part this may reflect older retired families and in part it may represent impoverished rural southern Negroes whose homeownership may be quite modest. In general, it is safe to conclude that Negroes of similar income are not accumulating an equity position in housing at the same rate as white families.

The tendency to owe mortgage debt, however, appears roughly equal for Negroes and whites of similar income. Since Negroes have a lesser tendency to own homes at a given level of income, this similarity in the fraction of the total population owing mortgage debt suggests clearly that if a Negro does own a home, the chances are greater that he has a mortgage on it than for a white homeowner with the same income.

Table 1. *Fraction of Population Holding Different Financial Assets, by Income Class and Race, 1967*

Income Class	Life Insurance		Savings Accounts		Stocks	
	Negro	Non-Negro	Nego	Non-Negro	Negro	Non-Negro
Under $3,000	54	49	13	44	0	11
$3,000 to $5,000	75	68	41	56	1	15
$5,000 to $7,500	85	80	52	62	5	21
$7,500 to $10,000	95	92	58	69	5	26
Over $10,000	100	96	89	79	30	45
Total	73	80	38	64	4	26

Source: Survey Research Center, University of Michigan.

Table 2. *Fraction of Population with Different Financial Liabilities, by Income Class and Race, 1967*

Income Class	Installment Debt		Mortgage Debt			
			Negro		Non-Negro	
	Negro	Non-Negro	Owners	Debt	Owners	Debt
Under $3,000	49	19	40	10	52	8
$3,000 to $5,000	59	39	29	8	54	28
$5,000 to $7,500	84	52	37	25	54	27
$7,500 to $10,000	71	60	50	39	68	46
Over $10,000	93	53	70	66	79	55
Total	64	46	40	20	63	37

Source: Survey Research Center, University of Michigan.

These data on the financial assets and liabilities shed new light on the economic achievements of Negro families. These data show that Negro families of comparable income have greater liabilities and fewer financial assets to meet these liabilities than whites. This finding suggests that the usually observed data on white-Negro income differentials actually understate differences in purchasing power, because the income figures do not indicate the relatively poorer net financial position of Negro families. The figures on assets and liabilities accentuate the problems of weak markets facing businessmen who limit themselves to the Negro community.

THE STRUCTURE OF NEGRO BUSINESSES AND THE OUTLOOK FOR ECONOMIC DEVELOPMENT

Having highlighted some of the limitations inherent in the Negro market, it might be helpful to see what types of enterprises have developed in this environment. For this purpose, only fragmentary information is available. One source relates to Negro owned and operated businesses in Washington, D.C., in 1967. (See table 3 attached.) These data show a heavy preponderance in the service area. The distribution of businesses within each category is also revealing:

1. Of the 1,249 businesses classified as services, 555 (or 44 percent) were barber shops, beauty salons or beauty schools, while 146 (or 12 percent) were drycleaning establishments.

2. Of the 473 retail businesses 240 (or 51 percent) were carryout shops, delicatessens, grocery stores, or restaurants. There were only two used car lots in this category and no new car dealers.

3. Of the 84 businesses in finance, insurance, and real estate, there were two banks, one finance company, seven insurance companies, one title company, and 73 (or 87 percent) were in real estate.

4. Of the 35 manufacturing companies, 28 (or 80 percent) were newspaper publishers, printers, or sign shops.

Thus, businesses in the Washington area are highly concentrated in areas such as barber shops, beauty salons, and drycleaning establishments where Negroes are servicing Negroes.

Table 3. *Distribution of Negro-Owned and Operated Business in Washington, D.C., 1967*

Type of Business	Number	Percent
Services	1,249	60.5
Retail	473	22.9
Contract construction	119	5.8
Transportation	82	4.0
Finance, insurance, and real estate . . .	84	4.1
Manufacturing	35	1.7
Wholesale	20	1.0
Total	2,062	100.0

Source: "A Directory of Negro-Owned and Operated Businesses in Washington, D.C." compiled by Small Business Guidance and Development Center, Howard University, 1967.

However, a second—and more important—conclusion emerging from these data is that these are not the types of enterprises which can serve as the mainsprings of economic development in the long run.

Table 4. *Distribution of Negro-Owned Enterprises by Number of Employees, National Business League Survey, 1969*

Category of Business	Number of Employees					
	1 to 4	5 to 10	11 to 20	21 to 30	Over 30	Total
Restaurants	44	9	1	0	0	54
Snack and carryouts	9	4	0	0	0	13
Grocery and supermarkets	70	7	4	0	1	82
Service station and auto repairs. . .	29	10	1	0	0	40
Laundry and drycleaning.	24	8	3	2	1	38
Beauty and barbershops	92	8	2	0	0	102
Total in 6 categories	268	46	11	2	2	329
Total, all businesses	452	83	21	3	5	564

This conclusion is also strongly supported by the results of a seven-city survey of Negro businesses conducted by the National Business League in early 1969. (See table 4 attached.) Of the 564 businesses reported in the survey, 329 (or 58 percent) were concentrated in six out of 67 industry categories. These six categories correspond closely to the local market oriented service operations in Washington, D.C., described above.

A careful look at the employment patterns within the specific categories of Negro business is useful. Of the 329 businesses in the six-industry group, 268 (or 82 percent) had four or less employees, while the corresponding figure for the entire sample was nearly as high—80 percent. Thus, these six categories are a good representation of employment patterns for the entire sample. The obvious conclusion from these figures are that Negro businesses are very small, indeed.

The small size of the average Negro business is, in part, due to a concentration in the types of enterprises which are traditionally quite small. Barber and beauty shops are small operations, and it is no surprise that 92 (or 90 percent) of the barber and beauty shops had four or fewer employees. What is more distressing is the tendency for Negro businesses to be small in operations which are not traditionally small. The category labeled grocery stores and super-markets is a good example. Of the 82 businesses in this category, 70—or 85 percent—had four or fewer employees, and only 1 had over twenty-one employees. Clearly the category labeled

grocery stores and supermarkets refers to very small grocery stores serving limited markets.

Employment figures present only one dimension of Negro businesses, and more information is possible through data on income and profits. (See table 5 attached.) The income and profit figures reflect the same general trends as the employment data. Of the 329 firms in the six-industry groups, 279 (or 85 percent) expected gross income in 1967 of $20,000 or less, while 455 (or 81 percent of the total sample) expected to be in this range. For estimated net profits, the picture was equally poor—with 290 (or 88 percent of the businesses in the six categories) and 474 (or 81 percent of all businesses)—expected a net profit of $5,000 or less. Of the 54 restaurants in the sample, 49 (or 91 percent) estimated net profits of $5,000 or less and the remaining 5 anticipated profits of between $5,000 and $10,000.

CONCLUDING COMMENTS

From this analysis, we can conclude that the prospects for economic development through Negro owned businesses dependent upon the type of infrastructure discussed above are not very encouraging. The asset and liability data presented above reinforce the already familiar income statistics, and together they show clearly that the Negro market is by no means a strong one. Consequently, entrepreneurs who limit themselves to these markets will be denied the

Table 5. *Distribution of Negro Owned Enterprises, by Size of
Estimated Income and Profit, 1967*

Category of Business	Estimated Gross Income					Estimated Gross Profit				
	Under $20,000	$20,000 to $50,000	$50,000 to $95,000	Over $95,000	Total	Under $5,000	$5,000 to $10,000	$10,000 to $20,000	$20,000 to $30,000	Over $30,000
Restaurants	48	4	1	1	54	49	5	0	0	0
Snack and carryout	11	1	1	0	13	13	0	0	0	0
Grocery and supermarkets. . .	62	10	2	8	82	75	4	2	1	0
Service station and auto repairs	31	4	3	2	40	31	5	4	0	0
Laundry and drycleaning	30	5	2	1	38	27	8	3	0	0
Beauty and barber shops . . .	97	3	0	2	102	95	6	1	0	0
Total in 6 categories . . .	279	27	9	14	329	290	28	10	1	0
Total, all businesses . . .	455	59	24	26	564	474	58	25	3	4

Source: National Business League Survey.

economies of scale which are a precondition of long-run economic development. The small firms spawned by these markets offer a limited potential for an expansion in the total number of job opportunities. The high concentration of these firms in service areas does not provide a margin of profit large enough for the accumulation of new capital, and it inhibits the development of the types of skills needed to compete successfully for executive positions in large corporations operating in a modern high technology economy.

As mentioned at the outset, my purpose in testifying today is not to demean small businesses which I feel do offer modest opportunities for some potential Negro entrepreneurs. Rather, my purpose has been to point out some of the serious economic pitfalls of a strategy based upon separatism and segregation. Economic separatism has been tried in the past, and it has failed to provide genuine opportunity for Negro businessmen—and it certainly has failed to provide economic well-being for our Negro population. I am personally convinced that the most promising path of economic opportunity for Negroes lies in full participation in an integrated national economy. This holds for Negroes who want to be businessmen as well as

for everyone else. The sooner we recognize this important lesson from the past, the quicker we can start to attack the real obstacles to the Negro's economic progress in the United States.

TESTIMONY

MR. BRIMMER. I should say that since this is mainly a personal statement on my own part, I am speaking for myself, and the Board did not address itself to this issue, since the invitation came to me directly.

Let me say at the outset my main interest in responding was to share with the committee an economic analysis of the environment in which minority businesses—and primarily Negro-owned businesses—have been operated and in which they are likely to operate in the foreseeable future. Thus, I will put aside many of the somewhat more exhilarating and fascinating issues which have been raised before this committee—and which surround this subject generally—such as the pride of ownership, cultural advantage, and so on, using business as one instrument. Instead, I would like to concentrate on the question of the potential of the Negro market and the role of small business as an instrument of economic development.

On the basis of my analysis of the economic evidence, I have concluded that we should be extremely cautious in advising and urging Negroes to seek careers as self-employed small businessmen. This is especially true if the expectation of success in these careers is based on the assumption that the businessman can conduct his affairs in a separate, all-black environment, protected from the competition of those firms that are active in the large national market.

In looking at the record, I concluded that in general, if a potential businessman wishes to restrict his efforts to small-scale, neighborhood detailing and the provision of relatively simple personal services, it is quite possible that he can make a living, although it is likely to be a rather modest living.

However, and this is one of the critical points, if he really desires to engage in manufacturing, construction, transportation, or wholesale trade, the prospects of success appear to be extremely dim if the firm's output is to be sold mainly in the limited market provided by the Negro community. Between these extremes, the outlook for success really becomes less and less promising as the scale and technical sophistication of the enterprise increase.

Mr. Chairman, in the last 2 or 3 years, on one or two occasions, I have tried to look at the rationale for Negro business and Negro markets in general. I concluded that Negro business, as we know it, is really the product of a situation which is roughly comparable to the existence of a protective tariff in international trade. In other words, because of segregation, the Negro community did not really have access to the market for many services, whereas it had relatively open access to the market for most goods.

So what we see is the erection of barriers as to services. Behind these barriers, there grew up opportunities for Negro businessmen to provide those services which Negro citizens could not acquire other places. These were primarily personal services—barber shops, funeral services, and so on—whereas the market for goods was generally open. This led to the result that you expect: In those occupations where Negroes could meet the demand behind a wall of segregation, there was heavy participation by Negro professionals and businessmen.

The opposite was true in the open part of the market. Thus, one should not be surprised when he looks around the country and finds very few Negroes running department stores, hardware stores, furniture stores, and similar places.

Again, the higher income which Negroes derived from offering services in this protected market favored concentration behind the wall of segregation. So it is here that one finds a high proportion of professionals—such as physicians, dentists, lawyers, ministers and so on.

What happened when the wall of segregation, especially in public accommodations, began to decline? Again, the result was exactly what you should expect with the removal of a tariff or other barrier in international trade. These weak industries, these weak enterprises, these protected professions, began to suffer immensely.

One of the most striking examples I have found of this adverse impact is the decline of the once prestigious and fairly good hotels which previously served Negroes on a segregated basis around the country. Go to any one of the large cities in the East or Midwest and look around the Negro community, and you are likely to find there is or was a hotel which has lost a good bit of its patronage as more and more of its former customers are now finding their way into the better accommodations downtown.

But the classic example, of course, is found in the life insurance industry. Sometime in the early 1880's, the nationwide life insurance companies began to use separate mortality tables for Negroes or did not sell them insurance at all. Here again were the conditions under which Negro insurance companies could grow up, and they did. So over the years, the insurance industry became the most promising and prosperous part of the Negro business community. But, from the mid-1950's on, when the large insurance companies began to compete for this patronage, began to scrap, as it were, the old mortality tables and look for customers, particularly among middle-class Negroes, the rate of growth of the Negro insurance companies began to decline. In some cases, there were absolute declines.

This impact of desegregation, as I have said, has been substantial. I have in the paper some rough evidence suggesting what has happened to the incomes of Negro businessmen who have been mainly concentrated in the retail field.

Essentially what these data say is that the businessmen who were concentrating in retail trade lagged behind substantially. While this was true for white businessmen who were self-employed in retail trade, it is even more true for Negro businessmen.

As I said at the outset, I think it would be highly desirable to look carefully at this legacy of racial segregation and subsequent desegregation, because I think it goes a long way toward shaping the environment in which Negro businessmen will have to operate, not only for today but for the near future.

I shall not bore the committee with the evidence describing the economic characteristics of the Negro community. You know these. What I would like to do for the next few minutes is ask you to look away from the income figures, which are widely known and appreciated. For example, we know that, roughly, the median family income in the Negro community is just about three-fifths that of white families. But actually, these income figures understate the relative weakness of the Negro market—the market for consumer goods in the Negro community as opposed to the market in the white community. It would be much better if we took a look at their respective financial positions—that is, financial assets and liabilities of the two communities. For this purpose, the data gathered by the Survey Research Center at the University of Michigan are quite helpful. I have summarized in tables 1 and 2 the evidence gathered in the center's survey for 1967.

The first thing you notice about this table, of course, is that there is a very high incidence of ownership of life insurance. This reflects my earlier comments about the availability of life insurance and the effort to sell it on the part of the Negro life insurance companies over the years. Increasingly, of course, a good bit of the coverage is in the larger white companies, but we see that the ownership of life insurance is much higher among Negroes than one would normally have expected.

The picture with respect to other financial assets is quite different. Negroes at virtually all levels of income are less likely to have savings accounts or stock. The lone exception appears in the over $10,000 income class, where Negroes rely heavily on savings accounts, though far less frequently on stocks. Though not shown in this table, the same Michigan survey—taken in 1967, showing income for 1966—reported that in 1966 Negro families obtained only 2 percent of their total money income from dividends, rent, interest, and trust funds—property, in other words—whereas for white families, the proportion was about 6 percent.

The most important data in table 1 are for the income categories between $5,000 and $10,000. I think the committee would be especially interested in this particular range of incomes. In this range, between $5,000 and $10,000, we find roughly 40 percent of all Negro families. Thus, here we will find the broadest based foundations for the Negro market. The asset data for families within this critical income range show that Negroes have considerably less financial accumulation than white families. This finding implies that these Negro families would not be as good potential customers as the income figures might suggest.

Liabilities, constituting the other side of the financial picture, are summarized in table 2. One is immediately struck by the fact that Negroes at all levels of income are much more heavily burdened with installment debt. The repayment of this debt represents a sizable claim on disposable income and thus makes a Negro family a poorer potential customer for additional goods and services than a white family of similar income who is less encumbered by installment debt payments.

I think it would be helpful, also, if the committee looked at the ownership of homes, but it tells roughly the same story. Again, the ownership incidence is less, but the incidence of mortgage indebtedness is somewhat higher.

Now I think these data on financial assets and liabilities shed new light on the economic achievement of Negro families. These data show that Negro families of comparable income have greater liabilities and fewer financial assets to meet these liabilities than whites. These findings suggest that the usually observed data on white-Negro income differentials actually understate differences in purchasing power, because the income figures do not indicate the relatively poor net financial position of Negro families. These figures on assets and liabilities accentuate the problems of weak markets facing businessmen who try to limit themselves to the Negro community alone.

Mr. Chairman, against that background, I have tried to get some feeling for the structure of Negro businesses and the outlook for economic development, which is one of the key questions before the committee. I have summarized in a table the main dimensions of the ownership of businesses in the city of Washington since it is clear that we have only fragmentary information on the internal characteristics of Negro businesses. If the committee wishes, we can come back to those data. They are summarized in table 3 and also in the text.

The most interesting conclusion to me is the very high concentration in services, and above all, a high concentration in those services where the average size of the business is quite small. This has serious implications from the point of view of the margin of profit and the ability to accumulate capital.

In order to get a better appreciation of this situation, I was able to share the results of a survey conducted in early 1969 by the National Business League. Mr. Berkeley Burrell, who is on the list to testify, either before me or after me, was kind enough to let me examine some of the unpublished data from that survey. I have summarized these in table 4 and table 5. They are available for the committee's use.

This survey covered 564 businesses—at least they have results tabulated from 564 businesses in seven cities around the country. I did not list the cities, but I think I remember them, Los Angeles, Atlanta, Chicago, Durham, Norfolk, Va., Cleveland, and Jackson, Miss.—these are cities which are quite representative of the characteristics of businesses owned and operated by Negroes.

I have tried to get some indication of the size of the enterprise and the relative profitability. The summaries shown suggest exactly what we would have expected—again, their high concentration in the services and especially on those activities which were restricted to Negroes in the economy as a whole.

The average size of business is very small indeed, less than four employees. In the typical case, the vast majority of the 564, for example—over 450—have less than four employees. But really, the interesting thing is to look at the profitability of the enterprise. These are summarized in table 5.

The income and profits figures reflect the same general trend as the employment data. We could look at some 329 firms in the six industry categories, mainly services, which account for the bulk of these businesses.

Of the 329 firms in the six industry groups, about 85 percent expect a gross income in 1967 of $20,000 or less. I think that is important. And the vast majority, again about four-fifths, expected a net profit of $5,000 or less.

I suggest, Mr. Chairman, and members of the committee, that the above analyses point toward the need to be cautious in encouraging minority groups to go into business. I would not want to suggest that there is no hope at all—quite to the contrary. I think with the kind of open-mindedness and preparation for hardship which this involves, the small scale retail business would provide some opportunities for a few businessmen.

On the other hand, I think the evidence suggests that it would be most unwise to encourage people to think that they can maintain a small business on a separatist basis, that they can do it free from competition from the outside. I am personally convinced that the most promising path of economic development for Negroes lies in full participation in an integrated economy. This holds for Negroes who want to be businessmen as well as for everybody else. I think the sooner we recognize this, the better we all will be.

That is the substance of what I have to share with the committee. . . .

MR. [SILVIO O.] CONTE. Mr. Brimmer, I must say that your statement is most discouraging. There is no doubt about your intelligence. You have come forth here with a statement filled with statistics, but you did not offer or propose one solution in the whole thing. I think, and there is a school of thought around here that feels, that the black man has become very impatient. He has waited a hundred years for equal rights and equal treatment. Finally, we have recognized these problems. There is little more that can be done in this area from the standpoint of additional legislation. Now he wants a piece of the action. After hearing your statement, if I were a black man, I would be darned discouraged. You have not given him any hope here that he is going to get a piece of the action.

MR. BRIMMER. Mr. Conte, I am not going to

sit here and tell you or this committee that I have solutions for you. I said at the very outset of my statement that I did not come before you to debate the quesion of who should have a piece of the action or the question of pride of ownership and prestige and image. When I got an invitation, I assumed I was being invited on the basis of somebody's presumption that I could make a contribution. That contribution is of the sort I have offered you.

I am an economist. As I said in my opening remarks, I prefer to deal with questions of economic analysis and leave these other questions to the Congress and to those who would wish to pursue them.

Having said that, I have no expectation whatsoever that small businesses of the sort I have seen, not only in the Negro community but in the community generally, are likely to be the principal instrument of economic development. I think it would be better, if you are looking for solutions, and I did not try to give solutions—if you are looking for solutions, you really ought to concentrate on the real potential and the capacity where you can find them. One of these steps which might contribute to a solution, and I certainly would not ask this committee to recall this, was suggested by me last December. In addressing myself to the question of the role which banks could play in urban economic development, I did suggest an approach of trying to mobilize the financial capacity of the large financial institutions of the country, especially the commercial banks, through what I called at that time a domestic version of an Edge Act corporation. They could mobilize their own resources and make funds available in the community which would help finance not only housing but business requirements, including equity. But the key point was that these had to be of sufficient size as to make a difference.

In other words, Mr. Congressman, I am uninterested in encouraging anybody to try to run piggy banks or small stores. I think this would not be a useful and meaningful service, either to them or to the country. So I am not optimistic about small business being the best way to undertake these enormous tasks which we find in our urban areas.

MR. CONTE. Big industry likewise could be mobilized to provide a bank of management and technical-know to a lot of minority people in this country and help them set up their own operations.

MR. BRIMMER. Well, Mr. Congressman, it looks as though you and I just have basically different philosophical views of the world. As far as I am concerned, owning your own little business is not the critical issue. If you want to be a businessman, it seems to me you ought to be interested in being in a business where you can make a difference. After all, being in a corporation is being in business. If you want a piece of the action, to use your language—the language I never use myself—if you really want to own a piece of American industry, you can own some stock. After all, that is what most people do who own a stake in business.

MR. CONTE. What are you going to buy that stock with? The only philosophical difference between you and me is that you will not even give it a chance. I want to give it a chance.

MR. BRIMMER. Mr. Congressman, I am quite certain that you and I could have a fascinating exchange on what should be the proper way to do it. I suggested that whatever path you choose, it might be helpful to have some information and that is what I have attempted to provide in my statement. . . .

MR. CORMAN. Governor, I would like to pose a question or two. I was rather surprised to hear the representative of the American Bankers Association this morning say there was no shortage of capital for minority small businessmen. Is that your observation? Private capital, I am talking about.

MR. BRIMMER. Since I did not hear that—

MR. CORMAN. I will make an observation, repeating him. What is your comment on that observation? Does it seem to you there is a little shortage of capital?

MR. BRIMMER. It is my impression, Mr. Congressman, that if a businessman has something to go along with the additional financial resources he might get from the bank, there is not any shortage. I find it difficult, however, to unravel what is in fact a bankable proposition and what is not. If I were a banker, I would be as interested in the technical and managerial capacity, and above all, the ideas being put forth as I would be in the balance sheet. So I cannot answer that, because I assume at a price, there would be capital.

MR. CORMAN. Let me get at it in a little

different way. Don't you think there are a lot of propositions that would have been bankable 3 years ago that are not bankable today because there are less funds today than there were 3 years ago?

MR. BRIMMER. Mr. Congressman, I hope that is true. If that is not true, much of what we have been doing has failed.

MR. CORMAN. My constituents would indicate that you have had great success.

MR. BRIMMER. May I turn that around and say on the other hand that there are a lot of bankers who find bankable, even in today's tight money situation, propositions that 3 years ago they did not find bankable, because they have acquired new skills themselves in looking at many of these minority business operations that do not have the kind of documentation of which a credit manager would look. So they are finding many of these bankable. So I would say it is cutting both ways.

MR. CORMAN. Governor, do you not think that the banks having limited capital to lend are still placing about the same priorities on it, and that is security of the loan and the return they get on it rather than the social impact?

MR. BRIMMER. Oh, I would say at the margin, they may be making a slight bit of difference, but I see no evidence that bankers are in fact revolutionizing their lending procedure so that now they are taking on great loads of paper that they would not otherwise have done.

MR. CORMAN. I expect that is close to accurate.

Recognizing, you know, that the world is not going to be changed by efforts of the Government or other groups interested in trying to develop black entrepreneurship, and I have always had and now have it statistically backed with the fact that a black neighborhood is not where anybody ought to go into business if he can get in some place else, but can't we use these programs for horizontal movement of Negro communities?

MR. BRIMMER. It would be my hope that not only we can, but that we would.

Why should a businessman who happens to be black or some other color go into business on the assumption that his only opportunity is in a limited market? If he wants to be in business, he ought to be interested in a marketplace. It seems to me he ought to be equally interested, if

anything more interested, in getting out of that immediate confine and out where the market is expanding much more rapidly. So not only would it be my expectation that you could use these programs, but that you would use these programs, in the way you suggest. . . .

MR. CORMAN. Would you say that these programs ought to have high on their priority of objectives for a horizontal movement?

MR. BRIMMER. I would think that any Government program, and here I am abstracting from whether it is a particular administration program in this area, ought to have as one of its prime objectives to maximize the benefits to the total community of the use of these resources. And given the analysis I have done, I am convinced that these yields would likely be higher by moving into some of the more promising enterprises, into bigger markets. Then it would follow from my analysis that one seriously would hope that this would be the case.

MR. CORMAN. I take it you are basing your answer almost entirely on the economics.

MR. BRIMMER. Exactly. As I said in the first paragraph of my statement, I deliberately set out to avoid debating these larger issues because I do not think the committee is interested in any hearsay views I may have. I do not work in the area of sociology, and I have not acquired any foundation on the basis of which I could have anything in the way of expertise on the subject to share with this committee.

MR. CHAIRMAN. Thank you, Governor.

MR. CORMAN. We very much appreciate your coming.

MR. BRIMMER. Thank you, gentlemen.

ADDITIONAL READINGS FOR CHAPTER 8

Andrew F. Brimmer, "The Negro in the National Economy," in John P. Davis (ed), *The American Negro Reference Book* (Englewood Cliffs, N.J.: Prentice-Hall, 1966), esp. pp. 291-334.

Flournoy A. Coles, Jr., *An Analysis of Black Entrepreneurship in Seven Urban Areas* (Washington, D.C.: The National Business League, November 1969).

Harold Cruse, *Rebellion or Revolution* (New York: William Morrow & Company, 1968), pp. 156-167.

———, *The Crisis of the Negro Intellectual* (New York: William Morrow & Company, 1967), pp. 305-336.

St. Clair Drake and Horace Cayton, *Black Metropo-*

lis: A Study of Negro Life in a Northern City, V. II, Revised and enlarged ed. (New York: Schocken Books 1962), esp. pp. 430-494.

Drexel Institute of Technology, *An Analysis of the Little Businessman in Philadelphia,* V. I (Philadelphia: Drexel Institute of Technology, 1964).

——, *The Census of Negro — Owned Businesses* (Philadelphia: Drexel Institute of Technology, 1964).

W. E. B. DuBois, *The Philadelphia Negro: A Social Study* (New York: Schocken Books, 1967), esp. pp. 115-126.

Economic Development Opportunity, Hearings Before the Select Committee on Small Business, United States Senate, 90th Congress, 2nd Session, on The Role of the Federal Government in the Development of Small Business Enterprises in the Urban Ghetto, Newark, New Jersey - May 24, 1968, New York, New York-June 17, 1968 (Washington, D.C.: U.S. Government Printing Office, 1968).

E. Franklin Frazier, *The Negro Family in the United States,* Revised and abridged ed. (Chicago: University of Chicago Press, 1966), esp. pp. 317-355.

Eugene D. Genovese, *The Political Economy of Slavery: Studies on the Economy and Society of the Slave South* (New York: Pantheon Books, Inc., 1965), esp. pp. 180-239 and 275-287.

Nathan Glazer and Daniel Patrick Moynihan, *Beyond the Melting Pot: The Negroes, Puerto Ricans, Jews, Italians and Irish of New York City* (Cambridge, Mass.: The M.I.T. Press, 1963), esp. pp. 1-85.

Jessie E. Gloster, *Minority Business Enterprise in Houston, Texas* (Houston, Texas: Department of Economics, Texas Southern University, September 1969).

Abram L. Harris, *The Negro as Capitalist: A Study of Banking and Business Among American Negroes* (Philadelphia: American Academy of Political and Social Science, 1936).

James M. Hund, *Black Entrepreneurship* (Belmont, Calif.: Wadsworth Publishing Co., 1970).

Robert H. Kinzer and Edward Sagarin, *The Negro in American Business* (New York: Greenberg, 1950).

Robert S. Lackey and H. Elliott Wright (eds.), *Black Manifesto: Religion, Racism, and Reparations* (New York: Sheed and Ward, 1969).

Gunnar Myrdal, with the assistance of Richard Sterner and Arnold Rose, *An American Dilemma: The Negro Problem and Modern Democracy* (New York, Harper & Row, Publishers, 1962), pp. 304-332.

National Conference on Small Business, H. Naylor Fitzhugh, ed., *Problems and Opportunity Confronting Negroes in the Field of Business* (Washington, D.C.: U.S. Department of Commerce, 1962).

V. V. Oak, *The Negro's Adventure in General Business* (Yellow Springs, Ohio: The Antioch Press, 1949).

Robert C. Puth, "Supreme Life: The History of a Negro Life Insurance Company, 1919-1962, *"Business History Review,* V. XLIII, N.1 (Spring 1969), pp. 1-20.

PACT, Incorporated, *Black Business in San Francisco: The Problems and the Solutions* (San Francisco; PACT, Inc., November 1968).

Allan H. Spear, *Black Chicago: The Making of a Negro Ghetto, 1890-1920* (Chicago: University of Chicago Press, 1967).

Charles Tate, "Brimmer and Black Capitalism: An Analysis," *Review of Black Political Economy,* V. 1, N. 1 (Spring/Summer, 1970), pp. 84-90.

Daniel C. Thompson, *The Negro Leadership Class* (Englewood Cliffs, N.J.: Prentice-Hall, 1963).

Urban America, Inc. and the Urban Coalition, *One Year Later: An Assessment of the Nation's Response to the Crisis Described by the National Advisory Commission on Civil Disorders* (Washington, D.C.: Urban America, Inc. and the Urban Coalition, 1969), pp. 4-28.

Booker T. Washington, *The Negro in Business* (Boston, 1907).

PART 3

THE ROLE OF BUSINESS
IN SOCIAL CHANGE

In Part 2 we described in some detail the unhappy relationship which has existed between business and the black community in the areas of employment, housing, retail merchandising, finance, and black business development. We now turn to the task of examining a number of contemporary programs and policy proposals intended to redress the negative imbalance which has been endemic to these areas of economic interface. No account of the story of black Americans and white business would be complete if it concluded simply with a catalogue of the miseries and malpractices of yesterday and today.

As a result of increased militancy (both peaceful and otherwise) by the black community, governmental pressures, and a fusion of social idealism and economic pragmatism on the part of business leaders, corporate managers (and others) have begun to reassess old patterns and practices and to propose and implement corrective measures. Naturally, what is genuinely effective has to be sorted out from merely self-laudatory public relations talk, or naively enthusiastic plans which avoid recognition of existing social and economic pathology. Also, new programs and policies by business concerning blacks are still at a seminal stage and the early glow of enthusiasm by business executives for "social responsibility" has faded as deep-seated problems have not disappeared as quickly as had been anticipated.[1] The difficulties are real, and progress is modest.

In searching the literature, we have uncovered a number of instructive reports of programs initiated by business firms to change both employment practices and housing conditions. Additionally, we have found some new, interesting and forcefully presented policy proposals (conjoining public and private sector action) relating to these two areas as well as others intended to improve the operations of financial institutions and enhance black economic development. Chapters 9, 10, 11, and 12 present some of these.

Let us turn now to the critical subject of employment. In his powerful and insightful study of black streetcorner men in Washington, *Talley's Corner,* Elliot Liebow observed that the central fact of life among lower-class blacks was the inability of the black man to earn a living and support his family. Liebow states:

> If there is to be a change in this way of life, this central fact must be changed; the Negro man, along with everyone else, must be given the skills to earn a living and an opportunity to put these skills to work.[2]

Earning a living has an importance far transcending the economic realm. To quote Liebow again:

> One of the major points of articulation between the inside world and the larger society surrounding it is in the area of employment. The way in which a man makes a living and the kind of living he makes have important consequences for how the man sees himself and is seen by others; and these, in turn, importantly shape his relationship with family members, lovers, friends and neighbors.[3]

Employment Policies

The quality of life of black Americans can only be enhanced by a dramatic improvement in the income, status, personal esteem, and financial security of the average man and woman. All four elements are directly dependent upon the meaningful and stable employment of blacks by the business community, the major source of jobs in American society. If essential changes are not forthcoming in the pattern of black occupations and employment mobility, there is little hope for a bright future for black—or white—Americans. It is in the area of employment that business has its greatest challenge and opportunity for creative social action.

A number of companies have demonstrated a recognition of this fact. The rate at which major firms in many industries hired new employees from black and Spanish-speaking minorities during 1969 is part of the story. According to a recent *Saturday Review* report:

In Los Angeles, 42 per cent of the first-entry hires made by the Bank of America were from minority groups. In Chicago, 48.9 per cent of the first hires made by the Illinois Bell Telephone Company were minority members. In the Detroit metropolitan area, the figures for the big three auto companies are as follows: Chrysler, 46 per cent from minority groups; Ford, 35 per cent; General Motors, 34.1 per cent. In Newark, New Jersey, Prudential Insurance Company reports that 46.5 per cent of all its first hires were from minority groups. In Philadelphia at Smith Kline and French Laboratories 29 per cent were from minority groups. For the Chemical Bank in New York, the figure was just under 50 per cent; for Consolidated Edison, 48 per cent; for the New York Telephone Company, 51 per cent. For Equitable Life, it was 42 per cent, and for New York Life, it was also 42 per cent[4]

However, all the hope one might take from the 1969 employment statistics just cited must be tempered by knowing that disproportionate shares of minority group employees do not last long on the job for one reason or another. As the *Saturday Review* report points out:

Good as this overall record is, there is another important aspect: The rate of turnover of the minority first hires in the first year ran from 20 per cent to well over 50 per cent. Nationally, banks and other financial institutions have a minority group turnover rate of from 35 to 60 per cent. Insurance companies run much lower. Public utilities in the big cities have a turnover of well over 40 per cent among first hires in the minority group classification.[5]

The selections which follow suggest several possible courses of action by the business community.

The first reading, "Proposed Solutions to the Problem of Cultural Bias in Testing," by Phyllis Wallace, Beverly Kissinger, and Betty Reynolds, discusses the removal of another employment barrier to blacks—inherent cultural bias in employment testing. At present, unsophisticated personnel men often use employment tests in ways which appall psychologists mindful of the technical problems of establishing reliability and validity. The authors explain the special measures which may be taken to achieve culture-free, culture-fair, and culture-equivalent tests. They also describe other steps the employer may take to free his recruitment and selection procedures of racial discrimination.

The next selection, "Guidelines for Affirmative Action in Equal Employment Opportunity," by Louis A. Ferman, offers a practical manual of advice on formulating, communicating, and administering an equal employment opportunity policy and its practices. The advice is well informed and realistically anticipates many problems commonly encountered in translating equal employment opportunity from pious hope to operating reality.

In "Successful Experience: Training Hard-Core Unemployed," Secretary of Labor James D. Hodgson, then an officer of Lockheed Aircraft Corporation, and Marshall H. Brenner, an industrial psychologist at Lockheed, report on that company's activities in recruiting and training hard-core unemployed at two of its plants. The authors compare the programs used at the two facilities and make a number of observations relevant to other companies.

A final and highly critical area of activity for business firms in the years ahead is the recruitment, promotion, job placement, and retention of black managers. The reader will recall the total absence of black executive officers in a 1970 study conducted by the Race Relations Information Center among nearly 3200 senior officers and directors of 50 of the nation's largest corporations. Only three blacks were included as directors on the boards of those firms.[6] An acid test of both the sincerity and effectiveness of business activities in the employment field will be whether the new generation of black M.B.A.'s who are now emerging from the nation's leading graduate schools of business in increasing numbers will achieve responsible decision-making positions within the business hierachy in the decade of the 1970s. No longer will business be able to use the "unavailability of qualified individuals" as an excuse for the paucity of black executives in American industry. In the final selection, "A Modest Proposal for the Abatement of Corporate Racism," James S. Spain, an executive with Allied Chemical Corporation and past president and board chairman of the Council of Concerned Black Executives, strongly criticizes the business community for its poor performance in recruiting and promoting black managers and makes a variety of suggestions regarding the implementation of a strong affirmative action program to correct these deficiencies.

The selections in this chapter do not purport to cover all of the areas of concern in improving the employment opportunities of black Americans. Other critical areas in addition to the recruitment, selection, and training of black employees include remedial education, orientation to work and the environment, the provision of counseling the supportive services, obtaining the cooperation of the labor unions, the location of jobs within reasonable geographical proximity to the black community, the opening up of white collar positions to black males, the retention of workers who are hired, and the appropriate role of the black community in the determination of the company's employment practices. Each of these problems has arisen in the past and is sure to confront management in the future.

NOTES

[1] See, e.g., Jules Cohn, "Is Business Meeting the Challenge of Urban Affairs?," *Harvard Business Review*, V. 48, N. 2 (March-April 1970), pp. 68-82.

[2] Elliot Liebow, *Tally's Corner: A Study of Negro Streetcorner Men* (Boston: Little, Brown and Company, 1967), p. 224.

[3] *Ibid*, p. 210.

[4] L.L.L. Golden, "It's Not a Matter of Choice," *Saturday Review* (May 9, 1970), p. 67.

[5] *Ibid*, p. 67.

[6] The R.R.I.C. study is reported in "Executive Suites—A White Domain," *San Francisco Chronicle*, October 1, 1970, p. 4.

PROPOSED SOLUTIONS TO THE PROBLEM OF CULTURAL BIAS IN TESTING

Phyllis Wallace, Beverly Kissinger, and Betty Reynolds

Most employers defined tests as an efficient device for choosing the most qualified applicants. Where Negro job applicants consistently score significantly below white job applicants a question should be raised about test scores as predictors of job performance. In an employment situation we would like to know whether differences between group means are also associated with performance on the criterion. Do the factors that depress test performance also depress trainability or whatever criterion is to be predicted? Psychologists have suggested ways in which the effect of cultural bias inherent in many aptitude tests can be alleviated for minority group applicants. Few of these proposals have been universally accepted, but most have been discussed in the professional literature on testing of minority groups and the culturally disadvantaged.

VARIANTS OF "CULTURE-FREE" AND "CULTURE-FAIR" TESTS

Culture-free tests. One such proposal is the development of tests which are free of cultural bias in their content and instructions. Dr. Robert Krug, who has written extensively on testing of minority persons, indicates that one of two conditions must be met before a test can be classified as "culture-free": either the test items are those which all people of all cultures have had equal opportunity and equal motive to learn, or the test items must possess complete

Reprinted from *Testing of Minority Group Applicants for Employment,* by Phyllis Wallace, Beverly Kissinger, Betty Reynolds (Washington, D.C., Office of Research and Reports, Equal Employment Opportunity Commission, March 1966), pp. 9-22. Footnotes omitted.

novelty for all people of all cultures. For all practical purposes these two conditions are almost impossible to meet and the idea is often rejected as unfeasible. Howard Lockwood of Lockheed Corporation states that many industrial psychologists agree that even if such a test could be developed, it would be useless in personnel selection. It is impossible, he maintains, to avoid measuring cultural influences, and if they were completely eliminated from all tests, the tests would measure, in essence, nothing.

Culture-fair tests. Dr. Krug, on the other hand, does not reject the idea entirely. He describes a "culture-fair" test as a modification of the "culture-free" idea. The assumption underlying the "culture-fair" tests is that there exists a set of test stimuli which are equally appropriate, that is, equal opportunity and motive to learn, for at least two cultural groups. Dr. Paul Schwartz, who headed an AID-sponsored aptitude test development project in West Africa, has done most of the research in this area. A "culture-fair" test or "culture-common test" developed by Schwartz for Nigerian and American children utilized a set of fruits and vegetables which were approximately equal in familiarity to both cultures.

Culture-equivalent tests. Dr. Schwartz also developed another variant of this concept called "cultural-equivalent" tests, denoting that two tests which are not identical may, in fact, be equivalent. In this case investigations were undertaken to discover cultural counterparts of tools and machines, cultural manifestations of mechanical principles, and cultural opportunities to acquire information of potential relevance to mechanical training. The argument of cultural equivalence rests on the demonstration that tests constructed in this way have been valid predictors of performance in Westernized training programs in shop mechanics, electrical repair, and the like. Development of similar tests in this country is impeded by lack of knowledge concerning the culture of southern Negroes, northern slum-dwellers of all races, or any other identifiable sub-groups. Dr. Ash asserts that so-called culture-fair tests do not measure aptitudes or characteristics significantly related to most ordinary measures of job success such as turnover, production or foreman ratings.

CREATIVITY TESTS

Another approach, adopted by Dr. Newton Metfessel and Professor J. J. Risser, of the University of Southern California, involves the use of tests to measure *creativity* rather than traditional intelligence tests. The latter sample only a relatively small portion of the factors which are involved in intellectual potential and have placed a premium on verbal comprehension and speed of response and emphasize convergent thinking, or the ability to select the one correct answer.

Creativity tests, on the other hand, stress divergent thinking or the ability to create new or original answers. They are, according to Metfessel, more suitable for the testing of the culturally disadvantaged and certain ethnic groups whose command of language is not highly developed.

These tests utilize the most common and familiar of objects in order to sample the testee's ability to recognize problems, and his originality, flexibility, and fluency of thinking. Tasks include suggesting improvements in a familiar device such as a telephone, or thinking of problems that might occur in the use of an object such as a candle. One test requires the subject to list as many uses as he can for a broom handle.

The tests are scored simply on the number of acceptable answers given by the subject. They seem to be as effective in predicting academic success as traditional intelligence tests and,

probably, would be as effective as the latter in predicting job performance.

DIFFERENTIAL SELECTION AMONG APPLICANTS FROM DIFFERENT SOCIO-ECONOMIC ETHNIC BACKGROUNDS

It has been proposed that, since prediction equations for job performance for most tests currently in use have been based on the performance of whites, different standards (separate test norms, conversion tables, prediction weights, etc.) be employed for Negroes and other culturally disadvantaged groups. This approach involves a technique known as the *moderator variable*. Applicants for a given job are divided into sub-groups, and selection procedures are applied differentially to members of the two groups. Applicants could be classified, for example, on the basis of a measure of socio-economic status, demographic data (such as percentage of Negroes living in the census tract from which the applicant is applying), and race.

Studies could then be undertaken to determine whether there is, in fact, a difference in the predictive efficiency of job tests as between high and low status groups. Difference in selection procedures for different ethnic groups do not mean a lowering of standards because the standards which count are standards of performance on the job, not the selection standards. Equally qualified persons may be selected from various ethnic groups by applying the standards which are appropriate to each group.

Lockwood has proposed the use of "cultural exposure" as a moderator variable. Examinees should be grouped homogeneously as to cultural exposure and these groups treated separately in validity studies. Cultural exposure is defined as the material things to which a person has been exposed and the attitudes to which he has been exposed and which he has acquired. Research would lead to a better identification of the culturally disadvantaged and to the utilization of their abilities through a refinement in prediction of training and occupational success.

A major investigation is under way by Dr. Richard Barrett to determine if the division of applicants into sub-groups improves the accuracy of prediction for members of both groups.

If selection is improved by applying different procedures to the high and low socio-economic groups, then the more talented would benefit, regardless of race. "It may also happen that dividing the group of applicants on the basis of race may lead to improved accuracy of predictions for members of both races. Such a result has far reaching implications for fair employment practices because *failure to treat the two races separately would, if current policies were followed, lead to discrimination against the more talented Negroes."* .

The overwhelming evidence is that the cultural background of the Negro in America today is so different from that of the white that his performance during the selection process can reasonably be expected to be different. It may be difficult to find an adequate sample of Negroes in most occupations in order to develop separate and suitable prediction equations for them. Lockwood also cautions against the use of a lower minimum score or separate standards of test performance for Negroes since it might tend to perpetuate the idea of race differences or race inferiority.

DUAL TEST STANDARDS AND COMPENSATORY TRAINING

The concept of a "dual standard" has some support among psychologists. Ash cites the work of Dr. Kenneth B. Clark of the City University of New York. Clark's work suggests that culturally deprived people who score low on tests may tend to overachieve on the job. In studying the college performance of students who scored low on college entrance tests, Clark found that for students from non-deprived environments, the tests were good predictors, and low college entrance test scores were accurate indicators of poor grades. On the other hand, students coming from deprived environments did significantly better in college than would have been predicted from the tests.

An experimental training program run by the Federal Department Stores in Detroit, Michigan, indicates that a lowering of required test scores will not necessarily result in a lower quality of job performance. The Federal Department Stores took 16 young people from culturally and economically deprived areas, all of whom had failed standard employment tests and were classified as "unemployable" and put them through a 10-week special training program. All 16 subsequently were employed, 14 at Federal and two elsewhere. The record of performance of all 14 employees at Federal exceeded what was predicted by standard sales aptitude tests. Some exceeded the company's minimum performance standards for new employees by "unbelievable margins." Re-test results one year later for the ten trainees still employed by Federal showed no significant changes in the scores as a group.

Although the Federal Department Stores experiment is considered one of the first of its kind in offering compensatory training for individuals with low test scores, the concept of "double-standard" has had wide acceptance for years in the fairly common practice of maintaining different norms for the sexes. Several popular tests which offer different sex norms are the Bennet, The Wonderlic, the Minnesota Paper Form Board, and the Thurstone Temperament Schedule.

It is generally agreed that some of these sex differences on tests are undoubtedly of environmental origin. Girls, are expected to score lower than boys on tests of mechanical information. It is also expected that girls will perform less effectively on tasks for which the Mechanical Information test is a predictor. This, however, does not prevent many companies from employing women in manufacturing tasks which require mechanical ability where they perform satisfactorily.

On the basis of these examples, it appears that a "double-standard" can be justified in some circumstances, though a double standard in job performance and hiring of less qualified applicants is usually rejected as not being effective. If it can be demonstrated that score X for Group A and Score K-k for Group B are associated with *identical* levels of performance on the job, then an employer might reasonably consider adopting a more flexible attitude toward test scores.

INTENSIFICATION OF RECRUITMENT

While there are significant differences in average performance, there is a considerable overlap in the distribution of test scores of whites and Negroes. It has been proposed, on the basis of this observation, that employers who wish to maintain their present standard of performance on their pre-employment tests, can increase their number of Negro employees by intensifying recruitment among Negroes in order to identify those whose test performance is equal to that of acceptable white applicants. Although this approach has merit in that it could provide employment for Negroes who are qualified but who do not apply for jobs in companies where they assume discrimination is practiced, it is not a solution to the testing problem. It ducks the question of the fairness of tests to those who fail because of cultural disadvantage, and it will not provide enough additional workers to satisfy present and future labor needs.

USE OF TEST SCORES AS ONLY ONE INDICATOR

One other practical solution similar in many respects to the "double-standard" is to use test scores as only one indicator among others in the hiring decision, with a clear awareness that, where the applicant has not shared in the predominant middle-class verbal culture, the test score significantly underestimates his potential. A difference of one point more or less cannot be expected to determine if an applicant will fail or succeed on the job. Other personal characteristics such as achievement, motivation, and dependability may be just as significant indicators of successful job performance, and they usually can be identified in each cultural group.

PROPER TESTING PRACTICES

Along with adoption of a more flexible attitude toward test scores, the most immediate improvement can be accomplished by an emphasis by the employer on proper testing practices.

(1) The employer could reconsider the relevance of the qualifications for employment to the specific job tasks required by his company. Many of these requirements are stated in terms of some generalized stereotypes, such as high school graduate, high IQ, or potential to advance to higher level jobs, and are quite extraneous to the requirements of that job. Tests should be professionally chosen to fit the distinctive features of both the industry and the background, education and other characteristics of the successful work force. It is unreasonable to insist that all lower level workers have potential for supervisory positions. An employer may eventually find that by adopting a more reasonable set of qualifications for each job, he will have access to a considerably larger source of workers who can perform capably and who will present him with fewer problems of employee frustration or labor turnover.

(2) Selection tests should be developed by reputable professional psychologists who are competent in conducting testing programs in an industrial setting.

(3) Pre-employment tests should be administered by personnel who are properly trained not only in the technical details of giving tests, but also in the orientation and handling of people in the testing situation. Members of disadvantaged groups tend to be particularly sensitive to any mannerisms that might be considered antagonistic, sarcastic, or condescending, and test administrators should be aware of this and be able by their behavior to alleviate a certain amount of test anxiety. A personnel manager at a recent testing conference complained that the number of Negro applicants for jobs in his company had fallen off by 80 percent after the company recently instituted a pre-employment testing program.

(4) A policy of re-testing "failure" candidates may gain for an employer many good employees who otherwise would have been eliminated by the first test. Many candidates, particularly members of minority groups, regard testing as a threatening situation and do not perform as well as they could. A second test would provide a more accurate indication of the true capability of a person who is less experienced with testing situations and who may have been intimidated by his first experience.

(5) Finally, the most important principle is *validation* of tests in order to confirm the relationship between test scores and on-the-job performance. There is general agreement that tests should not be used for a group which differs from the validation group. Validity is relative both to the criterion to be predicted and

to the group for which the prediction is to be made. Very few employers have validated their testing instruments. In a recent survey by the University of Wisconsin Industrial Relations Research Center, 152 companies which apply testing techniques were canvassed and only 7 percent reported that all their tests had been validated locally against on-the-job performance measures. Nearly 60 percent had validated *none* of their tests. The remainder reported that some but not all of their tests were validated.

Dr. Warren Ketcham, University of Michigan psychologist and vice president of Psychodynamics Research and Associates, has suggested that within-company norms should be used exclusively. This only requires that an applicant perform on tests as well as or better than persons who have done or are presently doing the job satisfactorily. The norm tables should then be used to rank applicants as substandard, low-average, average, high-average, or superior.

From recent discussions with research psychologists attached to large industrial concerns, it appears that many companies are developing ability tests which will measure the essentials required for training or employment, while keeping at a minimum the relevant aspects of culture. For a number of reasons, these findings may never be released for general consumption. One of the responsibilities of the Commission will be to encourage this type of research by the psychological profession. If the purpose of tests is to uncover talent and potential, irrespective of label, surely the Commission could not advocate a more commendable policy.

UNITED STATES AS A MODEL EMPLOYER

If the Equal Employment Opportunity Commission establishes basic guidelines on testing of minority group applicants, including a provision on validation of tests, it will require private employers to satisfy certain standards which the United States government, as a civilian employer, for the most part does not meet. Of some interest is the fact that the United States Employment Service has recently undertaken a program to develop aptitude measures that can be used to evaluate potential for literacy training, vocational training and occupational potential of the educationally deficient. Much of the research is designed to improve the General Aptitude Test Battery, GATB.

The U.S. government has set a fine example in its standardized testing program for the military where these tests have been completely validated. Testing in the Armed Forces serves a number of major programs, two of which are (1) to identify the number of personnel required in each skill and professional category, and (2) to identify each individual for training, upgrading, and utilization to his highest potential.

In order to maintain validity, test development activities are mainly serviced by professional job analysts, subject matter specialists, and test psychologists and validated in the working area. This systematic approach is essential to assure that the tests sample specific job functions in direct proportion to the importance of those functions to the job. As a result, job analysis provides not only a basis for test construction, selection and training, but also a means for increasing productivity and facilitating work.

RECOMMENDATIONS FOR TESTING GUIDELINES

The following recommendations are designed as a guide to help employers establish objective standards for selection, screening, and promotion of workers. These procedures should ensure that all qualified applicants are given equal opportunity for employment.

1. Job descriptions should be examined and their *critical* requirements established before tests are selected for screening applicants. 2. Tests used should be those developed by reputable psychologists. Such tests should be administered by professionally qualified personnel who have had training in occupational testing in an industrial setting.

3. Rigidly inflexible minimum scores should be re-examined in light of the considerable research under way on differential selection.

4. Test scores must be considered as only one source of information, and must be combined with other available data on performance such as motivation, leadership and organizational experience, self-sufficiency, and dependability.

5. Tests should be validated within the setting where they will be used. Validation should be for as many separate groups as possible in preference to one large heterogeneous group.

6. It may be advisable for employers who deal with applicants from culturally disadvantaged backgrounds to offer re-tests to candidates who are unsuccessful on their first try, since these people are less familiar with testing situations and may not perform as well as they are able.

GUIDELINES FOR AFFIRMATIVE ACTION IN EQUAL EMPLOYMENT OPPORTUNITY

Louis A. Ferman

The question must now be raised as to whether it is possible to arrive at a set of general principles which can be used as guidelines in the establishment of an affirmative action equal employment program. The term "guidelines" may seem somewhat gratuitous, in view of one important finding of the current study, viz., that such practices are significantly influenced by features unique to the employment situation of any particular firm. However, reference to general principles and to guidelines is justifiable if the following conditions are held in mind.

Viewed at one level, the twenty companies included in this study represent individual case experiences with the development and implementation of affirmative action policies and programs. There are many factors which differentiate these companies—industrial type, unit size, regional location, employment structure and community context. Any discussion of guidelines cannot neglect these different conditions and their ramifications for the content and determination of an equal employment opportunity program.

Less apparent than these obvious differences are commonalities of experience which vary with particular categories of interest (e.g., recruitment, placement, testing), suggesting that general conclusions regarding the structure and programming of equal employment opportunity activities are feasible. The differences noted above should not be allowed to overshadow this

Reprinted from *The Negro and Equal Employment Opportunities: A Review of Management Experiences in Twenty Companies,* by Louis A. Ferman, prepared for the Office of Manpower Policy Evaluation and Research (Washington, D.C.: U.S. Government Printing Office, December 1966), pp. 128-151.

fact. No suggestion will be made that any and all such principles are equally applicable to every case; rather, it is our conclusion that these experiences suggest guideposts that can be used to good effect by other employers, many of whom may be taking initial steps toward affirmative action measures.

Those who seek assistance by referring to the experiences of other companies with affirmative action programs should not accept their findings without reservation. Affirmative action is not a unitary term, nor is it one which can be disembodied from the particular circumstances of a company and a community. Techniques and strategies which others have found effective cannot be simply emulated. Because of differences in organizational structures and traditions, modifications are necessary. Affirmative action occurs in many shapes and forms, each of which may be peculiarly effective for a particular set of organizational conditions.

Finally, it has been a central thesis in the study that affirmative action does not result automatically from expressions of goodwill by company executives or from the issuance of a public policy statement. Although these are vital, a realistic and positive appraisal of the company's potential is the necessary ingredient. Careful assessment and programming can spell the difference between success and disillusionment.

In deriving general guidelines for affirmative action, we have not shied away from drawing upon the findings of other studies that have been concerned with the equalization of employment opportunities in American industry. In one sense this discussion reflects the cumulative experiences of many researchers and practitioners who have examined the problems, promises, fads and foibles of affirmative action programs. By dividing our discussion according to categories, we express our concern that an affirmative action program be viewed as multifaceted and touching upon all parts of the employment process, though perhaps not with equal degrees of emphasis.

FORMULATION OF AN EQUAL EMPLOYMENT OPPORTUNITY POLICY

Careful consideration must be given to the formulation of an equal employment opportunity policy. Rightly considered, this policy will (or should) provide the basic direction for the development of operating procedures to implement the affirmative action program. It represents a company commitment of major dimensions.

Two immediate considerations affect the formulation of an affirmative action policy in a company. First, it is true that many companies have had an explicit or implicit nondiscrimination policy for many years. Thus, the development of an affirmative action program may be viewed, not as a new policy, but as a continuation of an already existing one, with the new emphases reaffirming or clarifying management's commitment to equal employment opportunity objectives. However this may be, experiences have shown that no assumption should be made that a pre-existing policy statement is an adequate foundation for new emphases. Affirmative action does not just happen; objectives and operating procedures must be carefully thought out.

Second, companies vary in the degree of formality involved in the establishment of general employment policies. Some officials in companies which tend toward the informal pattern regard as moot the question whether the formulation of an equal employment opportunity policy should depart radically from usual procedures.

In either case there is little question that the company's top management needs to clearly state its affirmative action commitment in policy form. A relevant distinction in this respect can be made between policy statements and policy decisions. Policy statements serve a public relations function. The latter represent commitments of company resources to policy implementation. Policy decisions should clarify objectives and mandate an aggressive campaign for their achievement. The distinction is a viable one in that, while company tradition may not favor a written policy statement, there can be little question of the necessity of a policy decision.

Policy decisions should serve three basic purposes: (1) they should express the company's commitment to the goal of equal employment opportunity; (2) they should reflect realistic but definite targets to be achieved; and, (3) they should be couched in terms which leave no doubt about the company's intentions in the minds of the managers and supervisors who will be responsible for the operating program.

The following principles are generally applicable in the formulation of an equal employment policy:

(1) The policy should be developed with the full backing of top officials in the company, including the chief officer. This backing should not be only symbolic. Key executives should be involved both in formulating the basic policy and in establishing the operating procedures for its implementation.

(2) The equal employment policy should reflect an adequate appraisal of the company's potential for expanding minority group employment opportunities. Platitudinous statements are less important than a clear statement of objectives that are within the company's reach. Some companies which develop affirmative action programs will be employing their first Negro workers; others may have had Negro employees for a number of years, but in lower level jobs. The formulation of policy should consider both the company's present circumstance and its potential for change.

(3) The policy should be formulated in such a manner that it is recognized as a major policy commitment, rather than a low priority administrative item.

(4) An affirmative action program touches many, if not all, parts of the employment structure of a company, and there should be no doubt about the policy's application to all of these — hiring, placement, supervision, training, upgrading and promotion.

COMMUNICATION OF POLICY

There is a subtle distinction in terms which can be introduced to good effect. "Communicating the policy" and "announcing the policy" are not fully synonymous in meaning. The former encompasses the latter but contains much more. Here, we are primarily concerned with the more limited term, but it should be recognized that the communication of an equal employment policy is accomplished as much by actions as by public pronouncements. The time-worn phrase to the effect that "Action speaks louder than words" is well borne out in the experiences of those who have formulated and operated affirmative action programs. In fact, Negro and white workers and community members are often skeptical and suspicious that the policy may not be a firm commitment, and their reactions are not simply dispelled by paper communications.

None of the above should be construed as depreciating the importance of disseminating information about the equal employment policy. There is general agreement, however, that these communications should be carefully planned and controlled. In general, they should be targeted only to those persons and agencies which in some manner affect the policy's operation or control the flow of manpower supply to the company. An uncontrolled communication pattern, particularly with respect to organizations and media outside the company could possibly be detrimental in the sense that (a) it is viewed more as a public relations gesture than a sincere commitment, or (b) it results in job applications by minority group members who, in terms of numbers and/or qualifications, cannot be accepted for employment by the company. Many recommend that these media be used only when some significant accomplishments in the equal opportunity field have been made.

The strategies decided upon for communicating the policy ultimately depend upon company traditions and managerial styles. However, there are two key questions involved in the process of communications: (1) To whom should the policy be communicated? (2) What are the most effective means of communication? Neither can be answered by statements applicable to all situations, but the observations offered below incorporate suggestions that emerge from the experiences of many employers.

Communication within the company. The general suggestion is that personnel at all levels within the company should be informed of the policy and that all such announcements should carry the stamp of top management approval. This does not imply that the content and depth of information should be the same throughout, or that the same announcement is made to all at the same time. Most experienced employers advise the provision of advance information for supervisory personnel, the rationale being that this enables those who will directly administer the policy to act with confidence and authority. Nonsupervisory employees should also be made aware of the policy, although there is some disagreement as to how this is best effected. In most cases, a combination of formal and informal means have been used to disseminate information about the policy within a company.

A point not often made, but one which can be of significance in some communities, is communication of the company's nondiscrimination policy to job applicants when they appear at the employment office. Of course, this may already have been accomplished by the appending of an "Equal Opportunity Employer" notice in help-wanted ads or by signs appropriately placed in the employment office itself. But the inclusion of some statement about the company's stance on equal employment opportunity at the time of processing the job application can assure that the company's position is understood by the prospective employee.

Many employers recommend that any procedures established to process grievances concerning discrimination should be specified when the policy is announced. This type of action may serve two purposes: (1) It can again reflect management's commitment to an equal employment opportunity program as a reality rather than merely as an idea; (2) It may forestall the possibility of incidents arising from interracial friction moving outside the company gates and becoming "community incidents."

Communication of policy to the union. Most company executives who have engaged in the initial formulation and communication of an equal employment policy agree that any announcement to unions with which the company has collective bargaining agreements should be a simple and forthright statement of objectives. Some contend that even this is unnecessary, for such a policy is solely a managerial responsibility.

However this question is resolved, one point is fairly clear. It is quite possible that an affirmative action program may necessitate some modifications of practices that are relevant to union-management agreements. But these are matters of negotiation; and primary concern at this point is with the communication of a policy which, in effect, is unilaterally determined. The basic purpose of this communication, if attempted at all, is to solicit union support and cooperation.

Communication of policy to employment agencies and other sources of manpower supply. There are two points of reference for the guidelines here. On the one hand, there are sources of recruitment which a company may be regularly using (e.g. public and private employment agencies, vocational training schools, community high schools, colleges and universities), and these should be informed of the policy. In addition, the nature of an equal employment opportunity policy itself mandates the early establishment of contacts with possible new sources of recruitment (e.g. predominantly Negro high schools and colleges; Negro civic agencies).

In all the above cases, it should be emphasized that communicating the company's equal employment policy is an important component of affirmative action, *but it is only an initial step.* Those employers with experience concur in their judgment that such announcements by themselves produce few minority group job applicants. As stated previously, an equal employment policy is only a statement of intent until basic decisions are made to commit company resources to its implementation. Until this is done, it is only an imaginary program which will yield—as experience clearly shows—imaginary results. What are the most effective techniques for communicating the equal employment opportunity policy? The answer to this will vary according to availability of means, size of company and, not of least importance, managerial ingenuity. Some of the techniques that have

been used to good effect, often in combination, are:

(1) Orientation sessions with managerial and supervisory personnel. These meetings can fulfill several purposes: (a) They convey the message that top management considers the policy to be of major importance and is unequivocal in its commitment; (b) they provide an opportunity for lower-echelon managers and supervisors to raise pertinent questions about operating procedures, thus avoiding ambiguity and uncertainty about responsibilities; (c) they offer an opportunity to determine specific implications of the general guidelines typically established in policy formulations; (d) in companies of considerable size, they can provide assurance that information about the policy is uniformly disseminated in all units, and every supervisor is informed of his responsibilities under the program.

(2) A statement to the work group by the supervisor. Some recommend this strategy on the assumption that the immediate supervisor is in the best position to anticipate and deal with workers' reactions.

(3) A letter signed by the president or a vice-president and sent to every employee. This has one advantage in that it expresses the commitment of the chief officer or other top executive.

(4) A letter to managerial and supervisory personnel with copies posted on bulletin boards.

(5) Notices of the policy placed on the bulletin boards only.

(6) Inclusion of the policy statement in employee handbooks.

(7) Statements in memoranda, following the usual channels of transmittal.

(8) Statement and discussion of the equal employment policy in supervisors' handbooks.

(9) Articles regarding the policy (and particularly achievements) in company publications.

(10) Special publications explaining the policy and the program's objectives.

(11) Contacts through letters and individual visits by company representatives to outside agencies and groups to explain the company's policy and objectives.

Whatever methods are chosen to communicate the equal employment opportunity policy, past experiences suggest the following general rule. The content of the communication should be forceful but forthright and not convey an impression to present employees or others that the company is relaxing its standards of job qualification or performance.

ADMINISTRATION OF NONDISCRIMINATION EMPLOYMENT PRACTICES

The administration of an affirmative action policy incorporates two interdependent but distinguishable dimensions. On the one hand, there must be practices established which deal with specific components of the employment structure. On the other hand, the operating policy should be administratively organized and controlled in order to assure continuity of effort as well as feedback of information about progress and suggested modifications. At this point attention is focused on the latter emphasis.

How the administrative system for organizing and controlling affirmative action practices is established depends on several factors . . . . The existing corporate structure tends to set limits to the administrative practices and control procedures that are feasible. In some cases, administrative control is highly centralized, with little delegation of decision-making authority to operating units. In others, there is a strong tradition of decentralization and much delegation of administrative responsibility. The combined experiences of many employers suggest that affirmative action programs are most effective when they do not radically depart from established procedures of administrative control. This suggests that no single blueprint can be developed which is applicable to all companies.

The preceding point should not be construed as implying that administrative innovation is unnecessary for the development of an effective equal employment opportunity program. It may well be the case, particularly in companies which have had implicit or explicit nondiscrimination policies for many years, that a key problem to be faced will be inertia within the present system of activities. But innovation does not necessarily mean upheaval. Working on the assumption that the adoption of an equal employment policy does require some form of innovative activity, the following points may be instructive before moving on to more specific

considerations of administrative control. Administrative innovation may utilize one or another of the following modes for introducing change into the organization: (1) by establishing a new unit within the corporate structure, which is charged with primary responsibilities for implementing the new policy; (2) by interpolating new functions into existing corporate structure, thus improvising but not basically altering; and (3) by continuing with existing arrangements, under the assumption that no new inputs are necessary to bring about a desired state of affairs.

What are the arguments pro and con for each of the above three points? First of all, at a practical level it can be pointed out that the first pattern (establishing a new unit) is seldom found in companies that have developed equal employment opportunity policies. Only two instances of this were discovered in the present study, and in both cases the companies were of major size and had highly formalized and complex administrative structures. Each company previously used this procedure to introduce new programs that represented a major policy commitment. It is important to note, however, that in neither case were the administrative responsibilities for the equal employment policy completely isolated within the new unit. Rather, the delegated responsibilities were in the direction of coordination, performance review, and information feedback to other operating units.

Others have argued that the creation of new units, besides being costly and time-consuming, overestimates the innovative character of an equal employment opportunity program. The rationale underlying this argument is that, while in the initial stages there may be "crash efforts" to get the program moving, the ultimate goal should be to incorporate equal employment objectives into general employment procedures. Thus the creation of a new unit may give the impression that an equal employment program is distinct from the company's general practices. In addition, the argument is made that most phases of affirmative action must ultimately be carried out by operating units at all organizational levels, and disengaging control from these units may make it operationally inconclusive.

More commonly found are administrative

procedures of the second type (the interpolation of new functions into existing units), although concrete examples extend across a wide range of possibilities. Some conditioning factors are company size, geographical concentration or dispersion of installations, and degree of formalization and complexity of administrative structure. Typically, responsibilities for program coordination and storage of information relevant to minority group employment are lodged within a particular unit, but operating assignments are widely spread throughout the organization. The unit may also act as a central point for dealing with problems that arise occasionally but not continually (e.g., grievance and discipline problems that cannot be easily handled at their points of origin).

Arguments favoring this type of administrative organization point to its flexibility. Resources are definitely committed to an affirmative action program, but additional resources can be mobilized to meet needs and problems that often arise but are difficult to predict in advance. As relative emphases on program components shift over time (e.g., initial recruitment to training and upgrading), expertise relevant to specific issues can be brought to bear.

The third alternative neither alters structure nor extends functions. The implicit assumptions are that existing arrangements are adequate, and a simple statement of policy can stimulate movement toward implementation. But results may be disappointing; and most employers have found this strategy to be unsatisfactory in providing tangible evidence of affirmative action.

As noted previously, whichever general model is followed will depend partly on the company's capabilities as well as managerial style and level of commitment to affirmative action objectives. There are, however, several individual components of administration that must be considered under any circumstance, and these are treated below.

CREATING AN ADMINISTRATIVE STRUCTURE FOR AFFIRMATIVE ACTION

The cumulative experiences of employers who have formulated equal employment opportunity policies indicate that giving attention to the administration of affirmative action programs pays dividends in that it (1) clearly demonstrates management's commitment, (2) removes ambiguity about responsibilities under the policy, and (3) goes far in assuring a coordinated company effort.

In this section we shall discuss four important features of the administrative structure underlying affirmative action. We wish to emphasize again that no single pattern can be adopted without modifications which take into account unique company situations. To date, most of the pressures for affirmative action have been directed toward business firms of comparatively large size and, thus, much of our current knowledge about equal employment opportunity policies is dependent on reported experience of fairly large employers. Yet, demands for affirmative action are becoming more widespread and are affecting many companies with smaller, informal and less complex employment operations.

At the general level, the preferred method of instituting affirmation action, as discussed in the preceding section, will partially dictate administrative needs. The extent of *employer commitment* and *employer capability* for engaging in affirmative action are contingencies which condition the actual operating program.

Assignment of administrative responsibility. Earlier it was stated that affirmative action doesn't "just happen." It is the result of policy commitment, purposeful administrative practice and the assignment of administrative responsibility to carry through policy implementation.

The assignment of responsibilities for policy implementation should be made with the assurance that the implications of the policy are known and understood at all operating levels. How this is best accomplished depends upon several factors: (1) As noted earlier, a few large companies decided to create a new administrative unit to coordinate and oversee affirmative action practices. Others have chosen to extend the functions of already existing units to include administrative responsibilities to carry through the equal employment opportunity policy. Our evidence indicates that, for the most part, in companies using the second pattern, the responsibility is typically located within the personnel, industrial relations, or employee relations department, with the reporting system extending upwards to at least the vice-presidential level. It is true that some employers prefer not to program any assignments of personnel, but to allow the policy to act as its own stimulus. Our observations disclose that the ratio of success is lowest when this last alternative is chosen. In any event, the policy decision regarding equal employment opportunity should incorporate some guidelines concerning its administration. (2) Company size is also a variable which cannot be ignored. Generally speaking, larger companies have more complex administrative structures, and, while this may afford opportunities for more definitive programming of responsibilities, it also may mandate a more formal statement of objectives. This may be particularly true in the case of corporations which have central offices and local installations geographically dispersed. How the policy, as formulated at corporate headquarters, becomes translated into action at the local, or operating level depends upon the degree of equivalence in policy interpretation between company officials at both ends. Assigning definite responsibilities for coordinating and clarifying policy objectives can provide insurance against misinterpretation and delays in action.

Smaller companies with simpler and more informal administrative structures have some advantages in that administrative offices are usually more consolidated, and lines of communication are shorter. But there are possible pitfalls. The simpler and more informal pattern may lead to an unwarranted assumption that objectives and responsibilities are more clearly understood than they actually are. This is a danger to be guarded against.

(3) Although certain practices relating to affirmative action (e.g., coordination, performance review) may be centralized within a particular company unit, it is necessary for all managers and supervisors to share responsibilities for policy implementation. In most companies, a division of operating responsibilities will be clearly indicated. For example, line departments may be much closer to points of hiring and upgrading, while personnel or industrial relations officials may have greater expertise in recruitment. In one sense this is another way of saying that success necessitates the incorporation of affirmative action practices into the general employment structure, even in those instances where a unit is newly created to oversee the equal employment opportunity policy. *Assignment of responsibilities* and *coordination of efforts* are the keynotes.

Allocating resources for affirmative action. To be effective, an equal employment policy demands an allocation of company resources for its implementation. Many employers can testify that the simple statement of an equal employment policy is a sterile gesture which may lead to little, if any, results. Any or all of the following activities may be necessary: (1) The establishment of contacts with new sources of recruitment; (2) a review of current minority group employees, with a view to upgrading where possible; (3) the careful cultivation of community sentiments; (4) the review and possible modification of selection and testing procedures; (5) a re-examination of company-sponsored social activities; and (6) the desegregation of company facilities. None of these are accomplished without the investment of time, staff and resources.

Establishing a system for control and audit. What are the specific aspects of the administrative arrangements that need to be established for policy implementation. Many a well-intentioned employer has been disappointed by the meager results of affirmative action in his company. Besides the patterning of administrative responsibilities and the provision of resources, there must also be processes of control and auditing as inventories of progress. Of course, this is more easily said than done. A review of the three case examples discussed . . . [previously] clearly illustrates that existing corporate structure will place limits upon the control and auditing pattern followed.

In some cases, control can be very direct, although informal. This is best demonstrated by companies in which administrative control is not highly formalized and policy decisions by executive fiat are the rule rather than the exception. In companies with highly formalized, bureaucratic structures, control may be less direct but nonetheless effective. In companies which have highly decentralized patterns of administration, with great autonomy lodged in operating management, effective control, whether direct or indirect, is difficult to achieve. In this case, except for internal modification of employment structure or the presence of pressures applied directly to operating units, a control and audit system will be virtually impossible to develop.

In the present study, we found many concrete illustrations of policy control, extending from highly formalized paper systems to the very informal (e.g., personal visits or telephone calls to local managers or department heads); from the very coercive to the gently persuasive. But whether formal or informal, direct or indirect, in all companies which demonstrated some degree of effectiveness in affirmative action, identifiable patterns of control and auditing procedures were in evidence. In these companies, no assumptions were made that affirmative action practices would be self-starting.

Evaluating the effectiveness of affirmative action practices. Effectiveness in affirmative action can be measured by employment statistics which are useful indicators of progress or lack of progress. Every company included in the present study utilized some statistical reporting system of employment data. Most of the companies were reporting these data either as government contractors, as members of Plans for Progress, or on request from a local or state agency. It can be taken as axiomatic that a program of affirmative action must include a periodic inventory of employees by race. In large corporations, the reporting system may be quite formal with field reports submitted on a scheduled basis. In smaller firms, procedures may be less formal, even to the extent of reliance on personal observation by key officials. In any event, some systematic collection of employment data must be instituted as a check on progress. These data should contain, where possible, employment statistics by occupational level and data on promotion and upgrading. While there is little question of the need for employment statistics as baseline data, the more important question concerns the use to which these data are put. If, as is true in some cases, operating units send reports up the line to a staff office which acts only to store and or transmit the data to an outside agency, use of reports as self-corrective tools is virtually nil. Experience

has shown that reports can be used to good effect within the company, provided that the company's commitment to equal employment opportunity is firm and an administrative pattern for policy implementation has been established. Some of the functions fulfilled by audit systems are: (1) to provide for feedback of information to reporting units and to provide such units with a survey analysis of progress or lack of progress; (2) to provide a basis for further discussion about the policy with a view to finding out what has produced results and what has not; and (3) to provide suggestions for additional work at weak points (e.g., a step-up in recruitment efforts).

Admittedly, record-keeping is a chore, and one which many would prefer to avoid. Nonetheless, apart from some periodic inventory of employment, there is virtually no way to gauge the current situation or measure progress. In the preceding discussion, continuity of effort was emphasized as a key feature of affirmative action. The accumulation and feedback of information about minority group employment is a basic requisite for this process.

AFFIRMATIVE ACTION AND THE EMPLOYMENT STRUCTURE

The preceding discussion has emphasized the need for effective administrative control and direction of affirmative action practices. In this section several components of the employment structure are examined for their relationship to equal employment opportunities. Major emphasis is placed on recruitment procedures. The discussion proceeds on the assumption that affirmative action may require the addition of new employment practices, the extension or modification of others, or even the elimination of some.

RECRUITMENT

Recruitment is widely regarded as the most important component of affirmative action. An active recruitment effort generally involves two major approaches: (1) A re-examination of current recruiting practices to see if they are inadvertently discriminatory against minority group job applicants; (2) the establishment of contacts with new sources of manpower supply, particularly within the minority group community. Each of these is discussed below, from the standpoint of some specific strategies and techniques which employers have found effective.

(1) Current patterns of recruitment may be directly or indirectly discriminatory. This can occur, for example, when a company has come to depend heavily upon referrals from present employees. If the current work force is largely or completely composed of white employees, continued reliance on the personal referrals can perpetuate the exclusion of minority group members. Even in cases where minority group members are already employed by the company, if they are concentrated in unskilled jobs, personal referrals will generally produce few qualified minority group applicants for higher skilled jobs.

(2) Typically, companies come to rely on a few outside agencies for referral of applicants. In many cases these are private and public employment agencies which, in the past, may not have been productive sources for minority group referrals. This does not imply that they cannot be, and each should be clearly advised of the company's equal employment policy and affirmative action objectives.

(3) Contacts must also be established with special sources of recruitment which can assist in supplying referrals of minority group job applicants. In the early stages of an affirmative action program, it is advisable to place considerable emphasis on the cultivation of such contacts. How extensive these efforts should, or can, be is affected by a number of company conditions: (1) The manpower needs of the company, particularly with reference to the skill levels for which recruits are sought, will partially determine the character of the recruiting program. Larger companies are increasingly placing greater emphasis on finding Negroes with professional and technical skills. This is commendable, but the search for individuals qualified for lesser skilled entry level jobs should not be neglected. Nor should the possibility of upgrading present Negro employees be overlooked. (2) Special recruitment efforts will also be affected by the network of professional leaders and civic agencies available within the local minority group community. (3) The resources that can be allocated to special recruiting activities will vary

from company to company. Larger companies have some overall advantage in that corporate staff and local staff can coordinate their efforts, thus making the "talent search" national, regional, and or local.

Special recruiting procedures for affirmative action can incorporate a wide range of types, extending from the very indirect and impersonal to the very direct and personal. Some examples of indirect and impersonal procedures include: (1) The addition of an "Equal Opportunity Employer" slogan to advertisements in newspapers and other public media; (2) sponsorship of employment advertisements in journals or other publications catering to Negro or other minority group subscribers; and (3) the dissemination of information about the company's policy via company publications or trade journals. Many employers who have operated affirmative action programs feel that these techniques are useful and necessary, but effective only when used to complement more direct and personal contacts.

More direct or personal contacts are those which link the company to individuals and associations that are in touch with potential job applicants. There are many examples of these. (1) Some companies encourage their executives to serve on commissions, special committees, and boards of agencies that deal with minority group problems. Such civic activities have value, although they are no substitute for direct recruiting. (2) Some companies engage in the sponsorship or co-sponsorship of community programs and activities that are directly linked to the recruitment of minority group workers. These programs may be short- or long-range in perspective. Examples of the latter include: participation in high school "career day" programs; conducting students, teachers, and counselors on tours of company facilities; participation in work experience programs after school hours; and participation in job orientation and placement programs conducted by such agencies as the Urban League. (3) Requests for referrals from minority group organizations, such as Negro civic agencies and churches, or from minority group community leaders. Experienced employers recommend that the company's manpower needs and its selection standards be fully clarified to the individuals and organizations approached. Neglecting this may cause embarrassment and possibly antagonism. It should also be recognized that such persons and organizations are usually besieged with requests for referrals from employers. Singular reliance on this type of contact may prove disappointing. (4) Requests for referrals from vocational and educational guidance agencies may prove valuable, particularly with respect to agencies which have significant numbers of minority group clients. (5) Recruitment at high schools, training schools and colleges which have significant numbers of minority group members in the student body is a fairly standard strategy. Most experienced employers recommend working directly with placement officers in order to acquaint them with the firm's employment needs.

OTHER COMPONENTS OF EMPLOYMENT STRUCTURE AND AFFIRMATIVE ACTION

For employers who in the past have employed few or no minority group workers, recruitment is the *sine qua non* of affirmative action. Certainly, our most complete information about equal employment opportunity practices concerns recruitment strategies and techniques for increasing minority group employment. It is probable that most employers enjoy greater latitude for innovation and experimentation in matters of recruitment than in any other aspect of the employment process. But establishing an equal employment policy must not end with recruitment. To be effective, affirmative action must pervade the company's entire employment structure.

In this section other components of the company's employment procedures which affect and are affected by affirmative action practices will be treated. The discussion will be brief, and confined to major issues and questions that must be faced. Several points which could have been included here have been thoroughly discussed in earlier chapters, and those paths will not be retrod.

In the current study, employers generally concurred that affirmative action which deviates from established employment standards is self-defeating. The generally accepted principle seems to be that all phases of employment should be administered equitably, with individuals judged only by criteria that are job-related.

In sum, this is the meaning assigned to the term, equal employment *opportunity*. But the actual working out of the principle depends on the work, "equitably"—how it is defined and put into practice. What are some of the issues involved in assuring that all phases of employment are administered equitably?

There is considerable variation among companies as to the specific procedures used in accepting or rejecting job applicants. Many companies use combinations of personal interviews, aptitude and personality tests, records of past employment experiences, and personal references. Others rely mainly on the personal interview, typically informal in nature, with the evaluation of qualifications depending heavily on subjective impressions.

Whether formal or informal, complex or simple, selection procedures incorporate a series of reference points that are used in making decisions to accept or reject job applicants. Frequently, the specific techniques are products of tradition or convenience, and few attempts have been made to validate results as predictors of performance on the job. This is particularly true when tests are used which have been standardized on national samples. The important criterion for any technique is whether it is a valid predictor of job performance in the local situation.

The basic purpose of selection standards is objectivity in evaluation of qualifications and elimination of considerations that are unrelated to job performance. A new look at selection and testing procedures is an important component of affirmative action. This should include: (1) Frequent re-examination of testing procedures; (2) an appraisal of employment prerequisites to see if the standards are realistic and necessary; and, (3) a check on those who make hiring decisions to make certain that all applicants are equitably considered.

Few of the respondents in the present study considered job placement to be a major issue in minority group employment. Some did admit, however, to the exercise of caution when the "first" Negro was placed on the job, assuming that a successful pilot experience contributed to later favorable results. More frequently, the contention was made that management's firmness and determination to see that the equal employment policy was actively pursued proved to be the most important ingredient of success. Available evidence suggests that anticipations of employee resistance to the policy tend to be exaggerated, and weaknesses in the affirmative action program occur when management equivocates in its policy commitment or is administratively incapable of demanding compliance at operating levels.

Promotion and upgrading are important features of affirmative action practices. However, it is true that a company's capability in providing opportunities to minority group employees for promotion or upgrading may be limited by several conditions. Turnover rates may be low within a company, and, thus, few job openings will occur. In addition, procedures for promotion and upgrading may be partially determined by company-union contract agreements, particularly in cases where lines of progression and seniority rights in job bidding are rigidly determined. Some companies, however, are not so restricted and can be more flexible with respect to promotion and upgrading opportunities. No single pattern for affirmative action can be recommended, but the following techniques are some which have been used to provide greater opportunities for minority group employees: (1) Some companies have instituted reviews of the personnel files of current minority group employees to see if some may qualify as candidates for higher level jobs. This has proved to be particularly effective in cases where, because of local tradition, individuals may have been reticent to come forward on their own. (2) A reexamination of the seniority system and lines of job progression may disclose that minority group employees are "frozen" in certain departments and excluded from equitable consideration for promotion and upgrading. (3) In companies where promotion procedures are not formally prescribed, policies and practices should be periodically reviewed and audited to insure impartiality.

Opportunities for training are important features of affirmative action, in that training is often a requisite for job mobility. Much training in American industry is of an informal, on-the-job type, although two other types are frequently found—tuition-relief programs for employees who attend classes at some outside training installation, and apprenticeship training programs which are usually associated with preparation for entry into the skilled crafts. Affirmative action with respect to training opportunities should be twofold: (1) The equal employment policy should be administratively controlled so that qualified minority group employees are included in training programs. (2) Minority group employees should be actively encouraged to increase their skills and job potential through participation in available training and educational programs. The latter may necessitate counseling efforts expressly undertaken for this purpose.

Needless to say, the existence of segregated company facilities or company sponsorship of segregated social activities for employees gives the lie to any policy pronouncements. The experiences of many employers who have faced one or the other, or both of these problems, suggest that they are practices which are best eliminated with as little fanfare as possible.

In this section no attempt has been made to cover the gamut of possibilities and problems of affirmative action. Many suggestions can be gleaned from discussions in previous chapters. These points are clear, however: (1) Affirmative action touches upon all phases of employment within a company. Although recruiting processes are key features of affirmative action, the equal employment opportunity policy should be defined as covering all components of the employment structure. (2) Specific techniques of affirmative action will be effective only insofar as they are backed up and coordinated through a clear assignment of administrative responsibilities and program-auditing procedures. Inertia is, typically, the greatest obstacle to affirmative action.

POLICY IMPLICATIONS OF THE STUDY

Equal employment opportunities for Negroes is a subject that is beset both by complexity and by emotions. Any statement on the subject is bound to be challenged by any, or all, of the following interested parties: corporate decision-makers; union leaders, civil rights leaders; government policy-makers; or rank-and-file Negro and white workers. Nevertheless, it would be fitting to conclude with some thoughts on the development of equal employment opportunities for Negro workers.

It must be reasserted at the beginning of this discussion that this study *was not* an attempt to exhaustively survey the problems of equal employment opportunities for Negro workers in the country. The following remarks shall necessarily be circumscribed by the observations and insights gathered from a *very select* group of companies, their unions, and their white and Negro workers. The purpose was to uncover some of the basics that perpetuated or reduced discrimination against Negroes in twenty companies—not to discover the "cause" of all employment inequality that Negroes experience. Such remarks must necessarily involve suggestions and recommendations for social policy in this field, as well as suggestions for further research.

POLICY RECOMMENDATIONS

One of the key problems in implementing an equal employment opportunity program is to find a suitable basis for an intensive effort by management. This study suggests that this effort, if it does come, will be *within the framework of existing company employment practices*. In a free enterprise system, the expectation is that *voluntary action* will suffice to equalize opportunities but the experience in the 1960's has shown that such action must be complemented with *persuasive forces* from the outside to result in *extensive change*. Contract compliance machinery, for example, has now been in evidence for some time and has made a valuable contribution in developing effective equal employment opportunity practices in many companies.

In a broad sense, the equalizing of employment opportunities for Negroes requires the concerted and cooperative actions of a number of institutions in our society: business, labor, government and education. It is within this framework that the following specific policy recommendations are made.

IMPLICATIONS OF THE STUDY

The observations on the twenty companies in the preceding pages suggest a number of practices that might facilitate the recruitment, hiring and upgrading of Negroes in American indus-

try. Six of these practices deserve to be emphasized:

(1) *The principls of "outreach."* It is clear that the recruitment of Negro workers, particularly those with skill, require some degree of "outreach." Negro workers do not respond automatically when the hiring sign is out. Most companies in this study found it necessary to go to the Negro neighborhood, to the Negro school, or to the Negro church to recruit. However crude these attempts were, recruitment was facilitated by such activities.

The spatial and social ghettoization of the Negro makes it difficult for the company to gain direct access to the Negro worker through normal channels of recruitment. Successful recruitment requires the building of links between industry and the Negro community — its citizens and institutions. In early recruitment, the company must establish some roots in the Negro community. In some cases, there may be a company field office; more frequently there is systematic support for Negro agencies and organizations (e.g. the Urban League). The principle of "outreach" suggests, then, not only company recruiting in the Negro community but the sustained support of Negro organizations and structures that attempt to ameliorate Negro work problems.

But not only must "outreach" be practiced by the company, the principle must be adopted by all agencies, public and private, that are involved in the manpower process. The state employment service; the vocational school; job clinics—these do, little good if they are not physically and psychologically based in the Negro community. The detached worker from the social work agency who makes himself at home with the gang on the street should have a parallel in the manpower agencies if their prevocational services are to have any effect.

(2) *The need for job development.* The observations of the minority group practices in these companies suggest that special efforts must be made to fit Negro workers into the work force of a company. Special efforts may be minimal for skilled workers but in the case of nonskilled workers, the company and community agencies must engage in special job development. This may involve either (a) providing the worker with special job preparation—before employment or during employment—or (b) changing

the work requirements to make the Negro eligible for employment. In both cases more than simple job placement is required. There may be the need to provide the worker with special social skills for the job, or a more satisfactory transportation arrangement, or special tools and medical treatment. Extensive follow-up services (psychological, medical or vocational) may be required for an extensive period after he enters the job situation. In any case, there is a continuous need to sift and examine the demands of the job and the worker's needs in adopting to them. It is a serious mistake to feel that the job is complete when the Negro is recruited and hired. Usually, much remains to be done during the period of employment.

(3) *The need for job creation*. The equalizing of opportunities may demand a *total* review of the employment structure and the creation of new jobs. Employers in this study frequently found that when Negro workers could not qualify for job openings, some amelioration was possible by creating new jobs in which the worker could perform productively and enlarge his skills to qualify for a "regular" job. This strategy usually helped both employer and worker; the former by filling a portion of his manpower needs and the latter by providing work experience in a setting where job promotion or enlargement was possible.

(4) *The need to review testing and interviewing procedures*. Frequently, discrimination is *unintentional*, resulting from the perpetuation of traditional or outdated interviewing or testing procedures that eliminate many job applicants from consideration. It was a frequent experience that a re-examination of these practices and particularly their role in placement and promotion opportunities resulted in modification of job entry requirements.

(5) *The need to establish special procedures in upgrading or promotions*. Only a small number of the companies had established special aids in upgrading or promotions; and these were companies in high growth industries (electronics, heavy manufacturing). Two essential elements were present in these cases: (a) systematic review of worker job histories and (b) special counselling programs to advise workers of new job openings or chances for advancement.

(6) *The need for job rotation to increase*

opportunities for informal learning on the job. It was obvious from this study that Negroes are seriously disadvantaged in informal work learning opportunities. The Negro may be locked into a job because he has had no access to informal learning situations that pave the way for job mobility. The employer must develop mechanisms either through collective bargaining or changes in employment policy to insure rotation of jobs and equal access to informal learning.

SPECIFIC POLICY RECOMMENDATIONS

(1) *There must be a continued monitoring of progress in company equal employment practices by outside agencies which have statutory powers to inspect personnel records and employment practices and to effect change*. Experience with such monitoring systems suggests that they perform at least three important functions. First, they are a stimulus for personnel changes to avoid contract cancellation or legal action. Second, the monitoring records become source material for the company to examine and analyze its own practices, frequently initiating change in the name of increased efficiency of manpower policy. Finally, the records may act to locate and substantiate inadequacies in minority group manpower and stimulate remedial action (e.g. retraining).

(2) *There should be a national research or demonstration program designed to support experiments with personnel practices in minority group employment*. Such a program might be funded cooperatively by government, industry, private foundations and labor. Only a small number of companies at this time have access to the meagre information on company practices that work in employing the Negro in American industry. Such a program would be the source of new insight into the problem which could be transferred into application techniques. A program of this kind could also codify and disseminate the extensive knowledge on integration gleaned from the experiences of the armed services and federal agencies where there is a long and successful prototype of integration experience to follow.

(3) *There should be a program of subsidies developed cooperatively between the federal government and business to support changes in*

company employment structures. The development of a comprehensive equal employment opportunity program encompassing a wide range of employment practices is apt to be costly in terms of the resources—financial and personnel—that must be assigned to it. Faced with this "calculus of organization," resistance will frequently develop to sweeping changes, especially in the local plant, if such changes are detrimental to the cost structure. Although many managerial people have moral convictions in line with equality in employment, their commitment, both ideological and self-interest, to operate a viable, profitable establishment acts as a barrier. Experimentation with testing, new ways of recruiting, and development of adequate control systems—all of these are necessary to a sound equal employment opportunity program but are costly in time, talent and money. Faced with this problem, there is a tendency to develop a program that is within the cost structure of the firm, and the result is frequently inadequate.

One answer to this problem is a subsidy program for hiring and training of Negro workers. The Manpower Development and Training Act has On-the-Job Training provisions for training and it might be sufficient to enlarge these provisions; but beyond this there is a need to create a "Marshall Plan" to growing industries to provide an incentive for the recruitment and hiring of employees who may not be as productive or as well prepared as other employees. There are precedents for this; the cost-plus contracts of World War II and the Post World War II G.I. Bill. Such subsidies might overcome management resistance to the employment of less qualified job applicants.

Such a subsidy program should be conceived in its broadest sense. Special counseling programs to guide and encourage job mobility for Negroes would be supported by such a subsidy, as well as cooperative activities between the school and the firm. For example, the firm might be subsidized to hold special demonstration programs for minority group applicants to inform them of the job structure and work opportunities within the company. The firm should be encouraged to design an equal employment opportunity plan that is adequate, to assess its cost and then to seek support for its application. It is only in this framework of

subsidy that sufficient experimentation and innovation can occur to open new employment vistas for Negroes.

(4) *There should be a greater utilization of government training and maintenance facilities to train underskilled Negro youth.* One of the main problems in equalizing opportunities is the skill barrier. Negro youth are relatively less prepared than whites for rewarding mechanical work. Training opportunities outside the craft union apprenticeship system are poor and cannot narrow the gap. However, the federal government supervises extensive work training centers (army depots, shipyards) where such youth could be trained either on-the-job or after working hours. Such craft training would result in jobs in the public employment sector, if not in union-controlled employment.

(5) *There should be an extension of the compliance review concept to craft unions and other institutional structures involved in controlling the flow of manpower into the labor market.* There is a need to audit pre-occupational opportunities as well as employment opportunities. In many cases these organizations are the recipients of government aid programs which provide leverage, as well as the threat of publicity from unfavorable legal action.

(6) *There should be an extension of on-the-job training opportunities, as developed in the Manpower Development and Training Act.* Serious consideration must be given to increasing these opportunities in interested companies with particular emphasis on the use of Negro manpower. Serious study should be given to the conditions which have acted as barriers to the development of this kind of training. It is a subject on which management currently has much misinformation and reluctance. It might be worthwhile to consider changes in current On-the-Job Training philosophy and provisions to make them more appealing to management.

(7) *More data should be required in compliance review forms on employment practices (e.g. use of tests) and such data should be made available to local agencies as a basis for developing affirmative action in local companies.* One of the basic problems in interagency operations has been the necessity of local agencies to "find their own information to press affirmative actions." Since the data are collected regularly on the federal level, this involves needless duplication. Specific

policies and administrative procedures must be initiated to increase the liaison between federal and local agencies dealing with the same companies. Such an exchange of information would undoubtedly increase surveillance of small companies which are not adequately covered by federal agencies at the present time and so remain "invisible" in their minority group practices.

(8) *There should be some relaxation of the prohibition against reporting race data in the preoccupational period; the inability to obtain such data and the legal norms enforcing it prevent any effort to check the progress of minority group members in the job world.* Inability to obtain such data from integrated schools, for example, lessen the possibilities of determining the effectiveness of this kind of education for equalizing job opportunities.

(9) *More attention should be given in national manpower policy to the development of multiagency programs, combining employment training with community and emotional rehabilitation in equalizing opportunities.* One should recognize that lack of skill is only one consideration denying equal employment opportunities to the Negro. Frequently, his inability to meet health standards or gain access to adequate transportation may be equally serious drawbacks. More attention should be given to this type of preparation for the job world.

(10) *Serious research and consideration should be given to the prospects of subprofessional employment in industry for Negro youth, utilizing some of the concepts and theories from experiences in the public sector.* We are implying that certain jobs can be created from a redivision of labor in which Negroes with limited skills could be employed. Thus, the draftsman may do his job more efficiently with an attendant draftsman. The logic is that such employment would be part of a learning and employment situation in which job mobility would become possible.

(11) *More attention should be given to the use of the small business firm as a possible vehicle for the employment and or training of minority group members.* Little attention has been given to the role of small business firms in minority group employment. The aggregate employment potential of these firms is quite sizable. Three points should be noted. First, few of these firms are linked to regional or national minority group employment programs, excluded by the economics of their operation. Consequently, there is an inadequate information flow to them on company practices in equal employment opportunities. The information flow should be increased to involve them in equal employment efforts. It may well be that one solution is to expand the activities of regional EEOC offices from the single function of investigation to include information dissemination in small companies.

Second, few small business organizations *successfully* recruit and hire Negroes. Frequently, this is not the result of discrimination, but rather, that trained and skilled Negroes prefer the larger companies. It is possible that Negro applicants who are rejected for interview or test reasons in a large company might fill the manpower needs of the small company since (a) standards are usually lower and (b) there is less rigidity in employment criteria.

Finally, some of the small firms would make excellent training situations outside of the union apprentice system. For example, the tool-and-die shop historically was the training ground for learners in the trades, but finally ended training activities when "graduates" repeatedly quit the small shop to work in the large companies. It might be possible to renew this system for minority group members if some provisions could be made for a fixed period of guaranteed service in the shop.

Needless to say, these suggestions are aimed at revision of the opportunity structure for the Negro. This must be the guiding principle in minority group employment.

SUCCESSFUL EXPERIENCE: TRAINING HARD-CORE UNEMPLOYED

James D. Hodgson and Marshall H. Brenner

Industry in the United States now is facing up to a task of awesome proportions, the task of realizing the National Alliance of Businessmen's goals of finding jobs for 100,000 hard-core unemployed by June 1969 and for 500,000 by June 1971.

It is not so much the magnitude of the numbers that is overwhelming, but the nature of the task itself. Before the uneducated poor can become productive employees, they must be trained; and the training poses problems never previously encountered by business, in spite of its experience in developing individuals into productive workers.

Few people question the advisability of undertaking this effort or the enlightenment and dedication of those companies supporting the NAB program. It is a job that necessity dictates and conscience supports. It is a matter of American faith that even the toughest problems will yield to technological know-how and management expertise, once business puts its mind to it.

And yet it must be acknowledged that here we are moving into unaccustomed terrain where experience and technological competence are of uncertain help. Technology has awkward limitations when applied to such intangibles as human motivation and attitudes. The emerging discipline of systems analysis has yet to develop enough to cope with the unstructured problems of society. Industrial management remains an art whose techniques, though successful in some

situations, cannot always be counted on to work in others.

The company contemplating the prospect of undertaking training of the hard-core unemployed for the first time can therefore be excused for harboring lingering doubts about the methods it should employ, the expectations of success, and the nature of problems it will encounter. While there is no definitive body of experience to dissipate these doubts entirely, the hesitant executive may be partly reassured and can be instructed by the initial experience of others which is now being accumulated.

LOCKHEED'S EXPERIENCE

Before the NAB had launched its program, the Lockheed Aircraft Corporation sensed that hard-core unemployment might become the nation's major social problem. Wishing to make some contribution in this area, but proceeding cautiously, it began two experimental training programs in early 1967, maintaining careful documentation for later evaluation. While the final results are not all in, these programs have achieved a degree of success that surprised even some of the enthusiasts. Equally important, they revealed, along the way and on later analysis, lessons that may well prove helpful to other companies as business approaches the massive training effort looming ahead. In this article we describe in detail these programs.

No one contends that the programs have been wholly successful, and changes are even now under way as the result of the first year's experience. (We shall discuss those changes later.) The programs have demonstrated, how-

Reprinted from *the Harvard Business Review*, V. 46, N. 5 (September-October, 1968), pp. 148-156, by permission of the authors and the publisher. © 1968 by the President and Fellows of Harvard College; all rights reserved.

ever, that given careful preparation and a willingness to devote more time and attention than ordinarily demanded by training activities, the hard-core unemployed can be trained and integrated into an industrial work force.

Before launching into our report, we should say a word here about the term "hard-core unemployed." How hard is hard? The typical representative of this stratum of society in Lockheed's programs is a Negro with no useful skills, a record of many arrests, and a history of long periods without work, Considering the experience of U.S. industry at this point, that is pretty hard. But the typical trainee also is an adult who is somewhat motivated to work; he is not one of those totally unmotivated youths who have been among the main offenders in the burning and looting during the ghetto riots. These youths make up the "hardest core," and so far business has found them virtually unreachable as potential employees. As experience accumulates through programs like Lockheed's, perhaps techniques can be developed to solve this most critical part of the problem.

TWO DIFFERENT EFFORTS

Our company's programs took place in two locations, at the Lockheed-Georgia Company's main plant in Marietta, Georgia, and at the Lockheed Missiles & Space Company's main plant in Sunnyvale, California. With more than 20,000 employees each, these divisions are two of the three largest in the Lockheed Aircraft Corporation.

At the time the parent company launched this undertaking, these divisions were hiring. Each division formulated its program independently, according to the population available for hire and the kind of work for which it was hiring. Lockheed-Georgia, or GELAC, as it is commonly called in the company, aimed its efforts principally at the younger unemployed in Atlanta who would be willing to make the daily trip of about 15 miles to Marietta and who, the division felt, would be the best bets for longterm productivity. The Lockheed Missiles & Space Company (LMSC), on the other hand, directed part of its recruiting effort at Mexican-Americans who were field laborers on farms to the south, around San Jose. They were generally older, and most were heads of households with

Exhibit 1. *Trainee Characteristics in Lockheed Programs*

Characteristic	GELAC	LMSC
Median age	20	26
Percent from racial or national minority	73%	69%
Percent from families on welfare	60%	76%
Percent with police records	63%	40%
Percent with previous industrial work history	15%	21%
Median time in months since last regular employment (defined as job lasting more than 90 days)	6	7
Percent married	31%	57%
Percent heads of households	31%	82%
Median number of dependents	0	2
Median years' education	10	10

dependents. See Exhibit 1 for a comparison of the two approaches.

At GELAC, the sheet-metalwork training program was 12 weeks long, compared with 4 weeks at LMSC for three kinds of jobs. The reason for the difference is that sheet-metal training involves learning many skills and provides a basis for advancing to other work (e.g., many of the trainees later learned welding), while the training at LMSC was for specific jobs. In Exhibit II there is an outline of other characteristics of the programs that are different; we shall touch on them in due course.

GELAC PROGRAM

During 1967, 98 trainees entered the GELAC program. All were male, most were single, three fourths were Negroes, two thirds were 21 years of age or younger, and more than two thirds were school dropouts. The median time since the last employment was six months, and only about 10% had ever had experience in an industrial organization. Such experience as they had had was generally in low-paying service jobs like bus boy and short-order cook. About two thirds came from families on welfare, and about the same proportion had records of arrest. More than half had no more than a tenth-grade education. None would have met traditional company hiring standards.

Some preliminary screening was conducted. Applicants were sent from the Georgia State

Exhibit 2. *Lockheed Program Characteristics and Results*

	GELAC	LMSC
Length of training	12 weeks	4 weeks
Type of training	Classroom and vestibule	Classroom and vestibule
Training content	General sheet-metalwork skills	Specific training for general helper-factory; keypunch operator; electrical assembler
Stipend during training	$20–$35 per week, plus $5 per dependent, plus transportation (not on company payroll)	About $100 per week for those on company payroll; variable welfare payments for the remainder
• Interpersonal skills training	About 72 hours of psychodrama	None
Managerial training	None	None
Counseling	On an "exception" basis—that is, when absenteeism or need for discipline occurred	Personal and financial assistance provided as requested by trainees
Number entering training	98	111
Terminations from training		
Voluntary	18	1
Involuntary	10	2
Total	28	3
Number entering jobs	48*	108
Terminations from job		
Voluntary	0	5
Involuntary	4	5
Total	4	10

*The remainder of those trained were placed at other companies because of a personnel reduction at Lockheed.

Employment Service to the Atlanta Employment Evaluation and Service Center, where they were given a battery of standardized psychological tests for later research purposes. At this stage about 25% were rejected because of their failure to achieve a fifth-grade reading level. Training openings were available for about 50% of the remaining applicants, and selections were made on the basis of indications of interest and motivation as evaluated in interviews.

The training program was conducted in a regular training facility separate from the main plant. The building was equipped in much the same manner as the work stations the students would later find in the factory, and they were exposed as far as practicable to standard work routines—they were, for example, required to punch a time clock. The object of the sheet-metal instruction was to develop skills in such basic operations as drilling and riveting. No remedial education was offered, but the instruction was supplemented by an average of 70 hours of classroom work in blueprint reading and shop mathematics, according to individual needs, given largely in the first six weeks of training. The instructors in this supplemental job preparation were Lockheed training department personnel.

During the training period the students were not on the Lockheed payroll, but received government funds under a Manpower Development and Training Act contract. Single men received $20 a week, while heads of households received $35 a week plus $5 a week for each dependent. In addition, transportation costs were paid.

Of the 98 men who started the schooling, 70 completed it. For those who did not, the most common reason was loss of interest as evidenced by unacceptably poor attendance records. The company hired the first 43 to complete the program.

Unhappily, a decline in the work force late in 1967 took a heavy toll of the new employees. By the end of the year, most of them had been "bumped" out of work by layoffs dictated by the seniority procedure under the union contract. But by that time their qualifications were such that the company had little difficulty finding full-time jobs for about two thirds of them in the Atlanta area, in a similar line of work. The general level of skill and pay were slightly below those they had at GELAC, because the company's skill level and wages are higher than the Atlanta market's (wages are 25% to 35% higher). But in all cases the jobs obtained were much better than those the employees had ever had before their training. About one third of them did not immediately accept job offers, preferring not to work for "only" about $80 a week, but to wait for GELAC to recall them. GELAC has since offered reemployment to those who had recall rights.

The employees' average stay with Lockheed before being laid off was fourth months. There were no voluntary terminations, and only four dismissals—absenteeism, again, accounting for three of them. While this experience with only 43 employees over four months is admittedly limited, the termination rate of these workers was substantially below the usual rate for new hires. By way of comparison, at the Lockheed-California Company (the other of the three largest corporate divisions), a study found voluntary turnover to be 30% to 40% in the first six months, with dismissals accounting for an additional 5% to 7%; and about 80% of the terminations occurred in the first three months of employment.

LMSC PROGRAM

At about the same time as the GELAC program began, LMSC launched its experiment. This was really two programs in one, the Vocational Improvement Program, company organized and funded except for a small amount from Manpower Development and Training Act contracts, and the Welfare Reemployment Program, which is company-funded training for Santa Clara County welfare recipients.

The 80 VIP students were on the company payroll from the start of their schooling, they held the titles for the occupations for which they were being trained, and they immediately received the beginning rates of pay for those classifications. On the other hand, the 31 WRP students (most of them women) were selected by Santa Clara County welfare agencies; and in effect LMSC was just doing the training for the Welfare Department. They were not put on the payroll until the end of their training; during that time they continued to receive their welfare payments.

The trainees at LMSC differed somewhat in composition from those at GELAC, as we have indicated (see Exhibit 1). There are both men and women, they were somewhat older, and they were composed almost equally of Negroes, Mexican-Americans, and Caucasians. Of these, 60% had no more than a tenth-grade education. Two thirds of the women were either separated or divorced, and 83% were on welfare. Two thirds of the men had arrest records. The year before entering the program, 50% of the men and 72% of the women made $2,000 or less. Significantly, more than 80% of the total were heads of households, in contrast to only 31% in the Georgia program.

The applicants were obtained from 33 agencies in the San Francisco—Sunnyvale area, particularly the Urban League, the Mexican-American Opportunities Center, the Opportunities Industrialization Center West, and various skills centers. The low unemployment rate in the Sunnyvale area and the availability of other jobs made recruitment difficult. Even so, LMSC accepted only 13% of those applying.

Of the several hundred persons rejected for training, 70% were turned down because they were not "hard" enough or because their arrest records were too serious. While no formal reading requirement was imposed, the applicants had to meet four of these five criteria of "hardness": (1) school dropout, (2) unemployed head of household, (3) income less than $3,000 in the last 12 months, (4) poor work history, and (5) no primary working skills.

As for records of arrests, no exact set of criteria was established; each applicant's materials were evaluated in an investigation. But the protection of employees and property, as well as government security, had to be considered. So an applicant was unacceptable if his record contained evidence of crimes of violence (such as assault and battery), arson, drug usage or peddling of drugs, morals offenses (like child molestation and homosexuality), or numerous recent charges of theft. No one currently on parole was accepted. In respect to other offenses, their number and recency were considerations.

Initially, LMSC planned to have all VIP students take a prevocational training course at the Opportunities Industrialization Center West or at the East Bay Skills Center. The course is designed to improve communication and computational skills and attitudes toward work and to develop good grooming, health, and hygiene habits. Some, however, did not go through this program. Of those who started it, some did not complete it. The company supports such prevocational instruction, particularly when it is conducted by minority-group organizations like the Opportunities Industrialization Center. But lack of it appeared to have no adverse effect on either training performance or productivity.

Each member of the VIP and WRP groups underwent a four-week period of instruction in one of three job classifications: general helper-factory, electrical assembler, or keypunch operator. The training was conducted in LMSC's off-site training center. The rates of pay for the VIP group were: general helper, $2.64 an hour; electrical assembler, $2.68; and keypunch operator, $2.53. In addition, all received 24 cents an hour in cost-of-living pay. The different pay levels caused no noticeable resentment among the trainees, since the groups were isolated from each other during working hours. Moreover, there were very few keypunch operators.

Of the 111 persons who entered training, all but 3 completed it and became regular employees. By the end of 1967, only 10 had left the company. Of these, 5 resigned voluntarily, 4 were dismissed for poor attendance, and 1 was arrested and convicted of a felony. No one was terminated for inability to perform assigned work. The termination rate of 9% in 4 months was about the same as that of GELAC's smaller group of trainees.

A study comparing the LMSC group with 50 employees who met traditional hiring standards and entered the same occupations during the same period indicated no difference in ratings of quality and quantity of work. A larger proportion of trainees had more absences, but this difference was not statistically significant.

Judging from interviews with supervisors, the former trainees showed ability to perform on the job and little inability to adjust to supervision and fellow workers. The supervisors' most frequent complaint concerned poor attendance. Some supervisors were lavish in their praise. "Best-trained and most productive men I have ever received," commented one. Another said, "These men really want to work, they work hard, and the quality of their work is very good."

WHY THE PROGRAMS SUCCEEDED

Statistics, observation, and opinion all testify to the success of these programs. Two groups that were unable to meet traditional hiring standards were able to meet established performance standards and actually achieved a better-than-normal turnover record. Naturally, the question arises, "What made them succeed?"

It is impossible to give a wholly definitive answer to this question. Perhaps one of the least apparent reasons is one of the most important—the dedication and total commitment of those who were associated with the programs and who cared enough about them to do more than was required. Nevertheless, some reasons for success are evident to both instructors and observers:

• The training developed proficiency for specific jobs, jobs for which the trainees knew they were being prepared. The preparation had direct relevance to the performance required in the jobs, and the trainees were shown the relationship. The instructors made a constant effort to have them appreciate the relationship of training to the job requirements and understand the reasons for learning what they were being taught. Most instructors felt that this was extremely important for motivational purposes.

• The students were prepared for skill levels slightly above those required by the jobs for which they were being trained. T.E. "Jeff" Lyons, training manager at LMSC, puts it like this: "We knew the line would give us hell if we gave them unqualified people, so we gave them more than they needed." The deliberate over-training was the result of an early decision that aimed at more than merely passive acceptance of the program by supervisors. It was designed also to give trainees a feeling of confidence once they were on the job. The company reasoned that providing them with more-than-adequate skills would help them compete with other employees.

With one exception, so far as is known, this overtraining did not lead to dissatisfaction on the part of trainees because their tasks did not come up to their expectations. The exception was a man who did the lowest-level work as a general helper for two months. At that point he was promoted.

● The job instruction was by demonstration. Most poor and uneducated people have few associative hooks on which to hang new information. They do not learn well by association; they must be taught by showing, by doing, and by repetition. This is a standard approach for any kind of job instruction, but in the case of the hard-core trainee it must be done over and over. According to James McWilliams, instructor at LMSC, "We must teach by demonstration and by repetition. Show them—again and again." McWilliams and the other instructors agree wholeheartedly that nothing succeeds like patience.

● Recognition was frequent. The training was set up in small units of work. A prime reason for this is that a large number of units allows frequent opportunity for reassurance and recognition for accomplishing a task. In the words of James Greengrass, a GELAC instructor, "When they come to us, these fellows need confidence in themselves. They've been frequent losers in the past, and we have to help them get self-respect and make them want to come here—come here because there is something here of value to them. We make sure they develop the feeling of learning and its value, and one way is by rewarding them regularly."

● The trainees were given special personal help. Stanley Hawkins, an LMSC training supervisor, estimates that he spent up to 50% of his time on personal problems, ranging from bailing trainees out of jail in the middle of the night to working with creditors to get garnishments reduced. Trouble with transportation also

was a common problem; reliable autos do not figure among the assets of the poor. Such personal assistance was necessary so that trainees could concentrate on the instruction—not to mention show up for it.

The instructors were careful in their counseling to try to build strength, not suffocate it; to help the students deal with society, not deal with it for them. Aware that a sense of control over one's fate is closely related to minority group achievement, the instructors concentrated on helping the trainees help themselves. If a car broke down, for example, the instructor might help the owner get the money to fix it, but arranging for its repair was up to him.

● There were jobs in sight. It is important to have a job ready for successful trainees. It is just as important to get them to believe it, which is not easy. "They were suspicious of us initially," McWilliams says. "Many of them had experience with other programs before and felt that we were probably just another program getting in on the rush and that there wasn't anything at the end. When they realized that we meant what we said about having a job at the end of the road, they really got involved and motivated."

● The jobs were not dead-end jobs. At LMSC the trainees were placed only in positions that had opportunities for advancement beyond the entry level, and the former students have progressed in about the same ratio as "regular" employees. In a few cases they have received promotions faster or greater than usual. At GELAC, the trainees were originally placed according to their skills, as evaluated during their training. Some of them admittedly went into positions with limited advancement potential ("heavy janitors," for instance). Some, on the other hand, were put in jobs with greater-than-average promotional possibilities.

WHAT LOCKHEED LEARNED

For all the learning accomplished in the programs, perhaps it was the company and the company's supervisors and training personnel who learned the most. They gained understanding of people with whom they ordinarily have no contact; and they learned something about motivating them, training them, and helping them to succeed. Much of what they learned was common-sense things they "knew," but it took experience in the undertaking to make them realize their meaning and significance.

They learned that trainees require an enormous amount of attention to financial, family, and vocational problems, which are often so absorbing that they interfere with learning. They discovered that counseling was a much bigger part of the task than they had originally thought.

They learned that one way to ensure built-in motivation is to hire heads of households. This is considered to be one reason for the extremely low rate of dropouts during the training period at LMSC and voluntary terminations later. As Jeff Lyons puts it, "Drawing pay right away is important for the guy with kids to support."

They learned that what authorities on training and psychologists have been saying about the importance of individual differences is indeed true. In spite of this truth, school systems and industrial training programs alike have traditionally fed the same material at the same rate to many students. With the hard core this is impossible. A corollary is that they need much individual attention to make even satisfactory progress. According to Lockheed-Georgia Company instructor Rogers Gibson, "They're very reluctant to ask for help. You've got to keep an eye out and get to them before they do things wrong and get bad habits built up." Gibson believes that a very low student-teacher ratio, perhaps six to one, and a great deal of teamwork among instructors are essential.

They learned once again that tests are not always good predictors of success. At GELAC, where test batteries were administered for research purposes, efforts are now under way to determine the relationship between test results and demographic data and measures of successful performance. The tests investigated to date include the Army General Classification Test, the SRA Pictorial Reasoning Test, the Wide-Range Achievement Test (reading), and the general intelligence section of the General Aptitude Test Battery. Each of these tests was related to 5 measures of on-the-job success and 10 measures of success in the training program.

The measures of on-the-job success (ratings based on these were furnished by the instructor) were:

1. Attendance.
2. Quantity of work produced.
3. Quality of work.
4. Social adjustment to peers.
5. Adjustment to supervision.

The measures of training success (ratings were obtained weekly from the instructors) were:

1. Supervision required.
2. Demonstrated skill.
3. Initiative displayed.
4. Accuracy.
5. Lower time-loss between operations.
6. Knowledge of job.
7. Follow-through on assignments.
8. Performance under pressure.
9. Productivity (quality and speed).
10. Knowledge retained.

The only test that significantly related to any measure of success was the AGCT score, and it was *inversely* related to some of the measures of success in training.

They learned that some techniques can produce unexpectedly good results. Most of the trainees acted in a very withdrawn manner—they looked away when spoken to, they talked to the floor, and they failed to ask for help when they needed it. In an effort to give them more self-confidence, GELAC used the services of a specialist in psychodrama who conducted three two-hour sessions each week. He involved the trainees in role playing that required them to act out various situations in which they confronted each other, tried to persuade each other, and had to make immediate decisions.

The program appears to have accomplished its objectives; the former trainees themselves say (and the instructors agree) that the psychodrama experience gave them much more confidence in dealing with their instructors. Indeed, it may have succeeded too well. Many of them have become too "unsuppressed"; because they are unaware of what is appropriate on what occasions, they frequently act much like adolescents. Now the training instructors feel that the trainees must learn to control their self-confidence, or many supervisors may find them difficult to manage.

They learned that some special supervisory education is desirable where the trainees have been identified to supervisors as hard core before going on the job. This was the case at LMSC, where many managers and supervisors have difficulty communicating effectively with Negroes and Mexican-Americans because they are unable to understand their attitudes and cultures. At GELAC, on the other hand, the trainees were not singled out, and the supervisors did not know the difference between them and regular "new hires."

They learned to their surprise that it is very easy for instructors to lose their objectivity by getting too close to trainees. This is a lesson perhaps all professional people have to learn. The temptation to make too many allowances for disadvantaged students, because of sympathy for them, is sometimes overwhelming. As Robert Hudson, training manager for GELAC, explains it, "It's too easy for instructors to get too close to trainees and become too understanding. Instructors can get too involved with the difference between the trainees' initial level of skill and their level in training, instead of with the difference between where they are in training and where they have to be in order to be sucessful. If they don't meet the standard when they leave us, it's all been for nothing."

They learned (most importantly) that it has not all been for nothing. The programs in the two companies have convinced their managements that the disadvantaged and hard core can be trained to perform industrial jobs, and they can be moved into the factory as effective, well-adjusted members of the working team.

EXPANSION AND CHANGE

Lockheed is so convinced of the value of these programs that it is not only continuing them, but expanding them.

The corporation recently opened a subsidiary plant in San Antonio with the primary objective of providing training and employment for hard-core unemployed and underemployed persons. Most of the 100-odd employees will be Spanish-surnamed Americans. The subsidiary was established in connection with President Johnson's Test Program for Job Development—the so-called "test cities" program.

The current program at Lockheed-Georgia involves 200 persons. LMSC expects to turn out 200 graduates in a year-long contract with the U.S. Department of Labor that ends in April 1969. In addition, LMSC recently entered into a two-year agreement with the Bay Area Management Council, by which the Lockheed division will train hard-core unemployed for 41 companies in a consortium arrangement. And these companies, which include a bank, a seed company, several electronics companies, and the Southern Pacific Railroad, have pledged to provide 481 jobs. The Labor Department is funding this project too.

As Lockheed has gained more experience in these undertakings, improvements and refinements in the divisional programs have been introduced.

GELAC has altered the training structure on finding that the students could learn faster than was first assumed and could attain somewhat higher standards than originally established. Another reason for making changes stems from the nature of the work that some of them have eventually found themselves doing; as at LMSC, it has been necessary to find employment for some trainees elsewhere during slack times at GELAC, and many of the companies that have hired them put them into metalworking jobs other than sheet metal. So now the GELAC trainees get basic sheet-metal instruction earlier than before, and at the same time learn fundamental shop practices and disciplines. Then, during the second six-week period, if there is demand for them at GELAC, they receive further sheet-metal instruction and preparation in the Marietta plant's assembly techniques. Otherwise, during that period they get specialized instruction in other metalworking with a view toward employment elsewhere.

GELAC, deciding that a fifth-grade reading level was not necessary, has reduced its requirement to a second-grade level. The first indications (subjective, from instructors) are that the performance of persons hired under the new requirement does not differ in the first six weeks of training, but is slightly poorer in the second six weeks.

At LMSC, on-the-job training time has been extended from 330 hours over 10 weeks to 380 hours over 20 weeks, to improve funding arrangements and to permit training department personnel to observe and help the trainees for a longer time.

Also, in response to the demonstrated need, LMSC is developing a course in human relations for managers and supervisors. Its first students will be supervisors in the consortium companies who are scheduled to have minority-group employees assigned to their jurisdictions. Rather than appearing to dictate standards of behavior to the supervisors, the approach is to sound them out and try to get them to identify the problems which they expect to have. From this vantage point, it is hoped, some solutions can be arrived at.

At both GELAC and LMSC, professional counseling services have been expanded. The companies decided that the instructors and training supervisors should not be expected to handle so many of the trainees' frustrating financial and legal problems. LMSC has arranged for counseling help from the local Urban League and the Mexican-American Opportunities Center.

CONCLUDING NOTE

In spite of government aid, these ventures cost money, more money than the usual company-sponsored training program. At GELAC, Lockheed's cost per trainee was about $135, and at LMSC, about $770. The difference is due to the fact that federal funding would not pay wages at LMSC and that the local union was unwilling to give the required approval to the MDTA contract. Lockheed expects that in 1968 it will pay about 25% of the cost, or about $430 per trainee, including overhead. Out-of-pocket cost is estimated at $150 to $200 each.

But the cost represents an investment that should bring returns to society many times over. Considering only reduction of welfare expenditures, the programs have brought returns. If the trainees receiving welfare payments at the time of their employment at LMSC had instead comtinued on the public payroll through the year on the same basis as before, their welfare payments would have totaled $108,297.

But that, of course, is the least significant return from programs training the hard-core unemployed. If we measure the benefit in lives rebuilt, in the restoration of men and women to productivity, in reduced social tensions, and in strengthened human resources for the nation, the returns are incalculable.

A MODEST PROPOSAL FOR THE ABATEMENT OF CORPORATE RACISM

James S. Spain

Let there be no mistake about it: racism is a disease. As a severe mental aberration, it is as fully destructive of the mind's capacity to function properly as paranoia, schizophrenia or any other psychosis. Formally defined, racism is "the assumption that psycho-cultural traits and capacities are determined by biological race and that races differ decisively from one another, which assumption is usually coupled with the belief in the inherent superiority of a particular race and its right of domination over others." Lest anyone forget, it was this pernicious belief which produced the so-called Europeanization of the world during the age of exploration and colonialism, with its complete disregard for non-European cultural values, the wholesale slaughter of various aboriginal peoples and the introduction of black slavery into the Western Hemisphere. In more modern times, the professed belief in the superiority of one race over another led to the systematic destruction of European Jewry on one side of the Atlantic while on the other, it permitted the internment of Japanese-Americans in concentration camps during World War II.

Today, much closer to home, the evil of racism is nowhere more evident in one of its more virulent forms than in the relegation of black Americans to an inferior position in society by the dominant white majority simply because of their race; and in no area of American life is contemporary racism more glaringly obvious than in the management of business corporations where blacks, denied the opportu-

nity to attain positions of real authority and responsibility, function merely as eunuchs. I shall not tolerate as a valid objection to the preceding statement the fact that here and there, in this company or that, a few blacks do hold positions of some little responsibility; for the mere fact of the existence of this handful who have escaped complete castration simply serves to throw into sharper relief the sad condition of the overwhelming majority of blacks employed in pseudo-managerial positions who have felt the full mutilating effect of the racist's knife. Nor will I accept the facile arguments of whites who will undoubtedly protest that most whites in corporations have had to content themselves with positions of little or no authority or responsibility, for what we are concerned with here is the virtually total absence of blacks in the ranks of middle and upper-middle management, and the complete exclusion of blacks at the very top of the management structure. And most important of all, our concern is with the fact that whereas the individual white manager finds his growth checked at one level or another because of factors which have nothing to do with the color of his skin, blacks on the other hand have been prevented from realizing their potential precisely because of their color and nothing else.

It is my contention that until white Americans, individually and collectively, admit the existence of their illness, no progress will be made in curing it. White Americans must view their malady as they would a mangled leg, a damaged heart or a tubercular lung, and resolve to have the condition corrected before our national life can be made whole. In brief, until white Americans look their illness of racism squarely in the face as one would any other

Reprinted from *The MBA* Vol. IV, No. 7 (April-May 1970), pp. 17-20, 63-65, by permission of the publisher.

aberrant condition and make up their minds to deal with it for what it is, a crippling, life-sapping disorder, no substantial progress will be made in making available to black men and women the opportunity to participate meaningfully in all sectors of our national life. This is no less true of progress in the business world than it is of progress in any other sphere of activity. There are those naive souls, both black and white, who would sever one part of the problem from its other components and assert that the proper way to proceed is by dealing separately with securing of voters' rights, or with ending discrimination in housing or in education, or with the complex matters of welfare reform, feeding the hungry and providing for the delivery of desperately needed health services to the rural poor in the black belt of the South. In other words, say the advocates of this approach, progress should be sought on a piecemeal basis, with one part of the problem being attacked at a time, In reply, I declare that this approach is one of sheer nonsense, which not only fails to take into account the experience of the past but which also ignores the fact that securing social, political and economic justice for black Americans is an indivisible cause which no one has the right to delay by arbitrarily dividing it into segments and then establishing on a long-range basis a table of priorities which is never met anyway. As with certain forms of cancer, the attempt to eliminate racial injustice in one area of activity without simultaneously seeking to eliminate it in others merely has the effect of causing it to manifest itself in the untreated parts with a fresh virulence which foredooms to failure even the partial effort that is being made. Hence the lack of wide-scale, enduring success in the wake of voter registration drives, the promulgation of an open housing policy, crusades against illiteracy, poverty and hunger, and, the most spectacular failure of all among the plethora of programs launched in recent years, that of the National Alliance of Businessmen, which was solemnly undertaken to put an end to unemployment among the urban poor by giving everyone a job, any kind of a job so long as black adults and youth were kept too busy to foment riots and other civil disorders.

It seems to me that what is needed is for white Americans to at long last abandon the too facile and utterly unproductive approach of moving at random with the appointment of prestigious commissions of inquiry and the awaiting of voluminous reports whose recommendations and findings nearly everyone promptly ignores as soon as they have been published. It is time to cease forming urban coalitions, suburban task forces and all the other sick excreta of voluntarism which have served merely to confuse issues and to delay progress. It is high time that government at all levels put an end to the restructuring of agencies, the revision of anti-poverty programs and the shuffling and reshuffling of personnel to implement them or to delay their implementation, depending upon which political party is in power at the moment. If yet one more too-clever acronym is devised to describe still another inertia-oriented, ill-conceived and mismanaged program of social betterment I shall vomit.

What then, if there are to be no more commissions, reports, special programs, nor any other of the carnival tricks by means of which white Americans have deluded black Americans during the past decade, throwing sand in their eyes and reducing the matter of the improvement of their sad plight to an illusion of the now-you-see-it and now-you-don't variety? What is to be done to change once and for all a situation whereunder, according to information recently made public by the Bureau of Labor Statistics and the Census Bureau, a black with a high school diploma on the average is still unable to earn as much income as a white with an eighth-grade education; and while the national unemployment rate dropped steadily during the past decade, the black rate of unemployment remained steadily double the white rate; or while there was a slight relative gain in the income of a black family in comparison with whites in recent years, the actual dollar gain lags considerably behind that of whites? What is needed to change the prevailing state of affairs which has become so characterized by cynicism, hypocrisy, procrastination and a general decline of public, to say nothing of private morality? Vast numbers of Americans believe that the American system has reached such an advanced state of debilitation that it is beyond anyone's ability to reform its public and private institutions, that these institutions must be destroyed, the rubble cleared away and the ground prepared for the creation of new ones capable of responding in humane terms to contemporary needs.

I should like to suggest that there is yet time for what has always been the most vital and the most imaginatively alert and productive sector of our national life to come to the rescue of the people and to save the situation. I refer to the private business sector, that marvelously well-organized structure of men, money and machines which in the case of every emergency situation in our past history has played a very important if not a crucial role in resolving the crises which threatened either to paralyze or to destroy the life of the nation or some part thereof. We have always dealt more or less successfully with wars, depressions, floods, storms, forest fires, epidemics and other disasters mainly because the private business sector, either on its own initiative or in response to the prodding of legislative bodies or courts, became convinced of the seriousness of the situation and either refrained from doing certain things or began to do others which made available the necessary human and material resources necessary to stabilize a threat to the security of the nation's life. Even in those situations which have involved mainly our national prestige, the space and arms races for example, American industry has risen to the challenge and provided our national government with the means to produce and to stockpile at least as many deadly armaments as anybody else and to dazzle world opinion with daring space flights and landings on the moon. At this very moment, when pundits and sages are solemnly pronouncing that human beings are about to be buried beneath heaps of their garbage and filth of various kinds, the private business sector is rallying behind the cry of "Save the environment!" and gearing itself up to do deadly battle against untreated waste. But what good will it do to clean up the rivers, refresh the land, purify the air and cleanse the very sea itself, if Americans, particularly the young, remain convinced that it has only been done in order to permit the strong to continue to oppress the weak and to provide a cleaned-up base of operations from which to launch new warlike adventures like the pitiable debacle in Viet Nam, in other words, business as usual? Similarly, we presently see the beginnings of a massive national campaign to suppress the use of drugs, but I submit that this campaign will not only fail to limit the illicit use of drugs but will actually stimulate it, unless young people become convinced that they are being asked to preserve the wholeness of their minds, their bodies and their energy for something other than the perpetuation of a system of guilt-ridden evil which, in a thousand and one ways, they have been telling their elders during the past decade they want no part of. I submit further that yet another of our great national crusades, that which is being mounted to suppress crime and to restore law and order, will tend only to increase the so-called criminal propensities of the urban poor, unless something is done to persuade them that decent and honest attitude to life is something other than the system of social and economic oppression of which they have been the principal victims. It is folly to ask a man to be concerned about the quality of the air he breathes, the purity of the water he drinks or of the neatness of the earth he treads when the life he lives is but a species of death. It is worse than foolish to ask young people to cease using drugs, when each day of their lives presents their sensibilities fresh affronts in the form of adult indifference and apathy to human suffering, a request that they go docilely to die in an Asian swamp, or the knowledge that every five minutes an American child dies from the effects of malnutrition.

What can the private business sector do as its contribution towards restoring confidence in our system? With the utmost seriousness, I suggest that each businessman begin by examining his own conscience. If he is intelligent, he must needs be appalled by what he will find there in terms of the compromises of ordinary human decency he has made in the name of the preservation of "the traditional American way of life." He can only be ashamed by the numberless acts of discrimination he has committed against black people, either individually or collectively, as a representative of his class. He can only be filled with self-loathing and disgust by the recollection of all the acts of omission or of commission by means of which he has contributed to the creation of a situation wherein blacks feel that there is no place for them in business in any but the most insignificant kinds of jobs. He can only be ashamed by the number of times he has conspired and tacitly acquiesced in the conspiracy to prevent blacks from being accorded opportunities to grow and to develop as corporate line and staff managers on terms of complete equality with their white counterparts. I refuse to play the numbers game, because as a black man I am sick of it, and I regard it as being both degrading and dehumanizing. I shall not sink to the level of being primarily concerned with the paltry number of black men and women employed by American business corporations while neglecting to recall that even these few are employed in jobs which do not permit their talents and abilities to take full flight in terms of encountering and dealing with mind-expanding challenges. When one has repeated to one's self that blacks account for no more than one and one half percent of the personnel counted as officials and managers by major American corporations, and this after nearly ten years of Plans for Progress voluntary compliance with fair employment practices laws, what has one really accomplished except to remind one's self of the obdurate resistance of the system to meaningful change?

In my most honest moments, when I have thrown off all the fashionable blinders which businessmen wear these days to obscure the truth, when I have rid my thoughts of all the clever terms like qualified versus qualifiable which are bandied about to explain the absence of blacks in important positions in corporate life, I tell myself that we blacks are the victims of a cruel system of exclusion which permits whites with impunity to carry with them into their offices those private feelings which form the very core of their hatred of blacks and to make them the basis of their decisions concerning how far blacks will be permitted to advance up the corporate ladder. We are the victims of that weird amalgam of irrationalities and the reactions they produce which comprise the very heart of white American racism: the nameless and indescribable fear, the dread apprehensions and the terrible anxiety and unease which the mere sight of a black man excites in a white man. I submit, therefore, that as long as those American men who have the responsibility for managing the affairs of major business corporations permit their attitude towards black managers and professional employees to be determined by the sick fear that to accord to them true equality of opportunity means to run the risk that they may earn a place in executive

suites at top levels with appropriate compensation in terms of salaries and other benefits, and that this in turn means assuming the risk that this opens the way for them to somehow insinuate themselves into the world of private clubs and then living rooms, and ultimately—ghastly thought—into the sacred confines of white bedrooms and the arms of white women, the culmination of the whole sick fantasy of fatally projected evil, no real progress is likely to occur. We shall never get beyond the point where we are now of deluding ourselves with the whole silly charade of reporting statistics of alleged progress, of submitting cheerfully to compliance reviews and of evading substantial compliance with the law. Gradualism or tokenism, call it what you will. It all adds up to that state of affirs which leaves whites solidly in control of things and asking blacks to be patient and to wait another twenty or thirty years until they have proven their ability to participate meaningfully in the managerial process.

Since fantasy seems to be the order of the day, let us indulge in yet another and pretend that one fine morning we awakened to find not that a complete cure of institutionalized white racism had been effected but merely that a sufficient relenting of traditional views had occurred among business leaders to permit them to give serious thought to implementing a truly effective affirmative action program for the utilization of college-trained blacks in the management structure of the corporations they have been delegated to control.

What provisions should a really effective corporate program of affirmative action contain? Based upon my experience as Director of Urban Affairs for a major corporation, with responsibility for the creation and implementation of an equal employment opportunity program which emphasizes the preparation of college-trained black men and women for true upward mobility, I have concluded that in order to produce the desired result of increasing the number of blacks functioning at higher levels in the managerial structure, the affirmative action program must provide for the following:

1. The institution of a vigorous recruiting program on the campuses of both white and predominantly black colleges and universitities in order to insure a steady influx of business-oriented young blacks into the work force. The

greatest emphasis should be placed upon recruiting those young men and women who have earned MBA degrees or master's degrees in economics. In many cases, because the supply of black MBA holders is considerably less than the demand, recruiters often will have to settle for bright, highly-motivated bachelor's degree holders who have indicated an intention to complete graduate studies after becoming employed. The recruiters themselves should, in terms of either chronological age or their attitude toward blacks, be either young enough or sufficiently enlightened and progressive in their thinking to understand and to sympathize with the problems which the black college graduate has usually encountered in completing his education. Recruiters should be sent out in pairs, black and white. It is my opinion that retired black military men are among the least effective recruiters of black college graduates because of the rigidity of their views and their lack of receptivity to contemporary life styles. Similarly, men whose professional experience has been mainly in non-profit, civil rights and community-action type organizations are more likely than not to be very ineffective recruiters, simply because they lack in a very fundamental sense an understanding of the dynamics of a career in business and of what is required to function successfully in a profit-oriented environment. As a matter of policy and commitment, corporations should instruct their recruiters that they must be prepared to accept the *qualifiable* as well as the qualified black candidate.

2. The acceptance of the principle of hiring-in at all levels in the case of blacks as an integral part of the affirmative action program. This is necessary in order to accelerate the entry of blacks into those areas of a company's operations which are likely to be so-called "white islands" with no black representation.

3. The creation of an inventory of the supervisory and managerial potential of black employees as a device by which the progress of black professional and managerial employees can be audited on a regular and continual basis. This inventory should include the name of each black managerial and professional employee, his date of birth, his service date, his level of education, his initial work assignment in the company, his subsequent work assignments up-dated, special

training received on the job, and his last performance rating. It is this inventory which should form the basis for appraising the effectiveness of the efforts of white supervisors and managers in training and up-grading black managerial aspirants. It should be constantly emphasized that not merely the number of college blacks being trained and promoted is to be taken into consideration but also the quality of the training they are receiving and the nature of the responsibilities with which they are being entrusted at successive levels. Without delay, blacks at appropriate levels should be enrolled in all in-house training programs specifically designed to identify and to "annoint" those persons whose careers are going to be directed towards the very top echelons.

4. The establishment of a policy of accelerated promotion for blacks embodying the high-risk, high-reward concept in order to permit, on a proportionate basis, the closing of the gap between black and white representation in the ranks of management at a much faster rate than would otherwise be possible.

5. The institution of a special management development seminar as the general vehicle by means of which the steady growth and development of black managerial aspirants will be assured on a systematic basis. Every black managerial and professional college-trained employee in the company should be enrolled in this seminar, which ought to meet on a quarterly basis. Its purposes should be as follows:

a. To establish and maintain an effective and meaningful dialogue between company management and black managerial aspirants and professional personnel.

b. To provide a vehicle through which the junior men can learn and benefit from some of the experiences of successful black managerial and professional personnel.

c. To improve their managerial skills level so that the development and promotability of these employees can be enhanced and accelerated.

d. To encourage the junior men to help themselves by pursuing avenues of training and education which will help them maximize their potential.

e. To explore and to suggest solutions to the problems, both real and and imaginary, arising out of the confrontation of the traditional (white) business environment and its values by the black sub-culture and its values.

6. A special training program for middle and upper management (as a corollary to paragraph e. above) to explore and to suggest solutions to the problems, both real and imaginary, arising out of the confrontation of the traditional (white) business environment with the black sub-culture and its values.

7. The requirement that a report of employment by race and job category be submitted to the corporate office quarterly by all reporting units and subdivisions of the company so that numerical progress can be audited at regular intervals, to ensure that progress is being made in achieving stated goals in accordance with established target dates.

8. Financial and advisory support of special consortium-type university-level programs for accelerated graduate education in business for blacks, to ensure a consistent growth of the available pool of black managerial talent.

9. The utilization of carefully selected black executive search and management consulting firms as an additional source of candidates for specific jobs. Great care should be taken to employ the services of only those specialized firms which make a conscientious effort to supply properly qualified or qualifiable candidates with the requisite degree of experience and which make a bona fide attempt to achieve a suitable match between the candidate and the job requirements. In other words, those firms which, as a matter of principle, treat their black clients as human beings and not as chattels to be bartered or sold.

10. The appointment of the best qualified black person available to create, implement and audit at the corporate level the progress of the affirmative action program outlined above. The description of this official's duties should provide for regular briefings of middle and top management on the effectiveness of the program.

All that I am really advocating is the application of the principle of management by goals and objectives to the utilization of college-trained blacks in the management structure. I am merely insisting that the recommended affirmative action program be action rather than inertia-oriented. The Federal Department of Labor guidelines for the establishment of corporate affirmative action programs state that such programs should be designed to produce results that are both measurable and attainable. I submit that the program outlined above meets these requirements.

Leaders of industry, that is to say board chairmen and presidents of companies, must exert themselves to take action in this area beyond the mere issuance of equal employment opportunity policies and ceremonially subscribing to concepts like Plans for Progress, which all too easily become screens behind which to conceal inactivity and inadequacies in performance. Truly progressive business leaders should publicly support the enactment of federal legislation which will put teeth into the compliance powers of the Equal Employment Opportunity Commission. We suffer from a surfeit of slogans, gimmicks and publicity campaigns. What is needed now is meaningful activity which will produce measurable results.

If the Federal Government had taken firm measures to enforce school desegregation, one grade at a time, beginning in September of 1954, a substantial part of the problem would have been eliminated within 13 years. The same is true in the area of according real quality of opportunity to blacks to advance up through the ranks of management. It is my contention that enormous progress can be made if white business leaders resolve to treat this problem as seriously as any other situation requiring firm and well-reasoned policy direction and the enforcement of solutions dictated from the top.

Only the application of this kind of leadership will bring about meaningful and enduring progress in a situation where there has been so little advance that it can truly be said, to quote an old proverb, "The more things change the more they remain the same." In speaking of the new sense of urgency which characterized the struggle of black men and women in this country to achieve full equality, Martin Luther King, Jr. remarked a few years ago that "there is nothing in the world more powerful than an idea whose time has come." I submit that the time for sweeping changes in the ethnic composition of the ranks of top-level management has not only arrived, but is long overdue. The leaders of each of the various spheres of activity which make up our national life have the responsibility by virtue of their position and the authority entrusted to them to do all that is humanly possible in their respective areas to assist black people in their efforts to raise themselves from their inferior position to one of decency and true equality. I suggest then that we get on with the job or else let us proceed with the business of implementing a final solution to the black question. I modestly propose that with the technology we have at our disposal, thermonuclear-fired furnaces for example, the job can be done with an efficiency and dispatch that will make the activity of the Nazis in disposing of the Jews look like childish games. I think, however, that a *caveat* ought to be sounded here, for I am of the opinion that all black people will not docilely march off to extermination centers singing "We Shall Overcome." I suggest that there are those who will resist in a way that will make the uprising of the Warsaw ghetto seem like dancing around a Maypole.

ADDITIONAL READINGS FOR CHAPTER 9

American Management Association, *How To Employ the "Unemployable" Successfully,* Nora Percival, ed. (New York: American Management Association, Inc., 1969).

Ivan Berg, *Education and Jobs: The Great Training Robbery* (New York: Praeger Publishers, 1970).

———, "Rich Man's Qualifications for Poor Man's Jobs," *Trans-action,* V. 6, N. 5 (March 1969), pp. 45-50.

Robert O. Blood, Jr., *Northern Breakthrough* (Belmont, Calif: Wadsworth Publishing Company, 1968).

Gilbert Burck, "A New Business for Business: Reclaiming Human Resources," *Fortune,* V. LXXVII, N. 1 (January 1968), pp. 158-161, 198-200, 202.

"Business, Labor, and Jobs in the Ghetto," *Issues in Industrial Society,* V. 1, N. 1 (1969).

Joel T. Campbell, *Selecting and Training Negroes for Managerial Positions* (Princeton, N.J.: Educational Testing Service, 1964).

Alfonso J. Cervantes, "To Prevent A Chain of Super-Watts," *Harvard Business Review,* V. 45, N. 5 (September-October, 1967).

Peter B. Doeringer (ed.), *Programs to Employ the Disadvantaged* (Englwood Cliffs, N.J.: Prentice Hall, 1969).

Georges F. Doriot, Special Report to Management: *The management of Racial Integration in Business* (New York: McGraw-Hill Book Company, 1964).

Louis A. Ferman, Joyce L. Kornbluh, and J.A. Miller,

Negroes and Jobs: A Book of Readings (Ann Arbor: University of Michigan Press, 1968).

Eli Ginzberg (ed.), *Business Leadership and the Negro Crisis* (New York: McGraw Hill Book Company, 1968).

———, *The Development of Human Resources* (New York: McGraw Hill Book Company, 1966).

Joseph R. Goeke and Caroline S. Weymar, "Barriers to Hiring the Blacks," *Harvard Business Review,* V. 47, N. 5 (September-October 1969), pp. 144-149, 152.

Sar A. Levitan, Garth L. Mangum and Robert Taggart III, *Economic Opportunity in the Ghetto: The Partnership of Government and Business,* Policy Studies in Employment and Welfare Number 3 (Baltimore, Md.: The Johns Hopkins Press, 1970).

Garth L. Mangum, *The Emergence of Manpower Policy* (New York: Holt, Rinehart and Winston, Inc., 1969).

Leonard Nadler, "Helping the Hard-Core Adjust to the World of Work," *Harvard Business Review,* V. 48, N. 2 (March-April, 1970), pp. 117-126.

Paul H. Norgren and Samuel E. Hill, *Toward Fair Employment* (New York: Columbia University Press, 1964).

Max Oliva, S.J. "Selection Techniques and the Black Hard-Core Male," *Personnel Journal,* V. 49, N. 5 (May 1970), pp. 424-430.

National Industrial Conference Board, *Education, Training, and Employment of the Disadvantaged,* Studies in Public Affairs, No. 4 (New York: National Industrial Conference Board, 1969).

———, *Company Experience with Negro Employment* Studies in Personnel Policy, No. 201, Vs. I and II (New York: National Industrial Conference Board, 1969).

Arthur M. Ross and Herbert Hill (eds.), *Employment, Race, and Poverty* (New York: Harcourt, Brace and World, 1967).

George S. Odiorne, *Green Power: The Corporation and the Urban Crisis,* (New York: Pitman Publishing Corporation, 1969.)

Aaron L. Rutledge and Gertrude Zemon Gass, *Nineteen Negro Men* (San Francisco: Jossey-Bass, Publishers, 1968).

S. Prakash Sethi, *Business Corporations and the Black Man: An Analysis of Social Conflict: The Kodak-FIGHT Controversy* (Scranton, Pa.: Chandler Publishing Company, 1970).

Michael I. Sovern, *Legal Restraints on Racial Discrimination in Employment* (New York: Twentieth Century Fund., 1966).

James L. Sundquist, "Jobs, Training, and Welfare for the Underclass," in Kermit Gordon (ed.), *Agenda For the Nation* (Washington, D.C.: The Brookings Institution, 1968), pp. 49-76.

David Wellman, "The *Wrong* Way to Find Jobs for Negroes," *Trans-action,* V. 5, N. 5 (April 1968), pp. 9-18.

10 *What Business Can Do*

In the Housing Act of 1949, Congress established as a national housing goal, "a realization as soon as possible of a decent home and a suitable living environment for every American family."[1] That this goal has not been achieved for either white or black Americans is evidenced by the passage nearly twenty years later of the Housing and Urban Development Act of 1968.[2] This legislation reaffirmed the national goal quoted above, and called for the construction and rehabilitation within the decade of the 1970s of 26 million housing units, 6 million of these for low or moderate income families (about 20 million persons).

Inadequate housing has become part of the "American way of life" for many citizens, both black and white. Given the record high costs of land, labor, capital (including credit); the increase in population of approximately 50 percent (from 200 to 300 million) which is anticipated by the year 2000; the continuing physical deterioration of the present housing stock; the urban migration of the rural poor; and the increasing reluctance (and apparent inability) of the federal government to spend anywhere near the sums needed for a massive national housing program—to mention but a few factors contributing to our housing difficulties—the problem of providing satisfactory housing for our nation's families (particularly the poor) will be with us for the forseeable future. There is no single solution to the problem; a variety of public and private approaches is necessary.[3]

While poor Americans of all races are obliged to bear poor housing, black Americans will continue to be greatly overrepresented among the inhabitants of substandard dwellings, compacted into the most rundown areas of our nation's urban ghettoes and rural shanty towns. This is partly a consequence of the single fact that a greater proportion of blacks than whites comprise the nation's poor (whatever definition of poverty is utilized). Accordingly, even if there were no other factors operating, on the basis of family income alone blacks would be destined to occupy more units of substandard housing than would whites, since those persons with the lowest amount of income available for housing consumption will, perforce, be obliged to seek the lowest cost (and poorest) housing which is available. Public housing and government rent and interest subsidy programs provide some assistance to low-income blacks; not nearly enough, however, to alter the configuration. The housing needs of blacks can be satisfied only by concerted governmental and private sector action designed to address the housing problems of all poor Americans.

As we saw in Chapter 5, in addition to the problem of poverty and the virtual unavailability of adequate low-cost housing, blacks confront the problem of discrimination emanating solely from their blackness. Thus, poverty (itself largely a consequence of economic discrimination) and residential segregation have worked hand-in-glove to perpetuate the unavailability of decent housing for many black Americans. Accordingly, the business community's concern in the area of housing must address itself to the twin evils of poverty and discrimination.

The problem of discrimination is easier for the business community to resolve than that arising from the economics of poverty. What is unsolved here is that landlords, real estate brokers, building developers, and the financial institutions providing mortgage credit continue to make race a salient variable in providing housing resources for those persons seeking it. Race must become irrelevant to the determination of whether, where, and what type of dwelling a person will inhabit. The policies behind so-called "fair housing laws" should become *de facto,* not merely *de jure,* guidelines for the real estate, home building, and mortgage industries. Once this is accomplished, part of the housing problem encountered by black Americans will have been resolved.

The general business community has a role to play in eliminating discriminatory practices in housing by taking positive action against such practices and those who pursue them. Why do real estate brokers, landlords, and housing developers practice discrimination? What would make them abandon such practice? An important part of the answer to these questions is that discrimination has been profitable, or at least not costly, to those who provide housing. When discrimination is no longer profitable it is more likely to disappear. Accordingly, business can make discrimination unprofitable to the discriminator. IBM provides one illustration of how this can be done. In the first selection for this chapter, "Race, Jobs, and Cities: What Business Can Do," Jeanne R. Lowe describes how IBM, the giant of the computer industry, dealt with realtors in Lexington, Kentucky, who were not showing homes to IBM's black employees. Other initiatives by Armour and Company and LTV Aerospace, also discussed in the essay, indicate additional positive steps business firms can take to assist their minority group employees in finding housing in communities where they work.

How can business contribute to the betterment of living conditions in urban ghettoes by providing decent housing for blacks (and other poor Americans)? Eli Goldston in "BURP and Make Money" states that business can indeed find ways to make a profitable and socially useful contribution to urban housing rehabilitation. He describes the role of his firm, Eastern Gas and Fuel Associates, in the Boston Urban Rehabilitation Program. His article includes a useful catalogue of programs for improving urban housing conditions.

As we suggested earlier, there are no existing panaceas to the problem of providing decent housing for the poor. The spectrum of federal programs which has come into existence over the past few years is both a tribute to the ingenuity of urban planners and housing experts and an admission of the inadequacy of any single approach. While virtually all of these programs are predicated on federal financing, tax relief, or subsidies, recent approaches such as National Housing Partnerships, Operation Breakthrough, Model Cities, and, indeed, urban renewal, rely on the efforts and participation of the business community.[4]

Even more extensive efforts by both the federal government and business will be necessary if the goals of the Housing Act of 1949 are to become any more of a reality in the next two decades than they have in the more than twenty years since the legislation was passed. There are several approaches that can be taken. One approach is through the investment of corporate capital in housing developments intended for low-income people, just as has been done for middle- and upper-income families. We are aware that federal tax and subsidy policy will play an important part in determining the "art of the possible" for business investment in low-income dwellings. A related activity is increased private sector involvement in the rehabilitation of slum housing, as is described in the article by Eli Goldston. A few large corporations have also provided interest-free loan funds as "seed money" to help finance housing for low income families, assisted in bonding and hired black construction contractors, participated in joint ventures in the area of housing with black-owned construction firms and community corporations, and engaged in "turnkey" operations, whereby ownership of housing units built by the company is transferred over to minority community organizations after a relatively short pay-out period.

Business firms, particularly financial institutions, can use their "good offices" to convince the owners of ghetto real estate to adhere to housing code requirements which are often poorly enforced by governmental officials and usually ignored by the landlord; to lobby for the elimination of those code provisions which are anachronistic in view of new building technologies and thereby increase construction costs; and to apply pressure on craft unions to eliminate a variety of restrictive practices which have effectively raised the cost of housing and kept blacks out of many building trades.

Finally, a few firms have assumed the responsibility of providing transportation for inner-city residents to job locations far removed from their neighborhoods. As is pointed out in the final reading in this chapter, "Transportation and Poverty" by economists John F. Kain and John R. Meyer, the unavailability of suburban housing for most blacks conjoined with poor or nonexistent transportation from black neighborhoods to plant locations has frequently foreclosed employment opportunities for black Americans. The authors make a number of suggestions regarding private sector action which could contribute toward the alleviation of the transportation difficulties experienced by urban blacks.

These approaches are merely indicative, not inclusive, of possible courses of action open to business in increasing the quantity and quality of housing (and transportation) available to blacks. Housing segregation, the totally inadequate stock of decent living accommodations available for poor Americans, and poor urban transportation combine to limit severely the social and economic potential of black Americans.

NOTES

[1] Housing Act of 1949, 42 U.S.C., 1401 et seq, (1949).

[2] Housing and Urban Development Act of 1968, 82 Stat. 476 (1968).

[3] For general discussions of some of the roots of the national housing problem see sources cited in the list of Additional Readings which appear at the end of this chapter.

[4] The National Housing Partnership Program is an outgrowth of the 1968 Report of the President's Committee on Urban Housing (chaired by industrialist Edgar F. Kaiser) and provides for the formation of a consortium of major industrial corporations and financial institutions to construct low- and moderate-income housing. Certain tax incentives are provided for the private sector participants. "Operation Break Through" is a program sponsored by the Department of Housing and Urban Development to explore and develop new technologies for industrialized low-cost housing construction. Twenty-two industrial firms (out of 236 competing groups) were selected by HUD to build 2000 units of prototype housing at ten different sites throughout the country.

For additional discussion and critique of these programs, see, e.g., Morton J. Schussheim, "Housing in Perspective," *The Public Interest,* N. 19 (Spring 1970), pp. 18-30; Urban America, Inc., *Development Forum-5* (Washington, D.C.; Urban American, Inc., October 27 to 28, 1968), pp. 1-23; and Paul Ma, "Housing: New Techniques," *Federal Reserve Bank of San Francisco, Monthly Review* (June 1970), pp. 130-131.

RACE, JOBS, AND CITIES: WHAT BUSINESS CAN DO

Jeanne R. Lowe

The new Republican Administration will be asking business to lend a bigger hand than ever in initiating and carrying out private-sector, community-level "solutions" to America's urban-racial crisis. During the past year, two sets of private-sector approaches have already gained currency. One, now fashionable with some corporation executives and Black Power leaders, focuses on strengthening the ghetto: building up its fragile economic power through private training and employment of residents, locating new plants there, assisting businesses that will be owned by new "black capitalists," and, most recently, forming local development corporations.

The other solution, advocated principally by some builders and real estate developers, calls for decentralizing the ghetto into freshly minted, privately built New Towns: systematically encouraging much of its population to move to new, carefully integrated communities—complete with industry, variously priced housing, and white families—to be built mostly beyond existing metropolitan areas.

Both tacks are worthwhile and should be pursued. Indeed, almost any effort is better than allowing what now exists to continue. Nonetheless, these currently popular courses will produce only limited results in the immediate future. New Towns won't take shape in significant numbers before the 1980s, and not even then unless the Goverment begins an unprecedented kind of land-use planning right now. In fact, both solutions lean heavily on government assistance, be it to people, property, or corpora-

tion. And the former, an agonizingly slow process, is of questionable long-range worth.

Another approach, an intermediate or metropolitan strategy, which has been curiously overlooked by most urban-crisis solvers, appears far more practical and should receive the private sector's most serious consideration. Its objective is to encourage a substantial movement of Negroes into the metropolitan community and the economic mainstream, in the belief that the basic economic, educational, and environmental disadvantages of the Negro can be altered significantly only beyond the ghetto, where economic opportunity lies and where industrial job formation is taking place—in metropolis.

The metropolitan approach is uniquely dependent upon business and industrial initiative; it should appeal to those concerned with business-like methods and sound economic development. It requires minimal cash outlay, little subsidy or risk. Unlike most urban crisis schemes now being considered, it goes with and not against the basic, new technological and economic trends in the country. It appears to have the best chance of benefiting both the Negro and the businessman.

Since most population growth, economic activity, and construction during the next decade will take place in our metropolitan regions—though generally outside the old central cities—we must work within this framework. If this development is to be generally beneficial, instead of intensifying the present artificially maintained and ominous socio-economic-racial divisions, we shall have to put an end to the harmful, omnipresent, and now (under the 1968 Civil Rights Act) illegal discriminatory real estate practices which prevent black people from moving into the residential and economic mainstream, and which keep them isolated, underemployed, or unemployed in inner-city ghettos, far from where the jobs are going.

Manufacturers are uniquely capable of doing this: severing the suburban "white noose" around our core cities, making the metropolitan housing-real estate market work the same for the Negro as for the white, and forcing exclusionist suburbs, exurbs, and smaller cities to accept non-white and lower-income families in significant volume and in a harmonious manner.

This is not to ignore the importance of the new federal open-housing statute, which is just now being put into effect. The force of law has had relatively little effect, however, in stemming the ever deepening racial divisions that have grown in cities and states which have had strong laws against housing discrimination on their books for years. What the community wants and is willing to do will make the final difference. Here, business and industrial leadership can be decisive.

For, if industry comes, the home builders won't be far behind. The tract-developers depend on industrial locations, as do realtors, merchants, and other local businessmen in the chambers of commerce. Politicans seek out new industry; planning commissions offer zoning concessions. Bankers, public officials, and other powerful local business and interest groups look to industry for its payroll and tax base, as well as its community leadership. Industry can read them the law—if it wants. Also, of course, industry recruits and hires workers.

But industry, the major force in new urban development, commonly has been a too-willing, if perhaps unwitting, partner to the discriminatory and exclusionist practices which have divided our metropolitan areas and nation into the unequal "two societies" described by the National Advisory Commission on Civil Disorders. It has been spending billions of dollars on new plants in communities that not only welcome but seek out its newly landscaped, non-obnoxious factories and laboratories, with their large tax base and bank deposits and loans. These communities even change zoning laws or provide new facilities to accommodate industry, but too often exclude workers, not to mention the black and the poor.

Most manufacturers have not stopped to question the development of these extreme trends—with the accompanying high rate of unemployment or underemployment in ghettos and unfilled jobs in exurbia—or to ask whether it is natural and inevitable, and what might be done to alter it. The more public-spirited among those who have recently discovered the ghetto are concentrating on the ghetto (and its hard-core unemployed) as if all the answers lay there, rather than on looking at the situation closer to home. But it high time they took a hard look at how the housing market in their area works and at its effect. For the irrational, uneconomic disjuncture we have developed as a result of it is playing havoc with both our metropolitan tax base and labor supply, and is making it necessary for Washington to tax industry nationally to pay for remedies that might be at least partially mitigated locally through private or community-level correctives.

Manufacturers, like other leadership forces in our country, must face up to the causes of the growing concentration of black people in the core cities and their absence in the suburbs, and industry's own responsibility and ability to change the situation. Obviously, many black people face residential problems arising from poverty, different cultures, large families, and lack of education; many want to live with other black people or fear rejection and white hostility. But we do not sufficiently recognize how much of the ghetto problem has been created by the systematic practice of discrimination and denial of residence by realtors, home builders, mortgage bankers, and suburban communities—and is reinforced by unfounded, hard-dying fears of white homeowners over the supposedly adverse effect on property values of racial intrusion. Moreover, under our present crazy-quilt metropolitan system—with free-wheeling fiscal zoning by every tiny suburb, land speculation by private owners, excessive reliance on the property tax, and use of government housing subsidies in effect restricted to older cities—it is extremely difficult to build lower-priced housing in the suburbs. . . .

Sooner or later, the ghetto-improvers will have to admit what the Kerner Commission emphatically stated in its report's conclusion: "A Negro society largely concentrated within large central cities . . . will be permanently relegated to its current status, possibly even if we expend great amounts of money and effort trying to 'gild' the ghetto." Black Power will not become Green Power in the slums.

Equally important to the businessman concerned with sound economic development is the fact that land uses in many of our old manufacturing cities should change to accommodate growing operations in our emerging post-industrial economy that require face-to-face contacts and meeting places and institutional expansion. The metropolitan cores will be increasingly transformed into office and professional centers—headquarters for business, communications, and government—and will create more and more technical, managerial, and professional jobs—which too few inner-city Negroes can yet fill, and to which suburbanites must commute.

To pursue the present course will only worsen the present metropolitan disjuncture with its inherent inequalities. What can and must be altered are present demographic trends and restrictive real estate practices. For not even improved metropolitan transportation is a satisfactory alternative. A recent study concluded:

Commutation is not a practical solution for reducing the disparity between job location and the housing location of minorities: It is prohibitively expensive, excessively time-consuming; and the ghetto poor are in no position to maintain the automobile necessary for most commuters. . . . To commute from Hunter's Point in San Francisco to a job in suburban Contra Costa County in the East Bay area would cost $3 per day, consume four to five hours daily in travel time, and would involve three or four transfers.

Data about "reverse commutation" in the Philadelphia region makes the point. There, the central city lost 50,000 manufacturing jobs between 1951 and 1965, and the suburbs gained 215,000—although Philadelphia has the nation's most advanced industrial redevelopment program. Of the work force of 480,000 in the Philadelphia suburbs, only 1.8 per cent are non-white commuters from the city proper, and only 8.6 per cent of the employed non-whites who live in the city commute to suburban jobs.

The implications for industry are grim: since the now-urbanized Negro has been having children at a higher rate than the white, a growing proportion of our prime work force

will be non-white. And when 10 per cent of the national population is unable to qualify for or compete equally for jobs (or on-the-job training programs) —partly because of inability to be educated for them, or to move to appropriate jobs and training opportunities or to even hear about them—the free-market process upon which industry depends is not functioning, and industry will pay, directly and indirectly.

Even "equal opportunity employers"—commonly government defense contractors located in regions or communities with few minority residents—have failed to address themselves to the effect of residential exclusion on the chances of black persons for equal employment. This has been vividly documented in hearings of the U.S. Commission on Civil Rights.

Some companies have begun to recognize the connection between housing and job opportunities and have started to exercise their exceptional influence to eliminate residential barriers. The following examples show what can be done:

1) When IBM located its huge new typewriter plant in Lexington, Kentucky, in 1958, it was the first manufacturing facility of significance in the area. Lexingtonians' main concern then was whether the factory would frighten off the horses. Recently, IBM, an outstanding equal opportunity employer, began a new national policy of recruiting black employees for jobs at various levels—white collar, technical, managerial. In Lexington, however, the incoming recruits had trouble. Despite the state's open-housing statute, realtors were not showing them homes.

Last spring the chairman of the Lexington-Fayette County Commission on Human Rights pointed out to IBM's local plant manager that the company—which, with a work force of over 5,000, is the largest employer in the area—was not using the influence it could exert to stop discrimination in housing. IBM has a plan under which it guarantees the sale of employees' homes when they transfer to another location. In 1967, it guaranteed the sale of homes worth $4,000,000 in the Lexington area; realtor commissions on these sales amounted to some $240,000. Although this involved only some 200 homes, it affected the entire local real estate market, as each local realtor handled a number of sales.

In June, IBM's vice president for manufacturing in Lexington sent a short letter to the president of Lexington's First Security National Bank, which acts as the company's agency in listing homes for IBM under the guarantee plan. The letter reiterated a verbal agreement with the banker.

In the listing of such properties, First Security will communicate to such realtors that IBM's policy is to utilize only those realtors who provide their services to prospective purchasers without discrimination against such individuals because of race, color, religion, or national origin.

If you discover this policy is not being followed, please advise me.

The bank president sent the letter to the Real Estate Board, which sent a copy of it with an accompanying memo to participants in the local Multiple Listing Service stating that IBM Guarantee Plan Properties "will only be assigned to realtors who agree to observe the IBM policy."

Within two days after the IBM letter went out, one black IBM employee who had made no progress in finding housing after two weeks of effort received nine phone calls from real estate dealers. A local realtor stated that IBM's stand would carry more weight than either Kentucky's open-housing law or the recent U.S. Supreme Court decision banning discrimination in all housing. Galen Martin, executive director of the Kentucky Commission on Human Rights, points out: "Real estate people want someone else to give them the lead."

2) In 1964, Armour and Company moved its Kansas City plant operations to all-white Worthington, Minnesota, a town of 10,000 in the heart of rural America. Among the several hundred workers who were planning to transfer with Armour to Worthington were forty-five Negroes and several Puerto Ricans.

To facilitate employee relocation and retraining for the new plant, Armour's management in Kansas City formed a committee with the unions involved. This committee worked with community leaders in Worthington—bankers, realtors, and public officials—and asked their assistance in finding housing for incoming workers "without discrimination against minority members." They received this cooperation, and, in addition, the local churches, press, and business and fraternal clubs developed and carried out a community relations program

which was effective in creating a favorable climate. They also established a Housing Information Bureau to help the newcomers secure homes at a fair price and throughout the community. The result was the peaceful and harmonious settlement of Negro and other minority families in Worthington.

3) In labor-tight Dallas, LTV Aerospace Corporation, a major employer in the metropolitan area, found itself unable to fill assembly-line jobs at its aeronautics plant. To overcome this problem, it worked out a program with the State of Texas Employment Commission through which 750 industrially unskilled Mexican-Americans living 500 miles away in the Rio Grande Valley were trained for work in the Dallas plant. The commission paid the trainees' salaries with funds from the U.S. Department of Labor; LTV set up the training center and provided instruction. When the workers were ready to move to their new jobs in Dallas, the commission—working closely with LTV—paid their relocation expenses and acted as liaison in finding them housing. Both the company and the state agency prepared the community to welcome the new workers.

They have fitted well into both jobs and community, have had superior records of staying on the job, and have not encountered the many problems experienced by most unskilled newcomers to the city.

These examples and others make clear that when progressive industry understands the facts and implications of a seemingly insoluble "social" problem, it can do much to bring about necessary changes. Industry can have a major impact in breaking rigid residential patterns—making the real estate market function without discrimination and assuring the peaceful accommodation of minority families in new communities.

But if more working and lower-income families are to be enabled to live outside the central cities and ghettos, industry will also have to use its local community influence to facilitate the necessary construction of more moderate-priced housing in suburbs and new growth areas. It can get more suburban land rezoned for small lots and multiple dwellings; lend its prestige to the establishment of nonprofit corporations that will develop residential land banks, and use low-interest government housing programs in suburbia; and encourage formation of county-wide public agencies to use the rent-supplement program. Business leaders can urge states to assume a larger share of local education costs, which lead to exclusionist suburban zoning, and can discourage the establishment of new plants in communities that practice residential exclusion.

Such corporate measures do not, of course, preclude business support for other necessary kinds of action by both government and private institutions, within ghetto areas and beyond. But it is urgent for the modern corporation, particularly major industrial concerns, to recognize that their practices in communities where they are located, or plan to locate, can make a major difference in altering the racial divisions and inequities in America.

BURP AND MAKE MONEY

Eli Goldston

The delegation comes in—typically consisting of a financial expert, an administrator, and an engineering-operating man—asking us the standard business questions of men in their specialties. They represent a company whose corporate conscience is being nagged about social involvement, and they have heard that we have some expertise to share in the field of large-scale, low-income urban housing rehabilitation.

We have made this date with them; we have assembled in a conference room; and now the questions begin:

• The financial man wants to know how we arrived at the value of the equity, what the problems are in getting interim financing, what the interest rate is likely to be, whether any difficulties with bonding or insurance are expected, what a pro forma P&L statement looks like, and how the spillover tax shelter works.

• The administrator asks us to take him through the intricacies of the National Housing Act, to differentiate between Sections 221(d)(3) and 236, to show him the forms necessary for initial endorsement, to tell him what happens at the time of commitment, to describe the advantages of a limited partnership over a general partnership, and to offer an opinion on whether it is better to work directly or through a specially organized subsidiary.

• The engineering-operating man is naturally concerned with the actual work on the structures, invariably probing for information on new techniques or materials in housing rehabilitation which he has heard can achieve dramatic economies of time and money. He asks about

Reprinted from the *Harvard Business Review,* Vol. 47, No. 5 (September-October 1969), pp. 84-99, by permission of the author and the publisher. ©1969 by the President and Fellows of Harvard College; all rights reserved.

mass production approaches, prefabrication, the durability of materials, and the quality of workmanship.

These are important questions, and we answer them as well as we can, digging into our memories and files for information. When we have done our best with their questions, we ask some of our own:

What has been the ethnic succession pattern in the neighborhood you're talking about?

Can you tell us anything of family sizes, their economic levels, and the scope of the possible program with relation to the total community?

Is your mayor on speaking terms with not only the municipal renewal agency but also the regional FHA and HUD officials?

Is the city flexible and progressive with respect to its building code?

Are you acquainted with some local community (which usually means black) contractors, real estate operators, lawyers, and construction workers?

What are the attitudes and effectiveness of the neighborhood institutions, particularly any weekly newspapers?

This is when their education in the realities of urban housing rehabilitation begins to begin. It continues as we put on a slide show of the successes and mistakes of our project, the Boston Urban Rehabilitation Program (BURP).

Often they fail to grasp our point until later, perhaps at lunch, when the head of an all-black development team, invited to meet the visitors, instructs them on the benefits of double declining balance depreciation, and the black real estate manager describes his method of keeping tenants advised about the progress of the work.

Our most important message for visitors is that an understanding of the sociopolitical factors—particularly recognition of the ghetto's "do-it-ourselves" requirement—must come first, and the financial and legal questions come last.

Front-line experience in urban housing rehabilitation is clearly a sought-after commodity today. Since the announcement nearly two years ago of the participation by Eastern Gas and Fuel Associates and its subsidiary, Boston Gas Company, in BURP, nearly every day has brought a call or a letter asking for information, seeking an opportunity to come, hear, and see, or pleading for someone to fill a speaking engagement.

These inquirers want to learn about this first involvement of a major business organization in a joint housing venture with a number of small real estate developers and the federal government, where the motivations of both private profit and social good seem to have been merged successfully.

We say our participation in BURP demonstrates that it is possible to do well by doing good. We have done "well" by combining the tax benefits afforded to the parent by real estate investment with increased gas sales made by the subsidiary. We have done "good" by helping significantly in the effort to rehouse a major segment of Boston's black community.

OPPORTUNITY KNOCKING

These days, almost every publicly held U.S. company feels some unease concerning its role in the problem areas of our society. Thoughtful businessmen increasingly are examining corporate actions that may have contributed to the problems, and at the same time they are searching for ways for the corporation to serve— preferably highly visible ways.

More recently there has developed an equally vague awareness that in the problems lie opportunities. More and more businessmen accept the notion that no one really benefits from squalor and poverty. They believe that the deprived segments of our society present untapped markets—if only these segments could be helped to join the buying throng!

And if this questioning had not been selfgenerating, it would have been stimulated by the shared and expressed convictions of both major political parties that business must become more

directly involved in the solution of social problems. Augmenting these expressions of conviction are the federal government's many direct and subtle ways of exerting pressure and the demands of the more outspoken blacks.

Businessmen and public officials alike, for reasons that are almost self-evident, have settled on inner-city housing—especially the rehabilitation of substandard housing—as one of the first areas where the muscle and money of business can very effectively assist. Such diverse political figures as President Nixon and the late Senator Robert Kennedy have reached the same conclusion: corporate involvement in inner-city housing must be generated if we are to attack our urban problems effectively.

This is truly a task of great urgency and magnitude. According to a study by the Kaiser Committee in 1968, "about 7.8 million U.S. families—one in every eight—cannot afford to pay the market price for standard housing." The report also estimated that "6.7 million occupied units are substandard dwellings—4.0 million lacking indoor plumbing and 2.7 million in dilapidated condition."[1] Most informed persons agree that there are certainly 3.4 million units in our cities which need rehabilitation.

While the employment drive of the government-business alliance has set a target of hiring 600,000 hard-core unemployed over the next 10 years, the housing goal has been set at 6 million standard dwelling units over the same period—a rate astronomically beyond the present construction rates. This housing gap obviously is too wide for government alone to close.

The vague notion of market opportunity has crystallized for many companies in estimates of the need for new bathroom fixtures and kitchen appliances, wallboard, glass, hardware, and the whole range of building materials except for heavy framework essentials. The F.W. Dodge Company states that the current rehabilitation market represents a $12 billion opportunity (including the market for new and increased utility services in areas where the basic piping and wiring already has been installed).

RATIONALE FOR REHABILITATION

While the lure of involvement in new housing construction has been tempting, there is a powerful rationale for rehabilitation that seems particularly appealing to big business. Halting deterioration, preserving the preservable, and salvaging the structurally sound are concepts satisfying to the prudent businessman. He may be quite willing to destroy the dilapidated and build anew, but he likes to think that more can be accomplished for less by rehabilitation.

It also seems to be a speedier solution. With no need for site acquisition or clearance, installation of utilities, or major planning, design, and construction, the inventory of standard housing units could be rapidly swelled by refurbishing the old.

Finally, there is the argument that rehabilitation avoids displacement or dispersal of residents and preserves whole communities with their existing services.

Inasmuch as rehabilitation historically has been carried out by small contractors, big businesses have been encouraged to believe that they could effect vast economies by bringing to bear their know-how and technology. The convergence of all these pressures, lures, and changes in attitudes has resulted in the persuasion of a fair number of large companies to venture into the rehabilitation of middle- and lower-income housing. The best-known projects have been these:

• Warner & Swasey Company rehabilitated a 40-year-old apartment building in the Hough area of Cleveland into 13 living units with three bedrooms each.

• Smith, Kline & French Laboratories assisted the developer who rehabilitated 210 living units in 70 structures near the SKF factory and administration building in Philadelphia.

• Allegheny Housing Rehabilitation Corporation, financed by a number of Pittsburgh's major corporations, as a demonstration of financial feasibility rehabilitated 22 substandard row houses and provided 22 families with decent housing at rents only slightly higher than before.

• United States Gypsum Company, in a demonstration of modular prefabrication, rehabilitated in 48 hours a New York City tenement building containing 32 units by dropping preassembled kitchen and bathroom modules through a hole cut in the roof.

None of these early efforts, or others (to the extent that details have been made available),

seem to have been profitable. Of course, several were only demonstrations, but even their costs appear to have run very substantially over estimates. All of them also have been quite small in relation to the needs of their respective cities.

Beyond the marketing, operational, and social attractions of rehabilitation, however, there is the more sophisticated financial consideration of the "spillover" tax shelter in real estate investment which industrial companies have hitherto seldom considered in their analyses of profitability.

They are just now learning about this dynamic, which has motivated private investors in commercial and upper-income residential development for many years. They are discovering the relation of land values to cash flow, the leverage achieved by esoteric ways of financing (like "bobtailed mortgage debt"), and the benefits of capital gains at disposition.

The only major program of ghetto housing rehabilitation where all these considerations played a significant part in producing a profitable project is BURP. Since we encountered a wide range of the problems inherent in each facet of such involvement, made every possible mistake, and emerged with some solutions and many judgments, it is not surprising that companies contemplating ventures in housing want to hear about BURP.

LARGE DEMONSTRATION

What has come to be known as the Boston Urban Rehabilitation Program (BURP) had its genesis in the early fall of 1967, when the Department of Housing and Urban Development (HUD) decided to conduct a large demonstration of rehabilitation in the Roxbury-Dorchester section of Boston under Section 221(d)(3) of the National Housing Act of 1961.

The BURP designation was originally limited to describing the allocation of $24.5 million in federal funds to five private developer-sponsors to rehabilitate 2,000 apartment units in 101 buildings. It has since been extended by common usage to cover an almost contemporaneous rent supplement program involving 731 units in 30 buildings, with an allocation of $7.5 million, and two subsequent projects covering 217 units at a cost of $2.7 million. (Although rent supplement financing varies slightly, all other elements of the program are virtually identical.)

The central 2,000-unit award still is far and away the largest single allocation for rehabilitation the Federal Housing Administration has ever made. In the eight years since the FHA has had authority under Section 221(d)(3), only 9,000 dwelling units (including the 3,000 BURP units) have been rehabilitated under it in the entire nation. In that perspective BURP constitutes a very significant prototype.

"A controlled experiment" was how the then Secretary of HUD, Robert C. Weaver, described it. "What we seek here," he said, "is not only good dwelling units but the knowledge of how to produce them more quickly than ever before. . . . What are the human resources, the leadership ingredients, the building techniques— and perhaps as much as anything, what are the processing techniques that will reduce nine pieces of paper to one piece of paper."[3]

Our companies became involved initially because of the marketing interest of Boston Gas in the sales opportunities of such a vast rehabilitation program. (The inelegant acronym of the program name provided our subsidiary with the lighthearted slogan, "When you BURP, think gas!" It also led a housing expert, Charles Abrams, to challenge our electric utility competitor to match us in social responsibility with BELCH—Boston Edison Low-Cost Housing.)

Inquiries revealed the developers' need for equity cash to make their projects go. After extensive negotiation with the developers and discussions with FHA officials, Eastern Gas and Fuel Associates provided this money by the purchase of equity interests in limited partnerships in a majority of the units. Boston Gas received the fuel commitment by extending its low public housing rates to the buildings, thus meeting competitive fuel costs.

Boston Gas gained its largest single addition to gas load in recent years, while Eastern received the spillover tax shelter benefit. Neither return by itself would have justified our involvement commercially, but together the two showed a respectable profit.

With all its difficulties, BURP was successful by many standards. In 18 months, one seventh of the black population of Boston was rehoused in renovated units, with no increase in shelter cost. More than 400 black construction workers were employed at one time or another, and the majority of them were given some craft training. Two all-black development teams—contractors, lawyers, developer-sponsors, managers, and a majority of the investors—emerged to receive about 10% of the total BURP program.

LESSONS WE HAVE LEARNED

The challenge for us and HUD, as it is for the corporate teams that visit us, is to find the lessons of the BURP experience and determine what elements are transferable to other locations and other circumstances. In the jargon of housing specialists, to what extent is BURP replicatable? It is important that, when the inevitable national housing effort finally gathers force, the alliance of public direction and private execution functions to the benefit of our whole society.

We have thought deeply about the lessons of BURP, and we have learned from our mistakes. From the questions asked of us about our experience, we have an understanding of what corporate newcomers to this field need to know. Here are the key elements to consider and the advice we give our visitors.

TEST YOUR ATTITUDE

We tell our visitors first to examine more carefully their own approach and attitude to the problems in our cities, of which lack of housing is, after all, just one.

Astute urbanologists early in the renewal effort suggested that more important than all the particulars of a single program is the business community's recognition that it must, like Chaucer's clerk, be willing to "gladly . . . lerne and gladly teche" when it assumes a role in social action. As one of them, Webb S. Fiser, has written:

"The interests included must contain all the different business and industrial interests, labor, religious groups, professional groups, civic associations and minority interests, social agencies and educational institutions.

"Many businessmen have a natural repugnance toward this procedure. First of all, they are not accustomed to meeting with representatives of many of these groups and therefore feel uncomfortable. Also the perspective of many of these people will seem strange to business leaders; yet it is precisely the accommodation of these perspectives that is required for community consensus. . . .

"Second, businessmen will often want action and insist upon getting down to work. Bringing in a lot of other people creates the danger of delay. However, too great an emphasis upon action may get short-term results but is apt to build up opposition over the long haul. The only secure basis for community development is full consideration of all the important concerns of the community."[4]

As Fiser suggests, businessmen often assume that their economic power should automatically validate their ideas about the future of the community. This attitude offends the nonbusiness people, and in many community issues businessmen have demonstrated that they do not even perceive what their own long-run interests require, let alone what the public interest is.

A primary lesson of our experience was that involvement in housing rehabilitation means a long, slow, often frustrating and time-consuming process of give-and-take. It is a path that requires much listening and much adjusting, and is as likely to bring abuse and noisy public criticism as praise. The company president should not be surprised if, just at the time when he thinks he deserves community acclaim for helping to bring a vast rehabilitation program to the area, he is burned in effigy. I was—and (to make things worse, since I'm in the gas utility business) in oil!

But he must not let this deter him from the effort. The alternative could be an accelerating plunge of our cities into decay and violence and an ever-widening gulf between great segments of our population and the business-based economy that has accomplished so much.

FIND "GOOD EGGS"

A good omelet means starting with good eggs. Similarly, the starting point in rehabilitation is suitable structures to rehabilitate, and any company thinking of involvement in rehabilitation should first be sure that it has "good eggs." We therefore tell our visitors to look carefully at the neighborhoods under consideration to see if the pattern of population progression and sociological development seems to have left structures suitable for rebuilding.

The Roxbury-Dorchester section of Boston was originally a community of Yankee farmers. They were displaced in the early 1900's by Irish and Canadian immigrants. These in turn were succeeded by middle-class Jewish families, who moved to this "streetcar suburb" from downtown West End Boston as that area became Italian. Beginning in the late 1940's the black population of Boston expanded into Roxbury-Dorchester, which now is predominantly black.

The buildings are generally three-story brick apartment houses, with each entry serving six walk-up units. They were built in the mid-1920's many of them as investments by families who then lived in one of the apartments. This meant that the structures were well-built and well-kept as long as this sociological pattern prevailed.

The pattern began to change in the 1950's, and it changed more precipitously in the 1960's as the black population increased. Overcrowding and undermaintenance produced a dramatically rapid deterioration in condition. Since these properties were mostly owned by the original builder-owners' children, who had moved away from the neighborhood or even from the city, real estate managers, acting for absentee landlords, bled the properties. When tenants left, taking lighting fixtures, hardware, and even doors, the properties were boarded up rather than rehabilitated.

Among these apartment buildings there often stood wooden single- or multiple-family dwellings of about the same vintage, usually still owner-occupied and only beginning to show the neglect that comes from despair that the area is doomed to decay. The government hoped that if the apartment structures were renewed, the owners of these smaller dwellings would be encouraged to keep them up, and in this way the neighborhood would be saved.

The characteristics of the buildings in BURP make them more suitable for rehabilitation than most of the millions of "deteriorated" or "dilapidated" buildings that abound in our nation's cities. They were built as multiunit structures; their rooms are large enough to permit rehabilitation by installing "a box within a box"; their foundations and bearing walls are still sound;

and they also have adequate stairways and fire escapes.

Too often the inexperienced developer is tempted to try to convert large single-family town houses into apartments, or to try refurbishing buildings such as the so-called "old law" tenements in New York. In the first case, the large rooms, high ceilings, inadequate stairs, and so on, require too much rebuilding to be economic. In the other case, the tiny rooms neither meet present-day building code requirements nor permit the box-within-a-box technique that seems to be the best approach to rehabilitation.

It is cheaper by far, for instance, to "fur" over a cracked plaster wall and install gypsum board than to haul away the old plaster; the disposal of construction waste is a significant cost in a project. Similar handling of ceilings and floors provides a quick overhaul and a new appearance, and permits easy and inexpensive installation of new wiring and plumbing. The rule of thumb is to nail down and then cover up anything that doesn't smell, doesn't spontaneously combust, or doesn't contain live vermin.

There is a continuing debate among those experienced in rehabilitation as to how much to preserve and how much to renew. The answer must be an individual one, varying with the company and the project.

No nationwide survey seems to be at hand to spot the availability of potential rehabilitation structures. In some cities, such as Milwaukee, most of the lower-income residential properties are of a type that probably should be demolished or only modestly rehabilitated. The area of Boston selected for BURP offered residential housing almost ideal for rehabilitation. Out of the vast pool of "deteriorated" and "dilapidated" residential buildings (using the latest dual classification of substandard dwellings) there must be great numbers that would meet the test of economics that BURP has demonstrated. Without them, forget it.

KNOW YOUR GOVERNMENT

Any rehabilitation program of substance inevitably becomes the concern of the city's political structure. Its success or failure can easily affect the political fortunes of an administration or at least of certain elected officials. It must, in short, be welcomed, or at least tolerated, by officialdom.

Any business contemplating rehabilitation involvement on a large scale should carefully consider the attitude of the city government. For example:

Is it a project the mayor will endorse?

Will the city council favor or oppose it?

Are the assessors sympathetic to the idea of providing a greater supply of low-income housing through salvage of properties to which the city now holds tax title?

What is the approach of the city's building code enforcement agency to the use of new materials, new techniques, and new construction methods?

The last question is particularly crucial because building restrictions can be a serious impediment. It is important, for instance, to check out at an early stage whether the rehabilitated properties will be subject to current building code requirements or recognized as falling within a "grandfather" clause.

Many zoning, building code, and setback restrictions were developed in the 1940's and early 1950's, when the threat of urban blight was unknown or unappreciated. Their goal was the gradual elimination of existing nonconforming structures. In today's situation such restrictions are unrealistic if applied to the rehabilitation of 40-year-old buildings.

At least two favorable preconditions for rapid, economic implementation of a large housing program were present in Boston. Urban renewal in the city was lodged in a single agency, the Boston Redevelopment Authority (BRA), with centralized power and control that helped to cut red tape. Moreover, the city government had established a precedent for tax treatment of commercial property that would not impose a crippling hardship on rehabilitation. Such preconditions may not prevail in other cities.

Even so, BURP needed a sympathetic city administration to prevail over a difficult interregnum situation in the early days of the project. BURP was put together in the fall of 1967, shortly before city elections were to bring about a change of administration that included both the mayor and his urban renewal administrator. Fortunately the new mayor, Kevin H. White, moved quickly to name a new head of the BRA,

Hale Champion, who joined with the mayor in action to overcome the program's birth pangs.

Federal agencies: Valuable attributes are knowledge of and patience with the staffs and procedures of federal agencies involved in inner-city housing. Too often a businessman approaches these agencies belligerently with demands for instant action, then retreats in furor and frustration when they are not immediately met. Such an approach to a normal business transaction might very well produce negative results.

More important are a perspective on the procedures and a personal relationship with those handling the government's part of the processing. This can range from a first-name acquaintance with secretaries checking entries on forms to a top-level friendship that permits clearance of important policy points by telephone.

In the case of BURP one of the primary objectives set by HUD Secretary Weaver was to try to cut through lengthy procedures and greatly reduce the time required to process applications for FHA mortgage insurance commitments. This was achieved to the extent that paperwork which had taken other developers 18 months to move through the steps from application to commitment was now completed within two months.

With this evidence that it can be done, we suggest to businessmen approaching us for advice that they first try to get "BURP processing" for their projects, using whatever persuasive powers they can muster through the local government and local agencies (which are usually just as eager to move ahead quickly). The applicant must be willing to move as fast as he is asking the agencies to do, and to respond with dispatch to any request they may make.

WORK WITH THE COMMUNITY

Nowhere is the businessman less sure of himself or more apprehensive than in dealing with a community of blacks (or other minorities). And no aspect of involvement in inner-city housing rehabilitation is more important. Experience in dealing with minority groups on nonhousing issues is a far more valuable asset than knowledge of rehabilitation techniques or the ability to understand sophisticated real estate financing.

The businessman seeking involvement in inner-city work must not naively assume, as many have done, that his company's arrival with a completely developed program will be greeted with open arms. The corporation must understand that black communities today are no longer docile and complacent, but are outspoken and demanding in their aims and goals. They are protective of their neighborhoods ("our turf") and will no longer allow decisions that impinge on their destiny to be made without their representation and participation. White businesses must accept the fact that they will most likely be regarded as intruders.

Here the lesson of BURP is certainly instructive. Its twin goals of speed and size led to early oversights and mistakes that caused problems with many elements of the black community. To assemble almost 3,000 dwelling units without undue real estate speculation and complete the rehabilitation in record time, it seemed to be advisable for the FHA to move quietly in the beginning and to select established and experienced real estate and rehabilitation firms as private developers.

Furthermore, to heighten the impact of the program, it was determined that the announcement should be made with a splash and a show. Little did we know, but danger was waiting.

At the announcement luncheon, held in a black settlement house which represented the social work approach of an earlier generation, Secretary Weaver—himself a black—was interrupted and challenged by black militants as he tried to explain the program. They denounced BURP as another effort of slumlords, undertaken without consulting or considering tenants or the community, to profiteer in the ghetto.

In succeeding days an extreme cold wave, coinciding with eviction notices, brought an avalanche of public complaints of hardship. A glorious experiment appeared doomed before it started.

We tell our businessmen visitors, therefore, that their principal concern should be to find the way of genuine community acceptance. To this end, they need the best possible advice from the community itself.

This means competent black advisers with whom mutual confidence has been established by previous business relationships. Sometimes they are employees, sometimes customers, sometimes community leaders whose causes the company has aided. From them it is possible to get guidance about the groups and persons who are the focal points of persuasion in the community.

It is not easy to determine the power structure or to estimate how long it may prevail. While there is a more-or-less recognized leadership, there is also, as in all other communities—but perhaps more so in the black ghettos—significant new leadership appearing within short periods of times. A company must realize that its friends of today may be the *ancien régime* of tomorrow. Plans for Columbia University's gymnasium and Governor Nelson Rockefeller's state office building originally received support from the Harlem community but were later blocked after a turnover in community leadership.

In the case of BURP, where it was necessary to counter community opposition promptly, we found that established company relationships with the NAACP, various youth and employment groups, a community social service center, and especially the widely respected black operator of a school of fine arts were invaluable resources.

Local partners: A search for allies or partners acceptable in the ghetto community may turn a company toward nonprofit organizations. This direction, however tempting, can bring the frustrations of inexpert, spare-time participation. Or it could result in a more radical step, a kind of black socialism. Either outcome makes real accomplishment very difficult to achieve, though there is a valid role for nonprofit organizations in eventual ownership of properties rehabilitated by business.

The best solution is to find black entrepreneurs with commercial talent (if not scope of experience) and help them perform as much of the ghetto operation as possible, not as fronts for the company, but as principals or at least equal partners in a rehabilitation enterprise.

Such persons can be located; through black employees and friends, we were able to identify a number of local people with the instinct for commercial enterprise. Black sports figures or entertainers need tax shelter, and successful black contractors and real estate operators can be found—though their businesses may be small.

The danger is that the white businessman who is unacquainted with his black community will team up with the very sort of glib, politically or spiritually motivated, impractical black person whom he would instantly identify and avoid if the person were white.

Real estate rehabilitation is one of the most promising fields for black entrepreneurs. The cash needs in FHA programs are modest, so large pieces of property can be put in the hands of black owners with small cash payments. The work can be broken down into easily managed portions, and the economies of scale that make some projects more amenable to the large corporate approach do not apply here.

Moreover, big business can be the most help precisely in the aspects of the program where black businessmen are the most limited. The construction work can be subcontracted so that white companies can be brought in for more sophisticated parts of the job until black firms develop expertise. Because most black firms are too small to afford accountants, the black entrepreneur can use help in keeping adequate records.

Bonding in the usual way will be a special problem, but, again, big business can fill the gap, either by endorsement or by itself guaranteeing the construction performance of the entrepreneurs. Of course, the FHA is likely to be reasonably flexible on a mortgage increase to cover overruns based on improvements and additions beyond the minimum contract specifications.

The benefits of bringing along capable, though inexperienced, black entrepreneurs and helping them take on the projects themselves are incalculable. Here is the "piece of the action" that the black community now insists on having. Here is the best chance of community acceptance. Here is the hope for mutually respectful employee and tenant-landlord relationships. Here opens the possibility of the ghetto reclaiming itself. And, with confidence established in their own business ability, the black developer-sponsors can impartially consider the commercial interests of their tutors.

We have worked with several black developer-sponsor teams in Boston, helping them get organized, leading them through the paperwork, giving them legal, financial, and technical advice, and using our knowledge of city and federal agencies for their benefit. These black groups either have completed or are carrying out more than $5.5 million worth of rehabilitation projects in Boston, involving nearly 450 apartment units—far more than a token share of the rehabilitation work being done in the area. And they have chosen gas heat for all of these units.

CONSIDER YOUR TENANTS

An early concern of the developer should be a tenant audit, including, when possible, data on both family size and income level. With this information he can make adequate provision in his planning for size of families. Otherwise, he may find out after the job is finished that he underestimated the number of four-bedroom apartments that would be needed, giving him a severe relocation problem.

This happened with BURP. We failed to insist on a tenant audit, not realizing this was important even at the expense of speed of completion of the work. The result was that a number of so-called "oversized" families, previously permitted to crowd into inadequate quarters in unregulated structures, could not qualify under FHA regulations—either by size or income level—for the refurbished units. (I should add here that, by means of rent supplement contracts with HUD and of leased public housing contracts with the local housing authority, tenants with inadequate incomes can be accommodated.)

We also tell our business visitors to try their best to make sure that the structures to be rehabilitated follow FHA regulations on filling the needs of the present tenants. (This is conditioned to some extent by the necessity for secrecy in assembling the real estate, to avoid driving up prices.)

In planning for tenant occupancy, by the way, the sponsor may wish to weed out families who are chronically delinquent in paying their rent or have other undesirable characteristics. But it is unrealistic to expect that such tenant selection can be accomplished unilaterally. Tenant organizations, probably supported by community leaders, will insist on the right of first refusal for present occupants to return to the rehabilitated apartments.

If the sponsor decides to relocate many large families without first making suitable provision for them, he is headed for trouble. The public clamor, based on a claim of undeniable injustice, will undo any gains in bricks and mortar. A good relocation plan is a must.

Prepare yourself, we say too, for a great deal of negotiating and consulting with tenants. A tenants' council most likely will be organized, but our experience is that you can live with it comfortably, and perhaps it may even come to provide the self-regulation and control lacking in typical low-income rental situations. The sponsor may be surprised to discover a spirit of cooperation in the leaders of tenant groups—except on the subject of ability to pay rent. They usually recognize that it is in the tenants' interest to eliminate troublesome occupants and keep the buildings well maintained. So, tenant organizations, often headed by officious matriarchs, will support landlords who insist on cleanliness and good housekeeping.

In our case, the regular weekly meetings of the BURP tenants' council became in part a forum for educating tenants in landlords' problems. As tenants saw the damage to their own self-interest caused by recalcitrant neighbors, the council became useful as a final arbitrator of disputes.

In any event, a hard look at the tenant situation is a basic social precondition of business involvement in housing rehabilitation. And if trouble develops, the developer cannot necessarily depend on the courts to sustain what he considers to be a landlord's rights. As two experts on urban law and I recently wrote in the *Columbia Law Review:*

"With black militancy, community control, advocacy planning and all of the other social tides surging back and forth in low income communities, large scale undertakings of any sort cannot be successfully operated on the assumption that traditional legal rights, obligations and enforcement procedures will be heeded by anyone—even the courts."[5]

WATCH FOR LABOR PROBLEMS

As part of their understandable claims for a piece of the action, the ghetto residents will want some of the jobs created by the project. Here, again, the position of the black development team gives it a natural advantage over white developers; but to get the ghetto housing job done, the general contractors probably will require a majority of whites in some building trades for a long time to come.

In the meantime, as a partner of a black developer, the sponsor should prepare for confrontations with building trades unions and for the uncontrolled costs that result from use of pathetically unskilled black workers. Vandalism, at the least, will be the consequence if a satisfactory accommodation is not reached.

As for labor union problems, we can say that on the projects in which BURP was involved they were faced with firmness. When the union demanded the dismissal of nonunion blacks, it was refused, but the union was offered the opportunity to try to organize the workers. This offer was not immediately accepted, nor was our suggestion that they try to put white pickets at the job sites in the black community.

While it is likely that the situation in the building trades unions will gradually improve, it is nevertheless important to lose no time in building up a pool of capable, responsible black construction workers. One way in which the FHA can promote this effort is to take the lower productivity of unskilled workers into account in calculating mortgage commitments, perhaps with a productivity scale. Or else the government should provide training funds from other sources. To illustrate:

One of the principal white developer-sponsors in BURP attempted to satisfy community demands by employing a considerable number of blacks. Under FHA requirements, "prevailing wages" had to be paid. The result was almost catastrophic financially. Productivity was about one third that of skilled white workers. Expenses mounted while projects lagged.

Eventually the developer's training and apprenticeship programs began paying off in improved work performance. But project costs substantially exceeded mortgage limits, and efforts are even now being made to have these limits raised accordingly.

When contemplating a ghetto project of any size the prudent businessman should remember that the social requirement of hiring substantial numbers of unskilled black construction workers will cost him extra money.

TAKE CARE IN STAFFING

The range of these socioeconomic questions leads us naturally to ask our visitors if they have considered the staff necessary to handle the enterprise.

A fund of legal, financial, planning, and production expertise is necessary to interpret the National Housing Act, FHA regulations, and the Internal Revenue Code; to translate the titles and paragraphs into a housing package that makes financial sense; to lay out and oversee a program; to create a partnership of investors; to locate and acquire suitable properties; to find contractors; and finally to obtain the necessary money to launch the project. Only an organization with a strong profit motivation is likely to persist through this maze.

The missing element in most corporations that undertake these ventures is an urban affairs officer with enough experience to guide the company through the tangled and complex community problems and enough authority in the corporation to see that the right things are done in the right way. We say, be sure you have such a man.

ANALYZE THE $ AND SENSE

By this circuitous route we bring our visitors back to some of their original questions, particularly concerning the profit possibilities in urban housing rehabilitation. Now we are on ground familiar to them—profit and loss statements, balance sheets, tax returns, and so on—but even here, real estate financing is apt to be an unknown quantity.

Until recently, few of the larger, publicly held U.S. companies have taken much interest in real estate, particularly residential real estate. Most real estate owners have been individuals, partnerships, or smaller publicly owned syndications. Usually the tax shelter from real estate is more significant than the cash earnings or book earnings. Because of the relatively low book earnings, publicly held companies conscious of their earnings per share have shied from real estate investing.

In the early days of urban renewal a number

of major corporations did show an interest in the program, but largely for the purpose of exploring the possibilities of expanding the use of their products in the construction industry or the markets for their consumer goods. In the early 1960's, for example, the Aluminum Company of America and Reynolds Metals Company competed vigorously for urban renewal projects, and Westinghouse and General Electric also participated.

Concern remained, however, as to the impact of equity ownership on book earnings, the effect on traditional balance-sheet ratios of showing large mortgages in consolidated statements, the problems arising from rent controls, demands for open occupancy, and so on. Several major insurance companies, in fact, sold out large residential developments because they concluded that the public relations headaches exceeded the benefits to themselves.

Many of these objections can be overcome by investing in rehabilitation projects as a limited partner. With an interest of less than 50%, the investor is not required, under present accounting practices, to consolidate mortgages in his balance sheet or operating losses in his earnings statement. Also, he can remain anonymous to the tenants.

The principal factor in most speculative real estate developments is the spillover tax shelter, by which tax losses on cash-producing real estate can be used to reduce the taxes paid on income from other sources. The tax loss write-offs (rather large in comparison to the size of the equity investment) result from the interplay of two sets of legislation, the National Housing Act and income tax laws:

The Housing Act makes mortgage financing available on very favorable terms for a high percentage of the cost of acquiring and rehabilitating properties. As a result, relatively little in the way of cash equity investment is required. Offsetting this are rather strict legal restrictions on the distribution of cash earnings from these projects.

Section 167 of the Internal Revenue Code allows equity investors to take rapid depreciation on real estate improvements, whether paid for out of equity investment or out of mortgage borrowing. This write-off in turn, creates substantial tax losses for projects during their early years of operation. High tax-bracket investors, including corporations, who are limited part-

ners in such projects may carry these losses into their tax returns as offsets to taxable income from other sources.

221(d)(30) &236: Among the several sections of the National Housing Act concerning the financing of real estate projects, 221(d)(3) was the basis for underwriting the BURP projects. It provides among other things that, in the case of "for profit" sponsors, the FHA will insure mortgage financing for up to 90% of the total cost of a rehabilitation project. It also enables federal funds to be lent for this purpose at a 3% interest rate, repayable on a level debt service basis over 40 years.

The reader who is interested in the financial details of a typical BURP project can find them in the Appendix to this article.

In 1968 Congress amended the National Housing Act by the addition of Section 236 relating to low-income housing. It is similar in many respects to 221(d)(3). Under both programs 90% mortgage financing for limited dividend partnerships and 100% financing for nonprofit sponsors are authorized. Both sections limit the cash distributions to limited dividend developers to an amount that approximates 6% of the equity investment. Both are also subject to the HUD regulation that no more than 20% of the units in a given project may be leased to local housing authorities who, in turn, further subsidize rentals.

The two sections differ mainly in the form of the financing subsidy. Under 221(d)(3), mortgages are available either at or below market interest rates, with the latter salable to Ginnie Mae (Government National Mortgage Association). Section 236, on the other hand, permits developers to negotiate mortgages directly with lending institutions at market interest rates.

To cover the gap between tenant capacity to pay and interest expense at market rates, HUD pays a subsidy. Thus, the debt service paid by the mortgagor will vary from a minimum of 1% for the lowest income housing to 6%, depending on the tenants' income formula. Any balance between that figure and the market interest rate is made up by HUD in the form of an interest subsidy.

Section 236 also provides that on completion of rehabilitation the developers may sell to a nonprofit or cooperative entity, which can finance the purchase with a new mortgage at the then fair value of the project. This could permit a large enough mortgage to reimburse the seller for his entire investment, plus any taxes he incurs on the sale.

It is possible that, depending on treatment for tax purposes of the interest subsidy in the partnership accounts, the tax shelter created by a 236 project could be more favorable than a similar 221(d)(3) venture. The IRS has not yet clarified this.

'Jumping' partnership: Even without the opportunity to form a partnership with black athletes or entertainers who can use the tax shelter, a developer can still make a piece of the action available to the community through a so-called "jumping" partnership. Here is how it would work:

The partnership might include ghetto residents of modest means, who would be given a nominal interest—say, 10%. Since most of the tax shelter advantages will be realized by about the tenth year—and at that point certain tax recapture provisions will have run out—the partnership agreement would provide for automatic transfer of all or a large portion of the high tax-bracket partners' interest to the 10% partner early in the eleventh year.

Such a transfer would of course occur without payment to the 90% partner. However, this probably does not represent much of a sacrifice in terms of capital gains, since it is difficult at the outset to place a high residual value 10 years in the future on partnership interests in rehabilitation projects. (Section 236 allows limited dividend projects to be sold to nonprofit entities with enough increase in the mortgage to provide the sellers with much of the cost required to pay their taxes.)

The financing available under the National Housing Act provides other advantages. For one, only property in the project itself is subject to the mortgage lien; it does not extend to the general or limited partners beyond their initial investment. Therefore the equity in one project cannot be pledged to support the indebtedness of another project. This prevents pyramiding of the type that led to the downfall of at least one major real estate enterprise in the past decade.

RATIONALE FOR INVOLVEMENT

Over drinks at the club or on the way to the airport at the day's end, after a tour of the rehabilitated apartments, we turn our visitors back to the motivation for their visit. It came, they say, from a nagging feeling that their company ought to be tackling some of the problems of our society, and the sneaking suspicion that perhaps they might also make money at it.

It is true that there is a great need for business to establish its legitimacy as an influential social institution in a society that has begun reexamining all of its perceived premises and challenging all of its conventional wisdom. A well-conceived program of residential property rehabilitation seems to offer a company a highly visible opportunity to express its compassion while demonstrating its business competence.

In our own instance, since the time we finally got BURP back on track, our efforts have drawn extensive and continuing favorable publicity and also have shown a reasonable profit. They have not only helped to rehouse one seventh of the black citizens in our franchised territory, but they have also brought considerable pride and satisfaction to many of our employees and helped greatly in attracting an unusually high quality of young executive recruits. The project has even brought some investment in both our equity and debt securities by colleges which feared, perhaps, that their portfolios might be challenged by their students "in this increasingly questioning age," as one college treasurer put it.

What, then, out of all our studies of other projects and our experience in BURP, do we recommend to these visitors? We arm all of them with a barely portable library on BURP and on housing, but the advice we give is explicit: Stay out of it unless you're willing to work as hard and tenaciously at it as at any important business problem. Stay out of it unless you can answer the hard questions we've asked and unless you're prepared to provide enough of the right kind of staff for it.

Under existing social conditions, rehabilitating occupied lower-income residential property can be likened to performing a major operation without being able to anesthetize the patient. It is no game for amateurs, and anyone who approaches the operating table with warm compassion but without trained competence will soon prove to be both a quack and a failure.

Nevertheless, it has become increasingly clear that large companies which make the same preparations that they would for a venture into a new territory or with a new product can succeed in the once-unknown terrain of the low-income areas of our central cities. The successful ones are pragmatic in facing the social issues that inevitably tangle and can destroy the best-intentioned efforts.

Companies willing to take some financial and public relations risks, willing to train their own staffs to participate in the problem solving, and willing to depend on outside consultation for sensitizing themselves to the problems — those companies, and only those, are ready to plunge into residential rehabilitation on a scale commensurate with their resources.

Companies unwilling to do these things but concerned about the crisis of the cities should just send money. But such money won't buy what most of the bright young people you are hoping to recruit are seeking: a sense of belonging to an organization that has the compassion to direct its capacities toward the crisis of our cities and that also has the intelligence and energy to do it within the framework of the free enterprise system.

The real challenge is to do good for society while doing well for your business. You can concentrate on increasing your sales and earnings, you can build your plants in relatively remote suburban areas inaccessible to the black ghetto. Thus for a while you may divorce yourself from a chance to help your country in a time of grave crisis and, indeed, from a chance to participate in one of the most challenging business adventures in the world today.

Justice Oliver Wendell Holmes, Jr. put the issue accurately when he said: "Life is action and passion. I think it is required of a man that he should share the action and passion of his time at peril of being judged not to have lived."

NOTES

[1] President's Committee on Urban Housing, *A Decent Home*, report submitted December 11, 1968, pp. 7-8.
[2] Ibid., p. 21.
[3] Robert C. Weaver, "Preserving Neighborhoods," an address at Freedom House, Boston, December 4, 1967.
[4] *Mastery of the Metropolis* (Englewood Cliffs, New Jersey, Prentice-Hall, Inc., 1962), pp. 148-149.
[5] Curtis Berger, Eli Goldston, and Guido A. Rothrauff, Jr., "Slum Area Rehabilitation by Private Enterprise," *Columbia Law Review*, May 1969, p. 739.

TRANSPORTATION AND POVERTY

John F. Kain and John R. Meyer

Widespread concern about the problems of poverty and race has led to a proliferation of schemes for reducing the unemployment, increasing the incomes, and generally improving the well-being of disadvantaged groups in our society. Prominent among these are several that would use transportation to increase the employment opportunites of the poor. The concept that inadequate transportation must be numbered among the disadvantages of the poor and that improved mobility, particularly as it improves access to jobs, could increase their self-sufficiency was publicized widely in the aftermath of the Watts riots in 1965. The McCone Commission report on the causes of the riots concluded that "the most serious immediate problem [facing] the Negro in our community is employment. . . ." The commission suggested that, although a serious lack of skill and overt discrimination are major causes of high Negro unemployment, inadequate and costly public transportation also limit Negro employment opportunities:

Our investigation has brought into clear focus the fact that the inadequate and costly public transportation currently existing throughout the Los Angeles area seriously restricts the residents of the disadvantaged areas such as south central Los Angeles. This lack of adequate transportation handicaps them in seeking and holding jobs, attending schools, shopping and fulfilling other needs. (California Governor's Commission on the Los Angeles Riots, *Violence in the City—An End or a Beginning?* (Los Angeles, 1965), p. 65.

The McCone Commission, therefore, recom-

Reprinted from *The Public Interest,* No. 18 (Winter 1970), pp. 75-87, by permission of the authors and the publisher. Copyright 1970 by National Affairs, Inc.

mended that public transit services in Los Angeles be expanded and subsidized. (Its report was strangely silent about the possibility of improving access to jobs by reducing segregation in the housing market.) This recommendation attracted considerable public attention, and the federal government, through the Department of Housing and Urban Development, has sponsored some demonstration projects designed to ascertain if better and more extensive transit services between ghettos and employment centers would yield additional jobs for ghetto residents. The entire subject is very fashionable. But it is astonishing how little knowledge lies behind the popular political opinions it provokes.

A NEW PROBLEM?

In light of the new public awareness of the relation between poverty and transportation, it is appropriate to ask whether the problem itself is new. Obviously, poverty is no new problem; nor is it a growing problem. But when the relation between transportation and poverty is examined, it becomes apparent that something *is* new. Postwar changes in urban ecology and transportation systems, while conferring significant improvements on the majority, have almost certainly caused a *relative* deterioration in the access to job opportunities enjoyed by a significant fraction of the poor.

To be sure, many, if not most, poor continue to live in centrally located residential areas; and these are reasonably well served by public transit to the central business district, where one usually finds the highest density of job opportunities. But in the past two decades, new job opportunities have grown more swiftly *outside* this central business district. It is estimated that there may be 100,000 fewer low-income jobs in New York City than there are low-income workers. A similar pattern has apparently emerged in several other American cities. Living in a neighborhood well served by public transit to the central business district is therefore less of an advantage for lower-income groups today than it once was.

THE AUTOMOBILE AND THE POOR

Reflecting these and other changes in the post-war pattern of American urban living, the total number of passenger trips by mass transit has declined in every year since World War II. Much of the early post-war decline must be viewed against the abnormal conditions of wartime, when transit use was artificially swollen by restrictions on automobile use; transit patronage in 1953 was almost the same as in 1940 or 1941. But the decline in transit use has continued well past 1953, and today transit patronage is about two-thirds of what it was in 1940 or 1953, in spite of a considerable growth in urban population during the past decade.

This can be explained by the fact that a growing proportion of the urban population chooses to travel by automobile. To a considerable extent this results from steadily expanding auto ownership. In 1950, 6 out of every 10 United States households owned one or more private automobiles. By 1967, the figure was nearly 8 out of every 10. But of family units with incomes between $2,000 and $2,999 before taxes, only 53 per cent owned an automobile in 1967. The percentage of those with autos in the below-$2,000 bracket is, of course, much lower still.

The low levels of auto ownership among the poor reflect the fact that the automobile, though a near necessity in much of urban America, is a very expensive one. The high initial capital outlay and operating costs of a private automobile are a heavy strain on the budgets of low-income households. In general, then, when adequate transit services are available, low-income households can and do obtain substantial savings by foregoing auto ownership.

The acquisition of an efficient private auto-mobile (one without exorbitant maintenance costs) requires considerable financing, a chronic difficulty for the poor. Poor people, therefore, even when they own cars, generally own poor cars. Many of these are inadequate for long-distance commutation and expressway operation. Often they are also uninsured. Thus, statistics on car ownership among the poor, as adverse as they are, may paint a more favorable picture than is actually justified.

The dependence on public transit by the urban poor therefore continues to be very great. In the New York region, for example, less than 25 per cent of the households earning under $1,000 per year in 1963 used private automobiles to reach work; over 75 per cent used some form of transit. The proportions using automobiles were 57 per cent for those with incomes between $4,000 and $10,000 and 62 per cent for those with incomes over $10,000 per year.

Transit managements have made some effort to offset the steady decline in transit use by developing new markets. They have done this mainly by expanding route miles or services offered. The route miles of rapid and grade-separated rail transit service has increased about 2 per cent since 1945 and soon will increase further as new rail rapid transit systems under construction are completed. Route miles of all kinds of transit service, bus and rail, have risen nearly 20 per cent since 1955. In the same period, however, transit operators have curtailed the vehicle (revenue) miles of services offered by 20 per cent in response to decreases in ridership. To some extent this decline in vehicle miles of service has been offset by the use of larger vehicles with more seats. Nevertheless, the overall effect has been a reduction in the frequency and, therefore, the basic quality of the service rendered. In general, reductions in service offerings have been most severe on weekends and other off-peak periods (particularly evenings) and for commuter trains.

TRANSIT TO SUBURBAN JOBS

The effectiveness of the additional route miles, moreover, has been less than it might have been because modern bus transit tends to follow the same routes as the old streetcar lines. This means that a high percentage of services in most cities converge on the central business district. For an individual to make a trip from one point at the periphery of a city to another point at the periphery usually requires taking one radial line into the central business district and then transferring to another line to make the trip out to his destination. This arrangement tends to be costly for both operators and users. Bus lines operating through a central business district encounter congestion, with all that entails for increasing operating costs. For the user wanting to make a trip from one peripheral urban location to another, the radial trip to and from the CBD means a much longer and more time-consuming journey than is geographically necessary. Commuters at all income levels, therefore, tend to use automobiles for such trips. Even the poor tend to do so whenever they can make the necessary arrangements, either by owning an inexpensive car or by joining a carpool.

In general, conventional transit is at a performance disadvantage compared to driving or carpooling when serving thinly-traveled, long-distance routes between central city residences and suburban workplaces. Even when available, the transit service is often too little and too slow to compete with the automobile. Moreover, such transit service can impose dollars-and-cents handicaps that go beyond the direct costs in money and time of the commuter's trip itself. For example, conventional transit often adapts to limited demand by providing only peak-hour service between the suburban work places and centrally located residential areas. The worker must either catch the bus when it leaves exactly at closing time, or find some other mode of transportation, often at considerable additional expense. This means that the worker who depends on public transit cannot easily accept overtime employment. The unavailability of a worker for overtime work not only denies him a lucrative opportunity, but can involve costs to his employer as well. Limited public transit scheduling, for example, can make it difficult for the employer to stagger shifts or closing hours. (And staggered closing hours can be helpful in solving such other transportation problems as traffic congestion at peak commuter hours.)

It is therefore not surprising that transit operators serving suburban plants report that low-income workers frequently use transit only when obtaining their jobs and for the first few days or weeks of employment. Once the workers manage to save enough for the down payment on a car, or become acquainted with some fellow workers living near them, they drive to work or join a carpool. *If this is a common pattern, existing transit services may indeed be serving a critical function for low-income households, but one whose value is badly gauged by the fare box or by aggregate statistics on transit use.*

The basic problem, however, remains: efficient transit requires that large numbers of persons travel between the same two points at approximately the same time. The growing dispersal of workplaces and residences means that this condition is satisfied less frequently than before. As jobs, and particularly blue-collar jobs, have shifted from areas that are relatively well served by public transit to areas that are poorly served, employment opportunities for low-income households dependent on public transit service have been reduced. Increasingly, low-income workers are forced to choose between a higher-paying job that is inaccessible by public transit, and thereby pay more for transportation (e.g., by buying and operating an automobile), or a lower-paying job that is served by transit. To put it in somewhat different terms, low-income households now have at their disposal at most only a bit more, and oftentimes less, transit service than they once did for reaching what is, in effect, a much larger metropolitan region.

THE PROBLEM OF RACE

The dispersal of the job market and the decline of transit systems have created particular difficulties for low-income Negroes. If the job of a low-income white worker shifts to the suburbs, he is usually able to follow it by moving to a new residence. If not, he may be able to relocate his residence to be near a transit line serving his new suburban workplace reasonably well. The low-income Negro worker, however, may not be so fortunate. Regardless of his income or family situation, if his job moves to the suburbs, he may find it difficult to move out of the ghetto. That is, his residence may not easily follow his job to the suburbs. For him, the service characteristics, coverage, and cost of the transportation system can therefore be especially critical.

Unfortunately, conventional transit systems usually do not provide adequate services between the ghetto and suburban workplaces. The black worker, confined to ghetto housing near but not directly at the urban core, cannot readily reach many new suburban job locations by simple reverse commuting on existing transit systems. Existing public transit tends to connect suburban *residential* locations with the very core of the central business district; it may not pass through, or even near, new suburban industrial or office parks, just as it may also fail to pass through the ghetto.

If the ghetto resident is able to reach a suburban workplace at all by public transit, the trip may be expensive. If he is lucky, he may be able to join a carpool with a fellow worker and share the considerable expense of a long-distance auto trip from the ghetto. Here, too, the limitations on his residential options and the remoteness of most suburban workplaces from the ghetto reduce the possibilities of him making an advantageous arrangement.

THE POLICY QUESTIONS

Despite the public discussion and federally financed experiments that followed publication of the McCone Commission report, virtually nothing has been done so far to establish a factual basis for evaluating the utility of improved transportation in reducing urban poverty and unemployment. In particular, answers must be found to a number of questions. What effects do existing transportation policies have on income distribution? Are they the ones that were anticipated? Can transportation policy be an effective tool for expanding the opportunities and increasing the welfare of the disadvantaged? Should transportation be used this way? If so, what specific policies and programs should be adopted for achieving these purposes?

JOBS AND TRANSPORTATION

Inferior access to new jobs is by no means the only disadvantage of the ghetto resident. Indeed, in terms of his participation in the labor market, it may be much less important than other factors.

Thomas Floyd, who was deeply involved in the administration of demonstration projects in Watts and elsewhere, notes: "There is . . . reason to believe that some employers were using the transportation barrier as a convenient excuse for not hiring for other reasons. In addition to racial bias, there may be presumed or actual inadequate job skills or work habits". When the improved transportation services were provided, he observed, the jobs did not always materialize.

If transportation is but one of many factors influencing job opportunities, provision of more or cheaper transportation *by itself* is probably an inefficient method of reducing unemployment or increasing incomes. Effective measures to increase the opportunities, employment, and incomes of the long-term unemployed or underemployed must operate simultaneously on several fronts. Training, education, counseling, placement, and transportation programs complement one another. Most or all of these programs should have a role in any well-designed assault on employment problems, and any one of these programs in isolation could well fail because it lacked other essential services. On the other hand, simply putting all these programs into effect simultaneously would not guarantee results either. The different programs must be properly articulated and synthesized.

INCOME REDISTRIBUTION AND TRANSPORTATION

Subsidies for urban transportation have long enjoyed wide support on the ground that such subsidies help the poor. In spite of the fact that the poor generally are more reliant on transit than the rich, the truth of this proposition is less than self-evident.

Advocates of public transit subsidies need to be discriminating if the subsidies they support are actually to aid the poor. Many proposed new systems, such as the BART system in San Francisco and the transit extensions in Boston, will provide only nominal benefits for the poor. In fact, it is probable that both systems will have a highly regressive impact. They are to be subsidized out of the property tax, which is heavily regressive; and virtually all of the benefits will accrue to high-income, long-distance commuters traveling between high-income suburbs and central employment centers. They will do practically nothing to improve accessibility between centrally located ghettos and suburban employment centers.

In general, users of high-speed, long-distance rail commuter systems are among the wealthier classes of society. Local bus systems, by contrast, frequently serve large numbers of low-income users. Paradoxically, these local bus services rarely require large public subsidies. In fact, the available evidence suggests that local bus systems serving low-income and dense central city neighborhoods often make a profit, and often subsidize unprofitable long-distance commuter systems serving low-density, high-income neighborhoods.

Another anomalous fact is that a disporportionate number of taxi trips are made by poor persons. The explanation apparently is that many locations are simply inaccessible to carless households except by taxi. For many of the poor, occasional use of taxicabs as a supplement to transit and to walking is relatively economical compared with automobile ownership.

New York provides contrasting figures that illustrate this point. In New York, poor households do *not* make proportionately more taxi trips than middle-income families. The reason is that a smaller proportion of middle- and upper-income families own automobiles in New York than elsewhere. Moreover, the public transit system is much more extensive in New York than in most other cities and is thus a better substitute for taxicabs. In small cities and towns, however, taxicabs are sometimes the only form of public transit available to the poor. In these instances the poor and infirm may be almost the only users of taxicabs—because everyone else drives.

Thus, the apparently simple question of which income groups use which modes of transportation is a good deal more complex than is commonly imagined. Such hasty generalizations as "taxicabs are a luxury used only by the very rich"; "automobile ownership is limited to the well-to-do"; and "transit is used only by the poor" fail to hold up under scrutiny.

The mobility and transport choices of different income groups could be discussed more cogently if we had better measures of urban mobility. Unfortunately, the usual measure of "tripmaking" used in metropolitan transportation studies is poorly suited for defining mobility differences between different income classes. By definition, only vehicle trips (transit, truck, taxi, or automobile) and walk-to-work trips are counted as trips; walking trips other than those made to and from work are omitted. On average, such noncommuter walking trips are probably of far greater importance in low-income than in high-income neighborhoods. Poor people more often than higher-income people live in high-density neighborhoods where shopping, recreation, and employment are located close to home. Many trips that must be made by auto or transit in low density areas can conveniently be made by foot in high-density neighborhoods. Whether this means, as some believe, that the poor should be considered less mobile is not entirely clear.

In general, almost no data exist that describe how persons of different life styles, living at different urban densities and income levels, solve their personal transportation problems. Moreover, there is no hard information to demonstrate the existence of large and unfulfilled latent demands for alternative forms of transportation. Information on such matters is crucial for designing programs to improve the mobility of the poor and for evaluating the benefits of such programs as against their costs. Yet, to date, the information simply has not been gathered.

INDIRECT COSTS

Most observers agree that the indirect and secondary costs of major transportation investment, such as urban expressways and rapid transit, have not been given adequate consideration when choosing locations and alignment, designing facilities, and deciding whether construction is justified at all. At least two major kinds of such costs can be identified.

First, there are uncompensated costs imposed on individuals—residents, property owners, and businessmen—who are forced to move. These uncompensated costs commonly include not only the direct money outlays for moving but also losses engendered by destruction of cherished friendships, familiar environments, business relationships, and other intangibles.

Second, there are collective costs. These consist of adverse changes in the neighborhood or environment and largely affect those who are *not* required to move. It is sometimes remarked that the owners whose property is taken by eminent domain are often the lucky ones. Those located nearby, but not within, the right-of-way frequently suffer disruption and loss of value for which they receive no compensation. There can be no doubt that the building of a major highway or transit line through a residential area causes fundamental changes to the neighborhood. These changes may be either beneficial or harmful— quite often, they are both.

There is some evidence that the disruption may be greater if the highway or transit line is put through a tightly knit working-class community as opposed to a middle-class area. Some observers have argued that the working-class family is more immobile than the middle-class family, and more tightly linked to an extended family that typically lives within walking distance. If true, when a decision is made to carry out construction in a working-class neighborhood, greater aid may be needed to compensate displaced residents and to assist the reconstruction of their environment.

Unfortunately, few operational tools are available for improving route selection decisions by taking such broader social considerations into account. To do so, several hard questions must be faced. How much community-wide benefit from construction of a road should be sacrificed for these neighborhood and individual values? Can cash payments of whatever amount compensate residents for the real character of their loss? If they cannot reconstruct their present environment, would adequate resources allow the displaced to construct a different but equally satisfactory or better environment? Is the problem in question essentially unique, or is it typical of all or most low-income communities? If it is typical, the road builders' options are, of course, limited. Almost any alignment would impose comparable costs on the affected communities. The range of choice is then narrowed to whether the road should be built, which remedial actions should be taken to limit the displacement or damage, and how generously the damaged population should be compensated.

Existing compensation formulas and mecha-nisms, unfortunately, fail to compensate many losers altogether and provide many others with grossly inadequate compensation. These inadequacies are responsible for much of the current resistance to urban transportation construction. A few individuals are often required to bear a disproportionately large share of the costs of urban transportation improvements in order to provide benefits for all. In these circumstances, spontaneous community action to oppose the new construction is hardly surprising.

PROPOSED SOLUTIONS

Perhaps the most ambitious proposal for improving urban transportation services for the poor is to make public transit free, thereby eliminating income as a determinant of transit use. Clearly, though, this is inefficient. A large proportion of transit users are not poor, and free transit would subsidize the affluent as well as the poor. Moreover, the major difficulty facing the poor, and particularly the ghetto poor, is not that transit is too expensive, but that it is all too frequently unavailable in forms and services that are needed. In general, transit use seems far more sensitive to service improvements than to fare reductions, even for the poor. Nor is "free" transit particularly cheap. It has been estimated that, nationwide, the costs of free transit would be approximately $2 billion a year, assuming no increase in service.

Boston can be used to illustrate the comparative costs of free transit and service improvements for the poor. Until very recently, access between Boston's Roxbury ghetto and rapidly expanding suburban employment centers has been nonexistent for all practical purposes. The costs of providing transit services between all Boston's poverty areas (i.e., census tracts with median family incomes below $5,500 per year) and low-skill employment centers has been estimated at about $4.3 million annually. This is to be compared with an estimate of $75 million a year for free transit in Boston. The $4.3 million figure is, moreover, a total or gross cost; it would be less if any fare box revenues were realized. Furthermore, the million subsidy for free transit would not provide any significant improvement in transit service between central city poverty areas and suburban employment centers.

An increasingly popular view is that public transit systems, as currently constituted, are incapable of increasing the mobility of the poor. The argument is that the transportation demands involved in serving outlying workplaces from central city residences are too complex to be met adequately by any kind of public transit services at costs that are competitive with private automobiles. At two persons per car, for example, the cost of private automobile operation often is comparable to or lower than bus transportation in serving dispersed workplaces.

If so, it may be cheaper and more effective to provide some form of personal transportation for the poor. One such proposal, which its originator terms "new Volks for poor folks," is to rent, lease, or otherwise finance new or relatively new cars for low-income households. Cheap used cars are seldom low-cost cars. If the cost of automobile use is to be reduced for low-income groups, their cars must be relatively new; if they are to have such new cars, the cost of credit must be lowered. A related proposal is to assist those workers who live in central ghettos and work in the suburbs to sell transportation services to fellow workers. Such sales would help pay the purchase and operating costs of an automobile. In many cities, however, this proposal would encounter a number of institutional and legal barriers.

Of course, new cars for poor people will not help nondrivers, who are now estimated to make up 20 percent of the population over 17 years of age. In fact, any extension of automobile ownership among the able-bodied poor may only serve to further degrade public transit services for nondrivers. To provide mobility for nondrivers, some have advocated the development of so-called demand actuated systems. Different versions of this concept come under a variety of names or acronyms, including Taxi-bus, Dial-a-bus, DART, GENIE, and CARS. In all cases, however, the idea is to provide something approximating the point-to-point service of taxis, while achieving better utilization levels and load factors than transit vehicles can now achieve on fixed routes and schedules.

In these systems, vehicles intermediate in size between a taxicab and a conventional bus would be used to pick up and deliver passengers at specific origins and destinations. By use of electronic control and scheduling, it is claimed, loads could be assembled with a minimum of delay. Proponents believe these systems usually would have cost characteristics intermediate between the conventional bus and the taxicab. By providing more individualistic door-to-door service than public transit, these systems might be of particular use for the elderly and the infirm. Furthermore, if such systems have the advantages suggested, they might be a better and more politically acceptable solution to the problems of ghetto access than subsidies to extend ownership of private automobiles, particularly in older cities with high density central residential neighborhoods.

Indeed, were it not for franchise restrictions and prohibitions on group fares, taxicabs could improve their operating efficiency considerably without any technological improvements. Demand-activated systems are functionally identical with taxis, but have more sophisticated scheduling, control devices, and operating policies.

Indeed, many benefits would accrue to the poor if there were fewer restrictions on the provision of taxi and jitney services. A deregulated taxi industry would provide a considerable number of additional jobs for low-income workers. It has been calculated that removing entry barriers and other controls might expand the number of taxis by as much as two and a half times in most American cities. In Philadelphia, for example, deregulation could create an additional 7,400 jobs for drivers alone; if these jobs went to the poorest 20 per cent of the population, unemployment among these poor would fall by about 3.2 percentage points.

Taxi operation can also be an important income supplement for low-income households even where it is not a full-time job. A significant number of Washington's taxi drivers own and operate their own cabs on a part-time basis as a supplement to a regular job. The off-duty cab often doubles as the family car, thus substantially reducing the cost of auto ownership and increasing the mobility of residents of low-income neighborhoods.

A much expanded taxi and jitney industry could also provide an appreciable increase in urban mobility, particularly for the poor. Except for restrictive legislation, jitneys and taxicabs might now be providing a significant fraction of passenger service in urban areas. The greater number of taxis per hundred persons in Washington, D.C., an essentially unregulated city, and the sizable capital value of medallions (franchises to operate a cab) in New York, Boston, and several other cities, attest to a substantial latent demand for these services.

In short, simply providing larger subsidies to transit systems is unlikely to be an effective way of increasing the mobility of the poor. New systems seem needed, and there is some agreement on their characteristics. Such systems would normally use a smaller vehicle than conventional transit, would be demand activated rather than on fixed routes and schedules, and would provide point-to-point service or some close approximation of it. Such systems would most likely have somewhat lower passenger mile costs than do taxicabs (even those operating in unrestricted markets like Washington), but unit costs probably would be somewhat above those of current transit systems. In some instances, such services might merely supplement the more heavily used transit services; in others, they might replace such services altogether.

Ownership of these more ubiquitous systems might vary from place to place and from time to time. Where elaborate control and scheduling are required, a fleet might be necessary. In other instances, the services could be provided by large numbers of owner-operators working either independently or in a cooperative. Another possibility is nothing more complicated than organized carpooling, compensated or uncompensated.

Most such systems require very little long-lived investment. The most extensive capital requirements, of course, would be for the more elaborate, electronically controlled, demand activated systems. All would require major changes in institutions and regulatory frameworks. Fortunately, however, most also lend themselves to experimentation on a modest scale. Such experimentation could do much to improve our fund of information, which at this point is simply inadequate to support bolder policy initiatives.

ADDITIONAL READINGS FOR CHAPTER 10

Charles Abrams, *The City Is the Frontier* (New York: Harper & Row, Publishers, 1965).

David L. Birch, *The Businessman and the City* (Boston: Harvard University Graduate School of Business Administration, 1967).

Building the American City, Report of the National Commission on Urban Problems to the Congress and to the President of the United States, 91st Congress, 1st Senior (Washington, D.C.: U.S. Government Printing Office, 1969).

"The Conscience of the City," *Daedalus,* V. 97, N. 11 (Fall 1968).

A Decent Home, Report of the President's Committee on Urban Housing, December 11, 1968 (Washington, D.C.: U.S. Government Printing Office, 1969).

Anthony Downs, "Moving Toward Realistic Housing Goals," in Kennet Gordon (ed.), *Agenda for the Nation* (Washington, D.C.: The Brookings Institution, 1968), pp. 141-178.

Leonard F. Duhl (ed.), *The Urban Condition: People and Policy in the Metropolis* (New York: Simon and Schuster, 1963).

Richard W. Epps, "Suburban Jobs and Black Workers," Federal Reserve Bank of Philadelphia *Business Review,* (October 1969), pp. 3-13.

Webb S. Fiser, *Mastery of the Metropolis* (Englewood Cliffs, N.J.: Prentice-Hall, 1962).

George and Eunice Grier, *Equality and Beyond: Housing Goals and the Great Society* (Chicago: Quadrangle Books, 1966).

Chester W. Hartiman and Gregg Carr, "Housing the Poor," *Trans-action,* V. 7, N. 2 (December 1969), pp. 49-53.

Michael Harrington, "Can Private Industry Abolish Slums?" *Dissent,* V. 15, N. 1 (January-February 1968), pp. 4-6.

George K. Hesslink, *Black Neighbors: Negroes in a Northern Rural Community* (Indianapolis: The Bobbs-Merrill Company, 1968).

Jane Jacobs, *The Economy of Cities* (New York: Random House, 1969).

Verle Johnson, "Housing: Old Problems," *Federal Reserve Bank of San Francisco Monthly Review* (June 1970), pp. 125-129.

John F. Kain and John J. Persky, "Alternatives to the Gilded Ghetto," *The Public Interest,* N. 14 (Winter 1969) pp. 74-87.

Robert F. Kennedy, *To Seek a Newer World,* 2nd ed. (New York: Bantam Books, 1968).

Walter McQuade, "Mortgages for the Slums," *Fortune,* V. LXXVII, N. 1 (January 1968), pp. 162-163.

Harvey S. Perloff and Lowdon Wingo, Jr. (eds.), *Issues in Urban Economics.* (Baltimore, Md.: Published for Resources for the Future, Inc, by The Johns Hopkins Press, 1968).

Everett O. Robinson and John D. Johnston, Jr. (eds.), "Housing Part I: Perspectives and Problems, A Symposium," *Law and Contemporary Problems,* V. 32, N. 2 (Spring 1967), pp. 187-370.

Arnold Schucter, "Conjoining Black Revolution and

Private Enterprise," *White Power / Black Freedom: Planning the Future of Urban America* (Boston: Beacon Press, 1968), pp. 308-321.

Morton J. Schussheim, "Housing in Perspective," *The Public Interest,* No. 19 (Spring 1970), pp. 18-30.

Wallace F. Smith, *Housing, the Social and Economic Aspects* (Berkeley and Los Angeles: University of California Press, 1970).

Wilbur R. Thompson, *A Preface to Urban Economics,* (Baltimore, Md.: Published for Resources for the Future, Inc., by The Johns Hopkins Press, 1965).

Urban America: Goals and Problems, Subcommittee on Urban Affairs of the Joint Economic Committee, U.S. Congress (Washington, D.C.: U.S. Government Printing Office, 1967), pp. 292-303.

Urban America, Inc., *Development Forum-5* (Washington, D.C.: Urban America, Inc., October 27 and 28, 1968.)

Irvin H. Welfeld, "Toward a New Housing Policy," *The Public Interest,* N. 19 (Spring 1970), pp. 31-43.

As is true in the case of other areas of interface of the business and black communities, the inadequate performance of financial institutions in the ghetto emanates from a variety of sources, two of the most important being the economics of poverty and discrimination.

In the prologue to Chapter 7, we specified the most critical factors contributing to the credit drought which has existed in black communities. To summarize briefly: to the extent that black people are poor people, they suffer from the unwillingness of lending institutions to assume the risks and incur the costs of making small loans to low-income people. The only partial exception occurs, as we have seen, in the installment contract situation. The black ghetto businessman or the prospective homeowner has had virtually no reputable source of funds available to him. The economics of poverty operates against the black in the area of finance just as it does in the housing field.

Concerning discrimination, many lenders have taken the position that "black people just don't know how to handle money" in refusing categorically to make any but installment credit available to blacks. (In the installment credit situation the item for which credit is extended can be repossessed and sold to repay the loan.) Thus, irrespective of the personal and financial background of the prospective borrower and the purpose of the requested loan, blacks have been virtually excluded by their blackness from credit. Similarly, as we saw, insurance companies have often refused to provide coverage for black homes, black businesses and, at one time, even black lives. In many large cities today, black neighborhoods are still excluded ("red-lined") from coverage.

In some cases, public policy has provided tacit and even active support for inequitable treatment by the business community of black Americans. For example, in the past, public policy supported segregated housing by enforcing so-called "restrictive covenants" precluding sales of protected real estate to blacks and other minority group members, and tolerated discriminatory business behavior in the area of employment. Recently, however, some significant changes in public policy have occurred in employment, with enactment and rudimentary enforcement of equal employment opportunity legislation, and housing, with the passage of fair housing acts. These changes have had some impact in improving the operation of housing and employment markets by eliminating state sanction of discriminatory practices and providing pressure for alteration of traditional business practices.

Public policy is beginning to make a comparable impact on the operation of financial institutions in the ghetto. Truth-in-lending laws and the increasing willingness of courts to negate "unconscionable contracts" and to apply restrictions to the right of creditors to garnish or attach the wages of debtors are signs of an increasingly aggressive thrust of public policy into the regulation of financial institutions and their impact on the black (and other poor) communities. Some federal agencies, including the Small Business Administration, the Economic Development Administration in the Department of Commerce, the Office of Economic Opportunity, and the Model Cities Program in the Department of Housing and Urban Development, have provided small amounts of credit for black business enterprises, although these efforts, in terms of federal dollars committed, have been minimal in light of the critical need which exists. In summary, public policy, while changing somewhat, continues to lag in this area.

Because of the vast sums of moneys needed for significant improvement in the operation of financial institutions in the ghetto, new policy approaches on the part of federal and state authorities are imperative. Accordingly, most proposals for significant business initiatives in improving the flow of credit into the ghetto and for providing badly needed insurance coverage usually are interwoven with suggestions for changes in governmental policy regarding these problems. One approach was suggested by Senator William Proxmire in the Community Credit Expansion Act of 1969 which he introduced in the U.S. Senate. In the Act, Senator Proxmire proposed the establishment of a National Development Bank to increase the flow of credit to urban and rural poverty areas, and provided incentives for existing financial institutions to expand the amount of credit which they make available to these areas. The proposal was never enacted into law.[1]

In the first selection in this chapter, "Categorical Credit Incentives: A Statement," Theodore L. Cross, former editor of *Banker's Magazine* and a governmental advisor on minority business enterprise, proposes a variety of credit incentives—federally supported lending techniques administered by banks. These incentives are designed to promote liquidity, reduce risks, stimulate corporate deposits in slum area banks, build savings and thrift accounts in ghetto banks, form credit development corporations, and otherwise free the flow of "the mother's milk of business enterprise in the ghetto economy." When banks can offer credit at reasonable risk, they will do so at reasonable rates, Cross reasons. At such time as public policy and legitimate lending activity can facilitate a stronger flow of credit in the ghetto, the loan sharks, who now thrive, should be deprived of much of the function they now perform.

In "Conjoining Black Revolution and Private Enterprise," Arnold Schuchter examines the role that private industry can, and, in his opinion, should play in economic development within minority communities in terms of increasing the availability of capital for the establishment and growth of black enterprise. His discussion is especially valuable because of the emphasis he places on the combined role of business activity, governmental policy, and minority community decision making in enhancing the economic base of the ghetto.

The final reading, "The Provision of Insurance," is drawn from the Report of the President's National Panel on Insurance in Riot-Affected Areas and makes proposals to improve the presently inadequate insurance available to ghetto dwellers. Its recommendations also combine public policy and business action ". . . to assure property owners fair access to property [and other types of] insurance." The report proposes new laws and tax incentives, combined with industry pooling of risks, and better methods of preventing losses and marketing insurance in ghetto areas. Of particular interest is the proposal of a Fair Access to Insurance (FAIR) Plan.

Thus far, there has been some limited implementation of the suggestions made in the readings in this chapter.[2] Banks in a number of cities have begun to institute loan programs to assist black-owned businesses. In a few urban centers, notably San Francisco, Newark, and Philadelphia, a number of banks and industrial concerns have joined forces to provide debt capital for minority business enterprises. Some large business firms have formed Minority Small Enterprise Small Business Investment Companies (MESBICS) under a program instituted by the federal government in late 1969. A MESBIC is a small business investment company created by a corporation or other body with a minimum capital of $150,000 to be matched on a 2 for 1 basis by Small Business Administration funds, to provide a financial base for loans or loan guarantees for minority-owned small businesses. (The MESBIC concept has been criticized as inadequate for providing the large sums of capital needed for the establishment or development of substantial black businesses.)[3] Turning to the area of insurance, Congress provided in the Urban Property Protection and Reinsurance Act of 1968[4] that in order to be eligible for federal reinsurance provided by the legislation an insurance company must participate in the FAIR plan established in each state for which the company seeks federal reinsurance. A number of states have established FAIR plans (a type of "assigned risk" or pooled coverage) for certain categories of insurance coverage in ghetto areas.[5] To date, however, the coverage available under FAIR plans is limited in both amount and type of risk, and does not provide an adequate substitute for a normal insurance market in black neighborhoods.

The above programs are steps in the right direction toward improving the performance of financial institutions within black communities. However, they constitute only a patchwork of governmental and business effort rather than a comprehensive approach to restructuring the financial base of these communities and their inhabitants.

NOTES

[1]The reader is also referred to "GHEDIPLAN: Ghetto Economic Development and Industrialization Plan," by Dunbar S. McLaurin, from *Economic Development Opportunity,* Hearings before the Select Committee on Small Business, United States Senate, 90th Congress, 2d Session, on The Role of the Federal Government in the Development of Small Business Enterprises in the Urban Ghetto, Newark, New Jersey—May 24, 1968, New York, New York—June 17, 1968 (Washington, D.C.: U.S. Government Printing Office, 1968), pp. 245-257. GHEDIPLAN presents a creative approach for joint governmental, private sector, and grassroots efforts in the area of facilitating community economic development.

[2]A number of private sector programs intended to expand credit resources in minority communities are discussed in The Urban Coalition, *Consumer Credit and the Low Income Consumer,* Preliminary Report, researched and written by William G. Kaye and associates, Rockville, Maryland, for the Urban Coalition (November 1969).

[3]Richard S. Rosenbloom and John K. Shanks, "Let's Write Off MESBICS," *Harvard Business Review,* V. 48, N. 5 (September-October 1970), pp. 90-97.

[4]82 Stat. 476 (1968).

[5]For a discussion of the Pennsylvania Fair Plan, see George F. Reed, "The Question of Insurance," *The Business Lawyer,* V. 25, Special Issue (September 1969), pp. 165-172.

CATEGORICAL CREDIT INCENTIVES: A STATEMENT

Theodore L. Cross

CATEGORICAL CREDIT INCENTIVES: NEW LIQUIDITY FOR GHETTO-ORIGIN INSTALLMENT PAPER

A leading New York City bank is currently offering on television "A Red Rose Loan." With the loan proceeds the borrower also receives a red rose. Another bank fatuously offers "A Fairy Godmother Loan," and another "An Aladdin's Lamp Loan."

Banks can't feed out the installment credit fast enough in the normal economy.

There are no "Red Rose Loans" in Bedford Stuyvesant. What steps can be taken to get normal credit moving in the slum where income certainty does not exist, and where few people can sign a bankable unsecured note for five hundred dollars? How do we root out the loan sharks and other legally marginal lenders who destroy any possibility of building a reasonable system of installment credit?

Since the times of Jacob Riis, social workers have urged on us the edict of eliminating profit on credit in the ghetto. They assure us that criminal sanctions are the only method of rooting out the merchant credit-gouger and loan shark who take cruel advantage of the impoverished Negro's desperate desire to possess comforts enjoyed in the outside economy.

The nation's experience with legal prohibition of liquor alone should convince us that criminal penalties for violation of credit laws are almost always futile and naive. Enforced legal ceilings on interest rates do not reduce the

Reprinted from *Financial Institutions and the Urban Crisis*, Hearings Before the Subcommittee on Financial Institutions of the Committee on Banking and Currency, U.S. Senate, 90th Congress, Second Session, on Private Investment in the Inner City, Sept. 30 and Oct. 1-4, 1968, pp. 401-415.

Negro's determination for goods; he merely turns to the credit merchant or to the loan shark who exacts an even higher price for credit as compensation for the risks he assumes of arrest and prison.

When downtown commercial banks, motivated by considerations of social justice, boycott and refuse to discount commercial paper originating with ghetto merchants, the banks simply further freeze the meager patterns of credit in the ghetto economy—in favor of the illegal hip-pocket lender who will always supply the need.

Recent laws, enacted in many states, which restrict the negotiability and liquidity of installment paper taken in so-called "unconscionable" installment purchase transactions, have the same effect of excluding normal credit in the slums. Under these laws, low interest rate lending institutions, unable to distinguish what is and is not an "unconscionable" or fraudulent sale of merchandise, shy away from all commercial paper originating in the ghetto. The loan shark buys the paper and exacts his "toll."

Plainly, the objective is not to destroy the vestiges of low-cost bank credit that remain in the ghetto, but rather to build into the slum the normal patterns of reasonably priced credit that exist in the outside economy.

The approach I suggest is to create new incentives or profit opportunities for lenders which will result in the *export of low-cost credit from the normal economy into the ghetto*. This is achieved by compensating regulated commercial banks and finance companies for the extra credit risk they take in purchasing (discounting) installment loans which originate in poverty areas. If the legitimate lender's extra compensation incentive is sufficient, ghetto installment loans will become attractive to lenders; or at least they will be competitive with the "safe" loans available elsewhere. What bankers refer to as "soft loans" will become hard, negotiable and bankable.

Just as legalized sale of liquor drives out the bootlegger, the inflow into the ghetto of low-cost bank credit must inevitably drive out the credit-gouger and the loan shark whose cost of capital is too high to be competitive.

A bank or other regulated institution which purchases an installment loan contract originating in an eligible poverty area should be entitled to an additional income tax deduction (over and above its normal bad debt reserve deduction). This deduction should, on an annual basis, be equal to six percent of the face amount of the purchased loan. Such an arrangement yields the legitimate lender (normally a commercial bank or finance company in a 50 percent income tax bracket) a *three percent additional, after-tax yield on installment loans originating in ghetto areas*.

The cashier or auditor of the lending bank or finance company would be required to certify under oath, by endorsement on the loan paper, that to his best knowledge:

(a) The loan was made directly to a resident of an eligible poverty area and was secured by a first lien on new or used appliances, automobiles or other hard goods; or

(b) The loan was purchased from an automobile or hard goods dealer in an eligible poverty area and was so certified by the dealer.

The obvious criticism of this form of incentive is that the gouging ghetto appliance dealer is perfectly free not only to overcharge the customer but also privileged to "lay off" the loan on a downtown bank anxiously bidding for the commercial paper because it carries the special tax incentive. I suggest this will not hold true. The credit merchant can presently exact his toll of usurious interest rates (what black militants call the "color tax" because there is a shortage of normally priced credit in the ghetto. As soon as a massive supply of bank installment credit (say six percent discounted in advance) becomes available in the ghetto, it will drive out the credit merchant who will suddenly lose his monopoly over ghetto credit. If it becomes feasible for downtown banks to lend at competitive rates in the ghetto economy, new bank branches will open in the ghetto, and existing branches will

become aggressive lenders. New and normal credit market conditions will inevitably drive out the marginally legal ghetto lender who borrows at a high rate and charges a very high rate. If this precept is wrong, then we should all re-examine our high school texts on the laws of credit, supply and demand.

CATEGORICAL CREDIT INCENTIVES: REDUCING THE RISK ON "SOFT" COMMERCIAL LOANS

My friends on Wall Street tell me how to recognize a downtown money crisis: First mortgages are either unavailable or command interest rates of 12 percent, offerings of real estate move like molasses, business values crumble, risk capital evaporates, and finally grass grows in the streets.

If these conditions describe the Main Street crisis economy of 1933, they also describe actual conditions today in the Watts and Bedford-Stuyvesant ghettos.

In my judgment the *total lack of reasonable patterns of commercial credit is the single great obstacle to building business, commerce and the ownership of capital in the slums*. In the "main-stream economy," as the legend goes, the young man with a business idea borrows money from his rich aunt—probably without interest. In the ghetto economy nobody has a rich aunt—only the friendly ever present hip-pocket lender.

Patterns of discrimination aside, the credit profile of the ghetto business entrepreneur is non-banking because he is invariably undercapitalized and almost always lacks adequate marketing, production and administrative skills. There is no income certainty in his business, something credit men invariably require as a condition to making loans.

The commercial banks in the United States are frequently accused by militant blacks of "skimming off the cream" of commercial loan business and leaving the ghetto entrepreneur to the loan sharks. Skimming the cream is indeed the very business of banking. In the hierarchy of American lending institutions, banks are ordained by law to make low interest cost, almost risk-free, loans.

The risks of non-repayment of slum area business loans and the extra cost of servicing, collateralizing and frequently salvaging them, are so massive that the banker faces the same dilemma as any other businessman who would embark on programs for commercial enrichment of the ghetto. The ghetto economy has amassed such a pernicious array of risks, punishing any effort to introduce credit, *that there is no interest rate which is high enough to permit the banker to lend on a basis which is both fair to the ghetto borrower and to the owners of the bank. No liberalization of the banking laws to permit high risk slum area business loans can change or solve this problem.*

A few innovative banks, such as The First Pennsylvania Banking and Trust Company in Philadelphia, have made superb efforts to move commercial business credit into the ghetto. The successful program of this bank was not built on simple orders to lending officers to make ghetto loans. Negroes do not come into the branches of the First Pennsylvania Bank or into any bank. Nor is it practicable for the bank officers to physically solicit loans in the ghetto areas. The bank has found that the most effective method of implementing its Negro business lending program is to work through a loan clearing house which is located in the ghetto. In Philadelphia, this clearing house consists of a non-profit association organized by a group of Negro businessmen who actively recruit potential businessmen who need credit. The local group examines these loans from the standpoint of feasibility and rejects or recommends them to the bank. The primary function of the bank is to supply credit acting on the recommendation of people on the scene who understand the ghetto's special credit needs and risks.

This is a most effective program for forcing commercial credit into the ghetto. The program takes maximum advantage of the bank's economic power and, at the same time, negates the great disability which all banks share—an inherent reluctance of the loan officer on the platform to make a potentially "soft loan."

The bank takes the risk (actually, this is minor in relation to aggregate bad debt reserves), the bank supplies the capital, and the bank benefits in terms of greater city-wide business with the Negro community.

Negro businessmen need bank credit for all the usual purposes—business start-up expenses, equipment purchases and seasonal inventory requirements. Often, too, the Negro business needs credit for a special purpose which no downtown banker ever heard of.

Bankers in the main economy favor so-called "special purpose" loans, loans for new plant construction, acquisition of machinery or the expansion of markets. These are the loans that enrich and build the economy and are, therefore, often frequently exempted from voluntary credit restraints. However, loans to refund or pay off another loan or for the purpose of acquiring a business make no net addition to the economy and are looked on with less favor when credit is tight. In the ghetto economy there is a special and legitimate need for loans of the second type since slum businesses are often started up with short-term and high-cost credit. For the ghetto business, the interest rate, as we have seen, may be ten percent a week rather than ten percent a year. *Therefore, refunding or "clean up" loans are especially enriching the slum economy.* They should not be viewed with the same skepticism that they receive in banks downtown.[2]

A year or so ago most of the drugstores in Harlem were close to bankruptcy. This condition existed because a very large proportion of drugs purchased in the ghettos of Harlem and South Bronx are paid for under New York City's Medicaid or welfare program. At the time the City was several months behind in its paper work and disbursement. The druggists were stuck with stale customer accounts four or five months old. They carried these accounts receivable by borrowing at exhorbitant rates from the local hip-pocket lenders. Through the brilliant work of McKinsey & Company, Arthur Anderson & Co. and James Talcott, Inc., a refunding loan program was arranged under which the loan sharks were paid off and reasonably priced commercial finance credit was substituted. This incident illustrates that often Negro businessmen need commercial credit, not simply to start a new business, but *to save a perfectly sound existing business which is being strangled by a special and unusual credit need.*

Ironically the Small Business Administration rules have not permitted loans for refinancing small business where other creditors stand to take a loss. The S.B.A. has therefore neglected one of the most urgent commercial credit needs in the ghetto—the refunding loan.

Who are the potential lenders who are in a position to supply commercial business credit in the slum economy? Which institutions do not lend in the ghetto under present conditions—for sound business reasons unrelated to racial discrimination?

The American business economy is sustained by a vast and complicated network of commercial lenders. The twelve thousand commercial banks are the backbone of the system. Obviously the commercial banks operate under stiff regulatory restraints. In general, they make direct business loans only to established businesses having "bankable" credit. Long-term business and real estate loans come more often from the savings banks and life insurance companies—also highly regulated and restricted as to permissible loan risks.

The nation's strong and responsible personal loan companies have found it difficult to lend in slum areas where legal limits on interest rates do not cover the risks and expenses involved in making such loans. In some cases, these finance companies have shown remarkable mastery of skill in making high-risk loans. But the economic anarchy of the ghetto has more often bested them.

A most important group of business lenders are the commercial finance companies. Respected institutions such as James Talcott, Inc. in New York City specialize in high-risk "non-bankable" business loans. These lenders measure business credit risk in terms of interest rates of ten percent and higher. They are considered expert in evaluating the ability of marginal or undercapitalized business to repay a loan.

"Nimble" high-risk secondary lenders have been and are vital to the growth of the American economy. Unlike the bank loan officer who may be tied to tradition, the secondary lender or finance company in the ghetto scene often possesses greater competence in appraising the promise of a business which will be operating in a cultural and economic environment completely remote from his own experience. He possesses the capability of making a loan to an inexperienced Negro businessman and adequately insuring its repayment. He often has special experience in the loan "work-out"—salvaging a loan and a business that is in trouble, a common problem with slum area business loans. These special lending techniques are not acquired at American Bankers Association seminars.

The so-called "secondary lenders" are potentially more effective than commercial banks in operating in the anarchy of a slum economy. It is important that *legitimate secondary lenders be included in any program for introducing business credit into the slum economy.* Otherwise, the Mafia-financed loan sharks move in or retain their hold—and the cost of business credit escalates 1000 percent.

In recent years, some banks have developed an expertise with the high-risk or controlled risk loan. A few banks, like First National City, and Franklin National, in New York, and the First National of Boston, have moved into areas of risk financing which formerly belonged to the secondary lenders and commercial finance companies. Special departments in these and other banks have developed great agility in taking unusual banking risks with appropriate compensation in the form of higher interest rates. Because of such experience, these banks are ideally qualified to establish additional programs of commercial lending to businesses in the disadvantaged areas of their cities. The typically irregular and undercapitalized credit requirements of the ghetto present a rough but valuable proving ground for developing the skills of the loan officer trainee.

However, the hazards of the ghetto economy, and its income uncertainty, are so great that even the most venturesome banks and finance companies commit only taken business loans. Experience certainly teaches that government agencies such as the Small Business Administration cannot be relied on to perform any business or credit function which involves innovation or risk. *An automatic compensation credit incentive, predetermined yet unregulated, is necessary to force vital business credit into slum areas.*

This incentive cannot give the banker the high degree of "income certainty" that his directors and his examiners normally expect of commercial borrowers. The incentive cannot insure the lender against riots, fire or a business failure resulting in non-payment of the loan. However, the incentive goes far in compensating the lender for the extra risks involved, and overcomes many of the legitimate arguments against lending in the slum economy.

I suggest that any regulated lender such as a bank, insurance company or finance company making a loan to a business in an eligible poverty area, should be entitled to an additional income tax deduction (over and above its normal bad debt reserve allowance) on an annual basis of six percent of the face amount of the loan. This special credit incentive follows the pattern of the incentive which I also project for ghetto installment personal loans. It allows the corporate lender, who is normally in a 50 percent income tax bracket, an additional three percent after tax yield on commercial business loans made in eligible ghetto areas.

The special tax credit would be allowed even if the loan is secured by a mortgage—which would be the case for plants and supermarkets. The credit would not be allowed for loans for low-income housing where there is already a federal network of interest subsidies, rent supplements and loan guarantees.

However, the tax credit for loans for ghetto businesses would be allowed any lender who successfully processes a loan guarantee with the Small Business Administration. Such a perseverance should be rewarded with both the incentive and the repayment guarantee.

The application of compensating credit incentives to insurance company lenders, commercial finance companies, and banks—the only sector in our economy capable of supplying the missing link of leverage—is a vital part of my program for categorical corrective credit incentives.

By working toward an "enforced" federally-subsidized export of private commercial credit to the ghetto, we would not be building a separate Negro economy of apartheid, but developing conditions where the now undercapitalized and "underleveraged" businessmen in the slums can acquire the strength to market products in the rest of our economy. In time interest rates on risk credit in the slums of 50-to-250 percent annually will be replaced by those "tight money" rates of 7-to-10 percent that white businessmen now resent downtown. Hopefully, in time, there will be a reciprocating flow of commercial credit from all parts of our cities so that the now vivid distinction between the ghetto credit economy and the mainstream credit economy gradually will become blurred.

CATEGORICAL CREDIT INCENTIVES: STIMULATING CORPORATE DEPOSITS IN SLUM AREA BANKS

At the moment there are isolated examples of large corporations making deposits in ghetto area banks and subscribing to shares of newly organized interracial banks. However, in most cases these corporate programs are simply an act of charity.

The entire economy of the United States supports about 330 billion of bank deposits. There has been no visible shift of these funds to the 50-odd ghetto banking institutions whose total deposits are probably less than several hundred million dollars.

The object is to create conditions under which treasurers of national corporations, controlling billions of demand deposits will actually *need* to move funds into perfectly sound interracial banks operating in ghetto communities.

I suggest a program which is extraordinarily simple and should produce a positive, corrective impact.

I propose that any individual corporation or correspondent bank which maintains a deposit in any bank whose principal office[3] is located in an eligible poverty area[4] (defined as usual by the Secretary of Commerce) would be entitled to an annual federal income tax credit as follows:

(a) *For demand deposits* (non-interest bearing[5])—An annual tax credit for the depositor equal to ¼% of the average daily balance maintained as certified in writing at the end of the depositor's tax year by the cashier of the ghetto bank.

(b) *For time deposits*—An annual income tax credit for the depositing individual corporation or correspondent bank equal to 15% of the established interest rate on the time deposit. The tax credit would be limited to time deposits maintained for one year or more. This time deposit is more enriching to the ghetto economy than the demand deposit, since it more closely approximates permanent capital. This gives the ghetto bank greater flexibility in community loans.

(c) *Negotiable certificates of deposit or investments in ghetto bank debentures* issued by a ghetto bank would entitle the holder or owner at its year end to a tax credit equal to 15% of the established interest rate on the certificate of deposit or debenture.

It is not essential that the ghetto bank depositors be entitled to an increase in the present ceilings on federal insurance of bank deposits. The income tax credit for the depositor may be an adequate incentive to bring fresh capital funds into the ghetto economy. It can also be argued that any increase in federal deposit insurance for ghetto-domiciled banks would result in dislocations in markets for competing government securities and commercial paper.

There are many strongly-capitalized Negro banks. The country's bankers and corporate treasurers are nimble enough to evaluate the strength of the depository bank and do not need extra deposit insurance for their deposits.

The specific corrective tax incentives for deposits in ghetto banks should persuade large metropolitan banks to establish healthy correspondent relations and to move substantial deposit balances into slum-area-owned and controlled banks. The specific incentive should also lure demand and time deposits from the treasurers of the great national corporations. Portfolios managers of life insurance companies and other tax-paying financial institutions[6] will improve their investment performance by acquiring high yield tax-protected debentures issued by ghetto banks. Because of the new tax incentives available to depositors and investors, it is likely that credit markets will establish a low interest rate on debentures or certificates of deposit payable by ghetto banks. *This will give the ghetto bank a lower "cost of capital" and a borrowing cost "edge" which will permit it to lend aggressively in the high credit risk Negro community.*

Even the most progressive and nimble downtown banks have experienced great difficulty in "recruiting" Negro business borrowers. The tax incentive I propose for investments and deposits in resident ghetto banks not only provides new loanable funds for slum lenders, but also automatically delegates lending responsibility to on-the-scene bankers who have a better understanding and relationship with potential borrowers. Under a proper system of corrective and compensating interest rate incentives, money and capital that initially deserted the ghetto at the time of the exodus of the white middle class, and more recently as a result of riots and curfews, should begin to flow back home, chasing *a real and visible profit opportunity*.

CATEGORICAL CREDIT INCENTIVES: BUILDING SAVINGS AND THRIFT ACCOUNTS IN THE GHETTO ECONOMY

At the Negro-owned and controlled Freedom National Bank in the commercial center of Harlem, the average individual savings account (including commercial accounts which increase the average) is $600; but the large majority of the accounts are around $100. At a typical downtown thrift institution—The Dollar Bank for Savings, with branches all over New York City, the average savings account is $2,000 to $3,000.

The obvious point is that the usual generation of capital funds in the form of personal savings does not occur, since the slum dweller lives on an economic ragged edge where all money is spent to satisfy basic needs of human survival.[7] Even where discretionary funds can be squeezed out, the Negro, Puerto Rican, or Mexican-American is not convinced that if he saves today he can earn or spend more tomorrow.

The payment of interest as the conventional incentive to attract savings does not work. For a man who is borrowing from the credit merchants at a rate of 20 percent or more, an interest rate on savings accounts of double the normal 5 percent does not divert money from the numbers operator or make the difference between saving and spending.

Deferred gratification is one of the essential luxuries of the normal economy. The white man has confidence in a stable society; he is confident of his ability to hold a job; he knows his family is secure; he has an opportunity to invest and progress. The resident of the ghetto may also know that, in America, personal progress in business has frequently been the easiest route to social progress. Yet even if he puts money aside for savings, there still remain those crushing patterns of unequal business opportunity that stand in the way of his translating this capital into new business ventures, ownership of real equities, or other profit possibilities.

Individual aspirations exist, of course, but the opportunities are not visible— they do not act as a catalyst to personal savings. A television set that goes into a pawnshop at the time of financial crisis and is reclaimed when the welfare check arrives indicates only a weak and primitive instinct to put money aside for a rainy day. Instead of saving for new furniture, the slum dweller buys shoddy, second-hand tables or chairs. Instead of saving to buy anything, he borrows at usurious interest rates. There even are no savings in the form of food reserves in the home. The poor black invariably buys in small quantities.

In the undeveloped countries of Latin America and Africa, the major "disincentives" to personal savings are weak banks and national inflations that frequently wipe out 20 percent of personal capital in a few days. In this country bank deposits in Bedford-Stuyvesant are insured by Government agencies just as they are in Beverly Hills. The dollar is no weaker in Watts than it is on Wall Street. Yet excess business funds generated in the ghettos are promptly withdrawn and redeposited or invested in the more hospitable and stable economy outside the slum.

This failure of individuals, businesses or other ghetto-bound institutions to create an adequate pool of credit or capital in the urban slum is not compensated by capital exports from the outside. "Hit and run" capital moves into the slum every morning to settle up the accounts of the loan sharks and the numbers operators, but it always leaves before the end of the day.

There are simply no profit opportunities to overcome the chaotic economic "disincentives" which act as a barrier to the movement of established and permanent outside capital into the slum. Low business profit margins and skills, high real estate taxes, and marginal ability to repay loans have totally banished the inflow of investment, speculation and capital. Ironically, these "disincentives" have been compounded by threats of riots, burnings and curfews. These tragic dampers on profits have already caused a fresh and massive outflow of money from Watts, Hough, Newark, and other similar areas.

In the mainstream economy, a man with business talent or a product idea, who is shy of necessary front-end risk money to see it launched, turns to a number of sources of capital. The "seed money" may come from an affluent relative, a group of friends always on the lookout for capital gains, a friendly banker who is willing "to stretch a point," and (most importantly) that great American reservoir of risk capital—the markets for new security issues.

In the ghetto economy, *affluent* friends or relatives are rare. Discretionary investment funds are meager; the capital gains opportunity holds little allure. There are no security markets either in the ghetto or downtown for "new issues" to finance the start-up costs of black business enterprises. Branch offices of stock exchange houses were unknown in the ghetto until the announcement by Shearson Hammill and Co. in July, 1968 of plans to open a brokerage office in a converted furniture store on 125th Street in Harlem.

Therefore, all normal markets for "front-end" risk capital are excluded by the extra tariffs of risk and unprofitability in the ghetto. A witness testifying before the Senate Subcommittee looking into the poverty situation, stated that a large percentage of new businesses established by Puerto Rican Americans in New York City were initially financed with funds borrowed from loan sharks.

Therefore, at least in the hard-core areas, an almost total void of low cost credit and capital—the most vital ingredient for the development of business equities—is replaced by the staggering credit costs imposed by "credit-merchants" and "hip-pocket" lenders. These "six-for-five" loan-sharks finance purchases of appliances or clothing in the ghetto; but their astronomical rates prevent any form of borrowing for the purpose of developing either a healthy commercial enterprise or the ownership of capital or property.

The banker's ethic to the contrary, few people in the normal economy grow rich or even affluent through the simple process of faithfully and periodically depositing money in a savings account. A start toward affluence or wealth is more likely to come from the act of converting a stake of money or savings to a business or investment opportunity. The fund of savings is vital to the process of building personal wealth only when, by the owner's act of risk, it is converted into risk capital or "front-end" money necessary to start a business or to make a financial commitment.

The other wealth-producing factor of leverage—typically a line of credit from a bank—

operates only in conjunction with "seed money" or risk capital. It is rarely possible to start up a new business on borrowed money unless the owner supplies some element of margin money, equity or front-end money.

If the formation of risk capital is vital to the process of growing affluent in the normal economy, then it is necessary to either remove from the ghetto economy the forces that suppress the generation of internal savings, or export to the ghetto compensating profit opportunities in thrift accounts which adjust the economy in such a way as to virtually enforce the process of saving money.

The vices in the ghetto economy which crush the process of accumulating savings cannot be removed by simple legislative fiat, since they are the conditions of poverty itself. Obviously enough, savings do not occur in the slum economy primarily because people there are poor. But even when there are excess funds to put away savings do not develop because there is little motivation to save. *The motivation is absent because savings cannot be converted into a risk capital investment or new business opportunity.* The extra tariffs or costs of doing business in the slum, combined with the unusual weakness of the ghetto as a market for production, banish the opportunity to convert savings into risk capital for profit. While the normal economy is increasingly willing to accept and purchase production from the ghetto, it is not willing to absorb and recognize the extra markups which the added operating costs in the ghetto require its manufacturers to impose. Therefore, remaining patterns of discrimination by the white buyer against Negro goods, together with the ghetto resident's extra costs of producing or marketing the goods, discourages him from going into business—which, in turn, eliminates his motivation to save for a future business commitment.

Since the vital process of savings itself is such an urgent ingredient of the process of developing risk capital, I suggest a specific savings incentive program.

At first it would appear that a thrift incentive should be applied directly to the ghetto resident to encourage him to save. Such an approach might be a federally subsidized bonus to the ghetto saver in the form of a one percent, or one and one-half percent increment to the normal

five and one-half percent interest paid by the bank.

I suggest that if the ghetto purchaser is willing to completely disregard the interest charge on his installment purchases from the ghetto credit merchant (which frequently varies from 20 percent to 100 percent per annum), no reasonable additional credit to the interest column in a savings passbook will make the difference in the ghetto between saving money and turning it over to the numbers operator.

For this reason, and for reasons of more efficient administration, *the incentive is more effectively applied to the savings institution than to the saver.*

To persuade the resident of the ghetto to open and maintain a conventional savings account requires some marketing skill and maybe a little sorcery.

During the years after the 1933 Bank Holiday, when nobody trusted a savings bank, the banks showed great resourcefulness in coaxing the money back home. Banks advertised hard for savings; they merchandised savings by offering casseroles, clocks and sets of dishes. In the United Kingdom banks traditionally have merchandised savings by giving the depositor the option of applying one-half of his interest dividend to the purchase of national lottery tickets. Although banks cannot sell lottery tickets here, they do have access to trading stamps, television advertising, and a host of merchandising techniques which have never been used to encourage personal savings in ghetto areas.

In the normal economy thrift institutions, mutual funds, and insurance companies budget millions in advertising expense soliciting savings. I have explained earlier that *ghetto banking economics are so distorted that at the present time ghetto institutions actually discourage savings accounts.* The reason is that the low profit margins of ghetto banks is due in large part to the fact that they are plagued with high bookkeeping and administrative costs due to *the large number of small, active savings accounts with a very small percentage of more profitable demand deposits or checking accounts.* The typical ghetto saver may deposit fifty dollars on Monday, withdraw ten dollars on Friday, and perhaps even close out the account on Monday.

The small ghetto businessmen, particularly, use the savings account as if it were a checking account. Since banks are compensated for checks cleared on special checking accounts, and do not pay interest on checking accounts, the banks naturally tend to discourage small and active savings accounts, where interest is paid to the depositor and no charge is made for active deposits and withdrawals.

Therefore, I suggest that an incentive should be applied which compensates the ghetto savings institution for (1) the extra administrative costs of maintaining savings accounts in slum areas and (2) the extra marketing or promotional costs that are necessary to lure the money of ghetto savers into a passbook account, where it may ultimately be converted into risk capital, or even the purchase of a mutual fund share.

The incentive to ghetto area savings institutions would operate in the following way:

Every savings bank, savings and loan association, or commercial bank with its principal office or branch office in a poverty area as defined by the Secretary of Commerce would be entitled to a year-end income tax credit. The income tax credit would be one and one-half percent of the average savings account balance for the preceding year of all savings accounts in the institution held by individuals whose savings account applications at the time the account was opened showed them to be residents of the eligible poverty area.

The effect of the incentive is to give the institution an extra fund for promoting ghetto savings. It also compensates the bank in such a way that it will no longer tend to discourage the small, active savings accounts which are so costly for ghetto banks to maintain.

The incentive encourages formation of new conveniently located branch banks in the gray areas.

In states where permitted by law, the downtown banks will be more inclined to maintain mobile savings units operating in the slums.

The incentive will also have the effect of causing slum area banks to persuade the more affluent residents of the ghetto to transfer their savings accounts from downtown banking offices to slum area branches or independent interracial banks located in the ghetto.

The effect in all cases is a desirable infusion of capital into the slum banking community where it will be available for commercial and mortgage loans which enrich the ghetto economy.

Applying the incentive to an existing profit center—the ghetto savings institution—rather than to the ghetto saver himself has some political disadvantage. The charge will be made, inevitably, that the incentive is "a give away program for big banking interests who are already milking the ghetto economy." For those who care to listen to the truth it should be stated that the proposed thrift incentive is available only at bank offices located in the designated poverty areas. These are the banks that are willing to bear the crushing bad debt losses on ghetto loans and the extra costs of servicing ten small loans rather than one large one. These are the banks that are operating with twice the normal staff,[8] which the ghetto credit economy requires to stay in the banking business.

CATEGORICAL CREDIT INCENTIVES: CREDIT DEVELOPMENT CORPORATIONS

The commercial banks of America have approximately 334 billion dollars in loans and investments. In most cases these assets are safely invested in low risk loans and obligations. I have already suggested how, with due regard for the requirements of the bank examiner, some of these funds may be allocated to developing mortgages, secured loans, deposits and other bankable commitments in projects which enrich black slum areas.

As I have already outlined, the problem in getting a new business off the ground in a slum area—or saving it after it has run into trouble—is often a matter of securing risk capital or front-end money. This is the money that is first wiped out if something goes wrong. Also, under principles of leverage, this is the "margin" money, the spark of wealth, that builds at an incredible rate if the venture goes well.

There are almost *no institutional sources for risk capital of this sort*. Equity loans for "front-end" capital and second mortgages are illegal investments for life insurance companies and banks. Obtaining Small Business Administration guarantees on these loans is arduous and uncertain. Even where the lending institution is willing to reach into the ghetto for "soft loans," the loan officers are operating in a foreign economic environment where they are uncomfortable and inexperienced.[9]

Through the formation of a subsidiary high risk loan corporation, a bank, insurance company or syndicate of institutions can *make this "risk" money or margin money available to the slum community without the problems of control and regulation by banking supervisors and examiners.*

The prototype bank originated plan of this kind is the Citizens and Southern Community Development Corporation, formed by Georgia's one billion dollar Citizens and Southern National Bank. This subsidiary of the bank was capitalized in May of 1968 at one million dollars. It makes second mortgage loans and provides equity capital for new small businesses in the slums of Savannah. It will also lend second mortgage and equity money to slum dwellers to assist home purchases. The bank anticipates that in most cases total first and second mortgage payments will not be higher than the rents now being paid. This program is a brilliant innovation uniquely calculated to build ownership and equities in the ghetto. It should be emulated by other banks.[10]

A slightly different approach has been taken by the Interracial Council for Business Opportunity where main activities are in New York City. An ICBO Fund has been organized which plans to raise about $300,000 in capital funds. Unlike the Citizens and Southern National Bank plan, the ICBO Fund will not lend directly to Negro businesses. The Fund will guarantee repayment of such loans made by the banks that have agreed to participate in the program.[11] Through the use of the technique of the guarantee it is obvious that greater leverage is obtained. *The Fund estimates that $300,000 in capital will support one million dollars in Negro loan guarantees.* The ICBO Loan Guarantee Fund hopes to commit guarantees quickly—almost on the telephone. Its program puts private banks and businesses directly in the role of "recruiting" and funding loans to promising black businessmen. The guarantee eliminates the "soft" feature of the loans. They can be committed at rates prevailing outside the ghetto.

The ICBO program eliminates the two fundamental weaknesses of the Federal Small Business Administration loan program: (1) Administrative delays in making loan guarantees and

(2) Inability of the bureaucracy to recruit and recognize promising Negro borrowers.

The notion of a ghetto development lending institution with broad powers to make "free wheeling" risk loans and equity commitments in slum areas carries extraordinary potentials of leverage and enrichment. Potential sponsors of these projects should be encouraged through a specially tailored system of the incentives.

The incentive should be in the form of tax credits equal to a specified percentage of investments in any corporation formed to make commercial business loans or to take business equity positions in any poverty area as defined by the Secretary of Commerce:

1. Formed as a subsidiary (or as a joint venture with the incentive prorated).

2. Whether profit making or tax exempt.

3. Not in itself subject to regulation by any state or federal supervising agency.

CATEGORICAL CREDIT INCENTIVES: STOCK PLACEMENTS FOR "FRONT-END" BUSINESS INVESTMENT CAPITAL

I have already reviewed how meager money markets of the ghetto stubbornly fail and refuse to generate the credit money or leverage necessary to get even the smallest new business venture off the ground. For obvious reasons there is a parallel shortage in the ghetto of personal savings and discretionary funds for front-end risk money or "fliers" that aspiring entrepreneurs commit every day in the downtown "normal" economy.

The normal downtown markets provide extraordinary liquidity for even the small businessman who wants to "sell out" to a larger firm. In the ghetto economy, liquidity, the cornerstone of any market, has long since vanished. New ghetto real estate and businesses are assets frozen by the riots and the ensuing inability to obtain insurance. Federal programs have not helped. For many years the Small Business Administration has discouraged applications for the guarantee of loans to effect the transfer of ownership of a small business. Property sales in the ghetto have all the qualities of molasses.

Just as uncertain patterns of ghetto income and risks block bank and other credit from moving into the slum from downtown institutions, for the same reasons, the nation's underwriting industry *does not market new stock issues for financing new ghetto plants or real estate improvements.* A "hot new issue" of a Negro controlled enterprise is unknown on Wall Street—or for that matter on 125th Street in Harlem. There is no market whatsoever in either the downtown "normal" economy or the "subsidiary" ghetto economy for these stock placements. With one major exception the large downtown underwriters, brokerage firms and mutual fund salesmen are not present in ghetto areas.

The occasional new stock issue in Negro enterprises is not bought with any real expectation of profit. The investment is more often an act of philanthropy. A new stock issue in Harlem's Freedom National Bank was laboriously marketed in 1964, although Jackie Robinson, of Brooklyn's Dodgers' fame, was leading the team as Chairman of the Board of the bank.[12]

Mutual Real Estate Investment Trust (M—REIT), a publicly owned real estate trust formed for the purpose of buying all-white apartment buildings, and opening them up to all races, took two years to market its first share offering of four million dollars.

These efforts to market securities for enrichment of the ghetto stand in sharp contrast to the current frenzy of new issues in the main economy.

Hardly a week goes by where Wall Street, through the magical process of capitalizing earnings (or losses) does not make millionaires of men with new ideas for a restaurant franchise or an electronic product idea with a garage to manufacture it in.

Risk capital, obtained through the route of new stock issues, is a vital element in building of wealth and new businesses in the normal economy. Since new security issues are such an important catalyst of wealth in the "normal" economy, I suggest that capital incentives should be developed to start building normal patterns of new security issues for projects which will enrich the Negro slum economy.

Our income tax laws now permit any investor in a qualified Small Business Corporation to deduct in full against income any loss on the sale of stock in the corporation. This provision allows the security loss in full, even if it is "long term." You don't have to match the loss against other capital gains. This special income tax incentive was enacted several years ago in line with congressional policy to encourage risk capital investment in small business ventures.

I suggest that these special income tax privileges for small business corporations should be *expanded* for stock investment in small business corporations formed to build or develop new plants, office buildings, apartment houses, retail outlets or other new facilities in certified poverty areas. Losses in these security investments should be allowed in full against ordinary income plus an extra incentive deduction of 25% of the loss. Profits on resale of these stock investments should be taxed in the usual way but reduced by a special "poverty area" tax credit of 7% of the capital gain.

These tax incentives for new security issues should lure risk capital out of the normal economy and force it into the subsidiary economy. Newly provided risk capital can then combine with SBA and FHA-guaranteed long-term credits to build new strength and vitality into the commerce of the urban slums.

CATEGORICAL CREDIT INCENTIVES: NEW EQUITIES IN MINORITY OWNERSHIP

One of the most valuable efforts that a national corporation can undertake is the sharing of ownership of a slum area plant or facility with local residents and employees. A Montgomery Ward outlet in Hough enriches this community because it provides high quality low-cost merchandise to a community which is for the moment victimized by the gouging credit merchants. But the same national retail outlet is *doubly* enriching if shares in the Montgomery Ward subsidiary can be marketed to the Hough residents and employees of the stores.

I have been able to identify only very limited examples of industry efforts to sell in the slum *minority interests* in ghetto projects.

Originally Aerojet General's pilot tent manufacturing unit established in Watts after the 1965 riots planned to offer 49% of the stock in the unit to employees. So far this has not been accomplished and a piece work incentive plan has been established instead. Most of the present employees were formerly "hard-core"; they do not understand the value of equities. The stock plan must wait until the employees have acquired greater financial sophistication.[13]

In a joint venture with the U.S. Government and the District of Columbia's Model Inner City Community Organization, Fairchild Hiller has established in a converted warehouse an assembly operation for wiring harnesses and circuit boards in Washington's Shaw ghetto. Management will be almost entirely black. The subsidiary plans to sell stock and become a community-owned organization.

In March, 1967 Boston's nuclear testing firm of Edgerton, Germeshausen and Grier formed a new manufacturing unit, E.G. & G. Roxbury Inc., in the South Boston black community. This plant will be the nucleus of a project for training ghetto area workers in metal working, drafting and welding. Twenty-five percent of the stock of the subsidiary will be earmarked for employees. The ultimate goal, if the plan succeeds, is to sell the plant to the resident workers. In my opinion, if E.G. & G. is able to accomplish its objective, in whole or in part, the company will have opened vast new arteries of affluence in the Boston ghetto—far more enriching to the Roxbury slum and to the nation as a whole than equally expensive plans of handing out jobs to Roxbury residents who must commute to a suburban plant.[14]

Since minority interests *owned* by ghetto residents and employees build such valuable economic leverage and incentives among disadvantages citizens, I suggest a specific tax incentive to encourage similar programs.

The incentive should allow corporations a five year annual income tax credit equal to 10% of the annual carrying charges (interest, rent, plant maintenance, insurance and payroll), prorated for the percentage which the equity stock ownership initially marketed to ghetto residents or employees bears to the total stock ownership. For example, if the annual carrying charges of the ghetto subsidiary are $500,000 per year, and ten percent of the stock is marketed in the ghetto, the parent company would be entitled to an annual tax credit on its own income tax return of $50,000 for five consecutive years during which the plant is maintained.

Considering the extra costs and risks of establishing the plant in the ghetto in the first instance, the difficult process of marketing the stock (relieved perhaps by payroll withholding plans), the risk of bad press and black animosities if the plant is a failure, the incentive is not overly generous.

The parent company may choose to set aside the annual tax credit into a reserve fund for "voluntary" repurchases of the stock if the plant should fail.

If the United States Treasury can be convinced of the merits of a wealth-building ghetto experiment, the incentive may be sufficient to lure supermarket chains, oil companies, theatre chains and hotel companies into sharing equities in partnership with residents of the ghetto. If a highly innovative company such as E.G. & G. is willing to go it alone without incentives, the incentive may be sufficient to persuade others that a ghetto facility is a reasonable commitment of stockholder capital.

A SUGGESTED CONGRESSIONAL EXPERIMENT WITH "SELF-EXECUTING" REPAYMENT GUARANTEES FOR POVERTY AREA LOANS

I have suggested earlier in this statement that wealth builds in the normal "mainstreet" economy where two vital conditions exist: (1) a healthy supply of "front-end funds," "risk capital" or "margin money"; (2) an equally ample supply of "leverage," "debt financing" or "credit."

The first condition, the creation of front-end money, occurs only where there is "savings"— (funds exceeding normal living or staying in business expenses) which can be committed to a profit opportunity. In the normal economy, the simplest form of the first condition is margin money, the risk funds used to purchase, say, convertible bonds carried at a bank on a margin loan. The second condition of leverage, the margin loan itself, occurs only in an economy where *income uncertainty required by the lender can be reduced to an insignificant risk*. For example, in the normal economy there is virtually unlimited credit funds for a borrowing collateralized by U.S. Government bonds. A simple unsecured note of several hundred million, signed by IBM can be marketed at interest rates almost comparable to those accorded the notes of the United States Government. In both cases the credit status of the borrower is such that *income uncertainty is reduced to a practical zero*. The lender is *assured* of the payment of interest and the repayment of principal.

In the ghetto economy risk capital is not generated internally because there is virtually no discretionary income. Risk capital does not move in from the normal economy because the profit opportunities are nonexistent. In the slum economy the second condition—leverage or credit element is also almost entirely missing. There is no person or indigenous business enterprise whose patterns of income are sufficiently reliable that he can put his signature on a promissory note and reduce the holder's income uncertainty to a practical zero. The insurance company or banker says, "I have trust funds to lend or invest. Show me how you can reduce my income uncertainty to an acceptable level and I will furnish you with unlimited leverage and take delight in watching you grow rich."

The system I suggested earlier of *Categorical Corrective Credit Incentives* can be especially effective in moving front-end money or risk capital into the ghetto. Risk capital is readily attracted by profit opportunities which income tax incentives provide, as witnessed by the great success of Puerto Rico's *Operation Bootstrap*, which brought new industry to an island ghetto through the promise of long term income tax moritorium. But these incentives can operate on risk capital only where basic (almost risk free) credit is available to pay the major cost of a new plant or other entrepreneurial effort. However, the system of *Categorical Credit Corrective Incentives* is not capable in itself of creating the second condition, credit or leverage, where it is missing.

No income tax incentive can make "soft" loans bankable. If a bank or insurance company commits an 80% mortgage loan on a new shopping center in a hardened slum area, the institution's income certainty requirement is obviously missing. The deal "begs" for a guaranteed lease from Safeway or some other nationally recognized supermarket chain whose promise to repay is almost without risk. Without the lease guarantee the proposed supermarket loan remains "soft." Since the loan will not pass

the bank or insurance examiner, it will not be made in the first place.

If the established interest rate on the loan for the ghetto supermarket is, say 7% (the present prime rate on commercial mortgage loans) and if a 3% income tax credit is given the lender for each year the loan is outstanding, the overall loan yield is in effect equal to 9% (less some income taxes). Depending on various conditions, this may or may not be a sufficient after-tax yield to compensate a knowledgeable lender for the extraordinary risk in the loan. In all events, *the loan is not bankable*. Even if the income tax credit were 20%, bank and insurance examiners would not pass it because these institutions may lend policy holders' reserves and depositors' money only under conditions when income uncertainty, or risk of nonrepayment, is relatively low (1% or so). But regardless of how great the tax incentive, the ghetto supermarket loan is in fact 100% at risk from the day it is made.

The fundamental commercial credit problem in the ghetto is therefore inextricably linked with the fact that no one who resides there, or who engages in business or commerce there, has sufficient resources or adequately stable income, to reduce income uncertainty to a virtual zero. Riots and commerce killing curfews have now nailed this point down for good.

In the past, this problem of making "soft" commercial loans bankable or acceptable in a banker's portfolio (reducing income uncertainty to virtually zero) has been approached in a tentative way through the device of the Small Business Administration guarantee of loans to ghetto businesses. But we have seen that because of the inevitable encrustations of red tape and delays that have been developed, lenders and developers (the equity men with the front money) have been loath to deal with the government agency that promises the repayment of the loan. We have also seen that institutions such as the SBA, under Congressional prodding and scrutiny, has developed (perhaps through no fault of its own) very rigid and conservative loan guaranty policies. As a result SBA loans for new commercial ghetto projects are running at the snail's pace of $15,000,000 a year.

The answer to the problem does not lie in more federal agency loan guarantee programs. The solution is not necessarily to fund a new national development bank for loans in eligible poverty areas. These institutions will more than likely be subject to all the same delays, red tape and vast bureaucratic expenses that have infected similar loan guaranty programs in the past.

The solution, I suggest, lies in developing a system of *self-executing loan repayment guarantees* which will automatically insure repayment of certain loans for ghetto enrichment which Congress specifically designates as being in the interest of the United States. The system will also be tailored and constructed to provide adequate built-in safeguards to protect the Treasury against waste, scandal and fraud.

A program for a "federal blank check" or open-ended guarantee must obviously be approached with caution and experimentation. Unless the program is initially established as a demonstration or pilot effort resistance at all government levels will be formidable. I therefore suggest a preliminary test program be applied in the limited and isolated areas where the most abject poverty occurs—one or more of America's Indian reservations. In this manner the costs can be identified and limited and the results can be measured. If the program is feasible it can be extended to other poverty areas.

I therefore propose that loans to establish a new business or plant or commercial facility in or adjacent to an Indian reservation should automatically carry a *full repayment guaranty of interest and principal by the United States of America* under the following conditions and safeguards:

(a) The loan must be made by a bank, insurance company or other institutional lender regulated or supervised by state or federal law;

(b) If the loan is long term (more than a year) it shall carry an interest rate not to exceed that which is approved by Congress from time to time for FHA loans;

(c) If the loan is short term, the rate may not exceed one half of one percent of that paid on comparable U.S. Government notes;[15]

(d) The loan guaranty will not be effective until the regularly established auditors of the lending institution, and an independent licensed certified public accountant acting for the project sponsors, have certified to the lender that in their opinion the owners or sponsors of the new facility or plant have invested and paid for no less than 10% of the proposed cost of the commercial facility exclusive of working capital, inventory, pre-opening, training, advertising and other start-up expenses. Absent proof of fraud or collusion by the lending institutions, the auditor's certificates would be final and conclusive as to the validity of the Federal Government guarantee of repayment of the loan.

The program of self-executing loan repayment guarantees for facilities which enrich an Indian Reservation are designed to provide "the second condition" of leverage or credit. The "first condition" of front-end money or risk capital would be supplied by the *specific credit incentives* I have stipulated earlier for *any* new business investment in poverty areas.

The suggested program of self-executing loan repayment guarantees provides a method under which private industry, by *its own act,* may automatically commit the credit of the Federal Government to programs for rebuilding the ghetto economy may seem drastic. Indeed it is. The nation has barely survived a generation of laborious systems under which we have relied on thousands of federal loan approval officers to protect the Treasury from fraud and waste. Yet policemen of the federal agencies whose budgets are many millions of dollars have not succeeded in protecting the nation against waste of federal funds. Nor have they succeeded in building ownership of business equities in the ghetto. I believe that a combination of bank and institutional auditors (doubly safeguarded by licensed independent CPA's of project sponsors) are capable of doing an effective job of policing costs and honesty. Under a program for self-executing government guarantees, the administrative costs that are saved would more than compensate for any extra losses on ill-conceived loans.

NOTES

[1] Designated by the Secretary of Commerce.

[2] At an American Management Association Seminar in June, 1968, Thomas F. Murray, Vice President, Mortgages, of The Equitable Life Assurance Society of the United States, described the most valuable type of "refunding loans" which the Equitable is making on ghetto real estate: "Although at first glance we had assumed that the $83 million that was to be Equitable's participation in this

national program would be major investments, largely apartment houses and possibly some commercial structures, we soon found that the most expeditious way to get going was to invest in mortgages on one to four family residences. These mortgages usually permitted the owner or purchaser to obtain terms which were more favorable than were heretofore available, and often provided financing where none was obtainable before. We found, in many cases, that our mortgage refinanced a first and second, and possibly even a third mortgage whose combined monthly payments were practically impossible to meet for this Negro family that was seeking to establish itself as an owner in a community often characterized by absentee landlords. Very often our funds permitted the owner to rehabilitate his home, or he could use the decrease in monthly payments to modernize or improve his dwelling. We are delighted, accordingly, that our program has helped foster and support resident ownership in ghetto areas—nearly 85% of our funds have gone into this phase of our ghetto lending program."

[3]Ghetto branches of "Main Street" banks are excluded because their principal offices are not in an eligible poverty area. Deposits in ghetto branches of downtown banks are more likely to "run off" downtown and satisfy safer credit risks in the normal economy.

[4]There are about 53 Negro-controlled banks and loan associations headquartered in Negro ghetto areas including for example, Freedom National Bank in Harlem and Brooklyn's Bedford Stuyvesant, and Unity National Bank in Boston's Roxbury ghetto. Of course the incentive would apply to banks located in the impoverished Indian reservations in the South or Southwest or in any of the great rural poverty areas of Appalachia and Northern California.

[5]By almost universal law in the United States, a bank may not pay interest on demand deposits (usually checking accounts).

[6]Note that one of the most agressive depositors in ghetto banks is the *tax-exempt* New York Synod of the Presbyterian Church. *Without the impetus of tax incentives* the Church deposited $15,000 in Harlem's Freedom National in the Spring of 1968 and spread another quarter of a million dollars around in various slum-area banks and savings institutions.

The Executive Council of the Episcopal Church has performed well also. As of mid-July 1968 the Church has deposited $675,000 in forty-five ghetto banks. The only requirement is that the deposits be federally insured and that the institution be locally owned and managed for the benefit of those who live in the community.

At last count General Motors held cash and marketable securities of 2.3 billion dollars. There are no established figures of how much of it resides in ghetto banks—probably more than the combined capital and surplus of any one of them.

[7]The New York Times quotes a woman in Harlem who covers the point: "They keep on telling us, to take better care of our money, and to save it away and buy what is the best in the stores and do like they for dresses, and keep the children in school, and keep our husbands from leaving us. . . . Well, I'll tell you, they sure don't know what it's about . . . and let them start at zero the way we did and see how many big numbers they can become themselves. I mean, if you've got nothing when you are born, and you know you can't get a thing no matter how hard you try—well, then you dies with nothing. And no one can deny that arithmetic."

[8]Harlem's Freedom National Bank in Harlem employs 85. A normal non-ghetto bank the same size (30 million in deposits) employs half that many people.

[9]This is the reason cited by John Bunting, President of the First Pennsylvania Banking and Trust Company for insisting that most commercial loans in the Philadelphia ghetto be made through an intermediate agent or branch in the ghetto. Also you get the advantage of shifting the decisionmaking function on ghetto loans away from the hidebound lending officers downtown.

The First Pennsylvania Banking and Trust Company probably has as much knowledge and expertise in making, servicing and salvaging ghetto commercial loans as any bank in the country.

[10]The program was approved by the Comptroller of the Currency in late April 1968. The plan is therefore "legal" for any national bank. It is doubtful if any state regulatory authority would fault a state bank program of this sort provided it was reasonable in relationship to the sponsoring bank's capital funds. In the Citizens and Southern plan, the capital at risk is less than 1/10 of 1% of the total assets of the bank.

[11]The original participating banks were all in New York City: Bankers Trust Company, the Chase Manhattan Bank, Chemical Bank, New York Trust Company and Harlem's Freedom National Bank.

A similar guarantee fund, Puerto Rican Forum, Inc., has been established in New York City to help finance small businesses operated by minority group members. The fund is spearheaded by Manufacturers Hanover Trust Company and San Juan's Banco Popular de Puerto Rico under a foundation grant. The first loan of $6,000 at 7% simple interest was made by Manufacturers Trust Company in July 1968 to Tony Bonilla of 69 Irving Place, New York City for refinancing existing obligations of his printing shop. The fund guarantees half the loan on a prorated basis. The bank thus accepts one-half of the risk.

[12]The soliciting letter is hardly designed to excite stock traders downtown. It explained that Freedom National had been "planned as a community enterprise that will in every way belong to the people it is to serve. . . . Moreover, it is intended that these people shall be represented in the formation and administration of the policies of this bank to assure its role in helping to eradicate those financing practices that restrict the economic growth of the community and erode the money power of its members."

[13]Ed. note: A plan to transfer ownership of Watts Manufacturing Company, the corporation which was formed by Aerojet General, into the hands of its minority-group employees was announced in early 1970.

[14]Ed. note: E.G. & G. closed its Roxbury subsidiary in March, 1970 because of a lack of substantial orders, poor quality, and difficulties in training and keeping competent black managers. These difficulties resulted in continued losses for the parent company totalling about $5,000,000 since the subsidiary went into operation. Source: *The Wall Street Journal,* April 11, 1970, p. 14.

CONJOINING BLACK REVOLUTION AND PRIVATE ENTERPRISE

Arnold Schuchter

Hearings before the Senate Subcommittee on Executive Reorganization, the "Ribicoff Committee," [chaired by Senator Abraham A. Ribicoff], dwelled on trying to find out from businessmen what it would take to get them involved in creating jobs and housing in slum ghettos. The primary conclusion, reflected in subsequent legislation by Senators [Robert F.] Kennedy and [Jacob K.] Javits, was that the federal government must create a competitive, lucrative market in the slum ghettos, by increasing the yield on equity investment after taxes and by guaranteeing no risk of loss; in other words, guaranteeing a high profit yield after taxes for private equity capital. The Economic Opportunity Program (War on Poverty) was not altogether repudiated, but the consensus of testimony at the hearings, from both public officials and the private sector, was that the primary shortcoming of the anti-poverty program has been its failure to involve *and rely upon* the private enterprise system. This viewpoint was strengthened by the strong prevalent opinion that negligible additional financial help will come from the federal government as long as national resources are being diverted to Vietnam and for Cold War purposes.

Frequent references were made at the Senate hearing, by Senator Javits of New York and in testimony from private business persons, about the need for a Communication Satellite Corporation (COMSAT)-type corporation to build new housing in slum areas and develop new industry to expand employment opportunities.

It appears that the public has somehow been led to believe that COMSAT is a space-age public service corporation formed for social purposes. In fact, COMSAT is a private, profit-making corporation chartered by the federal government to hold a monopoly on U.S. development of, and participation in, the national and international communications satellite business. The social purposes of this type of corporation, if any exist, are in no way comparable to those required to undo the slum ghetto system. The profit potential of COMSAT is enormous. Here, *perhaps,* there is a valid analogy—in terms of the profit potential of corporate participation in slum renewal. Renewal of ghetto slums, however, cannot be compared to the investment attraction of COMSAT for the international communications carriers. This point should be elaborated further.

The international communications carriers were allotted (i.e., restricted to) 50 per cent of the outstanding voting stock of COMSAT. These corporations, especially A.T. & T., would have preferred 100 per cent of the voting stock, but a compromise had to be worked out to placate Congressmen outraged by a "no strings" billion dollar give-away. For instance, A.T. & T. was sold 2,895,750 shares of non-voting stock at $20 per share, valued at $57,915,000. The price range for COMSAT stock in 1965 and 1966 hit a low of $35 and a high of about $65.

Thus Senator Javits' remark, at the Ribicoff hearings, about COMSAT, by way of analogy to his proposed Economic Opportunity Corporation,[1] was somewhat naive and misleading: "We have seen in COMSAT that the people will invest in mixed government-business corporations." Furthermore, COMSAT is not, as Senator Javits described it, an example of "public-private financing" except in the sense that COMSAT benefited from over $470 million in government funds invested in space communications prior to COMSAT's inception. As David Rockefeller pointed out to Senator Javits at the Ribicoff hearings: "In the case of COMSAT, they [the public shareholders] have been led to believe, and there seems to be every reason to think that they are right, that this could be a profitable venture. In other words, a sound investment as well as a publicly desirable cause." Further aspects of this dialogue on the COMSAT model between Senator Javits and David Rockefeller, president of the Chase Manhattan Bank of New York, are quite illuminating:

SENATOR JAVITS. . . . would you go along with us in a COMSAT-type corporation? By that I mean, public-private financing. Let's forget about the division, how much, but a public-private board of directors with some public standards which it is required to meet, as well as considerable freedom in private sector operations, and essentially private sector management? Would you go along with us with that kind of company, perhaps national, certainly regional, for the service function—all kinds of training, all kinds of management, all kinds of technical assistance?

MR. ROCKEFELLER. If you carry the analogy to COMSAT one step further, this would mean the investment of funds by the public. COMSAT has an enormous number of public shareholders [actually 148,056 in December, 1966]. It seems to me that if they are going to be asked to put up their equity and their savings, many of them people of small means themselves, that they must understand clearly what they are getting into . . . I think it would be a great mistake to launch a venture in the housing field [like COMSAT], trying to attract similar funds, and then have the investing public discover that in point of fact this was not economically viable, and they were perhaps helping a good cause, but they weren't getting tax credit for it, and they were losing part of their savings, so that I think there is a very serious public responsibility to make sure that it does have economic justification, and that the public understands clearly when they invest what they are getting into.

SENATOR JAVITS. Would you believe, in your judgement—would an important section of American business leadership back such a company or even initiate, set it up? Could you gather around yourself or some other business leader enough American business to do something like this? After all, this is the practical implementation of your testimony and for people like myself, who are sitting here and contending that this is the way it ought to be done, it sounds pretty ridiculous, unless American business is really ready to move in and do it on some basis, and that is really what I am asking you.

MR. ROCKEFELLER. I am sure that there are business leaders who would be interested and glad to give it a good, hard look and see what could be put together and whether or not a viable type corporation could be established. Yes, I am sure they would go that far. Now, whether their conclusions would in their judgment justify their going further, I wouldn't know until I had studied it a lot more than I have.

With all their curiosity about the profit prospects of "slum business," industry is still wary and hesitant about making investment commitments. Spokesmen for industry have indicated that they are prepared to work on a contract basis for a nonprofit, mixed public-private corporation, or a public corporation that has urban rehabilitation as its primary objective. The semi-public or public corporation would establish a public consensus on the objective, raise capital funds, establish an effective demand for industry participation, and then, screen the private corporation from criticism if performance fails to meet standards, much the way NASA has performed for prime contractors in the space business. On the other hand, business has indicated its willingness to participate individually, if corporate profits are guaranteed. Thus far, very little public debate has focused on this point—that private sector support of the public good requires substantial profit-making incentives created by government.

There is an ironical twist to the emerging consensus about the "necessary" role of the private sector in renewing slum ghettos, as follows: plans and proposals for private industry involvement in slum ghettos have been precipitated and accelerated by ghetto riots and the prospects of future violence; at the heart of the riots is rebellion against dominance by white economic and political power; most plans for business investment in ghettos, with Senator Kennedy's tax credit plans at the head of the phalanx, stress devising organizational and market mechanisms for slum ghetto redevelopment which guarantee profits to white economic power interests in order to intensify their activities in the rebellious black ghettos. Thus, the aim of the latest thrust in the War on Poverty is "maximum feasible participation" of white economic power in the ghetto, and the result is likely to be reinforcement of the sense of dependency and powerlessness that provoked riots in the first place.

A further irony in the emerging business role in ghetto renewal is that the political leader who has shown the deepest understanding and most consistent regard for community development principles and practices in the ghetto areas— Senator Robert Kennedy—is the leading exponent of tax credit programs in ghetto housing and industrial development which tend to vitiate community participation and "self-governing power."

In December 1966, Kennedy announced the establishment of two parallel and cooperating corporations in Brooklyn: the Bedford-Stuyvesant Renewal and Rehabilitation Corporation and the Bedford-Stuyvesant Development and Services Corporation. The creation of both evolved out of extensive discussions with community groups. The nonprofit Renewal and Rehabilitation Corporation is responsible for developing and carrying out a program for physical, economic, and social development in Bedford-Stuyvesant (about 400,000 population) and to be operated "on a businesslike basis." This relatively new type of quasi-public organization seeks to become a parallel form of government in Brooklyn, New York, to function as the principal agent of community change in that area. It is in the process of drafting plans for housing, commercial and industrial development, education, health clinics, and so forth, all designed to consolidate and draw on self-help resources and federal grant-in-aid programs. Bedford-Stuyvesant is one of the areas selected by the city, and approved by HUD, for the Model Cities program.

The second corporation, the Development and Services Corporation, was created to assemble corporate leadership that could stimulate investment of private resources in program activities of the Renewal and Rehabilitation Corporation. The form of this second corporation apparently reflects several astute judgments: that the relationship of business resources to the community development corpora-

tion should be formalized and systematized through a parallel corporation, with specific commitments and responsibilities; that expert managerial advice for the community development corporation should be available when and as needed; and, for the foreseeable future, the community development corporation needed a powerful intermediator with the existing white economic and political power structure and its institutional resources.

Senator Kennedy's remarks before the Subcommittee on Executive Reorganization contain an excellent summary of the purpose of community development corporations: "The measure of success of this or any other program will be the extent to which it helps the ghetto to become a community—a functioning unit, its people acting together on matters of mutual concern, with the power and resources to affect the conditions of their own lives. Therefore, the heart of the program, I believe, should be the creation of community development corporations, which would carry out the work of construction, the hiring and training of workers, the provision of services, the encouragement of associated enterprises."

Against the background of this unique (for politicians) experience with creating community development structures in the ghetto and the remarkable perception of the purposes of community development, it is surprising that Senator Kennedy's proposed legislation for employment and housing development work *against* the community development concept. (Senator Kennedy's "Urban Housing Development Act of 1967[2] is discussed in . . . [an earlier chapter.]) Senator Kennedy's "Urban Employment Opportunities Development Act of 1967[3] is significant for three reasons: first, the use of tax credits to spur economic and job development for ghetto inhabitants is feasible, logical, and probably inevitable, regardless of who sponsors the tax credit plan; second, his plan, as of this writing, is the most carefully thought out and complete employment development plan utilizing tax credits; third, if Senator Kennedy, with his experience and background, sees no contradiction between his tax credit plan and community development approaches in ghettos, future public and private job development plans are even more likely to reflect the same misconception.

First, a brief summary of highlights of Senator Kennedy's "Urban Unemployment Opportunities Development Act of 1967." The plan would benefit poverty areas in Standard Metropolitan Statistical Area's (SMSA's) and persons living on Indian reservations. The program would be controlled, in terms of certification for eligibility, by municipalities. Federal participation and control would essentially be reduced to administration of compliance with standards set by the Department of Housing and Urban Development, the Department of Commerce, and the Department of Labor. The type of eligible industries would include manufacturers, producers, distributors, and construction firms—but not retailers. The industry receiving tax credits and subsidies would have to hire significant numbers of unskilled or semi-skilled workers from poverty areas, with no income criteria or unemployment criteria included in the legislation. Reflecting the intent to cater to enterprise with substantial investment resources, the legislation requires that companies must create at least fifty new jobs ("as a safeguard against insubstantial or fly-by-night operators"), and fill at least two-thirds of these jobs with residents of poverty areas, or other unemployed persons. The company's investment must be maintained for at least ten years in order to retain the tax credits. Citizen participation would consist of prior consultation with residents of the poverty area in which the industrial facility is to be located, culminating in a public hearing.

The provisions of the legislation are designed to create new jobs in manufacturing and services in ghettos (the latter through multiplier effect), in part, by overcoming transportation handicaps, and to bring symbols of entrepreneurial activity into poverty areas. In return for investing in industrial expansion in poverty areas, the plan is designed to afford investors *a minimum of a 50 per cent increase in their normal rate of return.*[4] The main tax credit benefits of Senator Kennedy's plan in relation to normal existing benefits under the tax code are summarized . . . [below].

Combined with existing corporate income tax and investment allowances, the above tax credits offer substantial inducements to corporations with surplus equity to invest, and a market that justifies expansion. Corporation income tax is high but tax and investment allowances have tended to reduce the percentage of corporation taxes to profits-before-taxes. Between 1952 and 1963, when the general corporation tax rate was 52 per cent, the percentage of corporation taxes to profits-before-taxes dropped almost 10 points, from 37.5 to 27.8 per cent. For those who argue that corporation income taxes are still too high, Senator Kennedy's plan is a small step in the right direction; for those who argue that corporation profits are too high, the plan does not add much weight to their position. From the viewpoint of the havenots in poverty areas, a good case might be made for the plan's amounting to outright bribery of the haves to share some of the leftovers with the have-nots.

For business and industry that stand to lose money in central cities if ghetto rebellion and

Kennedy Tax Plan	*Current Tax Code*
A 10 percent credit on machinery and equipment	7 percent investment credit
A 7 percent credit on costs of constructing a facility or leasing space	None
A carryback of 3 taxable years and a carryover of 10 years on capital losses	Capital gains can be carried forward for 5 years to offset capital losses
A useful life for depreciation of 66-2/3 percent of the normal useful life of real and personal property	Write-off period for depreciation allowance geared to actual replacement of assets by firm (to encourage faster write-offs)
A net operating loss carryover of 10 taxable years	Net operating losses can be carried back 3 years or, if not sufficient, carried forward 5 years
A special deduction of 25 percent of salaries paid to workers hired to meet requirements of the Act	None

rioting continue to grow, tax credit plans for ghetto investment at least offer a way to take positive action with a profit rationale. The assumption here is that altruism will not suffice even when supported by interests of self-protection. Frances Fox Piven, of the Columbia University School of Social Work, takes a much more cynical *realpolitik* view of the increasing political pressure to get corporations into the ghetto: "If Negroes were a powerful influence in city government they would be able to control redevelopment and all that it implies," Mrs. Piven says. "The corporate move into the slums is a way to sidestep the emerging Negro influence." Mrs. Piven poses a problem that will increasingly preoccupy the strategists of ghetto renewal: the corporate "invasion" of the ghetto could result in the Negro being better off economically, but at the expense of Negro political self-determination. Stating the problem somewhat differently; how do you put together enough White Power to do anything in slum ghettos without putting together too much White Power to do too much?

It is possible, of course, that a strategy of "corporate colonialism" may indeed be developing in the inner sanctum of Washington bureaucracy, with corporate leadership and trusted White House aides plotting to restore order and control in the ghetto by feeding thousands of black militants into the corporate machinery of subsidized jobs. It has probably occurred to HUD that its urban constituency is seriously jeopardized by the growing and turbulent hiatus between city hall and the ghetto. However, it is more likely that Mrs. Piven is both overstretching the "credibility gap" and overestimating the role of advanced political strategizing in Washington bureaucracy. Urban problem-solving has not yet reached the threshold of Cold War planning, alternative retaliatory strike strategies, and so forth. (I hate to think that the day may come when HUD borrows Defense Department strategy teams and computer experts to simulate counter-offense strategies and ghetto "kill ratios.") It is unlikely, therefore, that corporations have either volunteered or been chosen for the mission of bridging the political control gap between city halls and the ghettos in major urban centers afflicted by ghetto revolts.

The political pressure for corporate involvement in the ghetto comes from a much simpler and less conspiratorial combination of sources: desperation in the private sector over the inadequacies of government planning and programs; determination by public and private sectors to create a stopgap program to avert intensified racial violence in the Hot Summer of 1968, or more realistically, in 1969 and beyond; efforts by the Administration to avert serious pre-election rioting in the cities; general recognition that, given the complex root causes of ghetto turmoil and urban decay, remedies are remote, and the lead-time for planning, programming, and staging, very extensive. Businessmen throughout the nation are in fact deeply concerned, for more than self-interest reasons; they want to act effectively, but they really do not know what to do—safety and inexpensively.

The partnership between ghetto-dwellers and both federal and local government that abortively emerged under the Economic Opportunity Program now appears to be shifting to a partnership between large corporations, financial institutions, and government. As expressed by Bruce P. Hayden, Vice-President of the Connecticut General Life Insurance Company: ". . . any partnership approach to urban problems which involves government must be profit-oriented, if it is to do well and economically that which we want done. . . . If we can create an atmosphere in which a thousand Rouses,[5] of greater or lesser capacity, can attack the problems of American cities, and can be driven on by the possibility of substantial profit, we will have those men on the job."

Congress and the citizens of the United States must be wary of overconfidence in the capacities of our planners, developers, and industrial problem-solvers, of a hundred or a thousand extraordinary "Rouses," to design and implement "solutions" to the social and economic problems of the Negro masses. There is no question that, given the political will and consensus, the financial resources and the time required for organization and tooling-up, the United States Government could carve out attractive markets to "systems contractors," COMSAT's, and entrepreneur-developers to engage in large-scale city rebuilding and rehabilitation. However, in my judgment, this approach would prove unwise and disastrous, because it would ignore the basic "anti-colonialism" message of the ghetto rebellion. *A way must be found to attract and utilize private and public capital in order to vastly increase our present institutional capacity to involve and develop the human capital resources in Negro ghettos.* Negroes need the opportunity to participate fully in creating and controlling new and rehabilitated communities around new forms of political, social, and economic institutions—new not only for Negroes, but new for urban society in the United States. Institutional change in this country is lagging far behind our capabilities and standards for improving the quality of personal, social, and community life.

Everything we know about life in the black ghetto today demonstrates that, in the process of coping with social, economic, and other problems, the nature of the planning and development process itself is much more important than the end product, as far as ghetto-dwellers are concerned. Who provides the financial and technical assistance—public or private interests—is much less crucial than *how* that help is forthcoming. And it is not how efficiently the job is done that counts (when efficiency is judged by incomprehensible or alien standards such as intricate cost-benefit criteria); what counts is how many people benefit, and in what real and meaningful ways. (How many more people have freedom of choice today than yesterday? How many people exercised that freedom and did it actually pay off?) The question is not how many "Rouses" can be harnessed by profit and social purpose to bring about social and economic change in the ghetto. The question is how much Negro talent and human potential is rescued from ghetto oblivion through full participation in, and control over, community reconstruction.

Negroes know they have little or no inducements to offer to private investment in the ghetto. They have only two assets: their ability to generate fear of social disruption ("Burn, baby, burn") and the prospect of politically controlling major urban centers containing the centers of investment and trade. At the moment, these are the only "incentives" or bargaining tools that the ghetto market possesses. Political control through population growth is a bargaining tool that is relatively independent of Negro manipulation. As long as ghetto-dwellers possess no other significant bargaining instruments, no countervailing power, the threat of social

disorder will not be discarded as a major bargaining weapon, and violence is likely to occur again and again. And fear of social disruption and violence may undermine even the best program for attracting private industry into the ghetto. In my judgment, even though private enterprise is becoming aroused to its social responsibilities, and even with congressional provision of a generous tax incentives program, private enterprise will choose to participate primarily through capital investment rather than through direct participation (such as construction of new industrial or commercial facilities within ghettos). This opinion is supported, for instance, by the dialogue between Gerald L. Phillippe, Chairman of the Board of the General Electric Company, and Senator Robert Kennedy, at the Ribicoff Committee hearings.

First, Mr. Phillippe made a prepared statement to the Ribicoff Committee, highlighting the urgency of the so-called urban crisis, and describing GE's proposal to enter the "new cities industry," announced by GE in the summer of 1966.

MR. PHILLIPPE. . . . the quality of our whole national life depends on the quality of urban living. Neither industry nor any other segment of society can evade responsibility for doing its share to improve this quality . . . The challenges we face are of massive proportions—reminiscent of the grim challenge of Pearl Harbor just twenty-five years ago today. . . .

SENATOR KENNEDY. For instance, you have in Bedford-Stuyvesant a population of some 400,000. You have in Harlem a population of perhaps 400,000 or 500,000. What would be required for you to decide that you were going to build a plant in Bedford-Stuyvesant or Harlem or South Side Chicago or Watts, you or General Motors or Ford or any of the other large corporations or companies in the United States.

[After discussing general location requirements, Board Chairman Phillippe and Senator Kennedy discussed the threat of disorders and violence as deterrents to industry's locating in ghetto areas.]

MR. PHILLIPPE. I do not know, I have not investigated it, nor have any of our industrial relations people investigated it, but the record, if you are talking about climate right at the moment, the record of Harlem would not be particularly attractive to us, I would think.

SENATOR KENNEDY. Are you thinking particularly about violence?

MR. PHILLIPPE. Yes.

SENATOR KENNEDY. And the fact that there would be concern about this?

MR. PHILLIPPE. Yes. We would not like to walk into one of those things knowingly if we could avoid it. Now there might be some other motivations. There might be, if we could make some contribution to it, why we might consider it.

SENATOR KENNEDY. What you have talked about . . . the central market, the transportation of builders' supplies, the labor market and the cost of power . . . are not insurmountable problems as far as taking the kind of steps we are outlining.

MR. PHILLIPPE. Yes. They may not be.

SENATOR KENNEDY. I would think that if you could have some assurances, for instance, for the future . . .

MR. PHILLIPPE. Did you have on your list the climate in which we would be operating?

SENATOR KENNEDY. I will put that down. If you could have some assurances in connection with the labor supply and the training of people by the federal government, and if you could have some assurances as far as transportation in and out of the area, by the city, giving you certain guarantees regarding police protection and the environment under which people were working, you would have a market that really has been untapped as of the present time, first as far as workers is concerned, and, second, as far as purchasers are concerned.

MR. PHILLIPPE. A market for what, Senator?

SENATOR KENNEDY. All kinds of products.

MR. PHILLIPPE. For example, you could not make turbines in the middle of New York.

SENATOR KENNEDY. No, but I come back to this paragraph [in Mr. Phillippe's prepared statement] where you discuss the "more extensive market research into the needs of cities."

MR. PHILLIPPE. Oh, yes.

SENATOR KENNEDY. . . . let me ask you if anybody has ever asked you, across the country, to ever build a plant in any one of these areas?

MR. PHILLIPPE. Has anyone ever asked us to build a plant?

MR. SMITH (vice president for market and public relations). In any one of those areas?

MR. PHILLIPPE. In Stuyvesant?

SENATOR KENNEDY. Not just in Stuyvesant, but in any . . .

MR. PHILLIPPE. In any areas?

SENATOR KENNEDY. Ghetto areas.

MR. PHILLIPPE. Oh, yes.

SENATOR KENNEDY. Not just in any area but in any of the ghetto areas.

MR. PHILLIPPE. No, I do not believe so.

It is quite apparent from the above testimony that between the rhetoric about an "urban crisis" of the magnitude of "Pearl Harbor" and the justification and commitment to act, and between the tax incentive for large-scale industrial development in the ghetto and actual job creation, there is a gap filled with ambivalence, ambiguity, contradiction, and plain nonsense. Furthermore, it should be apparent that guarantees and assurances of tractable workers harmoniously adjusting to their nice new ghetto work environments are an improbable dream.

There is no structure of authority in urban centers that can guarantee to any corporation a cessation of hostilities in the ghetto. The ghetto is a trap for lower-income and lower-class Negroes. With sufficient income and dissolution of discrimination in housing, large numbers of Negroes would leave the Harlems and Bedford-Stuyvesants, still leaving a vast black proletariat in the inner cities. The question becomes, how do you gainfully employ lower-income lower-class Negroes, trapped for their lifetimes in one ghetto or another, in a manner that makes them content despite their lack of freedom? How do we make the Negro reservations under our apartheid system tolerably comfortable? If there is a rational answer to such fundamentally absurd questions, I suspect that major emphasis on direct investment by large corporations in industrial development in the ghettos is not that answer. . . .

Let us briefly recapitulate the logic of the argument for industrial development in the ghetto up to this point:

Male breadwinners in the ghettos need jobs, especially jobs which pay decent wages. Industrial job growth has a multiplier effect, generating new service and retail jobs. Industrial jobs, therefore, should be a primary target in ghetto economic development. These new jobs should be located in the ghetto, so as to be easily accessible and also to generate new secondary employment in the ghetto.

It requires substantial capital investment and entrepreneurial skill to produce large quantities of new industrial jobs. Large industry has lots of both. The most effective way to tap large industries' resources is to provide incentives for such industry to locate new plants in the ghetto.

These incentives must be sufficiently strong to compete favorably with alternative investment opportunities. The best proved incentive system for business development is the tax code. In recent years it has increasingly been used as an incentive to induce investment by level, location, type, and frequency over time. Based on past precedents, the tax code system can be modified and augmented by amendment to provide special incentives to achieve a worthwhile economic and social objective—in this case, investment by industry in the ghetto.

These tax credit incentives must (1) induce the investor to take more economic *and* social risks, but minimize the economic risks (manipulation of the social risks is problematic); (2) subsidize the *possibility* of a lower rate of return, but if the return on equity is normal, subsidize the *possibility* of higher than normal profits: and (3) induce the investor to spend money that normally would not be spent (e.g., training the hard-core unemployed).

In contrast to housing development, which involves the production of a social utility, the risks to profits for industrial development cannot be eliminated altogether by a guaranteed return on investment in industrial development. Operating losses can only be offset by liberal tax credits, and not eliminated—a critical difference when compared to housing investment protected wholly by government guarantees.

The only weakness in the above argument is its underlying premise—that the number one need in the ghetto is jobs. In my judgment, this is a false assumption. *The number one need in the ghetto is freedom of choice and, more specifically, community reconstruction and development through a black structured decision-making process,* a major by-product of this being a job for every person willing and able to work. One of the methods for community development is economic development, including the expansion of industrial employment. The method for expansion of industrial employment opportunities for Negroes within the territorial boundaries of the ghetto must be consistent with an economic development plan approved by the ghetto area's Community Development Corporation. The primary benefits of industrial development, capital accumulation, and profit benefits, as well as job benefits, must accrue to residents of the ghetto area.

Under Robert Kennedy's tax incentive plan for industrial development in the ghetto, private industry is being asked to play the role of an agent of economic and social change—beyond its capacity to support that role. Inspired by overconfidence in technology and power of "bigness," the Kennedy plan makes an assumption about the transferability of competence

from production engineering to social engineering that is more workable in Pakistan than in Harlem. In Pakistan, for example, private incentives, spurred by direct and indirect government intervention, do not have to contend with the social consequences of ghettoization. A pragmatic approach to the role of government and private enterprise, with good economic management on both sides, can produce significantly improved economic performance in an "underdeveloped" economy, such as we find in the ghetto or in Pakistan, if the powerful factor of racial segregation is not present. The existence of racial segregation, and the expectation that it will perpetuate for the foreseeable future, calls for a radically different approach to community and economic development: *a strategy designed for large, racially segregated Negro communities, convulsively seeking both self-government and freedom of choice to live beyond the ghetto.*

. . .

One of the most remarkable aspects of the modern corporation is that for all the creativeness, daring, and drive required to organize and operate a large-scale business firm, corporate managers, as a group, exercise negligible social initiative both locally and nationally. The public increasingly hears of business expanding its role in the War on Poverty: of insurance companies committing billions of dollars to wipe out slum housing; of business coalitions planning strategy for anti-Hot Summer activities, holding conferences to castigate welfare bureaucracies, and moving into rural and urban backwaters of hard-core unemployment to create jobs. But close examination of each of these efforts reveals not only the most minimal financial and social commitment commensurate with sound public relations, but, more surprising, an unbusinesslike acceptance of the status quo as the framework of operations, even when the status quo framework is at the root of the problem. However, business ideology is changing, slowly but perceptibly, toward more aggressive leadership in public affairs affecting urban development. But corporate America still has a long way to go before achieving effectiveness in relation to the black revolution evolving in major urban centers.

The separation of equity ownership and management has given to corporate institutions wide latitude for activities in the public interest, so long as these activities do not impede or impair profit-making operations. In the past few years, as the urban crisis became more visible as a result of ghetto riots, corporate rhetoric on social statesmanship has stressed its capabilities to operate effectively in the social sphere, with or without government partnership; but lately, there is increasing emphasis on the federal government as the market-maker and guarantor against risk for private participation in social uplift. This corporate rhetoric has tended to support the rejection of political centralism, by advocating that decision-making power be decentralized and vested in the locality. To the extent that corporations are successful in obtaining major responsibilities for urban development, the opponents of centralization of governmental power will have won a victory, though perhaps a Pyrrhic one. The unlimited scope of corporate activity, the limitations of both centralized and decentralized federal control and regulatory mechanisms, the metropolitanization of the most urgent domestic problems, the great lag in state and local government management capabilities, and many other factors, will operate in favor of a much more powerful corporate role in urban and human resources development at the national, state, metroregional, and local levels, as against a more significant role for local government itself.

A new phase of public-private enterprise partnership is taking shape around the problems and needs of urban ghettos. Because of the pace, complexity, scope, and intensity of technological and social change in urban America, specially organized institutions will be required to cope with the consequences of urbanization and ghettoization. Urban development and management will require mobilization of a vast number of highly trained administrators, technicians, researchers, project managers, and planners—quantities of the kind of talented manpower who normally shun public bureaucracies. One of the most significant outcomes of the urban crisis, therefore, will be increasing reliance on private enterprise to plan and carry out what traditionally have been public functions. Indeed, if this trend is not redirected, private enterprise will move into the position of deciding how and where this nation will live in the twenty-first century. The seventies will mark

the clear emergence of this quasi-public role for private enterprise.

Social critics like Michael Harrington take the extreme position that business methods and priorities are inapplicable to the crisis of the cities: "... when business methods are sincerely and honestly applied to urban problems, with very good intentions, they still *inevitably* lead to anti-social results" (italics mine). Harrington is saying more than that the allocation of resources dominated by economic criteria inevitably is antisocial in consequences. He states that the profit-making motive and social purpose are inherently incompatible, leading "straight to private alliances between self-interested executives and ambitious bureaucrats." Therefore, the duplicity and, possibly, dishonesty, of public and private management, according to Harrington, preclude public-private joint ventures to build and rebuild substantial portions of our metroregions.

No method of doing anything offers foolproof protection against anti-social institutional behavior. Even the collection of data can have anti-social consequences and certainly is not an ideologically neutral activity. Data collection for all governmental programs is politically biased in favor of the ideological interest of the data collection agency. The longer that an organization, like government, has been in the business, the stronger the vested interest in collecting data that can be interpreted favorably to the established institution, requiring no drastic adjustments in organizational structure or operating procedures. For this reason alone, the public domain should be opened to private enterprise, to force upon the public establishment systematic confrontation with its rationale and management system. Even if there were no poor people, no Negroes, Indians, or Mexican-Americans, "anti-monopoly" action against federal, state, and local government is desperately needed.

There is an abundant history, including and highlighted by the Economic Opportunity Program, of good intentions harnessed to nonprofit motives by "indigenous" poor people's organizations and nonindigenous rich people's organizations, resulting in more democratic but still pathetic results. Had these same people operated under the profit motive (perhaps paid on a piecework basis for successful project activities, with performance measured by reasonably meaningful criteria), the results probably would have been little better. For another example, social and economic research unencumbered by the profit-motive, under university or private foundation auspices, has made very little contribution to coping with the problems of urban living in a highly industrialized society burdened by a powerful legacy of racism. In fact, the latest badge of humility for "urbanologists" is to confess that they know very little about how our urban society actually works (and therefore, of course, millions of dollars more in applied research is needed, with some new innovative twists or "wrinkles," as they are termed by funding specialists).

The greatest menace to democratic control of planning in the ghettos is not the corporation seeking profit but inept and uninformed leadership and organization which result in continuous frustration and opens the way for exploitation and anarchism. Harrington does not give Negroes in the ghetto sufficient credit for becoming increasingly wiser about the diverse forms of economic and political "colonialism" to which they have been subjected. They are becoming well aware of the fact that, for example, "pilot" and "demonstration" projects in educational remediation and "enrichment" (so-called compensatory education) only serve to protect the school system from basic reforms in administration, teacher training, curriculum design, and so forth. However, there still remains among Negroes a huge gap between their increasingly sophisticated perception of underlying political power relationships and the lack of organizational, management, and programming skills to capitalize on this awareness. In my experience, Negroes in the ghettos, including incipient hard-core political leadership, would welcome the kind of technical and financial assistance that corporate enterprise could assemble, *if* the contractual terms and conditions of delivery and utilization can be satisfactorily established and then faithfully performed. These militant blacks, including savvy gang leaders, see frustration-crazed agitators and massive riots as undermining the potential for political and economic organization in the ghetto. They know, and white society must learn, that unless economic and political Black Power can be successfully organized in the ghetto to systematically direct ghetto manpower and profits into ghetto reconstruction, the social restraints on anarchic action will continue to disintegrate. *As of the moment however, there is no Black Power movement in the ghetto, just as there is no civil rights movement. There are only diverse and multiplying perceptions of the need for sufficient control, knowledge, and tools to crystallize power out of futility and wasted humanity.*

Contrary to Michael Harrington's convictions, the so-called "social industrialists," the corporate elite, are not incapable of grasping, intellectually and intuitively, the basic conflicts between corporate economic ideology, methods, goals, and processes and the Black Power concept of planning and development in urban ghettos. If so-called democratic planning institutions in the ghetto can be analytically described and humanly experienced, they can be understood sufficiently by corporate planners to enable them to work out a flexible, adaptable, but "businesslike" work program—one that allows plenty of margin for uncertainties and unknowns, one that respects the ideology and dynamics of evolving Black Power institutions. The critical prerequisites for the problematic matrimony between black revolution and private enterprise are: first, a vision of where blacks and whites are heading in urban America—one that can meaningfully encompass the aspirations of both races; and second, a new set of institutional vehicles, such as the Metroregional Development Corporation, the Urban-Grant University, and the Community Development Corporation, designed to pack a century of economic, social, political, and physical change into the span of a few decades.

NOTES

[1] A proposal for a federally chartered, mixed public-private corporation, with $600 million of stock issued to the public and $400 subscribed to by the federal government, for the purpose of financing any program designed to reduce urban or rural poverty approved by the directors and stockholders, with special emphasis on the application of business management techniques in the fields of job development, housing, and business development.

[2] S. 2100, 90th Congress, 1st Session.

[3] S. 2088, 90th Congress, 1st Session.

[4] Corporate earnings after tax on equity capital generally range between 5 and 10 per cent.

[5] James Rouse, developer of the new town of Columbia, Maryland.

THE PROVISION OF INSURANCE

President's National Advisory Panel on Insurance in Riot-Affected Areas

We propose a five-part program of mutually supporting actions to be undertaken immediately by all who have a responsibility for solving the problem:

—We call upon the insurance industry to take the lead in establishing voluntary plans in all states to assure all property owners fair access to property insurance.

—We look to the states to cooperate with the industry in establishing these plans; and to supplement the plans, to whatever extent may be necessary, by organizing insurance pools and taking other steps to facilitate the insuring of urban core properties.

—We urge that the federal government enact legislation creating a National Insurance Development Corporation (NIDC) to assist the insurance industry and the states in achieving the important goal of providing adequate insurance for inner cities. Through the NIDC, the state and federal governments can provide backup for the remote contingency of very large riot losses.

—We recommend that the federal government enact tax deferral measures to increase the capacity of the insurance industry to absorb the financial costs of the program.

—We suggest a series of other necessary steps to meet the special needs of the inner city insurance market—for example, programs to train agents and brokers from the core areas; to assure the absence of discrimination in insur-ance company employment on racial or other grounds; and to seek out better methods of preventing losses and of marketing insurance in low income areas.

—The fundamental thrust of our program is cooperative action. Thus, only those companies that participate in plans and pools at the local level, and only those states that take action to implement the program, will be eligible to receive the benefits provided by the National Insurance Development Corporation and by the federal tax deferral measures. We firmly believe that all concerned must work together to meet the urban insurance crisis. Everyone must contribute; no one should escape responsibility.

Our specific recommendations for a five-part program are:

FAIR PLANS

We recommend that the insurance industry, in cooperation with the states, institute in all states plans establishing fair access to insurance requirements (FAIR Plans).

A FAIR Plan assures every property owner in a state:

—Inspection of his property;

—Written notice of any improvements or loss prevention measures that may be required to make his property insurable; and

—Insurance if the property is adequately maintained according to reasonable insurance standards.

FAIR Plans make these assurances applicable to:

—All dwellings and commercial risks, including buildings and contents;

Reprinted from *Meeting the Insurance Crisis of Our Cities,* A Report by The President's National Advisory Panel on Insurance in Riot-Affected Areas (Washington, D.C.: U.S. Government Printing Office, January 1968), pp. 8–15.

and for these basic lines of insurance:
—Fire and extended coverage (damages from wind, hail, explosion, riot, civil commotion, aircraft, vehicle, and smoke);
—Vandalism and malicious mischief; and
—Burglary and theft.

FAIR Plans envision a substantial expansion of Urban Area Plans that have been in operation on a limited scale since 1960. Urban Area Plans generally cover only residential properties in limited geographical areas, offer only fire and extended coverage insurance, and have procedural inadequacies. Experience with Urban Area Plans demonstrates their promise, but also exposes their limitations. FAIR Plans will fulfill that promise.

One of the most notable extensions FAIR Plans will make over Urban Area Plans is to provide burglary and theft insurance as well as fire and extended coverage. What is commonly termed "burglary and theft insurance" encompasses a multitude of different coverages, each presenting difficult underwriting problems. This line of insurance has been a very minor part of total industry writings. It has been much more expensive to market, and increasing crime rates are making it even more expensive. The problems of burglary and theft insurance have received relatively little study, and the potential for improvement is great. While the ultimate answer to the problem lies in the reduction of crime and in loss prevention, FAIR Plans can provide the incentive to insurance companies to develop innovations in the burglary and theft line that will make the basic coverages more available to the public.

The major differences between Urban Area Plans and FAIR Plans have led us to formulate the new name, which has the added merit of conveying to the public the overriding purpose of the Plans.

We believe that FAIR Plans will:
—End the practice of "red-lining" neighborhoods and eliminate other restrictive activities;
—Secure for all property owners equitable access to all basic lines of property insurance; and
—Encourage property improvement and loss prevention by responsible owners.

FAIR Plans will also furnish accurate information to local and state governments on neighborhoods and on the condition of individual properties in poverty areas. We strongly urge forceful action at local levels to remedy the known environmental hazards of these areas. Action should include the development and enforcement of effective building and fire codes, the provision of more adequate police and fire protection, and the improvement of health, safety and related local services.

If the information produced by FAIR Plans leads to constructive governmental action, environmental hazards, which generate many of the insurance problems that make the FAIR Plans necessary, will be removed. Thus, FAIR Plans contain, in themselves, a broader implication. They serve as a stimulus to cure the basic conditions which have created the need for FAIR Plans at this time.

We recognize that the successful operation of FAIR Plans depends to a large extent on a sincere effort on the part of each insurance company to accept center city insurance risks.

We are confident that the insurance industry will take the steps required to help solve what is not only a complex and troublesome insurance problem, but a profound social problem.

FAIR Plans establish minimum standards that are essential to overcome center city insurance problems. Every state will develop and implement a plan in conformance with its own local institutions, and every state may, indeed, establish criteria beyond those suggested by the Panel.

The rates for insuring properties are an important aspect of FAIR Plans. Since the regulation of insurance rates is a state function, the states will bear the responsibility for the rates payable for properties insured under FAIR Plans.

We urge that, insofar as possible, the level of rates generally applicable in a state also apply to properties insured under FAIR Plans. Surcharges, if needed, should be permitted only for demonstrable hazards of the property itself. Wherever possible, there should be no additional rate for environmental hazards.

We recognize the need for flexible and adequate rates. A risk must bear an appropriate rate; if a property is significantly more hazardous than average, it must yield a commensurately higher premium. Nevertheless, we hope that the states will consider placing a maximum limit on surcharges. Excessive or discriminatory rates must not be permitted to undermine the goals of the FAIR Plans.

STATE POOLS OR OTHER FACILITIES

We recommend that states, in cooperation with the insurance industry, form pools of insurance companies (or other facilities) to make insurance available for insurable properties that do not receive coverage under the FAIR Plans.

State pools will supplement FAIR Plans. Some owners of well-maintained property will be unable to obtain insurance even after an inspection under the FAIR Plan. Although the property itself is in good condition, it may be adjacent to an extremely high fire risk, exposed to unusual crime hazards, or subject to other environmental hazards which presently make property uninsurable.

Owners of these properties, usually declined by individual insurance companies, must have fair access to insurance. The responsible owner who cares for his property must not be penalized because of his neighborhood. He must not be denied insurance for reasons beyond his control. To do so not only treats him unfairly, but encourages the spread of urban blight.

It is important to recognize the distinction between this property and uninsurable property that itself is in hazardous condition and cannot or will not be repaired by the owner. Uninsurable property of this latter sort should not be insured, but should, instead, be the object of renewal programs designed to revitalize blighted areas.

We recommend that state insurance pools be formed where necessary to insure well-maintained property, regardless of its location. A pool is an association of insurance companies that agree to share income, expenses and losses according to a predetermined arrangement. A pool may be voluntary if all but an insignificant part of the industry participates. In some states it may have to be mandatory to obtain the broad industry participation that is necessary.

State pools will:

—Guarantee to the property owner insurance if his property meets insurable standards, even when his property is subjected to environmental hazards;

—Provide a method of spreading equitably throughout the insurance industry the risks from environmental hazards unacceptable to a single company;

—Create a convenient facility for government financial assistance if it is needed to provide insurance for these risks.

Some states may well choose a different method to achieve the same results expected from pools. They may elect some other arrangement more suitable to their own local institutions—for example, a state insurance company to underwrite the properties directly or a state insurance fund to provide reinsurance for these risks. The point is, state pools or some other facility may be needed to achieve the goals of the FAIR Plans.

In some states, properties adversely affected by environmental hazards may be insignificant in number. They may be insured without the necessity of organizing a state pool. Diligent effort exercised by property owners and social responsibility exercised by state officials and the insurance industry—for example, by modifying underwriting standards—may succeed in providing adequate insurance through the FAIR Plans alone.

States that are uncertain whether a pool is necessary may wish to wait a year or two until they evaluate the data developed under their FAIR Plan. In this case, they would have the benefit of the experience of those states that have moved forward more rapidly with pool arrangements.

We recognize that very little is known about insuring core area risks under a pool arrangement. The experience of the Watts Pool is helpful; but since that pool is restricted to fire insurance at highly surcharged rates for commercial properties in a limited geographic area, it is not necessarily a model that can be used generally. Pooling, however, is a standard insurance arrangement, and there is every reason to expect that it can function effectively to handle center city insurance problems.

The underwriting standards of the pool should be set by the state insurance department after consulting with the insurance industry. All properties meeting reasonable standards of insurability should be accepted regardless of environmental hazards.

It is recognized that deductibles and other limits on liability may be needed in making insurance available through a pool.

Rates for property insured in the pool will be regulated by the states. Each state will determine its own appropriate pattern of rates. We recognize that flexible rates may be necessary. But we urge that the pool charge no additional rate for environmental hazards, and that, if surcharges are needed, they be subjected to a maximum limit in order to keep the premium costs within the means of the urban core resident.

It may well be that intensive loss prevention and educational campaigns, deductibles and other similar insurance devices, as well as prudent pool management, can make the pool profitable over a reasonable period of time.

We recognize, however, that the rates charged for pool risks and the type of risks undertaken by the pool may make recurring losses inevitable. Handling these losses might be resolved in a number of ways. If rates are adequate throughout a state to permit substantial profits by companies generally, companies might be assessed some portion of their underwriting income on non-pool property. Or, a state might itself provide funds from premium taxes or general revenues and subsidize to a certain extent the risks in the pool. Just as a state provides funds for other programs designed to revitalize core areas, it could consider its insurance pool as a related undertaking.

Another alternative for covering pool losses is for the state pool to apply to the National Insurance Development Corporation for financial backing against losses. In this event, federal as well as state funds would be available to spread the cost of subsidization.

NATIONAL INSURANCE DEVELOPMENT CORPORATION

We recommend that the federal government charter a National Insurance Development Corporation (NIDC) to undertake responsibility for a variety of vital but unfulfilled functions in support of the actions of private industry and states in the operations of FAIR Plans and state pools.

The National Insurance Development Corporation would have no shareholders, but rather directors appointed by the President and representing all the parties vitally interested in the inner city insurance problem—residents of urban cores, insurance industry representatives, state officials (including state regulators), federal officials, and members of the public. It would not seek to make a profit but to discharge important functions in making insurance more widely available to the public.

The Corporation would discharge these functions:

—Provide reinsurance against the risk of extraordinary loss from civil disorders, and thereby remove the burden from a single group of persons or segment of the insurance industry;

—Provide a source of reinsurance for state pools;

—Assess the performance of FAIR Plans, state pools, and other insurance programs designed to deal with the problems of the inner cities, by gathering information, analyzing data, and preparing studies for the benefit of the public, the industry, and government.

At the present time, standard insurance policies in many lines of insurance include coverage against loss from riots. We strongly believe that the insurance industry should continue to include this riot coverage in all lines of insurance in which it presently exists.

We believe that the riot risk should, however, be neutralized as a factor hampering the underwriting of insurance in center cities and the placement of private reinsurance. Accordingly, the NIDC would issue riot reinsurance to member companies which are participating fully in FAIR Plans and, where they exist, in state pools.

Any company desiring this riot reinsurance would pay a premium to the NIDC. The premiums paid in will provide a fund from which to pay losses should they occur. The companies would retain the primary coverage of riot damage. The NIDC reinsurance would cover only the contingency of very large losses.

Maintaining law and order is primarily a state and local responsibility. Thus, any state desiring reinsurance for riot risks located in that state would be required to accept a state layer of financial backup of some kind in the event that disorders actually take place in that state.

To the extent that losses on reinsured policies exceed the fund accumulated by company premiums and state contributions, the NIDC would have authority to borrow from the Federal Treasury amounts needed to pay for losses in excess of its assets up to whatever limit may be prescribed by Congress. The borrowings would be repaid by subsequent accumulations of premiums or by Congressional appropriations.

In addition, we recognize that there is great uncertainty as to how state pools will function, and how their financial aspects will be handled. We feel strongly, however, that pools should be undertaken now where they are required to meet urban core insurance problems. To aid the operation of state pools, the NIDC could receive direct appropriations for the purpose of helping the pools achieve their important objectives.

Finally, we recognize that our proposed program, like all new measures, will not be put into operation without difficulties. The program needs to be monitored to see that it is accomplishing its objectives, and this might best be undertaken by the NIDC.

The monitoring function includes:
—Collecting statistics on the operation of FAIR Plans and the state pools.
—Conducting surveys and studies in cooperation with state insurance departments and the insurance industry to assure that the program is achieving its objectives.
—Gathering statistics and preparing studies of reinsurance—especially alien reinsurance—and of direct insurance placed abroad.
—Publishing the results of studies and surveys and providing information and analysis to the public, the insurance industry, and state and federal governments.
—Making recommendations for any changes needed in the program to achieve its purposes.

TAX DEFERRAL MEASURES

We recommend federal legislation authorizing tax deferral measures to permit insurance companies participating in FAIR Plans and, where they exist, in state pools, to accumulate, as quickly as possible, more adequate reserves for "catastrophe losses."

Federal tax measures would operate as follows:
—The federal government would defer tax on any amount placed by insurance companies in special reserves to meet catastrophe losses. Any company desiring tax deferral must participate

in FAIR Plans and, where they exist, in state pools.
—That portion of the special reserve that would otherwise have been paid in taxes to the federal government would instead be invested in interest-free, non-transferable United States Treasury securities. Should the companies incur catastrophe losses, these securities could be redeemed for cash, which would then be available to pay the losses.
—Limits would be placed on the amount of funds that could be accumulated in the tax-deferred reserves. Funds set aside in pools and in special reserves which are later returned to the companies for general use would become taxable at the time of the return.

The states would authorize, within these limits, whatever reserves and premiums they determined to be desirable and appropriate. This action would trigger the federal tax deferral.

The Panel believes that when sufficient reserves are accumulated, the financial backup of government against catastrophe losses may no longer be necessary. Tax deferral measures therefore contain the promise of phasing out governmental support and restoring the entire enterprise to private hands.

OTHER NECESSARY STEPS

We recommend other measures to meet special problems of the urban core insurance market, specifically:

1. *Manpower Training Programs* to be sponsored by government to train residents of blighted areas as agents and brokers with special competence to handle the insurance needs of center city areas.

2. *Recruitment and Training Programs* to be expanded by insurance companies in order to attract residents of center city areas to fill personnel needs at all levels of the business.

3. *More Economical Methods of Marketing Insurance* to be studied by the insurance industry; for example, new forms of contracts, as well as new marketing and underwriting techniques designed to improve the insurance market in center cities.

4. *Better Procedures to Handle Policyholder Complaints* to be developed by state insurance

departments in order to have better records of complaints, cancellations, nonrenewals, and other statistics that measure insurance company performance.

5. *Research Programs* to be established by the insurance industry in cooperation with state pools and government to develop new loss prevention techniques and other methods of improving the insurance market in center city areas.

6. *More Refined Statistics* to be compiled by rating bureaus and insurance companies on loss experience in order to facilitate rate regulation and loss prevention.

7. *Lending Programs* to be accelerated in the urban core with particular attention to providing needed funds to small businessmen and other property owners for removal and control of fire and crime hazards.

8. *Contractors' Bid and Performance Bonds for Urban Core Businessmen* to be made more readily available to encourage construction work in these areas.

ADDITIONAL READINGS FOR CHAPTER 11

Andrew F. Brimmer, "The Banking System and Urban Economic Development," a paper presented at the 1968 Annual Meetings of the American Real Estate and Urban Economic Association and the American Finance Association, December 23, 1968.

"Business in the Ghetto," Proceedings, American Bar Association National Institute, April 11 and 12, 1969, *The Business Lawyer,* V. 25, Special Issue (September 1969).

Theodore L. Cross, *Black Capitalism: Strategy for Business in the Ghetto* (New York: Atheneum, 1969).

Economic Development Opportunity, Hearings before the Select Committee on Small Business, United States Senate, 90th Congress, 2nd Session, on the Role of the Federal Government in the Development of Small Business Enterprises in the Urban Ghetto, May 24, 1968 and June 17, 1968 (Washington, D.C.: U.S. Government Printing Office, 1968).

Eugene P. Foley, *The Achieving Ghetto* (Washington, D.C.: The Nation Press, Inc.) 1968).

Eli Ginzberg (ed.), *Business Leadership and the Negro Crisis* (New York: McGraw-Hill Book Company, 1968), pp. 95-120.

William F. Haddad and G. Douglas Pugh (eds.), *Black Economic Development* (Englewood Cliffs, N.J.: Prentice-Hall, 1969), especially article by Peter F. McNeish, "Where Does the Money Come From?", pp. 85-97.

Leland Hazard, "Thinking Ahead: Business Must Put Up," Harvard Business Review, V. 46, N. 1 (January—February 1968), pp. 2-4, 6, 8, 10, 12, 168-170.

Verle Johnston, "Financing the Inner City," in *Monthly Review* (Federal Reserve Bank of San Francisco, October 1969), pp. 199-210.

Louis O. Kelso and Patricia Hetter, *Two-Factor Theory: The Economics of Reality* (New York: Random House, 1967).

Robert F. Kennedy, "A Business Development Program for Our Poverty Areas," reprinted in Frederick D. Sturdivant (ed.), *The Ghetto Marketplace* (New York: The Free Press, 1969), pp. 193-209.

Walter McQuade, "Mortgages for the Slums," *Fortune,* V. LXXVII, N. 1 (January 1968), pp. 162-163.

Private Investment in the Inner City, Hearings before the Subcommittee on Financial Institutions of the Committee on Banking and Currency, United States Senate, 90th Congress, 2nd Session, on Private Investment in the Inner City, in the Fall of 1968 (Washington, D.C.: U.S. Government Printing Office, 1968).

Review of Small Business Administration's Programs and Policies—1969, Hearings before the Select Committee on Small Business, United States Senate, 91st Congress, 1st Session, on Review of Small Business Administration Financial Assistance Programs and Policies, June, July, and October 1969 (Washington, D.C.: U.S. Government Printing Office, 1969).

Richard S. Rosenbloom and John K. Shank, "Let's Write off MESBICS," *Harvard Business Review,* V. 48, N. 5 (September—October 1970) pp. 90-97.

Frederick D. Sturdivant, "Better Deal for Ghetto Shoppers," *Harvard Business Review,* V. 46, N. 2 (March—April 1968), pp. 130-139.

The Urban Coalition, *Consumer Credit and the Low Income Consumer*, Preliminary Report (Researched and Written by William G. Kaye and Associates, Rockville, Md., for the Urban Coalition, November 1969).

For the past several years there has been much discussion and considerable controversy within both the black and white communities regarding the economic role and potential of the black community in American society. The concept of black economic development has received the imprimatur of such disparate institutions as the Office of the President of the United States, the National Urban League, the Congress of Racial Equality (CORE), the National Business League, and the Nation of Islam (Black Muslims), as well as from a host of religious, fraternal, and business groups across the nation. Early in his administration, President Richard M. Nixon established the Office of Minority Business Enterprise within the Department of Commerce with the specific charge of coordinating federal efforts to assist black (and other) minority businessmen. While the performance of OMBE has been the subject of much skepticism and criticism, it is significant nonetheless that the President considered it necessary to institute as a specific aspect of federal policy the development of minority businesses. Other governmental agencies including the Small Business Administration, the Economic Development Administration, the Office of Economic Opportunity, and the Department of Housing and Urban Development have also been given the task of stimulating minority economic development.

Unfortunately, despite the full-blown rhetoric and the flurry of recent activity surrounding the economic development of minority groups—with greatest emphasis having been placed upon the economic aspirations and efforts of the black community—there has been little rigorous analysis of the following points:

1. The meaning of the concept of "black economic development" and whether there are specific characteristics which distinguish black economic development from economic development in general. There exists disagreement among economists whether black economic development relates solely to the establishment and growth of economic institutions owned and managed by blacks or refers also to an overall improvement of the economic base of the black community through an increase in aggregate employment and income of members of the community irrespective of the source of jobs and earnings. Moreover, does black economic development differ from simply creating black businesses? Similarly, there is some controversy concerning the meaning of "community." Does it refer to definable geographical areas, the totality of the black population wherever it is physically situated, or only those blacks who are poor?

2. The viability of the various models which have been proposed for black economic development. While many individuals—particularly whites—have used the expression "black capitalism" as a shorthand for black economic development, it is clear that the term is inappropriate to describe the economic philosophy of a substantial number of blacks. Indeed, capitalism has been viewed by some black leaders as the white man's "trick bag" and totally inappropriate for the black man. For example in his "Black Manifesto" which caused much controversy in April,

Development

1969, with its demand for $500 million in reparations to black people by white churches and synagogues, James Forman stated:

[W]e must separate ourselves from these Negroes who go around the country promoting all types of schemes for black capitalism....

[A]ny black man or negro who is advocating a perpetuation of capitalism inside the United States is in fact seeking not only his own ultimate destruction and death but is contributing to the continuous exploitation of black people all around the world. . . . [1]

In a somewhat more pragmatic vein, Roy Innis, national director of CORE, has asserted:

In the new focus on economic control, there has been much talk about something called "black capitalism." Many of our people have been deluded into endless debates centered around this term. There is no such animal. Capitalism, like socialism, is an economic and political philosophy that describes the experience of Europeans and their descendants— Americans. Blacks must innovate, must create a new ideology. It may include elements of capitalism, elements of socialism, or elements of either: that is immaterial. What matters is that it will be created to fit our needs. [2]

CORE has attempted to make this philosophy operative by emphasizing economic development under the leadership of community-owned development corporations, and by its sponsorship of the aborted Community Self-Determination Act. [3] This legislation calling for broad-based community ownership of industry was introduced before Congress in 1968 but failed to achieve passage. Obviously, a number of the approaches emanating from the black community cannot properly be called capitalistic.

Some of the suggestions for black economic development have called for black-owned and -managed businesses which are indentical with white enterprises (and, in some instances, are the result of collaborative black-white "turnkey" efforts), and which operate within an overwhelmingly white economy. Other approaches, including the Rev. Leon Sullivan's Opportunities Industrialization Center in Philadelphia, the Bedford-Stuyvesant Restoration Corporation in New York City, the Hough Development Corporation in Cleveland, and FIGHTON Inc., in Rochester, have concentrated on economic entities owned and managed (and with the profits going to) the community as a whole. In the extreme instance, there have been calls for the establishment of a separate black economy which would have no relationship with white America, except, possibly, in the area of foreign trade. On one point, however, there is consensus among black Americans. Black economic development cannot be restricted to the creations of "Mom and Pop" stores, but must result in the establishment of substantial financial, commercial, service, and industrial enterprises.

3. The problems and prospects which blacks face in their economic development

activities. These are conditioned by such factors as the possibility of changing the political, economic, social, and psychological conditions which thwarted black enterprise in the past; the availability of capital and entrepreneurial and management talent within the black community; the present structure of American industry and the ease or difficulty of market entry by new businesses; and the rate and directions of growth of the American economy in the years ahead.

4. In Chapter 8, we made the point that, in the past, the development of black enterprise was fostered but ultimately thwarted by various forms of economic segregation on the part of the white community in general and the business sector in particular. If past practices perpetuate themselves, the future of black economic development will be bleak. Accordingly, both blacks and whites must address the question of the appropriate role for white business and the white community in black economic development. A number of white corporations have been instrumental in establishing or facilitating the creation of black-owned and -managed businesses. Such firms include IBM, General Electric, Aero-Jet-General, Mattel Industries, General Motors, Litton Industries, Fairchild-Hiller, and Xerox. Such black firms as Watts Manufacturing Company, Progress Aerospace Enterprises, and Shindana Dolls have received various forms of corporate assistance. Some new enterprises have been owned and managed by blacks at the outset; others have been subsidiaries of the parent firm with black management and the provision of eventual transfer of ownership to black control. Other large corporations have also made available debt funding or served as guarantors of loans for black concerns. Still other businesses have provided technical assistance to new firms, and have entered into "shelter-contracts" guaranteeing to buy the output of incubating black industries. Some of the efforts are detailed in the selections which follow. Lest the reader receive an erroneous impression, however, while support of black economic development by the business community has been infinitely greater than in the past, the number of companies involved and the extent of their commitment in financial and manpower terms is still quite limited.

Yet, as Arnold Schucter's essay in Chapter 11 indicates, there are those within both the black and white community who have grave reservations regarding these forms of corporate involvement. Critics contend that these efforts result in neocolonialism in the ghetto; co-opt and usurp black control of their own economic destiny; inexorably tie black economic development to capitalism; cause the creation of some black enterprises which have no economic justification for existance other than the paternalistic umbrella provided by their corporate sponsors; raise the aspirations of many blacks to an unrealistic degree and destine many to disappointment and failure; sap the vitality and draw attention away from the efforts of black organizations which are attempting to "go it alone" in the economic development field; and permit business firms to avoid their obligations to employ and promote black employees. In a number of specific instances, these fears appear to have been well founded. Yet there are sufficient instances of collaboration which have been successful from the point of view of all participants to suggest that white business should continue, and, indeed, accelerate its participation in black economic development. However—and this is essential—collaboration must always be limited in time, place, and manner to approaches which are desired by, acceptable to, and compatible with the needs of the black community.

In addition to white business involvement, it should be obvious that substantial governmental assistance to black business is necessary if the growth of substantial minority enterprises is to take place. Government as a supplier of financing and credit, as a market, as a trainer of manpower, and as a provider of subsidies, are time-honored roles. In the selections which follow, several more radical suggestions for possible governmental action appear.

The first reading, "Black Economic Development," drawn from the Final Report of a Conference on Black Economic Development sponsored by the American Assembly in 1969, explores the social rationale of black economic development as well as several alternative approaches to its achievement, and makes a series of policy recommendations including the formation of a National Development Corporation. Richard F. America, Jr., a black economist, poses the question "What Do You People Want?" in the selection by that name. His response is that black people want economic power. To achieve economic power the author proposes a program of systematically transferring some of this nation's largest corporations to black ownership and operation. Banker Louis L. Allen challenges the America approach in his article, "Making Capitalism Work in the Ghetto," and argues that economic development—specifically capitalism—applies to blacks in exactly the same fashion as it does to all other Americans. He also examines the role of American business in the developmental process. Robert S. Browne, an economics professor and director of the Black Economic Research Center, implicitly responds to the Allen thesis in his essay, "Toward an Overall Assessment of Our Alternatives," and indicates the essential importance of new approaches to economic development to fulfill the aspirations of black men and women within the United States.

We suggest that the reader reread the selections which appear in Chapter 8, particularly those by Harding B. Young and James M. Hund, and Andrew F. Brimmer. Together with the essays presented here they suggest the complexity of the issues facing both black and white Americans in the critical area of the economic development of the black community within the United States.

NOTES

[1]See, "The Black Manifesto," reprinted in Robert S. Lecky and H. Elliott Wright (eds.), *Black Manifesto: Religion, Racism, and Reparations* (New York: Sheed and Ward, Inc., 1969), pp. 114-115.

[2]Roy Innis *"Separatist Economics:* A New Social Contract," in William F. Haddad and G. Doughlas Pugh (eds.), *Black Economic Development* (Englewood Cliffs, N.J.: Prentice-Hall, Inc., 1969), pp. 50-51.

[3]The Community Self-Determination Act of 1968, S. 3876, 90th Congress 2nd Session. Evaluations of the legislation are found in Kenneth H. Miller, "Community Capitalism and the Community Self-Determination Act", *Harvard Journal on Legislation,* V. 6, (1969), pp. 413-461, and Frederick D. Sturdivant, "The Limits of Black Capitalism," *Harvard Business Review* V. 47, N. 1, (January-February 1969), pp. 122-128.

BLACK ECONOMIC DEVELOPMENT

Thirty-Fifth American Assembly

After centuries of disenfranchisement and years of token progress in civil rights, black Americans are turning to economic development as a medium to secure the rights they have failed to gain.

Black economic development aspires to a condition of parity between the *haves* and *have-nots* in American society. It seeks a fair balance of economic power in terms of income, employment, accumulation of productive capital assets, and involvement at the managerial level of corporate enterprise. It aims, in short, at giving the black man what a succession of promising social measures has so far failed to give him—an equitable share in the American system.

Black economic development is not a panacea for the nation's racial ills. It is a vital thrust of the drive toward equality among the races—the logical culmination of a decade of disillusionment in which integration and employment programs by themselves were seen to have effected little improvement of the social order.

Having tested the programs for change and found them wanting, blacks now seek the opportunity to evolve their own options. It should be recognized that there can be no separate and autonomous black economy over the long run, for this would stifle the free commerce from which such an economy must draw its vitality, and it would thus be self-defeating. But blacks want effective control of the economic institutions in their own communities. This should not preclude general involvement elsewhere.

To do this most will initially need, in addition to their own talents, energies and efforts, the

Reprinted from *Black Economic Development.* Report of the Thirty-Fifth American Assembly, April 24-27, 1969, Arden House, Harriman, New York, pp. 4-9, by permission of the American Assembly, Columbia University.

advice, assistance and support of the white business community. The exclusion of blacks from business opportunity in the past has left them with neither the capital nor a reserve of trained, experienced, and immediately available talent upon which to build business structures in the present.

Negroes in America today who operate businesses of any considerable size are few indeed— fewer, in fact, than 40 years ago. The majority of black businesses are marginal operations. Between 1950 and 1960, black business ownership actually declined 20 per cent. Less than three per cent of all United States industry, less than two per cent of construction enterprises, less than one per cent of manufacturing are minority-owned. Of such businesses as blacks do own, 73 per cent operate within the strict confinement of their own community. Even in the black community, around 80 per cent of the gross volume of business is controlled by whites, the majority of them absentee owners. (From Small Business Administration estimates, 1968.)

So there is a huge gulf to be crossed. Yet evidence can be found in both black and white communities for cautious optimism. Here and there in the nation are signs of nascent movement toward fairer and more creative lending and bonding policies. A number of large corporations have recently created urban affairs divisions and are beginning to investigate ways and means of promoting and assisting black enterprises. A few corporations are already supporting black manufacturing ventures. The emergence of dynamic new black enterprises and the performance of the few spin-off ventures thus far formed are perhaps more encouraging. Black communities have developed a sharpened focus on capital formation. Many diverse attempts are being made within these communities to develop more job skills, more black managers, and new black enterprises.

But the commitment of the mass of the white business community still must be made. For example, even under the 90 per cent guarantees of the Small Business Administration, white financial institutions remain generally reluctant to make funds available to black enterprises. Only by recognizing its repressive role in the disparity of the economic order can business begin to make the fundamental change in operational behavior that is so urgently required. Given the willingness, the alert businessman working with the black community can find attractive opportunities and the promise of profit. Incentives such as tax allowances, write downs, and the like may stimulate his interest, yet he can enter into a relationship with black entrepreneurs in the sense of sharing a responsibility for change. The motives, pecuniary or compassionate, need not be mutually exclusive.

Black economic development is bound to no formula. It can proceed in a number of possible ways, including among others:

• Community-owned corporations supporting local enterprise and social services;

• Black-white partnership arrangements which may include provisions for gradual divestiture of interest by the white partner;

• Autonomous inner-city industries assisted, if necessary, by compensatory devices such as sheltered markets, guaranteed loans, and technical and managerial help from outside agencies and corporations;

• Location of branch operations of big business in the inner-city, especially where they are used to increase black involvement throughout the total enterprise.

Within the framework of a black-white alliance, inner-city entrepreneurs might also be able to evolve their own unique economic organizations such as cooperatives and profit-sharing ventures.

The long-range goal of black economic development is to generate the wealth to achieve social, political, and economic parity—in short, to enable the black community to build a more satisfying and self-sufficient life for its people and all Americans. The more immediate goal is to raise incomes.

The black entrepreneur does not lack ability or motivation. He lacks the experience and capital to reduce the risk factors in his enterprise. Above all, he lacks the opportunity that a reluctant financial and business community still denies him.

To insure and expedite parity within the system, The American Assembly makes the following recommendations:

1. It is urgent and critical that the national effort and emphasis designed to curtail poverty in our nation be intensified. Therefore the Assembly strongly urges the Administration and the Congress not to cut but to substantially expand current levels of federal participation in housing, community development, poverty, manpower, and educational programs.

Black economic development can not be considered apart from the problems which surround the black communities of this nation. Parity can not be achieved by robbing Peter to pay Paul. A well-coordinated, well-planned, and well-financed program must not only include adequate appropriations for economic development, but substantial appropriations which must be used to attack the root causes of resulting economic imbalance. A man who is poor, ill-housed, and untrained can not fully participate in a program for rapid economic growth.

2. The Assembly urgently calls upon the President, the Congress and the American people to reallocate budget funds in adequate volume to launch immediately a massive program of economic development, not unlike the Marshall Plan, to achieve rapidly emancipation for black and other minority Americans who have been denied the opportunity to participate equally in the rewards of the American economy.

3. The Assembly calls for the formation of a "National Development Corporation" and a variety of local development corporations, to carry out the mandate of the second recommendation.

This proposed Corporation, although chartered by the Congress, would be non-governmental, and operate as a quasi-public institution.

The Corporation would make effective use of available governmental resources, but not be dependent on yearly Congressional appropriations. It would have the authority to issue stocks and bonds for capitalization and expansion.

The Corporation would provide loan and equity capital for minority enterprises, provide technical assistance and managerial training, and conduct research and demonstration programs. It would participate in both secure and high risk ventures.

The Corporation would serve as a clearing house for local efforts and talent. It would not stifle, but rather encourage the development of locally based economic institutions with either similar or identical goals. Whenever possible, it would utilize local community institutions to carry out its work.

The Corporation would work closely and cooperatively with existing financial institutions.

It would also act as a knowledgeable catalyst to attract and involve industry and business in their program for economic development.

This Corporation should reflect the purpose for which it was recommended. We therefore urge the inclusion in the direction of this Corporation of sufficient numbers of representative black and other minority Americans to insure that it will be truly responsive to the wishes of the disadvantaged groups.

The Assembly recognizes that urban and rural economic development are interrelated. Therefore we believe it should be the responsibility of the Corporation to innovate new provisions for economic development in rural America.

The Assembly believes that the establishment of the Corporation can focus a national effort, remove the effort from the winds of politics, stimulate and assist local initiative and still have access to federal and private resources.

The Assembly recommends that present efforts by individuals and groups be continued and intensified. It further recommends the establishment of new community-based corporations through which private and public efforts may be coordinated and maximized by orderly plans for accelerated economic growth.

These plans must provide for maximum encouragement of individual private enterprise, including cooperatives, while at the same time recognizing total community needs.

4. These plans must also take into account the needs of the community as *defined* by the community.

Therefore the Assembly also recommends the creation of autonomous local development corporations with wide powers to raise and use private and public resources, and calls upon municipal governments and private institutions to stimulate the rapid development of these local corporations by the use of local purchasing powers, and other such devices, to channel economic prowess to the local community corporations.

The Assembly calls upon an organization such as the Urban Coalition to take the next step and organize the effort to draft and implement the blueprint for a "National Development Corporation."

5. The Assembly recommends the establishment of a loan "discount" mechanism to accelerate the involvement of financial institutions in the rapid expansion of black economic development. This could be done through a new network of federally chartered and financed regional "discount banks" that could function through use of the existing physical facilities of the Federal Reserve banks. These so-called "discount banks" would be prepared to purchase on presentation at face value without interest and without recourse to the seller, loans made to the black and other minority communities in urban and rural centers. The creation of such a system would provide added incentive and protection to those who enter this field of lending, and would expand existing loan guarantee programs. It would also be helpful to liberalize the existing discount practices at the Federal Reserve banks.

6. The requirements of surety companies for securing bonds are experience and sufficient working capital to execute construction projects under consideration. This generally means a small contractor must be able to provide sufficient working capital to carry his job to 20 per cent of completion before he is reimbursed. This lack of working capital is an insurmountable problem for small contractors and a constraint on their growth.

One device exists which will permit the smaller contractor to compete—the use of licensed builder's control companies. This service is currently available in the private sector at competitive prices with bonding companies. It provides support to the contractor and assures that the building project will be completed as planned.

Therefore we recommend a shift in private and governmental policy to a position which would permit the contractor the option of either obtaining a bond for a job or using the services of a local builder's control company. The Assembly recognizes this may require special regulations to protect the government's investment.

7. The Assembly recommends that a national effort be initiated to assist potential black entrepreneurs and to train and educate future executives. These programs can be initiated at the graduate business school level, and at the community level where, with the help of local industry, rapid business training programs can be developed. A continual flow of this trained talent will be needed to supply the demands of rapid economic growth.

8. The Assembly recommends that tax and other incentives be used, as they have been used and are now used, to interest traditional investors to participate in the rapid development of an under-utilized national resource.

Many new American industries—from oil to shipping—are afforded similar help in the national interest. The same theories underlying federal assistance to those industries must be applied in the case of black economic development. In the long run, both the nation and the economy will benefit from the stimulation of these enterprises and the concomitant development of these markets.

The Assembly also recommends that federal Special Impact monies be clearly earmarked for black economic development.

9. Black economic development also requires the immediate ending of racial discrimination in labor unions. Certain unions have been among the organizations most reluctant to permit members of minority groups to participate in the important task of rebuilding our nation. This must stop. The Assembly calls upon federal, state and local governments, the unions themselves, and the industries which contract with them, to provide equal opportunity for training and employment to minority groups.

It would seem imperative that all private and governmental efforts be used to relieve the overt and covert economic, social and political restraints which have served as effective barriers to full participation.

These barriers have been clearly identified. What remains now is to organize the effort to remove them.

"WHAT DO YOU PEOPLE WANT?"

Richard F. America, Jr.

In its November 19, 1967 issue *The New York Times* printed an editorial with the title "What Do the Negroes Want?" It said in part:

"Dr. Martin Luther King, Jr. . . . refers vaguely to [the Negroes' claim to] 'fulfillment of the rights to share in the ownership of property.' Mr. [James] Farmer declares that the Negro wants not merely jobs but 'jobs that bear his individual stamp and in industries where he commands power and a measure of ownership.' This is a hopelessly utopian claim that the United States has never honored for any other group. Impoverished Negroes, like all other poor Americans, past and present, will have to achieve success on an individual basis and by individual effort.

"American society is likely to accommodate Negro aspirations only as they express themselves in individual terms. It cannot be otherwise in a society that honors personal effort as its highest value and looks toward integration as its goal. Race, unlike poverty or the city, is a cultural or psychological concept, not one that can become a comprehensive basis for law or government policy."

The belief in the myth of rugged individualism; the espousal of black individualism while forgetting the history of public support for whites' special economic interests; the general ignorance of U.S. history—these attitudes, as reflected in the editorial, are widely held by white Americans. Many of them seem to have a weakness for suspending judgment and retreating to such shibboleths when contemplating the

Reprinted from *Harvard Business Review*, V. 47, N. 2 (March–April) 1969), pp. 103-112, by permission of the author and the publisher. © 1969 by the President and Fellows of Harvard College; all rights reserved.

changes necessary to sustain the nation's growth and realize its full potential.

What do black people want? Jobs, housing, and education, certainly. But, beyond that, the black community wants a secure economic base. Black people themselves, collectively and individually, must and can build much of that base, in profit-seeking and nonprofit forms.

Contrary to *The New York Times,* I maintain that race can indeed be made a basis for government economic policy explicitly favorable to black people, as it has long been favorable implicitly to whites. The fundamental inequities are collective and not individual, and must be dealt with collectively.

No program conceived to meet major domestic problems has been adequate. This is so because, among other reasons, none, not even the Freedom Budget and Domestic Marshall Plan, has sought to reallocate corporate power. No one has offered a program bold enough (however unsettling) to get at the fundamental inequities which even the most conservative voter and businessman, though he might deny it, must sense lie at the root of the country's present instability and disunity.

PROGRAM RATIONALE

Now, it will be argued in protest that some steps have been taken, and that is quite true. The movement to eliminate poverty and sub-standard health, housing, and education for 15 million black Americans seems destined to succeed if legislation already enacted is fully implemented. But the time elapsed between legislation, appropriation, and implementation of programs to full effect can be as long as a decade. If poverty is largely eliminated by, say, 1980, will the principal economic and political causes of urban unrest and racial conflict have been eliminated? Or are there other, currently secondary, considerations that will then assume primary importance?

There are many persons (Floyd McKissick and Senator Eugene McCarthy, for example) who define the black-white problem in the United States as a colonial problem. The colonial analogy is central and illumines a policy question that may prove even more intractable than the poverty question; indeed, in retrospect, by 1980 the latter may even appear relatively simple by contrast.

The colonial analogy permits perception of the black community as a "nation," systematically deprived of an opportunity to save and invest. It therefore can claim control of very little capital wealth. My basic assumption in this article is that, to treat the economics and politics of the race problem properly, this deficiency must be corrected.

The establishment and nurturing of small businesses, now being undertaken on an increasing scale, does not satisfy the need for significant economic independence and self-determination, which all emerging colonies require in order to prosper. Only large enterprises will satisfy that requirement, and they take a long time to develop.

All large businesses in the United States, with two or three exceptions, are owned and operated by whites. If relative economic parity is to be reached in one generation, some of these must be transferred to blacks. There are two additional elements in the rationale for corporate transfer:

1. *Influence in policy making*—It can be expected that black people will increasingly feel that white people, especially white businessmen, have had a disproportionate influence on the domestic and foreign affairs of this country. White businessmen have simply had too much to say about what goes on in this country. Domestic policy—including policy on problems in which the judgment of blacks is increasingly understood to be relevant, if not primary—is directly related to foreign policy. An example is domestic segregation and South Africa. U.S. foreign policy has always been made by the white establishment.

Black people, with certain exceptions like Senator Edward Brooke, have had no direct line of communication with the decision-making echelon. No black leaders of large businesses have such access, since there are virtually no such leaders. And on many of the critical world issues facing this country, new views are badly needed.

One orderly way to change this situation is to accelerate the belated development of comparably powerful groups of black businessmen whose perspectives on foreign and domestic questions would in all likelihood be somewhat different simply because of the racial difference.

It is reasonable to assume that black corporate leaders will introduce new variables and place new weights on old variables in the decision equations of industry and government. That may strike some white businessmen as a terrible prospect, but thoughtful consideration should lead to the conclusion that the introduction of this new element would be in the pluralistic tradition with which many historians credit the relatively consistent stability of the American economic and political experiment.

In short, black corporate leaders may be able to make a valuable contribution to high policy councils in the last quarter of this turbulent century. The entire nation would benefit from their presence.

2. *A 'countervailing' force*—The black-white problem in the United States can be framed in terms of John Kenneth Galbraith's concept of countervailing force. It may be necessary and desirable public policy from the white viewpoint, as it is already implicit black "policy," to foster the development of black corporate power as a force against continued mistreatment of blacks by white corporate and labor power, and against the continued political, social, and economic instablity which such mistreatment produces.

Massive mutual distrust is a factor between the races. Better economic and social conditions may reduce the level of distrust. But it is dangerous to assume that rising incomes and educational levels alone will be sufficient to dispel historic antipathies. On the contrary, they may just as easily inflame them, for we know that cultural, psychological, and political expectations will rise just as surely as economic expectations. A sense of relative collective political deprivation may persist when individual economic deprivation has been eliminated.

Secure and powerful black economic institutions, rather than simply mass individual affluence, would be the surest safeguard against feelings of collective powerlessness and against manifestations of continued white supremacy. Creating such institutions would be in the public interest.

For these reasons, a workable mechanism is required for the transfer of some major national corporations to black control.

PRECEDENTS FOR THE PROPOSAL

U.S. history does not lack for examples of the use of public resources in support of private activities when the results were expected to be in the public interest. There are ample precedents of public encouragement leading to private wealth.

Construction of the Western railroads, for example, was deemed so important to the development of both the Western region and the nation that private citizens were given extraordinary incentives to build the roads. Land was practically given away.

Examples of the transfer of technology from public to private hands are of course equally common. The development of commercial aviation benefited from publicly sponsored research and development. Currently, the government's aerospace research program is creating products and techniques for private exploitation, and the public is providing a substantial windfall to corporations in the process.

In each of these activities the public treasury has directly supported the development of large private enterprise; and, in the last two cases, the government has removed much of the development risk by turning over the corporations proven products and protected markets. The private benefits accrued after public subsidy of the substantial early costs.

The case of the aluminum industry is also pertinent. After World War II, the federal government concluded that the Aluminum Company of America was too big according to certain objective and subjective criteria. The federal approach, simply stated, was to force Alcoa to divest itself of some of its holdings or face direct competition from a corporation to be founded by the government. Alcoa chose to divest. The important point here is that the government considered the public interest to be sufficiently threatened by the monopolistic situation that it was determined to commit public resources to restore a measure of competition in the industry.

The white monopoly represented by *Fortune's* 500 largest companies might be similarly viewed. The total absence of any large black corporations in the United States is, to some extent, due to a kind of restraint of trade and "collusive" behavior over the years by almost all white institutions, including the government and the legal system. This has resulted in a situation contrary to the public interest.

Urban renewal: Perhaps the most relevant precedent for a transfer mechanism exists in the federal urban renewal program. The power of eminent domain has been relied on to secure land for restoration of certain areas and for essential public projects. A series of court tests has established that eminent domain may further be used to change a land use while title to the property passes from one private party, through the government, to another. The courts have ruled that such changing uses are sufficiently in the public interest to justify the exercise of eminent domain.

The process normally proceeds after extensive public hearings and with numerous safeguards and checks against abuse, although abuses are not unknown. The mechanism essentially consists of three elements:

1. The owner is compensated at full appraised fair market value for his property. This payment is made from the public treasury.

2. The property thus acquired is prepared for transfer. The preparation in the case of a new use for the land usually consists of clearance of structures, preparation of the ground for new construction, and placement of infrastructure, such as utility lines, street realignments, and curbing.

3. The property is sold to the developer, who ordinarily agrees to certain tenure, use, and design controls which are imposed by the developing authority.

The total cost of acquisition and preparation usually greatly exceeds the final sale price to the developer; indeed, it is not uncommon for property to be disposed of for as little as 5% of that total cost. This price, of course, is an even smaller percentage of what a developer might have had to pay to assemble the parcels in the open market without benefit of the public intermediary, assuming that the assembly could have been accomplished at all. The "net project costs" amount to roughly the difference between total acquisition and the disposition price. The public treasury absorbs the net project cost.

I propose that a variation on the mechanism used in urban renewal be employed to accomplish the transfer of major corporations or portions of them from white to black management and control.

ALTERNATIVE APPROACHES

It might be argued that a better, or at least a somewhat less bureaucratic, approach to developing large black industrial institutions should be developed.

Why not, for example, simply give the full purchase price to a group of black capitalists and let them proceed on their own toward acquisition? The problems of developing safeguards with that approach might be overwhelming. Or why not let the government directly set up large corporations in selected industries and turn them over to a black management group? The problems of altering industry structures and distorting existing competitive situations would be formidable.

While both approaches, or others, might be made operable, my proposed solution appears to be applicable with the least departure from precedent and the minimum disruption of normal financial and production arrangements for all parties directly or indirectly concerned.

It might be argued that black control could be achieved simply by bringing in black managers and accelerating their movement to the top, without disturbing ownership. This approach would probably not work. It is unlikely that the relationship between black management and a board of directors representing white interests would remain as harmonious as that between black management and a black-dominated board. Normal conflicts between management and the board would over time become exacerbated in the former case, in which racially based conflicts of interest, policy differences, and social objectives would be always potentially present, to the probable eventual detriment of the enterprise.

In transferring ownership of corporations, eminent domain, while not confiscatory, would not be a preferred method even if legal objections could be overcome. The process would require a congenial atmosphere and a high level of cooperation on the part of the original white owners and managers. The potential for obstruction or even sabotage is obvious, so proper incentives, indeed very attractive incentives, must be provided.

A brief aside is in order here. The process of black community development has two facets, one internal and the other external. If the external aspect were completely satisfactory—that is, if the white community moved to reform itself and initiate the needed programs—much of the benefit would be lost unless the black community were unified and able to carry out its part in the process.

For black people, then, the solution of certain internal problems is crucial. One of them is the degree of separatism which they should practice. Few in the black community would dispute that black people—not the white world, governmental or corporate—have the responsibility for internal planning. But the proposal in this article will be viewed as a much too conservative, perhaps even dangerous, step by some significant black analysts and activists who are separatists.

The converse of my statement about internal and external facets is not so. If internal problems are resolved and a high degree of unification is achieved, much white resistance will be effectively countered and eventually overcome. Black progress will not end if my proposal, or even others less far-reaching, is not put into action. Black self-help will accelerate and succeed; it will not be allowed to depend on white approbation.

TRANSFER MECHANISM

The process of corporate transfer should, if possible, be initiated by the candidate. An agency of the federal government created to facilitate such conveyances would issue a standing invitation to divest. Let's call it ACT (Agency for Corporate Transfer). It could be established in the Department of Commerce or the Office of the President.

The program should begin with a trial run, with perhaps three large companies transferred, one a year for three years. After the last transfer, two years of demonstration operations would be undertaken. At the end of the five-year test period it should be clear what program modifications would be required to improve the chances of success with subsequent transfers.

Two assumptions are implicit here: (1) there is a sufficient number of black capitalists with access to $1 million to $10 million to accomplish the program; and (2) there is a sufficient quantity of black managerial talent to run the tranferred concerns. These assumptions are sound, in my view; the money could be found, and the experience of personnel and management recruiting firms in the past five years suggests the existence of a sizable pool of unrecognized talent, particularly in government, education, and the military.

In each *Fortune* industry category (the 500 largest industrials, plus the 50 largest banks, utilities, and life insurance, merchandising, and transportation companies) might be set an ultimate target of 10% to come under black ownership and control by 1990. Adding 10% to the next 500 largest industrials makes a total of 125 companies to be transferred.

If there were no takers despite very attractive tax and other financial inducements, then, theoretically at least, criteria could be developed for identifying candidates for acquisition. Conglomerates, for example, might be approached to determine their interest in selling off portions. In the event of such an impasse, the initiative for opening discussions would fall to the government.

A climate in which no corporations would be interested in voluntary divestiture for purposes of simple liquidation or to take advantage of very attractive financial inducements would be a negative climate in any case. With such a total lack of interest prevailing, the necessary legislation for this program obviously never would be enacted in the first place.

So, discussion of a program requiring government initiative leads to a dead end for all practical purposes. Corporate transfer requires that the white business community understand its advantages, accept its premises, and concur

in its objective. Otherwise, the program is dead. But in that direction, as I have tried to suggest, lies severe uncertainty and social instability.

CORPORATE CANDIDATES

A difficulty might arise if the only offers of transfer come from marginal corporations or those whose prospects are dimming. It might be very tempting for a company with top management problems, or severe and chronic financial or labor problems, or obsolescent plant and equipment, or grim marketing problems to seize the opportunity to unload, perhaps even at a premium price. If offers from such companies are abundant in the early rounds, negotiations on selling price could be difficult.

Rejection of a few companies because of unsoundness or low potential, however, would cause them considerable embarrassment and would probably discourage offers from seriously troubled companies.

In seeking to develop black industry, the problem of competitiveness will be primary. There is little point in accomplishing the transfer of corporations whose activities are in no-growth or declining areas. On the other hand, companies on the technological frontiers like aero-space, ocean exploitation, and nuclear energy are unlikely to offer themselves. The first rounds of negotiations with manufacturers therefore are likely to involve stable, moderate-growth producers of consumer and industrial goods.

ACT might want to concentrate on industries at both ends of the competitive spectrum. An industry that is relatively "competitive," such as paper products or petroleum, will suffer less dislocation from a transfer of one or two of its major companies. Similarly, utilities and other monopolies should be readily transferable, since they are already heavily regulated and not in such delicate competitive balance as more oligopolistic industries, like autos and aircraft.

The opportunity of acquiring large businesses, incidentally, should certainly be extended to other groups in the United States whose situation vis-à-vis the white business world is similar to that of blacks: Puerto Ricans, Mexican-Americans, American Indians, and, to a lesser extent, Orientals. The government would have to have assurance first that the associates seeking transfer are qualified and would put the corporation to good use. This is the same as my suggested procedure with black groups, which I take up next.

BIDDING PROCEDURE

ACT would acquire a divesting corporation by paying a negotiated price for 51% of the common stock, after acceptance of a tender offer, with monies from the public treasury.

The availability of the corporation would then be made known to all interested parties through public media, and offers would be invited. In the case of a large manufacturer in which controlling interest could be purchased by ACT for $100 million, an offer of $1 million to $5 million should be sufficient to acquire that interest. The net acquisition cost—the difference between what ACT paid for the 51% interest and the purchasing group's offer—would be absorbed by the government. The portion of the majority interest not held by these entrepreneurs would be assigned by ACT to a nonprofit organization, which I shall describe later.

Initially, the competition from groups of eager entrepreneurs would be keen, but as bidding continued, the field could be expected to dwindle. When a small number of bidders, say three, remained, a set of rigorous criteria would be applied to determine the winner.

The principal criterion would be the ability of the bidding group to produce a management cadre with the potential for successful management of the company. The groups would be required to put together a team of black businessmen with the requisite training, background, general and specialized experience, and potential to fill the key management positions within a reasonable period of time, say 5 to 10 years. This would mean a team of 20 to 100 men with expertise in functional areas including marketing, finance, production, personnel, and so on. A typical team might average 35 years of age, with 10 years of business or noncommercial experience per man.

Objective tests of the team's capacity to enter the divesting company and industry and to learn the business within ten years would be required. Perhaps more difficult, some subjective analysis would be necessary so that the interpersonal dynamics between the divesting management group and the acquiring group's managers could be anticipated.

Obviously, the introduction of a group of black "fair-haired boys," taking over from white managers during a period of years, has the potential for triggering a variety of generally bad vibrations. The organizational behavior specialists would have their work cut out for them. It must be assumed, however, that in this situation—with a willing buyer, a willing seller, and competent managers, both black and white—these problems can be overcome.

Administrative and legal safeguards of a high order of effectiveness would be required because of the very large sums of money involved. Particularly important is a procedure for restraining the level of bidding. It might be tempting for competing bidders to seek outside capital in support of their 1% to 5% bids. In the case of a corporation in which controlling interest can be acquired for $100 million, white entrepreneurs might find it worthwhile to provide $50 million, $75 million, or even more to a black bidding group. In short, the price could be driven up to a level near the market price.

In that event, the black capitalists would become hardly more than a front for the whites, which would defeat the purpose of the program. A technique for certifying the source of all money must be employed, and full disclosure would be essential.

TRANSFER SAFEGUARDS

The mechanism will also have to protect the legitimate interests of minority stockholders who want to dispose of shares. ACT should stand ready to purchase their shares at the market price immediately before the announcement of the sale. On announcement, the stock market would probably discount the company's future earnings to take account of general uncertainty, the incoming and relatively inexperienced management, and similar factors. Small stockholders should not be penalized in this situation.

After the winning bidder has been selected, the stock would be immediately transferred. At this point, or perhaps even earlier, disgruntled minor stockholders might behave in such a way as to upset the management and the market. The government, through the Securities and Exchange Commission, would have to act to protect the corporation's securities from malevolent operators. Suspension of trading in case of panic selling or other abnormal market activities should be left to the judgment of the boards of the exchanges and the SEC.

The market's reassessment of the company's prospects is to be expected. Within a short time, if earnings hold up and operations continue normally, the market price should reflect the diminished uncertainty, and recovery should be complete.

RESTRICTIONS ON THE BUYERS

The purpose of this program is to contribute to the achievement of economic and political parity, not transform certain black capitalists into instant multimillionaires at public expense. But the purchase of, say, $100 million in stock for $1 million to $5 million would appear to have that effect. So the transfer mechanism must take care of that problem.

The safeguard likely to be most effective would take this form: members of the purchasing group would personally hold only that portion of stock which could have been acquired in the marketplace with the same amount of money as they actually expended. They would receive dividends only on those shares. The balance of the stock purchased by the government would reside in a nonprofit corporation with a community base, similar to the kind envisioned in several recent proposals advanced by black community groups, black spokesmen, and many politicians. It is commonly called a community development corporation (CDC).

Dividends, if any, on these shares would be paid to that corporation and could be used to fund a variety of public benefit projects in housing, health, recreation, and so forth—much as The Ford Foundation does with its Ford Motor Company dividends. If, however, in management's judgment the interests of the corporation would be best served by retention of earnings, that judgment should not be subordinated to the CDC's desire for cash; funding local public projects must remain secondary to the goal of sustaining competitive businesses.

The location of these nonprofit corporations and the communities to be benefited would be jointly determined by the new controlling group, by expressions of interest and capacity from local organizations, and by relevant government departments, such as OEO, Commerce, HEW, and HUD. As the controlling group desired, it would be free to purchase stock from the CDC within certain limits designed to prevent abuse or price manipulation.

Some provision would have to be devised either to make this large block of stock nonvoting for a period, to prevent interference from that quarter, or otherwise to restrict direct participation by the CDC in the direction of the company until a transitional period, perhaps two to three years, has been completed.

The entrepreneurial group should be allowed to exercise effective control through its shares at least until the success of the transfer is assured—probably five years in most cases. But the nonprofit corporation should have some representation on the company's board of directors at an early date.

It would be undesirable, however, to protect the directors of the corporation from any of their shareholders for any great length of time. Two or three years of nonvoting status might be suitable; but the CDC should be permitted to express its wishes prudently on some proportionate basis after that transitional period. Mutual respect between company and community corporation should ensure that no harm comes to the company's commercial interests from the CDC's pursuit of its noncommercial objectives. It can be predicted that the community group would not interfere unduly with the company's operations if interference threatened to harm its investment and dividend position.

Members of the acquiring group might be tempted to take advantage of market opportunities and withdraw at an early time. They should be permitted to do, but since the overriding purpose of the program is social, it seems reasonable to impose some limits on their freedom to trade their shares. Perhaps a moratorium of three years would be sufficient to prevent any manipulations.

OPERATIONAL QUESTIONS

So far as the company's operations are concerned, the period of accomplishing the transfer could run, as suggested earlier, five to ten years. The transition will introduce numerous uncertainty factors for the old management, for original board members who are phasing out, and for minority stockholders. Some means of reducing this uncertainty must be provided.

It will be necessary to allow the company to maintain normal operations while the old management is training the new. So the government should guarantee a minimum rate of return for the corporation and some negotiated level of sales and net income. This can be done through a government offer to purchase some quantity of the company's product (if it is a manufacturer) or through tax concessions.

The former approach is similar in intent to agricultural price supports, which are designed to maintain and protect certain economic activities in the belief that their continuation is in the public interest. Guaranteed markets or returns are also an element in U.S. government attempts to stimulate industrial development or investment in developing countries.

Tax concessions have been suggested recently by almost every nationally prominent politician as a means of inducing the participation of white private corporations in the solution of urban racial problems. Such a policy is undesirable because it would perpetuate the power imbalances that are at the root of these problems. Some kind of tax concessions are probably unavoidable, however, since private industry does have a role to play in treating physical and economic deterioration.

Tax incentives, if used at all, should be applied at least as extensively to the power problem as to the poverty or material deprivation problem. Indeed, the use of tax or other economic incentives to provide only housing, jobs, and so on, without using them to transfer corporate power, rewards white corporations for their past and current economic exploitation.

BLACK & WHITE MANAGERS

The terms of transfer will provide for the recruitment and employment of a potential senior management cadre of blacks. I do not envision that the important lower- and middle-management levels would be entirely black. Even if that were desirable, it would be virtually impossible in a complex, multidivision corporation. But the recruitment of management trainees and young accountants, engineers, and technicians should focus on black candidates having the potential for quick development. Many will be found in MBA programs at black and white universities.

Young whites should also be recruited. They would, of course, have to be men and women with special social orientations, but such persons are increasing in number. They of course would have to understand that, for good reason, the presidency and most other top management jobs would be filled by blacks after five to ten years and for the foreseeable future beyond that. This is not unlike the unspoken understanding that black MBAs and engineers have when entering large white corporations, and with less justification.

The problem with recruiting is not likely to be the absence of good white candidates. On the contrary, the problem is likely to be the attraction of droves of candidates with strong social motivations who anticipate an exciting five or ten years in an unusual, and therefore more interesting, industrial situation before making their normal career moves. Some screening out of young candidates with missionary motives may be necessary. There may be more of a problem with headhunting for white middle managers, because of their perceptions of risk; but, again, at this early conceptual stage we must rely on the organizational behavior specialists to work that problem out.

Since the program is designed to produce large corporations that are black-controlled and led, some whites (perhaps many) will find these circumstances uncongenial and leave. The effort will be better off without them. The policy of the program, however, must be that whites are welcome to participate in the operation of black economic institutions.

SOURCES OF OPPOSITION

Employee relations will obviously be a delicate area, but success here could make the companies models of innovative human relations programs. And, as I mentioned previously, passage of the enabling legislation presupposes a national climate favorable to the transfer program. Resistance in the white business and labor communities would be assumed to be moderate.

Even so, the first corporations transferred are likely to encounter displays of displeasure by employees, by the general public, or in the market. Boycotts, work slowdowns, strikes, even sabotage are possible.

Negotiations with unions and with all employees in candidate companies should precede transfer, and these groups should have a voice in the decision to transfer. The same should be true for other affected parties, such as financial counselors and bankers, manufacturers' representatives, dealers, suppliers, and principal customers. The involvement of all relevant groups would reduce the risk of direct resistance everywhere, except perhaps in the marketplace.

For this reason, it may be prudent to select, as the first companies transferred, manufacturers of producers' goods with relatively few customers and those with heavy government contracts.

After five or six years of experience beyond the demonstration stage, and with 25 or 30 large companies in the transfer pipeline, a manufacturer of cars, soaps and cosmetics, or household appliances might be chosen. When the housewife is ready to choose Brand X (Brand Black over Brand White) on its merits (or for whatever reasons housewives make those decisions), then the entire program may be considered to be a success.

Opposition from organized labor, particularly from craft unions, might pose serious problems if the transfer process were allowed to look like an attempt to break union power. A number of craft unions have been targets recently of black displeasure because of union resistance to entrance and upgrading of blacks. General union reaction would probably depend largely on which industries appeared to offer the earliest opportunities for corporate transfer.

CONCLUSION

After about eight corporations have been tranferred to black control each year for 15 years, the procedure would be discontinued, since by then blacks will have achieved economic parity roughly equivalent to their proportion of the population.

At an average purchase price of $100 million each, the total annual cost of the program, including administration and profit supports, should not run above $2 billion. In some years, however, it would exceed $2.5 billion if a giant or two should be transferred. A program with an annual cost of $2 billion that has the potential to contribute greatly to economic and social equality and stability is an effective program indeed.

Quantifiable benefits would presumably include most of those usually cited in assessing traditional social programs in housing, welfare, transportation, education, employment, and so forth. Such benefits are often realized from savings in public and private expenditures, and such savings might be realized from this program in a variety of ways.

But when the budget analysts have concluded with the cost-benefit arguments, the value of the program should rest on the political judgment that social progress depends on a reallocation of existing institutions—hence a redistribution of power—not merely on reallocation of resources in the form of educational dollars, or guaranteed income checks, or even job opportunities.

Only in this way can anything approaching economic parity be achieved in a satisfactory time—that is, in one generation. All other approaches are based implicitly on a policy of gradualism, which has been rejected by black people. Such a policy includes efforts of private enterprise to stimulate the growth of small, black-owned businesses in the black communities, which President Nixon (it appears at this time of writing) intends to concentrate on.

Would conservative and liberal politicians today support a plan going beyond the limited objectives of legislation promoting self-development, and designed to provide a measure of countervailing power to the black community? The answer is probably *no,* but in time the wisdom of such a course will, I think, become clear.

Meanwhile, the search for low-cost, supposedly nonthreatening solutions will continue with the implicit hope that somehow white economic supremacy can be maintained and no one will notice that the gross power imbalance remains despite the proliferation of new, small, black-controlled businesses.

A recent report by the Institute for Social

Research at the University of Michigan contained the finding (according to a newspaper editorial) that "most black Americans are seeking reform, not revolution," and the "changes they have in mind are essentially conservative in nature." It may be true that the changes most black people seek are conservative in principle.

But from the point of view of apprehensive white taxpayers and business leaders, the changes sought apparently are seen as very radical. Initially, the corporate transfer proposal may also be regarded as too radical by some, but its fundamentally conservative thrust should be obvious in light of the strong precedents.

In the 1930's much of the white business leadership, following the basically conservative direction of Franklin D. Roosevelt, supported stabilizing public and private policies that yielded a measure of power and wealth to labor. Though the circumstances are fundamentally different now (race rather than class being the basis of conflict), with enlightened conservatism a measure of institutional power will be yielded in order to secure for the nation the benefits of continuity and stability.

MAKING CAPITALISM WORK IN THE GHETTOS

Louis L. Allen

During a recent month, at least two dozen meetings, conferences, seminars, and orientation sessions were held in New York City on the subject of entrepreneurship and small business in the ghetto areas. Despite my interest in the subject, I did not attend a single one of the meetings. This was not because I knew all about the problem (I did not) but because I knew I would see the same faces, hear the same questions, and listen to the same answers that had long since become familiar to me from earlier meetings. Also, I was convinced that the ballroom of a plush midtown hotel was not the place to study or work on the problems of new business in dis-advantaged areas.

In trying to help the ghettos, we have followed the time-honored approach to business problem solving that was started 50 years ago with time and motion study—breaking a task down into its smallest, irreducible parts in order to analyze them further. This approach has led us to:

- Make an already difficult task much more complex by trying to "engineer" a magical, quick solution.
- Adopt labels for the problem and solution that direct our attention along false and misleading lines
- Look in the wrong places for someone or something to blame for the problem.
- Fail to talk with the people actually involved in ghetto business problems, while consulting with those who, though not directly involved, consider themselves spokesmen for the disadvantaged.

Reprinted from *Harvard Business Review*, V. 47, N. 3 (May–June, 1969), pp. 83–92, by permission of the author and the publisher. © 1969 by the President and Fellows of Harvard College; all rights reserved.

- Forget what are known to be the basic rules of capitalism.

The purpose of this article is to clear away the logjam in thinking about the economic development of slum areas. I shall elaborate on the points just mentioned, recount some experiences I have had with ghetto entrepreneurs, and summarize some of the practical lessons I have learned about investing in ghetto businesses. I call for a moratorium on conferences and meetings until we in management have something new and relevant to talk about. Such methods as decision trees, PERT, and planning models are not applicable to the problems at hand. What we are testing is the entrepreneurial spirit, which means that successful capitalists must go one at a time into the ghetto, find entrepreneurs, and work with them one at a time in the small businesses they seek to build.

EPIPHANY OF CAPITALISM

We are a jingle-writing and "sloganeering" people, we Americans. We like to tag everything with an acronym or a label, and this frequently gets us thinking along lines that we did not intend. Worse, with our aptness for phrasemaking, we sometimes mesmerize ourselves into assuming that since we have cleverly labeled something, we have somehow magically solved the problem it presents.

On occasions, the problem *does* go away. For example, as long as one fish product was called "horse mackerel," it could not be given away; now that it is called "tunafish," it's a very big seller. But the reverse can happen; the problem can be aggravated. For example, consider the label, "black capitalism." Although it is in current use, it is not appropriate to the circumstances, and its continued use will be dangerous. For "capitalism" is a word which describes a concept, a complex concept of many interwoven threads. Capitalism is an economic system in pretty much the same way that Christianity, Judaism, or Mohammedanism are religious schools of thought; that is, its basic appeal is that it can be universally applied, and the truths can withstand the closest scrutiny.

Capitalism can no more be adequately described by stating the color, racial origin, or religion of its practitioners than it can be described by the locality of its implementation— for example, Ohio capitalism as compared with New York capitalism. Its greatest strength is that it is, or should be, available to anyone, anywhere, anytime as a means to participate in an economic system, in the same way that Christianity, Judaism, or Mohammedanism can be practiced by all who want to believe in them. To use the term "black capitalism" is to demean those of its practitioners who are black.

It is true that there are many who have been and still are deprived of the opportunity to practice capitalism. But those who believe in this system, who have practiced it, and who have prospered from it must remember that there is no exclusivity in it. Exclusivity will change it— drastically and unfavorably.

The Epiphany is an annual feast celebrating the coming of the Magi with news for the Gentiles. What capitalism needs now is an "epiphany" of its own—many wise men who will bring its principles to those who need to know about them and who will remain with the initiates to make the principles work.

ILLUSION OF QUICK SOLUTIONS

Basic to a working understanding of capitalism is that it is built one step at a time by practitioners—not handed to them fully constructed. To talk about quick solutions is a terrible mistake because there are none.

An article in the March-April 1969 issue of HBR (Richard F. America, Jr., "'What Do You People Want?'" p. 103.) proposes that the government take over selected large corporations by eminent domain and give control of them to the black man. The author goes to some lengths to outline the ways in which this approach could be implemented, how payment could be made, how transition to black control could be effected, and so on. All of this explanation misses the point. My six-year-old son learned how to swim last winter at the local YMCA. But this summer I will still insist on his wearing a life jacket when he goes in a small boat. I will bet Richard F. America would do the same. Of course, the child may say he knows how to swim and does not need the life jacket.

Exactly the same principle holds in running a big business. No one can know how to manage a large corporation without experience in doing just that. Certainly experience in small company management is no substitute. America has outlined plans for an orderly transition of a few months time. I doubt how "orderly" the transition will be under the circumstances, and, in any case, the best of men could not learn to manage a big company in less than two years.

But the greatest oversight America has made is to give no thought to the customer. How many Ford customers would be lost if that company were turned over to blacks to own and manage? How many Maxwell House buyers would switch to other brands if that organization were one of the ones selected for black control? The problem with being a dictator and arranging things by decree, as America suggests, is that the decrees must cover all ramifications. America's proposals, I take it, ambitious as they may be, stop short of decreeing how many people are required to buy Fords and no other make, or to purchase only Maxwell House coffee.

Like a religion, capitalism can be practiced only on an individual basis. It is a matter of one man working at his task or working with a few or many others at an assigned or a selected task. If their work is to be successful, it must be done according to the rules. Capitalism cannot be legislated as suggested by America, nor does it offer any easy answers or comfortable compromises. To suggest that blacks take over a large corporation on a ready-made basis is very much akin to suggesting that the fox be placed in charge of the henhouse.

Capitalism can be made to work for the economically disadvantaged in our urban centers; it is working there now in many instances. But it requires new approaches, new commitments, and new efforts by everyone who has been a recipient of its great promises.

GETTING STARTED

What are the requirements of making capitalism work in a depressed urban area? My experience in financing new and small businesses for the economically disadvantaged has led me to conclude that we have been asking the wrong questions of the wrong people. The people who want to know about small business and capitalism in the ghetto are the people who live there and are trying to make decent lives for themselves and their families there. They do not attend the meetings at the Waldorf; they probably never have talked to anyone who has. Hence the first mistake we have been making is not listening to the right people. We have been listening instead to banquet table speakers.

And the questions we have been asking are wrong—for example, questions such as "What needs to be done?" If one has to ask that question, he will not understand the answer, which is simply that the knowledgeable businessman must go into a ghetto area and begin to work with a person there who aspires to something better than what he has.

THE MAKING OF A PRECEDENT

To illustrate that the need is to get on with the job, not discuss it further, let me tell you about the first investment in a ghetto business we made at Chase Manhattan Capital Corporation. While other businessmen may choose to make the jump into ghetto investing in a different way, they will have to be just as resolute as we were in this case:

As of several years ago, we had not yet begun a program of investing in small businesses in New York City. We had been going to all the conferences, reading all the articles and books, and getting very discouraged. It seemed to me hopeless to continue the meetings and conferences. I decided that the next applicant who walked into my office would get his financing.

I thought of an analogy about swimming. A man could learn all about the theories of bodies in a fluid medium, he could understand completely the skeletal and muscular functions of the human body, he could know all about the motor nerves, and everything else. But he could be dropped in the middle of a lake, and his knowledge would be of little comfort to him if

he sank to the bottom. What we needed was "swimmers"—not men who knew how and why a person could swim. We needed men who would invest a portion of their substance and their time, and generally assist those who could not get started without such help.

The next applicant at my office was a man in his late forties. He was from Jamaica. For 10 years he had been a furniture polisher and repairman for a large New York City hotel. And he wanted to be in business for himself. Over a period of two years he had saved about $10 per month until he had $250. With this he had bought some hand tools and made a payment on a very small store. It had been burglarized the very first night; all he possessed had been stolen.

When he had gone home that evening, his wife and ten-year-old daughter had prepared a dinner to celebrate the beginning of his business. They had no telephone, so he could not have called to let them know of the disaster. He told his wife and daughter what had happened. His daughter had got up and run to her room, he told me. He had started after her to comfort her when she came running back with an old brown envelope in her hands. She had thrown her arms around his neck, hugged him, and said, "That's all right, Daddy, I've saved some money and I want you to have it to start again." It was 12 cents in pennies.

The man in my office looked at me and said that he was not going to let his little girl down. We agreed to finance him. (Since then he has been struggling along; his business has not yet prospered by normal standards, but for him it has been a chance to be on his own and he is full of hope and enthusiasm.)

Once we had set a precedent of action for ourselves and broken the paralysis of discussion and inaction, we began to move in a serious way. That entrepreneur's firm was the first of many we have financed.

BREAKING AN OLD RULE

In the case just described, we put up all the money for the business. The man could not have saved enough in any case. That was the first way we changed our thinking about the problems associated with getting a business started in Bedford-Stuyvesant.

The tragedy of our citizens that live in the

ghetto is that they have no chance to save. The society in which they live does not permit saving, either implicitly or explicitly. They barely subsist on their low incomes and pay high prices for what they get. Because of the expense and lack of mobility, they are effectively denied the opportunity of going elsewhere. Since saving is the basis for accumulating capital, they simply cannot be expected to be in a position to provide any but the smallest part of the financial resources needed to get into business.

Would-be backers must make up their minds that they will have to relax or waive entirely the traditional requirement that an entrepreneur contribute part of the equity himself. If anyone wants to foster the start of capitalism in the economically disadvantaged areas, he must be ready and willing to put up all the money himself. There are no substitutes for this approach, in my experience. A lot of time is wasted and needless involvement undertaken looking around for "front money" to protect the investor's interest. That money is never there.

Bear in mind, too, that while the entrepreneur has no funds to get started, he has always faced very great odds. The level of his aspiration is high; yet he recognizes his prospects for achievement as low. If there is to be any chance for the success of such a venture, it must be constructed at the outset so he and any other principals will be the largest beneficiaries of any profits.

FALLACY OF THE GIVE-AWAY

Yet what we are discussing here is not a give-away program. This is one of the points where I disagree most vigorously with America's proposal. As I stated earlier, if the game is capitalism, it has to follow the rules. The only change is that here, because of the special circumstances, the investor must recognize the essential requirement of putting up all the money.

The investment should be made in capitalist terms. For instance, our typical financing at Chase Manhattan Capital Corporation is a ten-year loan with a five-year to seven-year moratorium on principal repayments. We form a corporation, issue *all* outstanding stock to the client, and take a detachable stock warrant for between 10% to 15% of the total capitalization.

At the same time we enter into a "put and call" arrangement with the founders according to which, after our original investment has been fully paid and discharged, they can "call" our warrant back for the pro-rated percentage of post-tax profits earned during the period of time the warrant has been outstanding. In other words, we will sell our right to, say 10% of the stock, for that amount of the company's net earnings. Under other circumstances we can "put" the warrant back to the founders at one half the rate of the "call"; or if there should be an underwriting, merger, or sale of the business, we can exercise the warrant and go along for the ride.

This is fair to all parties, it is businesslike, and it puts the founders in the driver's seat with respect to how the profits will be taken.

AN INVESTOR'S COMMITMENT

If we drop the requirement that the principals "come to the party" with some assets of their own to contribute, we must face some hard questions. One such question is inextricably involved with the general nature of business, especially small business. I regard it is an inalienable right of a businessman to be wrong—not stupid or careless, but just plain wrong. The uncertainties of business are such that the best plans can be laid waste regardless of the competence of the men who made the decisions.

Normally, however, the investor can protect himself. If he sees a decision going sour, he will turn to second lines of defense and commence working on them. But in the case of the typical small business in the ghetto, there is not going to be any second line of defense. To aggravate the matter, there will be no capital base which might absorb some of the trouble. All losses are going to come out of the funds provided by the investors. In this respect, a ghetto firm is a glaring example of a rule which impresses me more and more: the largest disadvantage of small size in business is the inability to absorb error.

This means that the investor must be willing, before he makes his original investment, to support the venture through at least one and probably many periods of crisis when all losses are in effect taken against funds provided by himself. All the deficits will come "out of his hide." It is a very discomforting thought!

How can anyone make a commitment like this? What must be considered, what weaknesses overlooked, what questions asked during the investigation and analysis of a loan or investment request? Indeed, what type of organization should even think about becoming involved?

NEED FOR A BROAD BASE

It seems to me that any organization formed for the exclusive purpose of assisting the establishment of capitalism in the major urban centers and in other economically disadvantaged areas of our country is doomed to failure from the start. It will certainly fail economically, and this in turn will cause it to fail in its objectives. The usual rule is that an investor should "go hunting where the ducks are," and, take it from me, there are no "ducks" in the ghetto. There are enough problems in running a business profitably if it is located in the best of places. When you add the additional problems found in the ghetto, the compound effect is often devastating.

This fact suggests the basic weakness of Senate Bill 3876—the proposed Community Development Corporation(CDC) Act. It would have an isolating effect. It will virtually eliminate participation by groups not centered in the areas (in other words, it will keep "whitey" out). This bill is a manifestation of the gap between aspiration and achievement that its backers are trying to fill. In their frustration the blacks think they need only money to bridge the gap—but in truth money is only part of their need. Those who would assist with financial aid cannot let the matter rest at that. They must not merely put up the cash and, then, in the manner of Pilate, "wash their hands" of these people. Ongoing counsel and direct assistance are cardinal to success.

To whom, then, should they be able to turn for help? I suggest that those who can help the disadvantaged gain a measure of self-control over their affairs by assisting them in starting businesses of their own are precisely those who have already had some success in doing this— that is, the "swimmers" of the capitalist world. Such help is the best possible way for the "swimmers" to direct some of their surplus profits and energies. My greatest fear is that if adequate help comes too late, or if we do not follow through with all our resources other than cash, those of us who did not take time to work on these matters may become like Barabbas and wander from place to place always wondering what will be the ultimate price of our oversight and how it will be exacted.

Companies that have a broader base of operations and are making profits in more fertile ground are the ones that can and should devote their energy, skill, and understanding to developing a new capitalism among the worthy people in disadvantaged areas. For example, at Chase Manhattan Capital Corporation we have gone ahead as we have, not because the fellow across the street was doing it—he was not—but simply because we have felt that the work has to be done.

Our objective is to have one third of the accounts in our portfolio vested in ghetto businesses. That may not be the right percentage, but it should give us a workable balance. We make good to very good profits in our general assignment of financing small businesses around the country. We are reasonably confident we can break even in our ghetto program. Although the latter requires a great amount of time in proportion to the dollar amount of investment, the results are exciting and seem to confirm the validity of our approach. We now have approximately 25% of our clients in this category.

ONE COMPANY'S APPROACH

We look at each investment opportunity with the hope that we can correctly identify and appraise the following:

1. The individual—his resourcefulness, his self-discipline, and his technical expertise.

2. The proposed business—its appropriateness to small size, the activities it will undertake to add value to its costs, its trading area, and its usefulness and social value to the neighborhood where it will be located.

3. The ability of our organization to give support in all areas, particularly during hard times, regardless of the size of investment.

There is no importance to the order of the list. Each category is part of the whole and adds either strength or weakness as the case may be. The list represents what we have found to be the important aspects of the failures and successes we have seen.

Our experience has been that when we find a person or group that meets the individual tests, has a proposition that meets the tests for the business, and leads us to feel reasonably confident that we will not lose faith, then we should go ahead with the support we can give in the way of capital and direct assistance; we believe we will not fail. We can provide the business with the resources needed to get over any periods of crisis or slowdown.

LESSONS & GUIDELINES

Now let me try to generalize from my company's experience and single out some of the things we have learned about backing a ghetto enterprise. These lessons may be useful to other investors who are new to this area.

DON'T OVERLOOK THE OBVIOUS

We have been surprised at how little can be taken for granted concerning an entrepreneur's business know-how. The following story will illustrate:

One man we financed seemed to meet all the tests. He was working very hard, and his receipts were right on target. Yet after several months there were nothing but losses for his business. We could not understand.

Since the young man on our staff who was working with this small businessman was as puzzled as we, it was decided that we would work up a complete audit of the business. As the work progressed, we continued to be perplexed because we could not pinpoint anything of sufficient magnitude to account for the poor results. After some more digging, we finally discovered the cause: our client was not adding anything to his costs to cover overhead!

You might think this such a simple error that it would be immediately apparent. But we had blinders on. On several occasions since then I have wondered how many other blinders we are wearing—how many other established concepts of business are so basic and routine that we are overlooking them. Why should we presume that

our client will know these things as intimately and instinctively as we do?

SEEK TO BE TRUSTED

The next problem is extremely difficult in some cases. I have no easy answers for it—I know only that the investor or consultant must be alert to the danger of not being trusted.

It is easy for us to explain the theory of business practices to our clients. We can help them in planning a sales campaign, in record keeping, in determining plant or office location, and in almost any technical aspect they may encounter. We have these services available either on our own staff or elsewhere.

Sometimes, however, our clients *do not believe us.* They doubt whether we are really interested in seeing them succeed even though we go to such great lengths to arrange the financing satisfactorily. We tell them that we want them to be successful because that is the only way we can make a profit. Yet cases like the following happen:

One black entrepreneur established a service business in a good community in central Long Island. He was experienced in the operations of the business from previous employment and was well recommended. We financed his operation and located the shop in a new shopping center. All the signals read "go."

After a couple of months, however, we began to have some serious questions about this client. The company's account was almost always overdrawn, although by small amounts. There was a series of meetings and phone calls when these matters were discussed in depth. Men from our staff balanced his checkbook and drew up an income-and-expense statement for him. On two occasions, when he clearly was not going to be able to cover his overdraft, we advanced temporary funds to cover it. At each meeting we emphasized that our interest was in helping him establish his business. We certainly gave evidence of this by continuing our support in the face of the irregularities.

Finally, at one of the meetings, we explained that the overdrafts had to stop. We suggested that a man from our staff visit the shop one night a week to issue checks. New checks would require two signatures including that of one of our men. This seemed acceptable to our client.

But the next day, before the new procedures could be implemented, new checks were drawn. And within 10 days the overdraft was at a new high point.

Earlier, when we had made our own examination of his accounts, we found that some funds had been drawn for noncorporate purposes. The man had used some money to pay for an operation for his mother-in-law. Some other money had been used to pay personal bills that predated the establishment of his business. Normally, the development of such evidence would have been sufficient for us to have called our loan. But in discussing these matters with us, he said that since it was his business he felt he should be able to use the funds as he saw fit. When we pointed out that this was not so, he said he understood and would conform to accepted business practice. We reconfirmed our desire to work with him. We reiterated our original belief that he had the makings of a good, small businessman, and told him he still had our support.

Now, with the new overdraft, our confidence was severely shaken. We found that he had drawn the checks immediately after our meeting and before the new check-signing procedures could be established, probably to get some last amounts out and paid while he alone could write a check. We called to say that the overdraft would not be covered by us, and we stated that we were sending the checks back because of insufficient funds. He promised to have a deposit made to cover the overdraft in the bank that afternoon.

A deposit was made that was more than sufficient to cover the overdraft. The checks were paid. But in five days the deposited check was returned because it had been drawn on a non-existent account at another bank. The deposited check was a complete fraud!

Now we went after the man in earnest. Again, a new deposit was made, large enough to cover all the old balance with some extra left over. And again, the same result; he had drawn the second check on a second bank against a second nonexistent account.

We finally arranged a meeting and told our client that we were calling our loan. He was contrite, apologetic, and full of remorse; he freely admitted all that he had done. But, and this is the point, he said he had done it because *he did not believe that we really were interested. He did not trust us!* He said no one had ever tried to help him before, so why would we be any different? He cited our suggestion of having two people sign checks; this proved to him that we wanted to take a good business away from him.

I have no idea how anyone can assure himself that he will be believed, that his partner will trust him. Yet this trust is cardinal to success; without it, no positive results can be predicted, and very probably the project will end in failure. It can be most difficult to gain the entrepreneur's trust if he comes from a background that will have conditioned him to expect the opposite. Such difficulties notwithstanding, a number of our clients have voluntarily told us that while they first approached us with distrust, they became convinced later that we were interested in their progress because they got help when they stubbed their toes. They realized that what we had told them was true—we could not prosper unless they first prospered. They saw that the way we constructed our financings effectively put the initiative in their hands and prevented us from making any real profits until after they had made profits for themselves.

DEAL IN TWO WORLDS

Related to the problem just described is the matter of appearances. The world of tall office buildings may affect the black entrepreneur from the ghetto in an unexpected way. For example:

One young man was highly recommended to us by several of the businessmen who had taught the first sessions of the local Workshop in Business Opportunities. I called him, and we set a date. It was not kept. We set another date and still another. Finally I reported all this to one of the business executives who had recommended the young man. The executive made several phone calls which did not give him the answers he wanted. Finally, he paid a visit to the young man's mother. He found out that the young man had only an old pair of blue jeans and a torn jacket. Each time he rode down on the subway and walked up to our building, he could not make himself go in. My executive friend helped the family get some new clothes for the young man, who then kept his appointment. We are working with him now, and I hope we will be able to help him get started.

The lesson is that those who of us who have "made it" are far removed from the world these applicants know. We must expect that as simple and obvious a fact as our physical surroundings will get a response (even though it may not be as pronounced as the one I have recounted). I think, on balance, that it is better to know this and be prepared to deal with it than to rent a shabby store and wear work clothes. It is essential that we be believed, and one cannot expect much belief if we start off with theatrics designed to put the client at ease.

GIVE DIRECT, PERSONAL HELP

Some problems lend themselves to all-encompassing solutions. For instance, mass programs have dealt effectively with such things as polio, chicken pox, anthrax, social security, and housing. But other problems must be solved on a one-to-one basis; that is, one problem solver working with one client. A cardiac patient needs this kind of attention; so does a small company president. When he runs into problems, his need is for direct help, usually of a consultative nature. He needs *individual* advice and guidance, not a management course.

A man who has gone into business for himself has in effect picked the president of his company. The chances of this selection being made according to any of the established precepts of personnel policy are remote. The selection has been made completely subjectively, by a man who is usually not qualified in executive selection and personnel practices. Yet it is the most fateful of all decisions that will affect the future of his small business.

INSIST ON REALISM

We decline some applications for help on the basis of inadequate preparation by the principals. Sometimes an applicant says he has heard we are helping men to get into business. We tell him that is correct. But when we ask what type of operation he is going to start, he replies that he does not care what it is, he just wants to be in business. Instead of rejecting such an applicant at the outset, we invite him in for a talk. Usually the meeting is not productive, but every now

and then we can suggest something constructive. For example:

We once talked to a man who had been a mechanic and filling station attendant. He had gone to work at the age of 12 in the South to help support his mother. Later, he moved to New York and found similar employment. At our suggestion he attended a school run by a major oil company and also joined the Workshop in Business Opportunities. Now, after nearly a year, he is ready to try something on his own.

We also turn down proposed enterprises that do not seem to lend themselves to small size. For example, we have had a number of inquiries about starting businesses such as garment manufacturing companies. In this day and age, a competitor in such an industry has little chance if he lacks a well-trained labor force and top-notch facilities. Of particular importance, the investor should insist that the entrepreneur *"start small."* The aspiring black businessman may want to go all the way in one jump (as Richard F. America proposes). He may think he can build a large market all at once. I feel that the investor should resist such tendencies. Let me illustrate:

In one case we considered, the principals of the new business had a potentially fine program, but they would not agree to start small; they insisted on forming a company that would immediately employ 50 people. Moreover, the market potential, in our view, was limited. The type of high fashion clothing the blacks proposed to make was a risky venture. The projected sales were far above what we considered attainable goals. Therefore we turned down the application.

The men went elsewhere and got their financing. The results were predictable. Overhead "ate them up," and the results were so poor that the investors refused to go further. The enterprise collapsed.

The failure of this business, in my view, did more harm than if it had never started. It will unquestionably hinder those investors from going ahead again soon, and it put a lot of people back on welfare after building up their hopes for something better. All the parties in the transaction were either unaware of, or chose to overlook, one of the most basic rules of the game of capitalism: one can have the most capable management, the best possible plant and equipment, the finest products, and adequate financing, but unless there is a customer there is no business. This is true with our largest and most successful corporations, and it is true with the small business in the ghetto.

TRADE OUTSIDE THE GHETTO

We encourage small businesses to trade outside the area where they are located. A case in point is a furniture and carpentry business we financed. It is located in the poorest section of Brooklyn near Flatbush Avenue. The few men who work at this business live within a block or two of the small shop from which they operate. Yet most of their jobs are done for homeowners and industry located in the well-to-do areas of Long Island. It is a struggling small business, but it brings fresh money to the ghetto area.

As long as the businesses located in the ghetto have their customers, or a majority of them, also located in the ghetto, capitalism will never reach its fullest potential. Could Detroit be so prosperous if most of the cars and trucks made there were sold only in Detroit? In this connection, it is worth noting that the Community Development Corporation legislation would very effectively eliminate any chance of trading outside the ghetto. This is one of the most urgent reasons why the whole program should be re-evaluated. The history of industrial development has always shown a heavy incidence of "foreign" investment as the basic capital on which a country has built its economy. It is going to be just as true with our urban ghettos.

Of course, exceptions should occasionally be made to this rule, as the following case indicates:

A group of about 30 mothers who were on welfare in the Fort Greene area of Brooklyn determined that they wanted to be free of welfare payments (on which they had been depending). The mothers formed a family day-care center where they and other mothers could leave their children and try to find work.

Seven were employed by the day-care center, which was funded by the appropriate state and local agencies. Eight found other work. Then the mothers at the day-care center and others who had not found work started to cook food for take-out orders. These take-out foods were an immediate success; the demand was greater than the supply. At this point the mothers came to see us:

There was a vacant luncheonette for rent in their neighborhood. We put up all the funds required to start the restaurant proposed by the women. It specialized in "soul food," which was especially popular with the people who live in that area. The mothers working at the restaurant remained on relief and drew no pay until the business was doing a volume sufficient to support them. We forecasted a period of about eight weeks for this volume to materialize. But business was so good that within three weeks the receipts were running nearly three times those expected. The business continues to thrive.

What an appropriate way for small capitalists to get started. In a case like this the investors know their funds will be used to establish the business, but not to support an overhead of payroll until the firm can make it on its own. The welfare authorities, on the other hand, continue to support the would-be entrepreneurs during the time they are building something that will eliminate the need for public support. I hope we can duplicate this procedure many times over.

EDUCATION IS CRUCIAL

Much of the frustration that undoubtedly results in the militancy and revolutionary fervor of many educated blacks can be traced to their inability to achieve anything meaningful despite their aspirations. After the Civil War and after World War I their hopes rose but their achievements did not. Again today, after the passage over the last eight years of sweeping civil rights legislation, the blacks have had their hopes built up only to find that they are still excluded from decision making at important levels. They still do not have the means for exercising an entrepreneurial spirit.

Indeed, with industry turning more and more to automation, with the widespread use of computers, and with the development of sophisticated techniques, the disadvantaged of our urban centers find it more and more difficult to prepare themselves for any kind of satisfying participation in significant affairs. We seem to have failed to develop adequate public schools in our urban centers. Up to about 15 years ago, the working class could sell its muscle with only a low degree of skill or specialized training being required. Now employment of this kind is growing less and less available. But we have taken only a few of the necessary steps to provide the required schooling facilities.

If members of the disadvantaged class are to be given the chance to work toward better positions, schooling must be considered an absolute essential of the process. A negative income tax and massive direct support would undoubtedly be very helpful. However, they would not provide for the acquisition of capital or help directly to establish a climate conducive to it. Know-how is required for that—and know-how requires education.

CONCLUSION

There have been enough conferences and meetings. We know right now all we need to know about the problem of developing entrepreneurship in the economically disadvantaged areas of our urban centers. Now there is just one great big pile of work to get on with.

Helping small businesses in these areas to get started and to prosper is no cure-all. It will not directly improve health standards, schooling, or housing. What it can and will do, if practiced broadly, will be to provide a significant number of deserving and aspiring individuals with the opportunity to try their hands at the capitalist game.

Those who would practice giving this help as investors and advisors should be the very ones who have themselves prospered as players in the capitalist game. It is true they will have to bend some of the rules a bit to fit special circumstances. But not very much bending is necessary. Moreover, the ghetto entrepreneurs themselves will be stronger and better qualified to "go it alone" if they are coached soundly and realistically.

Any program that would isolate small business in the ghetto or separate it from the mainstream of business affairs will fail. Any effort to donate capitalism ready-made must also fail. The best economic tool we have ever had is good, old-fashioned, no-nonsense capitalism. It is up to those of us who have learned it and prospered from it to pass it on to those who would use it if they could but learn how. Repeatedly, in the past, people succeeded and prospered if help was available when they needed it. It is time now for all of us to extend helping hands to our disadvantaged citizens.

ADDENDUM

The Editors, Harvard Business Review

FROM:
The HBR Editors
RE:
Making Capitalism Work in the Ghettos, by
Louis L. Allen,
HBR May–June 1969
It has come to our attention that, through no
fault of his, Mr. Allen distorted key points of
Richard F. America, Jr. in his criticism of Mr.
America's HBR article, "'What Do You People
Want?'" (March-April 1969).

America argued for shifting control of about
10% of our largest companies to black managerial groups, to redress "fundamental inequities"
in economic power now existing in this country.

He did not, contrary to Allen, propose that the
transfers be accomplished by the federal government through eminent domain. He maintained that the initiative must come from the
companies themselves, and the government
would act as the medium of transfer. Indded,
America stressed that his proposal "presupposes
a national climate favorable" to it.

Allen's article also misstates the recommended period of transfer of corporate operations.
It was not a few months, but five to ten years,

Reprinted from *Harvard Business Review,* V. 47, N. 5
(September–October, 1969), p. 158.

and the whole program would take a generation
to complete.

Allen questioned America's "oversight" in
ignoring the presumed adverse effect on sales of
a consumer products company that becomes
black-controlled. Anticipating such eventuali-
ties, America suggested that the initial candidates be manufacturers of producers' goods and
companies with large government contracts.
Then, after several years of experience, and with
general public acceptance of the program, consumer goods companies would join it.

Otherwise, the differences separating Allen
and America were mainly in points of view. The
former called the latter's proposal "a give-away
program," while the latter refers to it as a way to
make "government economic policy explicitly
favorable to black people, as it has long been
favorable implicitly to whites." America would
agree with Allen's statement that blacks "are
still excluded from decision making at important levels."

The misrepresentations in the Allen article
were a result of mis-information given to Allen
by us, while the America article was still in the
formative stage. We regret that America's argument has been inaccurately reported and that
Allen has been embarrassed by our error.

TOWARD AN OVERALL ASSESSMENT OF OUR ALTERNATIVES

Robert S. Browne

Aware and Concerned Brothers and Sisters—It is with great humility that I have accepted this invitation to deliver the keynote address for this important conference on Black Economic Development. We are all aware in what a critical period we black people in America now find ourselves. In the richest nation which the world has ever known, we find ourselves in a position of relative impoverishment. In a nation which boasts of its democratic processes, we find ourselves relatively powerless. In a nation which worships education as the magic key to success, our children are going unlettered. In an era of global nationalism, we are a people without a nation.

Obviously I have only begun to enumerate a few of the ways in which we are a disadvantaged people in this society. And indeed, there is nothing which I have stated which Frederick Douglass, or Booker T. Washington, or Dr. DuBois could not have declared with equal validity 69 or more years ago, as we entered upon this cataclysmic 20th century. Indeed, they did make many of these very observations to groups not unlike this one. But I feel there is a difference today—not merely the obvious difference that for us today is real whereas they are history—but a qualitative difference which derives from the differing mood of black people generally. I sense that today's blacks, and especially the younger ones, are a new breed of black person. I sense that the old passivity and dependency psychology has been replaced by a psychology of independent action and I sense that

Reprinted from *The Review of Black Political Economy*, V. 1, N. 1 (Spring/Summer, 1970), pp. 18-26, by permission of the author and the publisher.

the old gradualism has been replaced by a new urgency. And I also suspect that the several hundred people in this auditorium enjoy a capacity for implementation which far surpasses that of any audience which Douglass or Washington or DuBois ever addressed.

It might of course be argued that the obstacles to black achievement have increased at least as much as has our potential for achievement. I would not agree however. Our oppressors are probably no more vicious than they ever were; naturally their desperation can be expected to increase as they feel more threatened by our successes in fighting free from their grasp, but this is inevitable. Meanwhile, the general world situation has evolved in a manner more favorable to our cause. We have sympathetic allies in every corner of the globe, and modern communications insures that world opinion remains constantly apprised of the major happenings in our noble struggle.

However, lest I mislead you into thinking that my address will be cast in an optimistic vein, allow me to move on to some more sobering considerations. The subject of my talk is "the need for formulating an economic plan for Black people." What is an economic plan? The term initially gained its popularity from its usage by the Soviet Union.

In 1928, about a decade after the 1917 revolution, the Soviet Union announced that it was launching a 5 year plan for economic development. Since that time it has undertaken several more such plans, and the practice has been widely copied by other Socialist countries as well as by many non-socialist countries such as India and many of the smaller nations.

Indeed, such plans have become a regular part of the economic development process for a growing number of nations. Although differing in some details, the heart of these economic plans is the setting forth of specific goals to be achieved by a certain date, and some plan for attaining these goals. Goals are likely to be such things as: achieving a certain level of industrial productivity in designated categories, a certain level of agricultural production, a certain volume of exports, a certain rise in per capita income, lowering illiteracy by "x" percent, training "x" number of teachers, graduating so many doctors, etc. Obviously, such a plan must be internally consistent if it is to succeed, i.e., a large increase in agricultural production cannot be achieved unless plans are also made for producing (or importing) the necessary fertilizer, farm equipment, etc. Considerable research and data collection must precede the making of any economic development plan so that the goals will in fact be within the realm of possibility.

Does such an economic plan have meaning for black people in America? It seems to me that the answer is both yes and no. The answer is no because this type of a plan assumes the existence of a nation which has title to a cluster of contiguous resources and which exercises sovereignty over both itself as a community and over its members, who must feel themselves to be a part of this community. This sovereignty may be exercised either by consent or by coercion, but it must be effective if there is to be a nation. In effect, there must be a government with the power to govern. Short of this there can be no sovereignty, no nation, no economic development plan in the customary sense of the word.

Black America clearly fails all of these tests. The concepts of gross national product, imports and exports, agricultural or industrial output, etc., are not only not measurable for the black community; they have no meaning. In a rather crude fashion we can measure black purchasing power, the capitalization of black owned business establishments. And with extreme difficulty we might succeed in measuring black savings and black land ownership. Next year the census bureau will presumably attempt to measure the magnitude of the black population and will view with alarm its rate of increase, but I suggest that these magnitudes at present have little meaning in a national sense. It may be quite useful to get these measurements—indeed, urgent to do so—but the mere gathering of such data will not create the necessary conditions for nationhood or for an economic development plan. We are not yet a consciously cohesive community; we do not have sovereignty over ourselves as individuals; we do not have sovereignty over ourselves as a community. That is to say, we cannot draw up final rules for governing ourselves, for taxing ourselves, for conducting foreign relations and trading, for law enforcement, for property rights, for immigration and emigration, nor can we establish our own monetary unit. No, we are far from enjoying the basic prerogatives of nationhood, and despite the presence at this conference of some distinguished brothers who are doing ground-breaking work along these lines, I sense that this conference is not primarily to be concerned with the question of whether national sovereignty is desirable for blacks or how it can be achieved.

Rather, it seems to me, we have been brought here to discuss the more modest question of what is achievable by black people within the existing limitations of our NOT enjoying national sovereignty. That is, given the reality that we are, for the moment, inseparably attached to the larger, white, capitalistic American society, what are the most promising techniques which we can utilize to maximize black well-being.

Admittedly, this is a much more modest objective than the building of a black nation. It is clearly not an objective which will bring black people a major degree of control over their destinies. But it may put some additional bread on their tables and ease some chronic illnesses and therefore it is probably worth doing. For the achievement of this more limited objective I think that the concept of an economic plan can have considerable significance—obviously not the classical type of economic planning appropriate to an independent nation, but it is of the utmost importance that black people sit down and take inventory of where we are, where we hope to get to, and what series of steps seem most likely to get us there. Clearly, this conference did not convene in order to discuss simple band-aids which might be applied to some of the more painful sores on the black community. As a matter of fact, the white establishment has not been ungenerous with its band-aids—but any child knows that a band-aid is of little help when the limb is broken and bleeding profusely. Surgery may be necessary but short of that, major treatment is certainly called for. The task then of this conference, it seems to me, is to begin to prescribe that treatment. I am even hesitant to suggest that the conference should spend very much time diagnosing our malady, for we have been diagnosed thousands of times and I suspect that there is little new to be said on that count.

Essentially, the illness is that black people have no handle on the basic levers or sources of power in this country which I conceive to be six in number: (1) Accumulations of private wealth,—if you want to know who these families are I refer you to the May, 1968, issue of Fortune magazine, where most of them are listed together with an estimate of their assets. (2) Some 200 major corporations, most of whose annual incomes far exceed the budgets of most of the nations of Africa. The annual revenues of General Motors Corporation are larger than the gross national product of all but the top 15 of the nations of the world. (3) The military-industrial complex, centered in the Pentagon and obviously overlapping with the 200 largest corporations which I have just cited. (4) The federal and state governmental apparatus. (5) The federal legislative apparatus. (6) The crime syndicate. In deference to our host city I might add a close seventh—organized labor.

We lack access to these levers of control because of a combination of reasons, the main one being of course the history which we have experienced in this country. When the country was being divided up and raped, we were slaves. Indeed, we were part of the very property which was being divided and raped—literally. So we didn't get in when the melon was being cut and now almost the only way to get a really significant hunk of it is to wrest it away from someone else. We also lack access because we are numerically too small a group, and too dispersed, to have been able to seize control of any one of these levers. This lack of access to the instruments of power, supplemented by white America's vicious racial prejudice toward black people, has led to our perpetual impoverishment, our self-hatred and psychological insecurity, our

poor educational attainment, and our social disorganization.

If this diagnosis is correct, and I suspect that it is a diagnosis to which most blacks would subscribe, the question than arises: Should our attack be focussed on the causes of the malady or on the symptoms? Do we focus on raising black peoples' wages, enlarging their education and skills, overcoming their psychological insecurities, and building up their social organization? Or do we focus on the causes of our poverty and degradation, namely, our powerlessness, our lack of access to the levers of power in the society?

There will be a natural tendency to respond by saying "Attack the causes, not the symptoms." This is obviously what we usually do in medicine and I am quite sympathetic with this view. If only surface manifestations are changed while the underlying causes are left intact there is always the likelihood of a re-eruption of the malignancy. Realistically speaking, however, I see very limited possibility for our grasping the levers of control in this society. True, we have an excellent potential for exercising a sort of negative power, a limited veto so to speak, over how the white establishment uses its power. And we should work toward building this sort of negative power, essentially I suppose via the electoral process but not forgetting that our brothers in the streets have been rather creative about devising other techniques as well.

If we were to decide to go after the causes of our oppression, the sole avenue which might offer some hope for our grabbing a tenuous hold onto one lever of control, and an avenue which could serve a dual purpose of also helping us toward achievement of black nationhood, would be for blacks to capture control of one or more state governments. Unlike control of a municipality, control of a state government not only offers tremendous opportunities for developing an extensive corps of black technicians but also provides black people with a somewhat viable economic unit from which to build a tangible sense of community and of cultural autonomy. Where today are the black men who can design, build, and operate giant bridges, hydro-electric installations, water works and sewage disposal plants, massive port facilities, and other basic elements of the physical infra-structure of a modern society? If there are such people, and they can't be many, they are lost in a vast white ocean. There is no identifiable corps of blacks with these capabilities. Perhaps as a result, we have few blacks studying these skills. I have never forgotten how, in 1961, at the height of the Lumumba era, I was asked by an official of the Congolese government if I could recommend about 60 black mining engineers to come to the Congo to take over the direction of the Katanga mines from the Belgians. I hardly need to tell you that I was unable to produce even one such person. Indeed, as far as I could determine, there was no record of any blacks having finished from the Colorado School of Mines, which is perhaps the major institution for such study in this country. Mining engineering is of course only symbolic for an entire range of very basic technical activities which it would rarely occur to a black youngster to pursue, but which black possession of a state government might offer some access to. Hopefully, the Cleveland and Gary experiences, though they may be mere tokens of black control, and other black-run municipalities soon to come, will provide vitally needed opportunities for our black youth to gain some new skills and experiences. But a city is a relatively limited economic unit; it is usually not a viable financial unit these days; and physically a city is an extremely vulnerable unit in that it raises no food and is totally dependent on outsiders for its external communications. Thus it could not serve even as a symbolic homeland for black people—nor could a series of such enclaves. For me, the currently popular "parallel economy" concept takes on meaning not with black control of a series of geographically separated communities or cities but only with black control of a unit at least as large as a state. One avenue of effort by this conference then might be to explore the feasibility of a legal black takeover of one of the 50 states. Such a program would require extensive research and planning; it would require channeling millions of dollars into a concentrated voter registration drive in the designated state; the quiet buying up of large properties and the provision of an economic base for attracting black immigrants, etc. The New Towns provision of the Housing Act of 1968 might be of some use here, but needless to say, once the whites realized what was happening the resistance would be substantial. And let me reiterate that such an effort,

although I put if forth as a form of direct thrust for real power in America, would—even if highly successful—represent the accretion of only a modest amount of additional power for blacks. But it would enormously enhance our capability for further advance.

Let us, however, return to our consideration of whether we are better off to focus our attack on the causes of our disadvantage or on the symptoms. Can we launch an effective, direct attack on black poverty, black illiteracy, black insecurity despite our exclusion from the national power structure? I feel that we can. Our achievements will be of limited scope and will certainly not bring into being The Black Nation. But in putting some more bread on the table, in bringing us a greater degree of self-reliance, it will justify itself. It is in this sense that the numerous local development projects, small business programs, job training, consumer education, vocational guidance, school improvement and other community programs are all helpful. I believe such limited goals to be achievable because they do not threaten the superestablishment, the six power centers which I earlier specified. Achieving these limited goals may require expropriating some local landlords and businessmen, it may undermine some petty white racketeers and party hacks, it may deny some government-salaried jobs to some white middle class professionals, and it may weaken some racist union locals. But none of these groups are part of the national power structure anyway. The super-establishment, recognizing that blacks must be placated in some way, will be prepared to sacrifice the small fry local white exploiters so that it may continue uninterrupted with its global strategies. Thus we are presented an opportunity and a danger. The opportunity is to utilize our wits to exploit this willingness of the national power structure to meet some of our demands at the expense of the local exploiters. The danger is that we may find ourselves unwitting collaborators in a system which does long run damage to our self interest. It is a tricky bag in which we niggers find ourselves.

Certainly we must assume control of our communities. Certainly we must acquire ownership and control of income producing properties, and most especially those located within our communities. The real estate, the businesses, the public facilities, must belong to the community in some form or another. Racketeering, prostitution, the numbers—if they are to continue—must be put into the hands of the community. Education must be made more effective for black children. We must develop some industry. A larger portion of tax revenues must flow through our hands. I will not dwell on this because I suspect most everyone here agrees. But the implications of some of these demands cut many ways. Fifty per cent of federal tax revenues currently go into military expenditures. We are already getting a healthy share of the portion of these expenditures which go for enlisted men's salaries. Do we want to increase this share? Do we want to lobby Washington to award a few defense contracts to the black community so that we can make tanks and napalm to be used on black Africans—and on us? Do we want more of our black brothers in the State Department and the CIA if in fact it means that they will be flying about the world carrying out the Pentagon's repressive policies toward non-white nations?

What I am suggesting is that any significant economic development which we achieve will come about largely through political maneuvering, and we must therefore be very together and know exactly what we are doing. There is considerable resistance among black intellectuals to the concept of black capitalism and strong support for some sort of communal or cooperative ownership. This is desirable I think, but there is a risk of exaggerating the importance of such institutional differences.

In a capitalist, imperalist society, is a cooperatively owned Standard Oil Company likely to be any less exploitative than a privately owned one? If so, is it likely to succeed for very long? To repeat what I suggested earlier the amount of self-determination which we can achieve while remaining a part of white, capitalistic American society is extremely limited and we should clearly understand this. Otherwise, there is likely to be great disappointment. It is probably true that black control of our communities may provide us a much broader power base than we now have from which to attempt to make a leap to the power table. But it is far from being a guarantee that we can successfully make such a leap.

I do not bring you answers; if so, the Conference could be just about winding up now.

Rather, I bring you questions . . . questions which you must wrestle with today and tomorrow, and perhaps for some time to come. I have purposely avoided detailing specific actions which we might take, such as forming black construction unions, demanding a guaranteed income, channeling black savings into the community, and many other tasks which you will certainly be taking up in your workshops.

In developing plans for dealing with these specifics, however, may I point out that an economic plan is not a plan unless it comes to grips with the question of priorities. A shopping list of desirable things to be done is not a plan. To be a useful guide, the plan must have, first of all, clearly defined goals. [Frantz] Fanon, incidentally, in his revolutionary writings, placed great stress on the importance of being clear about your goals and being certain that the populace clearly understands the goals. Secondly, a development plan must have an overall logic, it must recognize the interdependence of each part with every other, it must state what is to be done first, what next, etc. Developing such a plan is an enormous task. It can't be completed in a week or a month, and in a sense such plans are never really completed because they must be flexible enough to change as the dynamics of the situation change. For blacks in America the question of an economic plan is further complicated by the fact that no group is likely to be given a mandate to draw up such a plan. Personal and institutional jealousies as well as valid ideological factionalism within the black community insures that no development plan will be accepted as satisfactory by all segments of the black population. It is a source of some distress to me that the head of one major national black organization intimately involved in economic development work complained to me that he had not been invited to attend this conference. I do not know if he was telling me the truth, but I do feel strongly that at this stage we should be inclusive. Nevertheless, this conference will have made an unprecedented contribution to black economic development if it seriously explores some of the grand issues which must necessarily be raised by such a planning effort.

For instance, it is believed that black people in the South have been selling their land holdings—sometimes rather substantial ones—

and moving to cities; an action which is perhaps justified from the point of view of the individual but which may be contrary to the best interests of blacks as a group. Such questions demand exploration and research. If it appears that such actions are in fact harmful to us then we might need to develop a fund to purchase such land and to decide its disposition on the basis of some rational black program. In exploring such an undertaking one should consider what resources blacks already have which might be useful. For example, there are a half dozen or more land grant Negro colleges in the South: Prairie View, Alcorn, A&T, Tennessee A&I, etc. What are these schools doing with regard to rural black populations? What should they be doing? What can we get them to do, and how? All such questions can be meaningfully explored as part of a black economic development plan.

On yesterday afternoon another national conference on black economic development opened in New York—organized by white academic and money interests. I attended yesterday's deliberations, which were participated in by about 30 white and 30 black persons from around the country. Obviously, a bi-racial conference of that nature has certain built-in inhibitions, a principal one being that black economic development cannot be discussed separately from black political development, and blacks don't easily discuss this with whites.

But within its limitations, the conference was instructive. One of the brothers who was there but who was also invited to be here summed up his dilemma by saying that he couldn't decide whether it was more instructive to listen to the folks who had the dough or to those who were trying to get it away from them. (Actually, we need people to do both.) The spectrum of black opinion at that conference is probably less broad than this audience here. But I did meet two or three beautiful cats whom I had never heard of before, and there are probably more whom I didn't meet. The same thing has already begun to happen to me here. I am really struck by the endless numbers of sharp, dedicated, together black guys who are appearing as if from nowhere. This suggests to me an additional benefit of an economic plan.

It is possible that the arduous task of forging an economic plan for black people, which would necessarily involve the intense interaction of most of these brothers with one another, could begin to produce the degree of unity which we so desperately need for the next stages of our liberation process.

In conclusion then, I suppose that the meat of my address has been that the first step in black economic development is not economic at all, but political. There is no question of "pulling ourselves up by our bootstraps." We have no bootstraps. We are starting with so few economic resources of our own that our tactic must be to utilize cleverly what strength we do have, namely, the political force of 25 million potentially united black minds, for extracting some economic resources from those who do have them. In many cases, of course, the resources morally belong to us anyway. But obtaining control of them will not be easy. A commitment even prior to the political one is implied in my statement, however, for I referred to our political force being based on 25 million potentially united black minds. Achieving a substantial degree of unity is an obvious prerequisite for rendering the political force effective as a lever for extracting resources. As Harold Cruse well said: our revolution must take place on three levels: cultural, political and economic. As this conference proceeds with its discussions focussed on economic issues I feel certain that the cultural and political—which is to say ideological—factors will inescapably impose themselves into your framework. It is inevitable and essential that they do so. But ideology is divisive as we all know, and can paralyze us totally. Therefore, as we begin this important work here this weekend I feel it to be of foremost importance that we recognize the tremendous implications of what we are about and that we approach our task soberly, humbly, and with a spirit of tolerance and black love.

I would urge that each of us concentrate our efforts on discovering what are the short run tasks that we can find common agreement on—irrespective of the fact that the brother who is pushing any particular program may indeed be our bitter personal rival or ideological opponent. Although we have had rather tragic experiences with black spokesmen and black cabinets in the past—whether Booker T. Washington, Mary McLeod Bethune, or the Civil Rights Leadership Conference, I can't help but feel that a great deal could be gained were we able to develop a united position on at least some aspects of how we would like to see government and private money used in the black community. This would be at least the beginnings of an economic plan.

Brothers and Sisters, what you do here this weekend may significantly influence where black people go from here. Shoulder your responsibilities well! UHURU!

ADDITIONAL READINGS FOR CHAPTER 12

Robert L. Allen, *Black Awakening in Capitalist America: An Analytic History* (Garden City, N.Y.: Doubleday and Company, 1969).

George E. Berkner, *Black Capitalism and the Urban Negro*, Occasional Paper Number 8 (Tempe, Arizona: Bureau of Business and Economic Research, College of Business Administration, Arizona State University, 1970).

"Black Capitalism, Problems and Prospects: A Special Issue," Saturday Review, V. LII, N. 34 (August 23, 1969).

"Black Self-Determination: A Debate," by Roy Innis and Norman Hill, *New Generation,* V. 51, N. 3 (Summer 1969), pp. 18-26.

Wayne G. Broehl, "A Less Developed Entrepreneur," *Columbia Journal of World Business,* V. V, N. 2 (March–April 1970), pp. 26-34.

Michael Brower and Doyle Little, "White Help for Black Business," *Harvard Business Review,* V. 48, N. 3 (May–June 1970), pp. 4-6, 8, 10, 12 14, 16, 163-164.

"Business in the Ghetto," Proceedings, ABA National Academy, April 11-12, 1969, *The Business Lawyer,* V. 25, Special Issue (September 1969).

Theodore L. Cross, *Black Capitalism: Strategy for Business in the Ghetto* (New York: Atheneum, 1969).

Laird Durham, *Black Capitalism: Critical Issues in Urban Management* (Washington, D.C.: published and distributed by Communication Service Corporation for Arthur D. Little, Inc., 1970).

Economic Development Opportunity, Hearings before the Select Committee on Small Business, United States Senate, 90th Congress, 2nd Session, on The Role of the Federal Government in the Development of Small Business Enterprises in the Urban Ghetto, Newark, New Jersey–May 24, 1968, New York, New York–June 17, 1968 (Washington, D.C.: U.S. Government Printing Office, 1968).

Richard W. Epps, "The Appeal of Black Capitalism," in Federal Reserve Bank of Philadelphia, *Business Review* (May 1969), pp. 9-15.

John T. Garrity, "Red Ink for Ghetto Industries," *Harvard Business Review,* V. 46, N. 3 (May–June 1968), pp. 4-16.

D. Parke Gibson, *The $30 Billion Negro* (New York: The Macmillian Company, 1969).

William F. Haddad and G. Douglas Pugh (eds.), *Black Economic Development* (Englewood Cliffs, N.J.: Prentice-Hall, 1969).

William L. Henderson and Larry C. Ledebur, "The Viable Alternative for Black Economic Development," *Public Policy,* V. XVIII, N. 3 (Spring 1970), pp. 429-449.

_____ *Economic Disparity: Problems and Strategies for Black America* (New York: The Free Press, 1970).

Jerome H. Holland, *Black Opportunity* (New York: Weybright and Talley, 1970).

"The Hough Development Corporation," *ICH Cases,* 13G 300-13G307 (Boston, Mass: Intercollegiate Case Clearing House, 1969).

James M. Hund, *Black Entrepreneurship* (Belmont, Calif.: Wadsworth Publishing Company, 1970).

Edward D. Irons, "Black Capitalism—1968," in Patricia W. Romero (ed.), *In Black America: 1968 The Year of Awakening* (Washington, D.C.: United Publishing Corporation, 1969), pp. 217-227.

Louis O. Kelso and Patricia Hetter, *Two Factor Theory: The Economics of Reality* (New York: Random House, 1967.)

Robert S. Lecky and H. Elliott Wright, *Black Manifesto: Religion, Racism and Reparations* (New York: Sheed and Ward, 1969).

Sar A. Levitan, Garth L. Mangum, Robert Taggart III, *Economic Opportunity in the Ghetto: The Partnership of Government and Business,* Policy Studies in Employment and Welfare No. 3 (Baltimore: The Johns Hopkins Press, 1970).

Robert B. McKersie, "Vitalize Black Enterprise," *Harvard Business Review,* V. 46, N. 5 (September–October 1968), pp. 88-99.

Kenneth H. Miller, "Community Capitalism and the Community Self-Determination Act," *Harvard Journal on Legislation,* V. 6 (1969). pp. 413-461.

David C. McClelland, "Black Capitalism: Making it Work," *Think* Magazine, V. 35, N. 4 (Armonk, N.Y.:IBM), July–August 1969, pp. 6-11.

_____ and David G. Winter, *Motivating Economic Achievement* (New York: The Free Press, 1969).

"Minority Enterprise," *Journal of Small Business,* V. 7, Ns. 2 and 3, combined issue (April–July 1969).

Harvey S. Perloff and Lowdon Wingo, Jr. (eds.), *Issues in Urban Economics* (Baltimore: published for Resources for the Future, Inc. by The Johns Hopkins Press, 1968).

Alvin N. Puryear, "Restoration: A Profile of Economic Development," *The MBA,* V. III (February 1969).

Martin Rein, "Social Stability and Black Capitalism," *TRANS-action,* V. 6, N. 7 (June 1969), pp. 4, 6.

The Review of Black Political Economy, V. 1, No. 1 (Spring/Summer 1970).

Review of Small Business Administration's Programs and Policies—1969, Hearings before the Select Committee on Small Business, 91st Congress, 1st Session, on Review of Small Business Administration Financial Assistance Programs and Policies, June 10, 11, 12, 20, 25; July 15, and October 15, 1969 (Washington, D.C.: U.S. Government Printing Office 1969).

Richard S. Rosenbloom and Robin Marris (eds.), *Social Innovation in the City: New Enterprises for Community Development* (Cambridge, Mass.: Harvard University Program on Technology and Society, 1969).

Arnold Schuchter, *White Power/Black Freedom: Planning the Future of Urban America* (Boston, Mass: Beacon Press, 1968).

——, *Reparations: The Black Manifesto and Its Challenge to White America* (Philadelphia: J. B. Lippincott Company, 1969).

Frederick D. Sturdivant, "The Limits of Black Capitalism," *Harvard Business Review,* V. 47, N. 1 (January—February 1969), pp. 122-128.

James L. Sundquist, "Jobs, Training, and Welfare for the Underclass," in Kermit Gordon (ed.), *Agenda for the Nation* (Washington, D.C.: The Brookings Institution, 1968), pp. 49-76.

Whitney M. Young, Jr., *Beyond Racism* (New York: McGraw-Hill Book Company, 1969).

PART **4**

WHITHER AN
AMERICAN DILEMMA?

13   *C o n c l u s i o n :*

In his introduction to *An American Dilemma,* Gunnar Myrdal placed the "Negro problem" into a broad societal perspective when he observed:

> *The Negro problem is an integral part of, or a special phase of, the whole complex of problems in the larger American civilization. It cannot be treated in isolation.* There is no single side of the Negro problem whether it be the Negro's political status, the education he gets, his place in the labor market, his cultural and personality traits, or anything else which is not predominantly determined by its total American setting. We shall, therefore, constantly be studying the American civilization in its entirety, though viewed in its implications for the most disadvantaged population group. [1]

Myrdal also pointed out that the "Negro problem" is basically the "white man's problem" since it is the "white majority group that naturally determines the Negro's place." [2] Although recent events have indicated that he imputed too great a degree of passivity to black Americans, his observations are as trenchant today as when he first made them a generation ago. The basic fact is that blacks constitute only approximately 11 percent of the population, and that nearly 85 percent of all Americans are white (Spanish American, Asian Americans, and American Indians constitute the remainder). Therefore, in population terms, the United States remains an overwhelmingly "white country." We have seen, moreover, that it has remained a "white country" in terms of the distribution of wealth, power, and status within the society. Black Americans—short of a successful revolution— will find it exceedingly difficult, if not impossible, to alter drastically the fundamental attributes of American society without the cooperation—at a minimum, the acquiescence—of the dominant white majority.

We have seen that the economic status of black men and women has been both a manifestation and a cause of their general position in American life. Whether that position will change substantially from the historic condition of negative imbalance to a situation of social, political, and economic parity will, in large measure, be decided by what occurs within the economic arena. We are not derogating the great importance of political organization and the ability of the political process to effect social change. In the past, other ethnic groups have used their control of governmental resources to enhance their economic positions (and their collective status). Rather, the point we are making is that economic and political power are closely related, and both are essential to social change. This relationship may be diagrammed as follows:

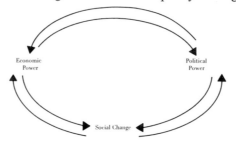

The Alternatives

Within the economic area, the behavior of business managers and their organizations holds much of the key to the future. Whether business firms pursue many of the programs and proposals suggested in Part 3, together with other initiatives which are equally or even more creative and innovative, will determine whether the manifold problems discussed in Parts 1 and 2 will be resolved. Indeed, as we have suggested, many of these problems have their contemporary origin at the multifaceted interface where black Americans meet white business.

The business community cannot resolve these problems alone. It does not have the resources, financial flexibility, expertise, or social legitimacy to act single-handedly. What is true of American business generally is particularly true of individual firms, no matter what their size.[3] Other institutions within our society, particularly local, state, and especially the federal government, have an essential role to play. We have emphasized throughout that business action and governmental activity must go hand in hand. It is our position, however, that without fundamental changes and initiatives by the business community in its relationship with the black community, there is little possibility of any real improvement in the socioeconomic status of black Americans.

The following chapter is entitled "Conclusion: The Alternatives" since, in our opinion, American society is confronted basically with two choices: *social progress* or *societal strife*. Either economic, political, and social change will take place peacefully and with "all deliberate speed," or violent change will occur, resulting in the demise of institutions basic to this society. The first alternative (social progress) holds out the promise of a society in which race will no longer be "outcome-determinative" in deciding the life-chances and life-style of American citizens, but instead, a society in which wealth and position are primarily a function of achievement.

Business institutions will either be catalytic agents in the change process or bear the risk of becoming anachronisms. Business may have to relinquish many of its traditional prerogatives and responsibilities to public authority as a result of its own failure to address itself to the fundamental problems confronting American society. The public will come to feel that it can no longer afford to have economic institutions which cannot or will not respond to pressing domestic needs.

Our most socially perceptive corporate leaders are keenly aware of this possibility. After reviewing a variety of problems—including that of race—confronting American society, Irwin Miller, chairman of the Cummins Engine Company observed:

We have an internal crisis that is in nature complex and pervasive, and in size and significance, ultimately mortal. It could destroy us. It also says that it is not too late to act, though it may very soon be too late. It says further that we cannot act slowly, as usually in the past we have been free to act. We cannot wait for a problem to become clearly desperate—and act by bits and pieces.

Instead we must act with a speed to which we have never been accustomed. We must act on all fronts because we have let crises pile up on us, and we must act with a degree of national commitment which in our history we have shown only in time of major war. The heart of the crisis and the fate of the outcome is to be found, therefore, . . . with business. This is a business and industry society. We are the "power group," the "lead group," the group that has a chance to show the way.[4]

Just as business has been quick to accept the credit for the favorable aspects of American society, so, too, it must inevitably shoulder the blame for the less than salutary conditions which exist.

In American society the conduct of economic activity has been "delegated" to the business sector. In other societies different socioeconomic alternatives are followed. Accordingly, other models are available *if* our existing institutions are no longer functional to the operation of the society. The possibilities for alterations of the present socioeconomic order range from extensive governmental regulation of present business organizations to total public ownership by the state. We are not suggesting that at present either of these contingencies has much popular support. However, if as the alternative to social conflict a basic restructuring of our economic organizations becomes necessary, this support could develop.

The second alternative (societal strife) holds out a very different prospect—a society where those in authority feel it necessary to counter violent demands for change by those who feel the social system cannot be altered peacefully with increasing suppression of personal liberties. A childish ditty, which contains much wisdom concerning the historic importance of race in American society, states:

If you're white, it's alright.
If you're yellow, it's mellow.
If you're brown, stick around.
If you're black, stay back!

Black people—and other people of color—are no longer willing to have a position within the United States of less than "alright," and they appear to have allies among significant numbers of young white Americans in their struggle for equality. Whether business will be operating within a friendly or a hostile environment during the decade of the seventies will partly be a function of the credibility it establishes within both groups who have expressed grave doubt concerning the willingness and ability of business to respond to critical social needs. If business is not responsive to the wide range of problems suggested in this book, we shall hear increasingly strident questions posed concerning the legitimacy of our "business society." While the large majority of blacks and young whites are prepared, and, in fact, desire, to work within the present framework of American society, they are willing to seek more radical alternatives if all else fails. If the social system cannot be altered by peaceful means, it will be altered by violence and repression. In short, there exists the potential for civil war within the United States if our domestic (and foreign) ills are not remedied in the near future.

It should be apparent that the second alternative is no alternative at all for American society. It is an invitation to tyranny which would be antithetical to the very concept of a democratic nation.

The readings in the final chapter examine alternative possibilities confronting American society. In "The White Race and Its Heroes," Black Panther leader Eldridge Cleaver points out some paradoxical problems facing white America. He looks at the antipathy developing between white youth (especially the more educated) and their elders as a result of the unwillingness of the former to accept the contradictions of American society. To these young people, the racial situation existing in this country encompasses the most blatant of these contradictions— poverty amidst affluence and social inequality in a "democratic" nation. We end the book with Gunnar Myrdal's concluding chapter in *An American Dilemma,* "America Again at the Crossroads." In this piece, Myrdal is optimistic that America will resolve its dilemma in the years ahead and offers valuable insights into the role that both individuals and institutions can play in making this resolution come to pass.

During the 1960s, we witnessed in America an increasing awareness of the alternatives confronting American business. Progress occurred on a number of fronts as a variety of key "firsts," took place. Unfortunately, however, the overall condition of negative imbalance between blacks and whites remained much the same. On occasion blacks—and their militant white supporters—vented their frustrations with "business as usual" by brief but destructive attacks on the existing social order. Which of the alternatives—social progress or societal strife—will predominate in the years ahead will depend ultimately on the attitudes and actions of *all* sectors of the black and white communities. It is our feeling, however, that the future relationship between black Americans and white business will provide much of the answer to the thorny questions facing American society as it confronts its dilemma.

NOTES

[1]Gunnar Myrdal, with the assistance of Richard Sterner and Arnold Rose, *An American Dilemma: The Negro Problem and Modern Democracy.* (New York: Harper & Row, Publishers, 1944), p. LXXVII.

[2]Myrdal, *An American Dilemma,* p. LXXV.

[3]For an excellent discussion at this point, see Robin Marris, "Businesses, Economics and Society," in Richard S. Rosenbloom and Robin Marris (eds.), *Social Innovation in the City: New Enterprises for Community Development* (Cambridge, Mass.: Harvard University Program on Technology and Society, 1969), pp. 19-49.

[4]Irwin Miller, "Business Has War to Win," *Harvard Business Review,* V. 47, N. 2 (March-April 1969), pp. 164, 168.

THE WHITE RACE AND ITS HEROES

Eldridge Cleaver

Right from the go, let me make one thing absolutely clear: I am not now, nor have I ever been, a white man. Nor, I hasten to add, am I now a Black Muslim— although I used to be. But I am an Ofay Watcher, a member of that unchartered, amorphous league which has members on all continents and the islands of the seas. Ofay Watchers Anonymous, we might be called, because we exist concealed in the shadows wherever colored people have known oppression by whites, by white enslavers, colonizers, imperialists, and neo-colonialists.

Did it irritate you, compatriot, for me to string those epithets out like that? Tolerate me. My intention was not necessarily to sprinkle salt over anyone's wounds. I did it primarily to relieve a certain pressure on my brain. Do you cop that? If not, then we're in trouble, because we Ofay Watchers have a pronounced tendency to slip into that mood. If it is bothersome to you, it is quite a task for me because not too long ago it was my way of life to preach, as ardently as I could, that the white race is a race of devils, created by their maker to do evil, and make evil appear as good; that the white race is the natural, unchangeable enemy of the black man, who is the original man, owner, maker, cream of the planet Earth; that the white race was soon to be destroyed by Allah, and that the black man would then inherit the earth, which has always, in fact, been his.

I have, so to speak, washed my hands in the blood of the martyr, Malcolm X, whose retreat from the precipice of madness created new room for others to turn about in, and I am now caught up in that tiny space, attempting a

maneuver of my own. Having renounced the teachings of Elijah Muhammad, I find that a rebirth does not follow automatically, of its own accord, that a void is left in one's vision, and this void seeks constantly to obliterate itself by pulling one back to one's former outlook. I have tried a tentative compromise by adopting a select vocabulary, so that now when I see the whites of *their* eyes, instead of saying "devil" or "beast" I say "imperialist" or "colonialist," and everyone seems to be happier.

In silence, we have spent our years watching the ofays, trying to understand them, on the principle that you have a better chance of coping with the known than with the unknown. Some of us have been, and some still are, interested in learning whether it is *ultimately* possible to live in the same territory with people who seem so disagreeable to live with; still others want to get as far away from ofays as possible. What we share in common is the desire to break the ofays' power over us.

At times of fundamental social change, such as the era in which we live, it is easy to be deceived by the onrush of events, beguiled by the craving for social stability into mistaking transitory phenomena for enduring reality. The strength and permanence of "white backlash" in America is just such an illusion. However much this rear-guard action might seem to grow in strength, the initiative, and the future, rest with those whites and blacks who have liberated themselves from the master/slave syndrome. And these are to be found mainly among the youth.

Over the past twelve years there has surfaced a political conflict between the generations that is deeper, even, than the struggle between the races. Its first dramatic manifestation was within the ranks of the Negro people, when college students in the South, fed up with Uncle Tom's hat-in-hand approach to revolution, threw off the yoke of the NAACP. When these students initiated the first sit-ins, their spirit spread like a raging fire across the nation, and the technique of non-violent direct action, constantly refined and ironed into a sharp cutting tool, swiftly matured. The older Negro "leaders," who are now all die-hard advocates of this tactic, scolded the students for sitting-in. The students rained down contempt upon their hoary heads. In the pre-sit-in days, these conservative leaders had always succeeded in putting down insurgent elements among the Negro people. (A measure of their power, prior to the students' rebellion, is shown by their success is isolating such great black men as the late W. E. B. DuBois and Paul Robeson, when these stalwarts, refusing to bite their tongues, lost favor with the U.S. government by their unstinting efforts to link up the Negro revolution with national liberation movements around the world.)

The "Negro leaders," and the whites who depended upon them to control their people, were outraged by the impudence of the students. Calling for a moratorium on student initiative, they were greeted instead by an encore of sit-ins, and retired to their ivory towers to contemplate the new phenomenon. Others, less prudent because held on a tighter leash by the whites, had their careers brought to an abrupt end because they thought they could lead a black/white backlash against the students, only to find themselves in a kind of Bay of Pigs. Negro college presidents, who expelled students from all-Negro colleges in an attempt to quash the demonstrations, ended up losing their jobs; the victorious students would no longer allow them to preside over the campuses. The spontaneous protests on southern campuses over the repressive measures of their college administrations were an earnest of the Free Speech upheaval which years later was to shake the UC campus at Berkeley. In countless ways, the rebellion of the black students served as catalyst for the brewing revolt of the whites.

What has suddenly happened is that the white race has lost its heroes. Worse, its heroes have been revealed as villains and its greatest heroes as the arch-villians. The new generations of whites, appalled by the sanguine and despicable record carved over the face of the globe by their race in the last five hundred years, are rejecting the panoply of white heroes, whose heroism consisted in erecting the inglorious edifice of colonialism and imperialism; heroes whose careers rested on a system of foreign and domestic exploitation, rooted in the myth of white supremacy and the manifest destiny of the white race. The emerging shape of a new world order, and the requisites for survival in such a world, are fostering in young whites a new outlook. They recoil in shame from the spectacle of cowboys and pioneers—their heroic forefathers whose exploits filled earlier generations with pride—galloping across a movie screen shooting down Indians like Coke bottles. Even Winston Churchill, who is looked upon by older whites as perhaps the greatest hero of the twentieth century—even he, because of the system of which he was a creature and which he served, is an arch-villain in the eyes of the young white rebels.

At the close of World War Two, national liberation movements in the colonized world picked up new momentum and audacity, seeking to cash in on the democratic promises made by the Allies during the war. The Atlantic Charter, signed by President Roosevelt and Prime Minister Churchill in 1941, affirming "the right of all people to choose the form of government under which they may live," established the principle, although it took years of postwar struggle to give this piece of rhetoric even the appearance of reality. And just as world revolution has prompted the oppressed to re-evaluate their self-image in terms of the changing conditions, to slough off the servile attitudes inculcated by long years of subordination, the same dynamics of change have prompted the white people of the world to re-evaluate their self-image as well, to disabuse themselves of the Master Race psychology developed over centuries of imperial hegemony.

It is among the white youth of the world that the greatest change is taking place. It is they who are experiencing the great psychic pain of waking into consciousness to find their inherited heroes turned by events into villains. Communication and understanding between the older and younger generations of whites has entered a crisis. The elders, who, in the tradition of privileged classes or races, genuinely do not understand the youth, trapped by old ways of thinking and blind to the future, have only just begun to be vexed—because the youth have only just begun to rebel. So thoroughgoing is the revolution in the psyches of white youth that the traditional tolerance which every older generation has found it necessary to display is quickly exhausted, leaving a gulf of fear, hostility, mutual misunderstanding, and contempt.

The rebellion of the oppressed peoples of the world, along with the Negro revolution in America, have opened the way to a new evaluation of history, a re-examination of the role played by the white race since the beginning of European expansion. The positive achievements are also there in the record, and future generations will applaud them. But there can be no applause now, not while the master still holds the whip in his hand! Not even the master's own children can find it possible to applaud him—he cannot even applaud himself! The negative rings too loudly. Slave-catchers, slaveowners, murderers, butchers, invaders, oppressors—the white heroes have acquired new names. The great white statesmen whom school children are taught to revere are revealed as the architects of systems of human exploitation and slavery. Religious leaders are exposed as condoners and justifiers of all these evil deeds. Schoolteachers and college professors are seen as a clique of brainwashers and whitewashers.

The white youth of today are coming to see, intuitively, that to escape the onus of the history their fathers made they must face and admit the moral truth concerning the works of their fathers. That such venerated figures as George Washington and Thomas Jefferson owned hundreds of black slaves, that all of the Presidents up to Lincoln presided over a slave state, and that every President since Lincoln connived politically and cynically with the issues affecting the human rights and general welfare of the broad masses of the American people—these facts weigh heavily upon the hearts of these young people.

The elders do not like to give these youngsters credit for being able to understand what is going on and what has gone on. When speaking of juvenile delinquency, or the rebellious attitude of today's youth, the elders employ a glib rhetoric. They speak of the "alienation of youth," the desire of the young to be independent, the problems of "the father image" and "the mother image" and their effect upon growing children who lack sound models upon which to pattern themselves. But they consider it bad form to connect the problems of the youth with the central event of our era—the national liberation movements abroad and the Negro revolution at home. The foundations of authority have been blasted to bits in America because the whole society has been indicted, tried, and convicted of injustice. To the youth, the elders are Ugly Americans; to the elders, the youth have gone mad.

The rebellion of the white youth has gone through four broadly discernible stages. First, there was an initial recoiling away, a rejection of the conformity which America expected, and had always received, sooner or later, from its youth. The disaffected youth were refusing to participate in the system, having discovered that America, far from helping the underdog, was up to its ears in the mud trying to hold the dog down. Because of the publicity and self-advertisements of the more vocal rebels, this period has come to be known as the *beatnik era,* although not all of the youth affected by these changes thought of themselves as beatniks. The howl of the beatniks and their scathing, outraged denunciation of the system—characterized by [poet Alan] Ginsberg as Moloch, a bloodthirsty Semitic deity to which the ancient tribes sacrificed their firstborn children—was a serious, irrevocable declaration of war. It is revealing that the elders looked upon the beatniks as mere obscene misfits who were too lazy to take baths and too stingy to buy a haircut. The elders had eyes but couldn't see, ears but couldn't hear—not even when the message came through as clearly as in this remarkable passage from Jack Kerouac's *On the Road*:

At Lilac evening I walked with every muscle aching among the lights of 27th and Welton in the Denver colored section, wishing I were a Negro, feeling that the best the white world had offered was not enough ecstasy for me, not enough life, joy, kicks, darkness, music, not enough night. I wished I were a Denver Mexican, or even a poor overworked Jap, anything but what I so drearily was, a "white man" disillusioned. All my life I'd had white ambitions. . . . I passed the dark porches of Mexican and Negro homes; soft voices were there, occasionally the dusky knee of some mysterious sensuous gal; the dark faces of the men behind rose arbors. Little children sat like sages in ancient rocking chairs.

The second stage arrived when these young people, having decided emphatically that the world, and particularly the U.S.A., was unacceptable to them in its present form, began an active search for roles they could play in changing the society. If many of these young people were content to lay up in their cool beat pads, smoking pot and listening to jazz in a perpetual orgy of esoteric bliss, there were others, less crushed by the system, who recognized the need for positive action. Moloch could not ask for anything more than to have its disaffected victims withdraw into safe, passive, apolitical little nonparticipatory islands, in an economy less and less able to provide jobs for the growing pool of unemployed. If all the unemployed had followed the lead of the beatniks, Moloch would gladly have legalized the use of euphoric drugs and marijuana, passed out free jazz albums and sleeping bags, to all those willing to sign affidavits promising to remain "beat." The non-beat disenchanted white youth were attracted magnetically to the Negro revolution, which had begun to take on a mass, insurrectionary tone. But they had difficulty understanding their relationship to the Negro, and what role "whites" could play in a "Negro revolution." For the time being they watched the Negro activists from afar.

The third stage, which is rapidly drawing to a close, emerged when white youth started joining Negro demonstrations in large numbers. The presence of whites among the demonstrators emboldened the Negro leaders and allowed them to use tactics they never would have been able to employ with all-black troops. The racist conscience of America is such that murder does not register as murder, really, unless the victim is white. And it was only when the newspapers and magazines started carrying pictures and stories of white demonstrators being beaten and maimed by mobs and police that the public began to protest. Negroes have become so used to this double standard that they, too, react differently to the death of a white. When white freedom riders were brutalized along with blacks, a sigh of relief went up from the black masses, because the blacks knew that white blood is the coin of freedom in a land where for four hundred years black blood has been shed unremarked and with impunity. America has never truly been outraged by the murder of a black man, woman, or child. White politicians may, if Negroes are aroused by a particular murder, say with their lips what they know with their minds they should feel with their hearts—but don't.

It is a measure of what the Negro feels that when the two white and one black civil rights workers were murdered in Mississippi in 1964, the event was welcomed by Negroes on a level of understanding beyond and deeper than the grief they felt for the victims and their families. This welcoming of violence and death to whites can almost be heard—indeed it can be heard—in the inevitable words, oft repeated by Negroes, that those whites, and blacks, do not die in vain. So it was with Mrs. Viola Liuzzo. And much of the anger which Negroes felt toward Martin Luther King during the Battle of Selma stemmed from the fact he denied history a great moment, never to be recaptured, when he turned tail on the Edmund Pettus Bridge and refused to all those whites behind him what they had traveled thousands of miles to receive. If the police had turned them back by force, all those nuns, priests, rabbis, preachers and distinguished ladies and gentlemen old and young—as they had done the Negroes a week earlier—the violence and brutality of the system would have been ruthlessly exposed. Or if, seeing King determined to lead them on to Montgomery, the troopers had stepped aside to avoid precisely the confrontation that Washington would not have tolerated, it would have signaled the capitulation of the militant white South. As it turned out, the March on Montgomery was a show of somewhat dim luster, stage-managed by the Establishment. But by this time the young whites were already active participants in the Negro revolution. In fact they had begun to transform it into something broader, with the potential of encompassing the whole of America in a radical reordering of society.

The fourth stage, now in its infancy, sees these white youth taking the initiative, using techniques learned in the Negro struggle to attack problems in the general society. The classic example of this new energy in action was the student battle on the UC campus at Berkeley,

California—the Free Speech Movement. Leading the revolt were veterans of the civil rights movement, some of whom spent time on the firing line in the wilderness of Mississippi/Alabama. Flowing from the same momentum were student demonstrations against U.S. interference in the internal affairs of Vietnam, Cuba, the Dominican Republic, and the Congo and U.S. aid to apartheid in South Africa. The students even aroused the intellectual community to actions and positions unthinkable a few years ago: witness the teach-ins. But their revolt is deeper than single-issue protest. The characteristics of the white rebels which most alarm their elders—the long hair, the new dances, their love for Negro music, their use of marijuana, their mystical attitude toward sex—are all tools of their rebellion. They have turned these tools against the totalitarian fabric of American society—and they mean to change it.

From the beginning, America has been a schizophrenic nation. Its two conflicting images of itself were never reconciled, because never before has the survival of its most cherished myths made a reconciliation mandatory. Once before, during the bitter struggle between North and South climaxed by the Civil War, the two images of America came into conflict, although whites North and South scarcely understood it. The image of America held by its most alienated citizens was advanced neither by the North nor by the South; it was perhaps best expressed by Frederick Douglass, who was born into slavery in 1817, escaped to the North, and became the greatest leader-spokesman for the blacks of his era. In words that can still, years later, arouse an audience of black Americans, Frederick Douglass delivered, in 1852, a scorching indictment in his Fourth of July oration in Rochester:

What to the American slave is your Fourth of July? I answer: a day that reveals to him, more than all other days in the year, the gross injustice and cruelty to which he is the constant victim. To him your celebration is a sham; your boasted liberty, an unholy license; your national greatness, swelling vanity; your sounds of rejoicing are empty and heartless; your denunciation of tyrants, brass-fronted impudence; your shouts of liberty and equality, hollow mockery; your prayers and hymns, your sermons and thanksgivings, with all your religious parade and solemnity, are, to him, more bombast, fraud, deception, impiety and hypocrisy—a thin veil to cover up crimes which would disgrace a nation of savages. . . .

You boast of your love of liberty, your superior civilization, and your pure Christianity, while the whole political power of the nation (as embodied in the two great political parties) is solemnly pledged to support and perpetuate the enslavement of three millions of your countrymen. You hurl your anathemas at the crown-headed tyrants of Russia and Austria and pride yourselves on your democratic institutions, while you yourselves consent to be the mere *tolls* and *bodyguards* of the tyrants of Virginia and Carolina.

You invite to your shores fugitives of oppression from abroad, honor them with banquets, greet them with ovations, cheer them, toast them, salute them, protect them, and pour out your money to them like water; but the fugitive from your own land you advertise, hunt, arrest, shoot, and kill. You glory in your refinement and your universal education; yet you maintain a system as barbarous and dreadful as ever stained the character of a nation—a system begun in avarice, supported in pride, and perpetuated in cruelty.

You shed tears over fallen Hungary, and make the sad story of her wrongs the theme of your poets, statesmen and orators, till your gallant sons are ready to fly to arms to vindicate her cause against the oppressor; but, in regard to the ten thousand wrongs of the American slave, you would enforce the strictest silence, and would hail him as an enemy of the nation who dares to make these wrongs the subject of public discourse!

This most alienated view of America was preached by the Abolitionists, and by Harriet Beecher Stowe in her *Uncle Tom's Cabin*. But such a view of America was too distasteful to receive wide attention, and serious debate about America's image and her reality was engaged in only on the fringes of society. Even when confronted with overwhelming evidence to the contrary, most white Americans have found it possible, after steadying their rattled nerves, to settle comfortably back into their vaunted belief that America is dedicated to the proposition that all men are created equal and endowed by their Creator with certain inalienable rights—life, liberty and the pursuit of happiness. With the Constitution for a rudder and the Declaration of Independence as its guiding star, the ship of state is sailing always toward a brighter vision of freedom and justice for all.

Because there is no common ground between these two contradictory images of America, they had to be kept apart. But the moment the blacks were let into the white world—let out of the voiceless and faceless cages of their ghettos, singing, walking, talking, dancing, writing, and orating *their* image of America and of Americans—the white world was suddenly challenged to match its practice to its preachments. And this is why those whites who abandon the *white* image of America and adopt the *black* are greeted with such unmitigated hostility by their elders.

For all these years whites have been taught to believe in the myth they preached, while Negroes have had to face the bitter reality of what America practiced. But without the lies and distortions, white Americans would not have been able to do the things they have done. When whites are forced to look honestly upon the objective proof of their deeds, the cement of mendacity holding white society together swiftly disintegrates. On the other hand, the core of the black world's vision remains intact, and in fact begins to expand and spread into the psychological territory vacated by the nonviable white lies, i.e., into the minds of young whites. It is remarkable how the system worked for so many years, how the majority of whites remained effectively unaware of any contradiction between their view of the world and that world itself. The mechanism by which this was rendered possible requires examination at this point.

Let us recall that the white man, in order to justify slavery and, later on, to justify segregation, elaborated a complex, all-pervasive myth which at one time classified the black man as a subhuman beast of burden. The myth was progressively modified, gradually elevating the blacks on the scale of evolution, following their slowly changing status, until the plateau of separate-but-equal was reached at the close of the nineteenth century. During slavery, the black was seen as a mindless Supermasculine Menial. Forced to do the backbreaking work, he was conceived in terms of his ability to do such work—"field niggers," etc. The white man administered the plantation, doing all the thinking, exercising omnipotent power over the slaves. He had little difficulty dissociating himself from the black slaves, and he could not

conceive of their positions being reversed or even reversible.

Blacks and whites being conceived as mutually exclusive types, those attributes imputed to the blacks could not also be imputed to the whites—at least not in equal degree—without blurring the line separating the races. These images were based upon the social function of the two races, the work they performed. The ideal white man was one who knew how to use his head, who knew how to manage and control things and get things done. Those whites who were not in a position to perform these functions nevertheless aspired to them. The ideal black man was one who did exactly as he was told, and did it efficiently and cheerfully. "Slaves," said Frederick Douglass, "are generally expected to sing as well as to work." As the black man's position and function became more varied, the images of white and black, having become stereotypes, lagged behind.

The separate-but-equal doctrine was promulgated by the Supreme Court in 1896. It had the same purpose domestically as the Open Door Policy toward China in the international arena: to stabilize a situation and subordinate a nonwhite population so that racist exploiters could manipulate those people according to their own selfish interests. These doctrines were foisted off as *the epitome of enlightened justice, the highest expression of morality*. Sanctified by religion, justified by philosophy and legalized by the Supreme Court, separate-but-equal was enforced by day by agencies of the law, and by the KKK & Co. under cover of night. Booker T. Washington, the Martin Luther King of his day, accepted separate-but-equal in the name of all Negroes. W. E. B. DuBois denounced it.

Separate-but-equal marked the last stage of the white man's flight into cultural neurosis, and the beginning of the black man's frantic striving to assert his humanity and equalize his position with the white. Blacks ventured into all fields of endeavor to which they could gain entrance. Their goal was to present in all fields a performance that would equal or surpass that of the whites. It was long axiomatic among blacks that a black had to be twice as competent as a white in any field in order to win grudging recognition from the whites. This produced a pathological motivation in the blacks to equal or surpass the whites, and a pathological motivation in the whites to maintain a distance from the blacks. This is the rack on which black and white Americans receive their delicious torture! At first there was the color bar, flatly denying the blacks entrance to certain spheres of activity. When this no longer worked, and blacks invaded sector after sector of American life and economy, the whites evolved other methods of keeping their distance. The illusion of the Negro's inferior nature had to be maintained. One device evolved by the whites was to tab whatever the blacks did with the prefix "Negro," We had *Negro* literature, *Negro* athletes, *Negro* music, *Negro* doctors, *Negro* politicans, *Negro* workers. The malignant ingeniousness of this device is that although it accurately describes an objective biological fact—or, at least, a sociological fact in America—it concealed the paramount psychological fact: that to the white mind, prefixing anything with "Negro" automatically consigned it to an inferior category. A well-known example of the white necessity to deny due credit to blacks is in the realm of music. White musicians were famous for going to Harlem and other Negro cultural centers literally to steal the black man's music, carrying it back across the color line into the Great White World and passing off the watered-down loot as their own original creations. Blacks, meanwhile, were ridiculed as *Negro* musicians playing inferior coon music.

The Negro revolution at home and national liberation movements abroad have unceremoniously shattered the world of fantasy in which the whites have been living. It is painful that many do not yet see that their fantasy world has been rendered uninhabitable in the last half of the twentieth century. But it is away from this world that the white youth of today are turning. The "paper tiger" hero, James Bond, offering the whites a triumphant image of themselves, is saying what many whites want desperately to hear reaffirmed: *I am still the White Man, lord of the land, licensed to kill, and the world is still an empire at my feet.* James Bond feeds on that secret little anxiety, the psychological white backlash, felt in some degree by most whites alive. It is exasperating to see little brown men and little yellow men from the mysterious Orient, and the opaque black men of Africa (to say nothing of these impudent American Negroes!) who come to the UN and talk smart to

us, who are scurrying all over *our* globe in their strange modes of dress—much as if they were new, unpleasant arrivals from another planet. Many whites believe in their ulcers that it is only a matter of time before the Marines get the signal to round up these truants and put them back securely in their cages. But it is away from this fantasy world that the white youth of today are turning.

In the world revolution now under way, the initiative rests with people of color. That growing numbers of white youth are repudiating their heritage of blood and taking people of color as their heroes and models is a tribute not only to their insight but to the resilience of the human spirit. For today the heroes of the initiative are people not usually thought of as white: Fidel Castro, Che Guevara, Kwame Nkrumah, Mao Tse-tung, Gamal Abdel Nasser, Robert F. Williams, Malcolm X, Ben Bella, John Lewis, Martin Luther King, Jr., Robert Parris Moses, Ho Chi Minh, Stokeley Carmichael, W. E. B. DuBois, James Forman, Chou En-lai.

The white youth of today have begun to react to the fact that the "American Way of Life" is a fossil of history. What do they care if their old baldheaded and crew-cut elders don't dig their caveman mops? They couldn't care less about the old, stiffassed honkies who don't like their new dances: Frug, Monkey, Jerk, Swim, Watusi. All they know is that it feels good to swing to way-out body-rhythms instead of dragassing across the dance floor like zombies to the dead beat of mind-smothered Mickey Mouse music. Is it any wonder that the youth have lost all respect for their elders, for law and order, when for as long as they can remember all they've witnessed is a monumental bickering over the Negro's place in American society and the right of people around the world to be left alone by outside powers? They have witnessed the law, both domestic and international, being spat upon by those who do not like its terms. Is it any wonder, then, that they feel justified, by sitting-in and freedom riding, in breaking laws made by lawless men? Old funny-styled, zipper-mouthed political night riders know nothing but to haul out an investigating committee *to look into the disturbance* to find the cause of the unrest among the youth. Look into a mirror! The cause is you, Mr. and Mrs. Yesterday, you with your forked tongues.

A young white today cannot help but recoil

from the base deeds of his people. On every side, on every continent, he sees racial arrogance, savage brutality toward the conquered and subjugated people, genocide; he sees the human cargo of the slave trade; he sees the systematic extermination of American Indians; he sees the civilized nations of Europe fighting in imperial depravity over the lands of other people—and over possession of the very people themselves. There seems to be no end to the ghastly deeds of which his people are guilty. GUILTY. The slaughter of the Jews by the Germans, the dropping of atomic bombs on the Japanese people—these deeds weigh heavily upon the prostrate souls and tumultuous consciences of the white youth. The white heroes, their hands dripping with blood, are dead.

The young whites know that the colored people of the world, Afro-Americans included, do not seek revenge for their suffering. They seek the same things the white rebel wants: an end to war and exploitation. Black and white, the young rebels are free people, free in a way that Americans have never been before in the history of their country. And they are outraged.

There is in America today a generation of white youth that is truly worthy of a black man's respect, and this is a rare event in the foul annals of American history. From the beginning of the contact between blacks and whites, there has been very little reason for a black man to respect a white, with such exceptions as John Brown and others lesser known. But respect commands itself and it can neither be given nor withheld when it is due. If a man like Malcolm X could change and repudiate racism, if I myself and other former Muslims can change, if young whites can change, then there is hope for America. It was certainly strange to find myself, while steeped in the doctrine that all whites were devils by nature, commanded by the heart to applaud and acknowledge respect for these young whites—despite the fact that they are descendants of the masters and I the descendant of slave. The sins of the fathers are visited upon the heads of the children—but only if the children continue in the evil deeds of the fathers.

AMERICA AGAIN AT THE CROSSROADS

Gunnar Myrdal

THE NEGRO PROBLEM AND THE WAR

The three great wars of this country have been fought for the ideals of liberty and equality to which the nation was pledged. As a consequence of all of them, the American Negro made great strides toward freedom and opportunity. The Revolutionary War started a development which ultimately ended slavery in all Northern states, made new import of slaves illegal and nearly accomplished abolition even in the South—though there the tide soon turned in a reaction toward fortification of the plantation system and of Negro slavery. The Civil War gave the Negro Emancipation and Reconstruction in the South—though it was soon followed by Restoration of white supremacy. The First World War provided the Negro his first real opportunity as a worker in Northern industry, started the Great Migration out of the South, and began the "New Negro" movement— though the end of the War saw numerous race riots and the beginning of a serious decline in employment opportunities. After the advances on all three occasions there were reactions, but not as much ground was lost as had been won. Even taking the subsequent reactions into account, each of the three great wars in the history of America helped the Negro take a permanent step forward.

Now America is again in a life-and-death struggle for liberty and equality, and the American Negro is again watching for signs of what war and victory will mean in terms of opportu-

"America Again at the Crossroads" in *An American Dilemma,* Twentieth Anniversary Edition, by Gunnar Myrdal, et al. Copyright, 1944, 1962 by Harper & Row, Publishers, Inc. Reprinted by permission of the publishers. Some notes omitted.

nity and rights for him in his native land. To the white American, too, the Negro problem has taken on a significance greater than it has ever had since the Civil War. This War is crucial for the future of the Negro, and the Negro problem is crucial in the War. There is bound to be a redefinition of the Negro's status in America as a result of this War.

The exact nature of this structural change in American society cannot yet be foreseen. History is not the result of a predetermined Fate. Nothing is irredeemable until it is past. The outcome will depend upon decisions and actions yet to be taken by whites and Negroes. What we can know definitely, however, are the trends as they developed up to the War and the changes so far during the War. On the basis of this knowledge, we can discern the gamut of possibilities for the future. If, in addition, we have some insight into the temper and inclination of the people who are both the actors and the spectators of the drama being staged, we can estimate which are the most probable developments.

. . .

THE DECAY OF THE CASTE THEORY

The problem of what would have occurred if there had been no war is now purely academic. The Second World War is bound to change all trends. But before we analyze the implications of the War for the Negro problem, we need to take a still broader perspective and ask: what has happened to white opinions on the Negro problem in the span of three generations since Emancipation?

In the South three generations ago white people had for their defense a consistent and respectable theory, endorsed by the church and by all sciences, printed in learned books and periodicals, and expounded by the South's great statesmen in the Capitol at Washington. The Negro's subordinate status was a principle integrated into a whole philosophy of society and of human life. The Negro was a completely different species of mankind: undeveloped, "childlike," amoral, and much less endowed with intellectual capacities than the white man; he was meant by the Creator to be a servant forever; if kept in his "place" he was useful or at least tolerable, and there he was also happy; "social equality" was unthinkable as it implied intermarriage which would destroy the white race and Anglo-Saxon civilization. Much of this theory—which acquired an elaborate structure to satisfy the specific needs to justify discrimination in various spheres of life—remained through Reconstruction, and it was again hailed in the Restoration of white supremacy. Indeed, much of it remained until a couple of decades ago. But now it is almost destroyed for upper class and educated people. Its maintenance among lower class and uneducated people meets increasing difficulties. *The gradual destruction of the popular theory behind race prejudice is the most important of all social trends in the field of interracial relations.*

It is significant that today even the white man who defends discrimination frequently describes his motives as "prejudice" and says that it is "irrational." The popular beliefs rationalizing caste in America are no longer intellectually respectable. They can no longer, therefore, be found in current books, newspapers or public speeches. They live a surreptitious life in thoughts and private remarks. There we have had to hunt them when studying the matter in this inquiry. When they were thus drawn out into the open they looked shabby and ashamed of themselves. Everybody who has acquired a higher education knows that they are wrong. Most white people with a little education also have a hunch that they are wrong. There is today a queer feeling of *credo quia absurdum* hovering over the whole complex of popular beliefs sustaining racial discrimination. This makes the prejudiced white man nearly as pathetic as his Negro victim.

The white man is thus in the process of losing confidence in the theory which gave reason and meaning to his way of life. And since he has not changed his life much, he is in a dilemma. This change is probably irreversible and cumulative. It is backed by the American Creed. The trend of psychology, education, anthropology, and social science is toward environmentalism in the explanation of group differences, which means that the racial beliefs which defended caste are being torn away. It also means, by implication, that the white majority group in power is accused of being the cause of the Negro's deficiencies and unhappiness. Authority and respectability are no longer supporting the popular beliefs. The beliefs are no longer nourished from above. Instead they are increasingly fought. There is a considerable time-lag between what is thought in the higher and in the lower social classes. But as time passes the lower social strata also will change their beliefs. These ideas are spread by the advance of education.

All of this is important. People want to be rational, and they want to feel that they are good and righteous. They want to have the society they live in, and their behavior in this society, explained and justified to their conscience. And now their theory is being torn to pieces; its expression is becoming recognized as a mark of ignorance.

On the other side of the caste gulf the development leads to increased bitterness. To the Negro the white man's trouble with his conscience cannot but seem to be insincerity or something worse. The Negro protest is rising, spurred by the improvement in education. The Negro group is being permeated by the democratic and equalitarian values of the American culture. Since at the same time there has been increasing separation between the two groups, Negroes are beginning to form a self-conscious "nation within the nation," defining ever more clearly their fundamental grievances against white America.

America can never more regard its Negroes as a patient, submissive minority. Negroes will continually become less well "accommodated." They will organize for defense and offense. They will be more and more vociferous. They will watch their opportunities ever more keenly. They will have a powerful tool in the caste struggle against white America: the glorious American ideals of democracy, liberty, and equality to which America is pledged not only by its political Constitution but also by the sincere devotion of its citizens. The Negroes are a minority, and they are poor and suppressed, but they have the advantage that they can fight wholeheartedly. The whites have all the power, but they are split in their moral personality. Their better selves are with the insurgents. The Negroes do not need any other allies.

This moral process had proceeded far when the Second World War broke out.

. . .

INTERNATIONAL ASPECTS

What has actually happened within the last few years is not only that the Negro problem has become national in scope after having been mainly a Southern worry. It has also acquired tremendous international implications, and this is another and decisive reason why the white North is prevented from compromising with the white South regarding the Negro. The situation is actually such that any and all concessions to Negro rights in this phase of the history of the world will repay the nation many times, while any and all injustices inflicted upon him will be extremely costly. This is not yet seen clearly by most Americans, but it will become increasingly apparent as the War goes on.

We mentioned in passing that the American Negro cannot help observing the color angle to this War. He is obviously getting vicarious satisfaction out of this perspective, and he is also testing some vague feelings of solidarity and allegiance to the cause of other colored peoples involved in the world conflagration. But this is a minor part of the international implications. The American Negro is thoroughly American in his culture and whole outlook on the world. He is also loyal to America, and there is no danger that he will betray it. This is at least certain in the short-range view, which covers this War and the coming peace. How the Negro would react if he were left dissatisfied and if later a new war were to be fought more definitely along color lines is more difficult to predict.

The main international implication is, instead, that America, for its international prestige, power, and future security, needs to demonstrate to the world that American Negroes can be satisfactorily integrated into its democracy. In a sense, this War marks the end of American isolation. America has had security behind the two protecting oceans. When now this isolation has been definitely broken, the historians will begin to see how it has always greatly determined the development of America. Statesmen will have to take cognizance of the changed geopolitical situation of the nation and carry out important adaptations of the American way of life to new necessities. A main adaptation is bound to be a redefinition of the Negro's status in American democracy.

It is commonly observed that the mistrust of, or open hostility against, the white man by colored people everywhere in the world has greatly increased the difficulties for the United Nations to win this war. Many old sins and stupidities are today staring back upon the white man, and he continues to commit them, though he now knows better. The treatment of the Negro in America has not made good propaganda for America abroad and particularly not among colored nations. That good American who has acquired such a rare understanding for the Asiatic people's mind, Pearl S. Buck, comments:

Japan . . . is declaring in the Philippines, in China, in India, Malaya, and even Russia that there is no basis for hope that colored peoples can expect any justice from the people who rule in the United States, namely, the white people. For specific proof the Japanese point to our treatment of our own colored people, citizens of generations in the United States. Every lynching, every race riot, gives joy to Japan. The discriminations of the American army and navy and the air forces against colored soldiers and sailors, the exclusion of colored labor in our defense industries and trade unions, all our social discriminations, are of the greatest aid today to our enemy in Asia, Japan. "Look at America," Japan is saying to millions of listening ears. "Will white Americans give you equality?"

And she assures her compatriots:

We cannot . . . win this war without convincing our colored allies—who are most of our allies—that we are not fighting for ourselves as continuing superior over colored peoples. The deep patience of colored peoples is at an end. Everywhere among them there is the same resolve for freedom and equality that white

Americans and British have, but it is a grimmer resolve, for it includes the determination to be rid of white rule and exploitation and white race prejudice, and nothing will weaken this will.[3]

This is perhaps an exaggeration. Perhaps the War can this time be won even without the colored people's confidence. But the absence of their full cooperation, and still more their obstructive activities, will be tremendously costly in time, men and materials. Caste is becoming an expensive luxury of white men.

It seems more definitely certain that it will be impossible to make and preserve a good peace without having built up the fullest trust and goodwill among the colored peoples. They will be strong after the War, and they are bound to become even stronger as time passes. For one thing, this is certain in so far as numbers are concerned. During the short span of the last three centuries, which include almost the entire epoch of white power expansion, the peoples of European stock increased sevenfold, while the others increased only threefold. The whites grew from a bare 100 millions, or a fifth of the globe's total, to over 700 millions, or a third of all mankind. The increase for the whites was fastest during the last century when they gradually became able to control deaths but had not as yet brought births under control. The whites are, however, now in the second phase of this dynamic sequence: the white birth rate is falling so fast that it is catching up with the relatively stable death rate. The population expansion of the whites is now slowing down, absolutely and relatively. Many of the Western nations, including America and all those other peoples on the highest level of industrial civilization, will probably start to shrink in population numbers within a few decades. The colored nations, on the other hand, are just entering the first stage where expansion is likely to be pushed by an increasingly improved control over death, and it is unlikely that the increase in birthe control will keep pace with the improvement of the control over death. The whites will, therefore, from now on become a progressively smaller portion of the total world population. If we except the Russian peoples, who are still rapidly increasing, the rapid change in proportion stands out still more dramatically.

Another broad trend is almost as certain, namely, that the "backward" countries, where most colored people live, are going to become somewhat industrialized. The examples of Japan and, more recently, of Russia and China give support to the view that in the future we shall see many backward countries industrialized at a tremendously more rapid rate than were the pioneer Western countries, who had to find out everything for themselves. The same examples illustrate also how such backward nations can advantageously use the newly created industrial apparatus for producing war materials, and they illustrate, too, how they can fight with them.

Particularly as Russia cannot be reckoned on to adhere to white supremacy, it is evident from these facts—though nobody in our countries seems to take it seriously—that within a short period the shrinking minority of white people in our Western lands will either have to succumb or to find ways of living on peaceful terms with colored people. If white people, for their own preservation, attempt to reach a state in which they will be tolerated by their colored neighbors, equality will be the most they will be strong enough to demand.

History is never irredeemable, and there is still time to come to good terms with colored peoples. Their race pride and race prejudice is still mostly a defensive mental device, a secondary reaction built up to meet the humiliations of white supremacy. This is apparent in the case of the American Negro. It probably holds true even for other colored people who have not yet had a taste of power. A Chinese propaganda leaflet assures the Americans:

Chinese nationalism or race-consciousness is essentially defensive in character. It has developed out of continuous fight for freedom, and has never been offensive.[3]

It should be apparent that the time to come to an understanding on the basis of equality is rapidly running out. When colored nations have once acquired power but still sense the scorn of white superiority and racial discrimination, they are likely to become indoctrinated by a race prejudice much more akin to that of the whites— a race prejudice which can be satisfied only by the whites' humiliation and subjugation.

MAKING THE PEACE

Americans in general are concerned with the task of making a constructive peace after the War. It is commonly understood that this task is fraught with immense and unprecedented difficulties and, particularly, that the flagrant mismanagement of international affairs by the great democracies in the period between the two World Wars, the devastation caused by the Second World War, the breaking up of the state structures of Europe, and the approaching liquidation of colonial imperialism in the Far East have created a psychological state in mankind which, aside from all physical and economic deficiencies, raises almost insurmountable obstacles for the peacemakers. Americans generally recognize also that the protection of the two oceans is gone forever, that American isolationism will never more be possible, that America is in world politics for better or for worse, and that this time it has to stick to the making and upholding of the peace which is yet to be written.

Americans also recognize that America has to take world leadership. The coming difficult decades will be America's turn in the endless sequence of main actors on the world stage. America then will have the major responsibility for the manner in which humanity approaches the long era during which the white peoples will have to adjust to shrinkage while the colored are bound to expand in numbers, in level of industrial civilization and in political power. For perhaps several decades, the whites will still hold the lead, and America will be the most powerful white nation.

America goes to this task with the best of intentions. Declarations of inalienable human rights for people all over the world are not emanating from America. Wilson's fourteen points were a rehearsal; Roosevelt's four freedoms are more general and more focused on the rights of the individual. The national leaders proclaim that the coming peace will open an age of human liberty and equality everywhere. This was so in the First World War, too. This time something must be done to give reality to the glittering generalities, because otherwise the world will become entirely demoralized. It will probably be impossible to excite people with empty promises a third time. It is commonly agreed, and taken as proved by the coming of this War, that peace cannot be preserved if the development of a democratic life in every nation is not internationally guaranteed and the possibility of oppression is not checked. It is anticipated that international agencies will be created to sanction such a development.

In view of the clarity and unanimity in America on these fundamental points, few white Americans fully realize all the obvious implications. I have, for instance, met few white Americans who have ever thought of the fact that, if America had joined the League of Nations, American Negroes could, and certainly would, have taken their cases before international tribunal back in the 'twenties. Some versatile Negro protest leaders are, however, familiar with the thought. After this War there is bound to be an international apparatus for appeal by oppressed minority groups. In America, Negro organizations like the N.A.A.C.P. are excellently equipped for such conspicuous litigation. It is, indeed, possible that such implications of the coming democratic peace, when they become better seen and publicly discussed, will act as deterrents and as a motive for isolationism in some American circles. But there is no way back. America is irredeemably in world politics.

Behind her two protecting oceans America has until now lived an exuberant and carefree life without having to bother much about its international reputation. Probably no other modern people has cared less about what impression it makes on other nations. The ordinary American might have been interested to know, but has not bothered much about, the fact that lynchings and race riots are headlines in Bombay; that Huey Long and Father Coughlin, the wave of organized crime during and after Prohibition, the fiscal bankruptcy of Chicago some years ago, the corrupt political machines in Philadelphia, the Dayton trial of Darwinism, provided stories for the Sunday papers in Oslo; that many men and women in democratic countries around the the entire world have had their first and decisive impression of American public life from the defense of Sacco and Vanzetti and the Scottsboro boys. Friends of America abroad have tried to make the picture of American life more balanced and more accurate by fixing public attention on the numerous good sides, on American accomplishments, on all the good intentions and on the favorable trends. But they have been only partly successful, and America itself has—until this War—never cared to advertise America abroad.

This—like America's openness to criticism, which is the positive side of this unconcernedness—is a sign of great strength, but it was the strength of a departed isolation. There was also ignorance behind the attitude. Aware of all the good things in his country and rightly convinced that, on the whole, they greatly outweigh all the imperfections, the ordinary American takes it for granted that America is liked and trusted abroad.

The loss of American isolation makes all this serious. America has now joined the world and is tremendously dependent upon the support and good-will of other countries. Its rise to leadership brings this to a climax. None is watched so suspiciously as the one who is rising. None has so little license, none needs all his virtue so much as the leader. And America, for its own security, cannot retreat from leadership.

There is, of course, another possible solution besides good-will, and that is power. In some quarters in America the observer finds exaggerated notions about the power which America's financial strength after the War will allow her. Americans have not commonly taken to heart what was conclusively proved by experience in the period between the two World Wars, namely, that, after the loans are given, the power belongs to the debtor and not to the creditor.

Military power, however, can be substituted for good-will. But America does not have the will or stamina for real imperialism. The farmer, the laborer, the merchant, the intellectual, in one word, the common man who ultimately makes political decisions is against suppression abroad. In the international field the Southerner is not unlike his Northern compatriot. All American adventures in imperialism give abundant proofs of halfheartedness and show again the power over the Americans of the American Creed. If America does not go fascist, American militarism will not be an adequate substitute for good-will.

The treatment of the Negro is America's greatest and most conspicuous scandal. It is tremendously publicized, and democratic America will continue to publicize it itself. For the colored peoples all over the world, whose rising influence is axiomatic, this scandal is salt in their wounds. In all white nations which, because of the accident of ethnic homogeneity or for other causes, have not been inculcated with race prejudice, the color of the victim does not provide any excuse for white solidarity. That this is so in Russia is well known and advertised. It holds true also in many other white nations.

AMERICA'S OPPORTUNITY

But these consequences of the present course of America's and the world's history should not be recorded only in terms of compelling forces. The bright side is that the conquering of color caste in America is America's own innermost desire. This nation early laid down as the moral basis for its existence the principles of equality and liberty. However much Americans have dodged this conviction, they have refused to adjust their laws to their own license. Today more than ever, they refuse to discuss systematizing their caste order to mutual advantage, apparently because they most seriously mean that caste is wrong and should not be given recognition. They stand warmheartedly against oppression in all the world. When they are reluctantly forced into war, they are compelled to justify their participation to their own conscience by insisting that they are fighting against aggression and for liberty and equality.

America feels itself to be humanity in miniature. When in this crucial time the international leadership passes to America, the great reason for hope is that this country has a national experience of uniting racial and cultural diversities and a national theory, if not a consistent practice, of freedom and equality for all. What America is constantly reaching for is democracy at home and abroad. The main trend in its history is the gradual realization of the American Creed.

In this sense the Negro problem is not only America's greatest failure but also America's incomparably great opportunity for the future. If America should follow its own deepest convictions, its well-being at home would be increased directly. At the same time America's prestige and power abroad would rise immensely. The century-old dream of American patriots, that America should give to the entire world its own freedoms and its own faith, would come true. America can demostrate that justice, equality and cooperation are possible between white and colored people.

In the present phase of history this is what the world needs to believe. Mankind is sick of fear and disbelief, of pessimism and cynicism. It needs the youthful moralistic optimism of America. But empty declarations only deepen cynicism. Deeds are called for. If America in actual practice could show the world a progressive trend by which the Negro became finally integrated into modern democracy, all mankind would be given faith again—it would have reason to believe that peace, progress and order are feasible. And America would have a spiritual power many times stronger than all her financial and military resources—the power of the trust and support of all good people on earth. *America is free to choose whether the Negro shall remain her liability or become her opportunity.*

The development of the American Negro problem during the years to come is, therefore, fateful not only for America itself but for all mankind. If America wants to make the second choice, she cannot wait and see. She has to do something big and do it soon. For two generations after the national compromise of the 1870's between the North and the South on the Negro problem, the caste status of the Negro was allowed to remain almost unchanged. It was believed by most well-meaning people that self-healing would work, that the Negro problem would come to solve itself by the lapse of time. George Washington Cable wrote in the 'eighties:

There is a vague hope, much commoner in the North than in the South, that somehow, if everybody will sit still, *"time"* will bring these changes.[4]

Two decades later, Ray Stannard Baker reported from the South:

All such relationships will work themselves out gradually, naturally, quietly, in the long course of the years: and the less thay are talked about the better.[5]

Most of the literature on the Negro problem continues to this day to be written upon this same static assumption.

We have given the reasons why we believe that the *interregnum,* during which the forces balanced each other fairly well, is now at an end. The equilibrium, contrary to common belief, was unstable and temporary. As American Negroes became educated and culturally assimilated, but still found themselves excluded, they grew bitter. Meanwhile the whites were in the process of losing their caste theory. The international upheavals connected with the two World Wars and the world depression brought these developments to a crisis. American isolation was lost. Technical developments brought all nations to be close neighbors even though they were not trained to live together.

We are now in a deeply unbalanced world situation. Many human relations will be readjusted in the present world revolution, and among them race relations are bound to change considerably. As always in a revolutionary situation when society's moorings are temporarily loosened, there is, on the one hand, an opportunity to direct the changes into organized reforms and, on the other hand, a corresponding risk involved in letting the changes remain uncontrolled and lead into disorganization. To do nothing is to accept defeat.

From the point of view of social science, this means, among other things, that social engineering will increasingly be demanded. Many things that for a long period have been predominantly a matter of individual adjustment will become more and more determined by political decision and public regulation. We are entering an era where fact-finding and scientific theories of causal relations will be seen as instrumental in planning controlled social change. The peace will bring nothing but problems, one mounting upon another, and consequently, new urgent tasks for social engineering. The American social scientist, because of the New Deal and the War, is already acquiring familiarity with planning and practical action. He will never again be given the opportunity to build up so "disinterested" a social science.

The social sciences in America are equipped to meet the demands of the post-war world. In social engineering they will retain the old American faith in human beings which is all the time becoming fortified by research as the trend continues toward environmentalism in the search for social causation. In a sense, the social engineering of the coming epoch will be nothing but the drawing of practical conclusions from the teaching of social science that "human nature" is changeable and that human deficiencies and unhappiness are, in large degree, preventable.

In this spirit, so intrinsically in harmony with the great tradition of the Enlightenment and the American Revolution, the author may be allowed to close with a personal note. Studying human beings and their behavior is not discouraging. When the author recalls the long gallery of persons whom, in the course of this inquiry, he has come to know with the impetuous but temporary intimacy of the stranger—sharecroppers and plantation owners, workers and employers, merchants and bankers, intellectuals, preachers, organization leaders, political bosses, gangsters, black and white, men and women, young and old, Southerners and Northerners—the general observation retained is the following: Behind all outward dissimilarities, behind their contradictory valuations, rationalizations, vested interests, group allegiances and animosities, behind fears and defense constructions, behind the role they play in life and the mask they wear, people are all much alike on a fundamental level. And they are all good people. They want to be rational and just. They all plead to their conscience that they meant well even when things went wrong.

Social study is concerned with explaining why all these potentially and intentionally good people so often make life a hell for themselves and each other when they live together, whether in a family, a community, a nation or a world. The fault is certainly not with becoming organized *per se*. In their formal organizations, as we have seen, people invest their highest ideals. These institutions regularly direct the individual toward more cooperation and justice than he would be inclined to observe as an isolated private person. The fault is, rather, that our structures or organizations are too imperfect, each by itself, and badly integrated into a social whole.

The rationalism and moralism which is the driving force behind social study, whether we admit it or not, is the faith that institutions can be improved and strengthened and that people

are good enough to live a happier life. With all we know today, there should be the possibility to build a nation and a world where people's great propensities for sympathy and cooperation would not be so thwarted.

To find the practical formulas for this never-ending reconstruction of society is the supreme task of social science. The world catastrophe places tremendous difficulties in our way and may shake our confidence to the depths. Yet we have today in social science a greater trust in the improvability of man and society than we have ever had since the Enlightenment.

NOTES

[1] *American Unity and Asia* (1942), p. 29.
[2] *Ibid.*, p. 25.
[3] *Contemporary China. A Reference Digest*, published by Chinese News Service, Inc. (August 10, 1942).
[4] *The Negro Question* (1890), p. 48.
[5] *Following the Color Line* (1908), p. 305.

ADDITIONAL READINGS FOR CHAPTER 13

Robert L. Allen, *Black Awakening in Capitalist America: An Analytic History:* (Garden City, N.Y.: Doubleday and Company, 1969).

Robert Albrook, "Business Wrestles With Its Social Conscience," *Fortune*, V. LXXVIII, N. 2 (August 1968), pp. 89-91, 178.

Peter Bachrach and Morton S. Baratz, *Power and Poverty: Theory and Practice* (New York: Oxford University Press, 1970).

Edward C. Banfield, *The Unheavenly City* (Boston: Little, Brown and Company, 1970).

Ivar Berg (ed.), *The Business of America* (New York: Harcourt, Brace and World, 1968).

—— and James W. Kuhn (eds.), *Values in a Business Society* (New York: Harcourt, Brace & World, 1968).

David L. Birch, *The Businessman and the City* (Boston: Harvard University Graduate School of Business Administration, 1967).

"The Black Revolution," Special Issue, *Ebony*, V. XXIV, N. 10 (August 1969).

Francis L. Broderick and August Meier (eds.), *Negro Protest Thought in the Twentieth Century* (Indianapolis: Howard W. Sams and Co., 1965).

"Business and the Urban Crisis," *Business Week*, N. 2005 (February 3, 1968), pp. 57-72.

Robert S. Browne, "The Case for Two Americas— One Black, One White," *The New York Times Magazine* (August 11, 1968).

Stokely Carmichael and Charles V. Hamilton, *Black*

Power: The Politics of Liberation in America (New York: Random House, 1967).

Kenneth Clark, "What Business Can Do for the Negro," *Nation's Business* (October 1967).

—— *Dark Ghetto: Dilemmas of Social Power,* (New York: Harper & Row, Publishers, 1965).

—— and Jeannette Hopkins, *A Relevant War Against Poverty: A Study of Community Action Programs and Observable Social Change* (New York: Harper & Row, Publishers, 1968).

Jules Cohn, "Is Business Meeting the Challenge of Urban Affairs?" *Harvard Business Review,* V. 48, N. 2 (March-April 1970), pp. 68-82.

"The Conscience of the City," *Daedalus,* V. 97, N. 4 (Fall 1968).

Robert Conot, *Rivers of Blood, Years of Darkness,* (New York: Bantam Books, 1967).

Harold Cruse, *Rebellion or Revolution* (New York: William Morrow and Company, 1968).

Allan T. Demaree, "Business Picks Up the Urban Challenge," *Fortune,* V. LXXIX, N. 4 (April 1969), pp. 103-104, 174, 179, 180, 184.

Theodore Draper, "The Fantasy of Black Nationalism," *Commentary,* V. 48, N. 3 (September 1969), pp. 27-54.

Peter F. Drucker, *The Age of Discontinuity: Guidelines to Our Changing Society* (New York: Harper & Row, Publishers, 1968).

W. E. Burghardt DuBois, *The Souls of Black Folks,* (Greenwich, Conn.: Fawcett Publications, 1961).

Leonard J. Duhl (ed.) *The Urban Condition: People and Policy in the Metropolis* (New York: Simon & Schuster, 1963).

Frantz Fanon, *The Wretched of the Earth* (New York: Grove Press, 1963).

Eli Ginzberg (ed.), *Business Leadership and the Negro Crisis* (New York: McGraw-Hill Book Company, 1968).

——, *The Negro Challenge to the Business Community* (New York: McGraw-Hill Book Company, 1964).

Nathan Glazer (ed.), *Cities in Trouble* (Chicago: Quadrangle Books, 1970).

——and Daniel Patrick Moynihan, *Beyond the Melting Pot: The Negroes, Puerto Ricans, Jews, Italians and Irish of New York City* (Cambridge, Mass: The MIT Press, 1963).

Kermit Gordon (ed.), *Agenda for the Nation* (Washington, D.C.: The Brookings Institution, 1968).

William A. Grier and Price M. Cobbs, *Black Rage,* (New York: Basic Books, 1968).

Hazel Henderson, "Should Business Tackle Society's Problems?," *Harvard Business Review.* V. 46, N. 4 (July-August 1968). pp. 77-85.

LeRoi Jones, *Home: Social Essays* (New York: William Morrow and Co., 1966).

Herman Kahn and Anthony J. Weiner, *The Year 2000: A Framework For Speculation on the Next Thirty-Three Years,* (New York: The Macmillan Company, 1967).

Lewis Killian and Charles Grigg, *Racial Crisis in America: Leadership and Conflict* (Englewood Cliffs, N.J.: Prentice-Hall, 1964).

Martin Luther King, Jr., *Where Do We Go From Here?: Chaos or Community* (New York: Harper & Row Publishers, 1967).

——,*Why We Can't Wait* (New York: Harper & Row, Publishers, 1963).

Sar A. Levitan, *The Great Society's Poor Law: A New Approach to Poverty,* (Baltimore, Md.: The Johns Hopkins Press, 1968).

Louis E. Lomax, *The Negro Revolt* (New York: The New American Library, 1962).

Raymond W. Mack, *Transforming America: Patterns of Social Change* (New York: Random House, 1967).

Malcolm X., *The Autobiography of Malcolm X* (New York: Grove Press, 1964).

Irwin Miller, "Business Has a War to Win," *Harvard Business Review,* V. 47, N. 2 (March-April 1969, pp. 4-6, 8, 10, 12, 164, 168.

Daniel P. Moynihan, *Maximum Feasible Misunderstanding: Community Action in the War on Poverty* (New York: The Free Press, 1969).

Raymond J. Murphy and Howard Elinson (eds.), *Problems and Prospects of the Negro Movement* 2nd. ed. (Belmont, Calif.: Wadsworth Publishing Company, 1968).

National Industrial Conference Board, *Business Amid Urban Crisis: Private-Sector Approaches to City Problems,* Studies in Public Affairs, No. 3 (New York: National Industrial Conference Board, Inc., 1968).

——, *National Conference on Corporate Urban Programs: An Investment in Economic Progress and Social Order,* Public Affairs Conference Report, No. 6 (New York: National Industrial Conference Board, Inc., 1968).

——,*The Urban Dilemma: Seven Steps Toward Resolution: Presentations Made to the Public Affairs Research Counsel,* Public Affairs Conference Report, No. 7 (New York: National Industrial Conference Board, Inc. 1969).

George S. Odiorne, *Green Power: The Corporation and the Urban Crisis* (New York: Pitman Publishing Corporation, 1969).

Talcott Parsons and Kenneth B. Clark (eds.), *The Negro American* (Boston: Beacon Press, 1964, 1965).

"Perspectives on Business," *Daedalus,* V. 98, N. 1 (Winter 1969).

Richard S. Rosenbloom and Robin Marris (eds.), *Social Innovation in the City: New Enterprises for Community Development* (Cambridge, Mass: Harvard University Programs on Technology and Society, 1969).

Report of the National Advisory Commission on Civil Disorders (New York: Bantam Books, Inc., 1968).

Bayard Rustin, "From Protest to Politics: The Future

of the Civil Rights Movement," *Commentary* V. XXXIX, N. 2 (February 1965), pp. 25-31.

Bobby Seale, *Seize the Time* (New York: Random House, 1970).

S. Prakash Sethi, *Business Corporations and the Black Man: An Analysis of Social Conflict: The Kodak-FIGHT Controversy* (Scranton, Pa.: Chandler Publishing Company, 1970).

—— and Dow Votaw, "Do We Need a New Response to a Changing Social Environment?" *California Management Review,* V. XII, N. 1 (Fall 1969), pp. 17-31.

Charles E. Silberman, "The Businessman and the Negro," *Fortune,* V. LXVIII, N. 3 (September 1963), pp. 97-99.

——,*Crisis in Black and White* (New York: Random House, Inc., 1964).

Jerome H. Skolnick, *The Politics of Protest* (New York: Ballantine Books, 1969).

"A Special Issue on Business and the Urban Crisis," *Fortune,* V. LXXVII, N. 1 (January 1968).

"Special Report: The War That Business Must Win," *Business Week,* (November 1, 1969), pp. 63-74.

"Toward the Year 2000: Work in Progress," *Daedalus,* V. 96, N. 3 (Summer 1968).

Clarence C. Walton, *Corporate Social Responsibilities* (Belmont, Calif.: Wadsworth Publishing Company, Inc., 1967).

"The War That Business Must Win," *Business Week,* N. 2096 (November 1, 1969), pp. 63-74.

Nathan Wright, Jr., *Black Power and Urban Unrest: Creative Possibilities* (New York: Hawthorne Books, Inc., 1967).

Whitney M. Young, Jr., *Beyond Racism* (New York: McGraw-Hill Book Company, 1969).

——,*To Be Equal,* (New York: McGraw-Hill Book Company, 1964).

LIST OF CONTRIBUTORS

LOUIS L. ALLEN, President, Chase Manhattan Capital Corporation, and specialist in small business formation.

RICHARD F. AMERICA, JR., Director of the Office of Urban Programs, Schools of Business, University of California, Berkeley, and economist specializing in black economic development.

ROBERT BLAUNER, Associate Professor of Sociology, University of California, Berkeley.

MARSHALL H. BRENNER, Industrial Psychologist, Lockheed Aircraft Corporation.

ANDREW F. BRIMMER, Member, Board of Governors, Federal Reserve System.

ROBERT S. BROWNE, Professor of Economics, Fairleigh Dickinson University, and Director of the Black Economic Research Center, New York City.

ANGUS CAMPBELL, Director, Survey Research Center, and Professor of Sociology, University of Michigan, Ann Arbor.

DAVID CAPLOVITZ, Professor of Sociology, Columbia University.

KENNETH B. CLARK, President, Metropolitan Applied Research Center Inc., and Professor of Psychology, City College of New York.

ELDRIDGE CLEAVER, Minister of Information, Black Panther Party for Self Defense, now living in Algeria.

PRICE M. COBBS, Assistant Professor of Psychiatry, University of California Medical Center, San Francisco.

THEODORE L. CROSS, formerly Editor, *The Bankers Magazine,* and consultant in the field of minority economic development.

W. E. B. DUBOIS, Sociologist and social activist who for over fifty years contributed by both his scholarship and leadership to the growth of nationalist feeling among American blacks. He died in Ghana 1963.

RALPH ELLISON, self-educated author, has taught literature at Bard College, University of Chicago and at Yale and Rutgers.

EDWIN M. EPSTEIN, Associate Professor of Business Administration and formerly Director of the Office of Urban Programs, Schools of Business Administration, University of California, Berkeley,

LOUIS A. FERMAN, Research director of the Institute of Labor and Industrial Relations, The University of Michigan—Wayne State University.

E. FRANKLIN FRAZIER, for many years Professor and Chairman, Department of Sociology at Howard University; first black President of the American Sociological Association. He died in 1962.

ELI GOLDSTON, President of Eastern Gas and Fuel Associates, Boston, Massachusetts.

WILLIAM GRIER, Assistant Professor of Psychiatry, University of California Medical Center, San Francisco.

DAVID R. HAMPTON, Associate Professor of Management, San Diego State College, California.

CLAIRE C. HODGE, Economic statistician, Office of Manpower and Employment Statistics, Bureau of Labor Statistics, U.S. Department of Labor.

JAMES C. HODGSON, Secretary, U.S. Department of Labor; formerly Vice President and Director of Industrial Relations for Lockheed Aircraft Corporation.

JAMES M. HUND, Professor and former Dean, School of Business Administration, Emory University, Atlanta, Georgia.

LEROI JONES, novelist, playwright, and essayist, and a leading militant among black intellectuals. His works include, *Home, The Slave,* and *Blues People.*

JOHN F. KAIN, Professor of Economics, Harvard University.

REV. MARTIN LUTHER KING, JR., winner of the Nobel Peace Medal; advocate of nonviolence in the struggle for racial equality. Assassinated in 1968.

BEVERLY KISSINGER, formerly a staff member of Office of Research and Reports, of the U.S. Equal Employment Opportunity Commission.

LOUIS E. LOMAX, author, journalist, and educator who wrote widely on the American racial scene.

JEANNE R. LOWE, Urban Affairs Editor, McCall's Magazine, and author of *Cities in A Race With Time*.

MALCOLM X (El-Hajj Malik El-Shabazz), black nationalist leader who left the Nation of Islam (Black Muslims) to form the Muslim Mosque Inc., and was considered to be one of most influential blacks of our times prior to his death in 1965.

JOHN R. MEYER, President of the National Bureau of Economic Research and Professor of Economics, Yale University.

GUNNAR MYRDAL, Professor Economics at the University of Stockholm.

NATIONAL ADVISORY COMMISSION ON CIVIL DISORDERS (KERNER COMMISSION)

CHAIRMAN: OTTO KERNER former governor of Illinois.

VICE CHAIRMAN: JOHN V. LINDSAY, mayor of New York City.

FRED R. HARRIS, U.S. Senator from Oklahoma.

EDWARD W. BROOKE, U.S. Senator from Massachusetts.

JAMES C. CORMAN, U.S. House of Representatives (California).

WILLIAM M. McCULLOCH, U.S. House of Representatives (Ohio).

I. W. ABEL, President, United Steelworkers of America (AFL-CIO).

CHARLES B. THORNTON, Chairman of the Board and Chief Executive Officer, Litton Industries Inc.

ROY WILKINS, Executive Director, National Association for the Advancement of Colored People.

KATHERINE GRAHAM PEDEN, Commissioner of Commerce, Kentucky.

HERBERT JENKINS, Chief of Police, Atlanta, Georgia.

HERBERT R. NORTHRUP, Director of the Industrial Research Unit and Chairman of the Department of Industry and Professor of Industry, Wharton School of Finance and Commerce, University of Pennsylvania.

THOMAS F. PETTIGREW, Social Relations, Harvard University.

PRESIDENTS' NATIONAL ADVISORY PANEL IN INSURANCE IN RIOT-AFFECTED AREAS

CHAIRMAN: RICHARD F. HUGHES, governor of New Jersey.

VICE CHAIRMAN: WILLIAM F. SCRANTON, former governor of Pennsylvania.

FRANK L. FARWELL, President, Liberty Mutual Insurance Company.

GEORGE S. HARRIS, President, Chicago Metropolitan Mutual Insurance Company.

A. ADDERSON ROBERTS, President, Reliance Insurance Company.

WALTER E. WASHINGTON, Commissioner (now Mayor), District of Columbia, former Chairman, New York City Housing Authority.

FRANK M. WOZENCRAFT, Assistant Attorney General in Charge of Office of Legal Counsel, U.S. Department of Justice.

WILLIAM PROXMIRE, U.S. Senator from Wisconsin.

BETTY REYNOLDS, formerly a staff member of the Office of Research and Reports, U.S. Equal Employment Opportunity Commission.

ARNOLD SCHUCHTER, urban renewal planning consultant, associated with Arthur D. Little Company, Cambridge, Massachusetts.

HOWARD SCHUMAN, Director of the Detroit Area Study and Associate Professor of Sociology, University of Michigan.

PAUL M. SIEGEL, Professor of Sociology, University of Michigan.

JAMES S. SPAIN, Manager, Equal Employment Opportunity and Urban Affairs, Allied Chemical Corporation, and Past President and Board Chairman of the Council of Concerned Black Executives.

PHYLLIS A. WALLACE, one of the nation's very few black women to receive a Ph.D. in economics, was former Chief of Technical Studies for the Equal Employment Opportunity Commission; presently she is Vice-President for Research of Metropolitan Applied Research Center Inc.

ROBERT C. WEAVER, President, Bernard M. Baruch College, City University of New York, and formerly Secretary, U.S. Department of Housing and Urban Development.

ROY WILKINS, Executive Secretary of the National Association for the Advancement of Colored People.

HARDING B. YOUNG, Professor of Business Administration, Georgia State University Atlanta; formerly Dean of the Graduate School of Business Administration of Atlanta University.

WHITNEY M. YOUNG, JR., Executive Director of the National Urban League since 1961; formerly Dean of the Atlanta University School of Work.

Index

J